Jamsa's 1001 DOS & PC Tips

About the Disk

The 3.5" disk that accompanies this book is jam-packed with information covered in the 1,001 tips in this book. On it, you will find utilities, batch file scripts, and other programs you can put to immediate use—over 250 such files!

As you are looking through the book, you will notice a special icon next to some listings or program names. This icon also appears to the side of this paragraph. It indicates a program or batch file script that is included on the disk. The name of the disk file is shown under the icon.

To begin using these files, all you need to do is copy them to your hard disk. To do this, create a directory called **1001DOS** (or any other directory name you desire). If you want to copy all the files from the diskette, you can use the XCOPY command. The following commands (entered from the DOS prompt) accomplishes both these steps:

```
C:\> MD  \1001DOS
C:\> XCOPY  B:\*.*  C:\1001DOS\*.* /S
```

You may need to replace the B and C drive designations with the proper ones for your system. You can also copy individual files from the diskette if you either have limited disk space or only want to use a few of them.

We hope you enjoy working with *Jamsa's 1001 DOS & PC Tips*. We trust you will discover, as many other readers have, that this book really is a computer user's best friend.

Minimum System Requirements: IBM PC, PC/AT, or 100% compatible computer system with 640Kb of RAM. If you are installing these programs on a hard disk (strongly recommended), you will need just under 2Mb of free space. If you plan on using the printer tips, you will need a printer.

Planting 1,001 Trees

I was reading another book recently when I encountered a note from the publisher about the number of trees required to produce a book such as this. I was astounded to learn it requires about 500 trees for every 10,000 books. That publisher had instituted a policy of planting 2 trees for every tree felled in the production of their book.

I was greatly impressed by this policy and have decided to follow suit. I hope that some day all publishers will do the same. For each 10,000 copies of *Jamsa's 1001 DOS & PC Tips* that are printed, my family and I will donate 1,001 trees for planting. If you would like to become involved in this effort, please write to:

The Basic Foundation
P.O. Box 47012
St. Petersburg, FL 33743

You can plant a single tree for only $5.00, or 1,001 trees for $255.00.

Jamsa's 1001 DOS & PC Tips

Kris Jamsa

Osborne **McGraw-Hill**

Berkeley New York St. Louis San Francisco
Auckland Bogotá Hamburg London Madrid
Mexico City Milan Montreal New Delhi Panama City
Paris São Paulo Singapore Sydney
Tokyo Toronto

Osborne McGraw-Hill
2600 Tenth Street
Berkeley, California 94710
U.S.A.

For information on translations or book distributors outside of the U.S.A., please write to Osborne McGraw-Hill at the above address.

Jamsa's 1001 DOS & PC Tips

1234567890 DOC 998765432

ISBN 0-07-881821-4

Publisher
Kenna S. Wood

Acquisitions Editor
Allen L. Wyatt

Associate Editor
Emily Rader

Project Editor
Cindy Brown

Technical Editor
Phil Schmauder

Copy Editors
Judy Ziajka
Janis Paris

Proofreader
Colleen Paretty

Indexer
Phil Schmauder

Illustrator
Susie C. Kim

Computer Designer
Fred Lass

Cover Design
Communications Design

In Memory of Grandpa Joe.
For his words of wisdom, lessons taught, friendship,
and love. He showed me 1,001 ways to view life.

Table of Contents

System

Memory

Tip

Keyboard

Tip

Disk

Tip

Directory

Tip

File

Tip

Batch File

GOTO Tip

Shell

Tip

Hardware

Tip

International

Tip

Printer

Tip

Maintenance

Acknowledgments

It won't take you long to realize that this book's content and layout is different from that of other computer books. Creating this book took the tireless effort and cooperation of a team of key individuals, each of whom helped pull "1001 pieces" together. It would be impossible for me to individually thank everyone who worked on this project in the small space provided, but you will become aware of their contribution as you read through each page of this book.

I cannot express my gratitude enough to Phil Schmauder, my technical editor and indexer. Phil is far and away the best in the business. This book could not have been done, and would not have been attempted, without Phil's assistance. I also need to thank Susie Kim, who has done a tremendous job with the artwork in this book. As with Phil, Susie's work is second to none.

PART 1

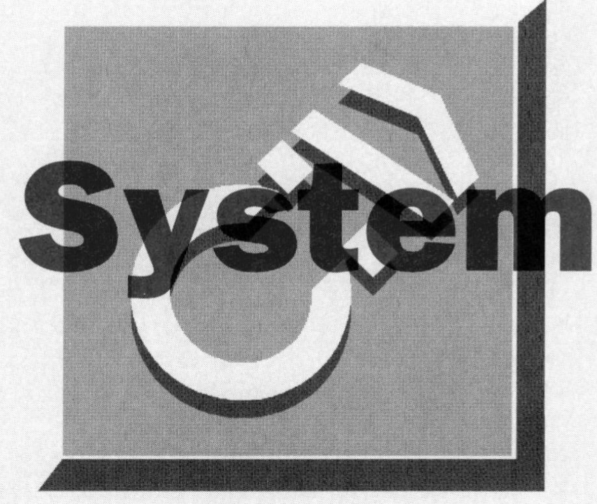

Keeping Other Users From Booting Your Hard Disk

You sometimes may want to keep other users from booting your system from your hard disk. The following DEBUG script file, LOCKOUT.SCR, creates a device driver named LOCKOUT.SYS that prompts you to enter a special passcode to access the system:

LOCKOUT.SCR

```
N LOCKOUT.SYS                <ENTER>
A 100                        <ENTER>
DB FF, FF, FF, FF            <ENTER>
DW 8000, 16, 21              <ENTER>
DB "LOCKOUT[{|"|}]         . <ENTER>
DB 0,0,0,0                   <ENTER>
CS:                          <ENTER>
MOV WORD PTR [12], BX        <ENTER>
CS:                          <ENTER>
MOV WORD PTR [14], ES        <ENTER>
RETF                         <ENTER>
PUSHF                        <ENTER>
PUSH AX                      <ENTER>
PUSH SI                      <ENTER>
PUSH DI                      <ENTER>
PUSH DS                      <ENTER>
PUSH BP                      <ENTER>
PUSH CS                      <ENTER>
POP DS                       <ENTER>
LES DI, [12]                 <ENTER>
ES:                          <ENTER>
CMP BYTE PTR [DI+2], 0       <ENTER>
JNZ 14B                      <ENTER>
CALL 152                     <ENTER>
ES:                          <ENTER>
MOV BYTE PTR [DI+0D], 0      <ENTER>
ES:                          <ENTER>
MOV BYTE PTR [DI+0E], 0      <ENTER>
ES:                          <ENTER>
MOV WORD PTR [DI+10], CS     <ENTER>
ES:                          <ENTER>
```

```
MOV WORD PTR [DI+3], 100 <ENTER>
POP BP                   <ENTER>
POP DS                   <ENTER>
POP DI                   <ENTER>
POP SI                   <ENTER>
POP AX                   <ENTER>
POPF                     <ENTER>
RETF                     <ENTER>
MOV AH, 0                <ENTER>
INT 16                   <ENTER>
CMP AH,44                <ENTER>
JNE 152                  <ENTER>
RET                      <ENTER>
                         <ENTER>
R CX                     <ENTER>
5C                       <ENTER>
W                        <ENTER>
Q                        <ENTER>
```

Use DEBUG as follows to create the device driver LOCKOUT.SYS:

```
C:\> DEBUG < LOCKOUT.SYS <ENTER>
```

In your CONFIG.SYS file, use a DEVICE or DEVICEHIGH entry as follows to install the driver:

```
DEVICE=C:\LOCKOUT.SYS
```

When you boot your system, the system will appear to stop. Press the F10 key to continue. If you want to change the driver to use a different key, change the value 44 in the following line to a differnt scancode:

CMP AH,44

To select the F9 function key, you would use the value 43. If you customize the driver, try booting the new driver from floppy disk to ensure that your change is correct before you install the driver on your hard disk.

An Automatic Restart Command

There may be times when one of your batch files makes changes to either your CONFIG.SYS or AUTOEXEC.BAT, after which you must restart your system. Using the following DEBUG script file RESTART.SCR, you can create a command file that automatically reboots your computer:

RESTART.SCR

```
N RESTART.COM <ENTER>
A 100         <ENTER>
MOV BX,40     <ENTER>
MOV DS,BX     <ENTER>
MOV BX,1234   <ENTER>
MOV [72],BX   <ENTER>
JMP FFFF:0    <ENTER>
              <ENTER>
R CX          <ENTER>
11            <ENTER>
W             <ENTER>
Q             <ENTER>
```

Use DEBUG as follows to create the RESTART.COM command:

```
C:\> DEBUG < RESTART.SCR <ENTER>
```

The following batch file ADDRAM.BAT saves the current CONFIG.SYS file to a file named CONFIG.SAV. The batch file then creates a new CONFIG.SYS file that installs a RAM drive. Last, the batch file uses the RESTART command to boot the computer.

```
@ECHO OFF
REM Save the current CONFIG.SYS
COPY \CONFIG.SYS \*.SAV
REM Create a new CONFIG.SYS containing RAMDRIVE.SYS
ECHO BUFFERS=30 > \CONFIG.SYS
ECHO FILES=30 >> \CONFIG.SYS
ECHO DEVICE=C:\DOS\RAMDRIVE.SYS >> \CONFIG.SYS
ECHO About to restart the system
PAUSE
RESTART
```

Installing Form-Feed Support for Print Screen Operations

As Tip 32 discusses, by pressing the SHIFT-PRTSC key combination, you direct the PC to print your screen's current contents. Unfortunately, a print screen operation does not eject the page containing the printout from your printer. The following DEBUG script file, PRTSCRFF.SCR, creates the memory-resident command PRTSCRFF.COM that automatically ejects the page from your printer:

PRTSCRFF.SCR

```
N PRTSCRFF.COM <ENTER>
A 100          <ENTER>
JMP 117        <ENTER>
DB 0,0,0,0     <ENTER>
STI            <ENTER>
PUSHF          <ENTER>
CS:            <ENTER>
CALL FAR [102] <ENTER>
MOV AH,0       <ENTER>
MOV AL,0C      <ENTER>
MOV DX,0       <ENTER>
INT 17         <ENTER>
IRET           <ENTER>
MOV AX, 3505   <ENTER>
INT 21         <ENTER>
CS:            <ENTER>
MOV [102],BX   <ENTER>
CS:            <ENTER>
MOV [104],ES   <ENTER>
MOV AX, 2505   <ENTER>
MOV DX, 106    <ENTER>
INT 21         <ENTER>
MOV DX,12      <ENTER>
MOV AX,3100    <ENTER>
INT 21         <ENTER>
               <ENTER>
R CX           <ENTER>
36             <ENTER>
```

```
W                    <ENTER>
Q                    <ENTER>
```

Use DEBUG as follows to create the command file PRTSCRFF.COM:

```
C:\> DEBUG < PRTSCRFF.SCR <ENTER>
```

To use PRTSCRFF, invoke it from the DOS prompt and then press SHIFT-PRTSC. If you are using 43- or 50-line mode, invoke the program FIXPRTSC.COM discussed in Tip 888 before invoking PRTSCRFF.COM.

Tip 4 Preventing a Reboot Operation

By pressing the CTRL-ALT-DEL keyboard combination, you direct DOS to restart. The following DEBUG script file, NOREBOOT.SCR, creates a command file named NOREBOOT.COM that disables the CTRL-ALT-DEL keyboard combination:

NOREBOOT.SCR

```
N NOREBOOT.COM <ENTER>
A 100          <ENTER>
JMP 161        <ENTER>
DB 0,0,0,0     <ENTER>
DB "NOREBOOT", 0          <ENTER>
DB "ALREADY INSTALLED"    <ENTER>
DB 0           <ENTER>
STI            <ENTER>
PUSH BP        <ENTER>
PUSH DS        <ENTER>
PUSH ES        <ENTER>
PUSH AX        <ENTER>
PUSH BX        <ENTER>
PUSH CX        <ENTER>
PUSH DX        <ENTER>
PUSH SI        <ENTER>
```

```
PUSH DI         <ENTER>
IN   AX, 60     <ENTER>
CMP  AL, 53     <ENTER>
JNE  151        <ENTER>
MOV  AX, 0200   <ENTER>
INT  16         <ENTER>
AND  AX, 000C   <ENTER>
CMP  AX, 000C   <ENTER>
JNE  151        <ENTER>
MOV  AX, 0E07   <ENTER>
INT  10         <ENTER>
MOV  AL, 20     <ENTER>
OUT  20, AL     <ENTER>
POP  DI         <ENTER>
POP  SI         <ENTER>
POP  DX         <ENTER>
POP  CX         <ENTER>
POP  BX         <ENTER>
POP  AX         <ENTER>
POP  ES         <ENTER>
POP  DS         <ENTER>
POP  BP         <ENTER>
IRET            <ENTER>
POP  DI         <ENTER>
POP  SI         <ENTER>
POP  DX         <ENTER>
POP  CX         <ENTER>
POP  BX         <ENTER>
POP  AX         <ENTER>
POP  ES         <ENTER>
POP  DS         <ENTER>
POP  BP         <ENTER>
PUSHF           <ENTER>
CS:             <ENTER>
CALL FAR [102]  <ENTER>
IRET            <ENTER>
MOV  AX, CS     <ENTER>
MOV  DS, AX     <ENTER>
MOV  ES, AX     <ENTER>
MOV  AX, 3000   <ENTER>
INT  21         <ENTER>
CMP  AL, 4      <ENTER>
```

```
JGE  183         <ENTER>
MOV  AX, 5100 <ENTER>
INT  21          <ENTER>
DEC  BX          <ENTER>
MOV  ES, BX      <ENTER>
MOV  DI, 8       <ENTER>
MOV  SI, 106     <ENTER>
MOV  CX, 8       <ENTER>
REP  MOVSB       <ENTER>
MOV  AX, 5200 <ENTER>
INT  21          <ENTER>
ES:              <ENTER>
MOV  AX, [BX][-2]         <ENTER>
MOV  ES, AX      <ENTER>
MOV  DI, 8       <ENTER>
MOV  SI, 106     <ENTER>
MOV  CX, 8       <ENTER>
REPE CMPSB       <ENTER>
JNE  1B7         <ENTER>
INC  BYTE PTR [120]       <ENTER>
CMP  BYTE PTR [120], 2 <ENTER>
JL   1B7         <ENTER>
MOV  BX, 0       <ENTER>
MOV  CX, 11      <ENTER>
MOV  DX, 10F     <ENTER>
MOV  AH, 40      <ENTER>
INT  21          <ENTER>
MOV  AH, 4C      <ENTER>
INT  21          <ENTER>
ES:              <ENTER>
MOV  AX, [0]     <ENTER>
CMP  AL, 5A      <ENTER>
JE   1CC         <ENTER>
ES:              <ENTER>
MOV  AX, [3]     <ENTER>
MOV  BX, ES      <ENTER>
ADD  BX, AX      <ENTER>
INC  BX          <ENTER>
MOV  ES, BX      <ENTER>
JMP  18E         <ENTER>
```

```
MOV  AX, 3509 <ENTER>
INT  21       <ENTER>
MOV  [102], BX <ENTER>
MOV  [104], ES <ENTER>
MOV  AX, 2509 <ENTER>
MOV  DX, 121  <ENTER>
INT  21       <ENTER>
MOV  AX, 3100 <ENTER>
MOV  DX, 200  <ENTER>
INT  21       <ENTER>
              <ENTER>
R CX          <ENTER>
200           <ENTER>
W             <ENTER>
Q             <ENTER>
```

After you run NOREBOOT, your computer will beep when you press the CTRL-ALT-DEL keyboard combination, as opposed to restarting DOS.

Use DEBUG as follows to build the command file NOREBOOT.COM:

```
C:\> DEBUG < NOREBOOT.SCR <ENTER>
```

Controlling the Cursor's Appearance

By default, the PC displays the cursor as a small thin line that appears at the base of characters on the current line. The PC represents the cursor using *scan lines*. The following illustration shows the default scan lines used by monochrome (scan lines 6 and 7) and color (scan lines 11 and 12) video displays:

Color	Monochrome
Scan lines 0-1	Scan line 0
Scan lines 2-3	Scan line 1
Scan lines 4-5	Scan line 2
Scan lines 6-7	Scan line 3
Scan lines 8-9	Scan line 4
Scan lines A-B	Scan line 5
Scan lines C-D	Scan line 6
Scan lines E-F	Scan line 7

Using the following DEBUG script file, CSRSIZE.SCR, you can customize your cursor size and appearance. Depending on your preference, you will need to assign different starting and ending scan line values to the CH and CL register. The following statements create the DEBUG script file CSRSIZE.SCR:

CSRSIZE.SCR

```
N CSRSIZE.COM <ENTER>
A 100         <ENTER>
MOV AH,1      <ENTER>
MOV CH,0   ; Starting scan line <ENTER>
MOV CL,7   ; Ending scan line   <ENTER>
INT 10        <ENTER>
MOV AH,4C     <ENTER>
INT 21        <ENTER>
              <ENTER>
R CX          <ENTER>
C             <ENTER>
W             <ENTER>
Q             <ENTER>
```

Use DEBUG as follows to create the command file CSRSIZE.COM:

```
C:\> DEBUG < CSRSIZE.SCR <ENTER>
```

To change the cursor size at a later time, you must edit the file CSRSIZE.SCR, assigning the desired scan lines to the CH and CL registers and then use the previous DEBUG command to rebuild the file CSRSIZE.COM. As an alternative, you might consider creating custom DEBUG script files for each cursor size you plan to use.

ANSI.SYS Slows I/O Operations

The ANSI.SYS device driver lets you select screen colors (see Tip 33), define keyboard keys (see Tip 311), or set the cursor position. To perform its processing, however, the ANSI.SYS device driver intercepts and examines each keystroke and each character written by DOS to the screen display. If you aren't using a specific feature of ANSI.SYS, do not install the driver. If you leave ANSI.SYS installed, each screen or keyboard I/O operation will take slightly longer.

On-line Help for DOS Commands

If you are using DOS 5, DOS provides you with two ways to get help about DOS commands. If you can't remember a specific command's name, type **HELP** at the DOS prompt. DOS will display a list and description of its commands as shown here:

```
C:\> HELP <ENTER>
APPEND   Allows programs to open data files in specified
         directories as if they were in the current directory.
ASSIGN   Redirects requests for disk operations on one drive to a
         different drive.
ATTRIB   Displays or changes file attributes.
BACKUP   Backs up one or more files from one disk to another.
.        .
.        .
.        .
VOL      Displays a disk volume label and serial number.
XCOPY    Copies files (except hidden and system files) and
         directory trees.
```

If you want help on a specific command, invoke the command with the /? switch. The following command, for example, displays help about the FORMAT command:

```
C:\> FORMAT /? <ENTER>
Formats a disk for use with MS-DOS.
FORMAT drive: [/V[:label]] [/Q] [/U] [/F:size] [/B | /S]
FORMAT drive: [/V[:label]] [/Q] [/U] [/T:tracks /N:sectors]
[/B|/S]
FORMAT drive: [/V[:label]] [/Q] [/U] [/1] [/4] [/B | /S]
FORMAT drive: [/Q] [/U] [/1] [/4] [/8] [/B | /S]
  /V[:label]  Specifies the volume label.
  /Q  Performs a quick format.
  /U  Performs an unconditional format.
  /F:size     Specifies the size of the floppy disk to format
(such as 160, 180, 320, 360, 720, 1.2, 1.44, 2.88).
  /B  Allocates space on the disk for system files.
  /S  Copies system files to the formatted disk.
  /T:tracks   Specifies the number of tracks per disk side.
  /N:sectors  Specifies the number of sectors per track.
  /1  Formats a single side of a floppy disk.
  /4  Formats a 5.25-inch 360K floppy disk in a
      high-density drive.
  /8  Formats eight sectors per track.
```

To use the /? switch to display help information on a specific command, you must be using DOS 5 or later.

A Faster COMMAND.COM Reload

COMMAND.COM is the DOS command interpreter, which contains the internal DOS commands and is responsible for executing the commands you type at the DOS prompt. To provide more memory for your programs, DOS divides COMMAND.COM into two parts: a resident section that always

resides in memory and a larger, transient section that can be overwritten by a large application program as shown here:

1024kb (1 Mb)	ROM-BIOS
960Kb	Reserved memory
768Kb	Reserved for video
640Kb	Transient COMMAND.COM
	Program memory
	Resident COMMAND.COM
	CONFIG.SYS entries
	DOS kernel
	BIOS communication area
1Kb	BIOS interrupt vectors
0Kb	

If a large application program overwrites the transient portion of COMMAND.COM in memory, the resident portion must reload the transient portion from disk. To locate COMMAND.COM on disk, DOS uses the environment's COMSPEC entry. By default, COMSPEC points to your boot disk's root directory or to the directory specified in the CONFIG.SYS SHELL= entry.

If your computer has extended or expanded memory available, you can use the memory to create a RAM drive to which you copy the file COMMAND.COM. Next, by assigning the COMSPEC entry to point to COMMAND.COM on the RAM drive, DOS can reload COMMAND.COM faster than if it had to use the slower hard disk.

To create a RAM drive in extended or expanded memory, see Tip 375. The reason you want to use extended or expanded memory is to prevent the RAM drive from consuming conventional memory. Place the following commands in your AUTOEXEC.BAT file to copy COMMAND.COM to your RAM drive and to assign the COMSPEC entry to use the RAM drive. These commands assume your RAM drive is drive D.

```
COPY C:\DOS\COMMAND.COM  D:
SET COMSPEC=D:\COMMAND.COM
```

Improving Performance by Turning Off Extended CTRL-BREAK Checking

By default, whenever DOS writes to your screen or printer, or reads from the keyboard, DOS checks whether or not you have pressed CTRL-C or CTRL-BREAK to end the current command. If you use a program that performs long calculations without performing input or output, it may take DOS considerable time to recognize a CTRL-C or CTRL-BREAK. Using the BREAK command, you can direct DOS to test for a CTRL-C more often. This testing is called extended CTRL-BREAK checking. To enable extended CTRL-BREAK checking, issue the following BREAK command:

```
C:\> BREAK ON <ENTER>
```

When you enable extended CTRL-BREAK checking, you increase the likelihood that DOS will recognize a CTRL-C or CTRL-BREAK sooner. Unfortunately, because DOS will test for a CTRL-BREAK more often, DOS will spend less time running your program, causing your system performance to decrease. Most users should leave extended CTRL-BREAK checking off. If you issue a BREAK command at the DOS prompt with no arguments as shown here, BREAK will display its current state:

```
C:\> BREAK <ENTER>
BREAK is on
```

If BREAK is currently on, use the following command to turn it off:

```
C:\> BREAK OFF <ENTER>
```

If BREAK was on, check your CONFIG.SYS file for an entry in the form BREAK=ON. If the entry exists, remove it. Likewise, check your AUTOEXEC.BAT for a BREAK ON command and remove the entry if it exists.

Which Executes First: BAT, EXE, or COM files?

When you create batch files, you must not assign the batch file the same name as an internal DOS command. For example, if you create a batch file named DATE.BAT, DOS will never execute your batch file, instead it will always execute the internal DATE command. Similarly, you should not assign a batch file the same name as an existing EXE or COM file. Using an existing name is only asking for confusion. However, should a batch file have the same name as an existing DOS command, the question becomes, "Which will DOS execute first: the batch file or the existing EXE or COM file?" As it turns out DOS does not define an execution order for BAT, COM, and EXE files. The first file DOS encounters will dictate which file DOS executes. If DOS encounters the batch file first, DOS will execute the batch file. Likewise, if DOS encounters the EXE file first, DOS will execute the corresponding program.

With this fact in mind, you can prevent users from running a specific command, such as FORMAT or FDISK, by creating a batch file with the same name and placing the batch files in directories that appear in the command path prior to the commands you want to suppress.

Documenting Your CONFIG.SYS File

Depending on your hardware configuration or the application programs installed on your system, the entries in your CONFIG.SYS file may differ greatly from those of other users. If you are using DOS 4 or higher, DOS lets you place remarks in your CONFIG.SYS file by using a REM statement that describe each entry's purpose. Consider the following CONFIG.SYS file:

```
BUFFERS=3
FILES=50
DEVICE=C:\DOS\HIMEM.SYS
DEVICE=C:\DOS\EMM386.EXE NOEMS
```

```
DOS=HIGH,UMB
DEVICEHIGH=C:\DOS\ANSI.SYS
DEVICEHIGH=C:\DOS\SMARTDRV.SYS
```

Using the REM statement, you can describe each entry as shown here:

```
REM Set the number of disk buffers to 3 because we are
REM using SMARTDRV for disk caching
BUFFERS=3

REM Reserve 50 file handles, they are needed for a database
FILES=50

REM Install support for extended memory
DEVICE=C:\DOS\HIMEM.SYS

REM Install support for using the upper-memory area—we don't
REM want to use expanded memory so include the NOEMS switch
DEVICE=C:\DOS\EMM386.EXE NOEMS

REM Load DOS into the high memory area and direct DOS to
REM reserve upper-memory blocks for device drivers and
REM memory resident commands
DOS=HIGH,UMB

REM Several batch files use ANSI.SYS escape sequences
DEVICEHIGH=C:\DOS\ANSI.SYS

REM Install disk caching support for faster performance
DEVICEHIGH=C:\DOS\SMARTDRV.SYS
```

With the entries described in this way, if you or another user later have to change CONFIG.SYS, you will better remember the existing entries. In addition to using REM to make CONFIG.SYS more understandable, the batch file also uses blank lines to improve its readability.

To use the REM statement within CONFIG.SYS, you must be using DOS 4 or higher.

Using the TEMP Environment Entry

By default, when you use the pipe (|) operator to redirect the output of one program to become the input of another, DOS creates two temporary files in your disk's root directory. Although users are normally unaware that these two temporary files exist, problems can arise if the disk is currently write-protected, or if the root directory is full, because both conditions prevent DOS from creating the files.

Beginning with DOS 5, you can specify the disk and directory within which you want DOS to create these two temporary files by using the TEMP environment entry. When you use the pipe operator under DOS 5, DOS first checks the environment for an entry in the form TEMP=. If DOS finds the entry, DOS creates the temporary files in the location specified. Otherwise, DOS creates the files in the root directory.

If you use the pipe operator regularly, you can improve your system performance by creating a RAM drive and assigning TEMP to use the drive. The RAM drive must be large enough, however, to hold the data written to the temporary files. Depending on how you use the pipe, you may have to experiment with different drive sizes.

Increasing Your Environment Size

The DOS environment contains information used by DOS, such as the command path or prompt, or possibly information used by application programs. Under DOS 5, the environment size starts at 256 bytes. As you add entries to the environment, DOS tries to expand the environment as necessary. The environment's entries must reside in consecutive memory locations. Unfortunately, when you install a memory-resident program such as FASTOPEN or MIRROR, the program may prevent the environment from expanding in the future as shown here:

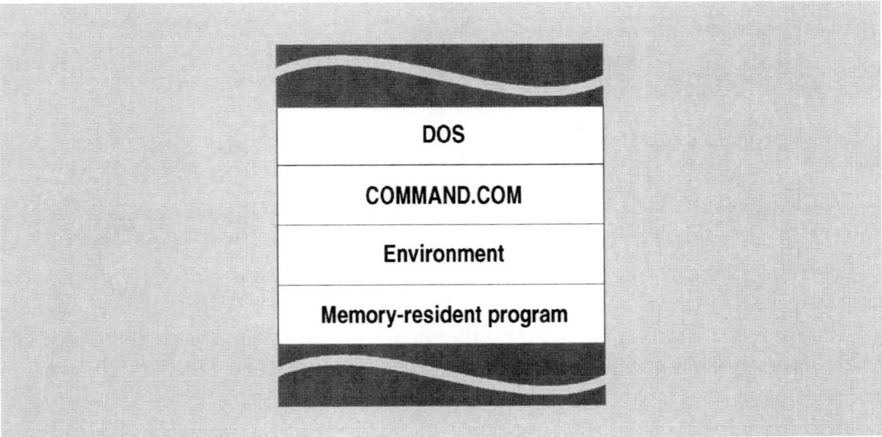

If you try to add an entry that can fit in the environment, and DOS is unable to expand the environment, DOS will display the following error message:

```
Out of environment space
```

If this message occurs, you can increase the amount of memory DOS initially allocates for the environment when your system starts by using the CONFIG.SYS SHELL entry. The SHELL entry /E switch lets you specify the environment size up to 32,768 bytes. The following entry allocates a 1,024 byte environment:

```
SHELL=C:\DOS\COMMAND.COM C:\DOS /E:1024 /P
```

Determining the correct environment size requires thought. If you make the environment too large, you will be wasting memory your application programs could be using.

Don't Call Technical Support Without Them!

Many users are often frustrated by the amount of time required to solve a problem when they call a company's technical support line for help. To save time and reduce your frustration, always have the following information available before you call technical support:

- The product serial number from your original disks or packaging.
- Your computer's BIOS type, version, and date, which is displayed when you first turn on your computer; your video type: monochrome, CGA, EGA, MCGA, or VGA; and ideally, the video board and monitor brand name.
- Your mouse type—serial or bus—as well as the version number of your mouse driver.
- Your DOS version.
- A current copy of your CONFIG.SYS and AUTOEXEC.BAT files. Use PRINT to print them.
- Your computer's current memory use. For DOS 4 or higher, issue the following MEM command: MEM /CLASSIFY > PRN.
- The amount of available disk space.
- Your printer type and connection (serial or parallel).
- A detailed description of the error, including a description of the error and a detailed list of the steps you performed to cause the error.

MORE15: A Timed MORE Command

Many users invoke the MORE command to view a file's contents one screenful at a time as shown here:

```
C:\> MORE < FILENAME.EXT <ENTER>
```

Likewise, users often redirect one program's output to become MORE's input as shown here:

```
C:\> DIR | MORE <ENTER>
```

When you use the MORE command, you must press a key each time you want to view the next screenful of information. The companion disk that accompanies this book provides the utility command MORE15.EXE which behaves similarly to MORE with the exception that if you don't press a key within 15 seconds, the program automatically displays the next screenful of information.

You can use MORE15 just as you would the MORE command. The following command, for example, uses MORE15 to display a directory listing a screenful at a time:

```
C:\> DIR | MORE15 <ENTER>
```

Likewise, this command displays a file's contents a screenful at a time:

```
C:\> MORE15 < FILENAME.EXT <ENTER>
```

MORE15.EXE

The utility program MORE15.EXE resides on the companion disk that accompanies this book.

ASCII and Extended ASCII Characters

Several tips in this book discuss the use of ASCII and extended ASCII characters. The companion disk that accompanies this book contains the utility program ASCII.EXE that displays the ASCII and extended ASCII character sets. To display the characters on your screen, invoke ASCII as shown here:

```
C:\> ASCII <ENTER>
```

To print an ASCII table, redirect ASCII's output to the printer as shown here:

```
C:\> ASCII > PRN <ENTER>
```

ASCII.EXE

The utility command ASCII.EXE resides on the companion disk that accompanies this book.

Changing the Number of Lines Your Screen Displays

By default your screen displays 25 lines of text, each containing up to 80 characters. If you are using an EGA or VGA monitor, you can select 43 (EGA) or 50 (VGA) line display. When you select one of these display modes, the PC will compress the text size, increasing the number of text lines. Place the ANSI.SYS entry in your CONFIG.SYS file and reboot. After your system starts, use one of the following MODE commands to select the desired number of text rows:

```
C:\> MODE CON LINES=43 <ENTER>

C:\> MODE CON LINES=50 <ENTER>
```

To restore the screen to 25 line mode, issue the following MODE command:

```
C:\> MODE CON LINES=25 <ENTER>
```

Not all programs support 43 or 50 line display, so you may have to toggle between 25 line and compressed mode. To use this command, you must have an EGA or VGA monitor.

Improving Performance by Turning Disk Verification Off

When the PC was first introduced, hard disks were much less reliable than they are today. Because of that, DOS included the VERIFY command, which directed DOS to ensure data written to disk was recorded correctly. To perform the verification, the disk controller typically reread the data written to disk and compared it to the original data. Because disk recording errors are rare, DOS does not automatically use disk verification. To use it, you must invoke the VERIFY command as shown here:

```
C:\> VERIFY ON <ENTER>
```

Although disk verification increases the likelihood of detecting a disk error, it does so at a large cost to performance. Because the disk is a mechanical device, it is much slower than your computer's electrical components. Unfortunately, when you turn on disk verification, you increase disk operations, decreasing system performance. Because disk record errors are very rare, you should turn verification off for normal operations using the following VERIFY command:

```
C:\> VERIFY OFF <ENTER>
```

If you later run a critical program such as a database or system back up, you can first turn disk verification on, run the program, and then turn verification off once again.

Turn Off Disk Verification and Extended CTRL-BREAK Checking in One Step

As discussed in Tip 9, extended CTRL-BREAK checking slows down your system's performance. Likewise, as discussed in Tip 18, verification slows down disk I/O operations, which also decreases your system's performance. Normally, you should turn both off. The following DEBUG script file, SLOWPOKE.SCR, creates the command file SLOWPOKE.COM that turns off extended CTRL-BREAK checking and disk verification in one step:

SLOWPOKE.SCR

```
N SLOWPOKE.COM <ENTER>
A 100          <ENTER>
MOV AX,2E00    <ENTER>
INT 21         <ENTER>
MOV AX,3301    <ENTER>
MOV DL,0       <ENTER>
INT 21         <ENTER>
MOV AH,4C      <ENTER>
INT 21         <ENTER>
               <ENTER>
R CX           <ENTER>
10             <ENTER>
W              <ENTER>
Q              <ENTER>
```

Use the DEBUG command as follows to create the command file SLOWPOKE.COM:

```
C:\> DEBUG < SLOWPOKE.SCR <ENTER>
```

Disabling AUTOEXEC.BAT

As discussed in Tip 444, using the CONFIG.SYS SHELL entry you can specify the directory that contains the command processor (COMMAND.COM) as well as the size of environment. Normally, the SHELL entry takes the following form:

```
SHELL=C:\DOS\COMMAND.COM C:\DOS /P
```

The /P switch directs DOS to execute the AUTOEXEC.BAT file at system startup. If the file does not exist, DOS instead executes the DATE and TIME commands. If you remove the /P switch from the SHELL entry, DOS will neither execute AUTOEXEC.BAT nor DATE and TIME.

Warning: If you disable AUTOEXEC.BAT in this way, invoking the EXIT command without first executing a second copy of the command, the processor will hang up the system.

Recording the Date and Time the System Was Last Booted

Sometimes you may want to know when the system was last booted. To find out, create a file named ENTER.DAT that contains a carriage return and line feed as shown here:

```
C:\> COPY CON \ENTER.DAT <ENTER>
<ENTER>
^Z   <ENTER>
            1 file(s) copied
```

Next, place the following lines in your AUTOEXEC.BAT to create a file named LASTBOOT.DAT:

```
DATE < \ENTER.DAT > LASTBOOT.DAT
TIME < \ENTER.DAT >> LASTBOOT.DAT
```

Each time your system starts, DOS will automatically create a new LASTBOOT.DAT file that contains the current system date and time. To display the boot information, use TYPE as shown here:

```
C:\> TYPE \LASTBOOT.DAT <ENTER>
```

Note that for simplicity, we have assumed the files ENTER.DAT and LASTBOOT.DAT reside in the root directory. A better solution would be to place the files in a different directory.

Determining the Correct Number of Disk Buffers

The CONFIG.SYS BUFFERS entry lets you specify the number of disk buffers DOS allocates at system startup. Use the BUFFERS settings listed in Table 22a according to your system type.

If you don't specify a BUFFERS entry, DOS uses the default value listed in Table 22b.

Table 22a. Recommended Disk Buffer Settings

System Type	Buffer Recommendation
8088	20
80286	25
80386	30
80486	35

Table 22b. Default Buffers Settings for Various RAM Configurations

System RAM	Default Buffers Setting
128Kb or less	2 for 360Kb disk 3 for disks larger than 360Kb
129Kb to 255Kb	5
256Kb to 511Kb	10
512Kb to 640Kb	15

If you are using the SMARTDRV disk cache, reduce the number of disk buffers to three as shown here:

```
BUFFERS=3
```

A More Flexible TYPE Command

The TYPE command lets you display an ASCII file's contents on your screen. TYPE lets you specify the name of only one file at a time and does not support wildcard characters. By creating the following batch file, MYTYPE.BAT, you can create a TYPE-like command that supports both multiple filenames and wildcards:

```
@ECHO OFF
:GET_NEXT_FILE
SHIFT
IF '%0'=='' GOTO DONE
FOR %%I IN (%0) DO TYPE %%I
GOTO GET_NEXT_FILE
:DONE
```

Using MYTYPE.BAT, the following command displays the contents of the files AUTOEXEC.BAT and CONFIG.SYS, one file after the other:

```
C:\> MYTYPE \AUTOEXEC.BAT \CONFIG.SYS <ENTER>
```

Likewise, this command displays the contents of every batch file in the current directory:

```
C:\> MYTYPE *.BAT <ENTER>
```

Sometimes Order Is Important

The CONFIG.SYS DEVICE entry lets you install a device driver such as ANSI.SYS or HIMEM.SYS or a mouse driver. When you install a device driver, DOS creates a chain of drivers in the order in which the drivers appear in your CONFIG.SYS file. Each time DOS must open one of these devices, DOS searches the chain of entries for the desired driver, so you want the device drivers you expect DOS to use most often as early in the list as possible.

When you place DEVICE entries in CONFIG.SYS, order the entries from most to least commonly used.

Turn Off Your System Only from the DOS Prompt

One of the most important rules you must remember is to turn off your computer only from the DOS prompt. If you turn off your computer while another program is active, you risk damaging your disk and files. Here's why. To reduce slow disk I/O operations, DOS writes its disk output to buffers in memory (the disk buffers created by the CONFIG.SYS BUFFERS entry). Normally, DOS writes the buffers to disk only when a buffer fills, the program ends, or the program specifically asks DOS to flush the buffers. So, although your program thinks it has written information to disk, the information

may still reside in a disk buffer. If you turn off your computer, the information will be lost. To avoid this possible data loss, always end your program and return to DOS before you turn off your computer. Do not, for example, turn off your computer from within Windows or the DOS shell.

When You Need an FCBS CONFIG.SYS Entry

Many users have an FCBS entry in their CONFIG.SYS file from long ago and may not remember why. When DOS was first released in 1981, DOS performed file input and output using file control blocks (FCBS).

In DOS version 2.0, DOS changed from file control blocks to file handles (the CONFIG.SYS FILES entry). To provide support for older programs that use file control blocks, DOS provides the CONFIG.SYS FCBS entry. Unless you are running a very old DOS program (pre-1985) you can remove the FCBS entry from your CONFIG.SYS file. In most cases, the entry is unnecessarily memory consuming. If you have a very old program that encounters file open errors, add an FCBS entry similar to the following:

```
FCBS=16
```

Note that historically, DOS replaced FCBS with file handles in DOS version 2 because the FCBS structure does not support subdirectories.

When You Need to Use the LASTDRIVE

DOS supports two types of disk drives: physical and logical drives. Physical drives are easy to understand; they are the disk drives such as drives A and C that are physically installed in your

computer. You can touch a physical drive. A logical drive, on the other hand, is a drive letter used to refer to a directory or RAM drive. The SUBST command (see Tip 453), for example, lets you abbreviate a directory name by using a logical disk drive letter.

By default, DOS supports only the drive letters A through E. If you want to assign other logical drive letters, you must use the CONFIG.SYS LASTDRIVE entry. The LASTDRIVE entry specifies the drive letter of the last logical drive you plan to use. DOS lets you use drives A through Z. The following LASTDRIVE entry selects drive M as the last drive:

```
LASTDRIVE=M
```

When you assign the LASTDRIVE entry, keep in mind that each logical drive entry consumes 80 to 96 bytes of memory. If you specify drive Z as the last drive entry, but you don't use very many logical drives, you are simply wasting memory.

Redefining DOS 5 Internal Commands

If a program or batch file has the same name as an internal DOS command, the program or batch file will never execute because DOS will always execute the internal DOS command instead.

However, if you are using DOS 5, you can use DOSKEY macros to redefine an internal DOS command. For example, the following DOSKEY macro redefines the TYPE command, allowing it to support wildcard characters and command-line parameters:

```
C:\> DOSKEY TYPE=FOR %I IN ($*) DO TYPE %I <ENTER>
```

If you want to disable an internal DOS command, you can do that as well. The following DOSKEY command directs DOS to ignore DEL:

```
C:\> DOSKEY DEL=ECHO. <ENTER>
```

If you don't want new users using various commands, you can turn the commands off by using DOSKEY in this way.

To use DOSKEY macros, you must be using DOS 5.

Generating an Escape Character

Several of the ANSI.SYS and HP printer tips presented in this book require the use of an escape sequence. Tip 34 describes how you enter an escape sequence by using the EDLIN editor. Tip 42 discusses how you would create an escape sequence by using EDIT. The following DEBUG script file ESCAPE.SCR creates a command file named ESCAPE.COM that writes the ASCII ESC character followed by the text you specify:

```
N ESCAPE.COM         <ENTER>
A 100                <ENTER>
MOV AH,2             <ENTER>
MOV DL,1B            <ENTER>
INT 21               <ENTER>
MOV BX,80            <ENTER>
INC BX               <ENTER>
CMP BYTE [BX],D      <ENTER>
JNE 109              <ENTER>
MOV BYTE [BX],24     <ENTER>
MOV AH,9             <ENTER>
MOV DX,82            <ENTER>
CMP DX,BX            <ENTER>
JG  11D              <ENTER>
INT 21               <ENTER>
MOV AH,4C            <ENTER>
INT 21               <ENTER>
                     <ENTER>
R CX                 <ENTER>
21                   <ENTER>
W                    <ENTER>
Q                    <ENTER>
```

ESCAPE.SCR

Use DEBUG as follows to create the command file ESCAPE.COM;

```
C:\> DEBUG < ESCAPE.SCR <ENTER>
```

Assuming you have installed the ANSI.SYS device driver, you can use ESCAPE as follows to select a blue screen background:

```
C:\> ESCAPE [44m <ENTER>
```

When you use ESCAPE, you must place the desired escape sequence one space after the ESCAPE command.

Automatic Fail on Critical Errors

A critical error occurs when DOS encounters a situation from which it cannot continue without user intervention. In most cases, when DOS encounters a critical error, DOS displays the familiar message shown here:

```
Abort, Retry, Fail?
```

If your CONFIG.SYS file contains a SHELL entry (see Tip 444), you can add the /F switch to direct DOS to automatically select the Fail option as shown here:

```
SHELL=C:\DOS\COMMAND.COM C:\DOS /P /F
```

Using the /F switch in this way, DOS automatically selects the Fail option when a critical error occurs. By directing DOS to automatically select the Fail option, you can prevent new users from becoming confused by the "Abort, Retry, Fail?" message.

Understanding the PC's Interrupt Vectors

As shown here, the first 1,024 bytes of conventional memory contain the PC's 256 interrupt vectors:

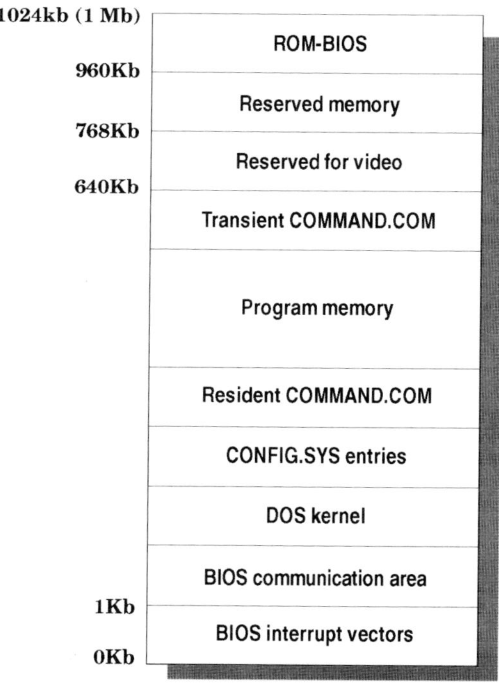

A vector is a 4-byte segment and offset address of the memory location containing the instructions the PC executes when a specific event occurs.

Table 31 lists the events that correspond to each vector.

Table 31. PC Interrupt Vectors and Their Uses

Interrupt Number	Purpose	Interrupt Number	Purpose
00H	Hardware divide by zero	1EH	Disk parameter table
01H	Hardware single step trap	1FH	Graphics character table
02H	Nonmaskable interrupt	20H	DOS terminate program
03H	Debugger breakpoint set	21H	DOS system services
04H	Arithmetic overflow	22H	Program terminate
05H	BIOS print screen	23H	DOS CTRL-BREAK
08H	IRQ0 clock tick	24H	DOS critical-error handler
09H	IRQ1 keyboard	25H	DOS disk read
0AH	IRQ2	26H	DOS disk write
0BH	IRQ3 COM2	27H	DOS terminate resident
0CH	IRQ4 COM1	28H	DOS idle
0DH	IRQ5 PC/XT hard disk or IRQ5 PC/AT LPT2	29H	DOS fast putchar
		2AH	MS-Net services
0EH	IRQ6 diskette	2EH	DOS primary shell program loader
0FH	IRQ7 LPT1		
10H	BIOS video services	2FH	DOS multiplex interrupt
11H	BIOS equipment list service	33H	Mouse services
12H	BIOS memory size service	40H	Diskette vector if hard disk present
13H	BIOS disk services		
14H	BIOS communication services	41H	Hard disk parameter table
		42H	EGA BIOS redirection
15H	BIOS miscellaneous services	43H	EGA parameter table
16H	BIOS keyboard services	44H	EGA character table
17H	BIOS printer services	4AH	PC/AT Int 70H alarm
18H	Invoke ROM-BASIC	5CH	NetBIOS services
19H	System reboot	67H	EMS services
1AH	BIOS time-of-day services	70H	IRQ8 PC/AT real-time clock
1BH	CTRL-BREAK handler	71H	IRQ9 PC/AT redirect of Int 0AH
1CH	Called by Int 08H handler		
1DH	Video parameter table	75H	IRQ13 PC/AT math coprocessor

The companion disk that accompanies this book contains a utility program named SHOWVECT.EXE that displays the current address for each of the PC's 256 vectors. To display the vectors, invoke the program from the DOS prompt as shown here:

```
C:\> SHOWVECT <ENTER>
```

If you periodically redirect the program's output to a file, you can use the COMP command to compare the current vector settings.

The utility command SHOWVECT.EXE resides on the companion disk that accompanies this book.

SHOWVECT.EXE

The Secret to Printing Your Screen Contents

The SHIFT-PRTSC keyboard combination directs your computer to print your screen's current contents. If your printer is attached to a serial port, you must first issue the following MODE command to direct DOS to use the serial port instead of LPT1:

```
C:\> MODE LPT1:=COM1: <ENTER>
```

If you want to print the contents of a screen that contains graphics, you must first issue the GRAPHICS command, which installs a memory-resident program to help print the graphics:

```
C:\> GRAPHICS <ENTER>
```

Selecting a Screen Background Color with ANSI.SYS

The ANSI.SYS device driver lets you increase video and keyboard capabilities provided by DOS. Using the ANSI.SYS device driver, for example, you can select the screen's background color. The ANSI driver uses various escape sequences to accomplish specific tasks. To select a screen background color, you must use the escape sequence Esc[ColorValuem. Table 33 lists the background color values.

Table 33. Background Color Values Supported by ANSI.SYS

Color Value	Background Color	Escape Sequence
40	Black	Esc[40m
41	Red	Esc[41m
42	Green	Esc[42m
43	Yellow	Esc[43m
44	Blue	Esc[44m
45	Magenta	Esc[45m
46	Cyan	Esc[46m
47	White	Esc[47m

Using the ESCAPE command discussed in Tip 29, the following commands select a red background:

```
@ECHO OFF
ESCAPE [41m
CLS
```

In this case, the escape sequence selects the red background, and the CLS command applies the color to the entire screen.

Creating an Escape Sequence with EDLIN

An escape sequence is a series of characters beginning with the ASCII escape character (ASCII 27).

Using the EDLIN line editor, you can create batch files that write escape sequences with ECHO, or you can create files that contain the escape sequence that you later display with TYPE or print. To create the escape character within EDLIN, you must hold down the CTRL key, press **V**, and then type the left bracket character.

Use the following steps to create a batch file named YELLOW.BAT that ECHOs the escape sequence Esc[43m to select a yellow background:

1. Invoke EDLIN with the filename YELLOW.BAT:

   ```
   C:\> EDLIN YELLOW.BAT <ENTER>
   New file
   *
   ```

2. Use EDLIN's Insert command to add the batch file command:

   ```
   *I <ENTER>
   1:*
   ```

3. Type the word ECHO followed by a space. Hold down the CTRL key and press **V**. Your screen will display the characters ^V as shown here:

   ```
   1:*ECHO ^V
   ```

4. Type the left bracket character [to complete the escape character:

   ```
   1:*ECHO ^V[
   ```

5. Finish the escape sequence by typing [**43m**, as shown here:

   ```
   1:*ECHO ^V[[43m <ENTER>
   2:*
   ```

6. End the batch file edit by pressing CTRL-C and issuing EDLIN's Exit command.

   ```
   2:*^C
   *E <ENTER>
   ```

The most common error users make when entering escape sequences with EDLIN is including only one left bracket [.

What Device Drivers Are Installed?

If you examine the contents of your CONFIG.SYS file, you can use the DEVICE entries to determine which device drivers you have installed. DOS, however, has two types of device drivers: those installed by the user, and those that reside in the DOS kernel itself. To view the names of all device drivers in your system, issue the following MEM command:

```
C:\> MEM /DEBUG <ENTER>
```

MEM will list the names of system device drivers and installed device drivers. For a disk to be bootable, the disk must contain two hidden files: IO.SYS and MSDOS.SYS. The file IO.SYS contains the system device drivers DOS uses for your screen, keyboard, disks, and printers.

To use the MEM command, you must be using DOS 4 or later.

A Quick Way to Perform Hexadecimal Addition and Subtraction

Many DOS commands work in hexadecimal format, the base-16 numbering system. Sometimes you may need to add or subtract two hexadecimal numbers. To perform hexadecimal calculations, invoke the DEBUG command:

```
C:\> DEBUG <ENTER>
```

When DEBUG displays its hyphen prompt (-), issue the DEBUG hexadecimal command (H) with the two numbers. For example, the following command adds and subtracts the hexadecimal values FE and F.

```
-H FE F <ENTER>
010D 00EF
```

The first value displayed is the result of the addition. The second number displayed is the result of the subtraction. Using DEBUG to perform such calculations is very straightforward.

Using the FOR Command from the DOS Prompt

Several of the tips presented in this book use the FOR command in batch files to apply a command to a specific set of files. DOS lets you use the FOR command from the DOS prompt as well as from within your batch files. When you use FOR from the DOS prompt, however, you place only one % (percent) sign in front of your variable names. If, for example, you want to display the contents of every batch file in the current directory, you would use FOR as follows:

```
C:\> FOR %I IN (*.BAT) DO TYPE %I <ENTER>
```

In this case, FOR will expand *.BAT into the corresponding filenames, invoking the TYPE commands one at a time with each name. Similarly, the following command directs FOR to display the contents of each batch file in the current directory, as well as each file with the TXT extension:

```
C:\> FOR %I IN (*.BAT *.TXT) DO TYPE %I <ENTER>
```

Is DOS in RAM or ROM?

Beginning with DOS 5, many notebook and laptop computers provide DOS in ROM (read-only memory) as opposed to on a disk that later gets loaded into RAM. The

following DEBUG script file, ISDOSROM.SCR, creates a command file named ISDOSROM.COM that returns the exit status value 1 for a ROM-based version of DOS and returns 0 otherwise:

ISDOSROM.SCR

```
N ISDOSROM.COM <ENTER>
A 100          <ENTER>
MOV AX,3001    <ENTER>
INT 21         <ENTER>
MOV AL,0       <ENTER>
CMP BH,8       <ENTER>
JNE 10E        <ENTER>
INC AL         <ENTER>
MOV AH,4C      <ENTER>
INT 21         <ENTER>
               <ENTER>
R CX           <ENTER>
12             <ENTER>
W              <ENTER>
Q              <ENTER>
```

The following batch commands illustrate how you might use ISDOSROM:

```
ISDOSROM
IF ERRORLEVEL 1 GOTO ROM_DOS
GOTO RAM_DOS
REM Other batch commands here
```

Determining Whether SHARE Is Installed

As Tip 346 discusses, if you are using DOS 4.0 and you are using a disk with partitions larger than 32Mb, you need to install the SHARE command. Likewise, if you are using Microsoft Windows and two or more of your programs share the same file, its a good habit to first install the SHARE command.

The following DEBUG script file, ISSHARE.SCR, creates the command file ISSHARE.COM that returns the exit status value 1 if share is installed and returns 0 otherwise:

```
N ISSHARE.COM <ENTER>
A 100         <ENTER>
MOV AX,1000   <ENTER>
INT 2F        <ENTER>
AND AL,1      <ENTER>
MOV AH,4C     <ENTER>
INT 21        <ENTER>
              <ENTER>
R CX          <ENTER>
B             <ENTER>
W             <ENTER>
Q             <ENTER>
```

ISSHARE.SCR

Use the DEBUG command as follows to create the command file ISSHARE.COM:

```
C:\> DEBUG < ISSHARE.SCR <ENTER>
```

Next, in your AUTOEXEC.BAT file, you can test whether SHARE is installed and, if it is not, install it, as shown here:

```
ISSHARE
IF NOT ERRORLEVEL 1 SHARE
```

If you are using DOS 5 and have support for the upper-memory area (see Tip 223), use the LOADHIGH command to invoke SHARE.

Do not invoke SHARE unless you are using DOS 4 with partitions larger then 32Mb or sharing files within Windows.

SHARE adds overhead with every read or write operation, which decreases your system performance.

Clearing the Screen with ANSI.SYS

Tip 33 explains how to set your screen's background color by using ANSI.SYS escape sequences. Tip 44 discusses how to use escape sequences to set the screen's foreground colors. In addition to letting you control screen colors, you can use an ANSI.SYS escape sequence to clean your screen display. Because most users use the CLS command, many don't understand why they would want to use the escape sequence Esc[2J to clear their screens.

Consider the following batch file REDBACK.BAT that uses the ANSI escape sequence Esc[41m to select a red background color:

```
@ECHO OFF
ECHO Esc[41m
CLS
```

After the ECHO command selects the red background color, the CLS command clears the screen, applying the color to the entire screen.

Although the batch file works, the use of CLS requires the batch file to execute an extra command, which decreases system performance. A better batch file would echo the escape sequence Esc[41m to select the red background and Esc[2J to clear the screen as shown here:

```
@ECHO OFF
ECHO Esc[41mEsc[2J
```

The previous batch files use the letters Esc to represent the unprintable ASCII escape character. In your batch files, however, you must insert the actual character as discussed in Tip 34.

Using CHKANSI, batch files can determine whether or not the ANSI driver is installed and, if not, display an error message to the user.

Is ANSI.SYS Installed?

Several of the tips presented in this book take advantage of ANSI.SYS escape sequences. If you are using DOS 4 or higher, your batch files can use the command CHKANSI.COM to determine whether the ANSI driver is installed. The following DEBUG script file, CHKANSI.SCR, creates the CHKANSI.COM command file:

```
N CHKANSI.COM <ENTER>
A 100         <ENTER>
MOV AX,1A00   <ENTER>
INT 2F        <ENTER>
AND AL,1      <ENTER>
MOV AH,4C     <ENTER>
INT 21        <ENTER>
              <ENTER>
R CX          <ENTER>
B             <ENTER>
W             <ENTER>
Q             <ENTER>
```

CHKANSI.SCR

If your batch file uses the ANSI escape sequences, the batch file should first invoke CHKANSI to ensure that the ANSI.SYS driver is installed. If the driver is installed, CHKANSI returns the value 1; otherwise, it returns 0. Use DEBUG as follows to create the command file CHKANSI.COM:

```
C:\> DEBUG < CHKANSI.SCR <ENTER>
```

Creating an Escape Sequence with EDIT

Tip 34 discusses how you enter an escape sequence with the EDLIN command. If you are using DOS 5, you will find the full screen editor, EDIT, much easier to use than EDLIN. Using EDIT, you can

quickly create simple batch files. One of the common tasks you may want to perform is entering an escape sequence. To create an Esc character using EDIT, hold down the CTRL key and press **P**. Next, press the ESC key. Edit will display a left arrow. Type the remainder of the escape sequence.

To use the EDIT command, you must be using DOS 5.

Upgrading to DOS 5

Many people ask what DOS 5 offers; in other words, is it worth the upgrade cost? The answer is yes. If you aren't using DOS 5, you should upgrade. First, DOS 5 provides a collection of very powerful memory management techniques that let you maximize your use of conventional memory. Second, DOS 5 provides several disk utility commands that have been available in the past only through third-party software packages. Third, the DOSKEY command improves command-line recall and lets you replace small batch files with faster, RAM-based macros that consume less disk space. Last, DOS 5 now supports disk partitions of up to 2 gigabytes in size. Table 43 lists the new commands introduced with DOS 5.

Table 43. Commands Introduced with DOS Version 5

DOSKEY	EXPAND	EDIT	LOADFIX
LOADHIGH	MIRROR	SETVER	UNDELETE
UNFORMAT			

Selecting a Screen Foreground Color with ANSI.SYS

Tip 33 discusses how you would select a screen background color by using ANSI.SYS. You can use the same escape sequence, Esc[colorm, to select a foreground color. Table 44 lists the foreground color values.

The escape sequence Esc[33m, for example, selects a yellow foreground color. The following batch file, GREENFG.BAT, uses the ECHO command to select a green foreground color:

```
@ECHO OFF
ECHO Esc[32m
CLS
```

In addition to letting you individually select foreground and background colors, the ANSI driver lets you specify both colors in the same escape sequence, by separating the color values with a semicolon. For example, the escape sequence Esc[44;37m selects a blue background and a white foreground color.

Table 44. ANSI.SYS Foreground Color Values

Color Value	Foreground Color	Escape Sequence
30	Black	Esc[30m
31	Red	Esc[31m
32	Green	Esc[32m
33	Yellow	Esc[33m
34	Blue	Esc[34m
35	Magenta	Esc[35m
36	Cyan	Esc[36m
37	White	Esc[37m

The batch files presented here used the characters "Esc" to represent the unprintable ASCII escape character. In your batch files you must use the actual escape character as discussed in Tip 34.

Generating an Escape Sequence with the PROMPT Command

Several of the tips presented in this book discuss the use of ANSI escape sequences for selecting screen colors (see Tip 33 and Tip 44). Using the PROMPT command's $E metacharacter, you can generate an escape sequence in your prompt. The following command uses the ANSI escape sequence Esc[colorm to select various screen colors:

```
C:\> PROMPT $e[44;37m$p$g$e[40m <ENTER>
```

To begin, the letters $e[44;37m select a blue background and a white foreground color. Next, the pg characters direct PROMPT to display the current drive and directory name in the prompt followed by the greater-than symbol. The letters $e[40m select a black background. Your system prompt then appears in blue and white.

Using ANSI.SYS Text Attributes

Tip 33 and Tip 44 explain how to use ANSI escape sequences to select foreground and background colors. In a similar way, you can use the escape sequence Esc[Attributem to select one of the text attributes, such as blinking or bold, that are listed in Table 46.

Table 46. ANSI.SYS Text Attribute Values

Attribute Value	Attribute	Escape Sequence
0	Attributes off	Esc[0m
1	Bold	Esc[1m
4	Monochrome underline	Esc[4m
5	Blinking	Esc[5m
7	Reverse video	Esc[7m
8	Black on black	Esc[8m

Using these text attributes and ECHO or PAUSE, you can enhance the messages your batch files display as shown here:

```
@ECHO OFF
ECHO Esc[1mThis message is bold
ECHO Esc[5mThis message flashes
ECHO Esc[7mThis message appears in reverse video
```

You can also use the escape sequences in your system prompt. The following PROMPT command, for example, displays your command prompt in bold:

```
C:\> PROMPT $E[1m$p$g$E[0m <ENTER>
```

Creating a Custom Prompt

The PROMPT command lets you select the prompt DOS displays each time it is ready for you to enter a command. Although most systems use a prompt that includes the current drive and directory, the PROMPT command provides several capabilities that let you design a custom prompt. The format of the PROMPT command is simply PROMPT *text*. The text can contain letters and numbers as well as a special set of characters called metacharacters that you must precede with a dollar sign. Table 47 lists the PROMPT metacharacters.

Table 47. DOS PROMPT Command Metacharacters

Metacharacter	Meaning
$B	DOS pipe character (I)
$D	Current system date
$E	ASCII escape character
$H	Backspace character
$G	Greater-than symbol (>)
$L	Less-than symbol (<)
$N	Current disk drive letter
$P	Current drive and directory
$Q	Equal sign
$T	Current system time
$_	Carriage return and line feed
$$	Dollar sign
$V	MS-DOS version number

Using the PROMPT command you can include multiple metacharacters in succession or within other text. The most common PROMPT command includes the PG metacharacters directing DOS to display the current drive and directory followed by a greater-than character (>). However, the following prompt illustrates the versatility of the PROMPT command. First, the following PROMPT command directs DOS to display the current date and time on one line followed by the current drive and directory on the next:

```
C:\> PROMPT $D $T$_$P$G <ENTER>
Fri 07-17-1992 12:49:04.38
C:\>
```

You issue this command from the DOS prompt or from within your AUTOEXEC.BAT file.

In a similar way, the following PROMPT command illustrates the use of the backspace character. The command erases the seconds and hundredths of seconds displayed in the current system time by the previous PROMPT command:

```
C:\> PROMPT $D $T$H$H$H$H$H$H$_$P$G <ENTER>
```

In this case, your prompt will appear similar to the following:

```
Fri 07-17-1992 12:49
C:\>
```

Experiment with the PROMPT command until you find a prompt that suits your needs. If you are using an ANSI.SYS device driver, see Tip 45 to learn how to incorporate colors into your system prompt.

System Startup Troubleshooting

When your system fails to start, you can check several items to isolate the source of the error:

- ❑ Are the computer and monitor plugged in? Verify that the outlets work by plugging in a different appliance.
- ❑ When you turn on your computer, can you hear the computer's internal fan whir? If not, your computer's power supply may be damaged and require servicing.
- ❑ Is your computer's monitor correctly attached to your computer's chassis? In addition to being plugged in to a wall outlet, the monitor must also connect to the computer chassis.
- ❑ Is your monitor's intensity correctly adjusted? The intensity controls the screen's brightness. If you cannot see text on your screen, the monitor's intensity may simply be set too low.
- ❑ Does your computer display a count of its internal memory on your screen? If not, or if the count does not complete, your computer is failing its memory or power-on self-test and requires servicing.
- ❑ Does your computer illuminate drive A's activation light in search of a disk in drive A? If not, your computer is failing its power-on self-test and requires servicing.
- ❑ Does your monitor display the following error message?

  ```
  Non-System disk or disk error
  Replace and strike any key when ready
  ```

  If so, your computer very likely contains a floppy disk in drive A. If so, remove the disk and press a key. If not, your hard disk does not contain the hidden files IO.SYS and MSDOS.SYS that DOS needs to start. Boot your system from floppy disk and use the SYS command to transfer the files to your hard disk.

Understanding DEBUG Script Files

The DEBUG command was originally introduced to help programmers locate errors, or bugs, in their programs. Today, several much more powerful debuggers are available for programmers. Although few programmers use DEBUG today, many users continue to use DEBUG to create custom command files. To create command files, most users create files called DEBUG script files that contain the commands users would normally type at the DEBUG prompt. This tip examines the commands consistently found in DEBUG script files.

Consider the following DEBUG script file, which creates a command file named BELL.COM that sounds the computer's built-in speaker:

BELL.SCR

```
N BELL.COM <ENTER>
A 100      <ENTER>
MOV AH,2   <ENTER>
MOV DL,7   <ENTER>
INT 21     <ENTER>
MOV AH,4C  <ENTER>
INT 21     <ENTER>
           <ENTER>
R CX       <ENTER>
A          <ENTER>
W          <ENTER>
Q          <ENTER>
```

To begin, the DEBUG's N command specifies the name of the file to which DEBUG will write the command file. Next, a command file contains several instructions that direct the computer to perform specific operations. The command A 100 directs DEBUG to enter the assembly language commands that follow, beginning at the hexadecimal offset 100. All of the commands you create using DEBUG will always start their instructions at offset 100.

Depending on the command's purpose, the assembly language's instructions will differ. Most, however, will end with the instructions MOV AH, 4C, INT 21, which tells DOS to end your command. The blank line that follows the last assembly language instruction is mandatory. Next, you must tell DEBUG the size of the command file.

The command R CX lets you assign the command's size (in bytes) to the CX register. The W command directs DEBUG to write the file to disk. Last, the Q command ends the current DEBUG session. When you redirect the contents of a DEBUG script file to the DEBUG command, DEBUG will process the script file's commands just as if you had entered them from the DEBUG prompt.

Using the Extended ASCII Box Characters

Tip 16 presents the ASCII command that lets you display the PC's ASCII and extended ASCII character set. The extended ASCII character set contains a set of characters, shown here, that you can use to create boxes:

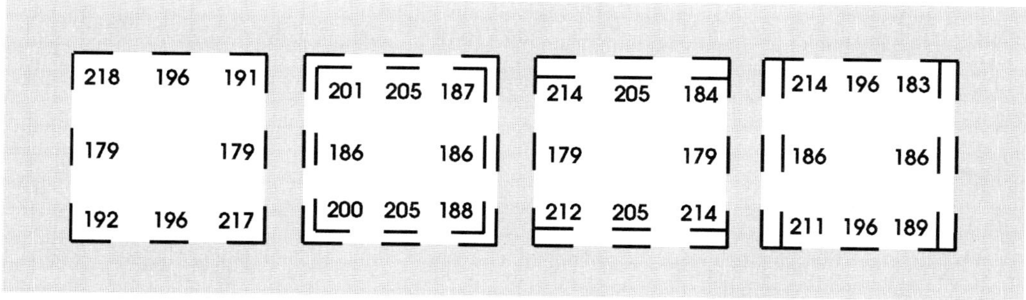

If you are listing menu-driven batch files, you can box menus by using the following characters with ECHO as shown here:

```
@ECHO OFF
ECHO
ECHO                MENU
ECHO
ECHO     PH Directory Listing
ECHO     F2 CHKDSK Command
ECHO     F3 Quit
ECHO
ECHO
```

If you are using a word processor to create your batch files, refer to the word processor's documentation to determine how to enter extended ASCII characters.

Taking a Critical Look at Your Command Path

Tip 446 discusses the importance of sequencing directories within your command according to the directory's likelihood of containing commonly used commands. Likewise, you should clean up and organize the files in the command path directories to achieve maximum performance. The following batch file, SHOWPATH.BAT, prints a listing of every file that resides in your command path:

```
@ECHO OFF
FOR %%I IN (%PATH%) DO DIR %%I > PRN
```

Invoke this batch file and take a critical look at the files each directory contains, organizing the directory's entries to improve performance.

To use the batch file SHOWPATH.BAT, you must be using DOS 3.3 or higher (to support named parameters).

Preventing Screen Burn-in

If the same image appears on your screen for a long period of time, it's possible for the image to actually become "burned into" your screen. A screen saver is a program that runs while your computer is inactive, either blanking the screen or displaying an image that continually changes, both of which prevent screen burn-in. In most cases, screen savers are memory-resident programs that consume memory and become active at fixed time intervals. At times, you may want

to simply activate a screen-saving program that runs while you are temporarily away from your PC. The following batch file, SAVER.BAT, creates a QBasic program that draws random spheres on your screen until you press a key:

```
@ECHO OFF
ECHO SCREEN 1  > SAVER.BAS
ECHO WHILE INKEY$ = "" >> SAVER.BAS
ECHO   X = RND * 320 >> SAVER.BAS
ECHO   Y = RND * 200 >> SAVER.BAS
ECHO   CLR = RND * 4 >> SAVER.BAS
ECHO   CIRCLE (X, Y), RND * 100, CLR  >> SAVER.BAS
ECHO   PAINT (X, Y), RND * 4, CLR  >> SAVER.BAS
ECHO WEND  >> SAVER.BAS
ECHO SYSTEM  >> SAVER.BAS
QBASIC /RUN SAVER.BAS
DEL SAVER.BAS
```

To use QBasic, you must be using DOS 5 or higher. If you are using an earlier version of DOS, change the batch file to use GWBASIC or BASICA.

Understanding Megahertz

When users discuss CPUs, they normally refer to the processor's speed in terms of megahertz (MHz). Here's what they mean. The CPU has a small built-in clock that controls how fast operations can occur within the processor. The processor's speed in megahertz describes how often the clock ticks per second. A CPU with.a clock speed of 20MHz ticks 20 million times per second. Likewise, a 33MHz CPU ticks 33 million times per second. On a 386 computer, for example, an ADD instruction takes 2 clock ticks. Obviously, the computer whose clock ticks faster can perform the instruction faster. Because programs are made up of many instructions, each of which requires a specific number of clock ticks, the CPU that ticks fastest executes the program fastest.

Low-Tech Adding Machine

Many users will tell you they use their computer as a calculator. However, doing so isn't as easy as it may seem. On its own, DOS doesn't provide a calculator. However, the following batch file, MATH.BAT, does:

```
@ECHO OFF
:LOOP
SHIFT
IF '%0'=='' GOTO RESULT
SET EXPRESSION=%EXPRESSION% %0
GOTO LOOP
:RESULT
ECHO PRINT %EXPRESSION% > MATH.BAS
ECHO SYSTEM >> MATH.BAS
QBASIC /RUN MATH.BAS
SET EXPRESSION=
```

To use MATH.BAT to perform calculations, invoke the batch file with the desired expression as shown here:

```
C:\> MATH 3.15*7.27 <ENTER>
```

By grouping expressions within parentheses, you can force operation precedence. For example, the following command adds the expressions that appear within the parentheses before performing the multiplication:

```
C:\> MATH  (2+3)*(4+1) <ENTER>
```

MATH.BAT uses QBASIC, which requires DOS 5. If you are using a different version of DOS, change the batch file to use GWBASIC or BASICA.

Using the SETVER Device Driver

When you upgrade to DOS 5, you may find that programs that were written to support a previous version of DOS now display the following message:

```
Invalid DOS version
```

To help you run these commands, DOS 5 provides the SETVER command. SEVTER intercepts a program's request for the current DOS version number and returns a version you have previously specified that lets the program run. For example, if you have a program named FOURONLY.COM that runs only under DOS 4, you would invoke SETVER as follows:

```
C:\> SETVER  FOURONLY.COM 4.0 <ENTER>
```

When you later invoke FOURONLY, SETVER will tell the program that it is running under DOS 4.0. Before you can use SETVER, you must install it as a device driver within your CONFIG.SYS file as follows:

```
DEVICE=C:\DOS\SETVER.EXE <ENTER>
```

If you are using the DOS 5 memory arrangement techniques, use DEVICEHIGH to install the driver.

Making Room for New SETVER Entries

Tip 55 describes the DOS 5 SETVER command and when you may need to use it. If you invoke SETVER with no parameters, SETVER will display its current program and version-number settings. SETVER stores its current program settings in the file SETVER.EXE. If, when you try to add a SETVER entry, SETVER has no more room to hold the entry, SETVER will display the following message:

```
There is no more space in version table for new entries
```

If this error message occurs, remove one or more of SETVER's entries that you don't need by using SETVER's /DELETE switch as shown here:

```
C:\> SETVER EntryName /DELETE <ENTER>
```

Catch That Bus!

Within your computer's chassis, communication between devices occurs over a collection of wires called a bus. When the original IBM PC shipped in 1981, the bus contained eight data wires that let devices exchange one byte of information at a time. When the PC AT was released in 1984, it brought with it a 16-bit bus that was named the ISA, or industry-standard architecture, bus. With the 386 computer came a larger, 32-bit bus called the EISA, or extended industry-standard architecture, bus. Regardless of the number of bits that a bus supports, the purpose of the bus is simply to exchange information via electronic signals. The more wires, the more information the bus can exchange in a shorter period of time. To support boards designed for each bus, older computers provided 8- and 16-bit bus slots. Today, newer computers also provide only 32-bit bus slots; however, the slots fully support 8- and 16-bit boards. If you are buying a board for your system, you need first to match the board type to your bus. In other words, if your computer has an ISA bus, you must use an ISA board.

If you are using an IBM PS/2 system, on the other hand, the PS/2 uses a unique 32-bit bus called the microchannel architecture, or MCA, bus. A board designed for an EISA bus will not work with the MCA. Likewise, boards designed for the MCA will not work in a clone that uses the EISA bus. As a result, you can't pull a board out of your PS/2 and use it in a clone, or vice versa.

Placing the Cursor at a Specific Row and Column

If your batch files display menus or other user messages, you may sometimes want the messages to appear at specific screen locations. Using an ANSI escape sequence, you can place the cursor at a

specific row and column position on your screen. The format of this escape sequence is Esc[Row;ColumnH. The following batch commands use the cursor positioning escape sequence to display a menu of options near the center of your screen:

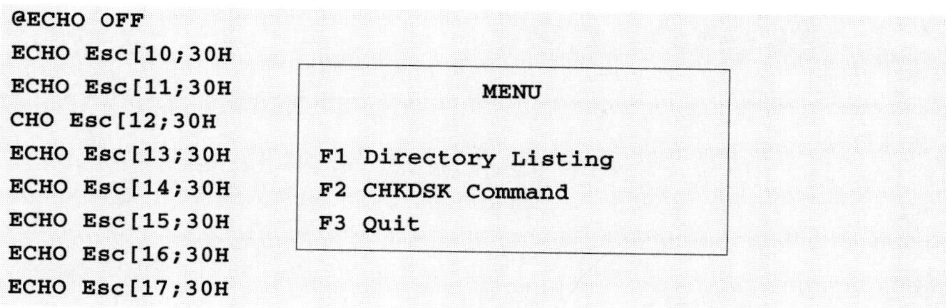

```
@ECHO OFF
ECHO Esc[10;30H
ECHO Esc[11;30H
CHO Esc[12;30H
ECHO Esc[13;30H
ECHO Esc[14;30H
ECHO Esc[15;30H
ECHO Esc[16;30H
ECHO Esc[17;30H
```

```
            MENU

F1 Directory Listing
F2 CHKDSK Command
F3 Quit
```

The preceding batch file uses the letters "Esc" to represent the unprintable ASCII escape character. Within your batch file, however, you must place the actual escape character as Tip 50 explains.

Moving the Cursor Up, Down, Left, or Right

Tip 58 explained how to use an ANSI escape sequence to move the cursor to a specific row and column position. The ANSI driver also provides four escape sequences that let you move the cursor's position left, right, up, and down. Table 59 lists these escape sequences.

Table 59. ANSI.SYS Cursor Movement Escape Sequences

Escape Sequence	Example	Movement
Esc[RowsA	Esc[5A	Moves cursor five rows up
Esc[RowsB	Esc[3B	Moves cursor three rows down
Esc[ColumnsC	Esc[2C	Moves cursor two columns right
Esc[ColumnsD	Esc[5D	Moves cursor five columns left

SX or DX: What's the Difference?

When you look at computer advertisements, you will see 386 and 486 computers listed as SX or DX machines. The SX machines are usually cheaper. Here's the difference: The 386 and 486 are both 32-bit processors. As Tip 57 explains, components within your computer communicate by sending electronic signals on a set of wires called a bus. The larger the bus, the more information the system can transfer at one time. The 386DX uses a 32-bit bus. The 386SX, on the other hand, uses a 16-bit bus, which slows down its data transfers. As a result, a 16MHz 386DX executes the same program faster than a 386SX. The 386DX and SX use an identical instruction set.

In a 486, the DX and SX both use a 32-bit bus. The 486DX, however, contains a math coprocessor, and the 486SX does not.

Displaying File or Command Output in Lowercase Letters

As Tip 442 discusses, using DOS 5 DIR /L switch lets you display a directory listing in lowercase letters. Similarly, the following DEBUG script file, LOWER.SCR, creates a command file named LOWER.COM that displays its redirected input in lowercase letters:

LOWER.SCR

```
N LOWER.COM    <ENTER>
A 100          <ENTER>
JMP 103        <ENTER>
DB '?'         <ENTER>
MOV AH,3F      <ENTER>
MOV BX,0       <ENTER>
MOV CX,1       <ENTER>
MOV DX,102     <ENTER>
INT 21         <ENTER>
CMP AX,0       <ENTER>
```

```
JE   12A        <ENTER>
MOV AL,[102]    <ENTER>
CMP AL,41       <ENTER>
JL   122        <ENTER>
CMP AL,5A       <ENTER>
JG   122        <ENTER>
ADD AL,20       <ENTER>
MOV DL,AL       <ENTER>
MOV AH,02       <ENTER>
INT 21          <ENTER>
JMP 103         <ENTER>
MOV AH,4C       <ENTER>
INT 21          <ENTER>
<ENTER>
R CX            <ENTER>
2E              <ENTER>
W               <ENTER>
Q               <ENTER>
```

To create the command file LOWER.COM, use the DEBUG command as follows:

```
C:\> DEBUG < LOWER.SCR <ENTER>
```

The following command, for example, displays the file CONFIG.SYS in lowercase letters:

```
C:\> LOWER < \CONFIG.SYS <ENTER>
```

Installing a Larger DOSKEY Buffer

Tip 305 describes how to track your commands by using the DOS 5 DOSKEY command; the number of commands you can track depends on the size of DOSKEY's memory buffer. Tip 343 describes how to replace simple batch files using DOSKEY macros; the number of macros you can create depends on their length as well as the size of the DOSKEY buffer. By default, DOSKEY uses a 512-byte buffer. To increase the size of the DOSKEY buffer, use the /BUFSIZE switch. The following DOSKEY command, for example, allocates a 2,048-byte buffer:

```
C:\> DOSKEY /BUFSIZE=2048 <ENTER>
```

DOSKEY lets you specify a buffer of up to 61,919 bytes. Most users will include a DOSKEY command in their AUTOEXEC.BAT file. If DOSKEY is already active, you can change the buffer size by combining the /BUFSIZE and /REINSTALL switches as shown here:

```
C:\> DOSKEY /REINSTALL /BUFSIZE=2048 <ENTER>
```

Be aware, however, that DOSKEY does not always behave as you might expect. See Tip 210.

DOS 5 Upgrade Users Beware

If you purchased and have installed the DOS 5 upgrade, be aware that unlike older versions of DOS, which let you build a new disk from scratch, the DOS 5 upgrade only lets you upgrade an existing system. If, for example, you inadvertently damage your hard disk, you may not be able to reinstall DOS using the upgrade. To prevent such a possibility, format a bootable floppy disk. Next, copy to the disk the following commands:

FORMAT.COM
FDISK.EXE
COMMAND.COM

Place this disk with your DOS 5 upgrade floppies. Should you ever need to rebuild your disk, you can partition your disk, format the disk as a bootable disk, and then perform the upgrade.

When to Use the CONFIG.SYS INSTALL Entry

If you are using DOS 5 and a 386 (or higher) computer, install DOS support for using upper memory blocks as discussed in Tip 223. Next, remove your CONFIG.SYS INSTALL entries, invoking the

identical commands from within AUTOEXEC.BAT by using LOADHIGH as discussed in Tip 225. If you are using DOS 4, using INSTALL to invoke memory-resident commands directs DOS to load the commands into memory before COMMAND.COM, a procedure less likely to restrict your environment entry's growth.

Understanding Your Environment Use

As Tip 13 discusses, DOS lets you increase the environment's size, either dynamically (if space exists) or by using the /E switch with the CONFIG.SYS SHELL entry. The companion disk that accompanies this book includes the utility command ENVUSE.EXE that displays the amount of memory currently allocated to the environment, the amount in use, and a message that describes whether or not DOS can dynamically increase the environment's size. To use ENVUSE, invoke the command from the DOS prompt as shown here:

```
C:\> ENVUSE <ENTER>
Environment block size 512 bytes
Environment space currently used 216
```

The utility command ENVUSE.EXE resides on the companion disk that accompanies this book.

ENVUSE.EXE

Testing for a Math Coprocessor

Depending on your existing software, you may need to include a command-line switch when you invoke a specific program if you want the program to use your PC's math coprocessor. The following

DEBUG script file, CHKMATH.SCR, creates a command file named CHKMATH.COM that returns the exit status value 1 if the PC contains a math coprocessor and returns 0 otherwise:

CHKMATH.SCR

```
N CHKMATH.COM <ENTER>
A 100         <ENTER>
MOV AX,40     <ENTER>
MOV DS,AX     <ENTER>
MOV AL,[10]   <ENTER>
AND AL,2      <ENTER>
JZ  10E       <ENTER>
MOV AL,1      <ENTER>
MOV AH,4C     <ENTER>
INT 21        <ENTER>
              <ENTER>
R CX          <ENTER>
12            <ENTER>
W             <ENTER>
Q             <ENTER>
```

Use DEBUG as follows to create the command file CHKMATH.COM:

```
C:\> DEBUG < CHKMATH.SCR <ENTER>
```

The following batch commands illustrate how you might use CHKMATH within a batch file:

```
@ECHO OFF
CHKMATH
IF ERRORLEVEL 1 SOMEPROG /MATH
IF NOT ERRORLEVEL 1 SOMEPROG
```

Understanding Exit Status Values

Several of the tips presented in this book take advantage of exit status values. One of the questions users commonly ask is how large can an exit status value be? An exit status value must fall in the range

0 through 255. If you examine one of the DEBUG script files, you will understand why. The last two instructions in most DEBUG script files are the following:

```
MOV AH,4C
INT 21
```

The DOS Int 21H function 4CH directs DOS to end the current program. When DOS executes this instruction, DOS returns the current value of the AL register as the exit status. Because AL is an 8-bit register, its value is restricted to the range 0 through 255.

Entering an Escape Character in WordPerfect

Tip 145 discusses how to create an ASCII file with WordPerfect. If you use this technique to create your batch files, you sometimes will want to enter an escape character (to generate an ANSI or LaserJet escape sequence, for example). To generate the escape character within WordPerfect, hold down the ALT key and type the number 27 from the numeric keypad at the far right of your keyboard. When you release the ALT key, a left arrow should appear. WordPerfect uses the left arrow to represent the escape character. Save your file as Tip 145 explains.

Are Your Interrupt Vector's Valid?

Tip 31 discusses the PC's interrupt vectors and their uses. When you run memory-resident programs, the programs typically change one or more of the vectors to point to the program itself. In some cases, application programs temporarily change one or more vectors, presumably restoring the vectors to their original settings before ending. If a program changes a vector and does not later restore it before

ending, your computer may experience errors whose causes are very difficult to detect. The companion disk that accompanies this book provides the utility program SHOWVECT that displays interrupt vectors (See Tip 31). If you experience errors after running a specified program, reboot your system, and print a copy of your current interrupt vectors as shown here:

```
C:\> SHOWVECT > PRN  <ENTER>
```

After you run the program, print a second listing of the vectors and compare. If a vector is different, you may have found the culprint. Next, issue the following MEM command to print a copy of your system's current memory use:

```
C:\> MEM > PRN  <ENTER>
```

Compare the addresses used by each vector to the memory addresses displayed by MEM to ensure the vectors point to memory that is in use.

Changing the Environment's Size

Tip 13 explains how to increase the size of the DOS environment at system startup by using the CONFIG.SYS SHELL entry. The companion disk that accompanies this book contains the utility program ENVSIZE.EXE that lets you dynamically change the environment's size, provided sufficient memory exists. To use ENVSIZE, simply specify the desired size in bytes as shown here:

```
C:\> ENVSIZE 8192 <ENTER>
```

Using ENVSIZE, you can even reduce the environment size. As is the case with the SHELL entry, you cannot increase the environment size beyond 32,768 bytes.

ENVSIZE.EXE

The utility program ENVSIZE.EXE resides on the companion disk that accompanies this book.

I/O Redirection and DOSKEY Macros

Several of the tips presented in this book show you how to create DOSKEY macros. As you create increasingly complex macros, you may sometimes need the macros to perform I/O redirection. If you include one of the DOS redirection operators in the macro definition, your DOSKEY command will fail. For example, the following DOSKEY command tries to create a macro named PRTDIR that prints a directory listing:

```
C:\> DOSKEY PRTDIR=DIR > PRN <ENTER>
```

When DOS encounters the output redirection operator, DOS does not place the operator in the macro. Instead, DOS assumes you want to redirect DOSKEY's output to the printer. To place a redirection operator in a DOSKEY macro, you must use one of the metacharacters listed in Table 71.

Using the $G metacharacter, the DOSKEY command to create the PRTDIR macro becomes the following:

```
C:\> DOSKEY PRTDIR=DIR $G PRN <ENTER>
```

To use DOSKEY macros, you must be using DOS 5.

Table 71. DOSKEY I/O Redirection Metacharacters

<table>
<tr><th>Metacharacter</th><th>Redirection Operator</th></tr>
<tr><td>$G</td><td>> DOS output redirection operator</td></tr>
<tr><td>GG</td><td>>> DOS append redirection operator</td></tr>
<tr><td>$L</td><td>< DOS input redirection operator</td></tr>
<tr><td>$B</td><td>| DOS pipe operator</td></tr>
</table>

Be Aware of EMM386.EXE When Using Windows 3.0

The device driver EMM386.EXE provides DOS with access to upper memory and, if necessary, lets you emulate expanded memory by using extended memory. If you are using Windows 3.0 and Windows displays a message saying that it cannot start in enhanced mode because of an invalid path for EMM386.EXE, change the CONFIG.SYS DEVICE entry for EMM386.EXE to include the /Y switch as shown here:

```
DEVICE=C:\DOS\EMM386.EXE  /Y=C:\DOS\EMM386.EXE  [other switches]
```

After you change the driver entry, restart DOS and then invoke Windows in enhanced mode.

TIP 73

Push In the Turbo Switch

Tip 53 discusses CPU clock speeds. When PC clock speeds first increased, some programs, such as computer games that relied on a specific clock speed, experienced errors. As a solution, many computers provide a switch or button on the front of the chassis that lets you run the computer at a slow or fast (often called turbo mode) clock speed. Today, almost every program you buy will run in the faster turbo mode. Thus, if your computer has a turbo switch, select it. Many switches have a small LED light indicating that turbo mode has been selected.

Generating a PC Siren

In Tip 49 you create a command file named BELL.COM that sounds the computer's built-in speaker. Using BELL.COM, your batch files can notify the user of system

events. Similarly, the following DEBUG script file, SIREN.SCR, creates a command file named SIREN.COM that generates a police-siren-like sound until the user presses a key:

```
N SIREN.COM   <ENTER>
A 100         <ENTER>
IN AL, 61     <ENTER>
OR AL, 3      <ENTER>
OUT 61, AL    <ENTER>
MOV CH, 10    <ENTER>
MOV AL, B6    <ENTER>
OUT 43, AL    <ENTER>
MOV AL, 0     <ENTER>
OUT 42, AL    <ENTER>
MOV AL, CH    <ENTER>
OUT 42, AL    <ENTER>
MOV BX, 8000  <ENTER>
DEC BX        <ENTER>
CMP BX, 0     <ENTER>
JNE 117       <ENTER>
MOV DL, FF    <ENTER>
MOV AH, 6     <ENTER>
INT 21        <ENTER>
JNZ 12E       <ENTER>
DEC CH        <ENTER>
CMP CH, 0     <ENTER>
JNE 108       <ENTER>
JMP 106       <ENTER>
IN AL, 61     <ENTER>
AND AL, FC    <ENTER>
OUT 61, AL    <ENTER>
MOV AH, 4C    <ENTER>
INT 21        <ENTER>
              <ENTER>
R CX          <ENTER>
38            <ENTER>
W             <ENTER>
Q             <ENTER>
```

SIREN.SCR

Use DEBUG as follows to create SIREN.COM:

```
C:\> DEBUG < SIREN.SCR <ENTER>
```

Within your batch files, you can use SIREN to notify the user of serious error conditions.

Selecting a Video Mode with ANSI.SYS

Tips in this book discuss how to use the ANSI.SYS device driver to select screen colors, define keys, and position the cursor. In addition, the ANSI driver lets you select one of the video modes listed in Table 75. To use ANSI.SYS to select a video mode, use the escape sequence ESC[=ModeValueh.

If you have a program that requires, but does not select, a specific video mode, or if the program leaves your system in a different mode, you can use the ANSI driver to select the correct mode.

Table 75. Video Modes Supported by ANSI.SYS

Video Mode	Description	Escape Sequence
0	25x40 monochrome text	Esc[=0h
1	25x40 color text	Esc[=1h
2	25x80 monochrome text	Esc[=2h
3	25x80 color text	Esc[=3h
4	320x200 4-color graphics	Esc[=4h
5	320x200 monochrome graphics	Esc[=5h
6	640x200 monochrome graphics	Esc[=6h
7	Line wrap enable	Esc[=7h
7	Line wrap disable	Esc[=7l
13	320x200 color graphics	Esc[=13h
14	640x200 16-color graphics	Esc[=14h
15	640x350 monochrome graphics	Esc[=15h
16	640x350 16-color graphics	Esc[=16h
17	640x480 monochrome graphics	Esc[=17h
18	640x480 VGA 16-color graphics	Esc[=18h
19	320x200 VGA 256-color graphics	Esc[=19h

Keeping Track of Your CMOS System Configuration

286 computers and higher keep track of specific hardware information, such as your video display type and disk drive types, in a battery-powered chip called the CMOS. Depending on your computer type, you can display or change CMOS settings by using a program provided on disk with your computer or by holding down a special key combination when your computer starts (see your hardware manual for the specific keys). Should you need to replace your CMOS battery (and eventually all batteries wear out), you will need to restore the computer's setup information. The companion disk that accompanies this book provides a program named SEESETUP.EXE that displays your computer's setup information on the screen. By redirecting the output of SEESETUP to the printer as follows, you can save a hard copy of your computer's settings:

```
C:\> SEESETUP > PRN <ENTER>
```

Place the printout in a safe location so if you ever need it, you will have it.

The utility program SEESETUP.EXE resides on the companion disk that accompanies this book.

SEESETUP.EXE

Saving Your Setup Information to Disk

In Tip 76 you learned how to display or print your computer's setup information by using the companion disk utility command SEESETUP.EXE. The companion disk also contains the utility command SAVECMOS.EXE that lets you save your CMOS settings to a file as shown here:

```
C:\> SAVECMOS Filename.Ext <ENTER>
```

If you ever need to restore the CMOS settings, you can do so by using the utility command LOADCMOS, which is also contained on the companion disk, as shown here:

```
A:\> LOADCMOS Filename.Ext <ENTER>
```

Tip 344 directed you to create an emergency backup disk for your system. You should place the utility command LOADCMOS.EXE on this disk along with a file containing your current CMOS settings.

SAVECMOS.EXE
LOADCMOS.EXE

The utility commands SAVECMOS.EXE and LOADCMOS.EXE reside on the companion disk that accompanies this book.

Converting Hexadecimal and Decimal Numbers

Many DOS commands use hexadecimal (base 16) numbers. Likewise, most DOS memory maps, PC ports, and interrupt vectors are expressed in hexadecimal format. The companion disk that accompanies this book contains a utility command called BASECHG.EXE that, given a hexadecimal value, displays the decimal counterpart, or vice versa. To view the decimal equivalent of the value 1FFH, for example, you invoke BASECHG as follows:

```
C:\> BASECHG 1FFH <ENTER>
511
```

If the value specified ends with the letter H, BASECHG converts it to decimal format. Otherwise, BASECHG converts the value from decimal to hexadecimal format. The BASECHG program supports only values commonly used by DOS. It does not support fractions such as 6.25.

BASECHG.EXE

The utility command BASECHG.EXE resides on the companion disk that accompanies this book.

Making Sure DOSKEY Is Correctly Installed

Tip 62 discusses how to create a larger DOSKEY buffer by using DOSKEY's /BUFSIZE buffers. Unfortunately, the first time you invoke DOSKEY to a create a macro, DOSKEY will use its default buffer size of 512 bytes. The following DEBUG script file, CKDOSKEY.SCR, creates a command file named CKDOSKEY.COM that returns the exit status value 1 if DOSKEY is installed and returns 0 otherwise:

```
N CKDOSKEY.COM      <ENTER>
A 100               <ENTER>
MOV AX,4800         <ENTER>
INT 2F              <ENTER>
CMP AL,0            <ENTER>
JE  10B             <ENTER>
MOV AL,1            <ENTER>
MOV AH,4C           <ENTER>
INT 21              <ENTER>
                    <ENTER>
R CX                <ENTER>
F                   <ENTER>
W                   <ENTER>
Q                   <ENTER>
```

CKDOSKEY.SCR

Use the DEBUG command as follows to create the command CKDOSKEY.COM:

```
C:\> DEBUG < CKDOSKEY.SCR <ENTER>
```

If you have a batch file that creates several macros, you can use CKDOSKEY as follows to determine whether DOSKEY is installed; if it is not, the batch file can install it with the correct buffer size as shown here:

```
@ECHO OFF
CKDOSKEY
IF NOT ERRORLEVEL 1 DOSKEY /BUFSIZE=2048
REM Other commands here
```

Traveling with or Mailing Floppy Disks

Users often ask if it is safe to send their disks through the X-ray machine at airports. Personally, I don't. Here's why. Although an X-ray cannot change the information recorded on your disks, the powerful electronic machines next to the X-ray machine, such as the motor that drives the belt that takes items through the machine, can, in theory, produce an electronic flux strong enough to damage your disk. There are many travelers who regularly send disks through the machines who have never lost a file. When I travel, I ask airport security to perform a hand check of my computer. I've never lost a file either.

If you are mailing diskettes, us a cardboard mailer designed specifically for disks. The mailer may contain a message stating it contains magnetic media. If necessary, add a message in bold print that directs the post office not to bend the package. Always make sure you keep copies of your disks until they successfully arrive at their destination.

Using the BIOS to Select the Video Mode

Tip 75 discusses how to use an ANSI escape sequence to set the current video mode. If you don't have the ANSI driver installed, you can select the video mode by using the ROM-BIOS. The following DEBUG script file, VIDMODE3.SCR, for example, creates a command file named VIDMODE3.COM that selects video mode 3:

VIDMODE3.SCR

```
N VIDMODE3.COM <ENTER>
A 100          <ENTER>
MOV AH,0       <ENTER>
MOV AL,3       <ENTER>
INT 10         <ENTER>
MOV AH,4C      <ENTER>
```

```
INT 21              <ENTER>
                    <ENTER>
R CX                <ENTER>
A                   <ENTER>
W                   <ENTER>
Q                   <ENTER>
```

Use DEBUG as follows to create the command file VIDMODE3.COM:

```
C:\> DEBUG < VIDMODE3.SCR <ENTER>
```

Table 81 lists the PC video modes and their corresponding values. By changing the command name specified in the previous DEBUG script file and by assigning a different mode value to AL, you can select a command file to specify any video mode you require.

Table 81. BIOS Video Mode Values

Video Mode	Description
0	25 x 40 monochrome text
1	25 x 40 color text
2	25 x 80 monochrome text
3	25 x 80 color text
4	320 x 200 4-color graphics
5	320 x 200 monochrome graphics
6	640 x 200 monochrome graphics
7	25 x 80 monochrome text
13	320 x 200 color graphics
14	640 x 200 16-color graphics
15	640 x 350 monochrome graphics
16	640 x 350 16-color graphics
17	640 x 480 monochrome graphics
18	640 x 480 VGA 16-color graphics
19	320 x 200 VGA 256-color graphics

Accessing the Command Line from Your DEBUG Script Files

Many of the DEBUG script files presented in this book allow the user to specify a command line when executing a command. For example, the following DEBUG script file, SHOWCMD.SCR, creates a command file named SHOWCMD.COM that displays the command line specified on the screen:

SHOWCMD.SCR

```
N SHOWCMD.COM         <ENTER>
A 100                 <ENTER>
MOV BX,80             <ENTER>
INC BX                <ENTER>
MOV DL, BYTE [BX]     <ENTER>
MOV AH, 02            <ENTER>
INT 21                <ENTER>
CMP DL,D              <ENTER>
JNE 103               <ENTER>
MOV AH,4C             <ENTER>
INT 21                <ENTER>
                      <ENTER>
R CX                  <ENTER>
13                    <ENTER>
W                     <ENTER>
Q                     <ENTER>
```

Use DEBUG as follows to create the command file SHOWCMD.COM:

```
C:\> DEBUG < SHOWCMD.SCR <ENTER>
```

Each time you execute a command, DOS creates a 256-byte buffer called the program segment prefix that it loads into memory immediately before the program (see Tip 100). One of the items in the program segment prefix (PSP) is the command line. DOS shows the command line at location 80 (hexadecimal). Actually, location 80 contains a count of the number of characters in the command line. The first command line character typically begins at offset 82 (location 81 normally contains a space character that separates the command and command line). After the last character in the command line, DOS places a carriage return (hexadecimal 0DH). If you invoke the command

SHOWCMD with the command line "This is a sample," DOS will store the command line at offset 80H as shown here:

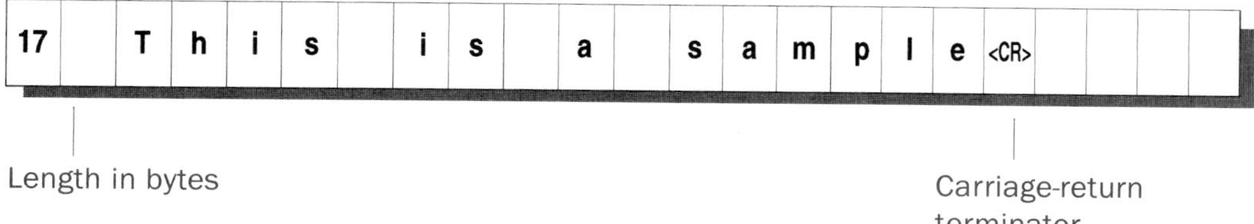

If you examine the assembly language instructions of the previous DEBUG script file, you will find that it simply displays characters until it encounters a carriage return.

Is the Mouse Driver Installed?

Almost all newer programs you purchase today provide mouse support. To use the mouse, you must first install a mouse device driver. Depending on your mouse type, the driver may require either a CONFIG.SYS entry or a memory-resident program. The following DEBUG script file, MOUSEAVL.SCR, creates a command file named MOUSEAVL.COM that returns the exit status value 1 if the mouse is installed and returns 0 otherwise:

```
N MOUSEAVL.COM     <ENTER>
A 100              <ENTER>
MOV AX,0           <ENTER>
INT 33             <ENTER>
CMP AL,0           <ENTER>
JE 10B             <ENTER>
MOV AL,1           <ENTER>
MOV AH,4C          <ENTER>
INT 21             <ENTER>
                   <ENTER>
R CX               <ENTER>
F                  <ENTER>
W                  <ENTER>
Q                  <ENTER>
```

MOUSEAVL.SCR

Use DEBUG as follows to create the command file MOUSEAVL.COM:

```
C:\> DEBUG < MOUSEAVL.SCR <ENTER>
```

The following batch file uses MOUSEAVL to determine whether the mouse driver is installed; if it is not, the file installs the driver residing in the diretory MICE:

```
@ECHO OFF
MOUSEAVL
IF NOT ERRORLEVEL 1 LOADHIGH C:\MICE\MOUSE.COM
```

In this case, if the mouse driver is not installed, the batch file uses the DOS 5 LOADHIGH command to install it.

Selecting Your Screen's Text Mode Border Color

In text mode, your screen contains a rectangular border area called the overscan region, shown here:

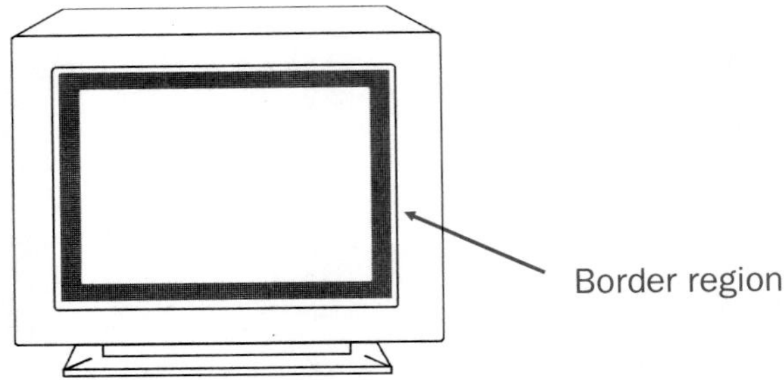

By default, the border area appears in black. The following DEBUG script file, BORDER.SCR, creates a command file named BORDER.COM that lets you assign the color of the border area:

```
N BORDER.COM    <ENTER>
A 100           <ENTER>
MOV AX,1001     <ENTER>
MOV BH,1        <ENTER>
INT 10          <ENTER>
MOV AH,4C       <ENTER>
INT 21          <ENTER>
                <ENTER>
R CX            <ENTER>
B               <ENTER>
W               <ENTER>
Q               <ENTER>
```

BORDER.SCR

Use DEBUG as follows to create the command file BORDER.COM:

```
C:\> DEBUG < BORDER.SCR <ENTER>
```

In this case, the DEBUG script file selects a border color of blue. To select a different color, change the DEBUG script file to assign to the BL register one of the color values listed in Table 84.

Table 84. Border Color Values for Use by BORDER.COM

Color Value	Color	Color Value	Color
0	Black	8	Dark grey
1	Blue	9	Light blue
2	Green	A	Light green
3	Cyan	B	Light cyan
4	Red	C	Light red
5	Magenta	D	Light magenta
6	Brown	E	Yellow
7	White	F	Bright white

Dumping Your BIOS Chip Date with DEBUG

When you experience hardware or software problems, a vendor may ask you for your BIOS type, version number, and date.

For compatibility purposes, most BIOS chips store their chip's creation date at location FFFF:0005 in memory. Using DEBUG you can display the BIOS date (if your BIOS stores its date in this area). To begin, invoke DEBUG from the DOS prompt:

```
C:\> DEBUG <ENTER>
```

Next, use DEBUG's D(ump) command as follows to display the contents of the memory area that contains the BIOS date:

```
-D FFFF:5 L 8 <ENTER>
FFFF:0000                30 39 2F-31 35 2F 38 39      09/15/89
```

To exit DEBUG, use the Q command:

```
-Q <ENTER>
```

Not all BIOS manufacturers place the BIOS date in memory.

What Is Baud, Anyway?

If you use a modem, or if you connect a printer to a serial port, you will have to specify a modem or serial port baud rate. Although most users know that baud has something to do with data transmission speed, most don't fully understand the term. When serial devices communicate, they do so over one wire, sending one bit of information at a time. For the devices to

communicate, the device sending the information must send bits at the speed the receiving device expects them. This transmission speed is referred to as the baud rate, often defined as the number of bits of data transmitted per second. Actually, however, baud rate defines the rate at which the transmitting device can place information on the wire, and the rate the receiving device samples the wire for new data. If you are using 1200 baud, for example, the receiving device samples the wire 1200 times per second, or approximately every millisecond.

Serial communication is not continuous, but rather occurs in bursts. In other words, the sending device says, "Here's some data, here's some more, here's the last." The receiving device, therefore, continuously samples the wire (at intervals defined by the baud rate), looking for new data. To help the receiver recognize new data, the sending device sends one or more start and stop bits that surround the data. Start and stop bits (and parity) can account for over 20 percent of the information sent per second, leaving 80 percent for data. Thus, at 1200 baud, you may actually send and receive only approximately 900 data bits per second; the remaining 300 bits are used for start, stop, and parity, as discussed in Tip 774 and Tip 787.

How Many Serial Ports Do I Have?

The PC uses serial ports to convert printers, modems, mouses, and other devices.

Tip 894 presents a utility command that returns, as an exit status, a count of the number of parallel ports contained within your PC. The following DEBUG script file, COMCOUNT.SCR, creates a command file named COMCOUNT.COM that returns, as an exit status value, a count of the number of serial ports in your PC:

```
N COMCOUNT.COM     <ENTER>
A 100              <ENTER>
MOV AX,40          <ENTER>
MOV DS,AX          <ENTER>
MOV AL,[11]        <ENTER>
MOV CL,1           <ENTER>
SAR AL,CL          <ENTER>
AND AL,7           <ENTER>
MOV AH,4C          <ENTER>
```

COMCOUNT.SCR

```
INT 21              <ENTER>
                    <ENTER>
R CX                <ENTER>
12                  <ENTER>
W                   <ENTER>
Q                   <ENTER>
```

Use DEBUG as follows to create the command file COMCOUNT.COM:

```
C:\> DEBUG < COMCOUNT.SCR <ENTER>
```

The following batch commands illustrate how you use COMCOUNT to determine the number of serial devices:

```
@ECHO OFF
COMCOUNT
IF NOT ERRORLEVEL 1 GOTO NO_SERIAL_DEVICES
IF ERROR LEVEL 1 GOTO SERIAL_AVAILABLE
REM other commands here
```

Using the BIOS to Determine the Current Video Mode

In Tip 81 you use a DEBUG script file to create a command file that lets you select the current video mode. The following DEBUG script file, VIDEOMOD.SCR, creates a command file named VIDEOMOD.COM that returns one of the video modes listed in Table 88 as an exit status value:

VIDEOMOD.SCR

```
N VIDEOMOD.COM      <ENTER>
A 100               <ENTER>
MOV AH,F            <ENTER>
INT 10              <ENTER>
MOV AH,4C           <ENTER>
INT 21              <ENTER>
```

```
                         <ENTER>
R CX                     <ENTER>
8                        <ENTER>
W                        <ENTER>
Q                        <ENTER>
```

Use DEBUG as follows to create the command file VIDEOMOD.COM:

```
C:\> DEBUG < VIDEOMOD.SCR <ENTER>
```

If you have a batch file that changes the current video mode, the batch file should first use VIDEOMOD.COM to determine and save the current video mode so it can restore the mode at a later time. The following batch commands, for example, save the current video mode in the named parameter %VIDEO_MODE%:

```
@ECHO OFF
VIDEOMOD
IF NOT ERRORLEVEL 1 SET VIDEO_MODE=0
IF ERRORLEVEL 1 IF NOT ERRORLEVEL 2 SET VIDEO_MODE=1
    :
    :
IF ERRORLEVEL 19 IF NOT ERRORLEVEL 20 SET VIDEO_MODE=19
REM other commands here
```

Table 88. Exit Status Values Returned by VIDEOMOD.COM

Exit Status	Video Mode	Exit Status	Video Mode
0	25x40 monochrome text	14	640x200 16-color graphics
1	25x40 color text	15	640x350 monochrome graphics
2	25x80 monochrome text	16	640x350 16-color graphics
3	25x80 color text	17	640x480 monochrome graphics
4	320x200 4-color graphics	18	640x480 VGA 16-color graphics
5	320x200 monochrome graphics	19	320x200 VGA 256-color graphics
6	640x200 monochrome graphics		
7	25x80 monochrome text		
13	320x200 color graphics		

Using Machine Code to Create Command Files

Many of the tips presented in this book use DEBUG script files to create commands. When you use DEBUG in this way, you can enter the command's instructions in assembly language, or you can enter the hexadecimal machine code values that represent each command. For example, the following DEBUG script file, BELL2.SCR, creates the command file BELL2.COM by entering machine code instead of assembly language instructions:

BELL2.COM

```
N BELL2.COM                                <ENTER>
E 100 B4 02 B2 07 CD 21 B4 4C CD 21        <ENTER>
                                           <ENTER>
R CX                                       <ENTER>
A                                          <ENTER>
W                                          <ENTER>
Q                                          <ENTER>
```

Use DEBUG as follows to create the command file BELL2.COM:

```
C:\> DEBUG < BELL2.SCR <ENTER>
```

When you read other books and magazines, you may encounter many DEBUG script files that use the hexadecimal machine code values. This book uses the assembly language format because it gives programmers and users wanting to understand how the command file works an opportunity to view the command's instructions. If you create a DEBUG script file using machine code and you want to view the corresponding instructions, invoke DEBUG with the command name as shown here:

```
C:\> DEBUG BELL2.COM <ENTER>
```

When DEBUG displays its hyphen prompt (-), use the command U 100 to view the command's instructions. By repeatedly issuing the U command, you can unassemble all of the machine code instructions into assembly language. Remember that the last two instructions in most command files are MOV AH,4C and INT 21.

Using Parameters in Your DOSKEY Macros

Several of the tips presented in this book use DOSKEY macros to replace batch files. Just as your batch files can access command line parameters using %1 through %9, DOSKEY macros can use the symbols $1 through $9. For example, the following CP macro abbreviates the COPY command by using $1 and $2:

```
C:\> DOSKEY CP=COPY $1 $2 <ENTER>
```

Macros do not have a command like that of batch files that provide a SHIFT command to move the contents of one parameter to another, which in turn lets you access more than nine parameters. However, using the $* metacharacter, you can access the macro's entire command line (minus the macro name). The following VIEW macro, for example, combines the $* metacharacter with FOR to display the contents of every file specified on the command line:

```
C:\> DOSKEY VIEW=FOR %I IN ($*) DO TYPE %I <ENTER>
```

Using the VIEW macro, you can include multiple filenames or wildcard characters as shown here:

```
C:\> VIEW \AUTOEXEC.BAT \CONFIG.SYS \BATCH\*BAT <ENTER>
```

To use DOSKEY macros, you must be using DOS 5.

Managing Your DOSKEY Macros

Several of the tips presented in this book make extensive use of DOSKEY macros. As the number of macros you create increases, you may have difficulty remembering all of the available macro commands. Using the DOSKEY/MACROS command shown here, you can list your current macros:

```
C:\> DOSKEY /MACROS <ENTER>
```

The following command uses DOSKEY to create a macro named MACROS that invokes the DOSKEY /MACROS command:

```
C:\> DOSKEY MACROS=DOSKEY /MACROS <ENTER>
```

If you want to delete a macro definition, invoke DOSKEY with the macro name as shown here:

```
C:\> DOSKEY MacroName= <ENTER>
```

If you want to delete all of your macros in one step, press the ALT-F10 keyboard combination.

To use DOSKEY macros, you must be using DOS 5.

Using DOSKEY to Execute Multiple Commands on the Same Line

By default, DOS lets you execute only one command at a time. However, if you are using DOS 5 and you have installed the DOSKEY command, DOS lets you execute several commands on the same line. To do so, you simply press the CTRL-T keyboard combination to separate the commands. Assume, for example, you want to execute the commands CLS, DIR, and DATE on the same line. To do so, you would type CLS, press CTRL-T, type DIR, press CTRL-T, type DATE, and press ENTER. Each time you press the CTRL-T keyboard combination, your screen will display the ASCII character 20 as shown here:

```
C:\> CLS ¶ DIR ¶ DATE  <ENTER>
```

To execute multiple commands at one time, you must be using the DOS 5 DOSKEY command.

Is This a VGA?

When you create batch files that will be distributed to other users, the batch files can't make assumptions about the video type. The following DEBUG script file, CHECKVGA.SCR, creates a command file named CHECKVGA.COM that returns the exit status 1 if the current system is using a VGA monitor and returns 0 otherwise:

```
N CHECKVGA.COM <ENTER>
A 100          <ENTER>
MOV AH,1A      <ENTER>
MOV AL,00      <ENTER>
INT 10         <ENTER>
CMP AL,1A      <ENTER>
JE 10E         <ENTER>
MOV AL,0       <ENTER>
JMP 110        <ENTER>
MOV AL,1       <ENTER>
MOV AH,4C      <ENTER>
INT 21         <ENTER>
               <ENTER>
R CX           <ENTER>
14             <ENTER>
W              <ENTER>
Q              <ENTER>
```

CHECKVGA.SCR

Use DEBUG as follows to create the command file CHECKVGA.COM:

```
C:\> DEBUG < CHECKVGA.SCR <ENTER>
```

The following batch commands illustrates how you can use CHECKVGA to test for a VGA monitor:

```
@ECHO OFF
CHECKVGA
IF ERRORLEVEL GOTO VGA_MONITOR
REM Other commands here
```

Temporarily Increasing the Environment Size

Tip 13 describes how to use the CONFIG.SYS SHELL entry to increase the environment size when DOS starts. In most cases, a user's environment will not exceed 512 bytes. Occasionally, however, such as when a large batch file makes extensive use of named parameters and thus requires a larger environment, you will need to exceed this size. If you use the CONFIG.SYS SHELL entry to increase the environment size, most of the environment will normally be unused, unnecessarily wasting memory. A better solution is to temporarily install a second command processor with the environment size needed. For example, assume the batch file needs a 2048-byte environment. You would use COMMAND as follows to create a secondary command processor with an environment of the required size that exists for the life of the batch file:

```
C:\> COMMAND /E:2048  /C BatFile <ENTER>
```

When the batch file ends, DOS will also terminate the secondary command processor. If you need the increased environment size to exist for several commands, invoke COMMAND with the environment size from the DOS prompt as follows:

```
C:\> COMMAND /E:2048 <ENTER>
```

DOS will load the secondary command processor. After you execute the commands you require, use the EXIT command to terminate the secondary command processor as shown here:

```
C:\> EXIT <ENTER>
```

Saving Your Macros to a Batch File

If you create several new DOSKEY macros you plan to use regularly, you can save the macros to a batch file, which you can invoke when you need the macros defined. To save the macros to a batch file, invoke DOSKEY as shown here:

```
C:\> DOSKEY /MACROS > BatFile.BAT <ENTER>
```

DOSKEY will place the macro definitions in the file as shown here:

```
LOWER=DIR $1 /L
WIDE=DIR $1 /W
SAFEDEL=DEL $1 /P
```

Next, edit the batch file, preceding each line with the DOSKEY command as shown here:

```
@ECHO OFF
DOSKEY LOWER=DIR $1 /L
DOSKEY WIDE=DIR $1 /W
DOSKEY SAFEDEL=DEL $1 /P
```

The batch file is now ready for use.

To use DOSKEY macros, you must be using DOS 5.

Is This an EGA?

TIP 96

Tip 93 creates a command file that lets you test whether the current display is a VGA. The following DEBUG script file, CHECKEGA.SCR, creates a command file named CHECKEGA.COM that returns 1 if the current monitor is an EGA and returns 0 otherwise:

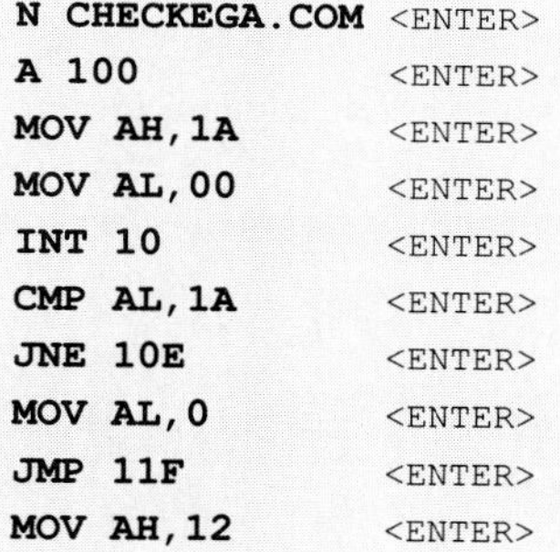

```
N CHECKEGA.COM <ENTER>
A 100          <ENTER>
MOV AH,1A      <ENTER>
MOV AL,00      <ENTER>
INT 10         <ENTER>
CMP AL,1A      <ENTER>
JNE 10E        <ENTER>
MOV AL,0       <ENTER>
JMP 11F        <ENTER>
MOV AH,12      <ENTER>
```

CHECKEGA.SCR

```
MOV BL,10        <ENTER>
INT 10           <ENTER>
CMP BL,10        <ENTER>
JNE 11D          <ENTER>
MOV AL,0         <ENTER>
JMP 11F          <ENTER>
MOV AL,1         <ENTER>
MOV AH, 4C       <ENTER>
INT 21           <ENTER>
                 <ENTER>
R CX             <ENTER>
23               <ENTER>
W                <ENTER>
Q                <ENTER>
```

Use DEBUG as follows to create the command file CHECKEGA.COM:

```
C:\> DEBUG < CHECKEGA.SCR <ENTER>
```

The following batch commands illustrate how you can use CHECKEGA:

```
@ECHO OFF
CHECKEGA
IF ERRORLEVEL 1 GOTO EGA_PRESENT
REM other commands here
```

TIP 97 When You Need EGA.SYS

As discussed in Tip 738, the DOS 5 shell lets you load several programs into memory and later switch among the programs as your needs require. If you are using an EGA monitor, you need to first install the EGA.SYS device driver before the shell's task swapper can correctly

save and restore your screen contents when you switch among tasks. The following CONFIG.SYS entry uses DEVICEHIGH to install the driver:

```
DEVICEHIGH=C:\DOS\EGA.SYS
```

If you are not using the DOS 5 memory management techniques, use the CONFIG.SYS DEVICE entry to install the driver.

You need to install the EGA.SYS driver only if you are using the DOS 5 task swapper with an EGA.

Print Screen Operations Whose Colors Match the Screen

By default, when you use the SHIFT-PRTSC keyboard combination to print your screen's current contents, the BIOS prints the image in reverse; in other words, the dark background becomes white, and the white text becomes black. If you need to perform print screen operations that use the same screen colors, you can issue the following GRAPHICS command:

```
C:\> GRAPHICS /R  <ENTER>
```

The GRAPHICS command will install memory-resident software that becomes active when you press the SHIFT-PRTSC key combination, printing your screen contents as desired.

Why Are Command Lines Restricted to 126 Characters?

As discussed in Tip 82, each time you execute a command, DOS places the corresponding command line at offset 80H within the command's program segment prefix. As shown here, DOS stores the length of the command line at location 80H:

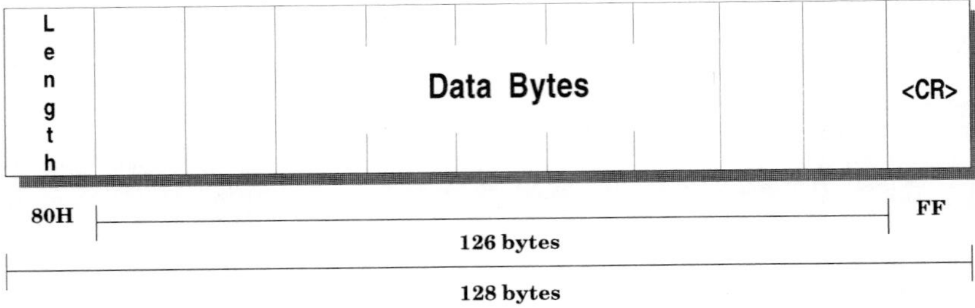

Likewise, DOS always includes the carriage return at the end of the command line. If you take these two characters into account along with the fact that the buffer can hold only 128 characters, the maximum command line becomes 126 characters.

Unfortunately, when you type commands at the DOS prompt, DOS lets you type only up to 127 characters before you must press ENTER. Because the command name is included within these 127 characters, very few commands take full advantage of the 126-character command line.

Understanding the Program Segment Prefix

As discussed in Tip 82, each time you run a command, DOS loads into memory a 256-byte program segment prefix (PSP). Within the PSP, DOS stores such information as the program's file table, which

tracks the program's open files, the program's command line, and the address of the program's environment entries. Take note of all the information the PSP provides, as shown here:

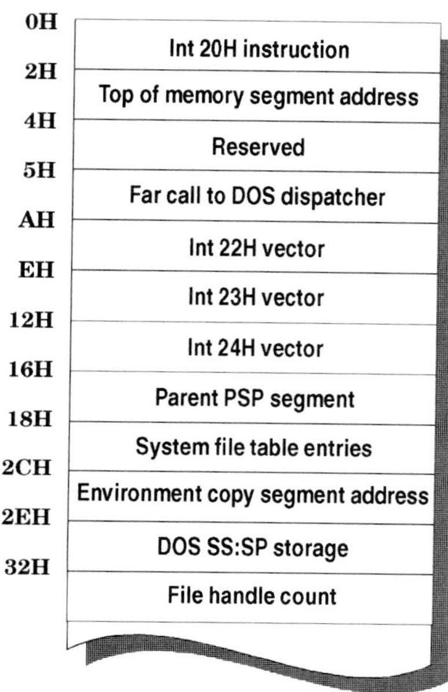

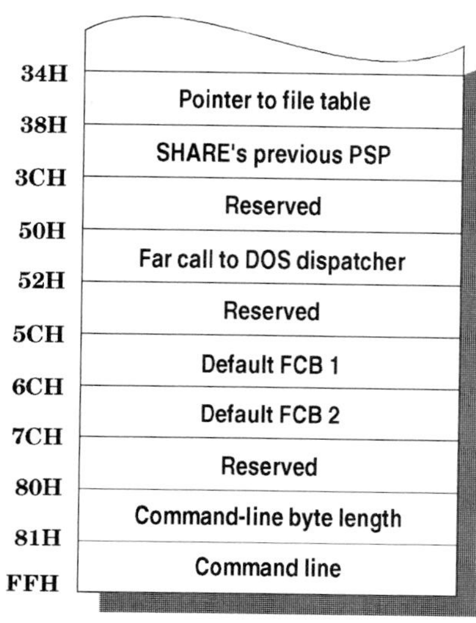

As the complexity of your DEBUG script files increase, take advantage of the information DOS places in the command's program segment prefix.

Using DEBUG to Display the Program Segment Prefix

Tip 100 discusses the fields found in the program segment prefix. Using DEBUG, you can examine the contents of the PSP. To begin, invoke DEBUG as follows:

```
C:\> DEBUG  This is a command line <ENTER>
```

When DEBUG displays its hyphen prompt (-), issue the following D(ump) command to view DEBUG's PSP:

```
-D 0 L 100 <ENTER>
```

Use the callouts listed here to identify the PSP fields:

```
115E:0000  CD 20 FF 9F 00 9A F0 FE-1D F0 4F 03 A4 0B 8A 03   . ........O.....
115E:0010  A4 0B 17 03 A4 0B 93 0B-01 01 01 00 02 FF FF FF   ................
115E:0020  FF FF FF FF FF FF FF FF-FF FF FF FF 51 11 4C 01   ............Q.L.
115E:0030  64 10 14 00 18 00 5E 11-FF FF FF FF 00 00 00 00   d.....^.........
115E:0040  05 00 00 00 00 00 00 00-00 00 00 00 00 00 00 00   ................
115E:0050  CD 21 CB 00 00 00 00 00-00 00 00 00 00 53 41 4D   .!...........SAM
115E:0060  50 4C 45 20 20 20 20 20-00 00 00 00 00 43 4F 4D   PLE     .....COM
115E:0070  4D 41 4E 44 20 20 20 20-00 00 00 00 00 00 00 00   MAND    ........
115E:0080  14 20 53 61 6D 70 6C 65-20 43 6F 6D 6D 61 6E 64   . Sample Command
115E:0090  20 4C 69 6E 65 0D 00 00-00 00 00 00 00 00 00 00    Line...........
115E:00A0  00 00 00 00 00 00 00 00-00 00 00 00 00 00 00 00   ................
115E:00B0  00 00 00 00 00 00 00 00-00 00 00 00 00 00 00 00   ................
115E:00C0  00 00 00 00 00 00 00 00-00 00 00 00 00 00 00 00   ................
115E:00D0  00 00 00 00 00 00 00 00-00 00 00 00 00 00 00 00   ................
115E:00E0  00 00 00 00 00 00 00 00-00 00 00 00 00 00 00 00   ................
115E:00F0  00 00 00 00 00 00 00 00-00 00 00 00 00 00 00 00   ................
115E:0100  00
```

1. Call to terminate vector
2. Segment address of program's top of memory
3. Call to Int 21H dispatcher
4. Int 22H vector
5. Int 23H vector
6. Int 24H vector
7. Parent PSP segment
8. Standard file handlers
9. Unused file handlers
10. Environment copy segment address
11. DOS SS:PP storage
12. Number of file handles (hex 14 = 20)
13. Pointer to file table
14. SHARE's previous PSP
15. Far call to DOS dispatcher
16. Drive for FCB 1
17. Filename for FCB 1
18. Drive for FCB 2
19. Filename for FCB 2
20. Length of command line
21. Command line
22. Carriage return

Make Sure You Install the Latest Drivers

To perform memory management, DOS 5 and Windows use the files HIMEM.SYS and EMM386.EXE. Because both products provide these two files, you need to make sure you are installing the latest software. To test HIMEM.SYS, issue the following DIR command:

```
C:\> DIR \HIMEM.SYS /S <ENTER>
```

DOS will display the name of each directory containing the file along with the file's directory entry. If more than one copy of the file exists, compare the files' date stamps. Edit your CONFIG.SYS file and place the directory name of the most current file in the corresponding DEVICE entry. Delete the duplicate file.

To begin this process for EMM386.EXE, issue the following DIR command:

```
C:\> DIR \EMM386.EXE /S <ENTER>
```

An Automatic Enter

Many commands display prompts such as "Press any key to continue...." or "Press Enter for more...." If you are executing these commands interactively from the keyboard, pressing ENTER to continue is easy. If you are running the command from a batch file, however, you may want the batch file to generate the ENTER key for you. The following DEBUG script file, ENTER.SCR, creates a command file named ENTER.COM that generates a carriage return:

```
N ENTER.COM    <ENTER>
A 100          <ENTER>
MOV AH,2       <ENTER>
MOV DL,D       <ENTER>
INT 21         <ENTER>
MOV AH,4C      <ENTER>
```

ENTER.SCR

```
INT 21          <ENTER>
                <ENTER>
R CX            <ENTER>
A               <ENTER>
W               <ENTER>
Q               <ENTER>
```

Use DEBUG as follows to create the command file ENTER.COM:

```
C:\> DEBUG < ENTER.SCR <ENTER>
```

If a program requires an ENTER key, you can redirect ENTER's output to the program as shown here:

```
ENTER | Program
```

The small DEBUG script file is an ideal candidate for a batch file to build "on the fly" as discussed in Tip 648.

Using Each Line of a File with a Specific Command

Tip 95 explains how to save your current DOSKEY macros to a batch file. In this tip, after you save your current macros you have to edit the file to place the word DOSKEY in front of each line in the file. To simplify this process, the companion disk that accompanies this book contains the command file FILECMD.EXE that executes a specific command for each entry in a file. For example, assume you save your current macros to a file named MACROS.DEF as shown here:

```
C:\> DOSKEY /MACROS > MACROS.DEF <ENTER>
```

You can then execute the DOSKEY command for each entry in the file by using FILECMD as shown here:

```
C:\> FILECMD MACROS.DEF DOSKEY <ENTER>
```

The utility command FILECMD.EXE resides on the companion disk that accompanies this book.

FILECMD.EXE

Trying to Save and Restore Environment Entries

If you have a batch file that uses several named parameters, or that changes one or more environment entries, you will probably want the batch file to restore the environment to its original settings before it ends. To do so, you might try to redirect the output of the SET command to a file, later processing the file using the utility command FILECMD as Tip 104 explains:

```
SET > ENVIRON.SET
REM Other commands here
FILECMD ENVIRON.SET SET
```

Although the FILECMD command successfully executes, your environment remains unchanged. The problem is that when FILECMD issues the SET command, SET changes FILECMD's copy of the environment, not COMMAND.COM's. As such, there is no easy way to restore the environment entries in one quick step.

Warm and Cold Boot Operations

Tip 2 presents the DEBUG script file RESTART.SCR that creates the command file RESTART.COM that performs a warm reboot operation. The PC performs a warm reboot operation when you execute

a CTRL-ALT-DEL keyboard combination. When you turn on your computer's power, the PC performs a cold boot. A cold boot differs from a warm boot in that a cold boot includes the PC's power-on self-test. The following DEBUG script file, COLDBOOT.SCR, creates a command file named COLDBOOT.COM that initiates a cold boot:

COLDBOOT.SCR

```
N COLDBOOT.COM <ENTER>
A 100          <ENTER>
MOV BX,40      <ENTER>
MOV DS,BX      <ENTER>
XOR BX,BX      <ENTER>
MOV [72],BX    <ENTER>
JMP FFFF:0     <ENTER>
               <ENTER>
R CX           <ENTER>
10             <ENTER>
W              <ENTER>
Q              <ENTER>
```

Use DEBUG as follows to create the command file COLDBOOT.COM:

```
C:\> DEBUG < COLDBOOT.SCR <ENTER>
```

Understanding ASCII

Tip 16 presents the utility command ASCII.EXE that displays the ASCII character set. Every character the computer prints or displays on your screen is represented in ASCII format. To help you better understand ASCII, the following batch file, UNDASCII.BAT, creates a BASIC program that prompts you for a line of text; the program then displays the ASCII values used to represent each character:

```
@ECHO OFF
ECHO INPUT "Type text and press Enter: ", T$ > UNDASCII.BAS
ECHO PRINT "The ASCII characters are: " >> UNDASCII.BAS
ECHO FOR I = 1 TO LEN(T$) >> UNDASCII.BAS
ECHO   PRINT MID$(T$,I,1) ASC(MID$(T$,I)) >> UNDASCII.BAS
ECHO NEXT >> UNDASCII.BAS
```

```
ECHO SYSTEM >> UNDASCII.BAS
QBASIC /RUN UNDASCII.BAS
DEL UNDASCII.BAS
```

Invoke the batch file from the DOS prompt as shown here:

```
C:\> UNDASCII <ENTER>
```

Type different letters, punctuation symbols, and even numbers. You will see the unique ASCII value for each.

The preceding batch file uses the DOS 5 QBASIC command. If you are not using DOS 5, change the batch file to use BASICA or GWBASIC.

Erasing an ECHO OFF Message

Most of the batch files presented in this book use the @ECHO OFF command to suppress command names. If you are not using DOS 3.3 or higher, you cannot precede ECHO OFF with the @ character. As a result, your screen will display the following message at the start of each batch file:

```
C:\>ECHO OFF
```

If you are using the ANSI.SYS device driver, you can use the following ECHO command to erase the ECHO OFF message:

```
ECHO Esc[1AEsc[80DEsc[K
```

The escape sequence moves the cursor up two lines and then erases the line's contents.

The following batch command file illustrates how you can erase the ECHO OFF message in this way:

```
ECHO OFF
ECHO Esc[1AEsc[80DEsc[K
```

```
ECHO The ECHO OFF message should not appear on your screen.
```

The ECHO commands just shown use the characters "Esc" to represent the unprintable ASCII escape character. In your batch files, you must use the actual character as Tip 34 discusses.

Turning the VGA Display On and Off

Tip 52 presents a BASIC program that displays random spheres on your screen, serving as a screen saver. Sometimes, however, you may want simply to disable the screen's display without actually turning the display off. The following DEBUG script file, VGACTL.SCR, creates two command files, VGA_ON.COM and VGA_OFF.COM, that turn your screen display on and off:

VGACTL.SCR

```
N VGA_OFF.COM    <ENTER>
A 100            <ENTER>
MOV DX,3DA       <ENTER>
IN  AX,DX        <ENTER>
MOV AL,0         <ENTER>
MOV DX,3C0       <ENTER>
OUT DX,AL        <ENTER>
MOV DX,3DA       <ENTER>
IN  AX,DX        <ENTER>
MOV AX,4C00      <ENTER>
INT 21           <ENTER>
                 <ENTER>
R CX             <ENTER>
13               <ENTER>
W                <ENTER>
                 <ENTER>
N VGA_ON.COM     <ENTER>
A 100            <ENTER>
MOV DX,3DA       <ENTER>
IN  AX,DX        <ENTER>
MOV AL,20        <ENTER>
```

```
MOV DX,3C0         <ENTER>
OUT DX,AL          <ENTER>
MOV DX,3DA         <ENTER>
IN  AX,DX          <ENTER>
MOV AX,4C00        <ENTER>
INT 21             <ENTER>
                   <ENTER>
R CX               <ENTER>
13                 <ENTER>
W                  <ENTER>
Q                  <ENTER>
```

Use DEBUG as follows to create the command files:

```
C:\> DEBUG < VGACTL.SCR <ENTER>
```

The following batch file, SAVESCR.BAT, uses VGA_OFF to turn off your screen display until you press a key. The batch file then uses VGA_ON to turn the screen display back on.

```
@ECHO OFF
VGA_OFF
PAUSE
VGA_ON
```

Correcting Misalignment in CGA Monitors

If you are using a CGA monitor and the characters do not appear centered on your screen, you can use the MODE command to correct the alignment. To move the characters left one position, issue the following command:

```
C:\> MODE ,L <ENTER>
```

If you need to move the characters to the right, replace the letter L in the previous command with R. If you are not sure how many positions you need to shift characters, invoke MODE by using R or L as follows:

```
C:\> MODE ,R,T <ENTER>
```

MODE will display a test pattern as shown here:

```
01234567890123456789012345678901234567899012345678901234567 89
Do you see the leftmost 0 (Y/N)?
```

If you can see the leftmost 0, type **Y**. Otherwise, type **N**, and MODE will shift the characters.

The MODE command can correct only CGA misalignment.

Some monitors provide an alignment knob that lets you manually adjust alignment.

Using Your Modem as an Auto-Dialer

If you have a Hayes-compatible modem installed in your system, you can actually use the modem to dial phone calls for you. To dial numbers in this way, you simply send the modem commands to the corresponding serial post. The easiest way to do so is by redirecting the output of the ECHO command. Assume, for example, that you want to dial the number 555-1212. If you have a pulse-dial phone, use the following command to dial the phone:

```
C:\> ECHO ATDT555-1212; > COM1 <ENTER>
```

If you have a rotary-based phone, issue the following command:

```
C:\> ECHO ATDP555-1212; > COM1 <ENTER>
```

When the phone call ends, issue the following command to disconnect the modem:

```
C:\> ECHO ATH > COM1 <ENTER>
```

Note that before you can use the your modem to dial the phone in this way, your modem and COM port must be set to the same baud rate. Most modem use 1200 baud by default. Use the following command to set your COM port to 1200 baud:

```
C:\> MODE COM1 1200 <ENTER>
```

An Auto-Dialer Rolodex

Tip 111 describes how to use your modem to automatically dial phone numbers. The following batch file, AUTODIAL.BAT, illustrates how you can create an automated dialer:

```
@ECHO OFF
MODE COM1 1200 > NUL
IF '%1'=='ALLEN' ECHO ATDT555-1212 > COM1
IF '%1'=='PHIL'  ECHO ATDT555-1111 > COM1
IF '%1'=='POLICE' ECHO ATDT911 > COM1
```

To auto-dial ALLEN, you would issue the following command:

```
C:\> AUTODIAL ALLEN <ENTER>
```

The batch file assumes that you are using a pulse-dial phone. If you are not, change ATDT to ATDP.

After you end the phone call, invoke the following batch file, HANGUP.BAT, to disconnect the modem:

```
ECHO ATH > COM1
```

Using ANSI.SYS Text Highlighting Attributes

Several of the tips presented in this book use ANSI escape sequences to control screen colors. In addition, the ANSI driver lets you control the attributes (such as blinking, reverse video, and intensity) used to display characters on your screen. To select text attributes, you use the same escape sequence you use to set foreground and background colors:

```
Esc[Attributem
```

Table 113 describes the text attribute values.

The following DOS PROMPT command uses the escape sequence to display the system prompt in reverse video:

```
C:\> PROMPT $E[7m$P$G$E[0m <ENTER>
```

Likewise, the following ECHO command uses the escape sequence to display a message with the blinking attribute:

```
ECHO Esc[5mImportant MessageEsc[0m
```

Table 113. ANSI.SYS Text Attribute Values

Attribute Value	Attribute
0	Normal attributes
1	High-intensity display
4	Monochrome underlining
5	Blinking
6	Rapid blinking
7	Reverse video
8	Invisible display

Performing Hexadecimal Multiplication and Division

Tip 36 explains how to use DEBUG to add and subtract hexadecimal numbers. The following batch file, HEXMATH.BAT, allows you to multiply (*) or divide (/) two hexadecimal values. To do so, invoke the batch file with the values as shown here:

```
C:\> HEXMATH FF * A <ENTER>
Result: 9F6

@ECHO OFF
IF '%1'=='' GOTO NO_PARAMS
IF '%2'=='' GOTO NO_PARAMS
IF '%3'=='' GOTO NO_PARAMS
ECHO ON ERROR GOTO MATHERROR > HEXMATH.BAS
ECHO RESULT& = &H%1  %2  &H%3 >> HEXMATH.BAS
ECHO PRINT "Result:"; Hex$(RESULT&) >> HEXMATH.BAS
ECHO SYSTEM >> HEXMATH.BAS
ECHO MATHERROR: >> HEXMATH.BAS
ECHO PRINT "Error in processing" >> HEXMATH.BAS
ECHO SYSTEM >> HEXMATH.BAS
QBASIC /RUN HEXMATH
DEL HEXMATH.BAS
GOTO DONE
:NO_PARAMS
ECHO Specify parameters separated by blanks (Example: FF + 1)
:DONE
```

This batch file uses QBASIC, provided with DOS 5. If you are using a different DOS version, replace QBASIC with GWBASIC or BASICA.

Toggling the Processor's Speed

As discussed in Tip 73, many PCs provide a switch or button that lets you select a faster or slower clock speed. If your system has a fast tasks mode, you should use it as often as possible. If your computer does not have a speed selection button, but if your CPU supports clock-speed switching and you are using the AMI BIOS chip, you may be able to toggle between the fast and slow processor speeds by using the following keyboard combinations:

CTRL-ALT +	Selects turbo mode
CTRL-ALT –	Slows processor speed

As Tip 324 describes, pin 5 of your keyboard cable contains a clock signal. When you use one of the preceding keyboard combinations, the AMI BIOS directs the keyboard controller to change the status of the clock line. If your CPU supports keyboard clock switching, it will change the CPU's clock speed.

How Many Video Lines Are Active?

As Tip 17 explains, you can use the ANSI.SYS driver to select a 43-line (EGA) or 50-line (VGA) display. Although DOS supports these display modes, many application programs may not. Thus, your batch files may need to change the display mode before running specific programs. If a batch file changes the video mode before running a program, the batch file should restore the original mode after the program ends. The following DEBUG script file, SCRLINES.SCR, creates a command file

named SCRLINES.COM that returns an exit status value of 25, 43, or 50 that corresponds to the number of lines currently displayed on the screen:

```
N SCRLINES.COM   <ENTER>
A 100            <ENTER>
MOV AX,40        <ENTER>
MOV ES,AX        <ENTER>
ES:              <ENTER>
MOV AL,[84]      <ENTER>
INC AX           <ENTER>
MOV AH,4C        <ENTER>
INT 21           <ENTER>
                 <ENTER>
R CX             <ENTER>
E                <ENTER>
W                <ENTER>
Q                <ENTER>
```

SCRLINES.SCR

Use DEBUG as follows to create the command file SCRLINES.COM:

```
C:\> DEBUG < SCRLINES.SCR <ENTER>
```

The following DEBUG commands use SCRLINES to save the current line count in the named parameter SCREEN_LINES:

```
@ECHO OFF
REM Default setting
SET SCREEN_LINES=25
SCRLINES
IF ERRORLEVEL 25 IF NOT ERRORLEVEL 26 SET SCREEN_LINES=25
IF ERRORLEVEL 43 IF NOT ERRORLEVEL 44 SET SCREEN_LINES=43
IF ERRORLEVEL 50 IF NOT ERRORLEVEL 51 SET SCREEN_LINES=50
REM Other commands here
REM Restore the original lines
MODE CON /LINES=%SCREEN_LINES%
SET SCREEN_LINES=
```

Using the DOS 5 Upgrade to Build a Bootable System

If you have purchased the DOS 5 upgrade, you can perform the upgrade only on a hard disk that contains a working version of DOS. If your hard disk does not contain a working version of DOS, you can first create a set of DOS 5 floppy disks that you can use to prepare your hard disk for the upgrade. To create the floppy disk-based DOS 5 system, place the DOS 5 upgrade disk in drive A and issue the following command:

```
A:\> SETUP /F <ENTER>
```

Depending on your disk type, DOS creates up to seven floppy disks. After the installation completes, place the floppy disk containing the FDISK command in drive A and partition your hard disk. When FDISK completes, place the floppy disk containing the FORMAT command in drive A and issue the following FORMAT command:

```
A:\> FORMAT C: /S <ENTER>
```

When FORMAT completes, you can perform the complete DOS 5 upgrade on your hard disk.

Restoring 25-Line Display Mode Without ANSI.SYS

Tip 17 describes how to use the MODE command in conjunction with ANSI.SYS to select 50 rows on a VGA monitor. Tip 119 and Tip 158 create the command files VGA_50.COM and EGA_43.COM that let you select 50- and 43-line mode without using ANSI.SYS. If you select 50- or 43-line mode, you can restore your screen to 25 lines by using the MODE command shown here:

```
C:\> MODE CO80 <ENTER>
```

In addition, the following DEBUG script file, VGA_25.SCR, creates a command file named VGA_25.COM that selects 25-line mode:

```
N VGA_25.COM   <ENTER>
A 100          <ENTER>
MOV AH,0       <ENTER>
MOV AL,3       <ENTER>
INT 10         <ENTER>
MOV AH,4C      <ENTER>
INT 21         <ENTER>
               <ENTER>
R CX           <ENTER>
0A             <ENTER>
W              <ENTER>
Q              <ENTER>
```

VGA_25.SCR

Use DEBUG as follows to create the command file VGA_25.COM:

```
C:\> DEBUG < VGA_25.SCR <ENTER>
```

Selecting 50-Line Display Mode Without ANSI.SYS

Tip 17 describes how to use the MODE command in conjunction with ANSI.SYS to select 50 rows on your video display. However, as Tip 6 discusses, installing the ANSI.SYS driver slows down every keyboard input and screen output operation. To address this problem, the following DEBUG script file, VGA_50.SCR, creates a command file named VGA_50.COM that sets a VGA monitor to 50-line mode:

```
N VGA_50.COM   <ENTER>
A 100          <ENTER>
MOV AH,0       <ENTER>
MOV AL,3       <ENTER>
INT 10         <ENTER>
MOV AX,1112    <ENTER>
```

VGA_50.SCR

```
MOV BX,0        <ENTER>
INT 10          <ENTER>
MOV AX,1200     <ENTER>
MOV BL,20       <ENTER>
INT 10          <ENTER>
MOV AH,4C       <ENTER>
INT 21          <ENTER>
                <ENTER>
R CX            <ENTER>
19              <ENTER>
W               <ENTER>
Q               <ENTER>
```

Use DEBUG as follows to create the command file VGA_50.COM:

```
C:\> DEBUG < VGA_50.SCR <ENTER>
```

To select 50-line mode, invoke the command from the DOS prompt as shown here:

```
C:\> VGA_50 <ENTER>
```

Understanding MIPs, FLOPs, and MFLOPs

As you read articles about computer performance or avertisements about newer high-end PCs, you may see the terms MIPS, FLOPS, or MFLOPS. Each of these terms describes the number of instructions or operations the PC can perform per second. MIPS is an abbreviation for millions of instructions per second; for example, a 2-MIPS machine can perform 2 million instructions per second. FLOPS is an abbreviation for floating-point operations per second; if your computer has a math coprocessor, its FLOPS rating will be high. MFLOPS, or mega-FLOPS, is an abbreviation for millions of floating-point operations per second; if you divide a computer's FLOPS value by 1 million, the result is MFLOPS.

You might think that the computer with the highest MIPS rating will be the fastest. However, ratings such as MIPS and MFLOPS are very dependent on the programs used and the conditions under which

the computers were run. It is possible for the same computer to have a 3-MIPS rating for one program and a MIPS rating of less than 1 for another, simply because of the instructions involved. Your system performance depends on a number of factors: processor speed, caching, memory speed, video speed, disk speed, and so on. If a salesperson tells you a machine has such-and-such a MIPS rating, say "great," and then ask to watch it run Windows.

What Are Multisynch Monitors?

As described in Tip 798, different video boards perform vertical and horizontal refresh operations at different rates. In the past, users simply attached CGA monitors to CGA video boards, EGA monitors to EGA boards, and so on. Unfortunately, with the development of VGA and Super VGA video capabilities, you cannot assume that the frequencies used by various video boards are identical. A multisynch monitor is a monitor capable of synchronization to a range of vertical and horizontal synchronization frequencies. Such a monitor is far more likely to be compatible with a range of video boards. When you purchase a video board, inquire about the board's VESA (Video Electronic Standards Association) and XGA compatibility. If a monitor is not VESA compatible or Super VGA or XGA compatible, you should probably shop for one that is.

Understanding Video Coprocessors

As described in Tip 767, a math coprocessor is a chip that can improve performance speed for programs that process complex mathematics operations. Similarly, a video coprocessor is a chip that can improve the performance spped of specific video operations. Unlike the math coprocessor that you install on your PC's motherboard, a video coprocesor typically resides on a video board; in other words, your video board either comes with a coprocessor, or it doesn't support one. As was the case with the math

coprocessor, a video coprocessor won't make every program faster—just those written to take advantage of it. The video coprocessor (like the CPU) has a set of specific instructions. If a program, such as Windows, is aware of the instructions, the program can use the coprocessor for faster screen updates; in fact, video coprocessors have been called Windows accelerators because of their impact on screen update rates. Before you buy a video board with a coprocessor, make sure the board is fully compatible with your software.

Understanding the PC's Modes of Operation

Depending on your PC type, your PC can run in one of three modes: real, protected, or virtual 8086 mode. Real mode corresponds to the mode of operation used by the original IBM PC (8088) and by DOS. In real mode, programs access physical addresses in memory. Real mode was designed to run one program at a time and does not, therefore, provide a way to protect one program from another. When the PC AT was released with the 286 in 1984, the chip supported two modes of operation: real and protected. By default, the 286 runs in real mode, which is the mode DOS requires.

Protected mode exists to let multiple applications run at the same time. In protected mode, programs don't address physical memory but, rather, virtual memory, which gives programs the impression they have an unlimited address space, regardless of the amount of memory actually present in the computer. To implement virtual memory, the operating system moves program instructions and data in and out of memory to disk as necessary. Because each program uses its own virtual memory, one program in memory cannot harm another. Unfortunately, DOS does not use protected mode. UNIX and OS/2 are protected-mode operating systems. Likewise, Microsoft Windows will run in protected mode.

The 386 introduced a third mode of operation: virtual 8086. In this protected mode, the operating system can simultaneously run several real-mode (or DOS) applications, each of which is unaware of the other, and each of which believes it is running in real mode on a PC by itself. Windows 386 Enhanced mode uses virtual 8086 tasks to run DOS applications in their own windows. Unfortunately, even though three modes of operation exist, DOS still uses real mode, the least powerful mode. The primary reason for this is to maintain compatibility with existing hardware and software. Over 90 million personal computers now run DOS; a large percentage of those can use only real mode.

Understanding CRC

CRC is an abbreviation for cyclic redundancy check, an error-detection technique employed by data communication software and disks. Tip 774 describes how the PC uses parity to detect single-bit errors. However, if two bits are in error, parity will not detect the error. CRC uses a more complex algorithm to detect errors. Here's a very simple example. Assume your modem is sending the ASCII characters for the word *DOS* to another system. A simple CRC algorithm could simply add up the values of each ASCII character as follows:

D	68
O	79
S	83
	——
	230

The sending modem also sends the CRC result (230) to the receiver. When the letter arrives at the receiver, the receiver too adds them up, comparing its CRC result with the sender's. If the values differ, an error has occurred, and the information must be resent.

As Tip 403 explains, your disk actually stores CRC information for each disk sector.

A Quick Lookup Table for the 8088 Instruction Set

Many of the tips presented in this book include the DEBUG script file, which contain assembly language instructions. To help you change or create your own DEBUG script files in the future, Table 125 lists the 8088 instruction set. For more information on each instruction, refer to your favorite assembly language book.

Table 125. The 8088 Instruction Set

AAA	INTO	JPO	RCR
AAD	IRET	JS	REP
AAM	JA	JZ	REPE
AAS	JAE	LAHF	REPNE
ADC	JB	LDS	REPNZ
ADD	JBE	LEA	REPZ
AND	JC	LES	RET
CALL	JCXZ	LOCK	RETF
CBW	JE	LODSV	ROL
CLC	JECXZ	LODSD	ROR
CLD	JG	LODSW	SAHF
CLI	JGE	LOOP	SAL
CMC	JL	LOOPE	SAR
CMP	JLE	LOOPNE	SBB
CMPSB	JMP	LOOPNZ	SCASB
CMPSD	JNA	LOOPZ	SCASD
CMPSW	JNAE	MOV	SCASW
CWD	JNB	MOVSB	SHL
DAA	JNBE	MOVSD	SHR
DAS	JNC	MOVSW	STC
DEC	JNE	MUL	STD
DIV	JNG	NEG	STI
ENTER	JNGE	NOP	STOSB
HLT	JNL	NOT	STOSD
IDIV	JNLE	OR	STOSW
IMUL	JNO	OUT	SUB
IN	JNP	POP	TEST
INC	JNS	POPF	WAIT
INSB	JNZ	PUSH	XCHG
INSW	JO	PUSHF	XLATB
INT	JP	RCL	XOR

Stepping Through a Command File's Execution with DEBUG

When you create your DEBUG script files, sometimes your command files simply don't work as you desire. When this occurs, you can use DEBUG as it was originally intended: to help you detect errors (bugs) in your program. To begin, create the file BELL.COM, using the DEBUG script BELL.SCR that Tip 49 describes. Next, use DEBUG to walk through each instruction's execution. To begin, invoke DEBUG as shown here:

```
C:\> DEBUG BELL.COM <ENTER>
```

When DEBUG displays its hyphen prompt, type **R** to display each register's contents:

```
-R <ENTER>
AX=0000  BX=0000  CX=000A  DX=0000  SP=FFFE  BP=0000  SI=0000 DI=0000
DS=236A  ES=236A  SS=236A  CS=236A  IP=0100   NV UP EI PL NZ NA PO NC
236A:0100 B402          MOV, AH,02
```

Issue DEBUG's (T)race command to execute the first instruction and redisplay the register's contents after the instruction's execution as follows:

```
-T <ENTER>
AX=0200  BX=0000  CX=000A  DX=0000  SP=FFFE  BP=0000  SI=0000 DI=0000
DS=236A  ES=236A  SS=236A  CS=236A  IP=0102   NV UP EI PL NZ NA PO NC
236A:0102 B207          MOV, DL,07
```

When the PC executes INT 21, it executes a series of instructions within the DOS kernel. Rather than single-stepping through these instructions with the T(race) command, issue DEBUG's P(roceed) command to bypass the DOS instructions:

```
-P <ENTER>
```

Use the T(race) and P(roceed) commands to traverse the remaining instructions. Following the last instruction, DEBUG will display a message informing you that the program has terminated successfully. Use DEBUG's Q(uit) command to exit DEBUG. By single-stepping through programs in this

way, you can examine the register contents after each instruction to verify that the instructions were executed correctly.

Monitoring the Flags Register While Debugging Your Script Files

The PC uses the flags register and its ability to indicate various machine states. Tip 126 discusses how to use DEBUG's T(race), R(egister), and P(roceed) commands to traverse your command files. Each time you issue one of these commands, DEBUG displays the flag register settings as shown here:

```
-R <ENTER>
AX=0000  BX=0000  CX=000A  DX=0000  SP=FFFE  BP=0000  SI=0000 DI=0000
DS=236A  ES=236A  SS=236A  CS=236A  IP=0100   NV UP EI PL NZ NA PO NC
236A:0100 B402          MOV, AH,02
                                              Flags register settings
```

Table 127 describes the meanings of the various flag register settings.

Table 127. Symbols Used in DEBUG to Represent System Flag Settings

Flag	Symbol If Set	Symbol If Clear
Overflow	OV	NV
Direction	DN	UP
Interrupt	EI	DI
Sign	NG	PL
Zero	ZR	NZ
Auxiliary carry	AC	NA
Parity	PE	PO
Carry	CY	NC

As you use DEBUG to trace your command's execution, watch how each instruction affects the flags. If your DEBUG script file contains conditional branches, use the table in Tip 125 to ensure you are using the correct branch instruction.

Identifying the Correct Branch Instruction

As you create your own DEBUG script files, you will eventually need the files to make their own decisions based on the result of the previous operation. To help you determine the correct branch instruction, use the instruction descriptions in Table 128.

Table 128. Branch Instructions to Test Specific System Flags

Branch Instruction	Description	DEBUG Flags for a Branch
JA	Jump if the first unsigned value is greater than the second.	NZ NC
JAE	Jump if the first unsigned value is greater than or equal to the second.	NC
JB	Jump if the first unsigned value is less than the second.	CY
JBE	Jump if the first unsigned value is less than or equal to the second.	ZR CY
JC	Jump if the carry flag is set.	CY
JCXZ	Jump if CX=0.	
JE	Jump if the values are equal.	ZR
JG	Jump if the first signed value is greater than the second.	PL NZ
JGE	Jump if the first signed value is greater than or equal to the second.	PL

Table 128. Branch Instructions to Test Specific System Flags (continued)

Branch Instruction	Description	DEBUG Flags for a Branch
JL	Jump if the first signed value is less than the second.	NG NZ
JLE	Jump if the first signed value is less than or equal to the second.	NG
JNA	Same as JBE.	
JNAE	Same as JB.	
JNB	Same as JAE.	
JNBE	Same as JA.	
JNC	Jump if the carry flag is clear.	NC
JNE	Jump if the values are not equal.	NZ
JNGE	Same as JL.	
JNL	Same as JGE.	
JNLE	Same as JG.	
JNO	Jump if the overlow flag is clear.	NV
JP	Jump if the parity flag is even.	PE
JPO	Jump if the parity flag is odd.	PO
JS	Jump if the sign flag is set.	NG
JZ	Jump if the value is zero.	ZR

Assigning Values to Memory Locations with DEBUG

Tip 89 uses the DEBUG E(nter) command to create a DEBUG script file. In general, the E(nter) command lets you assign byte values to a specific memory location. This tip explains how to use

DEBUG's E(nter) command so you can apply it in other tips presented in this book. To begin, invoke DEBUG with the command line "This is a test" as shown here:

```
C:\> DEBUG This is a test <ENTER>
```

Use the following DEBUG D(ump) command to display the command line:

```
-D 80 <ENTER>
```

Just as the D(ump) command lets you display values in memory, DEBUG's E(nter) command lets you assign values.

The easiest way to assign values is one byte at a time. To do so, issue DEBUG's E(enter) command with the desired address. The following command tells DEBUG you want to enter a byte at address 80H in the current data segment:

```
-E 80 <ENTER>
```

When you press ENTER, DEBUG will display the value currently stored in the memory location followed by a period. You can type the desired value (in hexadecimal format) or press the space key to leave the value unchanged, advancing to the next value. After you enter the last value, press ENTER. The following example uses the ENTER command to assign hexadecimal values for the ASCII characters D (44), 0 (4F), and S (53) to location 80:

```
-E 80 <ENTER>
nnnn:0080 0A.44 20.4F 69.53 <ENTER>
```

By using DEBUG's E(nter) command, you can create DEBUG script files. Tip 476 explains how to use E(nter) to rename root directory files and directories.

Discarding stderr's Output

Each time you run a program, DOS predefines five file handles: stdin, stdout, stderr, stdaux, and stdprn. DOS provides the stderr handle as a way for programs to display messages to the user's screen even when the user has redirected stdout to a file or device. Depending on your requirements, you sometimes may want to discard a message DOS would normally send to

stden. To help you do so, the companion disk that accompanies this book provides the utility program ERRTONUL.EXE that redirects stden's output to the NUL device and then invokes the command you specify. To use ERRTONUL, invoke your command from the DOS prompt or from within a DOS batch file as shown here:

```
C:\> ERRTONUL SomeProg [Parameters]
```

Errtonul fully supports I/O redirection. As shown here, however, to perform redirection you must use the DOSKEY metacharacters $G, $B, $l, and GG:

```
C:\> ERRTONUL SomeProg > PRN <ENTER>
```

ERRTONUL.EXE

The utility command ERRTONUL.EXE resides on the companion disk that accompanies this book.

What Is a File Handle, Anyway?

The CONFIG.SYS FILES entry specifies the number of files DOS can have open at one time. As Tip 82 briefly discusses, each time you execute a program, DOS creates a program segment prefix. The PSP contains a file table that tracks the files the current program has open. Each entry in this file table corresponds to a file handle. When a program opens a file, DOS returns a file handle indexed to the file table. The first five entries in the table correspond to the predefined handles stdin, stdout, stderr, stdaux, and stdprn. By default, the table can hold up to 20 entries; however, programs can ask DOS to increase the table size. Each table entry in the program's file table points to a larger system table that contains specific information about the files opened by all programs (memory-resident programs, DOS, and the current program). The following illustration shows the relationship among a file handle, program file table, and system file table:

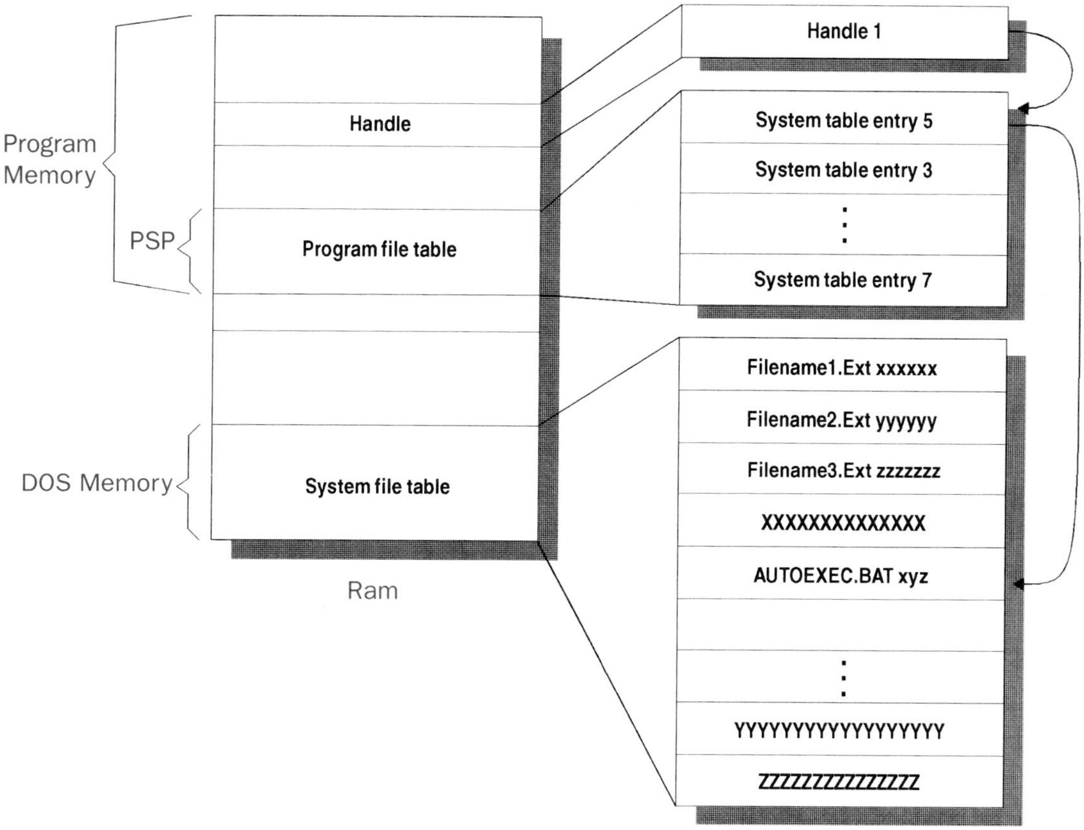

Program Memory
PSP
DOS Memory
Handle
Program file table
System file table
Ram
Handle 1
System table entry 5
System table entry 3
System table entry 7
Filename1.Ext xxxxxx
Filename2.Ext yyyyyy
Filename3.Ext zzzzzzz
XXXXXXXXXXXXXX
AUTOEXEC.BAT xyz
YYYYYYYYYYYYYYYYYY
ZZZZZZZZZZZZZZZ

The CONFIG.SYS FILES entry specifies the size of the system file table.

Redirecting stderr's Output to the Printer

Tip 130 describes how to use the utility command ERRTONUL to discard the output DOS would normally display on your screen with stderr by sending the output to the NUL device. Because the

messages that programs normally write to stderr are important error messages, a better alternative may be to redirect the messages to your system printer. The companion disk that accompanies this book contains the utility command ERRTOPRN.EXE that redirects stderr's output to LPT1. The following command illustrates how you would enter ERRTOPRN:

```
C:\> ERRTOPRN SomeProg <ENTER>
```

ERRTOPRN supports DOS I/O redirection, however, to perform redirection you must use the DOSKEY metacharacters $B,$G,$L, and GG.

ERRTOPRN.EXE

The utility command ERRTOPRN.EXE resides on the companion disk that accompanies this book.

Flushing Your DOSKEY Command Buffer

As discussed in Tip 305, the DOS 5 DOSKEY command lets you store your commands in a buffer so you can quickly recall and edit, or simply repeat, the commands. If you work in an office and need to leave temporarily, you may want to flush your DOSKEY buffers to prevent another user from viewing your previous commands. Also, if the number of commands in your buffer is large, locating a specific command in the buffer may be more work than simply retyping the command. By pressing the ALT-F7 keyboard combination, you can erase DOSKEY's command buffer.

To track commands using DOSKEY, you must be using DOS 5.

Vector Versus Raster Graphics

As you work with different screen images, you may encounter the terms vector, raster, and possibly, bit-mapped graphics. These terms describe how an image was created.

A vector is a line. A vector graphic is an image created using a series of lines. The following illustration shows a vector graphic:

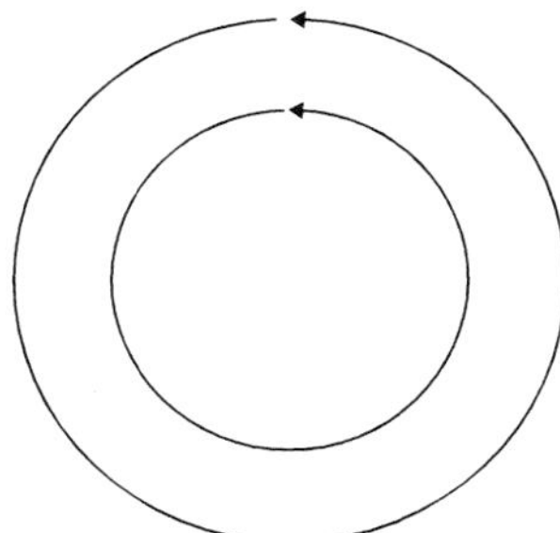

Because they are created using a sequence of lines, individual components of a vector graphic can easily be changed (moved, expanded, curved, and so on). Unfortunately, as vector images become more complex, the number of lines required to produce the image causes drawing the image to take considerable time.

Raster and bit-mapped graphics are one and the same. Raster graphics are images created using a series of dot patterns as shown here:

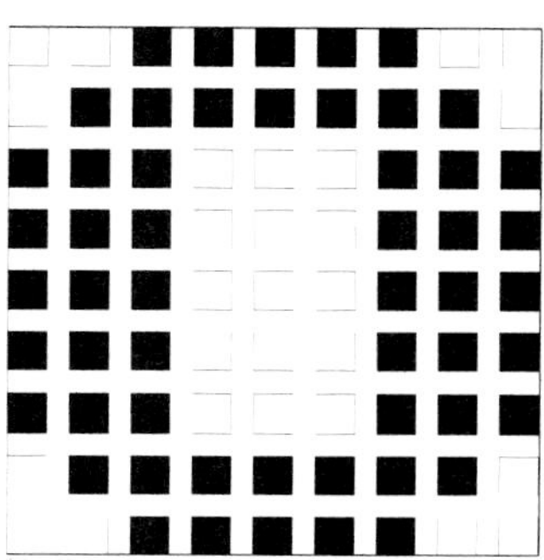

Raster graphics are normally used to represent images that require detail and sharpness such as a photograph. Raster graphics can often be displayed more quickly than vector graphics. However, because raster graphics require information about each image bit, they consume more disk space than vector graphics.

TIP 135 What Is Binary Coded Decimal?

As you read about different system and BIOS components, you will learn that some components store information in binary coded decimal, or BCD, format. A byte (8 bits) can represent 256 different values. When the BCD format is used, each byte holds a decimal value in the range 0 through 9.

For example, assume that a device stores the date 1993 in BCD format. To store these values, the device would use four bytes as shown here:

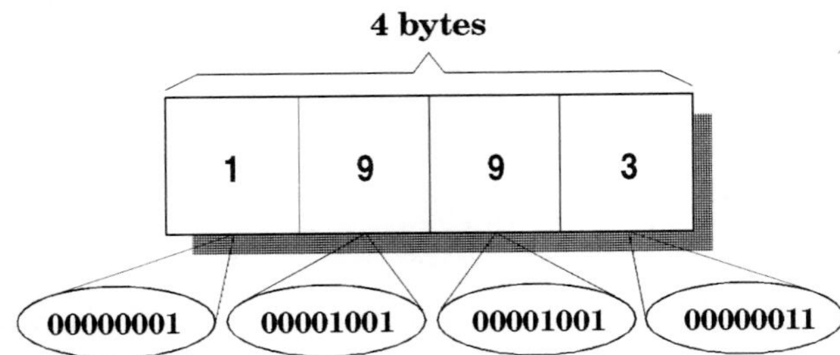

When BCD format is used, a byte value will never contain a value higher than 9. As you can see, the value in BCD format requires 4 bytes. In non-BCD format, the value can be represented in 2 bytes (16 bits). Thus, BCD format uses bits (binary) to code decimal values in the range 0 through 9. The PC's CMOS, for example, stores the date and time in BCD format.

Changing the DOS Switch Character

Something UNIX users find frustrating when working with DOS is that DOS and UNIX use different slashes to separate directory names. For example, in UNIX, you would represent the root directory's BIN subdirectory as /BIN. With DOS, however, the directory would be \BIN. DOS uses the forward slash (/) as its command-line switch character to tell DOS that the information that follows is a command option or qualifier. UNIX, on the other hand, uses a hyphen (-). If you are using DOS 3.3 or lower, the following DEBUG switch file, CHSWITCH.SCR, creates a command file named CHSWITCH.COM that changes the DOS switch character to a hyphen:

```
N CHSWITCH.COM <ENTER>
A 100          <ENTER>
MOV AX,3701    <ENTER>
MOV DL,2D      <ENTER>
INT 21         <ENTER>
MOV AH,4C      <ENTER>
INT 21         <ENTER>
               <ENTER>
R CX           <ENTER>
B              <ENTER>
W              <ENTER>
Q              <ENTER>
```

CHSWITCH.SCR

Use DEBUG as follows to create the command file CHSWITCH.COM:

```
C:\> DEBUG < CHSWITCH.SCR <ENTER>
```

After you invoke CHSWITCH, you can indicate switches by using the hyphen, and you can refer to directories by using forward slashes or backslashes. The following DIR command, for example, displays a wide directory listing of the DOS subdirectory:

```
C:\> DIR -W /DOS <ENTER>
```

Unfortunately, beginning with DOS version 4, most commands do not support switch character substitution.

Converting Environment Entries to Uppercase Format

The SET command lets you assign, remove, and display environment entries. When you place an entry in the environment with the SET command, SET converts the entry's name to uppercase letters but leaves the case of the entry itself unchanged. To place an uppercase entry value in the environment or to convert an existing entry's value to uppercase letters, you can use the utility command SETUPPER.EXE that resides on this book's companion disk. Treat the SETUPPER command just like SET. For example, the following batch file assigns the value specified in %1 to the entry FILE, first converting the value to uppercase format:

```
@ECHO OFF
SETUPPER FILE=%1
ECHO The value entered was %FILE%
```

If SETUPPER cannot add the entry to the environment, it returns the exit status 1; otherwise, it returns the value 0.

SETUPPER.EXE

The utility command SETUPPER.EXE resides on the companion disk that accompanies this book.

What's an MPC?

Tip 793 introduces multimedia, whose widespread use appears to be right around the corner. MPC is an abbreviation for multimedia PC. MPC is not a computer but, rather, a compatibility standard for multimedia products. If two products have the MPC logo, you can

consider the products to be compatible. The MPC standards, however, do specify the minimum requirements for a PC to be used for multimedia applications. At minimum, the system should have a 386SX processor with 2Mb of RAM, a 1.44Mb floppy drive, a VGA monitor, a CD-ROM, and a sound board and speakers. In addition, the computer must be running Windows 3.1 or the multimedia extensions to Windows 3.0. As you shop for multimedia equipment, watch for the MPC logo.

A Fast ANSI.SYS Screen Blanker

If you need to leave your system for a while but you don't want to run a screen saver program, a quick solution is to use the ANSI driver to select black text on a black background. To help you do so, the following DEBUG script file, B_ON_B.SCR, creates the command files B_ON_B.COM and W_ON_B.COM that let you display black-on-black text or white-on-black text as your needs require:

B_ON_B.SCR

```
N B_ON_B.COM   <ENTER>
A 100          <ENTER>
MOV AH,2       <ENTER>
MOV DL,1B      <ENTER>
INT 21         <ENTER>
MOV DL,5B      <ENTER>
INT 21         <ENTER>
MOV DL,38      <ENTER>
INT 21         <ENTER>
MOV DL,6D      <ENTER>
INT 21         <ENTER>
MOV AH,4C      <ENTER>
INT 21         <ENTER>
               <ENTER>
R CX           <ENTER>
16             <ENTER>
W              <ENTER>
N W_ON_B.COM   <ENTER>
A 10A          <ENTER>
MOV DL,30      <ENTER>
               <ENTER>
```

```
W                  <ENTER>
Q                  <ENTER>
```

Use DEBUG as follows to create the command files B_ON_B.COM and W_ON_B.COM:

```
C:\> DEBUG < B_ON_B.SCR <ENTER>
```

The following batch file, BLANKIT.BAT, uses B_ON_B.COM to select the black-on-black attribute and CLS to blank the screen. When you press any key, normal white-on-black screen colors take effect.

```
@ECHO OFF
B_ON_B
CLS
PAUSE
W_ON_B
```

Executing Multiple Commands in One Step

As described in Tip 92, using the DOS 5 DOSKEY command, you can issue multiple commands on the same command line. If you are not using DOS 5, or if you don't want to install DOSKEY's memory-resident software, you can use the companion disk utility command DO.EXE to execute several commands on the same command line. To use DO.EXE, simply place each command on the command line. If the command requires switches or parameters, enclose the command in double quotation marks as shown here:

```
C:\> DO CLS "CHDIR \DOS" "DIR /W" VOL <ENTER>
```

DO.EXE

The utility command DO.EXE resides on the companion disk that accompanies this book.

Use LOADHIGH with Environment Setting Commands

Several of the tips presented in this book describe commands that add or change environment entries. When you execute one of these commands, the command will attempt to increase the envionment's size, if necessary, to store the new entry. The following illustration shows an environment whose size can be expanded because of the available memory that immediately follows:

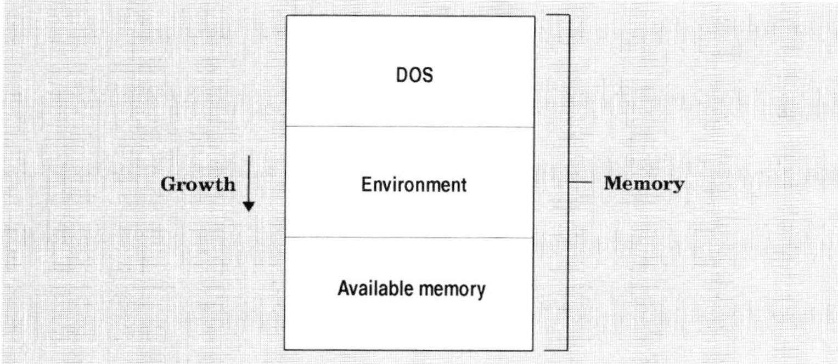

Unfortunately, when you execute commands that modify the environment, DOS normally loads the command in memory at the first available memory location as shown here, which may prevent the environment's growth:

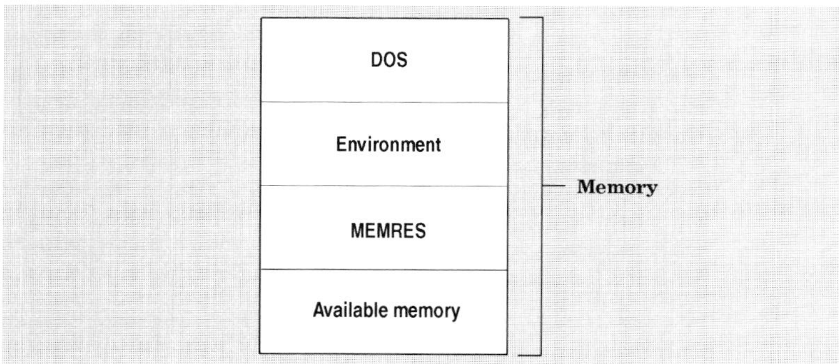

If you are using the DOS 5 memory management techniques, use LOADHIGH when you invoke the commands that modify the environment. LOADHIGH causes DOS to place the command into reserved memory, which allows the envionment to grow. The following batch file, for example, modifies the batch file DIR_COPY.BAT presented in Tip 685 to use LOADHIGH:

```
@ECHO OFF
SET CURRENT_FILE=
:LOOP
LOADHIGH NEXTFILE
IF '%CURRENT_FILE%'=='' GOTO DONE
:TRY_AGAIN
XCOPY '%CURRENT_FILE%' A:
IF ERRORLEVEL 1 GOTO DISK_FULL
GOTO LOOP

:DISK_FULL
ECHO Place a new floppy disk in drive A
PAUSE
GOTO TRY_AGAIN

:DONE
```

To use the LOADHIGH command, you must be using DOS 5 or later.

What Are Fractals?

The term fractal typically corresponds to a graphic image produced using fractal geometry. Fractals are typically used to draw multidimensional objects whose shapes are not smooth.

Although fractal creation is an exciting field for programmers, the use of fractals is appearing in many different fields of science. Fractals have unique goemetic relationships, and scientists have found that these same relationships occur in nature, such in the formation of clouds, waves, crystals, and so on. Using the computer, fractals allow researchers to model such objects.

Understanding WAV Files

As more systems add multimedia hardware, you will encounter different file types: for example, WAV files. As Tip 810 explains, sound is represented by an analog wave form similar to that shown here:

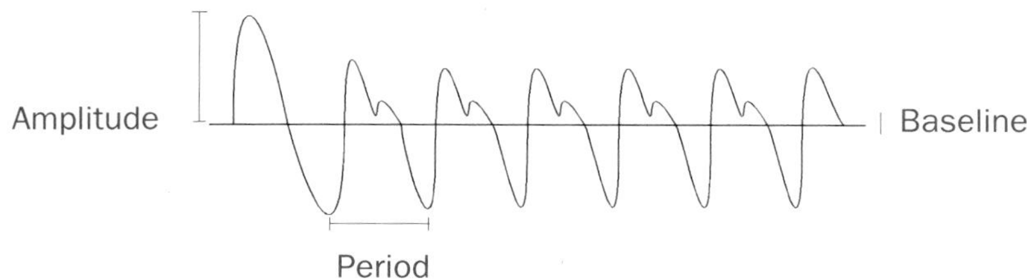

To store sound on disk, the PC digitizes the sound by taking samples of the sound at fixed time intervals. A WAV file is a file containing digitized sound. Sound can be sampled at rates of 11.025, 22.05, and 44.1KHz. Because of the amount of information required to represent sound, WAV files can become very large, very fast. In fact, digitized audio information sampled at a rate of 22.05KHz consumes storage at a rate exceeding 1Mb per minute! You can see that CD-ROM is almost mandatory for storing large WAV files.

Understanding the Video Overscan Region

Tip 84 creates a command file that sets your screen's border color. The border area is also called the overscan region. As Tip 798 shows, your monitor contains an electron gun that scans horizontally and then vertically across your screen, almost in a zig-zag fashion as shown here:

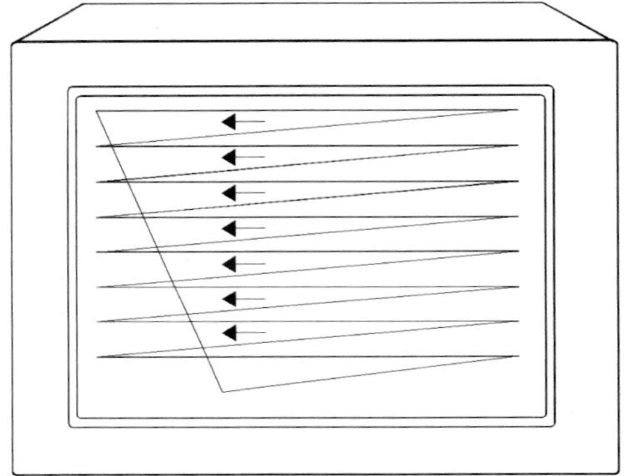

As you can see from the preceding illustration, the electron gun actually overshoots the edges of your screen display before reversing its direction. Normally, display of this signal is turned off in the overscan area. However, by enabling the signal's display and selecting a color for the region, you can direct the monitor to display a border color as in Tip 84.

Creating ASCII Files with WordPerfect

Most of the tips presented in this book that create ASCII files use either EDLIN or EDIT. If you are using WordPerfect 5.1, you sometimes may want to create a batch file or modify your CONFIG.SYS

file with WordPerfect. Both of these files must be ASCII files. To create an ASCII file using WordPerfect, invoke WordPerfect as shown here:

```
C:\> WP <ENTER>
```

Next, type the batch file commands. When you are done editing the file, press the CTRL-F5 keyboard combination. Next, select option 1 for DOS text (ASCII file), followed by option 1 to save the file; then type the batch file name. Press the F7 key to exit WordPerfect and do not save the file again.

What Are Video Display Pages?

To display text or graphics, programs place data in the PC's video memory. The amount of video memory in your system depends on your video board type. Table 146 specifies the amount of video memory used by each video adapter.

In most cases, the large amount of video memory is required to support high-resolution graphics. With a VGA monitor using 640-by-480 pixel resolution with 256 possible colors, 307,200 bytes of memory are required. In text mode, however, the display requires only 4000 bytes. To help you take advantage of available memory, CGA, EGA, VGA, and XGA cards let you divide the memory into logical screen displays called pages. At any time, only one video page's contents appears on your screen. However, programs can place information on the other video pages at any time, later switching between the pages to make the output appear instantaneous.

Table 146. The Amount of Video Memory Used by Each Video Adapter

Video Adapter	Video Memory
Monochrome	4Kb
CGA	16Kb
EGA	64Kb to 256Kb
VGA	256Kb to 1Mb
XGA	512Kb to 1Mb

The reason it is important for you to understand video pages is that many programs use video pages to produce fast video updates on your screen. Those programs that don't use video pages normally write their output to page 0. Should a program that uses video pages fail or end without restoring the screen to display video page 0, you won't be able to see the output of a program that writes its output to page 0.

If a program that you know works results in a blank screen or if its output simply doesn't appear, use the command file VIDPAGE0.COM created by the following DEBUG script file, VIDPAGE0.SCR, to select video page 0 and then run the program:

VIDPAGE0.SCR

```
N VIDPAGE0.COM <ENTER>
A 100          <ENTER>
MOV AX,500     <ENTER>
INT 10         <ENTER>
MOV AH,4C      <ENTER>
INT 21         <ENTER>
               <ENTER>
R CX           <ENTER>
9              <ENTER>
W              <ENTER>
Q              <ENTER>
```

Use DEBUG as follows to create the command file VIDPAGE0.COM:

```
C:\> DEBUG < VIDPAGE0.SCR: <ENTER>
```

To select video page 0, invoke VIDPAGE0 from the DOS prompt as shown here:

```
C:\> VIDPAGE0 <ENTER>
```

TIP 147 What Is Gray Scaling?

When you are printing color images, most printers (because they do not support color) have to convert the images to different shades of gray. The conversion of colors to gray shades is called gray scaling. To produce a shade, a scaling factor is used. By taking consistent percentages of the image's red, green, and blue colors, unique shades of gray are created. Normally, the percentages used are approximately 30 percent red, 60 percent green, and 10 percent blue. If you are

running a program such as Windows on a VGA monochrome monitor, the video BIOS will convert colors to gray shades to represent them on your screen.

Understanding the PC's Register Set

The PC stores your programs and data in RAM. To improve performance, the PC may provide a fast cache memory. In addition, within the CPU itself is a collection of fast temporary storage locations called registers. Because registers reside in the CPU itself, the processor can access their contents quickly.

The PC uses four types of registers: the segment, offset, general-purpose, and flags registers. The flags register stores information about the current machine state. Tip 149 discusses segment registers, and Tip 150 and Tip 151 discuss the PC's offset and general-purpose registers. The following illustration shows the PC's register sets:

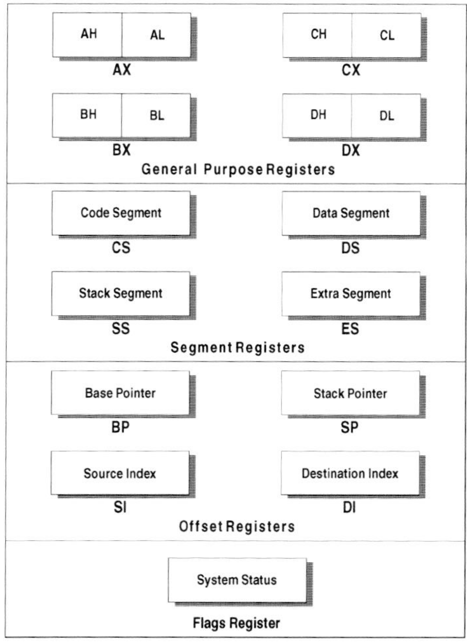

Several of the tips in this book discuss the PC's use of its various register types in detail. As you create and debug your own DEBUG script files, it's important that you understand how the PC uses these registers.

Understanding the PC's Segment Registers

A segment normally corresponds to a 64Kb region of memory. When you run a program, DOS creates a segment for your program's code (or instructions) and a second segment for your program's data. To keep track of the locations of these two segments, the PC uses code-segment register CS and the data segment register DS. In addition, as a program executes, it often needs to temporarily store information in an area called the stack. DOS allocates memory for a stack, assigning the start of the memory location to the stack segment register SS. The following illustration shows the PC's normal use of its primary segment registers:

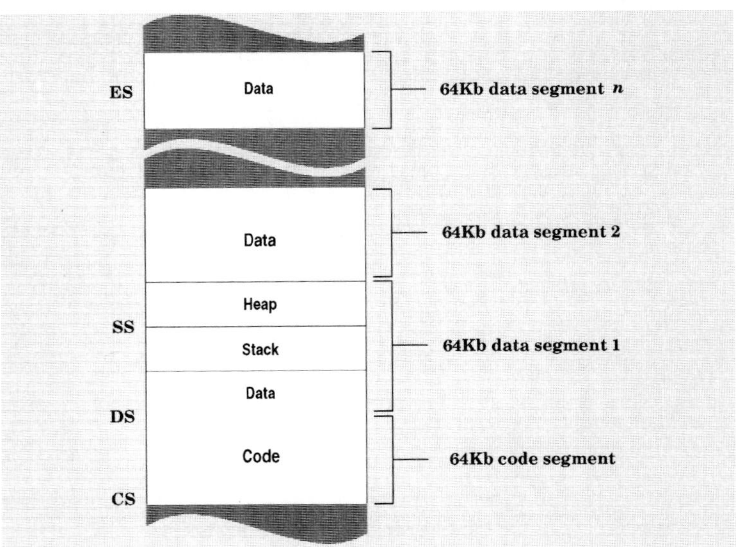

In some cases, a program requires an extra segment. Then the PC provides a fourth and final register called the extra segment register, or ES. Table 149 briefly describes each segment register.

Table 149. The PC Use of Each Segment Register

Segment Register	Purpose
CS	Stores the starting address of the current code segment
DS	Stores the starting address of the current data segment
SS	Stores the starting address of the current stack segment
ES	Stores the starting address of an extra segment

Understanding the PC's Offset Registers

As described in Tip 149, the PC uses segment registers to store the address of the start of a specific segment in memory. As your programs execute, however, they will eventually need to access specific locations within each segment. For example, when the program begins, it executes the first instruction stored at the start of the code segment. The second instruction, however, resides within the code segment. To access locations within a specific segment, the PC uses offset registers. The offset register contains a value from 0 through 65,535 that specifies a specific location within a segment. Offset 0 is the start of the segment, offset 1 is the second byte, and so on.

Within the code segment, the PC uses an offset register called the instruction pointer (IP) as an offset to the next instruction. Within the stack segment, the PC uses an offset register called the stack pointer (SP) as an offset to the last item stored in the stack. The following illustration shows an example of how the PC uses offset registers:

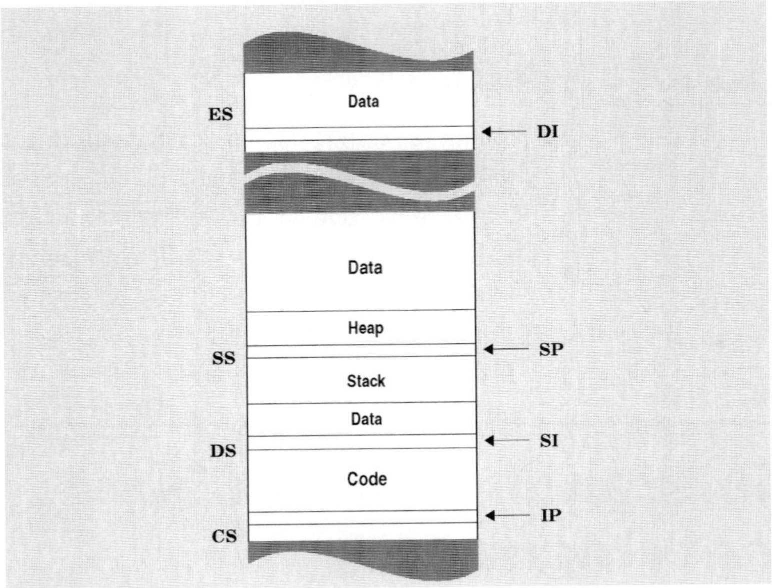

Table 150 lists the uses of the PC's offset registers.

Table 150. The PC's Offset Register Use

Offset Register	Purpose
IP	The PC's instruction pointer; contains the offset of the next instruction within the code segment (CS)
SP	The PC's stack pointer; contains the offset of the last data stored on the stack
SI	The PC's source index; contains the offset of data within the data segment (DS)
DI	The PC's destination index; contains the offset of data within the extra segment (ES)
BP	The PC's base pointer; holds the address of parameters passed on the stack

Understanding the PC's General-Purpose Registers

The PC's segment and offset register values combine to produce the address of specific locations in memory. In many cases, the PC uses registers to hold values it will use for mathematical operations or to hold the results of such operations. To hold such temporary values, the PC has four general-purpose registers named AX, BX, CX, and DX. General-purpose registers are just that—the PC can use them for almost any use. Each general-purpose register can hold up to 16 bits of data. In many cases, the PC needs to store only a byte (8 bits) of information at a time. The PC lets programs refer to the high and low bytes of each general-purpose register using the names shown here:

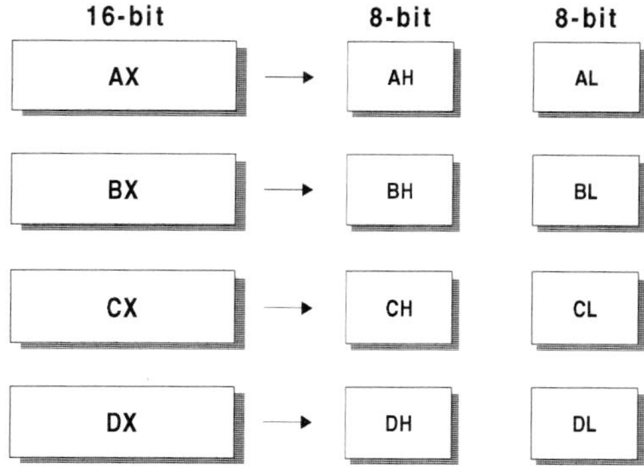

To access the high byte of the AX register, you would use the AH register (the H stands for high). To access the low byte of CX, you would use CL (the L stands for low). If you examine the DEBUG script files presented in this book, you will find assembly language statements that use the 8-bit and 16-bit register names.

What Is a PC Memory Model?

As described in Tip 149, DOS separates your programs into code and data segments. Depending on the program's size or the amount of data the program requires, the program may use several code or data segments. The number of segments the program uses defines the program's memory model. The choice of memory models is made by the programmer. Why should you care about memory models? First, knowledge of memory models will help you understand the difference between COM and EXE programs, and second, the knowledge will help you understand the register values you see when you debug command files with DEBUG. Table 152 lists the various DOS memory models.

A program's memory model has a definite impact on the program's execution speed. The more segments a program uses, the slower the program will execute. If you use one the DEBUG script files in this book to debug one of the COM files you created, you will find that DOS uses the same segment value for the code segment (CS) and data segment (DS) registers.

Table 152. DOS Memory Models

Model	Extension	Code Segments	Data Segments
Tiny	COM	1 shared code and data segment	
Small	EXE	1	1
Medium	EXE	1 or more	1
Compact	EXE	1	1 or more
Large	EXE	1 or more	1 or more

Do You Really Need the Mouse Driver?

Many software programs, such as the DOS 5 shell, support the mouse only if you have previously installed the mouse device driver. If you are using such programs, or if you have used such programs in the past, your AUTOEXEC.BAT file probably invokes the command MOUSE.COM, or your CONFIG.SYS file contains an entry for the MOUSE.SYS driver. Many newer programs, however, provide a built-in mouse driver. If you are using such programs, you may not need to install the mouse driver. Experiment with your applications by removing the driver using the REM statement as Tip 642. If your programs successfully use the mouse, leave the mouse driver uninstalled, freeing memory.

If Think You Have a Virus, Don't Panic

Tip 542 discusses computer viruses. If your computer begins to behave erratically, or if it displays a message telling you the disk has been infected, don't panic. Instead, follow these steps:

1. Turn off your computer and boot it by using the emergency floppy disk created in Tip 344.
2. Next, run a virus scan utility from a write-protected floppy disk. To place the utility on the floppy disk, you may have to use another PC. Use the virus scan utility to ensure that the other PC is not infected as well.
3. Depending on the virus scan program you are using, the program may be able to repair infected files. If it cannot, delete the infected files. Repeat the scan operation a second time just to be sure you've caught all infected files.

4. Use the virus scan utility to check all of your floppy disks. If you have a drawer full of used floppy disks, do not reuse any of the floppy disks until you have scanned them.
5. Do not restore backup files until you have scanned them as well.

If you use bulletin boards, or if you exchange files with other users, make sure you have and use a virus scan utility. Also, place the scan program on a write-protected floppy disk and store it with your emergency disks.

Disabling Your Phone's Call-Waiting Feature During Modem Operations

If your phone has call waiting, you've undoubtedly heard the beep while you are talking that tells you of an incoming call. If your modem uses the same phone line, it probably won't appreciate the incoming call notification and may even disconnect your current call. As a solution, before you initiate a call, disable call waiting by preceding the number you want the modem to dial with one of the entries listed in Table 155.

The commands will disable call waiting for the duration of the call. For example, to call (206)555-1212 on a touch-tone phone, your modem command will be ATDT *70, 206-555-1212.

By adding these entries to the autodialer as described in Tip 112, you can place phone calls without being disturbed by call waiting.

Table 155. Hayes Modem Commands to Disable Call Waiting

Phone Type	Command to Disable Call Waiting
Touch tone	ATDT *70,
Rotary	ATDP 1170,

Return to Traveler

With the recent boom in laptop and notebook computer sales, more and more businesspeople are traveling with PCs. To increase your chances of getting your PC back if it is lost or stolen, place a file in your root directory named REWARD.$$$. Include the following information in the file:

Name:
Address:
Home phone:
Work phone:
Reward for the return of this computer!

You may even want to display the file's contents as the last command in your AUTOEXEC.BAT.

Assigning a Key's Scancode to the Environment

Tip 316 discusses keyboard scancodes. Likewise, Tip 311 uses the ANSI.SYS driver to assign commands to keys by using the key's scancode values. To help you use a key's scancode, the companion disk that accompanies this book provides the utility command ENVSCODE.EXE that assigns the scancode for the key pressed to an environment entry named SCANCODE. The following batch commands tell the %SCANCODE% named parameter to display the scancode for the key pressed:

```
@ECHO OFF
ECHO Press any key
ENVSCODE
ECHO The scancode pressed was %SCANCODE%
```

If ENVSCODE successfully adds the environment entry, it returns the exit status value 0. If the environment is full, ENVSCODE returns 1.

ENVSCODE.EXE

The utility command ENVSCODE.EXE resides on the companion disk that accompanies this book.

Selecting 43-Line Display Mode Without ANSI.SYS

Tip 17 describes how to use the MODE command in conjunction with ANSI.SYS to select 43 rows with an EGA monitor. However, as Tip 6 discusses, installing the ANSI.SYS driver slows down every keyboard input and screen output operation. To address this problem, the following DEBUG script file, EGA_43.SCR, creates a command file named EGA_43.COM that sets an EGA monitor to 43-line mode:

EGA_43.SCR

```
N EGA_43.COM   <ENTER>
A 100          <ENTER>
MOV AH,0       <ENTER>
MOV AL,3       <ENTER>
INT 10         <ENTER>
MOV AX,1112    <ENTER>
MOV BX,0       <ENTER>
INT 10         <ENTER>
MOV AH,4C      <ENTER>
INT 21         <ENTER>
               <ENTER>
R CX           <ENTER>
12             <ENTER>
W              <ENTER>
Q              <ENTER>
```

Use DEBUG as follows to create the command file EGA_43.COM:

```
C:\> DEBUG < EGA_43.SCR <ENTER>
```

To select 43-line mode, invoke the command from the DOS prompt as shown here:

```
C:\> EGA_43 <ENTER>
```

Which Logical Floppy?

As Tip 378 discusses, if your computer only has one floppy drive, DOS lets you refer to it as drive A or drive B. If drive A is active and you reference drive B, DOS will display the following message:

```
Insert diskette for drive B: and press any key when ready
```

If you are creating a batch file, you can use the command A_OR_B.COM to determine which drive is active. If drive A is active, the command returns the exit status 1. If drive B is active, A_OR_B returns the exit status 2. The following DEBUG script file, A_OR_B.SCR, creates the command file:

```
N A_OR_B.COM   <ENTER>
A 100          <ENTER>
MOV AX,440E    <ENTER>
MOV BL,1       <ENTER>
INT 21         <ENTER>
MOV AH,4C      <ENTER>
INT 21         <ENTER>
               <ENTER>
R CX           <ENTER>
B              <ENTER>
W              <ENTER>
Q              <ENTER>
```

A_OR_B.SCR

Use DEBUG as follows to create the command file A_OR_B.COM:

```
C:\> DEBUG < A_OR_B.SCR <ENTER>
```

The following batch commands use A_OR_B.COM to determine the current drive; the Batch file then copies a file to the logical drive:

```
@ECHO OFF
A_OR_B
IF NOT ERRORLEVEL 2 COPY Filename.Ext A:
IF ERRORLEVEL 2 COPY Filename.Ext B:
```

By first testing for the logical drive, you ensure that DOS does not prompt you to insert a disk in the current logical drive.

Clearing the Screen in 43- or 50-Line Mode

Tip 158 and Tip 119 create the command files EGA_43.COM and VGA_50.COM that let you select a 43- or 50-line display. Unfortunately, depending on your DOS version, the CLS command may not clear the entire screen in these modes. The following DEBUG script file, CLRSCR.SCR, creates a command file named CLRSCR.COM that clears the screen in these modes:

CLRSCR.SCR

```
N CLRSCR.COM    <ENTER>
A 100           <ENTER>
MOV AH,0F       <ENTER>
INT 10          <ENTER>
MOV AH,0        <ENTER>
INT 10          <ENTER>
MOV AX,1112     <ENTER>
MOV BX,0        <ENTER>
INT 10          <ENTER>
MOV AH,4C       <ENTER>
INT 21          <ENTER>
                <ENTER>
R CX            <ENTER>
14              <ENTER>
W               <ENTER>
Q               <ENTER>
```

Use DEBUG as follows to create the command file CLRSCR.COM:

```
C:\> DEBUG < CLRSCR.SCR <ENTER>
```

A Redirection Option for On-the-Fly File Creation

Several of the tips presented in this book use ECHO with the DOS output and append redirection operators to build files on-the-fly as the batch file executes. For example, in Tip 709, the batch file MPAUSE.BAT creates a BASIC program using ECHO as shown here:

```
@ECHO OFF
ECHO DATA 262,1,294,2,330,2,350,2,392,2,440,2,494,1 > MPAUSE.BAS
ECHO DATA 494,1,440,2,392,2,350,2,330,2,294,2,262,1 >> MPAUSE.BAS

ECHO DO, >> MPAUSE.BAS
ECHO FOR I = 1 TO 14  >> MPAUSE.BAS
ECHO     READ FREQ, DURATION  >> MPAUSE.BAS
ECHO     SOUND FREQ, DURATION >> MPAUSE.BAS
ECHO NEXT I  >> MPAUSE.BAS
ECHO RESTORE >> MPAUSE.BAS
ECHO LOOP UNTIL NOT INKEY$ = ""  >> MPAUSE.BAS
ECHO SYSTEM  >> MPAUSE.BAS

ECHO %1 %2 %3 %4 %5 %6 %7 %8 %9
QBASIC /RUN MPAUSE

DEL MPAUSE.BAS
```

Normally, when you use these operators to redirect output, you place the text before the operator as shown here:

```
ECHO Text > Filename.Ext
```

However, DOS lets you also place the text you want to redirect after the filename as shown here:

```
ECHO > Filename.Ext This text is redirected!
```

Using this approach, you can improve the appearance of MPAUSE.BAT as shown here:

```
@ECHO OFF
ECHO >  MPAUSE.BAS  DATA 262,1,294,2,330,2,350,2,392,2,440,2,494,1
ECHO >> MPAUSE.BAS  DATA 494,1,440,2,392,2,350,2,330,2,294,2,262,1

ECHO >> MPAUSE.BAS DO
ECHO >> MPAUSE.BAS   FOR I = 1 TO 14
ECHO >> MPAUSE.BAS      READ FREQ, DURATION
ECHO >> MPAUSE.BAS     SOUND FREQ, DURATION
ECHO >> MPAUSE.BAS   NEXT I
ECHO >> MPAUSE.BAS   RESTORE
ECHO >> MPAUSE.BAS LOOP UNTIL NOT INKEY$ = ""
ECHO >> MPAUSE.BAS SYSTEM

ECHO %1 %2 %3 %4 %5 %6 %7 %8 %9
QBASIC /RUN MPAUSE

DEL MPAUSE.BAS
```

Displaying Device Driver Information

If you invoke the MEM /DEBUG command you can determine where your device drivers start in memory. Unfortunately, MEM does not tell you much more. Each device in your system has a specific attribute value whose bits describe the device. Table 162 lists the values of the device attribute bits when they are set.

Table 162. Device Attribute Bit Meanings

Bit	Meaning
0	Indicates that this character device is the standard input device
1	Indicates that this character device is the standard output device
2	Indicates this character device is the NUL device
3	Indicates that this device is the CLOCK$ device
4	Indicates that this character device supports fast character output via Int 29H
6	Indicates that this block device supports logical drive mapping, generic functions, or both
7	Indicates that this device supports IOCTL queries
11	Indicates that this device supports device-driver functions 0DH (open device), 0EH (close device), and 0FH (removable media)
13	Indicates that this device supports device-driver functions 10H (output until busy) or, if set for a block device, that DOS must supply the first FAT sector for calls to driver function 02H (build BPB)
15	Indicates that this device is a character device

Device drivers actually consist of two parts: a strategy routine and an interrupt handler. The strategy routine is nothing more than an address of a structure that specifies the operation DOS wants the device to perform. The interrupt handler is the actual software that performs the operations. To help you better understand your system's device drivers and the corresponding device attributes, the companion disk that accompanies this book provides the utility command DRVRINFO.EXE. As shown here, DRVRINFO displays information about each device driver and the corresponding device attributes:

Device	Units	Header Address	Attributes
NUL	.	nnnn:nnnn	1............1..
Block Device	3	nnnn:nnnn	....1...11....1.
:	:	:	:
XMSXXXX0	.	nnnn:nnnn	1.1..............

If your system experience errors, DRVRINFO gives you more information you can use to determine the error's cause.

The utility command DRVRINFO.EXE resides on the companion disk that accompanies this book.

DRVRINFO.EXE

Repeating a Command a Specific Number of Times

Tip 693 describes how to use the utility command RESULT.EXE that assigns the result of an expression to the environment entry RESULT. The companion disk also provides a second utility command, DO_DEC.EXE, that uses the RESULT environment to control the number of times a command executes. When the DO_DEC utility executes, it examines the value of the RESULT environment entry. If the entry is defined and contains a value greater than zero, DO_DEC executes the specified command. After the command completes, DO_DEC decrements RESULT's current value by 1. If the RESULT entry does not exist or contains a value less than zero, DO_DEC ends without executing the command. The following batch file uses DO_DEC to execute the DIR command five times:

```
SET RESULT=5
:LOOP
DO_DEC DIR
IF NOT %RESULT%==0 GOTO LOOP
```

The utility command DO_DEC.EXE resides on the companion disk that accompanies this book.

DO_DEC.EXE

Disabling the PC Speaker

TIP 164

There may be times when you want to turn off your PC's speaker. If you really want to disable the speaker, you can do so by unplugging the speaker cable. Unplug your computer and carefully remove the chassis cover. Next, as shown in the following illustration, locate the cable connected to the speaker and gently unplug it:

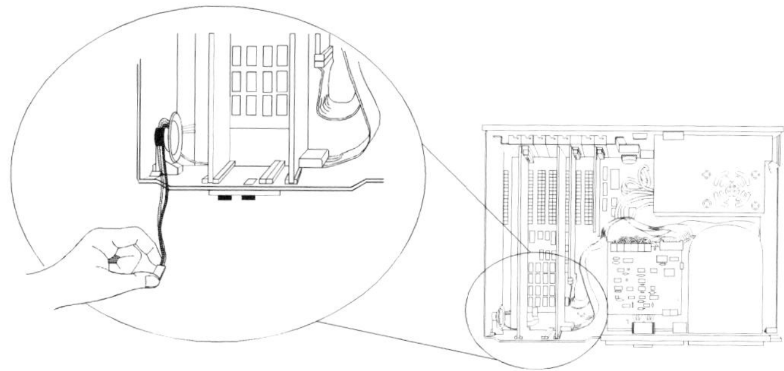

Because the PC no longer has a way of communicating with the speaker, beeps and other sounds are disabled.

Executing a Command a Specific Number of Times

For some applications, you may want to issue a certain command a specific number of times. For example, you may want to format five disks. The companion disk that accompanies this book provides the utility program DO_COUNT.EXE that executes a specific command a given number of times. For example, if an error occurs, the following batch commands use DO_COUNT to execute the BELL command three times:

```
@ECHO OFF
SomeProg
IF ERRORLEVEL 1 DO_COUNT 3 BELL
```

The format of the D0_COUNT command is as follows:

DO_COUNT Number Command [Parameters]

DO_COUNT.EXE

The utility command DO_COUNT.EXE resides on the companion disk that accompanies this book.

AT&T, MCI, Sprint? You Decide

When you make a long distance phone call, a specific phone company carrier provides service to the line. If you are traveling, for example, and you want to make a long distance modem call, charging the bill to your normal carrier can be difficult at best. However, if you are using a Hayes compatible modem, use one of the modem commands listed in Table 166, specifying the number you are calling for the letters yyy and substituting your phone credit card number for the letters xxx.

By using the modem commands shown, you can simplify your modem operations and get your best long distance phone rates.

Table 166. Modem Commands to Select Specific Long Distance Carriers

Phone Type	Company	Modem Command
Tone	AT&T	ATDT 102880,yyy,xxx
Rotary	AT&T	ATDP 102880,yyy,xxx
Tone	MCI	ATDT 102220,yyy,xxx
Rotary	MCI	ATDP 102220,yyy,xxx
Tone	Sprint	ATDT 103330,yyy,xxx
Rotary	Sprint	ATDP 103330,yyy,xxx

Assigning a Specific Line of a File to an Environment Entry

Several of the utility commands presented this book assign various values to environment entries. The companion disk that accompanies this book provides the utility command FILE_ENV.EXE that assigns to the FILE_LINE environment entry the value of a specific line of a file. For example, the following command assigns to the entry the contents of line 4 of your AUTOEXEC.BAT file:

```
C:\> FILE_ENV AUTOEXEC.BAT 4 <ENTER>
```

As your batch files become more complex, you will find FILE_ENV is very convenient. If the utility command successfully adds the environment entry, it returns the exit status value 0. If the environment is full, the utility returns the exit status value 1. If the line entry specified does not exist, the utility removes the FILE_LINE environment entry.

The utility command FILE_ENV.EXE resides on the companion disk that accompanies this book.

FIL_ ENV.EXE

Quieting Your Modem

To help you hear it dial the phone and to help you hear the target phone ring, most internal modems turn on their speaker. If you are using a Hayes-compatible modem, you can use the modem commands listed in Table 486 to enable and disable the modem's use of the speaker.

For example, to select high volume, issue the following modem command:

```
ATL3DT
```

Table 168. Modem Commands to Control the Modem's Speaker Volume

Modem Command	Description
L0	Lowest speaker volume
L1	Low speaker volume
L2	Medium speaker volume
L3	High speaker volume

When to Patch COMMAND.COM

Many books and magazines present tips that make modifications to COMMAND.COM. For example, they may change the CLS command to clear the screen, assigning a specific foreground or background color. As a rule, you shouldn't make modifications (called patches) to COMMAND.COM. In many cases, it's easy to make a subtle error that will prevent your system from later restarting. Also, if you find a documented patch, you need to ensure that the patch is valid for your DOS version. After you make the patch, you will then need to make it on every other system you use. Thus, I prefer to create small, customized DEBUG script files such as those presented in this book. With the memory management capabilities provided with DOS 5, memory-resident programs now are less of a memory-consumption problem. If you must modify COMMAND.COM, follow these steps:

- Always work from a bootable floppy while you test your patches. In this way, should an error occur, you can still boot your system from your hard disk.
- Place a copy of the nonpatched COMMAND.COM in a safe location should you need to restore it.
- Only after you are completely satisfied that your patch is correct, move the patched COMMAND.COM to your hard disk.
- Using REM, document your AUTOEXEC.BAT or CONFIG.SYS file, detailing the patch. Should a program you install not work, your patch may be the culprit.

Flushing the Environment

Sometimes, because a batch file did not clean up after itself or was ended prematurely, several unwanted entries may end up in your environment. To help you quickly remove these entries, the companion disk that accompanies this book provides the utility command FLUSHENV.EXE. The command removes all of the current environment entries. To use FLUSHENV, simply invoke it from the DOS prompt or from a DOS batch file as shown here:

```
C:\> FLUSHENV <ENTER>
```

After you invoke FLUSHENV, you will want to restore the PATH, PROMPT, and COMSPEC entries.

The utility FLUSHENV.EXE resides on the companion disk that accompanies this book.

FLUSHENV.EXE

Why You Can't Boot from Drive B

Each time your system starts, the BIOS searches drive A for a bootable floppy disk. If a bootable floppy disk is found, the BIOS boots from it; otherwise, the BIOS boots from your hard disk, drive C. If your system has two floppy drives, you will also see drive B's disk activation light briefly illuminate. However, the PC ignores drive B's contents. Why? When the PC illuminates drive B's disk light during startup, the PC is actually just testing the drive's motor as part of the power-on self-test. Thus, the

BIOS does not care what disk you have in the drive. If your disk drives are different sizes and you need to boot from a disk whose size matches drive B, you must open your chassis and exchange the ribbon cables connecting drives A and B to the disk controller. Depending on your BIOS type, you may also have to change your PC's setup configuration.

Bypassing the Keyboard Lock

As shown here, many PC's have a keyboard lock that lets you essentially lock keystrokes out of your PC while you are away from the system:

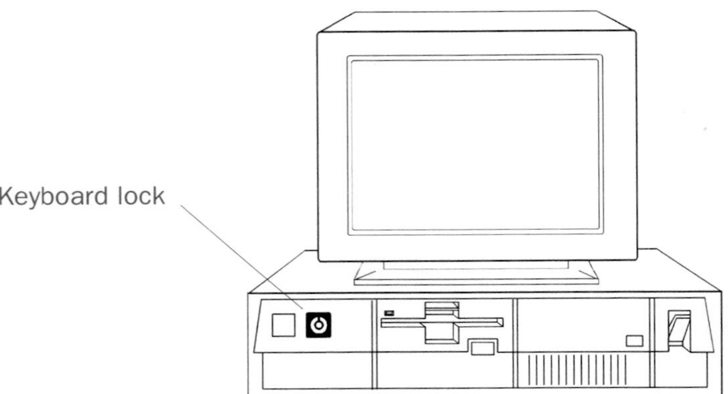

If your keyboard is locked and your key is misplaced, don't panic. By opening your computer's chassis and removing the cable from the lock to the motherboard, you can unlock the system. To do so, follow these steps. Unplug your PC and gently remove the chassis cover. Next, locate and disconnect the cable from the lock to the motherboard shown here:

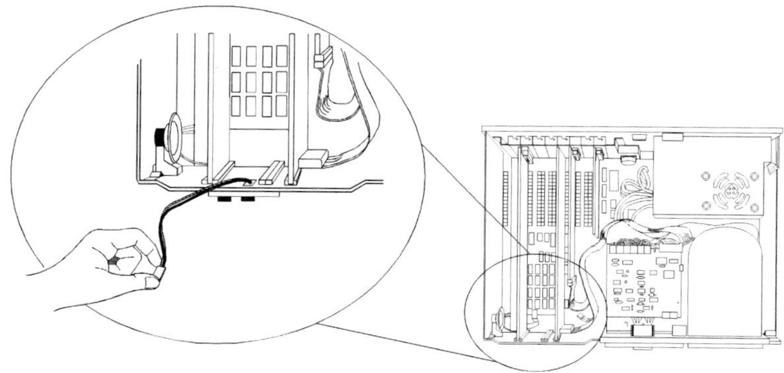

Replace the chassis cover and plug in your system. Your keyboard should now be fully operational.

Delaying Your Modem Dial

If you work in an office where a delay occurs before you get a dial tone, you may want to include a brief delay in your modem dialing commands. If you are using a Hayes-compatible modem, you can include a comma in your dialing commands to produce a delay. For example, if you work in an office where you must dial 9 and then wait for a dial tone, you can use the comma as shown here:

```
ATDT 9,555-1212
```

By default, most modems delay 2 seconds for each comma. However, using the modem's S8 register, you can specify a value in the range 1 to 255 seconds to change the amount of time each comma delays the dialing.

What Is NTSC?

As you examine advertisements for video boards and multimedia devices, you may encounter the term NTSC, an abbreviation for National Television Standards

Committee. In the United States, NTSC governs television and video playback standards. The current standard requires 525 scanlines, which the television displays 60 times per second. Updating is interlaced (see Tip 799), which means that only half of the frames are updated with each operation, yielding 30 full-frame updates per second. To produce video, RGB (red, green, and blue) signals are combined. The signal also contains audio.

As you can see, the NTSC standards aren't that rigorous when you apply them to a noninterlaced, high-resolution video card. Thus, don't purchase a video board or other device just because it supports NTSC standards. Instead, understand how those standards relate to your requirements.

Loading Programs High in Conventional Memory

If you are using DOS 5, you should use the LOADHIGH command to invoke the companion disk programs that modify the environment. If you use this command, DOS will load the programs into upper memory, leaving room for the environment's size to be increased. If you are not using DOS 5, you can use the SETSTRAT utility command presented in Tip 237 to select the last-fit low-memory strategy before loading the command, as shown here:

```
ECHO OFF
STRALAST
SomeCommand
STRAT1ST
```

In this case, the user has created two commands, STRALAST.COM and STRAT1ST.COM, that select the last-fit low-memory and first-fit low-memory strategies. By setting the memory strategy in this way, DOS will load the program as high in conventional memory as possible. As shown here, by loading the program high into conventional memory, you leave room for the environment to expand:

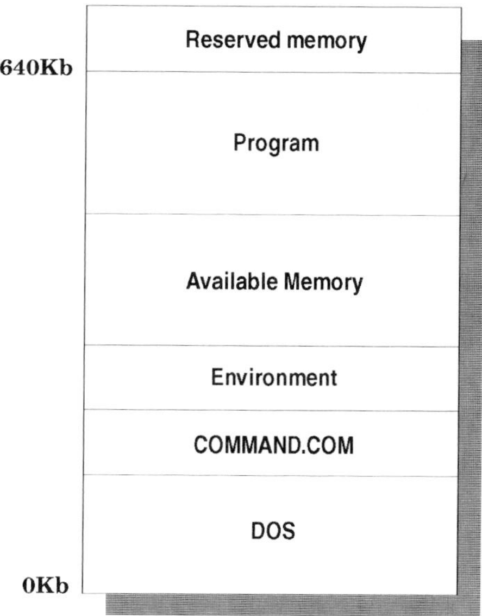

As you can see, before ending, the batch file uses the utility command STRAT1ST.COM to restore normal memory allocation.

Keeping Track of Boot Operations

You sometimes may want to perform a specific operation after the PC has booted a specific number of times. For example, you might want to invoke CHKDSK every fifth time the PC boots or invoke BACKUP every tenth time. To help you perform such operations, the companion disk that accompanies this book provides the utility command BOOTCNT.EXE that tracks the number of times your system has been booted, assigning the count to the environment entry BOOT_COUNT. The utility stores the count in a hidden root directory file named BOOT.CNT. The following batch commands illustrate how you might use BOOTCNT:

```
@ECHO OFF
BOOTCNT
IF %BOOT_COUNT%==5 CHKDSK
```

To reset the count to zero, edit the file, replacing the current number with 0. If BOOTCNT successfully adds the environment entry, it returns the exit status 0. If the environment is full, BOOTCNT returns the exit status 1.

BOOTCNT.EXE

The utility command BOOTCNT.EXE resides on the companion disk that accompanies this book.

Resetting the Boot Counter

Tip 176 uses the companion disk utility command BOOTCNT.EXE to track the number of times your system has been booted. BOOTCNT stores the boot count in a hidden root directory file named BOOT.CNT. To reset the count to zero, you can edit the value, changing the current value to 0. As an alternative, you can use the companion disk utility command RESETCNT.EXE, which zeros the boot count for you. The following batch commands invoke CHKDSK every fifth times the system starts, resetting the counter to zero:

```
@ECHO OFF
BOOTCNT
IF NOT %BOOT_COUNT%==5 GOTO CONTINUE
CHKDSK
RESETCNT
:CONTINUE
SET BOOT_COUNT=
REM other commands
```

RESETCNT.EXE

The utility command RESETCNT.EXE resides on the companion disk that accompanies this book.

Correcting Video Misalignment from within AUTOEXEC.BAT

Tip 110 explains how to use the MODE command to correct video misalignment on a CGA monitor. If your system's video display is misaligned, you will need to realign the video each time DOS boots. To do so, you can place the appropriate MODE command in your AUTOEXEC.BAT file, using ECHO and the DOS pipe to redirect to MODE the correct number of N characters to complete the alignment. The following command, for example, uses MODE to move characters two places to the right:

```
ECHO NN | MODE ,R,T
```

Displaying Only Filenames in the DOS Shell

By default, the DOS 5 shell displays a directory tree, file list, program list, and if the task switcher is active, a task list, as shown here:

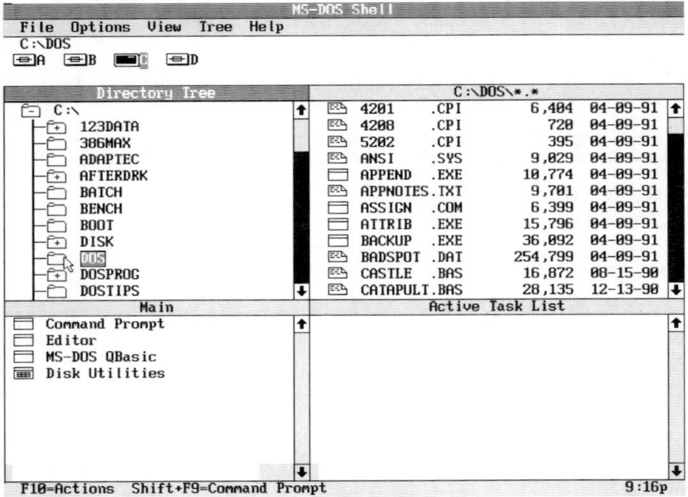

Sometimes, however, such as when you perform selective file copy, move, or delete operations, you may want to view only the file list. To display only the file list, select the shell's View menu and choose Single File List. The shell will display one file list similar to that shown here:

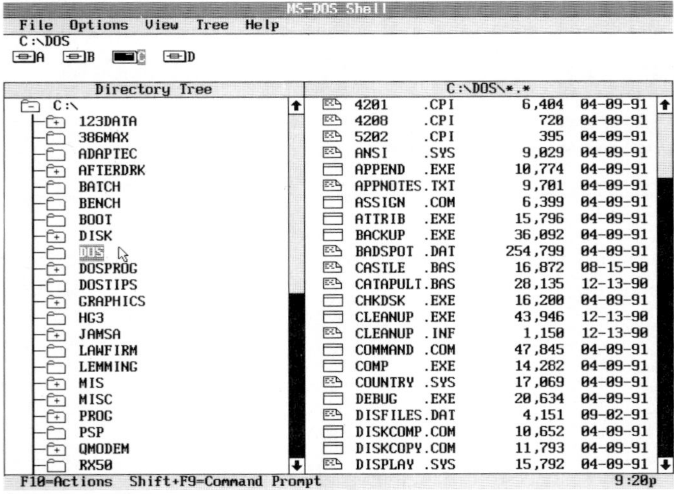

By only displaying a single file list in this way, you can view a greater number of directories or files in the current directory at one time. When you are ready to perform other shell operations, use the View menu to select your desired display format.

Controlling Your Modem Speaker

Tip 168 describes how to control your modem's speaker volume by using the commands L0 (low volume) through L3 (high volume). Sometimes, however, you may simply want to turn the speaker on or off. Table 180 lists modem commands that let you do just that.

The following modem command, for example, turns off the modem speaker during dialing:

```
ATM3DT 555-1212
```

Table 180. Modem Speaker Control Commands

Modem Command	Speaker Control
M0	Speaker is turned off.
M1	Speaker turns off when receiving a carrier signal.
M2	Speaker is turned on.
M3	Speaker turns off while dialing and while receiving a carrier signal.

Viewing All Available DOS Version Number Information

If you execute the VER command, DOS will display its major and minor version numbers as shown here:

```
C:\> VER <ENTER>
MS-DOS Version 5.00
```

In addition to the major and minor version numbers, DOS uses an OEM (original equipment manufacturer) serial number and, possibly, a user serial number. The companion disk that accompanies this book contains the utility command MOREVER.EXE, which displays more information about DOS as shown here:

```
C:\> MOREVER <ENTER>
Major: 5
Minor: 0
In ROM: No
In HMA: Yes
OEM Version: FF
User Serial Number: A0B1C2
```

If you are going to call a company's technical support line, first print a copy of MOREVER's output as shown here:

```
C:\> MOREVER > PRN <ENTER>
```

MOREVER.EXE

The utility command MOREVER.EXE resides on the companion disk that accompanies this book.

TIP 182 What TSR's Are Loaded?

Tip 162 uses the utility command DRVRINFO.EXE to display information about the device drivers loaded in your system. In a similar way, you may want to list the TSR programs. To do so, invoke the companion disk utility program SHOWTSRS.EXE as shown here:

```
C:\> SHOWTSRS <ENTER>
SHARE
PRINT
FASTOPEN
```

If you are going to call a company's technical support line, print a copy of SHOWTSR's output as shown here:

```
C:\> SHOWTSRS > PRN <ENTER>
```

To use SHOWTSRS.EXE, you must be running DOS 4 or higher. SHOWTSRS.EXE only displays the name of TSRs loaded in conventional memory.

The utility command SHOWTSRS.EXE resides on the companion disk that accompanies this book.

SHOWTSRS.EXE

Displaying Information with MSD.EXE

If you have Windows 3.1 installed on your system, you can use Microsoft's very powerful diagnostic tool called MSD.EXE. The easiest way to use the utility is to invoke it from the DOS prompt as shown here:

```
C:\> MSD <ENTER>
```

MSD will display its opening screen as shown here:

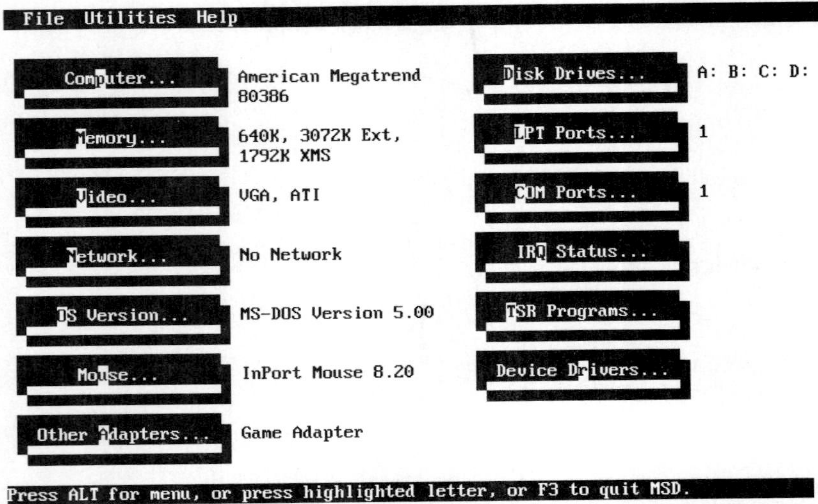

MSD provides you with several options that let you view information about specified system components. Several tips in this book discuss specific MSD options.

To use MSD.EXE, you must be using MS Windows 3.1.

What Is Your UART Type?

Tip 773 discusses UARTs (universal asynchronous receiver/transmitters) in detail. Your PC may have a 8250, 16450, or 16550 UART. The capabilities of each differs considerably. As Tip 183 explains, Windows 3.1 provides a utility program named MSD.EXE that displays system information. Using MSD, you can display your current serial port settings as well as each port's UART type. To do so, invoke MSD from the DOS prompt. When MSD displays its options menu, press C to display the COM port settings. MSD will display the settings as shown here:

COM Ports	COM1:	COM2:	COM3:	COM4:
Port Address	03F8H	N/A	N/A	N/A
Baud Rate	2400			
Parity	None			
Data Bits	8			
Stop Bits	1			
Carrier Detect (CD)	No			
Ring Indicator (RI)	No			
Data Set Ready (DSR)	No			
Clear To Send (CTS)	No			
UART Chip Used	8250			

OK

To use MSD.EXE, you must be using MS Windows 3.1.

Displaying Your System's IRQ Use

Tip 804 discusses your PC's IRQ use in detail. Tip 183 explains that if your system contains MS Windows 3.1, you can use the utility command MSD.EXE to display specifics about your system. To display information about your system's current IRQ use, invoke MSD from the DOS prompt. When MSD displays its options menu, type Q to select the IRQ settings. MSD will display the settings as shown here:

IRQ Status

IRQ	Address	Description	Detected	Handled By
0	1D42:0995	Timer Click	Yes	CAPTURE.EXE
1	1D42:1CE5	Keyboard	Yes	CAPTURE.EXE
2	0996:0057	Second 8259A	Yes	Default Handlers
3	0996:006F	COM2: COM4:	No	Default Handlers
4	0996:0087	COM1: COM3:	COM1:	Default Handlers
5	0B3A:02CD	LPT2:	InPort Mouse	MOUSE
6	0996:00B7	Floppy Disk	Yes	Default Handlers
7	0070:06F4	LPT1:	Yes	System Area
8	0996:0052	Real-Time Clock	Yes	Default Handlers
9	F000:EEE3	Redirected IRQ2	Yes	BIOS
10	0996:00CF	(Reserved)		Default Handlers
11	0996:00E7	(Reserved)		Default Handlers
12	0996:00FF	(Reserved)		Default Handlers
13	F000:EEEC	Math Coprocessor	No	BIOS
14	0996:0117	Fixed Disk	Yes	Default Handlers
15	F000:FF53	(Reserved)		BIOS

OK

If you are installing a new hardware board that requires you to select an IRQ value, use MSD.EXE to display the current settings so you can avoid conflicts.

Displaying Processor, Bus, and DMA Information

Several of the tips presented in this book discuss various processor and bus types and DMA and IRQ settings. As Tip 183 explains, if your system contains MS Windows 3.1, you can use the utility command MSD.EXE to display information about your system. To display processor and bus information, invoke MSD from the DOS prompt. When MSD displays its menu of options, type **P** to select Computer. MSD will display information about your computer as shown here:

```
                              Computer
     Computer Name: American Megatrends
 BIOS Manufacturer: American Megatrends
      BIOS Version: EXTENDED CMOS SETUP PROGRAM Ver - 1.50 ,(C)1988,
     BIOS Category: IBM PC/AT
     BIOS ID Bytes: FC 01 00
         BIOS Date: 03/03/89
         Processor: 80386
  Math Coprocessor: None
          Keyboard: Enhanced
          Bus Type: ISA/AT/Classic Bus
    DMA Controller: Yes
      Cascaded IRQ2: Yes
 BIOS Data Segment: None

                               OK
```

To use MSD.EXE you must be using Windows 3.1.

What Is APM?

If you work with a laptop or notebook computer, you have probably learned ways to conserve the computer's battery. APM is an abbreviation for advanced power management. APM is a software specification developed in conjunction with Intel that lets the operating

system make decisions about the computer's power use. By installing APM drivers, you can achieve up to 25 percent more battery life without changing your work habits. Both DOS 5.0 and Windows 3.1 support APM. If you own a laptop or notebook computer, or if you are considering one, ask your dealer about APM support.

Displaying Your COM Port Status

If you are connecting a device to a serial port, you need to ensure that you have set the correct baud rate (see Tip 86) and data communication parameters. To help you do so, the companion disk that accompanies this book provides the utility command SHOWCOM.EXE, which displays the settings of your COM ports as shown here:

```
C:\> SHOWCOM <ENTER>
Port        Baud        Parity        Data Bits   Stop Bits
COM1        1200          N               8           1
COM2        4800          E               7           0
```

If you are connecting serial devices, use SHOWCOM to help you troubleshoot.

The utility command SHOWCOM.EXE resides on the companion disk that accompanies this book.

SHOWCOM.EXE

Help for DEBUG Commands

Several of the tips in this book discuss techniques you can use within DEBUG to find errors in your DEBUG script files. When you are working within DEBUG, you

issue single-letter commands, such as A for assemble and D for dump. To display a description of DEBUG's commands, type a question mark (?) at DEBUG's hyphen prompt (-) and press ENTER:

```
-? <ENTER>
assemble      A [address]
compare       C range address
dump          D [range]
enter         E address [list]
fill          F range list
go            G [=address] [addresses]
hex           H value1 value2
input         I port
load          L [address] [drive] [firstsector] [number]
move          M range address
name          N [pathname] [arglist]
output        O port byte
proceed       P [=address] [number]
quit          Q
register      R [register]
search        S range list
trace         T [=address] [value]
unassemble    U [range]
write         W [address] [drive] [firstsector] [number]
allocate expanded memory         XA [#pages]
deallocate expanded memory       XD [handle]
map expanded memory pages        XM [Lpage] [Ppage] [handle]
display expanded memory status   XS
```

As you can see, DEBUG displays a brief description of each command's format.

Understanding DEBUG Command Fields

Tip 189 explains how to display a description of each DEBUG command. Several of the commands use addresses, some use ranges, and some ask for a list. To help you better understand the required information, Table 190 describes each command field, providing an example.

Table 190. DEBUG Command Field Names

Command Field	Description	Example
Address	A segment and offset combination, or simply an offset	D CS:0 D 100
Range	A starting and ending address, or a starting address and a length; to specify a length, precede the value with L	D 100 110 D 100 L10
List	A list of hexadecimal byte values separated by a space, comma, or tab; or a string of ASCII characters enclosed by single or double quotation marks	E DS:100 1 2 3 E DS:100 "Hello"
Value	A hexadecimal byte value	E 100 F
Port	A hexadecimal port value in the range 0 through FFFF	I 378
Drive	A hexadecimal drive value, where 0 is drive A, 1 is B,...19 is Z	L 100 2 0 1
First Sector	A hexadecimal value from 0 through FFFF that describes the first sector in a range of sectors	L 100 2 0 1
Number	A hexadecimal value that normally specifies a count	P 5
Pathname	An ASCII file or path name	N TEST.COM
Arguments	ASCII command-line arguments to be used with the command you are debugging	N TEST.COM A B C
Register	A register name of one of the PC's segment, offset, or general-purpose registers	R AX
#Pages	A hexadecimal value describing the number of expanded memory pages to allocate	XA F

Table 190 DEBUG Command Field Names (continued)

Command Field	Description	Example
Handle	A hexadecimal value corresponding to a specific expanded memory page	XD F
LPage	A hexadecimal value corresponding a logical expanded memory page number	XM 5 1 1
PPage	A hexadecimal value corresponding to a physical page number	XM 5 1 1

Generating Sounds with the PC Speaker

Several of the tips presented in this book have programs that cause the PC's built-in speaker to beep to notify the user of a specific event. The PC's speaker also can produce music. To produce a music sound, you must specify the sound's frequency in hertz (cycles per second) and the sound's duration. Table 191a lists the frequencies commonly used for musical notes.

For musical notes not listed in this table, approximate the note's frequency by doubling the corresponding note in the previous octave if you are moving up the scale or by halving the frequency if you are moving down the scale.

The sound's duration is measured in clock ticks that occur 18.2 times per second. Table 191b lists durations for common tempos.

See Tip 192 for an illustration of one way to generate music with your PC.

Table 191a. Frequencies for Common Musical Notes

Note	Frequency	Note	Frequency
C	131	C	523
D	147	D	587
E	165	E	659
F	175	F	698
G	196	G	784
A	220	A	880
B	247	B	988
C (Middle C)	262	C	1047
D	294	D	1175
E	330	E	1319
F	350	F	1397
G	392	G	1569
A	440	A	1760
B	494	B	1976

Table 191b. Sound Durations for Common Tempos

Tempo (Beats per Minute)	Duration in Clock Ticks
40 to 60	27 to 18
60 to 108	18 to 10
108 to 208	10 to 5

Generating Music

Tip 191 presents the sound frequencies and durations you can use to generate common musical notes. The easiest way to play such notes is by using BASIC's SOUND statement. The format of the sound statement is as follows:

SOUND Frequency, Duration

The following BASIC program, SCALES.BAS, uses the frequencies and durations listed in Table 191 to play the piano scales at various tempos:

```
DATA 262, 20, 294, 20, 330, 20, 350, 20, 392, 20, 440, 20, 494, 20
DATA 262, 10, 294, 10, 330, 10, 350, 10, 392, 10, 440, 10, 494, 10
DATA 262, 5, 294, 5, 330, 5, 350, 5, 392, 5, 440, 5, 494, 5
DATA 262, 1, 294, 1, 330, 1, 350, 1, 392, 1, 440, 1, 494, 1
DATA 494, 1, 440, 1, 392, 1, 350, 1, 330, 1, 294, 1, 262, 1

FOR I% = 1 TO 7
  READ FREQ%, DURATION%
  SOUND FREQ%, DURATION%
NEXT I%

FOR I% = 1 TO 7
  READ FREQ%, DURATION%
  SOUND FREQ%, DURATION%
NEXT I%

FOR I% = 1 TO 7
  READ FREQ%, DURATION%
  SOUND FREQ%, DURATION%
NEXT I%

FOR J% = 1 TO 2
  FOR I% = 1 TO 7
    READ FREQ%, DURATION%
    SOUND FREQ%, DURATION%
  NEXT I%
NEXT J%
```

If you are using DOS 5, use QBASIC to run the program as shown here:

```
C:\> QBASIC /RUN SCALES.BAS <ENTER>
```

If you are not using DOS 5, invoke the program by using GWBASIC or BASICA.

As you can see, the program simply reads and plays a specific number of notes and frequencies. By changing the DATA statements within the program, you can create and play your own songs.

Understanding MODE's Retry Option

When you use the MODE command to configure a serial port or parallel printer, one of the values you can specify is a retry option. The retry option tells DOS how to respond to device errors. Normally, when a device is busy or has experienced an error, DOS will perform a timeout on the operation it is executing. The following command, for example, uses MODE to select infinite retries for LPT1:

```
C:\> MODE LPT1 RETRY=P <ENTER>
```

When you select infinite retries, DOS will continue trying to complete an output operation—forever—if the device is busy or an error has occurred. If DOS becomes locked in such a loop, the only way to end the loop is by pressing CTRL-BREAK. Unless you have a very slow printer, you normally won't have a reason to select infinite retries. If your AUTOEXEC.BAT file contains a MODE command that selects infinite retries, keep in mind that should your system lock up, you can end the retry operation by pressing CTRL-BREAK.

Viewing Device Status Values

Several of the tips presented in this book use the MODE command to alter a device setting. Using MODE's /STATUS switch, you can display your current device settings as follows:

```
C:\> MODE /STATUS <ENTER>
```

Because MODE's status display will scroll past you quickly, redirect the command to MORE or to your printer as shown here:

```
C:\> MODE /STATUS | MORE <ENTER>
C:\> MODE /STATUS > PRN <ENTER>
```

Understanding Fail on Int 24

Many users have encountered the following error message but aren't sure what the message means:

```
Fail on Int 24
```

As you work with DOS, there are times when DOS cannot continue without your intervention, such as when the printer is off line or when a floppy drive is empty. Normally, when such an event occurs, DOS displays a message describing the error, followed by the following familiar prompt:

```
Abort, Retry, Fail?
```

The PC uses interrupts to temporarily suspend the task it is performing, so it can do something else. When DOS encounters an event for which it needs user intervention, DOS invokes interrupt 24 (abbreviated Int 24). As Tip 30 discusses, if you select the Fail option by typing F, the program will fail its current operation, possibly continuing its processing. If you select the Fail option and your screen displays the message "Fail on INT 24," DOS is simply telling you that the program could not continue after failing the operation.

Zero-Filling Memory

When you run a program, DOS loads the program's instructions and data into your computer's memory. Assume, for example, that you use a word processor to create a onfidential memo. After you store the memo on disk, a copy of the memo actually remains in your

computer's memory until it is overwritten by the next program. If you delete the memo from disk, you can use a third-party disk utility to overwrite the file, preventing it from being undeleted. However, using DEBUG, a user could examine your computer's RAM and find the memo. One way to remove the memo from memory is to turn off your computer (thus losing the contents of RAM). A second way is to use the companion disk utility ZEROMEM.EXE, which zeros out (fills with zeros) your PC's unused memory. To use ZEROMEM, invoke it from the DOS prompt as shown here:

```
C:\> ZEROMEM <ENTER>
```

If you are using the DOS 5 memory management techniques, invoke ZEROMEM by using LOADHIGH as shown here:

```
C:\> LOADHIGH ZEROMEM <ENTER>
```

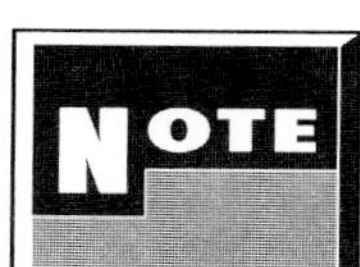

ZEROMEM does not zero upper-memory blocks but, rather, only conventional memory.

ZEROMEM.EXE

The utility command ZEROMEM.EXE resides on the companion disk that accompanies this book.

How DOSKEY Determines Macro Parameters

Tip 713 discusses how DOS batch files pass command-line parameters to arrive at the values assigned to %1 through %9. As Tip 713 explains, batch files use spaces, tabs, commas, semicolons, and equal signs as delimiters between parameters. DOSKEY macros, however, use only spaces and tabs as delimiters. The following DOSKEY macro, TESTMAC, lets you see DOS determines each parameter's value:

```
C:\> DOSKEY TESTMAC=ECHO 1 $1 2 $2 3 $3 4 $4 5 $5 6 $6 7 $7 8 $8 9 $9 <ENTER>
```

It is important to understand that even though DOSKEY macros provide capabilities similar to DOS batch files, the two are not identical in how they behave.

Using CTRL Characters in Your DOSKEY Macro Names

Unlike DOS filenames, which restrict you to a specific set of characters, DOSKEY macro names can be specified with CTRL characters. The following commands, for example, create several macros you can execute by pressing a CTRL-*key* combination followed by ENTER:

```
C:\> DOSKEY ^D=DIR *.* /S <ENTER>
C:\> DOSKEY ^K=DOSKEY /MACROS <ENTER>
C:\> DOSKEY ^L=DOSKEY /HISTORY <ENTER>
```

After you create these macros, you can use the ^D macro to display your directory listing as follows:

```
C:\> ^D <ENTER>
```

To use DOSKEY macros, you must be using DOS 5.

How Much DOSKEY Buffer Space Is in Use?

As described in Tip 62, DOSKEY's /BUFSIZE switch lets you control the size of the buffer in which DOSKEY stores macros and your previously entered commands. By default, DOSKEY uses a 512-byte

buffer. The following batch file, DOSKEYSZ.BAT, displays the approximate number of bytes of the buffer that DOSKEY is currently using:

```
@ECHO OFF
DOSKEY /MACROS /HISTORY > DOSKEY.SZ
DIR DOSKEY.SZ | FIND "DOSKEY"
DEL DOSKEY.SZ
```

To use the DOSKEY commands you must be using DOS 5 or higher.

How Much Environment Space Is in Use?

Tip 13 describes how to use the CONFIG.SYS SHELL entry to increase your environment size. The following batch file, ENVIROSZ.BAT, displays the approximate number of bytes currently used by environment entries:

```
@ECHO OFF
SET > ENVIRON.SZ
DIR ENVIRON.SZ | FIND "ENVIRON"
DEL ENVIRON.SZ
```

Specifying Comment Lines in CONFIG.SYS

Tip 642 describes how to use REM statements in CONFIG.SYS to explain each entry's purpose. A second way to place comments in CONFIG.SYS is by using the undocumented COMMENT= entry.

COMMENT, which is supported by DOS versions 2 through 5.0, lets you specify a series of letters; if the letters appear at the start of a line, the line contains a comment (or remark). For example, the following CONFIG.SYS uses COMMENT to specify that lines beginning with the word *NOTES* are comments and can be ignored:

```
COMMENT=NOTES
NOTES Specify the number of file handles
FILES=30
NOTES Specify the number of disk buffers
BUFFERS=25
```

Why do you need COMMENT when you can use REM? Assume, for example, that you want to start DOS without installing DEVICE drivers. Using COMMENT, you can direct DOS to ignore DEVICE entries as shown here:

```
COMMENT=DEVICE
```

Actually, you can probably get away with simply using the following:

```
COMMENT=DE
```

How to Find Undocumented Commands and Switches

Several of the tips presented in this book discuss undocumented commands and switches. You can use two techniques to find such undocumented features yourself. The first technique uses the utility command VIEWASCI, presented in Tip 611, to search your command files for ASCII text. The following command, for example, uses VIEWASCI to examine FDISK.EXE:

```
C:\> VIEWASCI C:\DOS\FDISK.EXE <ENTER>
```

Search the output of the VIEWDISK command for text beginning with a slash (/switch), which indicates a command-line switch. Then, provided your disk is backed up, experiment with the switch to see what it really does.

The second way to search for switches is to load a command file into DEBUG and then use DEBUG's Search command to look for a switch. The following DEBUG commands search FDISK for switches:

```
C:\> DEBUG C:\DOS\FDISK.EXE <ENTER>

-S 0 L FFFF "/" <ENTER>
```

DOSKEY Supports Virtually Any Macro Name

DOS lets you use characters, numbers, and a few special characters in your filenames. DOSKEY macros, however, let you use any character, letter, or keyboard symbol. As Tip 493 explains, you can even use CTRL characters in your macro names. The following DOSKEY commands take advantage of DOSKEY's naming flexibility:

```
C:\> DOSKEY \=CD \ <ENTER>
C:\> DOSKEY .=DIR <ENTER>
```

The first macro lets you select the root directory by typing the slash character and pressing ENTER as follows:

```
C:\SOMEDIR> \ <ENTER>
```

The second macro lets you display the current directory's files by typing a period and pressing ENTER.

Traveling Faster Through Text in EDIT

If you use EDIT, the DOS 5 full-screen text editor, you know you can use your arrow and PAGE UP keys to quickly move the cursor throughout the text. In addition, you can use the keyboard combinations listed in Table 204. As the size of your files increases, you will find these keystrokes convenient.

Table 204. Keyboard Combinations for Fast Text Traveling Within EDIT

Key Combination	Function
Arrow keys	Move cursor one position
PGUP	Moves cursor up one text screen
PGDN	Moves cursor down one text screen
HOME	Moves cursor to the beginning of the line
END	Moves cursor to the end of the line
CTRL-LEFT ARROW	Moves cursor one word to the left
CTRL-RIGHT ARROW	Moves cursor one word to the right
CTRL-ENTER	Moves cursor to the beginning of the next line
CTRL-Q-E	Moves cursor to the top line of the window
CTRL-Q-X	Moves cursor to the bottom line of the window
CTRL-W or CTRL-UP ARROW	Scrolls text up one line
CTRL-Z or CTRL-DOWN ARROW	Scrolls text down one line
CTRL-HOME or CTRL-Q-R	Moves cursor to the beginning of the file
CTRL-End or CTRL-Q-C	Moves cursor to the end of the file
CTRL-PGUP	Scrolls text left one screen
CTRL-PGDN	Scrolls text right one screen

Changing the Prompt for Programs that Let You Shell to DOS

Many commands, such as Windows and the DOS shell, let you temporarily exit to the DOS prompt so you can issue DOS commands. However, you should never turn off your system or restart DOS while such programs are active. Instead, you should execute an EXIT command to return to the program so you can properly end it. To help you remember to use EXIT, change the system prompt to something like this before executing a program that allows you to shell out:

```
Use EXIT to Return to XXX
C:\>
```

The following batch file, DOSH.BAT, changes the prompt and invokes the DOS shell. After the shell ends, the macro restores the prompt.

```
@ECHO OFF
SET SAVE_PROMPT=%PROMPT%
PROMPT Use EXIT to return to Shell$_$P$G
DOSSHELL
PROMPT %SAVE_PROMPT%
SET SAVE_PROMPT=
```

If you temporarily exit the shell, the new prompt will appear. When you permanently exit the shell, the original prompt will appear. By changing the prompt in this way, you reduce the chances that a user will turn off the computer while temporarily "shelled out" of a program.

Controlling Which Command DOS Executes

In some cases two or more programs have the same name. If the directories that contain these programs are both defined in the command path, DOS will always execute the command whose directory appears first in the path. The following batch file, RUN.BAT, lets you control which of the programs execute. To run a program named UNDELETE.EXE, for example, you would use RUN.BAT as follows:

```
C:\> RUN UNDELETE.EXE <ENTER>
```

The batch file will search the command path for a matching command. If a match is found, the batch file will display the following message:

```
RUN C:\PATHNAME\UNDELETE.EXE   (Y/N)?
```

If you type Y, the batch file will execute the command. If you type N, the batch file will continue its search. The following commands implement RUN.BAT:

```
@ECHO OFF
IF '%1'=='' GOTO DONE

ECHO ECHO Run %%1 (Y/N)? > ASKIT.BAT
ECHO YESORNO >> ASKIT.BAT
ECHO IF ERRORLEVEL 1 %%1 >> ASKIT.BAT

FOR %%I IN (%PATH%) DO IF EXIST %%I\%1 CALL ASKIT %%I\%1

DEL ASKIT.BAT
:DONE
```

The batch file works very well if your current path is fairly short. However, if you have six or seven names in your path, the FOR command may actually exceed the 126-character DOS command length restriction. If this occurs, the batch file will fail. To avoid this problem, you may want to test the length your path by using the companion disk utilty LENGTH.COM presented in Tip 688 and then proceed accordingly.

Support for Hercules Graphics Cards

If your video card is a Hercules graphics card and you have experimented with the QBASIC sample programs provided with DOS 5, you may have encountered problems. If you plan to use QBASIC with a Hercules card, invoke the DOS 5 MSHERC command, which installs memory-resident software to support the Hercules card, as follows:

```
C:\> MSHERC <ENTER>
```

If you also have a color adapter, include the /HALF switch as shown here:

```
C:\> MSHERC /HALF <ENTER>
```

If you are using DOS 5's memory-management capabilities, invoke MSHERC with the LOADHIGH command. DOS will then place the memory-resident software into upper memory, not consuming conventional memory that your programs can put to better use.

Is a CD-ROM Driver Installed?

Tip 398 discusses CD-ROM drives in detail. To use a CD-ROM drive under DOS or Windows, you need to install the device driver MSCDEX.EXE, which contains the Microsoft (MS) CD-ROM extensions (EX). If you are troubleshooting a CD-ROM installation, use the companion disk utility CHMSCDEX.EXE, which checks whether the MSCDEX driver is installed and, if it is, displays the driver's version number as shown here:

```
C:\> CHMSCDEX <ENTER>
Driver version 2.21
```

If the driver is not installed, the program will display a message stating so. If you are using CHMSCDEX from within a batch file, the utility returns the exit status value 1 if the driver is installed and returns 0 otherwise.

The utility command CHMSCDEX.EXE resides on the companion disk that accompanies this book.

CHMSCDEX.EXE

On a Network, Ask Before Changing LASTDRIVE

Tip 27 discusses the CONFIG.SYS LASTDRIVE entry, explaining that each drive you reserve consumes from 80 to 96 bytes. Normally, if you aren't using the drives for directory substitutions with SUBST, you should change the letter of the last drive to a letter closer to the beginning of the alphabet. However, if your system is connected to a network, don't change LASTDRIVE without first asking your network administrator. Many network programs map network drives to specific drive letters. If you change LASTDRIVE, you may eliminate necessary drive letters and so cause such commands to fail.

Be Aware of DOSKEY /REINSTALL

Tip 62 describes how to use DOSKEY's /REINSTALL switch to change DOSKEY's current settings. Although the switch lets you change DOSKEY's current settings, an apparent bug can cause an extra copy of DOSKEY to remain in memory after the operation. If you use the /REINSTALL switch a second time, you get a third copy of DOSKEY, and so on. If you want to change DOSKEY's settings, plan on restarting DOS.

Understanding OCR

OCR is an acronym for optical character recognition. OCR is the process of scanning a printed page and converting the resulting bitmap into a character file you can edit with a word processor. The OCR process begins with the scanning process. After the scanner produces a bitmap file, special OCR software is run that analyzes the bitmap, attempting to map its pixels to characters. This software can quickly convert most scanned pages containing typed text. After the software completes its character mapping, it typically invokes a spell-checker that corrects most of the errors encountered in the mapping process. Afterward, you may have to edit the file to perform a manual cleanup.

OCR software programs are some of the most sophisticated in the industry; even inexpensive programs purchased for a hand-held scanner do an amazingly good job. Most OCR packages, however, still provide only minimal capabilities for converting hand-written text.

Swapping Mouse Buttons

If you are left handed, working with a right-handed mouse within the DOSSHELL can be frustrating. To swap the mouse buttons, edit the file DOSSHELL.INI, which resides in the DOS subdirectory. Locate the line for the swap-mouse entry. Change the setting from disabled to enabled to swap the mouse buttons. The next time you start the shell, your change will be in effect.

Using the Mouse with EDIT

If you have a mouse driver installed, you can use the mouse within EDIT, the DOS 5 screen editor, to quickly position the cursor, select menu options, invoke EDIT's online help, or select text. To position the cursor for editing, simply aim the mouse pointer at the text location and click. If the file you are editing is large, you can use the mouse to click the scroll bar that appears to the right of your screen to travel through the file. To select a menu option, simply click the desired menu and then click the desired option. If you click your mouse's right button, EDIT will invoke its online help. To select text for a cut-and-paste operation as discussed in Tip 572, place the mouse pointer at the start of the desired text. Then hold down the mouse button and drag the mouse pointer to the end of the desired text.

Keeping Track of Your Current Position Within EDIT

If you are using EDIT, the DOS full-screen editor, to edit a large file, you sometimes may want to know your current position within the file. EDIT provides two ways for you to track your position. One way uses the vertical scroll bar that appears at the right edge of your screen. The bar contains a small block that you can use to determine your relative position within the file. If the block appears near the top of the scroll bar, your current position is near the beginning of the file. If the block is at the middle or bottom of the scroll bar, you are near the middle or end of the file.

A second way to determine your position is to look at the lower-right corner of your screen, where two numbers appear, separated by colons. The first number tells you the current line number. The second number tells you the current column number.

PART 2

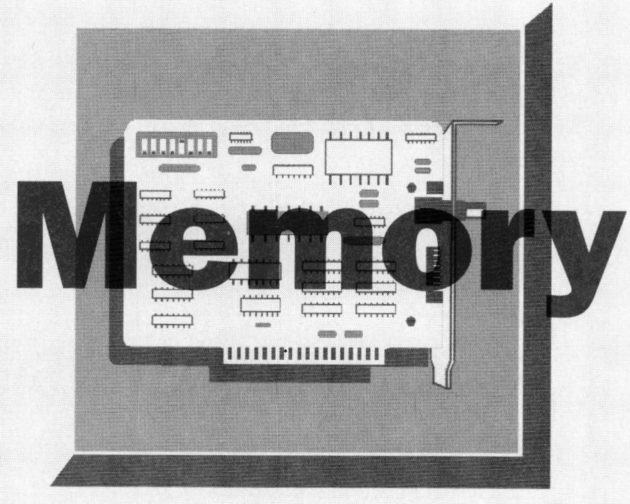

Memory

Understanding Conventional Memory

A PC can hold three different types of memory: conventional, extended, and expanded memory. Tip 220 explains extended memory. Tip 219 explains expanded memory.

This tip concentrates on conventional memory, the first 640Kb of memory used by every PC type (8088, 286, 386, or 486). The conventional way your computer uses its first 1Mb of memory is illustrated in Tip 31.

When the IBM PC was first released in 1981, most computers had 256Kb of memory or less. Today most computers now hold 640Kb. This memory area is where DOS and your programs reside. The 384Kb memory area between the top of conventional memory and 1Mb is called reserved memory; it contains the computer's video address space, ROM-BIOS code, and an unused area originally reserved for other hardware devices. Regardless of your computer type, the first 1Mb of the address space is the same.

Because DOS programs must reside in the 640Kb conventional address space, it is important that you make as much of this memory available as you can. Beginning with version 5, DOS provides several memory management techniques you can use to maximize your computer's available conventional memory (see Tip 222 and Tip 256).

What Kinds of Memory Do I Have?

Tip 215 discusses conventional memory, while Tip 189 discusses extended memory and Tip 178 discuss expanded memory. To determine which types of memory your computer contains and the amount of each memory type, use the MEM /CLASSIFY command as shown here:

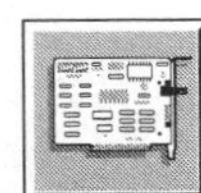

```
C:\> MEM /CLASSIFY <ENTER>

Conventional Memory :

  Name              Size in Decimal         Size in Hexidecimal
-------------     ---------------------   -------------------
  MSDOS             44144      ( 43.1K)        AC70
  HIMEM              1072      (  1.0K)         430
  EMM386             6848      (  6.7K)        1AC0
  ANSI               4192      (  4.1K)        1060
   .                  .           .             .
   .                  .           .             .
   .                  .           .             .
  COMMAND            2880      (  2.8K)         B40
  SMARTDRV          26768      ( 26.1K)        6890
  SHARE              6192      (  6.0K)        1830
  FREE                 64      (  0.1K)          40
  FREE                 64      (  0.1K)          40
  FREE                224      (  0.2K)          E0
  FREE             541744      (529.0K)       84430

Total  FREE :      542096      (529.4K)

Total bytes available to programs: 542096   (529.4K)
Largest executable program size:   541744   (529.0K)

    655360 bytes total EMS memory
    262144 bytes free EMS memory

   3538944 bytes total contiguous extended memory
         0 bytes available contiguous extended memory
   2015232 bytes available XMS memory
           MS-DOS resident in High Memory Area
```

In this case, MEM displays information about the computer's conventional, expanded, and extended memory use.

To use the MEM command you must be using DOS 4 or higher.

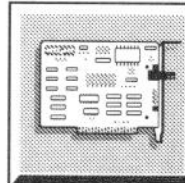

Freeing Conventional Memory by Moving FASTOPEN's Buffers

As Tip 460 discusses, the FASTOPEN command can improve your system performance by decreasing the number of slow directory search operations that DOS must perform. If you are using FASTOPEN and your computer has expanded memory available (see Tip 219), you can move FASTOPEN's buffers (each FASTOPEN buffer consumes 48 bytes of memory) to expanded memory, freeing conventional memory for program use. To place the FASTOPEN buffers into expanded memory, invoke FASTOPEN using the /X switch as shown here:

```
C:\> FASTOPEN C:=50 /X <ENTER>
```

The Purpose of the DOS 5 LOADFIX Command

If you are using DOS 5 and take full advantage of memory management techniques, you may be able to free so much memory that DOS actually loads programs into memory beneath the 64Kb address space. Periodically, a program cannot run when loaded this low in memory and, as a result, displays the following message:

```
Packed file corrupt
```

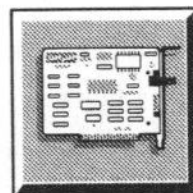

Should this message appear, use the DOS 5 LOADFIX command. The following LOADFIX command, for example, loads the program PROBLEM.EXE above the 64Kb address space:

```
C:\> LOADFIX PROBLEM.EXE <ENTER>
```

To use the LOADFIX command, you must be using DOS 5.

Understanding Expanded Memory

As discussed in Tip 215, DOS programs are restricted to the 640Kb conventional memory region. When the IBM PC was first released, among the most successful user applications were spreadsheet programs.

As the size of user spreadsheets increased, it didn't take long before users needed more memory space. Because the 8088 processor used a 20-bit address to reference memory locations, the 8088 was physically prevented from addressing memory locations above 1Mb. Even if a PC contained several megabytes of memory, the PC had no way to access it. Luckily, three companies (Lotus, Intel, and Microsoft) got together and created the expanded memory specification, a hardware and software solution that tricked the PC into using memory beyond its 1Mb limitation.

The term EMS is used to describe the expanded-memory specification. EMS combines a special memory board, called an expanded memory board, and a software device driver, typically called an EMS driver. Here's how the expanded memory board and software trick the PC into using memory beyond 1Mb. To begin, the EMS driver allocates a 64Kb-region of the reserved memory that resides above 640Kb and beneath 1Mb. The driver divides this memory region into four 16Kb pieces called physical pages, as shown here:

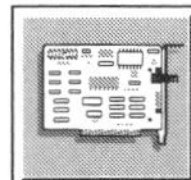

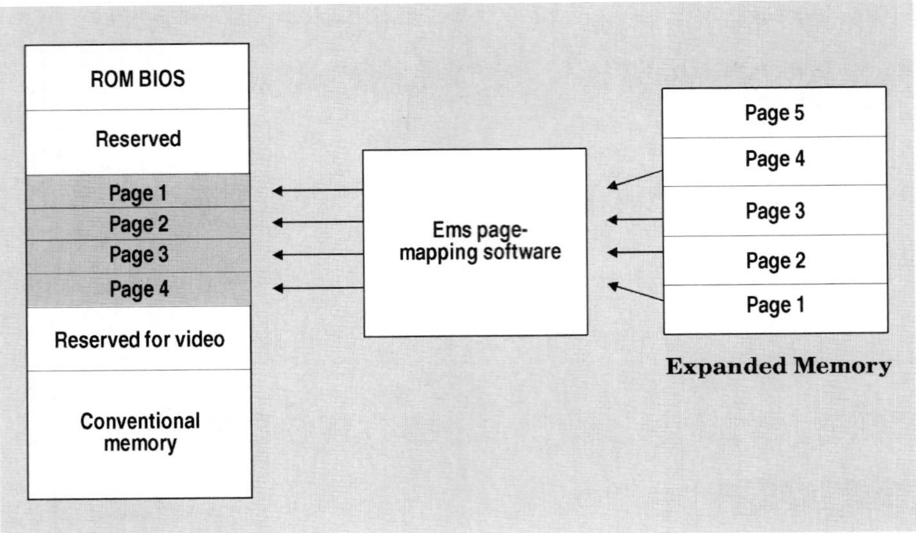

Next, programs written to support expanded memory divide their data (a spreadsheet for example) into 16Kb logical pages, which they then load into the expanded memory board. When the program needs to use a specific piece of data, the program maps the data's logical page from expanded memory to one of the physical pages.

The data is not actually copied from expanded memory. Instead, the expanded-memory board contains locations called ports in which the EMS software places the number of a logical page residing on the expanded memory that responds when a physical page is accessed. For example, depending on the current mappings, a reference to physical page 1 may result in an access to logical page 1, 2, 3, or even 1000. Luckily, programs keep track of mapping so users don't have to. However, because only four physical pages exist, programs must perform a considerable number of page mappings and remappings to access different pieces.

Although this page mapping lets your computer access memory beyond 1Mb, it adds considerable system overhead, which slows down your program execution. Because of this system overhead, given a choice, you should use extended memory as discussed in Tip 220. Unfortunately, unless you are using a 286 or higher, your system cannot use extended memory and must use expanded memory instead.

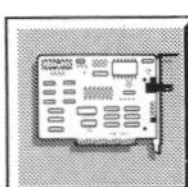

Understanding Extended Memory

Tip 215 discusses the PC's use of conventional memory. Tip 219 discusses expanded memory. The third type of memory used by 286 and higher computers is extended memory. The original IBM PC (an 8088 machine) used 20-bit addressing, which restricted its memory range to 1Mb. The 286, on the other hand, uses 24-bit addressing, which allows it to access up to 16 megabytes of physical memory. The 386 and 486 use 32-bit addressing, which lets them access more than 4 gigabytes of physical memory. Unfortunately, you will run out of money long before you can place 4 gigabytes of memory in your system.

Because these systems can access memory beyond 1Mb, we refer to the memory as extended memory. In other words, the memory extends your PC's memory capabilities beyond 1Mb. Because extended memory uses the PC's natural addressing capabilities, extended memory is much faster than expanded memory, which combines hardware and software to trick the computer into using memory beyond the 1Mb address space.

Table 220 describes the three fundamental memory types.

Under DOS, programs reside in your computer's conventional memory. Expanded and extended memory hold only data, not program instructions.

Table 220. PC Memory Types

Memory Type	Characteristic
Conventional	The first 640Kb of memory used by all PC types.
Expanded	A hardware and software technique that tricks the PC into accessing memory beyond 1Mb. Used by all PC types, although it was developed primarily for the 8088. Holds data only.
Extended	Memory beyond 1Mb addressable by 286, 386, and 486 machines. Extended memory holds data only.

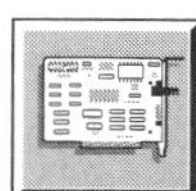

Accessing Extended Memory with HIMEM.SYS

As discussed in Tip 220, if you are using a 286 or higher computer, your computer can hold data in extended memory. Before you can use extended memory, you must install the HIMEM.SYS device driver provided with DOS 5 or Microsoft Windows. Unless you install the HIMEM.SYS device driver, DOS has no way of knowing your computer contains extended memory, let alone how to use it. If you have extended memory and are using DOS 5, place the following entry near the start of your CONFIG.SYS file:

```
DEVICE=C:\DOS\HIMEM.SYS
```

If you are using Windows, compare the date and time stamp of the file HIMEM.SYS provided by Windows with that of the HIMEM.SYS file provided by DOS. Install the newer HIMEM.SYS file and remove the older file from your disk to free disk space. Many of the DOS 5 memory management techniques rely on the HIMEM.SYS device driver. As such, the DEVICE entry for this driver must appear early in your CONFIG.SYS file.

Freeing Conventional Memory by Using the High-Memory Area

If your computer contains extended memory and you are using DOS 5, you can free conventional memory for your program's use by moving the DOS kernel (the core DOS program) to the first 64Kb

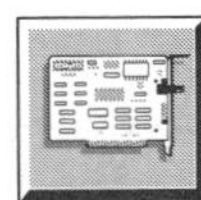

segment of extended memory: the high-memory area. The following illustration shows the high-memory area:

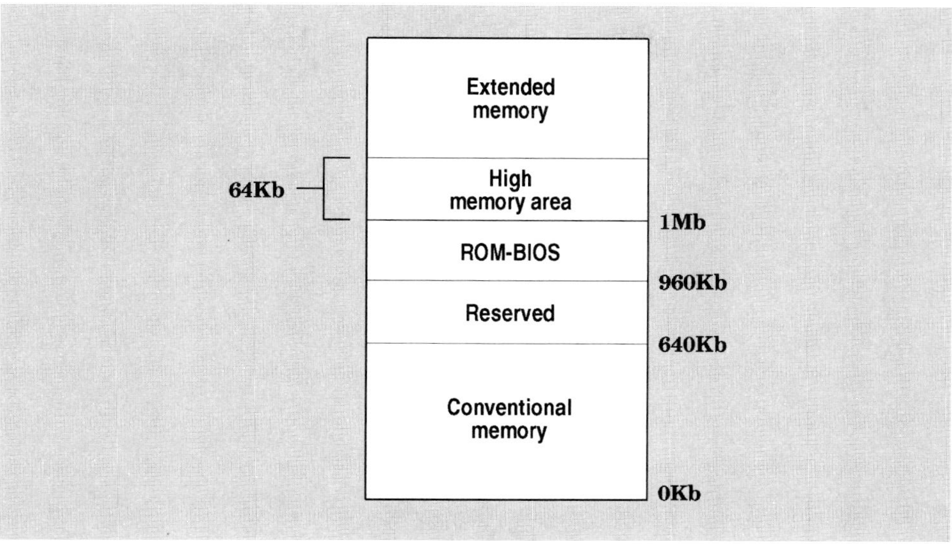

Using the DOS=HIGH entry in your CONFIG.SYS file, you direct DOS to move the kernel from conventional memory to the high-memory area. Because the kernel requires over 40Kb, you can free considerable memory.

The DOS=HIGH entry must follow the HIMEM.SYS device driver entry as shown here:

```
DEVICE=C:\DOS\HIMEM.SYS
DOS=HIGH
```

To use the DOS=HIGH CONFIG.SYS entry, you must be using DOS 5 or higher.

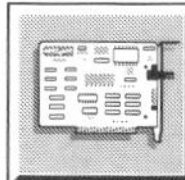

Understanding Upper-Memory Blocks

As discussed in Tip 223, the 384Kb region of memory between 640Kb and 1Mb is often called reserved memory. As shown here, the low end of reserved memory contains the PC's video memory, and the high end contains the ROM-BIOS:

BIOS
Available upper memory
Hard memory
Available upper memory
Video memory
Conventional memory

Much of reserved memory, however, remains unused.

If you are using DOS 5, you can direct DOS to use portions of reserved memory (called upper-memory blocks) for memory-resident commands as well as device drivers. By using upper memory in this way, you free conventional memory for your program use. Before you can use upper memory, however, you must place the DOS=UMB entry in your CONFIG.SYS file and install the EMM386.EXE device driver.

To use the EMM386.EXE device driver and to thus use upper memory, you must be using a 386 or higher computer. As discussed in Tip 222, the CONFIG.SYS DOS= entry also lets you load DOS into the high memory area. Most users will place the following entry in their CONFIG.SYS file:

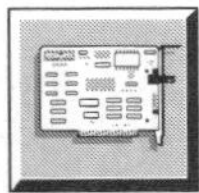

```
DOS=HIGH,UMB
```

In this case, the DOS= entry loads DOS into the high-memory area and tells DOS you will be using upper-memory blocks (UMBS). The EMM386.EXE device driver services two purposes. First, it allows 386 or higher machines with extended memory to trick DOS into believing the computer also has expanded memory (see Tip 219). Second, it gives DOS access to the upper-memory area. To use EMM386 only for access to the upper-memory area, install the device driver by using the NOEMS switch as shown here:

```
DEVICE=C:\DOS\EMM386.EXE NOEMS
```

After you install DOS support for the upper-memory area, you can take advantage of the DOS 5 DEVICEHIGH (see Tip 224) CONFIG.SYS entry as well as the DOS 5 LOADHIGH command (see Tip 225).

To use upper-memory blocks for device drivers and memory-resident commands, you must be using DOS 5 and a 386 or higher computer.

Freeing Conventional Memory by Moving Device Drivers

When DOS starts, it loads the device drivers you specify in CONFIG.SYS into conventional memory. As discussed in Tip 215, conventional memory is the 640Kb region within which DOS must load your programs. If you are using DOS 5 and a 386 or higher machine, you can free conventional memory by moving your device drivers to the upper-memory area discussed in Tip 223. To do so, you simply change your CONFIG.SYS DEVICE entries to DEVICEHIGH. The following CONFIG.SYS illustrates how you would install the device drivers ANSI.SYS and MOUSE.SYS into upper memory:

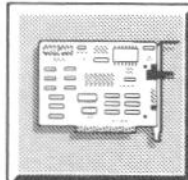

```
DEVICE=C:\DOS\HIMEM.SYS
DEVICE=C:\DOS\DMM386.EXE NOEMS
DOS=HIGH,UMB
DEVICEHIGH=C:\DOS\ANSI.SYS
DEVICEHIGH=C:\MICE\MOUSE.SYS
```

The entries for HIMEM.SYS and EMM386.EXE must be DEVICE entries because prior to these entries, support for upper memory does not exist. When DOS encounters a DEVICEHIGH entry, DOS will try to load the driver into the upper-memory area. If there is not enough upper memory to hold the driver, DOS will load the driver into conventional memory just as if you had used the DEVICE entry. The ability to move device drivers to upper memory in this way is one of DOS 5's best features, and definitely one you should take advantage of.

To use the DEVICEHIGH entry to load device drivers into upper memory, you must be using DOS 5 and a 386 or higher machine.

Increasing Available Conventional Memory by Moving Memory-Resident Commands

Most users install one or more memory-residents commands each time their system starts. Normally, DOS loads these commands into conventional memory immediately after the resident portion of COMMAND.COM, as shown here:

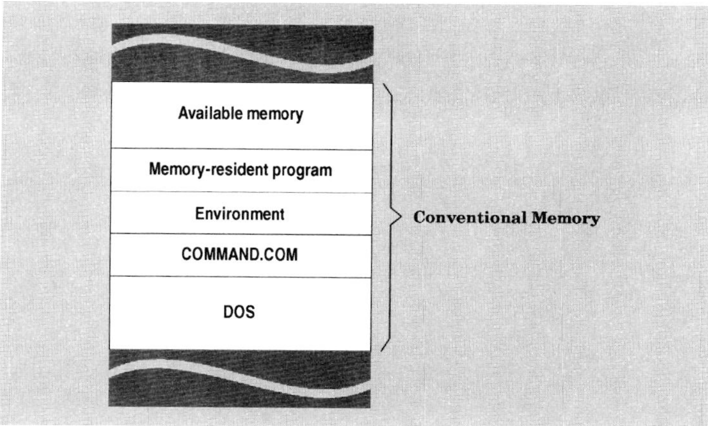

If you are using DOS 5 and have a 386 or higher machine, you can direct DOS to load memory-resident programs into the upper-memory area (see Tip 223) by using the LOADHIGH command. By placing memory-resident commands into upper memory in this way, you free conventional memory for your program use. After you have added the CONFIG.SYS entries required for using the upper-memory area, change your AUTOEXEC.BAT file to use LOADHIGH to install memory-resident programs. For example, the following AUTOEXEC.BAT file loads the FASTOPEN, PRINT, and SHARE commands:

```
@ECHO OFF
PATH C:\DOS
FASTOPEN C:=50
PRINT /D:LPT1
SHARE
```

Using the LOADHIGH command, the identical AUTOEXEC.BAT file becomes the following:

```
@ECHO OFF
PATH C:\DOS
LOADHIGH FASTOPEN C:=50
LOADHIGH PRINT /D:LPT1
LOADHIGH SHARE
```

If your CONFIG.SYS file contains INSTALL entries, remove the entries using LOADHIGH to invoke the same commands from within AUTOEXEC.BAT.

To use the LOADHIGH command, you must be using DOS 5.

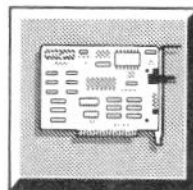

Pretending You Have Expanded Memory Available

Tip 219 describes expanded memory in detail. Likewise, Tip 220 discusses extended memory. Because expanded memory is slower than extended memory, you should use extended memory whenever possible. If you are using a 386 (or higher) computer with extended memory and you have a very old application program that supports only expanded memory, you can use the EMM386.EXE device driver to trick DOS into believing a portion of your extended memory is actually expanded. The following DEVICE entry uses EMM386.EXE to allocate 1024Kb of extended memory for use as expanded memory:

```
DEVICE=D:\DOS\EMM386.EXE  1024
```

The EMM386.EXE driver lets you allocate from 16Kb to 32,768Kb (32Mb) of extended memory for use as expanded memory. You should set aside memory to be treated as expanded memory only if you have a specific application program that requires it. Otherwise, you are wasting your extended memory.

The driver EMM386.EXE is provided with DOS 5. If you are using DOS 4, see Tip 276.

Using Shadow RAM

Your computer's BIOS is a hardware chip containing the PC's basic input and output routines (for the keyboard, video, disk, and so on). The BIOS is often called the ROM-BIOS because it resides in your computers read-only memory (ROM). Unlike your computer's

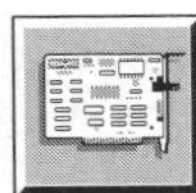

random-access memory (RAM), which loses its contents when you turn off your computer, the contents of ROM always remain the same. When your computer needs to perform a basic input or output operation, your computer executes instructions stored in ROM. Unfortunately, compared to RAM, ROM is much slower. Thus, executing instructions that reside in ROM takes longer than executing instructions that reside in RAM. Some computer's, therefore, let you copy contents of ROM to the faster RAM, later mapping memory accesses to ROM to the faster RAM. Because this RAM holds a copy of the PC's ROM, it is called shadow RAM. Not all PC's support shadow RAM; you need to check with your manufacturer. If your computer does support shadow RAM, using the shadow RAM may improve your system performance. The HIMEM.SYS /SHADOWRAM switch, shown here, lets you turn shadow RAM on and off:

```
DEVICE=C:\DOS\HIMEM.SYS  /SHADOWRAM:ON
```

The driver HIMEM.SYS ships with DOS 5 and Microsoft Windows.

Understanding Cache Memory

Users are commonly confused by discussions of disk and memory caches. If you look at a computer advertisement, you may see cache memory listed as one of the features. Tip 259 discusses the disk cache created by the SMARTDRV.SYS device driver. Here's the difference between the two cache types: Within your computer's CPU are a set of temporary storage locations called registers. Because registers reside within the CPU itself, the processor can access them very quickly. Unfortunately, there are only four general-purpose registers. Thus, to access data, the processor normally has to get the data from RAM, a much slower process. To reduce the overhead of getting data from memory, some computers provide a very fast cache memory that sits between the processor's registers and normal RAM as shown here:

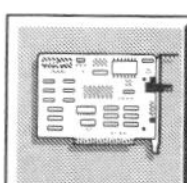

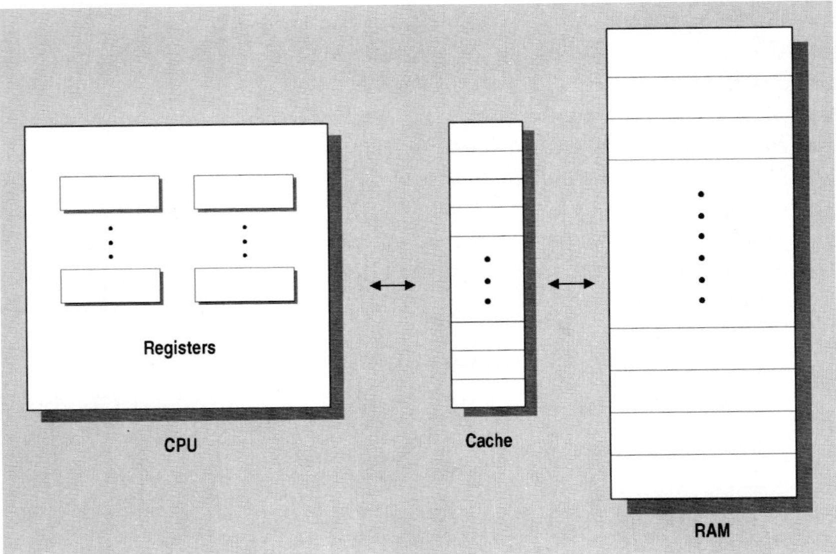

When the processor needs data, the processor first searches the high-speed cache. If the data is present, the processor uses it. Otherwise, the processor retrieves the data from the slower RAM, moving the data into the cache memory in case the data is needed a second time. Because groups of program instructions and data tend to be accessed in succession, the cache does not just move the one piece of data or the instruction currently requested. Instead, the cache moves a group of surrounding instructions and data and so increases the likelihood that the contents of the next memory request will be found in the cache. The amount of the data or the number of instructions the cache actually moves depends on the implementation. However, because memory references tend to access groups of program instructions and data, the fast cache memory significantly reduces memory-access overhead.

Because the fast cache memory is expensive and because of architectural considerations, the amount of cache memory provided is normally in the range 256Kb to 512Kb. The goal of cache memory isn't to hold everything, but rather, to hold the items you repeatedly use. If you are shopping for a PC, find out the size as well as the speed of the system's internal cache. In most cases, the larger and faster the cache, the better your system performance.

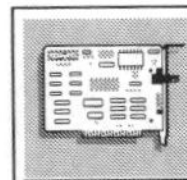

Understanding Zero Wait State Memory

When you look through computer advertisements, one of the features faster computers list is zero wait state memory. Here's why zero wait state memory is desirable. Accessing memory, whether to read the information currently stored or to write new information, takes time. When you purchase memory chips, the chips have a defined access time that typically ranges between 40 and 150 nanoseconds.Your computer's operations are defined in terms of clock ticks. If your memory access time is not fast enough to keep up with your CPU, the processor must waste a clock cycle waiting for the memory access to complete. Although you may have a fast processor, the wait states will severely degrade your system performance. If you are shopping for a new system, make sure to get a system that provides zero wait states. In most cases, the system uses a fast internal cache to reduce or eliminate wait states.

Understanding Memory Types

Your computer uses random-access memory (RAM) as well as read-only memory (ROM). When you get ready to purchase RAM for your computer, the salesperson may ask you if you want DRAM, SRAM, or even possibly VRAM. Here are the differences: DRAM (dynamic RAM) is the most common (and least expensive). Unfortunately, DRAM is also the slowest. To store information, DRAM chips must have their contents periodically refreshed (rewritten), normally at 2- to 3-millisecond intervals. There are times, therefore, when a data access operation is delayed because a refresh operation is in effect. In addition, after the memory controller reads information from a storage location, the information must be rewritten. Today, most DRAM chips are 1-megabit chips with an access time of approximately 80 nanoseconds.

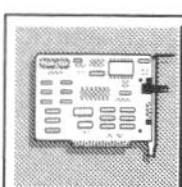

SRAM (static RAM) chips are much faster than DRAM chips, typically with an access time of 30 to 40 nanoseconds. SRAM chips do not require refreshing or write-after-read operations. Unfortunately, SRAM chips don't have the storage capacity of DRAM chips. The most common SRAM chips are 256 kilobits. A common use for SRAM chips is for a high-speed cache.

VRAM (video RAM) chips improve performance for video operations because they are dual ported, which allows them to be simultaneously read from (by the video controller) and written to (by the memory controller). If present in your system, VRAM would reside on your video card.

As you shop for a computer, you will run into each of these memory types. Use the speeds and storage capacities listed here to help you better understand each system's memory use.

Verifying the Amount of Conventional Memory Installed

Your batch files may sometimes invoke a program that require a specific amount of conventional memory or knowledge of how much conventional memory the system contains. The following DEBUG script file, CONVINST.SCR, creates a command file named CONVINST.COM that returns, as an exit status, the amount of conventional memory installed in the system. The exit status is the system's conventional memory size divided by 16. (The status is a value in the range 0 to 40.)

CONVISNT.SCR

```
N CONVINST.COM <ENTER>
A 100          <ENTER>
INT 12         <ENTER>
MOV CL,4       <ENTER>
SAR AX,CL      <ENTER>
MOV AH,4C      <ENTER>
INT 21         <ENTER>
               <ENTER>
R CX           <ENTER>
A              <ENTER>
W              <ENTER>
Q              <ENTER>
```

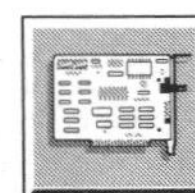

Use DEBUG as follows to create the command file CONVINST.COM:

```
C:\> DEBUG < CONVINST.SCR <ENTER>
```

The following batch commands use CONVINST.COM to verify that you have 640Kb of conventional memory:

```
@ECHO OFF
CONVINST
IF ERRORLEVEL 40 ECHO 640Kb present
IF NOT ERRORLEVEL 40 ECHO Less than 640KBb
```

Determining Which Programs Are Consuming Your Conventional Memory

Tip 241 explains how the MEM /DEBUG lets you see the device drivers and programs that currently reside in your computer's memory and their starting addresses in memory and their size. Unfortunately, when you use the /DEBUG switch, MEM displays these values in hexadecimal (base 16) format. If you are using the DOS 5 memory management techniques to load programs into upper memory, you can get a better feel for a program's memory requirements by using the MEM /CLASSIFY command, which displays program sizes in decimal format as shown here:

```
C:\> MEM  /CLASSIFY <ENTER>

Conventional Memory :

  Name                Size in Decimal         Size in Hex
-------------      ---------------------    -------------
  MSDOS              44144        ( 43.1K)         AC70
  HIMEM               1072        (  1.0K)          430
  EMM386              6848        (  6.7K)         1AC0
  ANSI                4192        (  4.1K)         1060
    :                   :              :              :
```

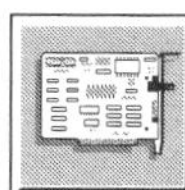

```
 :                        :            :             :
  COMMAND              2880        (  2.8K)         B40
  SMARTDRV            26768        ( 26.1K)        6890
  SHARE                6192        (  6.0K)        1830
  FREE                   64        (  0.1K)          40
  FREE                   64        (  0.1K)          40
  FREE                  224        (  0.2K)          E0
  FREE               541744        (529.0K)       84430
Total  FREE :        542096        (529.4K)

Total bytes available to programs : 542096    (529.4K)

Largest executable program size :   541744    (529.0K)

   655360 bytes total EMS memory
   262144 bytes free EMS memory

  3538944 bytes total contiguous extended memory
        0 bytes available contiguous extended memory
  2015232 bytes available XMS memory
          MS-DOS resident in High Memory Area
```

Viewing the program sizes in decimal format makes selecting the best programs to load into upper memory easier.

When You Need to Use STACKS

Depending on your hardware devices, sometimes a hardware device may interrupt DOS while DOS is performing a specific task, requesting DOS to temporarily suspend the task at hand to service the device. For DOS to later resume its previous operations, DOS must store information describing the current task in a memory area called a stack. DOS starts with a fixed amount of stack space. If interrupts occur so often that the stack space fills, DOS will display the following message, and your system will halt:

```
Fatal:  Internal Stack Failure, System Halted
```

Should this message occur, you need to add a STACKS entry to your CONFIG.SYS file. The format of the STACKS entry is as follows:

```
STACKS=NumberOfStacks,StackSize
```

Table 233 lists the default stack sizes. In most cases, the following entry should be more than sufficient:

```
STACKS=8,512
```

If you are trying to maximize your available memory, and your computer does not have an asynchronous device such as a network or modem that is working in the background, try setting the STACKS entry to 0,0.

Table 233. Default STACKS Entries

PC Type	Stacks Entry
PC, XT, Portables	0,0
Others	9,128

Avoiding Memory Conflicts

Hardware devices communicate with your computer through electronic mail boxes, or ports. Each port has a unique address. When you add new hardware to your system, you need to avoid port address conflicts. In a similar way, some devices use fixed locations in your computer's memory. For simplicity, the memory addresses above 640Kb and 1Mb are usually considered to be reserved. Actually, only pieces of this memory area are used, depending on your hardware type. Table 234 lists the memory regions used by different hardware devices.

When you install different hardware devices or device drivers (such as EMM386.EXE), you may need to specify a memory range. You can use Table 234 to avoid memory conflicts.

Table 234. Memory Use for Different Hardware Devices

Address Range	Device
A000H-C000H	EGA and VGA video memory
B000H-B200h	Monochrome video memory
B800H-BC00H	CGA video memory
C000H-C400H	EGA BIOS
C000H-C800H	VGA BIOS
C800H-CC00H	Hard disk controller
F000H-FFFFH	BIOS

Tip 235 Is Expanded Memory Available?

Tip 219 discusses expanded memory in detail. Before your programs can use expanded memory, you must install an expanded memory device driver. The companion disk that accompanies this book contains the utility command EMSAVAIL.EXE that returns the exit status value 1 if an EMS driver is installed and returns 0 otherwise. If you have a program that lets you control its use of expanded memory, you can use EMSAVAIL to test for expanded memory and then invoke the program by using the correct switches as shown here:

```
@ECHO OFF
EMSAVAIL
IF ERRORLEVEL 1 SOMEPROG /EMS_SWITCH
```

EMSAVAIL.EXE

The utility command EMSAVAIL.EXE resides on the companion disk that accompanies this book.

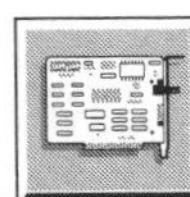

Understanding the Memory Allocation Strategy

By default, when your programs ask DOS for a region of memory, DOS searches the memory for the first available region that is large enough to satisfy the request. This memory allocation strategy is called first fit. If you are creating your own programs, or if you are installing memory-resident programs, you sometimes may want DOS to use a different allocation strategy. Table 236 lists the DOS memory allocation strategies.

Table 236. DOS Memory Allocation Strategies

Strategy Name	Value	Description
First fit low	00H	The default strategy. DOS selects the first block in conventional memory that satisfies the request.
Best fit low	01H	DOS selects the block of conventional memory whose size most closely matches the request.
Last fit low	02H	DOS selects the last memory block in conventional memory that satisfies the request.
First fit high only*	40H	DOS selects the first block in reserved memory that satisfies the request. If no block is found, the request fails.
Best fit high only*	41H	DOS selects the block of reserved memory whose size most closely matches the request. If no block is found, the request fails.
Last fit high only*	42H	DOS selects the last block of reserved memory that satisfies the request. If no block is found, the request fails.
First fit high first*	80H	Similar to first fit high only, but if no block is found, DOS performs first fit.
Best fit high first*	81H	Similar to best fit high only, but if no block is found, DOS performs best fit.
Last fit high first*	82H	Similar to last fit high only, but if no match is found, DOS performs last fit.

Note: * indicates that DOS 5 is required.

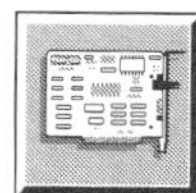

Tip 237 presents the utility command SETSTRAT.COM that lets you set the allocation strategy. Tip 238 presents the utility GETSTRAT.COM that returns the current memory allocation strategy as an exit status value.

Selecting a Memory Allocation Strategy

Tip 236 discusses DOS memory allocation strategies in detail. The following DEBUG script file, SETSTRAT.SCR, creates a command file named SETSTRAT.COM that lets you select an allocation strategy:

SETSTRAT.SCR

```
N SETSTRAT.COM     <ENTER>
A 100              <ENTER>
MOV AX,5801        <ENTER>
MOV BX,0           <ENTER>
INT 21             <ENTER>
MOV AH,4C          <ENTER>
INT 21             <ENTER>
                   <ENTER>
R CX               <ENTER>
C                  <ENTER>
W                  <ENTER>
Q                  <ENTER>
```

Use DEBUG as follows to create the command file SETSTRAT.COM:

```
C:\> DEBUG < SETSTRAT.SCR <ENTER>
```

In this case, the DEBUG script file selects the best-fit low strategy. To select a different strategy, edit the previous DEBUG script file and assign one of the values listed in Table 237 to the BX register, and use DEBUG to create a new command file. Depending on your needs, you might create command files for each strategy.

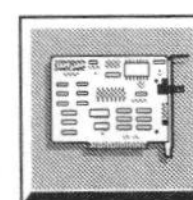

Table 237. Memory Allocation Strategy Values

Strategy	Value
First fit low	0
Best fit low	1
Last fit low	2
First fit high	80
Best fit high	81
Last fit high	82
First fit high only	40
Best fit high only	41
Last fit high only	42

Determining the Current Memory Allocation Strategy

Tip 236 discusses DOS memory allocation in detail. Tip 237 tells you how to create a command file that lets you select a specific stratigy. The following DEBUG script file, GETSTRAT.SCR, creates a command file named GETSTRAT.COM that returns one of the exit status values listed in Table 238 to indicate the current memory allocation strategy:

```
N GETSTRAT.COM     <ENTER>
A 100              <ENTER>
MOV AX,5800        <ENTER>
INT 21             <ENTER>
MOV AH,4C          <ENTER>
INT 21             <ENTER>
                   <ENTER>
R CX               <ENTER>
9                  <ENTER>
W                  <ENTER>
Q                  <ENTER>
```

GETSTRAT.SCR

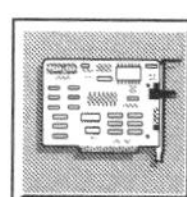

Table 238. Exit Status Values Returned by GETSTRAT.COM for Various Memory Allocation Strategies

Exit Status	Memory Allocation Strategy
0	First-fit low
1	Best-fit low
2	Last-fit low
64	First-fit high only
65	Best-fit high only
66	Last-fit high only
128	First-fit high
129	Best-fit high
130	Last-fit high

Use DEBUG as follows to create the command file GETSTRAT.COM:

```
C:\> DEBUG < GETSTRAT.SCR <ENTER>
```

Controlling Who Gets the High-Memory Area

Tip 223 explains the high-memory area and its use under DOS 5. To use the high-memory area, you must install the HIMEM.SYS device driver. Normally, most users will install the DOS kernel in the high-memory area, moving it from conventional memory. Depending on your applications, you may want to place a different program in this area. By default, DOS allocates the high-memory area on a first-come, first-served basis. When a program allocates memory from the high-memory area, DOS allocates the entire high-memory area to the program. In other words, two different programs can't have memory allocated from the high-memory area. The first program that asks for it, gets it. Using the HIMEM.SYS /HMAMIN switch, however, you can control which program receives control of the high-memory area by specifying the minimum amount of memory a program must request (in Kb) before DOS will allocate the high-memory area to it. The following CONFIG.SYS DEVICE

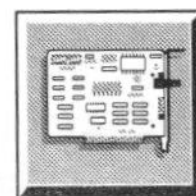

entry, for example, restricts the allocation of the high-memory area to programs requesting 48Kb or more.

```
DEVICE=C:\DOS\HIMEM.SYS /HMAMIN=48
```

In most cases, you can control who gets access to the high-memory area by simply sequencing your command execution. For those cases where you can't control the allocation in this way, the HIMEM.SYS /HMAMIN switch may provide a solution.

Is the High-Memory Area Available?

With the advent of DOS 5's memory management techniques, more memory-resident programs will emerge that allow you to take advantage of the high-memory area. Tip 223 discusses how DOS allocates the high-memory area. The companion disk that accompanies this book contains the utility command HIMEMAVL.EXE that returns the exit status value 1 if the high-memory area is available and 0 if it has already been allocated. If you have a memory-resident a command that lets you include switches for the high-memory area, you can test for the high-memory area's allocation as shown here:

```
@ECHO OFF
HIMEMAVL
IF ERRORLEVEL 1 SOMEPROG /HIGH_MEMORY_SWITCH
IF NOT ERRORLEVEL 1 SOMEPROG
```

The utility command HIMEMAVL.EXE resides on the companion disk that accompanies this book.

HIMEMAVL.EXE

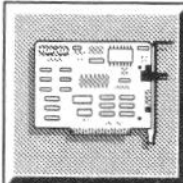

Understanding MEM /DEBUG

The MEM /DEBUG command displays detailed information on your computers memory use, as shown here:

```
C:\> MEM /DEBUG <ENTER>

  Address      Name          Size       Type
  -------      --------      ------     ------
  000000                     000400     Interrupt Vector
  000400                     000100     ROM Communication Area
  000500                     000200     DOS Communication Area

  000700       IO            000A60     System Data
                  CON                     System Device Driver
                  AUX                     System Device Driver
                  PRN                     System Device Driver
                  CLOCK$                  System Device Driver
                  A: - C:                 System Device Driver
                  COM1                    System Device Driver
                  LPT1                    System Device Driver
                  LPT2                    System Device Driver
                  LPT3                    System Device Driver
                  COM2                    System Device Driver
                  COM3                    System Device Driver
                  COM4                    System Device Driver

  001160       MSDOS         0013D0     System Data

  002530       IO            002A50     System Data
                HIMEM        000430      DEVICE=
                  XMSXXXX0                Installed Device Driver
                EMM386       000CA0      DEVICE=
                  $MMXXXX0                Installed Device Driver
                             0005D0      FILES=
                             000100      FCBS=
                             000200      BUFFERS=
```

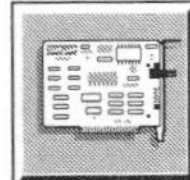

```
                              000480       LASTDRIVE=
                              000BC0       STACKS=
  004F90       MSDOS          000040      System Program

  004FE0       COMMAND        000940      Program
  005930       MSDOS          000040      — Free —
  005980       COMMAND        000200      Environment
  005B90       MSDOS          000040      — Free —
  005BE0       MSCDEX         00B5D0      Program
  0111C0       MEM            0000F0      Environment
  0112C0       MEM            0176F0      Program
  0289C0       MSDOS          077620      — Free —
  09FFF0       SYSTEM         028E40      System Program

  0C8E40       MSDOS          000020      — Free —
  0C8E70       MSDOS          003160      — Free —
  0CBFE0       SYSTEM         001020      System Program

  0CD010       IO             003790      System Data
                 ANSI         001060       DEVICE=
                   CON                      Installed Device Driver
                 SBPCD        002710       DEVICE=
                   MSCD001                  Installed Device Driver
  0D07B0       SMARTDRV       006890      Program
  0D7050       MSDOS          008FA0      — Free —


    655360 bytes total conventional memory
    655360 bytes available to MS-DOS
    584992 largest executable program size

   3538944 bytes total contiguous extended memory
         0 bytes available contiguous extended memory
   2224128 bytes available XMS memory
           MS-DOS resident in High Memory Area
```

When you invoke MEM, you may find its output hard to understand. Here's why. First, MEM displays sizes and addresses in hexadecimal format. If you convert the size of Interrupt Vector from hexadecimal (400H) to decimal (1024) format, the size makes sense. As discussed in Tip 31, the first 1,024 bytes of memory contain the ROM-BIOS interrupt vectors.

Next, MEM does not display addresses in the traditional segment and offset format. Instead, MEM displays the actual physical address in hexadecimal format. If, for example, you drop off the last 0 of

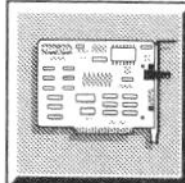

the address specified, you can determine the corresponding segment. For instance, the address 001160 corresponds to segment 116. Likewise, address 002530 corresponds to segment 253.

Avoiding Conflicts in the Upper-Memory Area

Tip 223 discusses the upper-memory area within which DOS 5 lets you load memory-resident commands and device drivers. To use the upper-memory area, you must install the EMM386.EXE device driver. To use the upper-memory area, the driver allocates unused memory regions that were originally reserved for memory-mapped devices. Depending on your hardware configuration, the memory allocated for use as an upper-memory block may sometimes conflict with the memory required for a device. Using the X= switch, you can direct the EMM386 driver to exclude the use of an address range. For example, the following DEVICE entry installs the EMM386 driver, directing it to exclude the memory range D000 through D800 from use as upper-memory blocks:

```
DEVICE=C:\DOS\EMM386.EXE NOEMS X=D000-D800
```

If your system hangs or behaves erratically when you use the upper-memory area, check your hardware documentation to ensure that a network card or other device does not require memory that may conflict with an upper-memory block and then, if necessary, use the X=switch to exclude the memory range.

Loading Drivers into Upper-Memory that Allocate Additional Memory

Tip 224 discusses the use of the DEVICEHIGH command to load device drivers into upper memory. When you use DEVICEHIGH, DOS loads the driver into the first upper-memory block large enough to hold the driver. If the driver later tries to allocate additional memory, the driver will fail. In such cases, you can use the DEVICEHIGH SIZE= entry to specify the amount of memory the driver

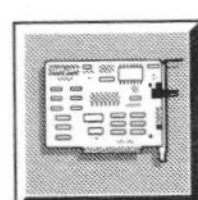

requires. In most cases, you will have to get this information from the manufacturer. The format of the SIZE entry is as follows:

```
DEVICEHIGH=DRIVER.EXT  SIZE=HexValue <ENTER>
```

You must specify the size as a hexadecimal (base 16) value. The following example uses the SIZE entry to install the MYBOARD driver with 8Kb of memory:

```
DEVICEHIGH=C:\MYBOARD.SYS SIZE=2000
```

If Possible, Place SMARTDRV.SYS in Extended Memory

Tip 374 describes the /A switch lets you install SMARTDRV.SYS in expanded memory instead of extended memory. As discussed in Tip 219, because expanded memory must continually map pages, it is much slower that extended memory. Thus, for best performance, place the SMARTDRV buffer in extended memory. Before you can use extended memory, you must install the HIMEM.SYS device driver, so make sure the SMARTDRV.SYS entry follows the HIMEM.SYS entry in your CONFIG.SYS file. Also, if you must use expanded memory, the SMARTDRV.SYS driver must follow your expanded memory driver in CONFIG.SYS.

Viewing Your Expanded Memory Use

As discussed in Tip 226, the EMM386 driver lets you use extended memory to emulate expanded memory. In addition, EMM386 provides you with access to the upper-memory area, which you can use for device drivers and other memory-resident commands. When your system starts and DOS loads

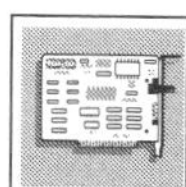

the EMM386 driver, the driver displays configuration information that typically scrolls past you faster than you can view it. Although the MEM command will tell you the basics about your expanded memory use, MEM really does not provide specifics. However, depending on the version of EMM386.EXE you are using, if you invoke EMM386 from the DOS prompt, the driver will display specifics as shown here:

```
C:\> EMM386 <ENTER>

MICROSOFT Expanded Memory Manager 386  Version 4.41
Copyright Microsoft Corporation 1986, 1991

  Available expanded memory . . . . . . . .  256 KB

  LIM/EMS version . . . . . . . . . . . . .   4.0
  Total expanded memory pages . . . . . . .    40
  Available expanded memory pages . . . . .    16
  Total handles . . . . . . . . . . . . . .    64
  Active handles  . . . . . . . . . . . . .     1
  Page frame segment  . . . . . . . . . . . D000 H

EMM386 Active.
```

To use EMM386.EXE, you must be using a 386 or higher computer and have previously installed HIMEM.SYS.

Controlling Expanded Memory Use with EMM386

As discussed in Tip 226, the EMM386.EXE driver lets you emulate expanded memory by using extended memory. Likewise, as discussed in Tip 223, the EMM386 driver also provides you with access

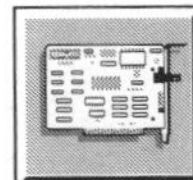

to the upper-memory area. If you are not using the upper-memory area (your CONFIG.SYS file contains DOS=NOUMB) and you are using EMM386 only to emulate expanded memory, you can invoke EMM386 from the DOS prompt to turn expanded memory support on or off. The following command, for example, turns off expanded memory support:

```
C:\> EMM386 OFF <ENTER>
```

To enable expanded memory support at a later time, invoke EMM386 with ON as shown here:

```
C:\> EMM386 ON <ENTER>
```

If you are testing programs that use expanded memory, using EMM386 to turn expanded memory support on and off in this way is more convenient than continually rebooting. Unfortunately, when you turn expanded memory support off, EMM386 does not relinquish its extended memory. In addition to using ON or OFF, you can invoke EMM386 with AUTO to direct EMM386 to provide expanded memory support only if a program requests it.

To use EMM386.EXE, you must be using a 386 or higher computer and have previously installed HIMEM.SYS.

If You Don't Have Extended Memory, Don't Install HIMEM.SYS

Tip 220 discusses extended memory in detail. Before you can use extended memory, you must install the HIMEM.SYS driver. Without HIMEM.SYS, DOS has no way of knowing that your computer's extended memory exists. If your computer does not have extended memory, do not install HIMEM.SYS; doing so will waste memory unnecessarily.

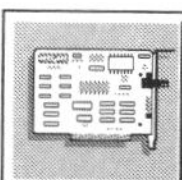

Using Memory Efficiently When You Install a RAM Drive

Tip 375 describes how to install and use a RAM drive. The examples in that tip use the CONFIG.SYS DEVICE entry to install the driver. If you are using the DOS 5 memory management facilities, use DEVICEHIGH to install the driver to conserve conventional memory as shown here:

```
DEVICEHIGH=C:\DOS\RAMDRIVE.SYS  128  [Other switches]
```

If you have extended or expanded memory, use the /E or /A switch to install the drive in the appropriate memory area. If you leave the RAM drive in conventional memory, you may actually decrease your system performance by consuming memory better used by your application programs. As discussed in Tip 219, the continual mapping of expanded memory makes it slower than extended memory. Thus, if you have a choice, place your RAM drive in extended memory for better performance.

Bypassing the Power-On Self-Test Memory Count

When you turn on your computer's power, the PC begins its power-on self-test and the PC displays a count of its working memory on your screen. Depending on the amount of memory your PC contains, the memory count can be quite time consuming. Thus, most new BIOS chips let you bypass the memory test by pressing the ESC key. Because memory errors are rare and because there will be times when you let the memory test complete (because you turn on your computer and walk away), bypassing the startup memory test by pressing ESC normally does not pose a threat to your system and will save you considerable time. Note that some BIOS chips let you press a key other than ESC to bypass the memory count. If pressing the ESC key has no effect, refer to the manual that accompanies your computer.

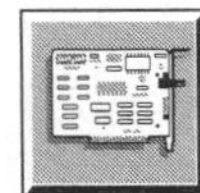

Is DOS in High or Conventional Memory?

Tip 222 describes how to use the DOS 5 DOS=HIGH CONFIG.SYS entry to load DOS into the high-memory area. If the high-memory area is available, DOS will use it; otherwise, DOS will load itself into conventional memory. The following DEBUG script file, ISDOSHI.SCR, creates a command file named ISDOSHI.COM that returns the exit status value 1 if DOS is in high memory and returns 0 if it is in conventional memory:

```
N ISDOSHI.COM <ENTER>
A 100         <ENTER>
MOV AX,3000   <ENTER>
INT 21        <ENTER>
CMP AL,5      <ENTER>
JL  117       <ENTER>
MOV AX,3306   <ENTER>
INT 21        <ENTER>
AND DH,10     <ENTER>
JZ  117       <ENTER>
MOV AL,1      <ENTER>
JMP 119       <ENTER>
MOV AL,0      <ENTER>
MOV AH,4C     <ENTER>
INT 21        <ENTER>
              <ENTER>
R CX          <ENTER>
1D            <ENTER>
W             <ENTER>
Q             <ENTER>
```

ISDOSHI.SCR

Use DEBUG as follows to create the command file ISDOSHI.COM:

```
C:\> DEBUG < ISDOSHI.SCR <ENTER>
```

The following batch file commands illustrate how you would use ISDOSHI:

```
@ECHO OFF
ISDOSHI
```

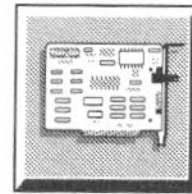

```
IF ERRORLEVEL 1 GOTO HIGH_MEMORY
GOTO LOW_MEMORY
REM Other commands here
```

Be Aware of the Weitek Coprocessor Memory Requirements

If you are using a Weitek math coprocessor and DOS 5, you may have experienced conflicts between the coprocessor and DOS 5 memory management techniques. First, the coprocesor will not work if the high memory area is not available. Thus, you cannot use the CONFIG.SYS entry DOS=HIGH to load the DOS kernel into high memory if you want to use the coprocessor. Second, if you are using the EMM386.EXE driver, you need to install support for the driver by using the W=ON switch as shown here:

```
DEVICE=C:\DOS\EMM386.EXE  [Other Switches] W=ON
```

Handling DMA Conflicts with EMM386.EXE

Tip 776 discusses direct memory access devices in detail. If you are using the EMM386.EXE device driver, you may periodically encounter memory conflicts. If such a conflict arises, use the EMM386 D= switch to increase the amount of memory available for DMA transfers. By default, the driver reserves 16Kb (0=16). The driver lets you increase the amount of memory up to 256Kb. The following entry, for example, reserves 64Kb for DMA:

```
DEVICE=:\DOS\EMM386.EXE  [Other Switches] D=64
```

Avoiding Machine Conflicts with Address Line 20

As Tip 222 explains, placing the DOS=HIGH entry in your CONFIG.SYS directs DOS to load itself into the high-memory area. When your system starts, DOS may display the following message:

```
High Memory Area Unavailable
```

Or your system may hang without starting DOS. In either case, check to see whether your computer matches one of the computers listed in Table 253. If it does, place a corresponding /MACHINE switch in your CONFIG.SYS HIMEM.SYS entry.

The following HIMEM.SYS entry specifies support for a PS/2:

Table 253. HIMEM.SYS Machine Entries

Machine Name	Value	Description
AT	1	IBM PC AT
PS2	2	IBM PS/2
PT1Cascade	3	Phoenix cascade BIOS
HPVECTRA	4	HP Vectra A and A+
ATT6300PLUS	5	AT&T 6300 Plus
ACER1100	6	Acer 1100
TOSHIBA	7	Toshiba 1600 and 1200XE
WYSE	8	Wyse 12.5 MHz 286
TULIP	9	Tulip SX
ZENITH	10	Zenith ZBIOS
AT1	11	IBM PC AT
AT2	12	IBM PC AT (alternative delay)
CSS	12	CSS Labs
AT3	13	IBM PC AT (alternative delay)
PHILIPS	13	Philips
FASTHP	14	HPVECTRA

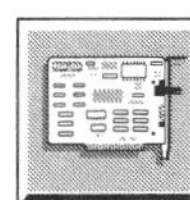

```
DEVICE=C:\DOS\HIMEM.SYS /MACHINE:PS2
```

You need the the HIMEM.SYS /MACHINE switch when the code HIMEM.SYS uses to toggle on and off address line 20 (A20) conflicts with the machine's BIOS.

Tip 270 describes address line 20 (A20) in detail.

Understanding the DOS 4 Install Entry

If you are using DOS 4, the DOS documentation recommends that you use the CONFIG.SYS INSTALL entry to install the KEYB, FASTOPEN, NLSFUNC, and SHARE memory-resident commands. Here's why.

If you invoke these commands from the DOS prompt or from within your AUTOEXEC.BAT file, DOS loads the commands into memory above COMMAND.COM as shown in this illustration:

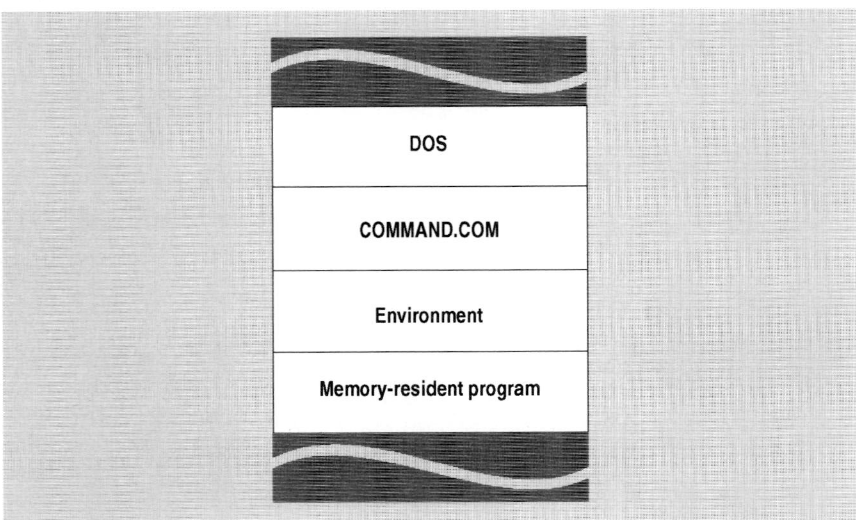

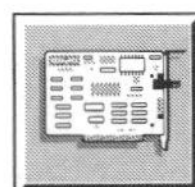

As a result, the commands immediately restrict the environment's future growth. If you instead use INSTALL to load these commands, DOS will place the commands beneath COMMAND.COM, which allows the environment to grow as future needs change.

What Upper-Memory Blocks Are Available?

As you decide which drivers and memory-resident programs you want to install in upper memory, consider each program's size and the size of the available upper-memory blocks. To display the upper-memory block sizes, invoke the MEM command using the /CLASSIFY switch as shown here:

```
C:\> MEM /CLASSIFY <ENTER>
```

To print a copy of the available memory blocks, redirect MEM's output to the printer as shown here:

```
C:\> MEM /CLASSIFY  PRN <ENTER>
```

What Does DOS=HIGH Really Do?

As discussed in Tip 223, the DOS=HIGH CONFIG.SYS entry directs DOS to load itself into the high-memory area. The best way to understand the files this entry affects is first to boot DOS in low memory. Then issue the following MEM. command:

```
C:\> MEM /DEBUG > PRN <ENTER>
```

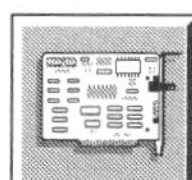

Next, restart DOS using the DOS=HIGH entry. Repeat the previous MEM /DEBUG command. When you compare the two printouts, you will find that DOS has loaded part of IO.SYS, MSDOS.SYS, the CONFIG.SYS BUFFERS, and the resident-portion of COMMAND.COM into the high-memory area.

TIP 257 Understanding Addressing Capabilities

As discussed in Tip 215, the original IBM PC could not address memory locations above 1Mb. An 80286 computer, however, can address up to 16Mb of physical memory, and 80386 and 80486 computers can address up to 4Gb of physical memory. What causes the differences? Each CPU uses a fixed-size address bus. As discussed in Tip 57, a bus is simply a group of wires. An 8088 computer, for example, uses a 20-bit bus. To determine the number of memory locations a 20-bit bus can address, determine the value of a 2 raised to the 20th, which is 1,048,576. An 8088 computer, therefore, can address 1,048,576 different address locations, or 1Mb.

To better understand this process, assume your PC uses a two-line address bus. As shown in Table 257, the 2-bit bus can address four different locations.

Similarly, a 3-bit bus could access 8 memory locations (2^3). An 80286 computer uses a 24-bit bus. If you raise 2 to the 24th (2^{24}), the result is 16Mb. The 80386 and 80486 computers use a 32-bit address bus, which means they can access 2^{32}, or 4,294,967,296 different memory locations!

Table 257. Memory Locations Addressable by a 2-Bit Bus.

Bus 1 Value	Bus 2 Value	Address Location
0	0	0
0	1	1
1	0	2
1	1	3

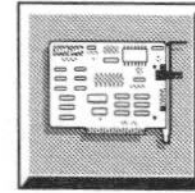

Understanding Flash Memory

The PC employs two primary types of memory chips: RAM and ROM. RAM holds your program's instructions and data as they execute. The PC can both read from and write to RAM. When you turn off your computer's power, the contents of RAM are lost. ROM is your PC's read-only memory. Unlike RAM, your computer's ROM does not lose it contents when power is lost. Your computers BIOS, which takes control when your computer starts, resides in ROM. As its name implies, your computer can only read the contents of ROM.

Recently a new memory technology, flash memory, has been gaining notice. Flash memory is best viewed as a cross between RAM and ROM. Like ROM, flash memory retains its contents when your PC's power is off. Like RAM, your PC changes the flash memory's contents. In addition, flash memory can be read with an access time approaching 80 nanoseconds.

Although flash memory has been touted as a replacement for disks, such technology is still a few years away. Unlike RAM, whose contents you can modify a byte at a time, the entire flash memory board must be updated at once. Currently, this operation can take several seconds. In addition, the contents of flash memory can be erased and rewritten only a fixed number of times. Although manufacturers will guarantee several thousand such operations, this number is not high enough to justify disk replacement. In the near term, flash memory will probably be used for programmable BIOS chips that let users easily upgrade their systems from floppy disks as upgrades become available.

Viewing SMARTDRV's Status

If you are using SMARTDRV.EXE version 4, you can invoke SMARTDRV from the DOS prompt to display the current status as shown here:

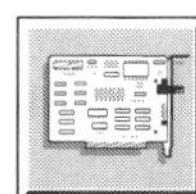

```
C:\> SMARTDRV <ENTER>
Microsoft SMARTDrive Disk Cache version 4.0.091
Copyright 1991,1992 Microsoft Corp.

Cache size: 1,048,576 bytes
Cache size while running Windows: 524,288 bytes

            Disk Caching Status
drive   read cache   write cache   buffering
--------------------------------------------
  A:       yes          no            no
  B:       yes          no            no
  C:       yes          yes           no

For help, type "Smartdrv /?".
```

As you can see, SMARTDRV displays its version number, cache sizes, and buffering techniques. SMARTDRV's read cache contains the sectors you have previously read as well as read-ahead sectors that SMARTDRV anticipates you will use. The write buffer is a write-behind buffer. In other words, when a program writes to a disk for which write buffering is active, the information is written to SMARTDRV'S buffer as opposed to disk, which causes the operation to complete very quickly. SMARTDRV, in turn, makes sure that the data is then written to disk. (Tip 259 discusses write-behind caching in detail.) The buffering option specifies whether the corresponding disk requires double buffering. Under Windows 3.0, depending on your disk controller type (for instance, if you are using a SCSI controller), you might want SMARTDRV to double buffer data, meaning SMARTDRV first writes data to conventional memory and then tries to write the data to disk. SMARTDRV double buffers data in this way to prevent a bus error from causing data loss. If you are using Windows 3.1, you can disable double buffering to improve performance speed.

To display SMARTDRV's current settings, you must be using SMARTDRV version 4 or higher.

Flushing SMARTDRV's Write-Behind Buffer

Tip 259 discusses SMARTDRV version 4's write-behind buffering in detail. When SMARTDRV performs write-behind buffering, it does not instantly write data to disk. Instead, SMARTDRV writes the data to disk within 5 seconds. To ensure that SMARTDRV has flushed its write-behind buffers, from the DOS prompt you can invoke SMARTDRV with the /C switch as shown here:

```
C:\> SMARTDRV /C <ENTER>
```

In fact, you might want to include this command in your TURNOFF.BAT batch file that you run before you turn off your PC. This command will ensure that the SMARTDRV buffers are flushed before you turn off your system's power.

To use the /C switch, you must be using SMARTDRV version 4 or higher.

Understanding Cache Hits and Misses

Tip 228 discussed the difference between memory and disk caches. Two terms commonly used with both cache types are "cache hits" and "cache misses." As discussed, when data is needed, the PC first looks in the cache. If the data is present, a cache hit occurs, meaning the data can be instantly accessed. If the data is not present, a cache miss occurs and the data must be accessed from the slower storage media. If you are using SMARTDRV version 4, you can invoke SMARTDRV from the DOS prompt using the /S switch to view its ratio of cache hits to cache misses as shown here:

```
C:\> SMARTDRV /S <ENTER>

Microsoft SMARTDrive Disk Cache version 4.0.091
```

```
Copyright 1991,1992 Microsoft Corp.

Room for 128 elements of 8,192 bytes each
There have been 68,105 cache hits
    and 8,487 cache misses

Cache size: 1,048,576 bytes
Cache size while running Windows: 524,288 bytes

            Disk Caching Status
drive   read cache   write cache   buffering
-------------------------------------------
  A:        yes           no            no
  B:        yes           no            no
  C:        yes           yes           no

For help, type "Smartdrv /?".
```

The number of cache hits tells you the number of times the SMARTDRV buffer contained the data DOS requested, which eliminated a slow disk read operation. The number of cache misses specifies the number of times the data was not present and had to be read from disk.

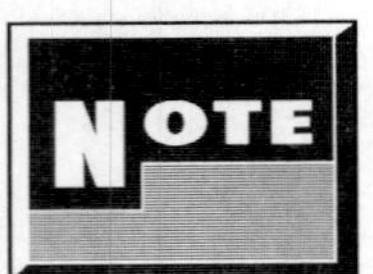

To use the /S switch, you must be using SMARTDRV version 4 or higher.

Understanding Memory Interleaving

As described in Tip 229, wait states occur when the processor cannot continue because memory is not ready. One way computer designers reduce the length of wait states is by interleaving memory. Conceptually, memory is a long, continuous bank of memory chips with a controller that is responsible for accessing, storing, and refreshing the chips. Interleaved memory is divided into multiple banks, with individual controllers as shown in the following illustration:

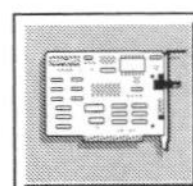

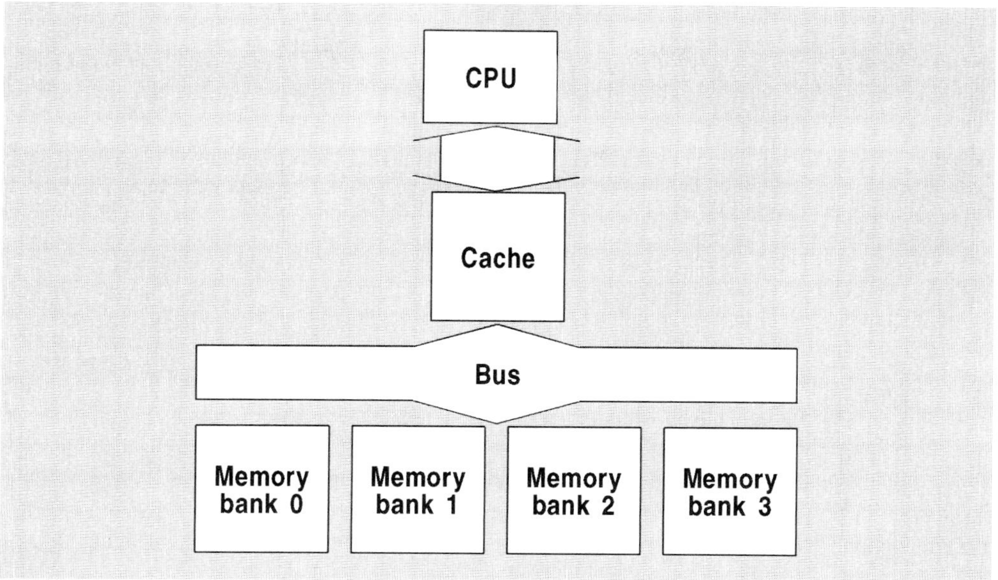

If a program needs to read words one through four, for example, each controller can quickly read its individual word, placing the data on the memory bus at the correct time. In the traditional (noninterleaved) system, the first word would be read and refreshed (delay 1), the second read and refreshed (delay 2), and so. Using interleaving, as bank 1 refreshes its data, bank 2 is providing data. By overlapping operations in this way, wait states are minimized.

What Is Dual-Ported Video Memory?

To display images on your screen, the PC places values that represent the image in the computer's video memory. Your video board, in turn, uses these values to display the information on the screen. As the following illustration shows, video memory can essentially be viewed as a pipe in which the PC places (or writes) data and from which the video board reads the data.

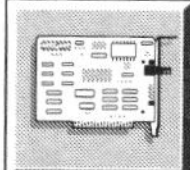

As complex windowing and multimedia operations become more common, dual-ported video memory, or VRAM, will become a necessity. Unfortunately, you can't just replace your existing DRAM chips with VRAM; you'll need a new video card.

Understanding Memory Speeds

When you purchase memory for your computer, you need to pay attention to memory chip speeds. Memory chip speeds are measured in nanoseconds, typically in the range 60 to 150 nanoseconds for DRAM chips and as low as 25 nanoseconds for SRAM chips; the lower the speed, the faster the chip. Memory chip speeds differ depending on your PC's processor speed. As a rule, you can use faster chips. However, faster memory chips are more expensive, and on their own, faster memory chips won't make your computer faster. Instead, the speed of your computer's internal clock controls the system's speed. Memory chips have their speeds printed on the chip's outer case.

Buying Memory Chips

When you buy memory, you need to be concerned with the memory Type, speed, and configuration. Tip 230 discusses memory types such as DRAM and SRAM. Tip 264 discusses memory speeds. In the past, users added memory to their system by adding memory cards as illustrated here. Depending on your memory needs, the board could be partially or entirely full (populated). Switches on the board specify the amount of memory present.

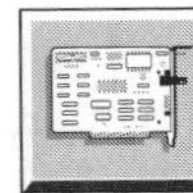

Today, memory commonly resides on small modules called SIMMs (single in-line memory modules) or SIPPs (single in-line pin packages) that connect to specific motherboard slots as shown here:

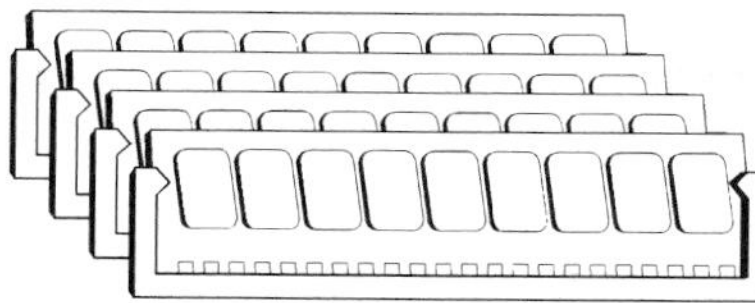

Because of increases in memory storage capacities, the smaller SIMMs and SIPPs often hold as much memory as the older expansion boards.

Regardless of your memory board type, you need to purchase chips of a specific size, such as 64Kb, 256Kb, or 1Mb. The documentation that accompanies your board or computer will tell you the chip sizes supported. Normally, you must use only one chip size; you can't mix sizes. Some boards, however, let you mix chip sizes in different banks. The chip's size specifies the number of bits the chip holds, not the number of bytes. To store 256Kb, you actually have to purchase nine 256K chips—the first eight chips store the data, and the ninth chip is used for parity information.

Understanding Memory Banks

As discussed in Tip 265, you can add memory to your system by using an extension board or SIMMs and SIPPs. When you add memory to an expansion card, each row of memory chips you insert forms a bank of memory.

If you are using a 286 or 386SX system, the processor moves data 16 bits at a time on the data bus. When you add memory to these systems, you must do so two banks (16 bits) at a time. The 386DX and 486 systems, on the other hand, move data 32 bits at a time. When you install memory on these systems, you should do so four banks at a time. There are SIMMs that support 36 bits (32 data and 4 parity) per module. Depending on your board type, you may be able to place different-sized chips in different banks. To do so, however, you will have to configure the board by using its DIP switches. For more information on this, refer to the documentation that accompanies your memory board.

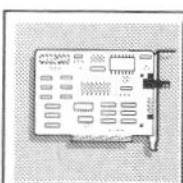

Install System Board Memory First

Almost all PC's have memory slots on the motherboard, called system board RAM. This memory directly connects to the CPU so it doesn't have to share a data bus with other devices. As a result, system board memory provides a much faster response than memory on an expansion board. Examine your motherboard for empty memory slots; when you are ready to add memory, fill the system board memory slots first.

Installing SIMMs

As the following illustration shows, a SIMM typically has notches at both ends that you use to lock the module into place:

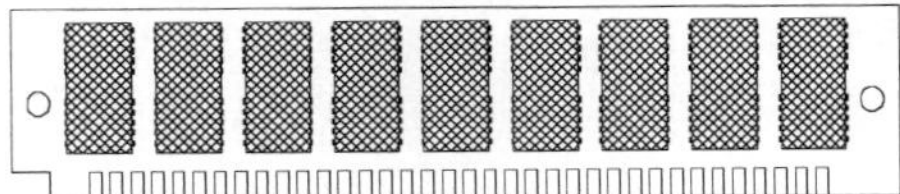

To insert a SIMM, note the proper chip orientation and then gently slide the SIMM into the socket at a 45-degree angle. Then stand the chip up, and it should snap into place. Should you ever need to remove the SIMM, open the locks, push the tabs from the notches, and gently slide the SIMM out.

Understanding DOS 20-Bit Addressing

The original IBM PC used 20-bit addressing and so could address up to 1Mb. To address different memory locations, the PC divides memory into segments, each of which can be 64Kb. A segment can start at any 16-byte boundary in memory. For example, segments can start at locations 0, 16, 32, 48, and so on up to 1,048,560. The PC uses a 16-bit address to hold the segment address.

When a program runs, its data is stored in one or more 64Kb segments. Within this large segment, the PC uses offsets to find specific pieces of information. For example, your first name might be located at offset 2, your age at offset 10, and so on. The programs you run keep track of these segments and offset locations. When the PC addresses a specific location, it must place the desired address on its 20-bit address bus. To do so, the PC combines the 16-bit segment address and 16-bit offset address to form a 20-bit address that specifies a location in the range 0 through 1,048,575. For example, assume the desired data is at segment 2H, offset 5H (storage location 16 * 2 + 5, or 37). The segment and offset registers will contain the hexadecimal values 0002H and 0005H. The PC first shifts the segment address one hexadecimal position to the left (0002H becomes 0020H). Next, the PC adds the values as shown here:

```
   0020H
 + 0005H
 ------------
   0025H
```

If you convert hexadecimal value 25H to decimal format, the result is 37, which matches the memory location previously specified. Had the data been stored at segment 400H, offset 127H, the PC would have calculated the 20-bit address as follows:

```
0400  becomes    4000H
               + 0127H
               ------------
                 4127H
```

By shifting the segment address and adding the offset in this way, the PC can address the entire 1,048,576 bytes in its address space.

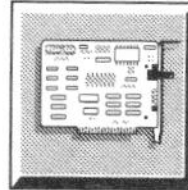

What Is Address Line A20?

The original IBM PC uses 20 address lines (lines A0 through A19). The 286 computer has 24 lines, and the 386 and 486 computers have 32. In fact, in real mode, 286 and higher computers can use the twenty-first address line, A20. Beginning with DOS 5, DOS allows use of line A20, which creates the high-memory area (the first 64Kb above 1Mb).

Because older real-mode programs were not written to support the high-memory area, many took advantage of the fact that, when the PC addressed memory in the range FFFF:0010H through FFFF:FFFF (the high-memory area), the PC would automatically wrap the addresses to the start of memory. To support such programs, DOS disables A20 when it runs a program. If the program addresses a location in the range just specified, the address will wrap, just as it would on a standard 8088. When the program needs to use one of the DOS services, DOS enables the use of the A20 line, which provides access to the DOS kernel. After DOS enables A20, the line remains in use until the program ends. Programs, therefore, must ensure they do not subsequently use addresses in the high-memory area or expect such addresses to wrap because they would overwrite DOS.

Why DRAM Chips Store More Bits than SRAM Chips

Tip 230 discusses static and dynamic RAM chips. DRAM chips can store considerably more information than SRAM chips. Here's why. Depending on the chip's design, SRAM chips require four to six transistors to store each bit. DRAM chips, on the other hand, use capacitors to store bits. A capacitor may require only one or two transistors. Thus, depending on the chip designs, storing a bit with SRAM will require at least twice as many transistors (and possibly up to six times as many) as with DRAM. Because each transistor takes up physical space, the SRAM chip can't hold the same number of bits. Unfortunately, although using capacitors reduces the number of transistors required, capacitors also produce the need for DRAM refresh.

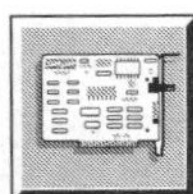

Understanding Why DRAM Chips Are Slower than SRAM Chips

As discussed in Tip 273, DRAM chips use capacitors to store bits. The advantage capacitors provide is that they can store a bit using only one or two transistors, and designers can squeeze more information into a DRAM chip. Capacitors store an electric charge. In the case of a bit, a charged capacitor corresponds to the value 1, and an uncharged capacitor corresponds to the value 0. Unfortunately, the only way to determine a capacitor's status is to discharge it. After the capacitor's charge is known, capacitors that contained a 1 (charged) must be recharged. Because the drain and recharge operations take more than one cycle, DRAM chips are slower than SRAM chips.

Why DRAM Chips Need Refreshing

Tip 230 discusses static and dynamic RAM. DRAM chips require periodic refresh operations, but SRAM chips do not. Here's why. To store one bit of information, SRAM chips use from four to six transistors to create a flip-flop, which retains its setting (0 to 1) until specifically changed. DRAM chips, on the other hand, store a bit by using a capacitor. A capacitor is simply a device that can hold an electric charge. For 1 bits, the capacitor is charged, and for 0 bits, it is not. Unfortunately, unlike flip-flops, whose values change only on command, capacitors lose their charge over time through leakage. Worse yet, the amount of time the capacitor can hold its charge is only a few milliseconds. So to prevent the bits from disappearing, DRAM chips must be refreshed regularly.

In older PCs, the processor was regularly interrupted to coordinate refresh operations. Although the processor employed its DMA chip to preform the refresh operation, the constant interruptions decreased system performance. Today, DRAM chips contain their own refresh circuitry, which takes the processor out of the loop, improving your system performance.

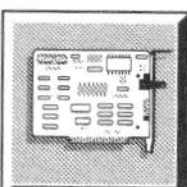

Decoding Memory Chips

If you examine memory chips, you will find their names printed on the chip's packaging. The following illustration shows several memory chips and their names:

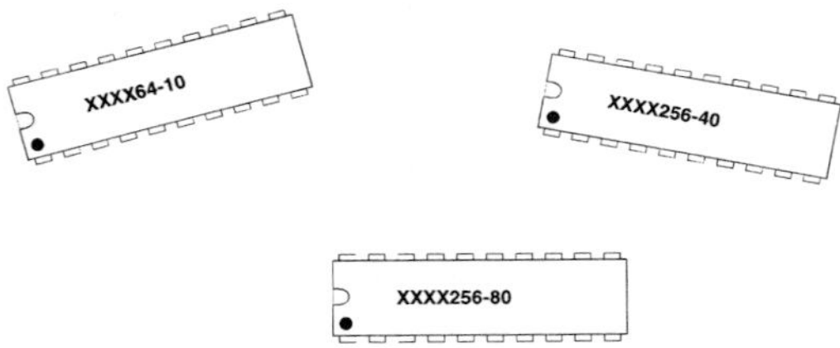

The chip name describes the chip's speed and storage capacity. Here's how you decode the names. Most memory chip names begin with two digits you can ignore. The digits that follow, up to a hyphen or other separator, indicate the chip's storage capacity. Using the chip names shown in the preceding illustration, you can determine that the chip capacities are as follows:

XXXX64-10	64K
XXX256-40	256K
XXX256-80	256K

The last two digits of the chip name specify the chip's speed. Again using the chip names in the preceding illustration, the chip speeds are as follows:

XXXX64-10	100 ns
XXX256-40	40 ns
XXX256-80	80 ns

Should You Purchase a Third-Party Memory Manager?

Using the DOS 5 memory management techniques, you can free considerable conventional memory by moving device drivers and memory-resident programs. To perform these memory management operations, you must use the DOS device drivers HIMEM.SYS and EMM386.EXE. If you read computer magazines, you will see reviews of third-party memory managers such as Quarterdeck's QEMM386 and Qualitas' 386MAX. In general, because these products focus solely on memory management, they will outperform the DOS drivers. They will not only execute faster, but they will let you free even more conventional memory. The advantage the DOS drivers provide is that they free considerable memory, and they do so for no extra cost. However, if you must fully maximize your memory management, try using one of these third-party products.

Using Expanded Memory with DOS 4

Tip 219 discusses expanded memory in detail. If you are using PC DOS version 4, XMA2EMS.SYS device driver provides access to expanded memory. To use the driver, place it in your CONFIG.SYS file as shown here:

```
DEVICE=C:\DOS\XMA2EMS.SYS [parameters]
```

The driver specifically supports the expanded memory adapters listed here:

IBM 2Mb expanded memory adapter
IBM PS/2 80286 expanded memory adapter /A
IBM PS/2 80286 memory expansion option
386-based systems using the XMAEM.SYS driver

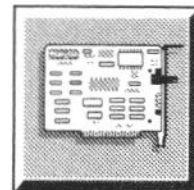

The XMAEM.SYS driver is required only if you are using DOS 4 and you are not using a third-party expanded memory driver.

DOS 4 Expanded Memory on a 386

As described in Tip 276, DOS 4 provides the XMA2EMS.SYS device driver for expanded memory support. If you are using a 386 computer that does not have expanded memory, you can use the XMAEM.SYS device driver, which uses extended memory to simulate expanded memory. You must install XMAEM.SYS in your CONFIG.SYS file before the XMA2EMS.SYS driver as shown here:

```
DEVICE=C:\DOS\XMAEM.SYS [SIZE]
DEVICE=C:\DOS\XMA2EMS.SYS [parameters]
```

The XMAEM.SYS driver lets you specify the amount of extended memory the driver can use. By default, the driver uses 1Mb (the minimum size). The maximum is 32Mb. You must specify the size in 16Kb increments.

The XMAEM.SYS driver is required only if you are using DOS 4 and you are not using a third-party expanded memory driver.

Are You Using SETVER?

Tip 55 presents the DOS 5 SETVER device driver, which lets you specify the version number you want a specific program to return if asked by DOS. If you don't have programs that need SETVER, don't install the driver; doing so wastes memory. If your

CONFIG.SYSfileinstallsSETVERanditdoesn'tcontainaREMstatementthatexplainswhy,invoke SETVERfromtheDOSpromptasshownhere:

```
C:\> SETVER <ENTER>

WIN200.BIN       3.40
WIN100.BIN       3.40
WINWORD.EXE      4.10
EXCEL.EXE        4.10
HITACHI.SYS      4.00
MSCDEX.EXE       4.00
   :              :
ZFMT.SYS         4.01
TOPSRDR.EXE      4.00
```

If none of the programs SETVER lists are programs you use, remove the SETVER entry; otherwise, if you use SETVER, use the DEVICEHIGH entry (if possible) to install it.

The SETVER command requires DOS 5.

Minimizing FCBS Support

Tip 26 discusses the CONFIG.SYS FCBS entry. By default, DOS provides support for four file control blocks if you don't specify otherwise. Because you will probably never require these file control blocks, you can free additional memory by selecting the minimum number of file control blocks with this CONFIG.SYS entry:

```
FCBS=1
```

Before you restart your system, invoke MEM or CHKDSK to determine the amount of available memory. Next, add the FCBS=1 entry to your CONFIG.SYS and reboot. Invoke MEM or CHKDSK a second time to see the amount of memory now available.

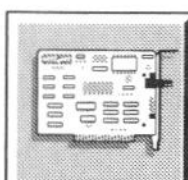

DOS Always Rounds the Environment Size Up

Tip 13 discusses how to increase your environment size by using the CONFIG.SYS SHELL entry. DOS lets you specify an environment size of up to 32,768 bytes. When you specify an environment size, DOS always rounds your size up to a value that is evenly divisible by 16. For example, if you specify the environment size 200, DOS will round the size up to 208. The reason for the rounding is that DOS allocates memory in 16-byte paragraphs. An environment size of 200 would require 12 1/2 paragraphs. Because DOS doesn't work with half paragraphs, DOS rounds the number of paragraphs to 13 (13 * 16 = 208). To best manage memory allocation, choose an environment size that is evenly divisible by 16.

Understanding the HIMEM.SYS /INT15 Switch

Tip 221 discusses extended memory and the use of the HIMEM.SYS device driver to access extended memory; to provide access to extended memory, HIMEM.SYS actually switches between real mode and protected mode and back again. The BIOS for 286 and higher computers provides a second way to access extended memory interrupt 15H (Int 15H). Although the Int 15H interface to extended memory is seldom used, you may encounter an older program that uses this approach. If you run an older program in which your attempts to access extended memory fail, you may need to use the HIMEM.SYS /INT15 switch that allocates a memory buffer between 0 and 64Kb for the Int 15H interface. For example, the following CONFIG.SYS entry allocates a 32Kb buffer:

```
DEVICE=C:\DOS\HIMEM.SYS /INT15=32
```

In addition to knowing when to use the /INT15 switch, you also need to know when you don't. If you encounter an /INT15 switch with your HIMEM.SYS entry without a remark explaining why it's needed, try working without it. In most cases, the switch is probably only causing your PC to consume memory unnecessarily.

A Pictorial View of Your System's Memory Use

Tip 215 discusses your computer's conventional memory use in detail. If your system contains Windows 3.1, you can use the program MSD.EXE to display system information. One of the items MSD can display is a visual presentation of your computer's conventional and upper-memory use. To display information about your system's memory use, invoke MSD from the DOS prompt. When MSD displays its menu of options, press **M** to select the Memory option. MSD will display a box illustrating your system's memory use as shown here:

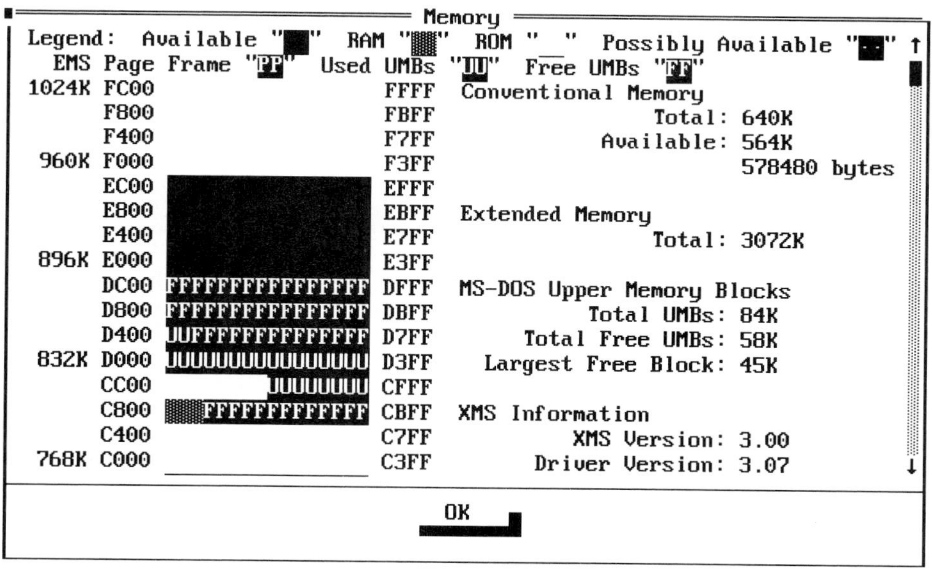

Use the legend that appears at the top of the box to understand the symbols used to describe your memory use. If you have a mouse, you can use the scroll bar at the right of the box to scroll through memory; otherwise, use your keyboard arrow keys.

To use MSD.EXE, you must be using Windows 3.1.

Viewing Memory Blocks with MSD.EXE

Tip 282 explains how to view your computer's upper-memory use with the Windows 3.1 utility program MSD.EXE. MSD also lets you display information identifying which program, driver, or DOS data structure is using a specific area of memory. To view this information, invoke MSD from the DOS prompt. Next, select the Utilities menu and choose Memory Block Display. MSD will display a detailed map of your system's memory use as shown here:

```
Allocated memory:                                     Memory map:

 Free Memory          EA7D     22560                  FC00
 MGR.EXE              E765     12656                  F800
 MGR.EXE              E747       464                  F400
 MGR.EXE              E644      4128                  F000
   HITACHIA           E32D     12656                  EC00 FFFFFFFFFFFFFFFF
   SETVER             E312       416                  E800 UUUUUUUUUFFFFFFF
   SJII               E155      7104                  E400 UUUUUUUUUUUUUUUU
   RAMDRIVE           E10A      1184                  E000 UUUUHUUUUUUUUUUU
   ANSI               E003      4192                  DC00 PPPPPPPPPPPPPPPP
 System Data          E001     25632                  D800 PPPPPPPPPPPPPPPP
 Excluded UMB Area    CFFE     65568                  D400 PPPPPPPPPPPPPPPP
 Free Memory          CCF8     12368                  D000 PPPPPPPPPPPPPPPP
 MGR.EXE              C8F7     16384                  CC00 UUUFFFFFFFFFFFFF
 MGR.EXE              C8E4       288                  C800     UUUUUUUUUUUUU
 Excluded UMB Area    9FFF    167488                  C400
 Free Memory          8032    130240                  C000

                                  Close
```

If you are using a mouse, use the scroll bar that appears to the right of the box to move through memory; otherwise, use your keyboard's arrow keys.

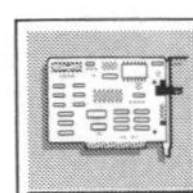

Browsing Through Memory with MSD.EXE

If your system contains MS Windows 3.1, you can use the utility command MSD.EXE to display information about your system. Using MSD, you can browse specific areas of your computer's ROM. To begin, invoke MSD from the DOS prompt. Next, select the Utilities menu and choose Memory Browser. MSD will display a box listing several memory regions you can browse as shown here:

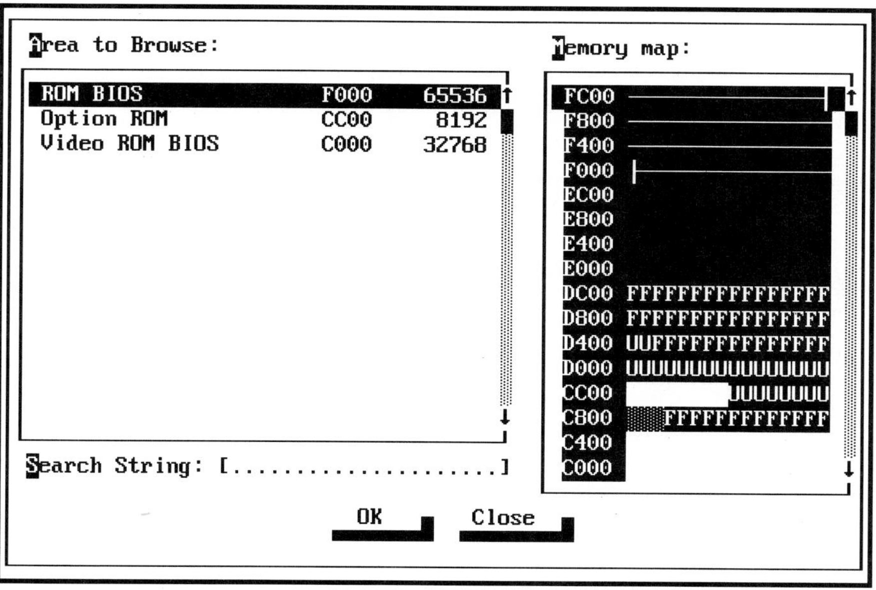

Using your mouse or the keyboard arrow keys, select the desired region and press ENTER. MSD will display a box listing addresses in the region and the region's corresponding contents as shown here:

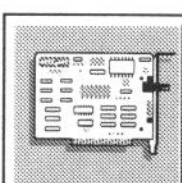

```
═══════════════════════════ ROM BIOS ═══════════════════════════
F000:3453 =1 DMA WAIT STATE   01=2 DMA WAIT STATE   10=3 DMA WAIT STATE
            11=4 DMA WAIT STATE 8 BIT DMA WAIT STATES EMR BIT   0=DISABL
          E   1=ENABLE CLK BIT   0 -> DMA CLK = SCLK/2   1 -> DMA CLK =
          SCLKVERSION/PROCESSOR CLOCK/NMI SOURCE PROCESSOR CLOCK
F000:73E0 System Configuration (C) Copyright 1985-1989, American Megatre
          nds Inc,.
F000:D621 CMOS SETUP (C) Copyright 1985-1989, American Megatrends Inc,.
           Date (mn/date/year):
F000:000A o02/15/89SETUP PROGRAM FOR C&T 386 CHIPSET(C)1988, American Me
          gatrends Inc.All rights reserved.1346 Oakbrook drive, Suite-12
          0,Norcross, GA 30093, Phone-(404)-263-8181.
F000:2E11 EXTENDED CMOS SETUP PROGRAM Ver - 1.50 ,(C)1988, American Mega
          trends Inc.    Prev/Next Window -
F000:8000 333388886666----0123AAAAMMMMIIII Date:-03/03/89 (C)1985-1989,
          American Megatrends Inc. All Rights Reserved. 1346 Oakbrook Dr
          ive, Suite-120, Norcross, GA-30093, USA.Phone-(404)-263-8181.
F000:E2D0 0000000000000000(C)1987 American Megatrends Inc.386-BIOS (C)19
          89 American Megatrends Inc

                                OK
```

If you are using a mouse, use the scroll bar that appears along the right edge of the box to move through the region; otherwise, use your keyboard arrow keys.

Displaying and Controlling Expanded Memory from Within DEBUG

If you are experiencing problems with a program that uses expanded memory, invoke DEBUG and issue the XS command to display the expanded memory status. If expanded memory is not installed, DEBUG will display the following screen:

```
-XS <ENTER>
EMS not installed
```

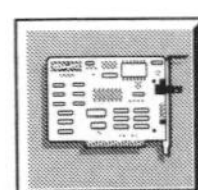

If this message appears, you've solved the problem. If expanded memory is installed, DEBUG will display the following screen:

```
-XS <ENTER>
Handle 0000 has 0018 pages allocated

Physical page 05 = Frame segment 4000
Physical page 06 = Frame segment 4400
   .      . . . .   .      .
   .      . . . .   .      .
   .      . . . .   .      .
Physical page 02 = Frame segment D800
Physical page 03 = Frame segment DC00

  18 of a total   28 EMS pages have been allocated
   1 of a total   40 EMS handles have been allocated
```

DEBUG provides three other commands, listed in Table 285, that deal specifically with expanded memory.

If the expanded memory driver is active, try issuing the following DEBUG commands:

```
-XA 5 <ENTER>
-XD Handle_Value_Returned_By_XA <ENTER>
```

If any of the commands fail, the problem is your expanded memory driver, not the software. In this case, double-check your driver entry in CONFIG.SYS and reboot.

Table 285. *DEBUG's Expanded Memory Commands*

DEBUG Command	Function
XA	Allocates expanded memory pages
XD	Deallocates expanded memory pages
XM	Maps a logical expanded memory page to a physical page

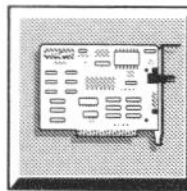

Is Your AMI BIOS Consuming RAM?

If you are using an AMI BIOS, one of the setup options corresponds to the BIOS scratch RAM. The setup screen gives you two options for scratch RAM (numbered options 1 and 2). If you are using DOS, select option 1 to direct the BIOS to use the BIOS stack area at location 0030:0000. If you were to select option 2, the BIOS would allocate 1K of conventional memory that would not be used.

Zero-Filling Extended Memory

Tip 196 describes how to use the companion disk utility command ZEROMEM.EXE to zero out conventional memory. In a similar way, the utility command ZEROEXT.EXE lets you zero-fill the unused portion of extended memory. To use ZEROEXT, invoke it from the DOS prompt as shown here:

```
C:\> ZEROEXT <ENTER>
```

If you have an application that uses extended memory and you are working with sensitive data, use the ZEROEXT utility to zero out extended memory.

ZEROEXT.EXE

The utility command ZEROEXT.EXE resides on the companion disk that accompanies this book.

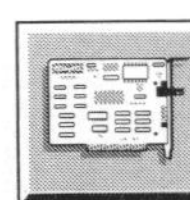

Displaying Information About Expanded Memory

Tip 219 discusses expanded memory in detail. Expanded memory allocates 16Kb pages, called physical pages, in reserved memory. Your programs allocate regions of expanded memory called logical pages. If you are using EMS 4.0, your physical pages are not restricted to 16Kb. Pages whose sizes differ are called raw pages. When a program allocates expanded memory, the EMM driver returns a unique value, called a handle, that the program must specify each time it references the logical pages.

To help you better understand your system's expanded memory use, the companion disk that accompanies this book provides the utility program EMMSTATS.EXE that displays information about your use of expanded memory as follows:

```
C:\> EMMSTATS <ENTER>
EMM functional
EMM version number 4.0
Total number of pages 40
Number of available pages 16
Number of raw pages 40
Total handles in the system 64
Number of active handles 1
```

If a program that uses expanded memory fails, run EMMSTATS to determine the current settings.

The utility command EMMSTATS.EXE resides on the companion disk that accompanies this book.

EMMSTATS.EXE

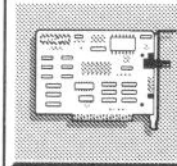

Listing Your Expanded Memory Physical Page Addresses

Tip 219 discusses expanded memory in detail. The EMS driver normally allocates four 16Kb pages in the reserved memory. If you are using an EMS driver whose version number is 4.0 or higher, however, the driver can allocate raw pages (whose size is not necessarily equal to 16Kb and that reside outside of the 64Kb EMS buffer). When you add hardware devices, you need to ensure that the device memory does not conflict with memory that the EMS drive is allocating. If a conflict exists, you can use switches when you install the EMS driver to direct it to help you detect conflicts. The companion disk that accompanies this book provides the utility program EMSPAGES.EXE that displays the current base addresses for the physical pages as shown here:

```
C:\> EMSPAGES <ENTER>
EMM functional
Page frame address D000
Number of mappable pages 29
Page 5 Segment Base Address 4000
Page 6 Segment Base Address 4400
Page 7 Segment Base Address 4800
Page 8 Segment Base Address 4C00
Page 9 Segment Base Address 5000
Page A Segment Base Address 5400
Page B Segment Base Address 5800
Page C Segment Base Address 5C00
Page D Segment Base Address 6000
Page E Segment Base Address 6400
Page F Segment Base Address 6800
Page 10 Segment Base Address 6C00
Page 11 Segment Base Address 7000
Page 12 Segment Base Address 7400
Page 13 Segment Base Address 7800
Page 14 Segment Base Address 7C00
Page 15 Segment Base Address 8000
Page 16 Segment Base Address 8400
Page 17 Segment Base Address 8800
Page 18 Segment Base Address 8C00
```

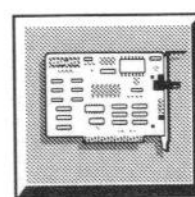

```
Page 19 Segment Base Address 9000
Page 1A Segment Base Address 9400
Page 1B Segment Base Address 9800
Page 1C Segment Base Address 9C00
Page 4 Segment Base Address C800
Page 0 Segment Base Address D000
Page 1 Segment Base Address D400
Page 2 Segment Base Address D800
Page 3 Segment Base Address DC00
```

In this case, the driver supports raw pages, which can reside at different memory locations. By using EMSPAGES to determine the base of each page in use, you can avoid page and hardware address conflicts.

The utility command EMSPAGES.EXE resides on the companion disk that accompanies this book.

EMSPAGES.EXE

Displaying Information About Your Expanded Memory Board

Tip 219 discusses expanded memory and expanded memory boards in detail. If your system uses an expanded memory board and you want to determine whether the board is compatible with a specific program, run the compansion disk utility program EMSBOARD.EXE to display information about your board as shown here:

```
C:\> EMSBOARD <ENTER>
RAW Page size (paragraphs) 1024
Number of alternate register sets 7
Mapping context area save size 120 bytes
Number of register sets for DMA use 0
Only one DMA register set is available
```

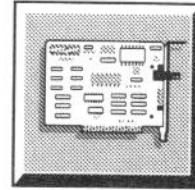

Although most of the information the EMSBOARD utility program displays will not be meaningful to most users, you can provide the information to a program's technical support representative to help determine whether your EMS board is compatible the program.

EMSBOARD.EXE

The utility command EMSBOARD.EXE resides on the companion disk that accompanies this book.

TIP 291

Configuring SHARE

As Tip 346 discusses, if you are using DOS 4.0 and have a hard disk with partitions larger than 32Mb, you need to install the SHARE command. Likewise, if you are running Windows and sharing files between programs, you also should install SHARE. When you install SHARE, DOS loads memory-resident software that monitors every file I/O operation. To keep track of its file locking information, SHARE creates two tables: one containing information about shared files and one containing file locks. By default, SHARE allocates 2,048 bytes of memory to hold the file information and provides support for 20 locks. In the file information table, SHARE stores 11 bytes of file-sharing information, plus the file's complete path name.

Using SHARE's /F and /L switches, you can specify the amount of memory SHARE can allocate for the file information table as well as the number of locks. The following SHARE command, for example, allocates 4,096 bytes of memory to hold the file table and specifies support for 40 locks:

```
C:\> SHARE /F:4096 /L:40 <ENTER>
```

If you increase the size of the file table or the number of locks, you also increase the amount of memory SHARE will consume. However, if you are using the DOS 5 memory management techniques, you can use LOADHIGH to load SHARE and its tables into upper memory.

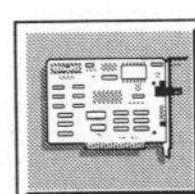

Loading DOS into High Memory Moves Disk Buffers Too

Tip 22 discusses DOS disk buffers. Each disk buffer consumes 528 bytes of memory. Assume, for example, that your CONFIG.SYS entry contains the following entry:

```
BUFFERS=30
```

In this case, DOS will consume about 15Kb of conventional memory. If you load DOS into high memory, however, DOS will load the disk buffers (as many as will fit) into high memory as well. Thus, if you use 40 disk buffers or less, DOS consumes only 512 bytes of conventional memory for disk buffers.

Invoking MODE with LOADHIGH

In Tip 32 you use the MODE command to redirect output destined for LPT1 to COM1, as shown here:

```
C:\> MODE LPT1:=COM1 <ENTER>
```

In Tip 110 you use MODE to adjust screen alignment for a CGA monitor. To perform these operations, MODE installs memory-resident software. If you are using the DOS 5 memory management techniques, you can use LOADHIGH to invoke MODE, placing the memory-resident software into upper memory, rather than conventional memory, as shown here:

```
C:\> LOADHIGH MODE LPT1:=COM1 <ENTER>
```

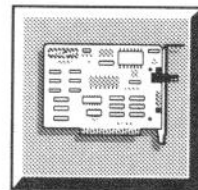

PART 3

Keyboard

Improving Your Keyboard's Response Rate

Beginning with DOS 4, the MODE command lets you control your keyboard's response rate. By increasing the response rate, your computer appears to become more responsive. The keyboard uses two rates to determine how fast keys are repeated. The typematic delay specifies how long you must hold down a key before the corresponding character repeats. The typematic delay value ranges from 1 to 4 corresponding to the rates shown in Table 294a.

The lower the typematic delay, the faster the character repeats. The typematic rate controls the speed at which characters repeat when you leave a key depressed. The value for the typematic rate ranges from 1 to 32 as shown in Table 294b.

For the fastest keyboard response, use the following MODE command or place the command into your AUTOEXEC.BAT file:

```
C:\> MODE CON: RATE=32 DELAY=1 <ENTER>
```

Before you issue this command, hold down a key and note how long it takes your computer to repeat the key. After you execute the MODE command, perform the same test and note your performance improvement.

To use the MODE command to control the keyboard's response rate, you must be using DOS 4 or higher.

Table 294a. Keyboard Typematic Delays

Typematic Delay	Delay in Seconds
1	0.25
2	0.50
3	0.75
4	1.00

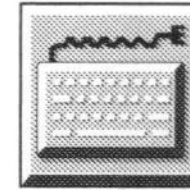

Table 294b. Keyboard Typematic Rate Values

Repeat Rate	Characters per second	Repeat Rate	Characters per second
1	2.0	17	8.4
2	2.1	18	8.6
3	2.3	19	9.2
4	2.5	20	10.0
5	2.7	21	10.9
6	3.0	22	12.0
7	3.3	23	13.3
8	3.7	24	15.0
9	4.0	25	16.0
10	4.3	26	17.1
11	4.6	27	18.5
12	5.0	28	20.0
13	5.5	29	21.8
14	6.0	30	24.0
15	6.7	31	26.7
16	7.5	32	30.0

A Faster Keyboard in One Command

If you are using DOS 4 or later, you can use the MODE command to set the keyboard's response rate. In a similar way, regardless of your DOS version, you can use the following DEBUG script file, FASTKEYS.SCR, to create the command file FASTKEYS.COM that maximizes your keyboard's response rate in one easy step:

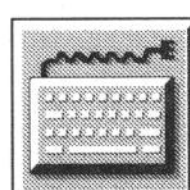

FASTKEYS.SCR

```
N FASTKEYS.COM <ENTER>
A 100          <ENTER>
MOV AX,0305    <ENTER>
XOR BX,BX      <ENTER>
INT 16         <ENTER>
MOV AH,4C      <ENTER>
INT 21         <ENTER>
               <ENTER>
R CX           <ENTER>
B              <ENTER>
W              <ENTER>
Q              <ENTER>
```

Use the DEBUG command as follows to create the command file FASTKEYS.COM:

```
C:\> DEBUG < FASTKEYS.SCR <ENTER>
```

Next, invoke the FASTKEYS command from the DOS prompt or add it to your AUTOEXEC.BAT file to maximize your keyboard's responsiveness.

TIP 296 Creating a Larger Keyboard Buffer

By default, the PC uses a 16-character keyboard buffer, into which it places the characters corresponding to the keystrokes you type at the keyboard. If you type keys faster than the PC uses them, the keyboard buffer will fill, and your computer will beep each time you type a key, informing you that it has ignored the keystroke. The companion disk that accompanies this book contains a utility program named MOVEKBD.EXE that creates a 64-character keyboard buffer. To install the larger keyboard, invoke the MOVEKBD command from the DOS prompt or from within your AUTOEXEC.BAT file. If you are using DOS 5 and have support for the upper memory area, invoke MOVEKBD using the LOADHIGH command. The keyboard buffer must reside in the 64Kb BIOS data area that begins at segment 0040H. Depending on your CONFIG.SYS entries and memory-resident programs, there may not be memory available in this region for a larger keyboard buffer.

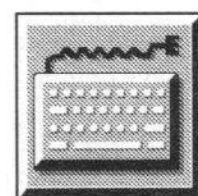

The command file MOVEKBD.EXE resides on the companion disk that accompanies this book.

MOVEKBD.EXE

Quickly Repeating Your Last Command

Each time you type a command at the DOS prompt, DOS places the command in a buffer whose contents you can quickly recall by using the F1 and F3 function keys. For example, issue the DIR command as shown here:

```
C:\> DIR <ENTER>
```

When the command completes, press the F1 key. DOS will recall the first letter of the command, the letter D. Press F1 again, and DOS will recall the letter I. When you press F1 a third time, DOS will recall the letter R. Press ENTER to repeat the command. This time when the command completes, press F3. DOS will recall the entire previous command in one step.

Sometimes you may need to edit the previous command, adding or deleting text. To do so, press the F1 key to the desired location to delete letters in the command buffer and then press the DEL key the appropriate number of times. After you have deleted the characters, use F1 or F3 to display the rest of the previous command line. To insert characters, press the F1 key to move to the desired location, press the Ins key, and type the desired text. Press the F1 or F3 keys to append the remainder of the previous command buffer.

Canceling the Current Command

Many times, after typing a command but before pressing ENTER, users decide they don't really want to execute the command. DOS provides several ways to proceed. First, you can simply press the

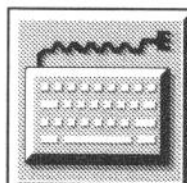

BACKSPACE key to erase the command. Depending on the command's length, however, using BACKSPACE may be time consuming. Second, you can cancel the command by pressing the CTRL-C keyboard combination. The fastest way to cancel the command, however, is to press the ESC key followed by ENTER. When you press the ESC key, DOS will display the backslash character (\) and will ignore the command. (If you have DOSKEY loaded, DOS will erase the command.) For example, the following command illustrates how DOS will respond when you cancel the DATE command:

```
C:\> DATE\ <ENTER>  (The Esc key generates the character \)

C:\>
```

Making an Enhanced Keyboard Behave like a Conventional Keyboard

A conventional and an enhanced keyboard are shown here:

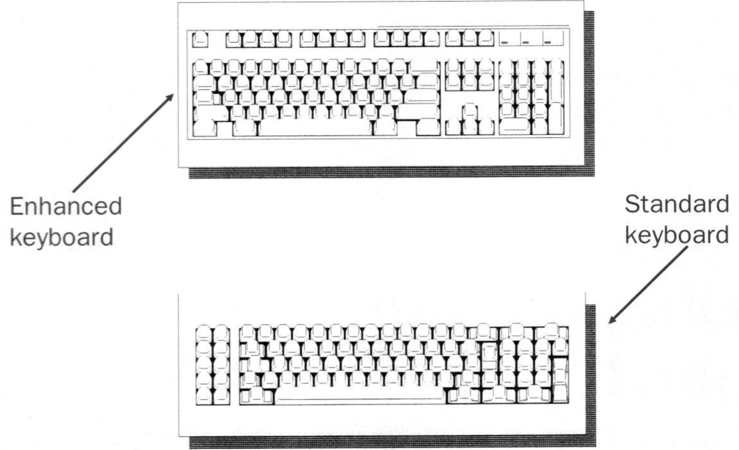

If you are running an older program, the program may not support the enhanced keyboard's capabilities.

Using the CONFIG.SYS SWITCHES entry with DOS 4 or higher, you can direct DOS to treat an enhanced keyboard as a conventional keyboard. When you press one of the enhanced keyboard keys, DOS will translate the keystroke into a conventional keyboard equivalent. To direct DOS to use or treat an enhanced keyboard as conventional in this way, place the following entry in your CONFIG.SYS file:

```
SWITCHES=/K
```

If you are using the ANSI.SYS device driver, install the ANSI.SYS driver with the /K switch as shown here:

```
DEVICE=C:\DOS\ANSI.SYS /K
```

To use the SWITCHES=/K entry, you must be using DOS 4 or higher.

Temporarily Suspending a Program's Output

As discussed in Tip 15, you can use the MORE command to display a program's output a screenful at a time. In addition to using MORE, you can use the CTRL-S keyboard combination to temporarily suspend a program's output. For example, issue the following ATTRIB command to display the names of every file on your disk:

```
C:\> ATTRIB C:\*.* /S <ENTER>
```

As the filenames scroll past you on the screen, press the CTRL-S keyboard combination to temporarily suspend the output. To resume the output, press any key. To later suspend the output, press CTRL-S again. Using the CTRL-S keyboard combination in this way gives you more control over when you suspend output than the MORE command does.

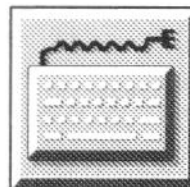

Using Part of the Previous Command Line by Pressing F2

As discussed in Tip 297, the F1 and F3 function keys let you quickly repeat the previous command. Similarly, you can quickly select part of the previous command line by using F2. When you press F2, DOS copies the contents of the previous command buffer up to, but not including, the character you type immediately after pressing F2. For example, suppose you issue the following DIR command:

```
C:\> DIR \DOS <ENTER>
```

Where the command completes, press F2 immediately followed by the backslash character (\). DOS will immediately copy the previous command line up to (but not including) the backslash, as shown here:

```
C:\> DIR
```

You can now type a filename or directory or simply press ENTER to execute the DIR command.

Now assume you issued the following command:

```
C:\> DIR \DOS\FOMAT.COM <ENTER>
```

By pressing the F2 key followed by M, you can quickly recall part of the previous command as shown:

```
C:\> DIR \DOS\FO
```

You can now press the INS key, type the letter **R**, and press F3 to recall the remainder of the previous command line.

Locking the Keyboard

If you work in an office, you may sometimes want to leave your computer for a moment. The companion disk that accompanies this book contains a utility command named KEYLOCK.EXE that clears your screen and locks the keyboard until you type a specific

password. When you invoke KEYLOCK, it will display a message asking you to type a password as shown:

```
Enter Password:
```

As you type the password, the corresponding letters will not appear. After you press ENTER, the screen will clear. When you return to the computer, type your password and press ENTER. If you type the correct password, the program will end, redisplaying the DOS prompt. By combining KEYLOCK and NOREBOOT (see Tip 4), you can prevent a user from accessing your system using CTRL-ALT-DEL. However, a user can restart your system by cycling the computer's power.

The utility program KEYLOCK.EXE resides on the companion disk that accompanies this book.

KEYLOCK.EXE

Stuffing the Keyboard Buffer

The companion disk that accompanies this book contains the utility program KEYSTUFF.EXE that lets your batch files place characters into the keyboard buffer before executing a command. In so doing, the subsequent command behaves as if you had typed the keys at the keyboard. To use KEYSTUFF, place the keystrokes (up to 16 unless you have increased the buffer size—see Tip 296) in the command line as shown here:

```
KEYSTUFF Letters
```

In addition to normal letters, KEYSTUFF lets you include the symbols specified in Table 303 to generate a specific character. KEYSTUFF supports only enhanced keyboards.

The following command, for example, stuffs the keyboard buffer with the word *Yes* followed by a carriage return:

```
KEYSTUFF Yes\R
```

Table 303. Character Symbols Supported by KEYSTUFF.EXE

Symbol	Character
\R	Carriage return
\T	Tab

KEYSTUFF.EXE

The utility program KEYSTUFF.EXE resides on the companion disk that accompanies this book.

Previous Command Editing with F4

Tip 301 described how to use the F2 function key to edit the previous command. In a similar way, you can use the F4 function key to edit the previous command line. When you press the F4 key, DOS recalls the previous command line, beginning with the first occurrence of the character you type after pressing the F4 function key. For example, assume you issue the following command:

```
C:\> DIR \DOS\FORMAT <ENTER>
```

Next, press the F4 key and type **F**, followed by the F3 key. DOS will display the FORMAT command as shown here:

```
C:\> FORMAT
```

You can now edit or execute the command.

Command-Line Editing with DOSKEY

If you are using DOS 5, the DOSKEY command lets you recall and quickly repeat your previously entered commands. To install the DOSKEY command, invoke DOSKEY as shown here:

```
C:\> DOSKEY <ENTER>
```

DOSKEY places each command that you enter into a list it stores in memory. After you install DOSKEY, you can quickly recall commands by using your keyboard's UP ARROW and DOWN ARROW keys. In addition, you can quickly recall the oldest command in the buffer by pressing the PGUP key and the latest command by pressing PGDN. If you press the F7 function key, DOSKEY will display all of the commands in the buffer, each preceded by a line number. If you then press F9, DOSKEY will display the following message prompting you for the line number of the desired command:

```
C:\> Line number:
```

Type the desired line number and press ENTER. DOSKEY will display the corresponding command.

The number of commands DOSKEY can hold depends on the size of the DOSKEY buffer. See Tip 62 to learn how to increase the DOSKEY buffer size.

To use DOSKEY, you must be using DOS 5.

Flushing the Keyboard Buffer

When you create a batch file that contains several commands, the user sometimes may intentionally or accidentally type more keystrokes than are necessary but which the program subsequently uses.

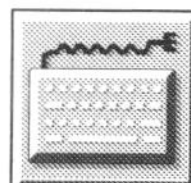

Because the PC buffers the extra keystrokes, subsequent commands in the batch file may attempt to use them.

The following DEBUG script file, KBDFLUSH.SCR, creates a command file named KBDFLUSH.COM that your batch files can use to empty the keyboard buffer.

KBDFLUSH.SCR

```
N KBDFLUSH.COM <ENTER>
A 100          <ENTER>
MOV AX,C06     <ENTER>
MOV DL,FF      <ENTER>
INT 21         <ENTER>
MOV AH,4C      <ENTER>
INT 21         <ENTER>
               <ENTER>
R CX           <ENTER>
B              <ENTER>
W              <ENTER>
Q              <ENTER>
```

Use the DEBUG command as follows to create the command file KBDFLUSH.COM:

```
C:\> DEBUG < KBDFLUSH.SCR <ENTER>
```

By invoking KBDFLUSH in your batch file before critical commands, you can prevent keystrokes in the keyboard buffer from affecting the command.

Turning Off NumLock

Some computers start with the NUMLOCK key enabled. Before you can use your keyboard's arrow keys, you must disable NUMLOCK. Likewise, some programs require that NUMLOCK be enabled. The following DEBUG script file, NUMLOCK.SCR, creates a command file named NUMLOCK.COM that toggles the NUMLOCK key's current state:

```
N NUMLOCK.COM      <ENTER>
A 100              <ENTER>
MOV AX,40          <ENTER>
MOV DS,AX          <ENTER>
XOR BYTE [17],20   <ENTER>
MOV AH,4C          <ENTER>
INT 21             <ENTER>
                   <ENTER>
R CX               <ENTER>
E                  <ENTER>
W                  <ENTER>
Q                  <ENTER>
```

NUMLOCK.SCR

Use the DEBUG command as follows to create the command file NUMLOCK.COM:

```
C:\> DEBUG < NUMLOCK.SCR <ENTER>
```

If your computer starts with NUMLOCK enabled, you can place the NUMLOCK command in your AUTOEXEC.BAT file to toggle the setting off.

Toggling the Caps Lock Key

Tip 307 teaches you how to toggle the NUMLOCK key by using the NUMLOCK utility command. You can create a utility command, CAPSLOCK.COM, that toggles the CAPSLOCK key. The following DEBUG script file CAPSLOCK.SCR creates the command file CAPSLOCK.COM:

```
N CAPSLOCK.COM     <ENTER>
A 100              <ENTER>
MOV AX,40          <ENTER>
MOV DS,AX          <ENTER>
XOR BYTE [17],40   <ENTER>
MOV AH,4C          <ENTER>
INT 21             <ENTER>
                   <ENTER>
R CX               <ENTER>
```

CAPSLOCK.SCR

```
E                          <ENTER>
W                          <ENTER>
Q                          <ENTER>
```

Use DEBUG as follows to create the command file CAPSLOCK.COM:

```
C:\> DEBUG < CAPSLOCK.SCR <ENTER>
```

Each time you invoke CAPSLOCK, the command will toggle the key's current state.

Toggling the SCROLL LOCK Key

Several older programs use the keyboard's SCROLL LOCK key to suspend and enable scrolling. When the SCROLL LOCK feature is active, most keyboards display a small LED light. The following DEBUG script file, SCROLL.SCR, creates a command file named SCROLL.COM that toggles the current setting of the SCROLL LOCK key:

SCROLL.SCR

```
N SCROLL.COM          <ENTER>
A 100                 <ENTER>
MOV AX,40             <ENTER>
MOV DS,AX             <ENTER>
XOR BYTE [17],10      <ENTER>
MOV AH,4C             <ENTER>
INT 21                <ENTER>
                      <ENTER>
R CX                  <ENTER>
E                     <ENTER>
W                     <ENTER>
Q                     <ENTER>
```

Use DEBUG as follows to create the command file SCROLL.COM:

```
C:\> DEBUG < SCROLL.SCR <ENTER>
```

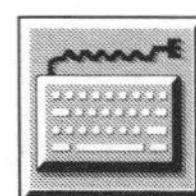

Editing the Current Command with F5

Tip 297 discusses how to edit the previous command line using the F1 and F3 function keys. Tip 301 and Tip 304 illustrate the use of F2 and F4. Sometimes, as you type a command, you may realize you have made a typographical error. By pressing the F5 function key, you can edit the current command. For example, assume you mistype the command FORMAT A: as shown here:

```
C:\> FOMAT A:
```

If, before pressing ENTER, you press the F5 function key, DOS will display the @ character at the end of the command, letting you edit the command line with the function keys F1 through F4 as well as INS and DEL. In the case of the previous command, DOS will display the following:

```
C:\> FOMAT A:@
_
```

By pressing the F1 key twice, you can recall the letters FO. Next, by pressing INS, you can add the letter R. By pressing F3, you can create the correct command as shown here:

```
C:\> FOMAT A:@
     FORMAT A: <ENTER>
```

By using F5 in this way, you can quickly correct the current command line.

If you are using the DOSKEY command and you press F5, DOSKEY will clear the current line rather than display a line beneath the current command. You can then use the function keys as just discussed to edit the command.

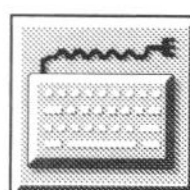

Redefining Keys with ANSI.SYS

Several of the tips presented in this book illustrate how you use ANSI.SYS to assign screen colors. In addition, ANSI.SYS lets you assign values to different keystrokes. To assign a value to a keystroke, you must use the following escape sequence:

```
Esc[ScanCode;"Text"p
```

Table 311 defines the scancodes for function keys F1 through F12.

For example, the following escape sequence assigns the DIR command to the F9 function key:

```
Esc[0;67;"DIR"p
```

When you press the F9 function keys, the ANSI driver will display the DIR command on your screen. To execute the command, press ENTER. If you want DOS to automatically execute the command when you press the key, you first include a carriage return in the text you assign to the key (see Tip 45).

Table 311. Scancode Values for Function Keys F1 *through* F12

Key	Key Only	SHIFT+Key	CTRL+Key	ALT+Key
F1	0;59	0;84	0;94	0;104
F2	0;60	0;85	0;95	0;105
F3	0;61	0;86	0;96	0;106
F4	0;62	0;87	0;97	0;107
F5	0;63	0;88	0;98	0;108
F6	0;64	0;89	0;99	0;109
F7	0;65	0;90	0;100	0;110
F8	0;66	0;91	0;101	0;111
F9	0;67	0;92	0;102	0;112
F10	0;68	0;93	0;103	0;113
F11	0;133	0;135	0;137	0;139
F12	0;134	0;136	0;138	0:140

Entering a Carriage-Return with EDLIN

Tip 34 tells you how to enter an escape character within EDLIN by using CTRL+V[. Tip 631 gives you several ways to echo blank lines within a DOS batch. Using EDLIN, you can quickly place line-feed characters after an ECHO command by pressing CTRL-V followed by J. For example, the following batch file uses the line-feed character with ECHO to skip three lines:

```
C:\> EDLIN SKIPIT.BAT
New file
*I
    1:*@ECHO OFF
    2:*ECHO About to skip three lines ^VJ^VJ^VJ
    3:*ECHO Done
    4:*^C
*E
```

To generate the ^V characters, hold down the CTRL key and press V. When you execute this batch file, you will see the two messages separated by three blank lines.

Defining Function Keys with the PROMPT Command

In Tip 311 you learned how to assign commands to function keys by using ANSI escape sequences. Using the PROMPT command, you can generate the escape sequence required not only to assign a command to a function key, but also to include the carriage-return character with the command that directs DOS to automatically execute the command when the key is pressed. The easiest way to use PROMPT to assign commands to keys is from within a DOS batch file. The following batch file, F9_F10.BAT, assigns the CLS command to F9 and the DIR command to F10:

```
PROMPT $E[0;67;"CLS"$_p
PROMPT $E[0;68;"DIR"$_p
PROMPT $P$G
```

Note that the batch file does not use the ECHO OFF command. If you turn echoing off, the prompt is never displayed, and the escape sequences have no effect. The first two PROMPT commands use the $E metacharacter, which generates an escape sequence, and $_, which produces a carriage return and line feed. The last PROMPT command simply restores the prompt to the drive letter and directory name followed by a greater-than symbol.

TIP 314 Allowing Batch Files to Respond to the Keyboard State

As your batch files execute, you may sometimes want the batch file to respond to various key states, such as the depression of the CTRL key. The following DEBUG script file, CHKCTRL.SCR, creates a command file named CHKCTRL.COM that returns the exit status 1 if the CTRL key is depressed and 0 if it is not depressed:

CHKCTRL.SCR

```
N CHKCTRL.COM <ENTER>
A 100         <ENTER>
MOV AX,40     <ENTER>
MOV DS,AX     <ENTER>
MOV AL,[17]   <ENTER>
AND AL,4      <ENTER>
JZ  10E       <ENTER>
MOV AL,1      <ENTER>
MOV AH,4C     <ENTER>
INT 21        <ENTER>
              <ENTER>
R CX          <ENTER>
12            <ENTER>
W             <ENTER>
Q             <ENTER>
```

Use DEBUG as follows to create the command file CHKCTRL.COM:

```
C:\> DEBUG < CHKCTRL.SCR <ENTER>
```

The following commands illustrate how you might use CHKCTRL within your AUTOEXEC.BAT file to prevent the execution of the file's commands if you are pressing the CTRL key:

```
CHKCTRL
IF ERRORLEVER 1 GOTO DONE
REM Other commands here
:DONE
```

To test for depression of other keys, such as ALT or SHIFT, change the value 4 in line 6 of the previous DEBUG script file to one of the values listed in Table 314.

Table 314. Values for Testing for Various Keyboard Key States

Key	Value
Right SHIFT	1
Left SHIFT	2
ALT	8
SCROLL LOCK	10
NUM LOCK	20
CAPS LOCK	40
INS	80

Appending Text from the Keyboard to an ASCII File

You sometimes may want to quickly append text to an ASCII file, such as a CONFIG.SYS entry or a batch file command. Using the COPY command you can do just that. Assume, for example, you want to append the entry DEVICE=\SUBDIR\MOUSE.SYS to your CONFIG.SYS file. To do so, invoke the copy command by using the plus (+) operator as shown here:

```
C:\> COPY CONFIG.SYS+CON CONFIG.SYS <ENTER>
```

The command directs COPY to append the text you type to the end of the file. When you press ENTER, your screen will display the following:

```
C:\> COPY  CONFIG.SYS+CON  CONFIG.SYS <ENTER>
CONFIG.SYS
CON
```

Type the entry you desire and press ENTER. After the last entry, press the F6 (end-of-file) function key followed by ENTER. COPY will update the file as shown here:

```
C:\> COPY CONFIG.SYS+CON  CONFIG.SYS <ENTER>
CONFIG.SYS
CON
DEVICE=C:\SUBDIR\MOUSE.SYS              <ENTER>
^Z                                      <ENTER>
    1 file(s) copied
```

Understanding Keyboard Scancodes

Every key on your computer has a unique value associated with it, called a scancode. The following illustration shows these scancode values, in decimal format:

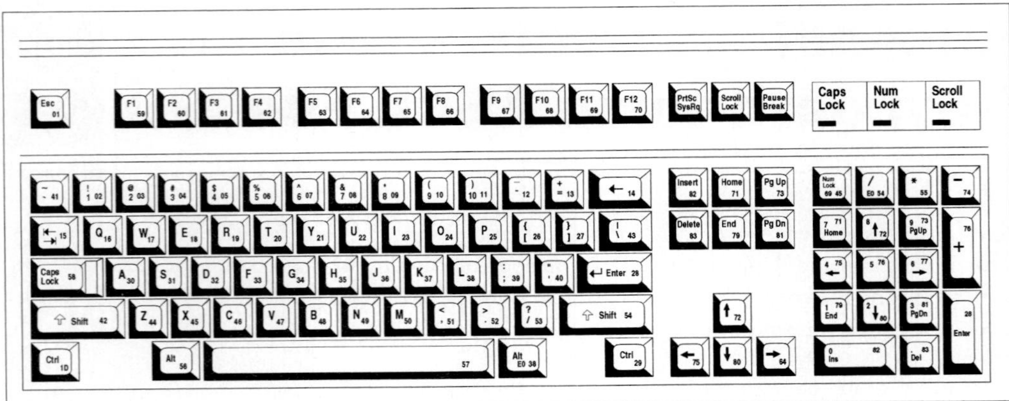

As Tip 317 discusses, you can create DEBUG script files that let your batch files use scancodes to test for specific keys. Tip 311 discusses how to use scancode values within ANSI escape sequences to assign different values (such as DOS commands) to different keyboard keys.

Processing Keyboard Scancodes

Tip 316 explains that every key on your keyboard has a unique value called a *scancode*. The following DEBUG script file, GETSCAN.SCR, creates a command file named GETSCAN.COM that returns as an exit status the scancode value of the key pressed:

```
N GETSCAN.COM <ENTER>
A 100         <ENTER>
XOR AH,AH     <ENTER>
INT 16        <ENTER>
CMP AH,0      <ENTER>
JE 100        <ENTER>
MOV AL,AH     <ENTER>
MOV AH,4C     <ENTER>
INT 21        <ENTER>
              <ENTER>
R CX          <ENTER>
10            <ENTER>
W             <ENTER>
Q             <ENTER>
```

GETSCAN.SCR

Use DEBUG as follows to create the command file GETSCAN.COM:

```
C:\> DEBUG < GETSCAN.SCR <ENTER>
```

The following batch commands illustrate how you would use GETSCAN to prompt the user for a yes or no (Y/N) response:

```
@ECHO OFF
ECHO Do you want to print a directory listing (Y/N)?
```

```
:LOOP
GETSCAN
IF ERRORLEVEL 21 IF NOT ERRORLEVEL 22 GOTO YES
IF ERRORLEVEL 49 IF NOT ERRORLEVEL 50 GOTO NO
GOTO LOOP
:YES
DIR > PRN
:NO
```

Checking for a Keystroke

Depending on your batch file's processing, you may sometimes need the batch file to periodically check whether the user has pressed a key. The following DEBUG script file, CHECKKEY.SCR, creates a command file named CHECKKEY.COM that returns 1 if the user has pressed a key and returns 0 otherwise:

CHECKKEY.SCR

```
N CHECKKEY.COM <ENTER>
A 100          <ENTER>
MOV AH,B       <ENTER>
INT 21         <ENTER>
AND AL,1       <ENTER>
MOV AH,4C      <ENTER>
INT 21         <ENTER>
               <ENTER>
R CX           <ENTER>
A              <ENTER>
W              <ENTER>
Q              <ENTER>
```

Use DEBUG as follows to create the command file CHECKKEY.COM:

```
C:\> DEBUG < CHECKKEY.SCR <ENTER>
```

The following batch file commands repeatedly display a directory listing until the user presses a key:

```
@ECHO OFF
```

```
:LOOP
DIR
CHECKKEY
IF NOT ERRORLEVEL 1 GOTO LOOP
```

Command Editing with DOSKEY

Tip 305 discusses how you can quickly recall your previous commands if you have installed the DOSKEY command available with DOS 5. After you display the desired command, DOSKEY lets you edit the command, if necessary, before you press ENTER to execute it. Table 319 lists the DOSKEY editing keys.

Table 319. DOSKEY Command Editing Keystrokes

Keystroke	Function
LEFT ARROW	Moves the cursor one character to the left
RIGHT ARROW	Moves the cursor one character to the right
HOME	Moves the cursor to the start of the command
END	Moves the cursor to the end of the command
CTRL-LEFT ARROW	Moves the cursor one word to the left
CTRL-RIGHT ARROW	Moves the cursor one word to the right
CTRL-HOME	Deletes the characters from the current position to the start of the command
CTRL-END	Deletes the characters from the current position to the end of the command
DEL	Deletes the character at the current cursor position
BACKSPACE	Deletes the character to the left of the cursor
INS	Toggles insert mode
ESC	Erases the command

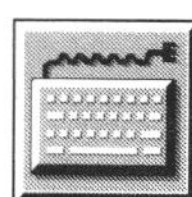

To edit commands with DOSKEY, you must be using DOS 5 and have installed DOSKEY's memory-resident software.

Directing ANSI.SYS to Treat Enhanced Keys as Distinct

Tip 299 discusses the difference between standard and enhanced keyboards. There you learned that by using the ANSI.SYS /K switch, you can direct the ANSI driver to ignore the extended keys. On the other hand, if you install the ANSI driver using the /X switch as shown here, you direct the ANSI driver to treat enhanced keys as distinct from their standard keyboard counterparts:

```
DEVICE=C:\DOS\ANSI.SYS /X
```

When you use the /X switch, you must use different scancode values to reference the enhanced keys. Table 320 lists the scancodes you should use for each key.

Table 320. Scancode Values for Standard and Enhanced(*) Keys When Using the ANSI.SYS /X Switch

Key	Key Only	SHIFT+Key	CTRL+Key
HOME	0;71	55	0;119
UP ARROW	0;72	56	0;141
PGUP	0;73	57	0;132
LEFT ARROW	0;75	52	0;115
RIGHT ARROW	0;77	54	0;116
END	0;79	49	0;117
DOWN ARROW	0;80	50	0;145

Table 320. Scancode Values for Standard and Enhanced(*) Keys When Using the ANSI.SYS /X Switch

Key	Key Only	SHIFT+Key	CTRL+Key
PGDN	0;81	51	0;118
INS	0;82	48	0;146
DEL	0;83	46	0;147
*HOME	224;71	224;55	224;119
*UP ARROW	224;72	224;56	224;141
*PGUP	224;73	224;57	224;132
*LEFT ARROW	224;75	224;52	224;115
*RIGHT ARROW	224;77	224;54	224;116
*END	224;79	224;49	224;117
*DOWN ARROW	224;80	224;50	224;145
*PGDN	224;81	224;51	224.118
*Ins	224;82	224;48	224;146
*DEL	224;83	224;46	224;147

Simulating an Active Shift Key

Depending on your programs, you sometimes may need to type in several keys' shifted components (for example, the characters !, @, #, $, and so on that appear in your keyboard's top row). The following DEBUG script file, SHTOGGLE.SCR, creates a command file named SHTOGGLE.COM that toggles the keyboard's current shift state:

```
N SHTOGGLE.COM     <ENTER>
A 100              <ENTER>
MOV AX,40          <ENTER>
MOV DS,AX          <ENTER>
XOR BYTE [17],1    <ENTER>
MOV AH,4C          <ENTER>
```

SHTOGGLE.SCR

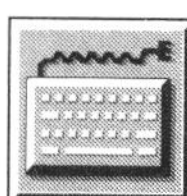

```
INT 21          <ENTER>
                <ENTER>
R CX            <ENTER>
E               <ENTER>
W               <ENTER>
Q               <ENTER>
```

Use DEBUG as follows to create the command file SHTOGGLE.COM:

```
C:\> DEBUG < SHTOGGLE.SCR <ENTER>
```

The following batch commands use SHTOGGLE to turn on SHIFT key emulation, execute a command, and then turn off SHIFT key emulation:

```
@ECHO OFF
SHTOGGLE
SomeProg
SHTOGGLE
```

Assign a Printer Form-Feed Operation to ALT-P

Tip 878 explains how to create the command file FFLPT1.COM that sends a form-feed character to the printer to eject the last printed page. Tip 311 explains how to assign commands to key combinations. Using the ANSI driver, the following escape sequence assigns FFLPT1 to the ALT-P keyboard combination:

```
Esc[0;25;"FFLPT1"p
```

By assigning FFLPT1 to ALT-P in this way, you can use SHIFT-PRTSC to print the screen's contents, and ALT-P to eject the page. The following batch file uses the PROMPT command to assign FFLPT1 to ALT-P:

```
SET SAVE_PROMPT=%PROMPT%
PROMPT $E[0;25;"FFLPT1$_"p
```

```
PROMPT %SAVE_PROMPT%
SET SAVE_PROMPT=
```

Obtaining a Key's Scancode

Tip 311 describes how to assign commands to keyboard scancodes by using the ANSI.SYS driver. Tip 317 describes how to create a command file that returns the scancode of the key pressed. As you create batch files that use scancodes, you can invoke the companion disk utility program SHOWSC.EXE to display the scancode for the key press as shown here:

```
C:\> SHOWSC  [F10 key pressed]
Scancode is 0;68
```

The utility command SCANCODE.EXE resides on the companion disk that accompanies this book.

SCANCODE.EXE

Understanding Your Keyboard Cable

Keyboard plugs are constructed so that there is only one way to correctly plug them in. You must align the plug's pins with the slots on the keyboard port so there is a snug fit between cable and connector.

Keyboard plugs typically consist of six pins. Each pin's function is shown here:

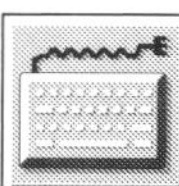

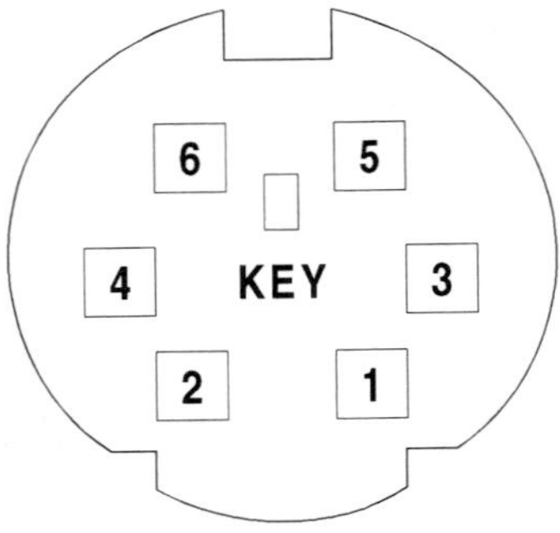

Pin	Use
1	Data
2	Not Used
3	Ground
4	Power
5	Clock
6	Not used

Understanding the Keyboard Buffer

Each time you press a key, the BIOS places the keystroke's ASCII value and scancode into a region in memory called the keyboard buffer. By default, the PC uses a 32-byte buffer that can hold 16 characters and scancodes. This buffer is stored at location 40:001E in the BIOS data area. Assume, for example, that you type the letters "Hello." The PC will place the ASCII characters and their scancodes in the buffer as shown here:

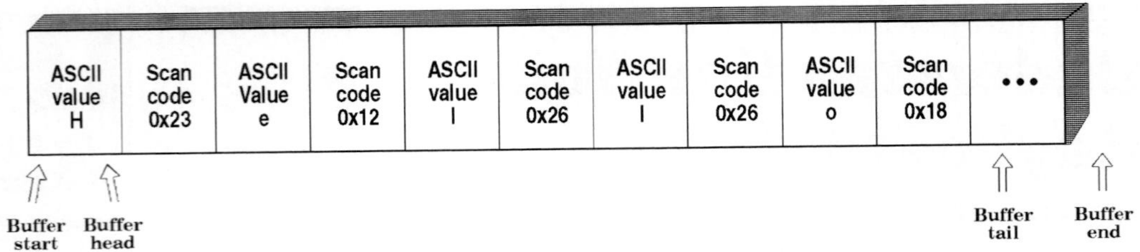

If you type characters faster than the PC can process them, the buffer will become full, and each time you press a key, the PC will beep to inform you that it is ignoring the keystroke. Tip 296 presents a utility command that lets you increase the size of the keyboard buffer. To manage the keyboard buffer, the BIOS uses the memory locations described in Table 325.

Table 325. BIOS Memory Locations Used to Manage the Keyboard Buffer

Memory Location	Contents
40:80	Contains the offset address (relative to segment 40H) of the start of the keyboard buffer
40:82	Contains the offset address (relative to segment 40H) of the end of the keyboard buffer
40:1A	Contains the offset address (relative to segment 40H) of the next unread character in the keyboard buffer
40:1C	Contains the offset address (relative to segment40H) of the next available storage location in the keyboard buffer

The keyboard buffer is called a circular buffer because the starting location of the buffer can change over time. The following illustration shows two different keyboard buffer scenarios—one in which the keyboard buffer is full, and the other in which it is empty. Note how the pointers described in Table 325 change or remain the same in each situation.

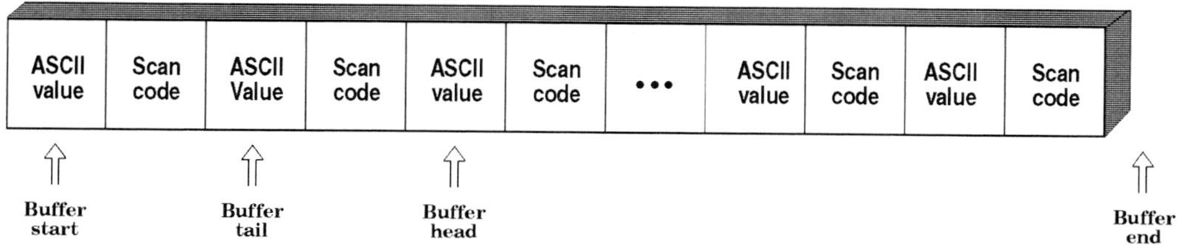

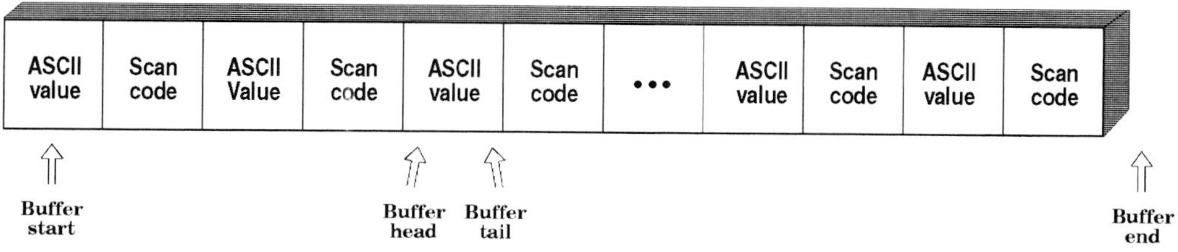

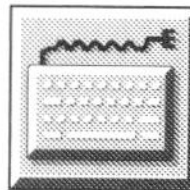

Better Understanding the Keyboard Buffer

Tip 325 describes the keyboard buffer and the memory locations the BIOS uses to manage the buffer. To help you better understand the processing involved, the companion disk that accompanies this book contains the utility command KBDINFO.EXE. The program begins by displaying information about your keyboard buffer as shown here:

```
C:\> KBDINFO <ENTER>
Keyboard buffer starts at 001e
Keyboard buffer ends at 003e
Keyboard buffer head 002e tail 002e
Keyboard buffer size 32
```

Next, the program asks you to type a few characters. The program gives you ten seconds to type. Type a few letters but do not press ENTER. The program then displays the keyboard buffer's ASCII and scan key.

KBDINFO.EXE

The utility command KBDINFO.EXE resides on the companion disk that accompanies this book.

Is This an Enhanced or Standard Keyboard?

Tip 299 illustrates the 84-key standard keyboard and the 101/102-key enhanced keyboard. If you are creating a batch file that uses the ANSI driver to assign commands to various keystrokes, the batch file may need to determine the keyboard type. The following DEBUG script file, KBDTYPE.SCR, creates a command file named KBDTYPE.COM that returns the exit status value 1 if an enhanced keyboard is being used and returns 0 if a standard keyboard is being used:

```
N KBDTYPE.COM <ENTER>
A 100         <ENTER>
MOV AX,40     <ENTER>
MOV DS,AX     <ENTER>
MOV AL,[96]   <ENTER>
AND AL,10     <ENTER>
JZ  10E       <ENTER>
MOV AL,1      <ENTER>
MOV AH,4C     <ENTER>
INT 21        <ENTER>
              <ENTER>
R CX          <ENTER>
12            <ENTER>
W             <ENTER>
Q             <ENTER>
```

KBDTYPE.SCR

Use DEBUG as follows to create the command file KBDTYPE.COM:

```
C:\> DEBUG < KBDTYPE.SCR <ENTER>
```

The following batch commands illustrate how you might use KBDTYPE.COM:

```
@ECHO OFF
KBDTYPE
IF ERRORLEVEL 1 GOTO ENHANCED_KEYBOARD
GOTO STANDARD_KEYBOARD
REM Other commands here
```

Controlling DOSKEY's Insert and Overstrike Modes

When you use DOSKEY to edit commands, you can use the Ins key to toggle between insert and overstrike modes. If you find that you typically want to use insert mode more often than overstrike

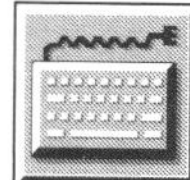

mode, or vice versa, you can use DOSKEY's /INSERT and /OVERSTRIKE switches to select one of the modes as DOSKEY's default mode. For example, the following DOSKEY command selects insert mode as DOSKEY's default mode:

```
C:\> DOSKEY  /INSERT <ENTER>
```

Each time you display a command for editing, DOSKEY will begin the edit in insert mode. By pressing the Ins key, you can toggle to overstrike mode as required.

Understanding the Keyboard Controller

Your PC's BIOS resides on a ROM chip. Your keyboard also has its own ROM-based processor, called the keyboard controller. The keyboard controller resides in the keyboard, with complementary circuitry in your computer. Although the keyboard controller's primary purpose is to interpret scan codes, the keyboard controller may also manage the A20 address line (see Tip 270) and the processor speed (see Tip 53).

If you experience system lockups or other intermittent errors while running Windows in protected mode, examine your keyboard controller to see whether it has a date or version number. If it does, verify that the controller is compatible with protected-mode operations.

Temporarily Shifting the Numeric Keypad Keys

The NUMLOCK key controls the behavior of your numeric key pad. When NUMLOCK is on, pressing the numeric keypad keys results in numbers. When NUMLOCK is off, pressing the keys positions the

cursor. Depending on your application, continually toggling the NUMLOCK key can be time consuming and frustrating. As an alternative, you can hold down the SHIFT key to reverse the key's current state. For example, if NUMLOCK is off, holding down a SHIFT key and pressing the numeric keys generates numbers. In some cases, using the SHIFT key in this way, as needed, may be faster or easier than toggling NUMLOCK.

Automating Keyboard Definitions

Tip 311 describes how to assign definitions to keyboard keys by using the ANSI.SYS device driver. The following batch file, AUTODEFN.BAT, asks the user for the desired definition. The batch file uses the utility command ASK_USER presented in Tip 687 to assign the user's response to the environment entry USER. Next, the batch file prompts the user to press the key or keyboard combination for the key to which the definition is to be assigned. The batch file uses the ENVSCODE utility presented in Tip 157 to assign the scancode to the environment entry SCANCODE. Last, the batch file writes an escape sequence to assign the definition.

```
@ECHO OFF
ASK_USER Enter the desired definition:
ENVSCAN Press the corresponding scancode:
ECHO Esc[%SCANCODE%;"%USER%"p
SET USER=
SET SCANCODE=
```

Getting Around a Stuck or Broken Key

If one of your keyboard keys breaks, sticks, or experiences some other problem, you will have to get the keyboard repaired. In the meantime, however, you can use the ANSI.SYS driver to work around the key. As discussed in Tip 311, you can use an escape sequence to redefine a keyboard key. Assume, for example, your S key sticks. The following escape sequence redefines the ALT-A keyboard combination as the lowercase "s" key and ALT-B as the uppercase "S" key:

```
Esc[0;30;115p
Esc[0;40;83p
```

Using the ANSI.SYS driver in this way, you can work around most keyboard errors.

TIP 333 Using the HOME and UP ARROW Keys to Change Directories

If you spend coniderable time traversing your directory tree, you might consider using the following batch file CDKEYS.BAT to assign "CHDIR \" to your HOME and "CHDIR .." to your UP ARROW key as shown here:

```
SET SAVE_PROMPT=%PROMPT%
PROMPT $E[0;71;"CHDIR \$_"p
PROMPT $E[0;72;"CHDIR ..$_"p
PROMPT %SAVE_PROMPT%
SET SAVE_PROMPT=
```

After you invoke this batch file, you can press the HOME key to select the root directory or the UP ARROW key to move up one level in the directory tree.

Because most application programs bypass the DOS keyboard services, redefining the HOME and UP ARROW keys in this way will not affect your programs.

TIP 334 Turning the ENTER Key On and Off

If you work in an office, you sometimes may want to walk away from your PC and prevent other users from entering commands. To do so, you can use the ANSI driver to redefine the ENTER key. The

following batch file, ENTEROFF.BAT, disables the ENTER key by assigning it the value of the BACKSPACE key:

```
@ECHO OFF
ECHO Esc[0;28;13p
ECHO Esc[13;8p
```

In this case, the batch file not only redefines the ENTER key, but also the ALT-ENTER keyboard combination. When another user tries to press ENTER to execute a command, the ENTER key will be ignored. However, if you need to press ENTER, you can use the ALT-ENTER keyboard combination. When you later want to use ENTER, execute the following batch file, ENTERON.BAT, to restore the key's normal use:

```
@ECHO OFF
ECHO Esc[13;13p
```

To execute the batch file, type its name at the DOS prompt and press ALT-ENTER. If you execute the ENTEROFF batch file from your AUTOEXEC.BAT file, you prevent users from gaining access to your system by rebooting.

Keyboard Swapping

Most users get used to the feel and response of their keyboards. Moving to a system that uses a different keyboard type can be frustrating. In many cases you can bring your old keyboard with you. However, the keyboards being exchanged must use the same connector types. The following illustration shows the two most common keyboard connectors:

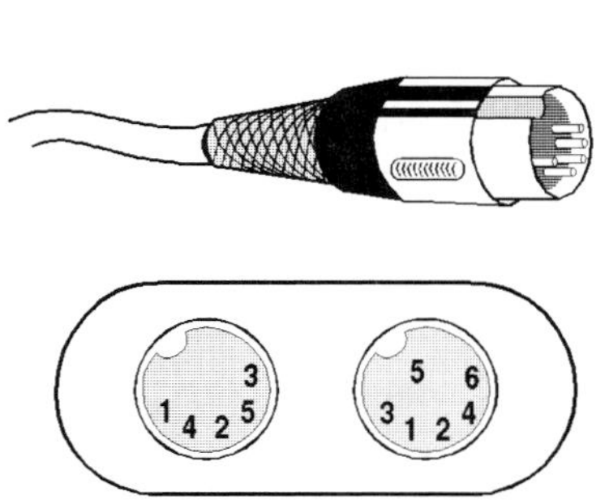

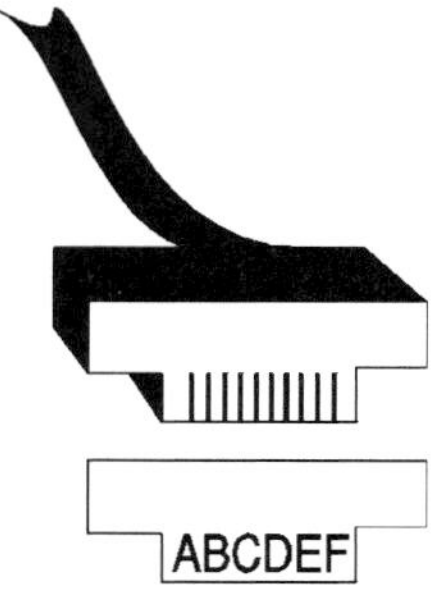

If you are moving to an XT system, you may run into BIOS compatibility problems. If your keyboard does not work, you may need to configure the keyboard as an XT-type keyboard. As shown here, most newer keyboards have DIP switch settings that let you configure the keyboard:

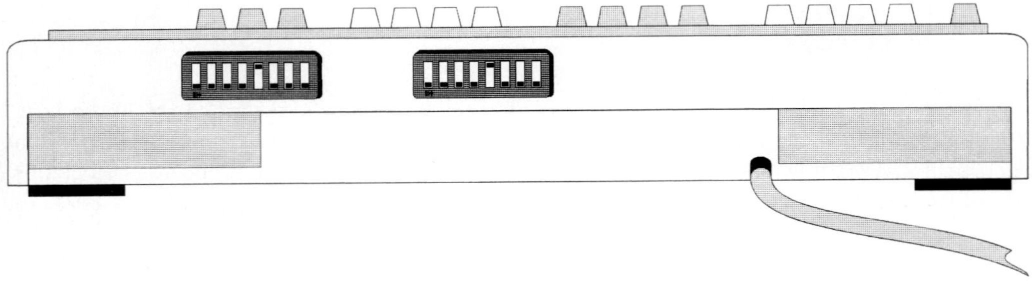

If you experience problems, refer to your keyboard manual for the proper DIP switch settings for your system.

Making Room for Your Keyboard

By the time many users set up their PCs on their desks, they no longer have any workspace. To help these users, several companies sell PC stands similar to the one shown here, under which you can slide your keyboard when it is not in use:

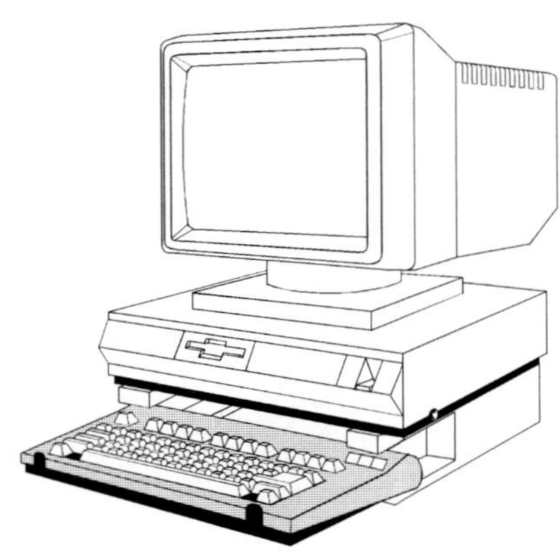

Using such a PC stand, you can slide your keyboard out when you need it and slide it back in, out of the way, when you don't.

Sore Wrists? Check Your Keyboard Height

If your PC is sitting on a table or noncomputer desk, chances are your keyboard is too high, which places considerable strain on your wrists. Ideally, your keyboard should be at a height of 26 to 28 inches from the floor. If your keyboard is higher than that, raise your chair, if you can, to a height that minimizes the upward bend of your wrist while you type. Improper keyboard height is a major cause of carpel tunnel syndrome, which produces pain and numbing of the wrists.

Keyboard Pads Reduce Wrist Strain

As discussed in Tip 337, improper keyboard height is a major contributor to wrist strain. Place your hands on your keyboard. If your wrists bend up, you are placing unnecessary strain on your wrists. One way to reduce this strain is to purchase a keyboard wrist pad, shown here:

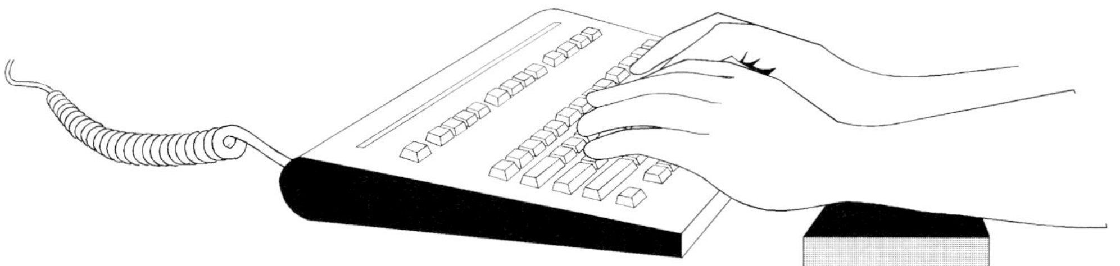

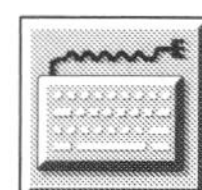

The pad elevates your wrists to a position that minimizes strain.

Understanding How Dust, Spills, and Smoke Can Effect the Keyboard

The following illustration shows a keyboard key in both its normal and depressed positions:

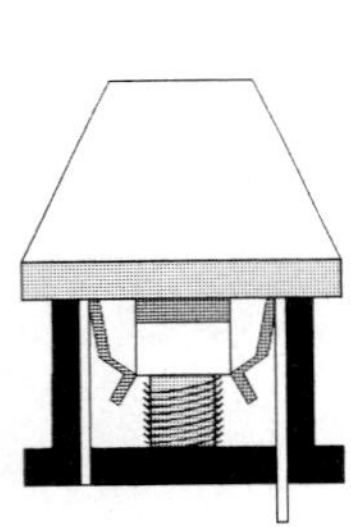

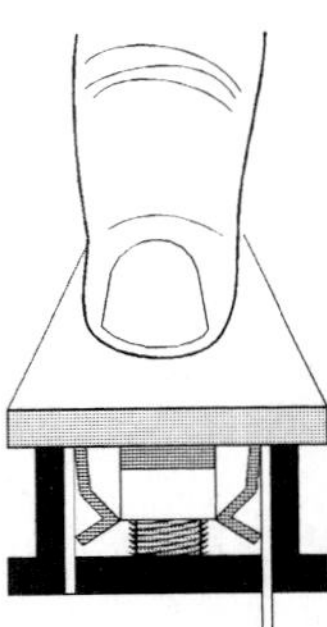

Over time, dirt and dust can accumulate inside your keyboard keys. In some cases, the dirt may lodge between the key and its contact, preventing the key from functioning properly. Should one of your keys fail to respond, you can probably pop the key off and gently use a screwdriver to clean out the dirt particles. As discussed in Tip 963, you will probably do more harm then good if you regularly pop keys off for cleaning. Instead, because such keyboard problems are rare, treat them as they occur.

PART 4

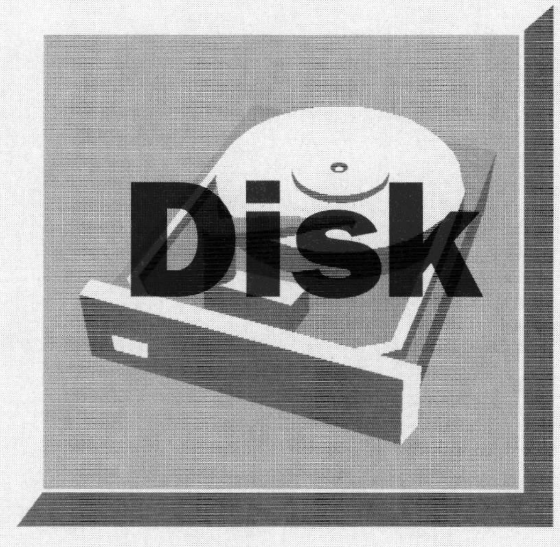

Finding a Misplaced File

As the number of files you store on your disk increases, you sometimes may misplace or can't find a file. If you are using DOS 5, you can use the following DOSKEY command to create a macro named WHEREIS that searches your disk for the file specified:

```
C:\> DOSKEY WHEREIS=DIR \$1 /S /B <ENTER>
```

To locate a specific file, use WHEREIS as follows:

```
C:\> WHEREIS FILENAME.EXT <ENTER>
```

The macro fully supports DOS wildcards. If you plan to use WHEREIS regularly, add the previous DOSKEY command to your AUTOEXEC.BAT file.

To use DOSKEY, you must be using DOS 5 or higher.

Faster Disk Formats

Most users have a collection of old floppy disks that they periodically reuse. If the floppy disk contains many directories of files, you may find that reformatting the disk is faster than individually deleting directories. If you are using DOS 5, the /Q switch directs FORMAT to perform a quick format operation that, rather than physically reformatting each of the disk's tracks and sectors, simply initializes the disk's root directory and file-allocation tables as if the disk were empty. Because a quick format operation does not actually format the disk, it completes very quickly. However, you can perform a quick format operation only on a previously formatted disk. The following command directs FORMAT to quick format the disk in drive A:

```
C:\> FORMAT A: /Q <ENTER>
```

To use FORMAT's /Q switch, you must be using DOS 5.

Saving the Partition Table with MIRROR

The first cylinder of every hard disk contains the master boot record, which holds information about the disk's partitions. If your hard disk contains several partitions, the master boot record contains information describing each partition's size and starting cylinder. To minimize the effect of a disk error, the MIRROR command lets you save the master boot record to a floppy disk. To begin, create a bootable floppy—one that contains the system (/S)—using FORMAT as shown here:

```
C:\> FORMAT A: /S <ENTER>
```

Next, use the following MIRROR command to copy the master boot record to the floppy disk:

```
C:\> MIRROR /PARTN <ENTER>
```

MIRROR will prompt you for the drive containing the floppy disk to which you want the information written. Type the drive letter and press ENTER. MIRROR will create a file named PARTNSAV.FIL on the floppy. Next, copy the file UNFORMAT.COM from the DOS directory to the floppy disk. If you ever need to restore the partition table information, you can do so by using the following FORMAT command:

```
A> UNFORMAT /PARTN <ENTER>
```

Label the disk with the label Disk Partition Information and place it in a safe location.

To use MIRROR and UNFORMAT to save and later restore partition table information, you must be using DOS 5.

Saving Disk Space with DOSKEY Macros

As discussed in Tip 503, a small file actually consumes a cluster of space on your disk. Many users have small batch files they use on a regular basis. If you are using DOS 5, you can convert many small batch files to DOSKEY macros. For example, the following batch file DATETIME.BAT contains three commands:

```
CLS
DATE
TIME
```

Using DOSKEY, you can create a macro that serves the same purpose:

```
C:\> DOSKEY DATETIME=CLS $T DATE $T TIME <ENTER>
```

As you can see, the macro separates commands using the $T metacharacter. By converting small batch files to macros in this way, you can define the macros from within your AUTOEXEC.BAT file. Once you do so, you can free disk space by deleting the batch files.

To use DOSKEY macros, you must be using DOS 5.

Creating an Emergency Floppy

One of the most important steps you can take to reduce the impact of an errant command is to create a bootable floppy disk containing the files you will probably need to correct the error. Use the FORMAT /S switch to create the bootable floppy disk as shown here:

```
C:\> FORMAT A: /S <ENTER>
```

If FORMAT does not copy the file COMMAND.COM to the floppy disk, do so yourself. Next, depending on your DOS version, copy the following files to the floppy disk:

RESTORE.COM
BACKUP.COM
UNDELETE.EXE
UNFORMAT.EXE
FDISK.COM
FORMAT.COM
EXPAND.EXE

Write-protect the floppy and store it in a safe location.

Parking Your Hard Disk While It Is Not In Use

When your computer is on, your hard disk spins at 3,600 revolutions per minute. During this time, your disk's read/write head floats just above the disk's surface. If someone violently bumps or moves your computer while the disk drive is spinning, the read/write head may come into contact with the disk's surface, causing a disk crash to occur. When a disk crash occurs, the read/write head scrapes off the disk's magnetic surface, spreading particles across the surface and destroying your disk's contents at the same time. When your computer is off, your disk quits spinning, and the read/write head gently comes to rest on the disk's surface.

Depending on your disk type, some disks provide an unused track that serves as a landing zone. Many disks, however, set the read/write head down on the last track used, possibly on top of your data. To reduce the amount of damage to data should a disk crash occur, many users park their disk drive's

read/write head before they turn their computer off, or when they know the drive will not be used for an extended period of time. Parking the disk drive means moving the read/write head over an unused track. Should the head come in contact with the track, the head is not in direct contact with your data. Many newer hard disks automatically park the drive when you turn off your computer's power. Use the following DEBUG script file, PARKHEAD.SCR, to create the utility command PARKHEAD so you can park your disk at any time:

PARKHEAD.SCR

```
N PARKHEAD.COM <ENTER>
A 100          <ENTER>
MOV AH,8       <ENTER>
MOV DL,80      <ENTER>
INT 13         <ENTER>
JC 110         <ENTER>
MOV AH,C       <ENTER>
MOV DL,80      <ENTER>
INT 13         <ENTER>
JMP 117        <ENTER>
MOV AH,9       <ENTER>
MOV DX,11B     <ENTER>
INT 21         <ENTER>
MOV AH,4C      <ENTER>
INT 21         <ENTER>
DB 'Controller failed to respond correctly-heads not parked.$'<ENTER>
               <ENTER>
R CX           <ENTER>
54             <ENTER>
W              <ENTER>
Q              <ENTER>
```

To create the PARKHEAD.COM file, use DEBUG as follows:

```
C:\> DEBUG < PARKHEAD.SCR <ENTER>
```

Invoke PARKHEAD.COM before you turn off your computer's power, or when your disk will not be used for a long time. PARKHEAD.COM moves the read/write head to your disk's last track, which most often is an unused area.

Why DOS 4.0 Requires SHARE for Disks Larger than 32Mb

If you are using DOS version 4.0 and you have a hard disk partition larger than 32Mb, you need to install the SHARE command to prevent possible disk corruption. DOS version 4.0 was the first DOS version to support disk partitions larger than 32Mb.

Unfortunately, an error in version 4.0 occurs when older programs that use file control blocks perform disk I/O. Because the file control block structure does not support partitions larger than 32Mb, a program using file control blocks can theoretically write its data (in error) to any location on your disk, overwriting existing data! The SHARE command intercepts and corrects such disk I/O operations, preventing this type of error. If you are using DOS 4.0 and have a disk partition larger than 32Mb, place the following entry in your CONFIG.SYS file:

```
INSTALL=C:\DOS\SHARE.EXE
```

Correcting Fragmented Files with DOS

As discussed in Tip 457, fragmented files decrease your system performance. The easiest way to correct fragmented files is by using a third-party disk utility. However, if you don't have such a utility, you can correct fragmentation using the BACKUP, FORMAT, and RESTORE commands. To begin, create a bootable floppy disk by using the FORMAT command as follows:

```
C:\> FORMAT A: /S <ENTER>
```

Next, copy the RESTORE and FORMAT commands to the floppy disk. Then, perform a complete disk backup operation (see Tip 354). *Only* if the backup operation is successful, format your disk as shown here:

```
A> FORMAT C: /S <ENTER>
```

After the FORMAT operation completes, issue the following command to RESTORE the files:

```
A> RESTORE  A:  C:\*.*  /S <ENTER>
```

The files will now reside in contiguous storage locations.

Recovering Lost Files and Pieces of Files

Over time, if you turn off your computer while your computer is running, or if you lose power to your computer while you are working, files may become broken or damaged, resulting in lost pieces of the file on your disk. Using the CHKDSK command shown here, you can determine whether such errors exist on your disk:

```
C:\> CHKDSK /F <ENTER>
```

If such damaged files exist, CHKDSK will display the following message:

```
nnn lost allocation units found in n chains.
Convent lost chains to files (Y/N)?
```

If such a message appears, type Y and press ENTER. CHKDSK will create one or more files in the disk's root directory containing the lost pieces. The files have names in the form FILE0000.CHK, FILE0001.CHK, and so on. Use the TYPE command to display each file's contents. If the file contains useful text, rename the file or merge the file into another by using an editor. If the file's contents are not understandable, delete the file to free disk space. If the file's contents appear to be a program file, you may have to reinstall your program to make it run properly.

A Disk's Data Storage Capacity Is Less than the Disk's Size

Table 349a lists the sizes of the most commonly used floppy disks in bytes.

Table 349a. Commonly Used Floppy Disk Sizes

Disk	Size in Bytes
360Kb	368,640
720Kb	737,280
1.2Mb	1,228,800
1.44Mb	1,474,560
2.88Mb	2,949,120

However, if you try to store a file containing 368,640 bytes on a 360Kb disk or a file containing 1,228,800 bytes on a 1.2Mb disk, the operation will fail. Why? To store information on your disk, DOS divides the disk into four parts. Every disk begins with a 512-byte boot record, followed by one or two file-allocation tables and a root directory. After these three items comes the space for your files. Table 349b lists the amount of space DOS uses for these items for the disk types listed in the preceding table.

When you want to know how much information a disk can hold, use the data value specified in Table 349b.

Table 349b. DOS Disk Space Usage for Commonly Used Disk Types

Disk	Boot	File-Allocation Records	Root Table	Data Directory
360Kb	512 bytes	2,048 bytes	3,584 bytes	362,496 bytes
720Kb	512 bytes	3,072 bytes	3,584 bytes	730,112 bytes
1.2Mb	512 bytes	7,168 bytes	7,168 bytes	1,213,952 bytes
1.44Mb	512 bytes	9,126 bytes	7,168 bytes	1,457,664 bytes

Keep UNFORMAT and UNDELETE in Mind When You Share Disks

In the past, users freely exchanged floppy disks containing files they wanted to share. Because DOS 5 provides an UNDELETE and UNFORMAT command, you need to be sure the disk does not contain deleted files the user receiving the disk can undelete, such as a confidential office memo. If you are using DOS 5, use the following FORMAT command to overwrite all the information on a disk before you copy to the disk files for another user:

```
C:\> FORMAT A: /U <ENTER>
```

The /U switch directs FORMAT to perform an unconditional format operation on the disk that cannot be unformatted.

Understanding the Master Boot Record

As discussed in Tip 369, you must divide your hard disk into one or more partitions. The disk stores partition information in the very first sector of your disk in a region called the master boot record. When the PC starts, it reads the master boot record to identify which partition it should boot from. In some cases, users place multiple operating systems such as DOS, UNIX, and OS/2 on their disks. The master boot record specifies the cylinders containing each operating system's partition and identifies the partition from which to boot. The master boot record can store information for up to four partitions. Each of the 4 entries in the master boot record consumes 16 bytes, as shown here:

Offset	Field
00H	Boot flag: 00H Not boot, 80H Boot partition
01H	Beginning head
02H	Beginning sector
03H	Beginning cylinder
04H	File system type
05H	Ending head
06H	Ending sector
07H	Ending cylinder
08H	First sector
0CH	Sector count
10H	

When your computer starts from the hard disk, the PC loads the master boot record into memory and then passes control to the first instruction contained in the boot code, which begins the startup process. Using the partition information, the PC then reads the corresponding boot sector from the partition from which it is to boot.

Removing Semi-Dangerous Commands from a New User's Disk

If you are setting up a system for a new user, you might want to consider removing commands such as FORMAT, RECOVER, and FDISK from the user's disk. New users have a habit of executing commands to find out what the commands do. If you don't want to remove the commands, move them to a different subdirectory that is not in the command path or disable the command by using a DOSKEY macro. If you use DOSKEY to remove commands, you can display a message, such as the following, to the user saying that you have intentionally removed the commands from their disk:

```
C:\> DOSKEY DEL=ECHO DEL has been disabled—See Bob Jones
```

If you remove commands from the user's disk, consider creating a batch file that explains to the user why the commands don't exist. For example, the following batch commands could be placed in the batch file FORMAT.BAT:

```
@ECHO OFF
ECHO For safety, FORMAT has been disabled—See Bob Jones
```

By displaying messages to the user in this way, new users with a DOS book won't be frustrated and discouraged when commands don't work.

Tip 353 Tricking Software into Using Your Hard Disk

Many older programs, in particular game programs, often assume that your program disk resides in drive A. Even when you place the software onto your hard disk, the program still looks for the files on drive A. In some cases, you can trick the program into using the hard disk by using the ASSIGN command. To use ASSIGN in this way, place the software in a directory on your hard disk.

Next, issue the following ASSIGN command to trick DOS into using drive C instead of drive A:

```
C:\> ASSIGN A=C <ENTER>
```

After you issue this command, any disk references for drive A are routed by DOS to drive C. When you run the program, it should find the desired files on drive C. After you are done using the program, issue the following ASSIGN command to restore normal disk operations:

```
C:\> ASSIGN <ENTER>
```

Tip 354 Backing Up Your Entire Disk

One of the most important operations you should perform monthly (ideally more often) is to back up your entire hard disk to floppy disks. Before you begin the backup operation, you should first make sure you have a sufficient number of floppy disks. To determine the number of disks required, invoke the CHKDSK command as shown here:

```
C:\> CHKDSK <ENTER>
Volume DOS 5 DISK  created 04-18-1992 4:43p
Volume Serial Number is 16F6-3B73

 200065024 bytes total disk space
   4280320 bytes in 4 hidden files
   1634304 bytes in 381 directories
 165556224 bytes in 8162 user files
  28594176 bytes available on disk

      4096 bytes in each allocation unit
     48844 total allocation units on disk
      6981 available allocation units on disk

    655360 total bytes memory
    541744 bytes free
```

Next, subtract the number of bytes available on your disk from the total disk space to determine the amount of disk space in use:

Space in use = Total disk space – Bytes available

To determine the number of floppy disks required, divide the disk space in use by the storage capacity of your floppy disks. Table 354 lists the capacities.

Number of floppies = Space in use / Floppy disk capacity

If you have the number of disks required and the disks are already formatted, issue the following command to back up your entire disk:

```
C:\> BACKUP C:\*.* A: /S <ENTER>
```

Table 354. Disk Storage Capacity for Commonly Used Disks

Disk	Data Storage Capacity
360Kb	362,496 bytes
720Kb	730,112 bytes
1.2Mb	1,213,952 bytes
1.44Mb	1,457,664 bytes

If the floppy disks are not formatted, you can include the /F switch directing BACKUP to format the floppy disks before it performs the backup operation.

Testing Whether a Drive Is Ready

When DOS tries to use a floppy drive and the drive does not contain a disk, DOS displays the following error message:

```
Not ready reading drive A
Abort, Retry, Fail?
```

The following DEBUG script file, A_EMPTY.SCR, creates a command file named A_EMPTY.COM that returns the exit status value 0 if drive A contains a disk and is ready for use, and 1 if the drive does not contain a disk or the drive latch is not closed:

A_EMPTY.SCR

```
N A_EMPTY.COM <ENTER>
A 100         <ENTER>
MOV AX,2524   <ENTER>
MOV DX,113    <ENTER>
INT 21        <ENTER>
MOV AH,1C     <ENTER>
MOV DL,1      <ENTER>
INT 21        <ENTER>
MOV AX,4C00   <ENTER>
INT 21        <ENTER>
MOV AX,4C01   <ENTER>
INT 21        <ENTER>
              <ENTER>
R CX          <ENTER>
18            <ENTER>
W             <ENTER>
Q             <ENTER>
```

Use DEBUG as follows to create the command file A_EMPTY.COM:

```
C:\> DEBUG < A_EMPTY.SCR <ENTER>
```

The following batch commands illustrate how your batch files might use A_EMPTY.COM:

```
REM Check if drive A contains a disk
A_EMPTY
IF ERRORLEVEL 1 GOTO NO_DISK
COPY FILENAME.EXT A:
GOTO DONE
REM Other commands
```

If by changing lines 1 and 7 of the DEBUG script file to the following, you can create a command filename B_EMPTY.COM that checks drive B's status:

B_EMPTY.SCR

```
N B_EMPTY.COM <ENTER>
A 100         <ENTER>
MOV AX,2524   <ENTER>
MOV DX, 113   <ENTER>
INT 21        <ENTER>
MOV AH,1C     <ENTER>
MOV DL,2      <ENTER>
INT 21        <ENTER>
MOV AX,4C00   <ENTER>
INT 21        <ENTER>
MOV AX 4C01   <ENTER>
INT 21        <ENTER>
              <ENTER>
R CX          <ENTER>
18            <ENTER>
W             <ENTER>
Q             <ENTER>
```

Flushing the Disk Buffers

DOS uses disk buffers to reduce the number of slow disk I/O operations it must perform. Tip 2 presents the RESTART utility, which reboots your system. Before you

invoke the RESTART command, you may want to force DOS to flush its buffers to disk with the DISKFLSH utility. The following DEBUG script file, DISKFLSH.SCR, creates the command file DISKFLSH.COM:

DISKFLSH.SCR

```
N DISKFLSH.COM <ENTER>
A 100          <ENTER>
MOV AH,0D      <ENTER>
INT 21         <ENTER>
MOV AH,4C      <ENTER>
INT 21         <ENTER>
               <ENTER>
R CX           <ENTER>
8              <ENTER>
W              <ENTER>
Q              <ENTER>
```

Use the DEBUG command as follows to create the command file DISKFLSH.COM:

```
C:\> DEBUG < DISKFLSH.SCR <ENTER>
```

The following commands illustrate how you might use DISKFLSH:

```
@ECHO OFF
DISKFLSH
RESTART
```

Restart Your System After Correcting Fragmentation

Tip 457 discusses disk fragmentation in detail. Tip 347 describes how you can eliminate disk fragmentation by using the BACKUP, FORMAT, and RESTORE commands. Although these three DOS commands help you eliminate fragmentation, using them can be time consuming. As an alternative, most users purchase a third-party disk utility program that quickly corrects fragmentation.

If you use such a third-party utility, restart your computer by using the CTRL-ALT-DEL keyboard combination as soon as the utility completes. By restarting your system in this way, you eliminate possible errors from memory-resident disk utility programs such as FASTOPEN, which records specific information about your disks that DOS later uses. Depending on your disk utility software, information on your disk may be moved without FASTOPEN's knowledge. When DOS later needs to open a file, FASTOPEN may give DOS incorrect information about the location of a file, causing a disk error. By restarting your system in this way, FASTOPEN starts with a new set of valid disk locations. For more information on FASTOPEN, see Tip 460.

Performing a Safe Format Operation

Beginning with version 5, DOS includes the UNFORMAT command that helps you recover an inadvertently formatted disk. To assist UNFORMAT, the FORMAT command in DOS 5 automatically performs a safe format operation. This means FORMAT records key information about the disk you are formatting on the disk. Should you later need to unformat the disk, the UNFORMAT command will use this information to rebuild the disk.

Note that in some cases (such as when the disk is nearly full), FORMAT may not be able to store the information UNFORMAT needs to unformat the disk. When this occurs, FORMAT will display the following message:

```
Drive A error. Insufficient space for the MIRROR image file.
```

If an error occurs in creating the format recovery file, FORMAT displays this message:

```
This disk cannot be unformatted.
Proceed with Format (Y/N)?
```

Should this message appear, and you wish to perform the default safe format, continue the operation only if you are sure you have the correct disk in the drive.

Safe FORMAT operations only occur when you are using DOS 5.

Replacing FORMAT's /4 Switch with /F

For years, users have been confused by when they need to use FORMAT's /4 switch when they format floppy disks. Here's the rule: If you have a 1.2Mb floppy disk drive, but you want to format a 360Kb diskette, you need to include the /4 switch as shown here:

```
C:\> FORMAT A: /4 <ENTER>
```

If you are using DOS 4 or higher, a solution that may be easier to remember is to use FORMAT's /F switch, which lets you specify one of the disk sizes listed in Table 359.

The following FORMAT command, for example, uses /F to format a 360Kb in drive A:

```
C:\> FORMAT A: /F:360 <ENTER>
```

Table 359. Disk Sizes Supported by FORMAT's /F Switch

160	160K	160Kb			
180	180K	180Kb			
320	320K	320Kb			
360	360K	360Kb			
720	720K	720Kb			
1200	1200K	1200Kb	1.2	1.2M	1.2Mb
1440	1440K	1440Kb	1.44	1.44M	1.44Mb
2880	2880K	2880Kb	2.88	2.88M	2.88Mb

Verifying the Contents of Mirror's Disk File

The DOS 5 MIRROR command lets you save your disk's file allocation table and root directory to a file on a disk that can be used by UNFORMAT to rebuild your disk should an inadvertent format operation occur. As you change or create files, DOS may update the contents of your disk's file allocation table, making the information previously stored by MIRROR obsolete. Obviously, the more often you invoke the MIRROR command, the more likely that its disk information will be up to date. Using the UNFORMAT command with the /J switch as follows, you can determine whether MIRROR's file is up to date or obsolete:

```
C:\> UNFORMAT C: /J <ENTER>
```

If the file is up to date, UNFORMAT will display the following message:

```
The system area of drive C has been verified to agree with the
MIRROR image file.
```

If the file is obsolete, UNFORMAT will display the following message:

```
The system area does NOT agree with the MIRROR image file.
```

If this message appears, invoke the MIRROR command to bring the file up to date.

Understanding Sector Interleaving

A disk drive's information storage area is divided into tracks and sectors. The number of sectors on the disk depend on the disk type. For simplicity, we normally assume that a track's sectors are numbered consecutively from 1 to however many sectors the track holds.

Within the drive, a hard disk spins at 3,600 revolutions per minute. In the past, slower computers could not keep up with the disk. Assume, for example, that a program needed the information stored in sectors 1 and 2. The PC first read the information in sector 1. Unfortunately, by the time the PC was ready for sector 2, the sector had already spun past the disk's read/write head, and the PC had to wait for the disk to spin a complete revolution before it again reached sector 2. To avoid such rotational delay's, disk drives separated consecutively numbered sectors, a process called interleaving. The following illustration shows a disk with an interleave factor of 2 and a disk with an interleave factor of 3:

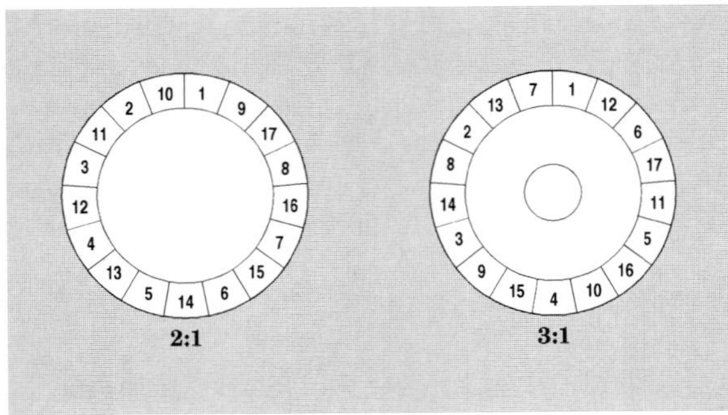

Interleaving sectors in this way reduces sector misses. Several software programs exist that let you determine and set your disk's interleave factor. Be aware that the wrong interleave factor can severely impact your system performance.

How Many Disks Will an Incremental Backup Operation Require?

Tip 532 discusses incremental backup operations, which back up only those files you have created or changed since the last backup operation. If you are using DOS 5, you can use DIR to determine the number of disks the backup operation will require. An incremental backup operation copies only those files whose archive attribute is set. The following DIR command uses the /A switch to display the name of every file on your disk whose archive attribute is set:

```
C:\> DIR C:\*.*  /S /A:A  <ENTER>
```

After DIR displays the last filename, DIR will display a count of the number of names displayed and the total disk space required, as shown here:

```
Total files listed:
     nnnn file(s)  nnnnnnn  bytes
```

To determine the number of floppy disks required, divide the disk space that the files require by your floppy disk's storage capacity.

$$\text{Number of disks} = \frac{\text{Disk space consumed}}{\text{Floppy disk capacity}}$$

What's In a Disk Controller Name?

When the PC needs to use your hard disk, the PC communicates with a disk controller that resides on a board inside your computer's chassis. There are several different disk controller types: RLL, MFM, SCSI, ESDI, and IDE. RLL and MFM are abbreviations for run-length limited and modified frequency modulation, two techniques the drive uses to record information on the disk. Most older hard disks use RLL and MFM controllers. SCSI, pronounced "scuzzy," is an interface technique that lets you easily attach an external hard drive. Tip 786 discusses the SCSI interface in detail. As the tip explains, you can attach several different types of devices besides disks to a SCSI port. ESDI is an abbreviation for enhanced small device interface. ESDI disks are much faster and can store much more information than RLL or MFM disks. However, they are also more expensive. The disk controller is a card containing the electronics that oversees disk operations. IDE (integrated drive electronics) disks have a built-in controller and do not require a controller card. When you purchase a hard disk, you need to make sure that the drive is compatible with your existing controller card, or if not, that you also purchase the correct controller. Don't be intimidated by disk controller types. In general, view them as nothing more than names that describe specific disk capabilities.

Increasing the Storage Capacity of Your 3 1/2-Inch Disk

The following illustration shows a 3 1/2-inch floppy disk. At the lower-left of the front side of the disk is the disk's high-density notch. If a notch is present, the disk is a high-capacity (1.44Mb) disk. If no notch is present, the disk is a 720Kb floppy.

In general, the primary difference between a 720Kb and a 1.44Mb floppy is that the 720Kb floppy stores information on only one side of the disk. If you have a 1.44Mb drive, several companies sell devices that let you "punch out" the high-density notch. When you remove the notch in this way, your disk will store information on both sides. If you use this technique, however, be very careful to make sure you have removed all bits of plastic that could later fall off the disk and into your drive. Such plastic could damage your drive or other disks.

Understanding the Boot Record

The first sector of every DOS disk contains a boot record. If the disk is bootable, the boot record contains the instructions required to start DOS. If the disk is not bootable, the boot record contains instructions that display the following message:

```
Non-System disk or disk error
Press any key to continue...
```

In addition to these instructions, the boot record contains information that describes the disk's layout to DOS. The following illustration shows the boot record fields:

Offset	Field
00H	JMP Instruction
03H	OEM name
0BH	Bytes per sector
0DH	Sectors per cluster
1EH	Number of reserved sectors
10H	Number of file allocation tables
11H	Number of root directory entries
13H	Total disk sectors
15H	Media descriptor
16H	Sectors per file allocation table
18H	Sectors per track
1AH	Number of heads
1CH	Number of hidden sectors
20H	Huge sector count
24H	Drive number
25H	Reserved
26H	Extended boot record signature
27H	Volume serial number
28H	Volume label
36H	File system type
3EH	DOS loader

When DOS uses a disk for the first time, DOS reads the disk's boot record to determine the disk's layout (number of sectors, sectors per clusters, and so on).

Tip 366 presents a utility command that displays the boot record fields of the current disk. Tip 367 discusses how to view your disk's boot record fields from within DEBUG.

Displaying the Contents of Your Disk's Boot Record

Tip 365 describes the fields contained in your disk's boot record. DOS reads these fields the first time it must use the disk, to determine the disk's layout and storage capacity. To help you better understand the boot record, the companion disk that accompanies this book contains the utility command BOOTINFO.EXE that displays your boot record fields. To display the current disk's boot record, invoke BOOTINFO from the DOS prompt as shown here:

```
C:\> BOOTINFO <ENTER>
OEM Name MSDOS5.0
Bytes per sector 512
Sectors per cluster 8
Number of reserved sectors 1
Number of file allocation tables 2
Root directory entries 512
Media descriptor F8
Sectors per file allocation table 191
Sectors per track 32
Number of heads 15
Number of hidden sectors 32
Total number of sectors 391168
Volume serial number 16f6-3b73
Volume DOS 5
File system FAT16
```

To print a copy of the disk's boot record contents, redirect BOOTINFO's output to your printer as shown here:

```
C:\> BOOTINFO > PRN <ENTER>
```

The utility command BOOTINFO.EXE resides on the companion disk that accompanies this book.

BOOTINFO.EXE

Dumping the Boot Record in DEBUG

Tip 365 discusses the contents of the boot record that resides in the first sector of every DOS disk. Using DEBUG you can read and display the boot record's contents as discussed here. To begin, invoke DEBUG from the DOS prompt. When DEBUG displays its hyphen prompt (-), issue one of the L(oad) commands listed in Table 367.

Table 367. DEBUG L(oad) Commands for Reading a Disk's Boot Sector

Disk Drive	Load Command
A	L 0 0 0 1
B	L 0 1 0 1
C	L 0 2 0 1
D	L 0 3 0 1

Next, issue the command D 0 L 200 to display the entire sector. The following illustration shows the various boot record fields:

```
-L 0 2 0 1 <ENTER>

-D 0 L 200 <ENTER>
                  1                    2                  3    4    5
21C4:0000  EB 3C 90 4D 53 44 4F 53-35 2E 30 00 02 08 01 00   ..MSDOS5.0.....
           6   7     8    9  10     11    12       13
21C4:0010  02 00 02 00 00 F8 BF 00-20 00 0F 00 20 00 00 00   ........ ... ...
              14     15            16           17
21C4:0020  00 F8 05 00 80 00 29 73-3B F6 16 44 4F 53 20 35   ......)s;..DOS 5
                                         18
21C4:0030  20 20 20 20 20 20 46 41-54 31 36 20 20 20 FA 33         FAT16   .3
21C4:0040  C0 8E D0 BC 00 7C 16 07-BB 78 00 36 C5 37 1E 56   .....|...x.6.7.V
21C4:0050  16 53 BF 3E 7C B9 0B 00-FC F3 A4 06 1F C6 45 FE   .S.|.........E.
21C4:0060  0F 8B 0E 18 7C 88 4D F9-89 47 02 C7 07 3E 7C FB   ....|.M..G...|.
21C4:0070  CD 13 72 79 33 C0 39 06-13 7C 74 08 8B 0E 13 7C   ..ry3.9..|t....|
21C4:0080  89 0E 20 7C A0 10 7C F7-26 16 7C 03 06 1C 7C 13   .. |..|.&.|...|.
21C4:0090  16 1E 7C 03 06 0E 7C 83-D2 00 A3 50 7C 89 16 52   ..|...|....P|..R
21C4:00A0  7C A3 49 7C 89 16 4B 7C-B8 20 00 F7 26 11 7C 8B   |.I|..K|. ..&.|.
21C4:00B0  1E 0B 7C 03 C3 48 F7 F3-01 06 49 7C 83 16 4B 7C   ..|..H....I|..K|
21C4:00C0  00 BB 00 05 8B 16 52 7C-A1 50 7C E8 92 00 72 1D   ......R|.P|...r.
21C4:00D0  B0 01 E8 AC 00 72 16 8B-FB B9 0B 00 BE E6 7D F3   .....r........}.
21C4:00E0  A6 75 0A 8D 7F 20 B9 0B-00 F3 A6 74 18 BE 9E 7D   .u... .....t...}
21C4:00F0  E8 5F 00 33 C0 CD 16 5E-1F 8F 04 8F 44 02 CD 19   ._.3...^....D...
21C4:0100  58 58 58 EB E8 8B 47 1A-48 48 8A 1E 0D 7C 32 FF   XXX...G.HH...|2.
21C4:0110  F7 E3 03 06 49 7C 13 16-4B 7C BB 00 07 B9 03 00   ....I|..K|......
21C4:0120  50 52 51 E8 3A 00 72 D8-B0 01 E8 54 00 59 5A 58   PRQ.:.r....T.YZX
21C4:0130  72 BB 05 01 00 83 D2 00-03 1E 0B 7C E2 E2 8A 2E   r..........|....
21C4:0140  15 7C 8A 16 24 7C 8B 1E-49 7C A1 4B 7C EA 00 00   .|..$|..I|.K|...
```

1. JMP
2. OEM Name
3. Bytes per sector 200H=512
4. Sectors per cluster
5. Number of reserved sectors
6. Number of file allocation tables
7. Number of root directory entries 200H=512
8. Total disk sectors 0=>disksize>32 Mb
9. Media descriptor
10. Sectors per file allocation table BFH = 191
11. Sectors per track ZOH = 32
12. Number of heads FH = 15
13. Number of hidden sectors ZOH = 32
14. Huge sector count SOF800H = 391,168
15. Drive number
16. Serial number
17. Volume label
18. File system type

After you are done viewing the boot record, issue the Q command to exit DEBUG. Do not, at any time, issue a W(rite) command. Doing so may damage your disk or files.

How Many Floppy Disks Are Present?

As your batch files increase in complexity, they sometimes may need to know the number of floppy disk drives available. The following DEBUG script file, FLOPCNT.SCR, creates a command file named FLOPCNT.COM that returns an exit status that corresponds to the number of floppy disk drives in the current system:

```
N FLOPCNT.COM <ENTER>
A 100         <ENTER>
MOV AX,40     <ENTER>
MOV DS,AX     <ENTER>
MOV AL,[10]   <ENTER>
MOV CL,6      <ENTER>
SAR AL,CL     <ENTER>
ADD AL,1      <ENTER>
MOV AH,4C     <ENTER>
INT 21        <ENTER>
              <ENTER>
R CX          <ENTER>
12            <ENTER>
W             <ENTER>
Q             <ENTER>
```

FLOPCNT.SCR

Use DEBUG as follows to create the command file FLOPCNT.COM:

```
C:\> DEBUG < FLOPCNT.SCR <ENTER>
```

The following batch commands use FLOPCNT to determine whether any floppy disk drives are present:

```
@ECHO OFF
FLOPCNT
IF NOT ERRORLEVEL 1 GOTO NO_FLOPPIES
```

```
GOTO FLOPPYS
REM Other commands here
```

Understanding Disk Partitions

When the PC XT was first released in the early 1980s, common hard disk sizes ranged from 5 to 10Mb. Thus, DOS was initially designed to support hard disks of up to 32Mb. As larger hard disks became affordable, users soon had disks larger than 32Mb. Unfortunately, DOS still did not provide support for disks larger than 32Mb. As a solution, DOS provided the FDISK command that let you divide your disk into smaller regions called partitions. If you are using DOS 4, DOS lets you exceed the 32Mb size by using partitions of up to 512Mb. If you are using DOS 5, your partition size can range up to 2Gb (two gigabytes, or 2 billion bytes). However, if you are using DOS 3.3 or lower, you must use partitions of 32Mb or smaller. If your disk is larger than 32Mb, you must divide the disk into two partitions: a DOS partition and an extended partition. The DOS partition cannot exceed 32Mb. This is the partition from which DOS will start. The extended partition can consume the rest of your disk. However, you must divide the extended partition into logical disk drives, whose size cannot exceed 32 Mb. The logical drives are named drives D through Z, depending on the size of the logical disk as well as the size of your extended partition. The FDISK command lets you control partitioning and logical drives.

Displaying the Master Boot Record's Contents

Tip 351 describes the master boot record that contains your disk's partition information. To help you better understand the master boot record's contents, the companion disk that accompanies this book

contains the utility command SHOWMAST.EXE that displays the contents of your disk's partition table entries. To use SHOWMAST, invoke it from the DOS prompt as shown here:

```
C:\> SHOWMAST <ENTER>
Partition 0
    DOS partition > 32Mb
    Beginning cylinder 0
    Ending cylinder 814
    Sector count 391168
Partition 1
    Not used
Partition 2
    Not used
Partition 3
    Not used
```

If you want to print a copy of the partition information, redirect SHOWMAST's output to your printer as follows:

```
C:\> SHOWMAST > PRN <ENTER>
```

The utility command SHOWMAST.EXE resides on the companion disk that accompanies this book.

SHOWMAST.EXE

Saving Partition Information

Tip 342 explains how to save your disk's partition table entries (or master boot record) to a floppy disk by using the DOS 5 UNFORMAT /PARTN command. If you are not using DOS 5, the companion disk that accompanies this book provides the utility commands SAVEPART.EXE and REST-PART.EXE that save and later restore the partition entries to or from floppy disk. To save the partition information to the floppy disk in drive A, invoke the SAVEPART command as follows:

```
C:\> SAVEPART <ENTER>
```

Place the floppy disk in a safe location. Should you ever need to restore your disk's partition information, invoke RESTPART as shown here:

```
A:\> RESTPART <ENTER>
```

SAVEPART.EXE
RESTPART.EXE

The utility commands SAVEPART.EXE and RESTPART.EXE reside on the companion disk that accompanies this book.

Creating a Secondary, or Read-Ahead, Cache

If you are using a 286 or higher computer that has extended memory, you should install SMARTDRV to perform disk caching as discussed in Tip 374. If you cannot take advantage of SMARTDRV and you are using DOS 4 or higher, you can improve your system performance by creating read-ahead buffers with the CONFIG.SYS BUFFERS entry. A read-ahead buffer is a memory buffer within which DOS reads subsequent disk sectors in anticipation of their use. DOS lets you specify from 1 to 8 read-ahead buffers. The following CONFIG.SYS entry, for example, allocates 30 disk buffers and 4 read-ahead buffers:

```
BUFFERS=30,4
```

The 30 disk buffers store previously read sectors in anticipation of their reuse. The read-ahead buffers contain sectors the program has not yet used, but that DOS anticipates the program may use. Each read-ahead buffer consumes approximately 512 bytes of memory. If you are using SMARTDRV, do not use read-ahead buffers.

To use read-ahead buffers, you must be using DOS 4 or higher.

Installing DOS Error Messages on Floppy-Disk-Based Systems

To better utilize memory, COMMAND.COM loads only some error messages into memory while reading others, as necessary, from the file COMMAND.COM on your disk. If you are running DOS 4 or 5 from a floppy-disk-based system and DOS encounters an error for which it needs to read a COMMAND.COM error message, DOS will read the drive that originally contained the boot disk. If the disk contains COMMAND.COM, DOS will display the correct error message. If the disk does not contain COMMAND.COM, DOS will display one of the following messages:

```
Parse error

Extended error
```

Using the /MSG switch with the CONFIG.SYS SHELL entry as shown here, you can direct COMMAND.COM to load all of its messages into memory at system startup to avoid such errors:

```
SHELL=COMMAND.COM /P /MSG
```

Although using the /MSG switch eliminates possible error message problems, loading the error messages consumes memory. Thus, use the /MSG switch only if you are running DOS from a floppy-disk-based system.

To use COMMAND.COM's /MSG switch, you must be using DOS 4 or higher.

Reducing Disk I/O Operations Using SMARTDRV.SYS

Because of a disk's slow mechanical nature, a performance goal is always to try to reduce the number of slow disk input and output operations. The CONFIG.SYS BUFFERS entry lets you establish memory buffers that DOS uses to reduce the number of disk operations. If your are using extended or expanded memory, however, you can create a much larger disk buffer (sometimes called a cache) by using the SMARTDRV.SYS device driver. Using SMARTDRV.SYS provides several advantages over DOS buffers:

- SMARTDRV lets you create a buffer of up to 8Mb in size.
- The SMARTDRV buffer does not consume conventional memory.
- SMARTDRV allows programs to dynamically adjust the buffer size as memory becomes scarce.

The format for installing the SMARTDRV.SYS driver is as follows:

```
DEVICE=C:\DOS\SMARTDRV.SYS [BufferSize][MinimumSize][/A]
```

The BufferSize parameter specifies the size of the SMARTDRV buffer in Kb. The buffer size can range from 128 through 8192Kb (8Mb). The default buffer size is 256Kb. As discussed, if memory becomes scarce, programs (such as Windows) can reduce the buffer size to free memory. The MinimumSize parameter specifies the minimum size to which the buffer can be reduced. The /A switch directs DOS to install the buffer in expanded memory as opposed to extended. The following CONFIG.SYS entry allocates a 2Mb buffer:

```
DEVICE=C:\DOS\SMARTDRV.SYS  2048
```

If you are using DOS 5 memory management techniques, use DEVICEHIGH to install the driver.

If you install SMARTDRV.SYS, reduce the number of DOS disk buffers to three as shown here:

```
BUFFERS=3
```

Used Correctly, RAM Drives Are Wonderful

A RAM drive is a simulated disk drive that resides in your computer's fast electronic memory. A RAM drive, like your floppy and hard disk drives, has a unique drive letter that you use to access the drive. Unlike your floppy and hard disk drives, the RAM drive stores information only temporarily. If you turn off your computer or restart DOS, the information the RAM drive contains is lost. Because the RAM drive is electronic, as opposed to mechanical, RAM drives are much faster than the fastest hard drive. If you have a program that creates temporary files, directing the program to use the RAM drive significantly improves performance.

The RAMDRIVE.SYS device driver lets you create a RAM drive. The format of RAMDRIVE.SYS is as follows:

```
DEVICE=C:\DOS\RAMDRIVE.SYS [DiskSizeKb [SectorSize [Entries]]] [/A|/E]
```

The DiskSizeKb parameter specifies the desired RAM drive size in Kb. The size can range from 16 to 4096Kb. The default size is 64Kb. The SectorSize parameter specifies the size of the RAM drives sectors in bytes. Valid sector sizes are 128, 256, and 512 bytes. The default sector size is 512 bytes. The Entries parameter specifies the number of root directory entries the RAM drive supports as a number from 2 through 1024. The default number of entries is 64. The /A switch directs DOS to install the drive in expanded memory. Likewise, /E directs DOS to install the RAM drive in extended memory. If you don't specify /E or /A, DOS installs the RAM drive in conventional memory.

The following RAMDRIVE.SYS entry installs a 128Kb RAM drive in conventional memory:

```
DEVICE=C:\DOS\RAMDRIVE.SYS 128
```

This RAMDRIVE.SYS entry also creates a 1-Mb RAM drive in extended memory:

```
DEVICE=C:\DOS\RAMDRIVE.SYS  1024  /E
```

When you restart your system, RAMDRIVE.SYS will display the RAM drive's corresponding drive letter on your screen. Normally, the RAM drive is assigned the next available drive letter. Assuming that the RAM drive uses the drive letter D, you can copy files to it as shown here:

```
C:\> COPY FILENAME.EXT  D: <ENTER>
```

You can select the RAM drive as the current drive as follows:

```
C:\> D: <ENTER>
D:\>
```

In other words, you can treat the drive like any other. Remember, however, that if you create or change a file on the RAM drive, you must save the file to your hard or floppy disk, or the file's contents will be lost when you turn off your computer.

Restoring an Entire Disk

Tip 559 descibes how to restore a specific file from your backup disks. If you ever need to restore all of the files on your hard disk, place a diskette containing RESTORE in drive A and issue the following command:

```
A:\> RESTORE A:  C:\*.* /S <ENTER>
```

When RESTORE prompts you for a floppy disk, place the first backup diskette in drive A. When RESTORE prompts you for the next diskette, place the second disk in drive A, following this process for each of your backup disks.

If Disk Space Is Tight, Disable MIRROR's File Delete Tracking and Delete MIRROR's Disk Image Files

As described in Tip 508, the MIRROR command lets you improve the likelihood of undeleting files by placing information about each file you delete in the hidden file PCTRACKR.DEL that resides in your disk's root directory. If your disk space is running low and you need to temporarily free some space, you can disable MIRROR's file delete tracking and delete the file PCTRACKER.DEL. The size

Table 377. Default File Sizes for PCTRACKR.DEL

Disk Size	Default Entries	Default File Size
360Kb	25	5Kb
720Kb	50	9Kb
1.2Mb	75	14Kb
1.44Mb	75	15Kb
20Mb	101	18Kb
32Mb	202	36Kb
>32Mb	303	55Kb

of the file depends on the number of entries you directed MIRROR to track. Table 377 lists the default sizes.

To delete PCTRACKR.DEL, perform these steps. First, disable MIRROR's file tracking by invoking MIRROR with the /U switch:

```
C:\> MIRROR /U <ENTER>
```

Next, remove the file's system attribute:

```
C:\> ATTRIB -S PCTRACKR.DEL <ENTER>
```

Use DEL to delete the file as shown here:

```
C:\> DEL PCTRACKR.DEL <ENTER>
```

Next, if your root directory contains the file MIRROR.FIL, remove the file's read-only attribute and delete the file:

```
C:\> ATTRIB -R MIRROR.FIL <ENTER>
C:\> DEL MIRROR.FIL <ENTER>
```

Last, use the following commands to delete the file MIRORSAV.FIL:

```
C:\> ATTRIB -R -S -H  MIRORSAV.FIL <ENTER>
C:\> DEL MIRORSAV.FIL <ENTER>
```

EDIT your AUTOEXEC.BAT and temporarily comment out (with the REM statement) the MIRROR command so these files are not created the next time your system starts. As soon as you have available disk space, start using MIRROR once again.

To use MIRROR, you must be using DOS 5.

Understanding Logical Drive Names

DOS lets you use more than one logical drive letter to refer to floppy disk drives. For example, if your computer only has one floppy drive, you can refer to the drive as either A: or B:. If drive A is active and you reference drive B, DOS will display the following message asking you to insert the floppy disk you want DOS to use in drive B:

```
Insert diskette for drive B: and press any key when ready
```

When you later reference drive A, DOS will display a similar message prompting you to enter drive A's floppy disk. Assume, for example, you have a floppy disk containing a file you want to copy to another floppy disk. One way to perform the copy operation is to first copy the file to the hard disk and then to copy it to the second floppy disk. However, because your computer uses the logical drive letters A and B to reference your floppy drive, you can perform the file copy operation as follows:

```
C:\> COPY A:FILENAME.EXT  B: <ENTER>
```

As DOS needs each floppy disk, it will display a message prompting you to insert the correct disk.

Creating a Customized Logical Disk Drive

As discussed in Tip 378, DOS lets you use more than one logical drive name to refer to floppy disk drives. The DRIVER.SYS device driver lets you create a new logical drive name for an existing floppy drive. In addition, the driver lets you select the drive's storage capacity. For example, if drive A is a 1.2Mb floppy drive, you can create a logical drive, possibly drive D, that provides a 360Kb drive. You can use DRIVER.SYS to create a smaller compatible drive, but you cannot use it to increase a drive's storage capacity. The following DRIVER.SYS entry, for example, assigns drive A (physical drive 0) a 360Kb logical drive that uses the next available drive letter:

```
DEVICE=C:\DOS\DRIVER.SYS  /D:0 /F:0
```

After you restart your system, you can use either logical name to refer to the floppy drive.

For more information on the available drive types, refer to DRIVER.SYS in your DOS documentation.

How Much Disk Space Do Specific Files Consume?

When users need to copy files from their hard disk to a floppy disk, they often want to know how many disks the files will require. You also may sometimes need to know how much hard disk space a set of files consumes. Using DIR, you can determine the amount of disk space consumed by specific files in a directory. For example, to determine the amount of current directory space consumed by files with the BAK extension, you would issue the following command:

```
C:\> DIR *.BAK <ENTER>
```

After DIR scrolls the filenames past you on the screen, DIR displays a count of the number of files displayed as well as the amount of disk space the files consume:

```
nn file(s)  nnnnn bytes
```

If you are using DOS 5, the following DOSKEY macro, CONSUME, displays the total number of bytes consumed on your entire disk by a particular type of file:

```
C:\> DOSKEY CONSUME=DIR \$1 /S  | FIND "file(s)" <ENTER>
```

To determine the amount of space consumed by EXE files, for example, you would use CONSUME as follows:

```
C:\> CONSUME *.EXE
```

To use the DIR /S switch and to create DOSKEY macros, you must be using DOS 5.

Changing a Floppy Disk's Characteristics with DRIVPARM

Tip 379 explains how to create a logical drive by using the DRIVER.SYS device driver with characteristics that differ from those of the original drive. The CONFIG.SYS DRIVPARM entry lets you change an existing drive's characteristics, though as with DRIVER.SYS, you can't use DRIVPARM to increase a drive's storage capacity. The following DRIVPARM entry, for example, converts a 1.2Mb drive to a 360Kb drive:

```
DRIVPARM=/D:0 /F:0
```

For more information on DRIVPARM, refer to your DOS documentation.

Does This Partition Exceed 32Mb?

As Tip 346 explains, prior to DOS 4, the largest disk partition size DOS supported was 32Mb. Starting with DOS 4, DOS supported disk partitions up to 512Mb. Under DOS 5, the partition size can reach 2Gb. Unfortunately, although DOS supports larger partition sizes, not all applications (in particular, disk utilities) do. The companion disk that accompanies this book includes the utility command HUGEDISK.EXE that returns the exit status value 1 if the current disk partition exceeds 32Mb and returns 0 otherwise. The following batch commands illustrate how you might use HUGEDISK to determine whether the current partition size exceeds 32Mb:

```
@ECHO OFF
HUGHDISK
IF ERRORLEVEL 1 GOTO 32MB_OR_BIGGER
REM Other commands here
```

The utility command HUGEDISK.EXE resides on the companion disk that accompanies this book.

HUGEDISK.EXE

Is This Drive Local or Remote?

Each day, more computers are attached to local area networks to share information and resources. On a network, you may work with local disks that reside in your computer or with remote network-based disk. There are many commands (such as UNDELETE, UNFORMAT, FORMAT, and RECOVER) that you should not use with a network drive. The following DEBUG script file, TSTLOCAL.SCR, tests the current drive to determine whether the drive is local or remote; if the drive is local, TSTLOCAL returns the exit status value 1, and if the drive is not local, it returns 0:

TSTLOCAL.SCR

```
N TSTLOCAL.COM <ENTER>
A 100          <ENTER>
MOV AX,4409    <ENTER>
MOV BL,0       <ENTER>
INT 21         <ENTER>
AND DX,1000    <ENTER>
JZ 111         <ENTER>
MOV AL,0       <ENTER>
JMP 113        <ENTER>
MOV AL,1       <ENTER>
MOV AH,4C      <ENTER>
INT 21         <ENTER>
               <ENTER>
R CX           <ENTER>
17             <ENTER>
W              <ENTER>
Q              <ENTER>
```

Use DEBUG as follows to create the command file TSTLOCAL.COM:

```
C:\> DEBUG < TSTLOCAL.SCR <ENTER>
```

The following batch commands illustrate how you might use TSTLOCAL:

```
@ECHO OFF
TSTLOCAL
IF ERRORLEVEL 1 GOTO LOCAL_DRIVE
GOTO NETWORK_DRIVE
REM Other commands here
```

From Which Disk Did DOS Start?

As your batch files become more complex, you sometimes may need to know the disk from which DOS booted, perhaps to locate COMMAND.COM, AUTOEXEC.BAT, or CONFIG.SYS. The following DEBUG script file, BOOTDISK.SCR, creates the command file BOOTDISK.COM that returns the boot disk as an exit status value (0 = A, 1 = B, 2 = C, and so on):

```
N BOOTDISK.COM <ENTER>
A 100          <ENTER>
MOV AX,3305    <ENTER>
INT 21         <ENTER>
MOV AL,DL      <ENTER>
MOV AH,4C      <ENTER>
INT 21         <ENTER>
               <ENTER>
R CX           <ENTER>
B              <ENTER>
W              <ENTER>
Q              <ENTER>
```

BOOTDISK.SCR

Use DEBUG as follows to create the command file BOOTDISK.COM:

```
C:\> DEBUG < BOOTDISK.SCR <ENTER>
```

The following batch commands illustrate how you can use BOOTDISK to create the named parameter %BOOTDISK% that contains the boot drive specifier:

```
@ECHO OFF
BOOTDISK
IF ERRORLEVEL 0 IF NOT ERRORLEVEL 1 SET BOOTDISK=A:
IF ERRORLEVEL 1 IF NOT ERRORLEVEL 2 SET BOOTDISK=B:
IF ERRORLEVEL 2 IF NOT ERRORLEVEL 3 SET BOOTDISK=C:
REM Other commands here
```

BOOTDISK.COM requires DOS 4 or higher.

Is the Current Media Fixed or Removable?

As your batch files become more complex, they sometimes may need to know specifics about the current disk. In Tip 644 you can create a command file that returns the disk's media description value

as an exit status value. In Tip 383, you can create a command file that tests whether the current drive is local or remote. The following DEBUG script file, TSTFIXED.SCR, creates a command file named TSTFIXED.COM that returns the exit status value 1 if the current disk used fixed media and returns 0 otherwise:

TSTFIXED.SCR

```
N TSTFIXED.COM <ENTER>
A 100          <ENTER>
MOV AX,4408    <ENTER>
MOV BL,0       <ENTER>
INT 21         <ENTER>
MOV AH,4C      <ENTER>
INT 21         <ENTER>
               <ENTER>
R CX           <ENTER>
B              <ENTER>
W              <ENTER>
Q              <ENTER>
```

Use DEBUG as follows to create the command file TSTFIXED.COM:

```
C:\> DEBUG < TSTFIXED.SCR <ENTER>
```

The following batch commands illustrate how you might use TSTFIXED:

```
@ECHO OFF
TSTFIXED
IF ERRORLEVEL 1 GOTO FIXED_MEDIA
GOTO REMOVEABLE_MEDIA
REM Other commands here
```

Understanding Write Precompensation

If you install a hard disk, or if your computer's CMOS battery runs out of power, you will eventually have to define your disk's characteristics, as Tip 76 explains. Depending on your disk type, you may

have to enter a write precompensation value (for example, MFM controllers require write precompensation).

Your disk divides its storage area into concentric tracks. Each track is further divided into sectors. Every track on your disk contains the same number of sectors. Thus, the data stored on inner tracks is stored much closer together (more densely) than data on the outer tracks. Because bits are stored on the disk magnetically, the inner tracks can experience problems caused by the magnetic attraction and repulsion of closely stored bits; in other words, two neighboring bits may tend to either pull together or push apart. To compensate for this bit behavior, some controllers place bits closer together or further apart so their attraction or repulsion pulls the bits into the correct locations. A disk's write precompensation value specifies the cylinder at which the drive must begin this compensation. The documentation that accompanies your disk should specify the correct value for the cylinder location.

Understanding Low-Level Disk Format Operations

When you purchase a computer, one of the operations the manufacturer typically performs for you is low-level formatting of your hard disk. A low-level format operation prepares your disk for use. The operation differs greatly from that of the FORMAT command that prepares a disk for use by DOS. The low-level format operation defines disks tracks and sectors. After low-level formatting has been applied to a disk, you can use the FDISK command to partition the disk and then the FORMAT command to prepare the disk for use by DOS.

The low-level format operation also specifies damaged disk locations so they are not used. If you examine the case of your hard disk in your computer's chassis, you will find a certificate describing the disk's bad locations. The disk manufacturer identified these areas by performing a surface analysis of your disk's surface. The individual performing the low-level format operation must be aware of these values so they can be entered.

The low-level format operation also identifies the disk's sectors interleave factor (see Tip 361).

Normally, you won't have to perform a low-level format operation. However, if your disk starts to experience errors that persist after you format the disk using the FORMAT command, you may need to perform low-level formatting. Before you do so, however, save as much information from your disk as you can; low-level formatting is a destructive operation. Next, perform a surface analysis to identify disk locations that can no longer store information. Write down the locations displayed. See Tip 388 for the steps you must perform next.

Performing a Low-Level Format Operation

Tip 387 discusses low-level hard disk formatting in detail. The only time you should need to perform low-level formatting on your disk is if you start experiencing a number of disk errors that formatting the disk with FORMAT won't correct. If you are using a disk controller other than an IDE, you can perform low-level formatting on your disk with software that accompanies the disk, a third-party software utility, or possibly, one of the DEBUG commands listed here. If you are using an IDE drive, you are probably out of luck. Normally, low-level formatting can be performed for IDE drives only at the factory, which means you may have to return the disk. Before you begin low-level formatting, make sure you have saved any files you can from your disk. Also make sure you know the disk's bad blocks.

In addition to letting you access your system's setup information by pressing a specific key when your system starts, some BIOS chips let you access built-in diagnostics that include a low-level formatting option. If your system does not provide such access, you may have received a floppy disk that contains low-level format software. If so, you can use the software to begin the low-level format operation. If you don't have such software, refer to the documentation that accompanies your disk to find a DEBUG Go (G) command that initiates a low-level format operation on your disk. Next, place a bootable floppy disk that contains DEBUG in drive A. If the documentation does not tell you how to initiate low-level formatting, call your retailer and ask for the correct steps. If you cannot find a DEBUG command that will initiate the low-level format operation, Table 388 lists several such commands that commonly initiate such operations.

If your system hangs when you issue one of the commands, press CTRL-ALT-DEL to restart your system and try the next command. If the DEBUG command is correct, you will see a menu-driven program you can use to initiate low-level formatting. If your disk has been misbehaving sporadically and your low-level format operation provides a surface analysis option, run the option to determine whether your disk contains any new defects. The surface analysis may require several hours. After the analysis ends, enter the known defects and initiate the low-level format opeartion.

Table 388. DEBUG Commands That May Initiate Low-Level Formatting

Memory Location	DEBUG Command
C800:0	G C800:0 <ENTER>
C800:5	G C800:5 <ENTER>
C800:CCC	G C800:CCC <ENTER>

What Is the Disk Landing Zone?

When your computer is turned on, your hard disk spins at 3600 RPM. The disk's read/write head floats just above the disk's surface. When you turn off your computer, the disk slows down, and the read/write head comes to rest on the disk's surface. To prevent the head from coming to rest on an area or your disk that contains data, many drives provide a designated landing zone as shown here:

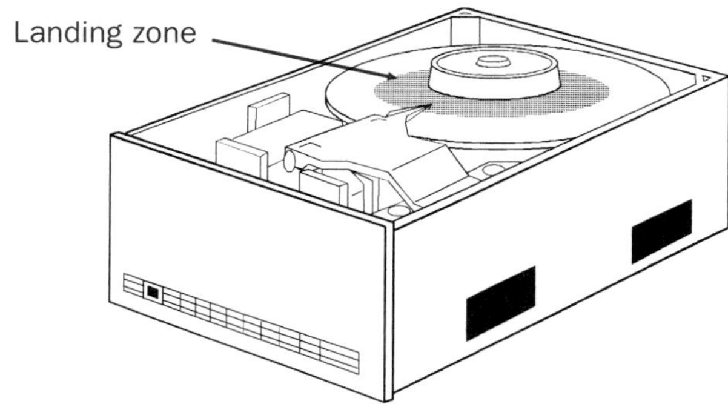

When you define your disk's characteristics during setup you may have to specify a landing zone. Normally, the landing zone corresponds to the disk's last track. If your disk does not have a landing zone, use the PARKHEAD utility presented in Tip 345 to park your disk heads before you turn off your computer's power.

What's My Number?

Each disk in your system is assigned a physical disk number that DOS and the BIOS use to access the disk. Drive A, for example, is physical drive 0, and drives B and C are physical drives 1 and 2. The following DEBUG script file, PHYSICAL.SCR, creates

the command file PHYSICAL.COM that returns the current drive's physical drive number as an exit status value:

PHYSICAL.SCR

```
N PHYSICAL.COM <ENTER>
A 100          <ENTER>
MOV AH,19      <ENTER>
INT 21         <ENTER>
MOV AH,4C      <ENTER>
INT 21         <ENTER>
               <ENTER>
R CX           <ENTER>
A              <ENTER>
W              <ENTER>
Q              <ENTER>
```

Use DEBUG as follows to create the command file PHYSICAL.COM:

```
C:\> DEBUG < PHYSICAL.SCR <ENTER>
```

The following batch commands use PHYSICAL to determine the current drive, assigning the drive to an environment entry name PHYSICAL_DRIVE:

```
@ECHO OFF
PHYSICAL
IF ERRORLEVEL 0 IF NOT ERRORLEVEL 1 SET PHYSICAL_DRIVE=A:
IF ERRORLEVEL 1 IF NOT ERRORLEVEL 2 SET PHYSICAL_DRIVE=B:
IF ERRORLEVEL 2 IF NOT ERRORLEVEL 3 SET PHYSICAL_DRIVE=C:
IF ERRORLEVEL 3 IF NOT ERRORLEVEL 4 SET PHYSICAL_DRIVE=D:
REM Other commands here
```

Reducing the Amount of Disk Space MIRROR Consumes

As discussed in Tip 508, if you invoke the DOS 5 MIRROR command from within your AUTOEXEC.BAT file, MIRROR will make a copy of your disk's root directory and file allocation table each

time your system starts. MIRROR stores this information in the file MIRROR.FIL. Should you need to unformat your disk at a later time, UNFORMAT will use the information in this file. By default, before MIRROR saves a copy of your disk's current information, MIRROR copies the old file to a file named MIRROR.BAK. Thus, should your computer restart after an inadvertent disk operation, you can use the older MIRROR copy to rebuild your disk.

If your disk space is at a premium, you can use MIRROR's 1 switch to direct MIRROR to overwrite the previous file as opposed to making a backup copy. If you use the /1 switch, however, you might want to give the user a chance to cancel the MIRROR command when the system starts to prevent MIRROR from overwriting the current file. One way to do so is to precede MIRROR with a PAUSE command shown here:

```
REM Starting commands
ECHO About to execute MIRROR
PAUSE
MIRROR /1
REM Other commands
```

If the user does not want to execute MIRROR, the user can press CTRL-C to end the batch file.

A second alternative that eliminates the user's need to press any key is to use the DELAY10.COM command presented in Tip 640, which gives the user time to press CTRL-C to cancel the batch file.

Combine SMARTDRV and FASTOPEN for Best Performance

Tip 374 discusses how you can use SMARTDRV.SYS to create a disk cache to reduce disk I/O operations, which in turn improves your system performance. Tip 460 discusses how you can use the FASTOPEN command to reduce directory search operations. FASTOPEN and SMARTDRV perform complimentary operations; you should use both for best performance. SMARTDRV.SYS reduces the number of disk sector read operations your PC must perform by buffering the sectors your programs have used in case the program needs to reuse them and by reading ahead the sectors it anticipates you may need. FASTOPEN, in turn, reduces the number of slow directory search operations DOS must perform for files you use more than once.

What Is a Form Factor?

A disk's form factor is a value that describes the disk's geometry: number of tracks, sectors, and so on. The DRIVER.SYS device driver and the CONFIG.SYS DRIVPARM entry let you specify form-factor values. Table 393 lists common form-factor values.

The advantage of using form-factor values is that you can quickly specify the desired drive type without having to know the drive's sector, track, or head use.

Table 393. Common Form-factor Values

Form Factor	Drive Type	DRIVPARM	DRIVER.SYS
0	360Kb	Yes	Yes
1	1.2Mb	Yes	Yes
2	720Kb	Yes	Yes
5	Hard disk	Yes	No
6	Tape drive	Yes	No
7	1.44Mb	Yes	Yes
8	CD-ROM	Yes	No
9	2.88Mb	Yes	Yes

Understanding the Information BACKUP Places on a Floppy Disk

Tip 354 explains how to make a complete backup copy of your disk. Tip 532 describes how to perform an incremental backup operation, which copies only those files created or changed since the last backup

operation. After you back up files to a floppy disk, the only way to access the files on the floppy disk is by using RESTORE. You can't, for example, use COPY to restore a file from the floppy disk. Here's why. Rather than individually copying the files to the floppy disk, BACKUP stores the files in a file named BACKUP.nnn, and it stores information about the files in a file named CONTROL.nnn. CONTROL.nnn contains information about each file as shown here:

```
C:\> DIR A: <ENTER>
 Volume in drive A is BACKUP  001
 Volume Serial Number is 2E3E-15E0
 Directory of A:\

BACKUP   001    1456128 07-19-92    2:26p
CONTROL  001       1229 07-19-92    2:26p
        2 file(s)     1457357 bytes
                            0 bytes free
```

The only commands that understand the format of these two files are BACKUP, which creates the files, and RESTORE, which uses these files to place a file back on your hard disk.

Obtaining Support for Newer Disks When Using an Older BIOS

If you are using an older 8088 or possibly even an older 80286 computer, your computer's BIO'S may not support a new disk drive type, such as a 3 1/2-inch disk. If you add such a drive to your system, the PC may treat the drive as a different drive type, such as a 360Kb-drive, for example. Beginning with DOS 5, the CONFIG.SYS DRIVPARM entry (see Tip 381) and the DRIVER.SYS device driver (see Tip 379) allow you to include the /I switch, which provides the necessary support. For example, if you add a 720Kb floppy drive (as drive B) to a system that does not recognize the drive, you would use the /I switch with DRIVPARM as follows:

```
DRIVPARM /D:1 /F:2 /I
```

Why You Normally Can't Apply Low-Level Formatting to IDE Disks

To locate specific tracks on a hard disk, many newer disk drives record mapping information, called *servo data*, on the disk. When the drive needs to access track 70, for example, the drive uses the servo data to find the track. In the past, many drives designated an entire disk platter specifically for storing servo data. Many IDE drives now embed the servo data between the data tracks as shown here:

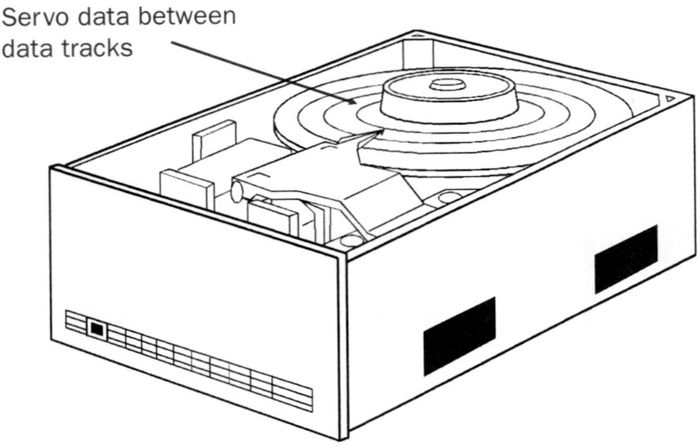

Unfortunately, most IDE controllers cannot perform low-level formatting on this servo information. As a result, low-level formatting can be applied to the disk only at the factory. Recently, a few software packages have emerged that can perform low-level formatting on a select group of IDE drives. If your IDE requires low-level formatting, check with your computer's manufacturer about the availability of such software.

Improving Performance with a Caching Disk Controller

If you use programs that are disk-use intensive, you can improve your system performance by upgrading to a caching disk controller. In short, a caching disk controller is nothing more than a disk controller with memory in which it can store sectors from the current track. For example, the following illustration shows the possible disk controller contents if your disk reads a sector from the first track:

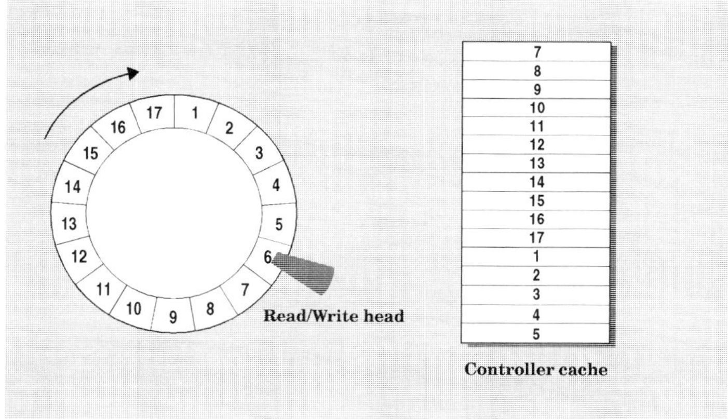

In general, as a sector passes the read/write head, the controller buffers the sector in anticipation of its use. Should the computer need to use one of the sectors, the controller has the sector immediately available. The advantage of using the caching controller as opposed to caching software such as SMARTDRV is that all of the overhead occurs within the disk controller.

The primary disadvantage of a caching controller is cost; caching controllers are more expensive than caching software. However, if performance speed is paramount to you, consider adding a caching controller to your wish list.

If you upgrade to a caching controller, make sure first that the controller is fully compatible with your system.

Thinking of Buying a CD-ROM?

For years people have used compact discs (CDs) in their stereos to play music. In the past few years, computer users have starting purchasing CD-ROM drives for their computers, not to play music, but instead to access the hundreds of megabytes of information a CD-ROM contains. A multivolume encyclopedia, for example, can be stored on one or two CDs. A single CD can store over 650Mb (300,000 pages). The coming of multimedia—and the amount of disk space required to store voice and video data—makes CD-ROM almost mandatory. CD-ROM drives come in two types: internal and external. The following illustration shows the two types:

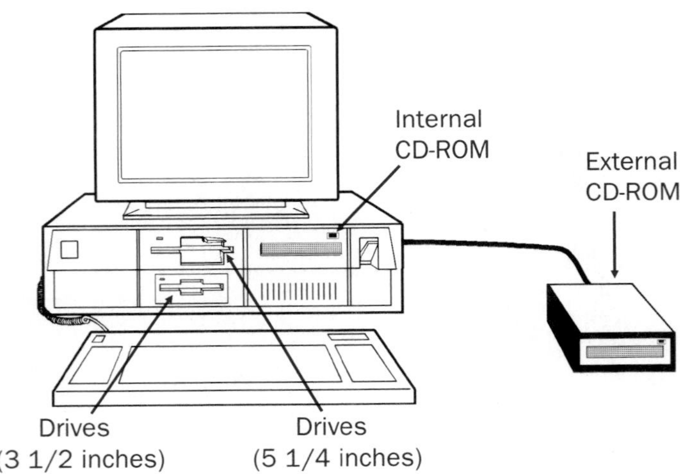

If you plan to purchase a CD-ROM, make sure you get Microsoft's CD-ROM extensions device drivers. If you are planning to use the CD-ROM for multimedia, the drive needs to support a sustained transfer rate of 150Kb per second. As discussed in Tip 794, the CD-ROM drive requires considerable power. Make sure your existing power supply can support it.

How a CD-ROM Stores Data

Many people are confused by how a CD-ROM actually stores information. Users typically think the disc contains information in the form of a laser or stored light. Actually, the CD-ROM stores information by placing microscopic pits in the disc, each of which represent one bit of information. If you examine the disc, you will see that the entire disc appears very reflective. When you place the CD in a drive, the drive reflects light off of exact locations on the disc. The CD's shiny locations reflect well. The pits, however, do not. By measuring the differences in reflections, the drive can read the information the disc contains.

To store information on a CD, the information (the pits) are essentially stamped into the disc. The disc is then sealed to protect it from fingerprints and most scratches, which explains why you don't feel the pits. Because the pits can be placed so closely together, the CD has tremendous storage capacity. However, because the disc's contents cannot be changed, the disc becomes a read-only, or ROM, device.

In the near future, CDs will be as common as floppy disks are today. Thus, it's important that you begin to understand their use today.

How Does a WORM Device Differ from CD-ROM?

WORM is an abbreviation for write-once, read many. A WORM device is similar to CD-ROM in that, once it is written, its media cannot be changed. Also, like CD-ROM, WORM devices read information by reflecting light off of the media. Information is stored on a CD-ROM by stamping a series of pits into the disc, where each pit represents a bit. Users, therefore, cannot record their own information on a CD-ROM.

A WORM drive normally costs 10 to 15 times as much as a CD-ROM drive because the WORM drive contains built-in lasers that let you record information on the disc one time. To record

information, the WORM drive lasers darken the pit areas on the disc, as opposed to actually pitting the disc. If you have large amounts of data that you must archive forever, such as large, company databases, a WORM drive is ideal. For the typical user, however, a WORM drive cost is still prohibitive.

What Is a Magnito-Optical Drive?

Tip 398 discusses CD-ROM discs and their advantages, such as capacity and durability. Tip 400 discusses WORM discs, their similarity to CD-ROM, and their ability to be written to once by the user. Ideally, the future will bring a medium with the capacity and longevity of CD-ROM and the modificability of magnetic disks. Currently, the medium closest to achieving these goals is magneto-optical storage. Like, magnetic disks, magneto-optical drives store information magnetically on disk. Unlike magnetic drives, these drives use lasers to record and read the data. As such, the drive can do so much more precisely, greatly increasing the disk's storage capacity. Current usable storage capacities are near 500Mb. Unfortunately, the storage technology is still slow when compared to current hard drives.

Understanding Disk-Speed Components

When you shop for a hard disk, you will encounter such terms as average access time, seek time, and latency, which relate to system performance. The average access time is the amount of time the drive normally takes to read or write the data you requested. When you purchase a new hard disk, you should buy one with an access time of 20ms or less. The average access time is calculated as follows:

Access time = Seek time + Latency + Transfer time + Controller overhead

The seek time is the time required to move the disk heads to the desired track. Because the distance (number of tracks) between successive seek operations varies, manufacturers typically advertise seek times that correspond to a movement across one-third of the disk. Seek times are measured in milliseconds.

Latency is amount of time the drive must wait for the desired sector to spin past the read/write head. Use the following equation to determine the disk's average latency:

$$\frac{3600 \text{ revolutions}}{1 \text{ minute}} x \frac{1 \text{ minute}}{60 \text{ seconds}} = \frac{60 \text{ revolutions}}{1 \text{ second}}$$

1 revolution = 0.0166 seconds

1/2 revolution = 0.00833 seconds, or 8.3ms

The transfer time is the amount of time required to transfer a sector to or from disk. Typically, transfer rates range from 2 to 4 megabits per seconnd. The controller overhead is the amount of time the disk controller requires to perform its processing, which is typically only a few milliseconds.

Understanding What Really Gets Stored on Disk

Conceptually, when you think about a disk's contents, you think only of tracks and sectors. Actually, the drive stores considerably more information about the disk's sectors. The following illustration shows the information the drive stores for each sector:

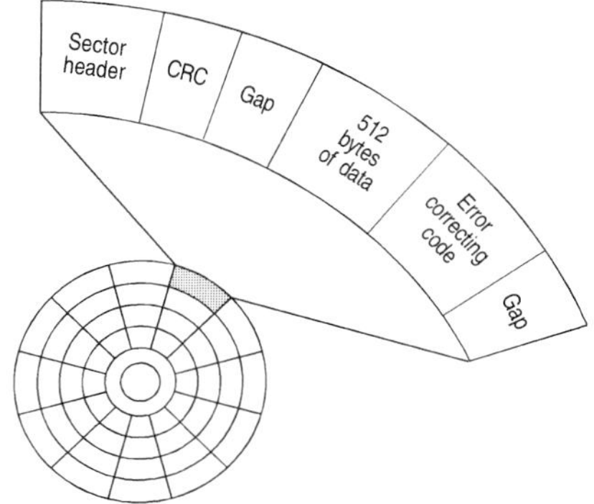

The sector header contains sector addressing information such as the side, track, and sector numbers. In addition, this header may contain specific information about a sector's state (usable or damaged). Immediately following the sector information is the CRC value, which helps the controller detect errors in the header. Following the CRC value is a small gap that gives the disk controller time to change from reading to writing. Next is the sector of data, followed by error-correcting code (ECC) that the controller may be able to use to rebuild the data section should an error occur. Following the ECC is a gap that separates the current sector from the next sector, which again allows the controller to change from reading to writing. The transition gap before the sector header is required because the only time the controller writes sector headers is during a low-level format operation.

Understanding Reduced-Write-Current Cylinders

Tip 386 discusses write precompensation and its use on the inner cylinders of your disk. Because of the bit density on these inner cylinders, the disk controller must perform write precompensation. In addition to performing write precompensation, many disk drives use reduced-write-current cylinders. A drive stores information to the disk by magnetizing the information on the disk. To do so, the disk applies electronic currents to specific parts of the disk. On the outer cylinders, there is little chance that the current targeted for one bit will affect another bit. However, to prevent current spillover on the denser bits of the inner cylinders, the drive reduces the current. The cylinder at which this current reduction occurs is called the reduced-write-current cylinder.

Understanding File Allocation Table Entry Sizes

Tip 503 describes how DOS stores the files on your disk by using disk clusters. Tip 405 describes how DOS stores information about each cluster's status in a disk structure called the file allocation table,

or FAT. The size of the file allocation table depends on the nuber of clusters on the disk. Table 405a lists FAT sizes for commonly used disk sizes.

Table 405a. FAT Sizes for Commonly Used Disks

Disk Size	Sectors Per Cluster	Sectors Per FAT	FAT Entries
360Kb	2	2	354
720Kb	2	3	713
1.2Mb	1	7	2371
1.44Mb	1	9	2847

The FAT serves as the road map to your file's clusters on disk. Every disk, therefore, must have a FAT. In fact, to prevent a single disk error from rendering your disk unusable, DOS normally places a second, backup, FAT on the disk; should the first FAT become damaged, DOS uses the second. Because one or more FATs reside on every disk, DOS tries to minimize the amount of disk space the FATs consume to give you more disk space for your files. One way DOS reduces the FAT sizes for disks that use less than 4,096 clusters is by representing the cluster numbers with 12-bit rather than 16-bit numbers. Thus, a 12-bit number can represent values in the range 0 to 4,095, since 2 raised to the power of 12 is 4,096. Here's how using 12-bit FAT entries saves disk space. If the FAT contains 4,096 entries and each entry requires 12 bits, you can calculate the number of sectors required to store the FAT as follows:

$$4{,}096 \times 12 \text{ bits} = 49{,}152 \text{ bits per FAT}$$

$$49{,}152 \text{ bits} \times \frac{1 \text{ byte}}{8 \text{ bits}} = 6{,}144 \text{ bytes per FAT}$$

$$6{,}144 \text{ bits} \times \frac{1 \text{ sector}}{512 \text{ bytes}} = 12 \text{ sectors per FAT}$$

If each FAT entry requires 16 bits, the FAT's sector consumption is as follows:

$$4{,}096 \times 16 \text{ bits} = 65{,}536 \text{ bits per FAT}$$

$$65{,}536 \text{ bits} \times \frac{1 \text{ byte}}{8 \text{ bits}} = 8{,}192 \text{ bytes per FAT}$$

$$8{,}192 \text{ bytes} \times \frac{1 \text{ sector}}{512 \text{ bytes}} = 16 \text{ sectors per FAT}$$

As you can see, using a 12-bit FAT saves four sectors per FAT. DOS places two copies of the FAT on each disk, so using a 12-bit FAT results in a savings of eight sectors. Table 405b lists the use of clusters for various disk partition sizes.

Table 405b. Cluster Use for Various Disk Partition Sizes

Disk Size	Cluster Type
360Kb	12 bit
720Kb	12 bit
1.2Mb	12 bit
1.44Mb	12 bit
2.88Mb	12 bit
0Mb < 16Mb	12 bit
> 16Mb	16 Bit

Understanding Sector Translation

Your computer records information about your hard disk in the CMOS setup information. Most systems support up to 47 different drive types. The drive type specifies the number of heads, sectors, and cylinders; the landing zone; and the disk's write precompensation cylinder. When you purchase a disk, your BIOS provides a disk type that matches your disk. If the BIOS does not provide a matching drive type, you can possibly upgrade your BIOS to one that supports the drive, use a third-party software program to supplement the available types, or use one of the existing drive types. If you choose the last option, however, you must choose a smaller-capacity drive, which means you will be wasting disk space. If you select a smaller drive type, make sure the type's head and sector valves correspond to your drive. Some IDE drives support sector translation, which lets them behave as if they were the drive type selected. To perform sector translation, the drive's controller converts BIOS logical sectors into its corresponding physical sectors. If your drive supports sector translation and its drive type is not listed in the BIOS setup options, use the disk type whose storage capacity is the closest to (but still less than) that of your disk.

FAT You Don't Want to Lose

Tip 349 shows the items DOS places on every disk: The boot record, one or more file allocation tables, the root directory, and space for your data. The file allocation table, or FAT, is the road map DOS uses to track your files. As discussed in Tip 503, DOS divides your disk into groups of multiple sectors called clusters or allocation units. Each time you store information in a file, DOS allocates one or more clusters to hold the file. The file allocation table tracks which clusters are in use, which are available for use, and which were marked as unusable by FORMAT. The following illustration shows an empty disk. As you can see, each file allocation table entry contains the value 0, which indicates that the cluster is available for use.

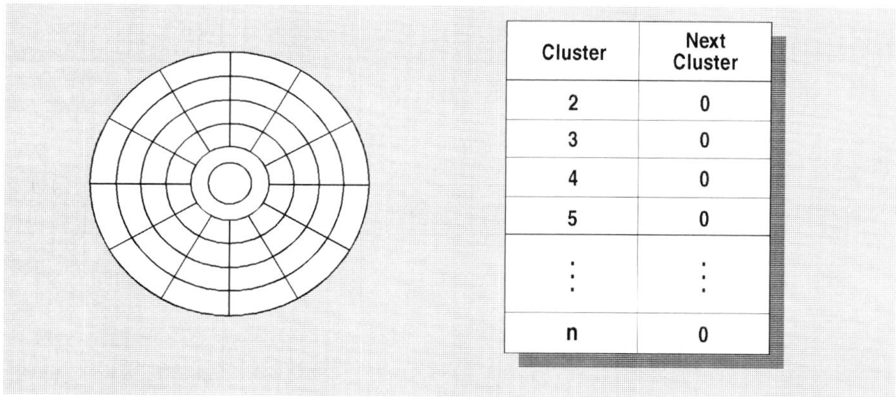

Cluster	Next Cluster
2	0
3	0
4	0
5	0
⋮	⋮
n	0

Assume that you create the file ONE.DAT that contains one cluster of data. DOS will allocate the first available cluster to the file (the first available cluster is always cluster 2). In the FAT, DOS marks the cluster as in use. In this case, as shown in the following illustration, DOS assigns the entry value FFF8, which tells DOS that the cluster is the file's only and/or ending) cluster.

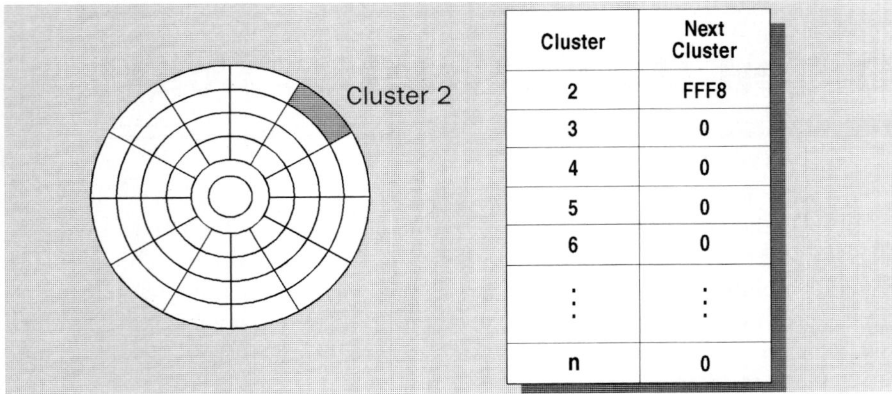

If you later increase the file's size beyond one cluster, DOS will allocate the next available cluster for the file, which in this case is cluster 3. When a file has multiple clusters, DOS creates a cluster chain. As the following illustration shows, if you start with cluster 2, the entry points to cluster 3, whose entry is FFF8, which tells DOS that it is the ending cluster.

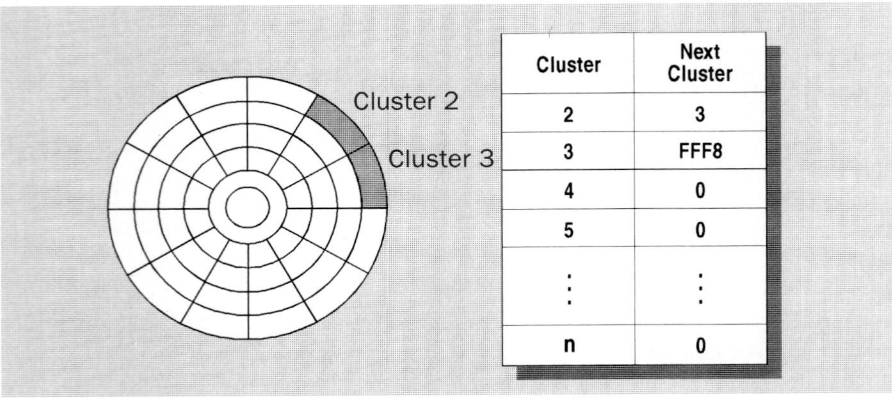

Next, assume you create a second file, named TWO.DAT, which requires one cluster. DOS will assign file cluster 4. If you later increase the size of your original file ONE.DAT, DOS will assign file cluster 5, which is the next available cluster. The following illustration shows the file allocation table state following these two operations:

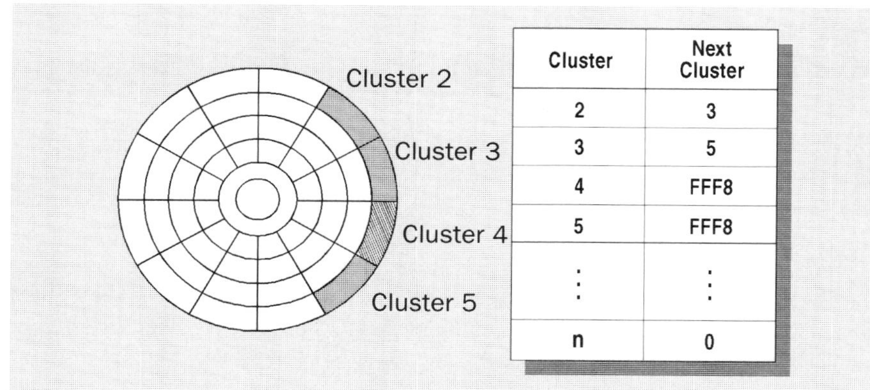

Cluster	Next Cluster
2	3
3	5
4	FFF8
5	FFF8
⋮	⋮
n	0

A Bad File Allocation Table

Tip 407 discusses the file allocation table in detail. The FAT provides DOS with a road map to which disk clusters correspond to which files on your disk. DOS stores the file allocation table on disk. Thus, the FAT is susceptible to disk errors that could destroy its contents and make it impossible for DOS to access your files. To reduce the possibility of such a disk error damaging your disk's FAT, DOS normally places two copies of the FAT on your disk. If the first copy gets damaged, DOS will use the second copy. You can determine the state of your file allocation table by using CHKDSK. If the first FAT has been damaged, CHKDSK will display the following error message:

```
File allocation table bad drive n:
```

Should this error message occur, immediately back up your files. If the backup operation is successful, format your disk to try to correct the error. If the error disappears, restore the disk's files from the backup disk. If the error persists, perform low-level formatting of your disk as discussed in Tip 387.

Using the utility command BOOTINFO presented in Tip 366, you can determine the number of file allocation tables on your disk as well as the number of sectors the FATs consume.

How DOS Tracks Damaged Locations on Your Disk

Tip 407 discusses the file allocation table in detail. The FAT tracks the clusters assigned to each file, the clusters available for reuse, and damaged clusters marked unusable by the FORMAT command. The following illustration shows a disk with two damaged clusters: 3 and 7. Within the file allocation table, DOS indicates the damaged cluster by using the value FFF7.

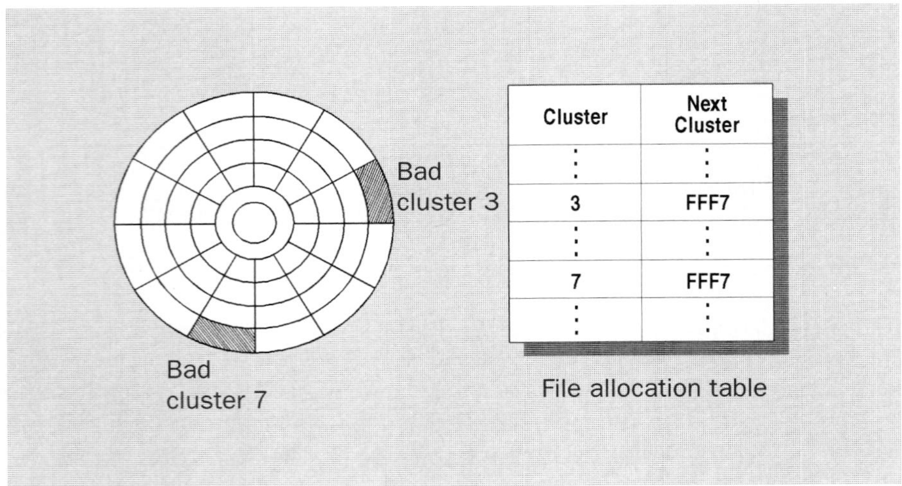

By marking each damaged cluster in this way, FORMAT ensures that DOS won't allocate a damaged cluster to a file for storing information. When you execute the CHKDSK command, CHKDSK examines the file allocation table for entries marked FFF7. CHKDSK uses these entries to determine the number of damaged sectors on your disk and then displays the following message:

```
nnnn bytes in bad sectors
```

The only time a cluster gets marked as unusable is during a disk format operation. If DOS tries to read or write a sector and the operation fails, DOS will not mark the clusters as damaged until the next format operation.

How Do the Damaged Disk Locations Identified by Low-Level Formatting Correspond to FORMAT's Bad Clusters?

Tip 387 discusses low-level disk format operations, which let you enter known disk defects and search your disk for others. The low-level format operation lays out your disk's sectors and tracks. If a low-level format operation identifies a disk defect, it skips the defect and assigns the next consecutive sector to the next usable location. When the low-level format operation completes, it considers every sector usable. The FORMAT command, in turn, examines each sector to ensure that the sector can be read from and written to. If a sector fails, FORMAT marks the sector's corresponding cluster as unusable. Thus, the defects recorded by the low-level format operation and the clusters marked as invalid by FORMAT are not related. In addition to examining each sector, FORMAT also writes the disk's boot record, file allocation tables, and root directories to the disk.

The Ideal Floppy Disk Drive

If you don't already have 5 1/4- and 3 1/2-inch drives, or if you do and you need one of the slots for a tape drive or CD-ROM, a new disk drive type provides the ideal solution. As shown here, the drive combines 5 1/4- and 3 1/2-inch drives into a half-height form factor.

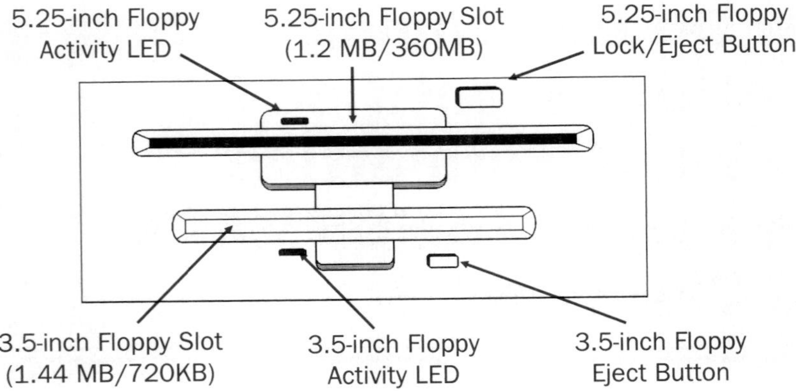

Depending on how you cable the drives, you can select which drive you want as drive A or B. The drive should be fully compatible with your existing controller and does not require unique device drivers.

TIP 412 What Are Hard Disk Cards?

If your hard disk is running out of space, or if you want an easy way to back up key files, consider purchasing a hard disk card. As shown here, a hard disk card is an expansion board that contains a drive controller and disk. Hard disk cards can range in size from 70Mb to more than 100Mb.

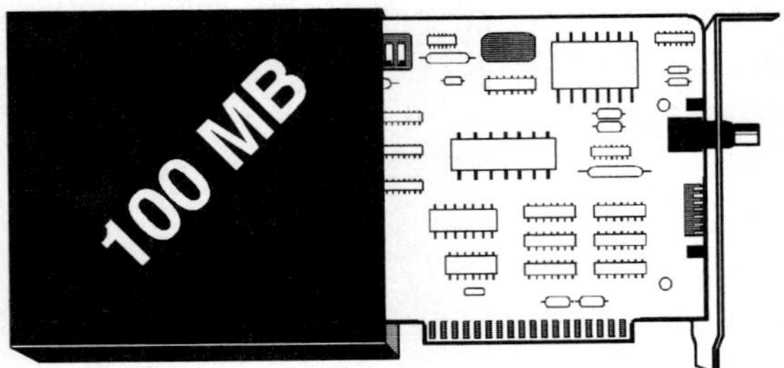

Depending on your board and the size of the disk drive, the hard disk card may require one-and-a-half or two expansion slots. If the board requires only one-and-a-half slots, you can still place a half-length card next to the hard disk card. Because they require time and floppy disk management, most users fail to perform backup operations each day. If you install a hard disk card, you can quickly copy key files to a second drive at the end of the day. Although such a backup file won't protect your files from fire or theft, it at least puts a copy of them on a second disk, preventing the information from being lost or destroyed by an errant DOS command or a disk failure.

Unwrite-Protecting 3 1/2-Inch Disks

Many users have older software programs stored on write-protected 3 1/2-inch disks. To prevent users from accidentally overwriting the disk's contents, many software companies removed the disk's write-protect shutter from the disk. If you no longer need the information stored on these disks, you can make the disks writable by applying a piece of dark electrical tape or a write-protect tab for a 5 1/4-inch disk over the write-protect opening as shown here:

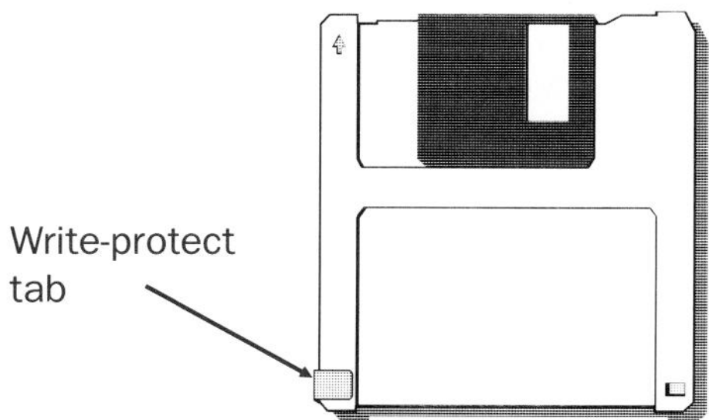

To determine whether a disk is write-protected, a 3 1/2-inch drive sends a light through the disk's write-protect opening. If the light passes through the opening, the disk is write-protected. By placing dark tape over the disk's write-protect opening, you prevent the light from passing through.

Permanently Write-Protecting a 3 1/2-Inch Disk

If you are preparing a 3 1/2-inch disk for a new user and you don't want the user to be able to change the disk's contents, remove the disk's write-protect shutter as shown here:

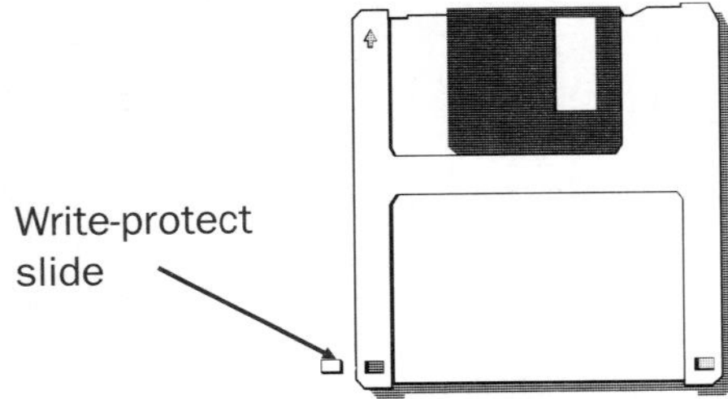

To determine whether a disk is write-protected, a 3 1/2-inch drive sends a light through the disk's write-protect opening. If the light passes through the opening, the disk is write-protected. By removing the write-protect shutter, you ensure that the user cannot accidently make the disk writeable. Should you ever need to change the disk's contents, see Tip 413.

Cleaning Floppy Drives

Like all of your PC's components, your floppy disk drives are susceptible to dust and smoke. Thus, depending on your computer's environment, you should clean the

floppy drives every three to six months. Most computer stores sell floppy drive cleaners, which look much like a floppy disk. Rather than containing a magnetic disk, the cleaner contains a soft pad to which you can apply a cleaning solvent. Normally, you insert the disk cleaner into the drive for a few seconds. As the cleaner spins in the drive, the cleaner removes dust and other particles. If your drive begins to experience errors with a number of floppy disks, try cleaning the drive. Normally, however, you can easily go six months without cleaning the drive. In fact, most drives are never cleaned.

Organizing Your Disks with a Disk Caddie

Almost all users have used 5 1/4- or 3 1/2-inch disk storage cases, like those that come with new packages of disks, to hold their floppy disks. Unfortunately, most users use the cases only for long-term disk storage.

When most users work, you can normally find floppy disks strewn across their desks. Unfortunately, many of their disks are later damaged by spills, by the telephone, or by objects being placed on top of them. Luckily, for about $5 you can purchase a disk rack that attaches directly to your monitor or chassis as shown here:

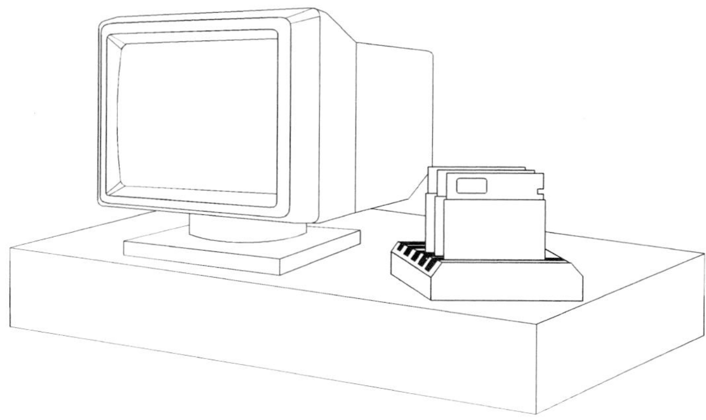

Not only does the rack keep your disk organized, it reduces the possibility of disk damage. You should, however, still use the covered disk cases for long-term floppy storage.

If you use a disk rack, do not place your phone, external speakers, or other devices near the rack.

Bringing Bent Disks Back to Life

If your letter carrier has a Macintosh, which uses 3 1/2 inch disks, he or she may not appreciate the fact that bending a 5 1/4-inch floppy disk in half and squeezing the disk into your mailbox is not a good solution. Luckily, however, you can often bring such bent floppies back to life. If the disk is only slightly bent, you may be able to smooth out the disk jacket by gently moving the disk against a straight edge, such as your desk. If the jacket is crushed, you may be able to gently remove the disk from the damaged jacket and place it in a different jacket. To do so, follow these steps:

- Using a sharp blade such as an Exacto knife, carefully cut back the fold along one of the jacket edges of the damaged disk and of an unused floppy disk. Unfold the edge so you can remove the media.
- Touching the disk media as little as possible (ideally, not at all), slide the disks out of their jackets.
- Again touching the damaged floppy as little as possible, gently insert the disk into the second jacket. Carefully tape the edges of the disk jacket closed.

If you have been careful and are lucky, DOS can now read the disk's contents, letting you copy it to another disk.

Reducing the Possibility of Formatting a Disk Accidentally

Depending on your DOS version, you FORMAT command may first prompt you to type the disk volume label before it will format your hard disk. If your DOS version provides this capability, use the LABEL command to assign a label to your disk. The label can contain up to 11 characters. To reduce the possibility of format your disk accidentally, place the ALT+255 character at the end of the label name. Tip 506 discusses the ALT+255 character in detail. Use the LABEL command to assign the volume label to your disk:

```
C:\> LABEL <ENTER>
```

Understanding the Extra Hidden File

To be bootable, a DOS disk must contain the two hidden system files I0.SYS and MSDOS.SYS. If you invoke the CHKDSK command, CHKDSK will report the number of hidden files on your disk as shown here:

```
nnnn bytes in 3 hidden files
```

In many cases, CHKDSK will report three hidden files rather than two. In most cases, the third hidden file is actually your disk's volume label. Prior to version 5, DOS stored the volume label as a hidden root directory entry. Beginning with DOS 5, however, DOS stores the volume label in the disk's book sector. Thus, if you are trying to determine what the third hidden file on your disk is, it's probably the volume label.

Compressing Everything on Your Disk

If you are like most users, you can probably fill up any size of hard disk. Unfortunately, constantly upgrading your hard disk can become expensive. One popular solution to the disk storage problem is compressing all the information on the disk on the fly and then decompressing the data later when you need to use it. Tip 509 presents two utility commands provided on this book's companion disk that let you compress and later decompress files as you require.

You can also use third-party disk products that compress everything written to your disk. One of the most popular is a product named STACKER. If you have available hardware slots, you can install a STACKER board and a device driver that work together to compress and decompress all disk I/O operations. If you don't have an available slot, you can also buy a version of STACKER that comes as software. The advantage of the hardware board is speed and less memory consumption. Both versions support DOS as well as Windows. If you find yourself in a disk space crunch, STACKER may help you solve the problem. However, like all good things, STACKER's disk compression does add system overhead, which slows your disk I/O operations.

Understanding Disk Serial Numbers

Beginning with DOS version 4, the FORMAT command adds serial numbers to your disks. When you issue the DIR command, DIR displays the disk's serial number as shown here:

```
C:\DOS> DIR <ENTER>

 Volume in drive C has no label
 Volume Serial Number is 16F6-3B73
 Directory of C:\DOS
```

If you copy a floppy disk by using the DISKCOPY command, DISKCOPY will assign a different serial number to the copy. Some programs check the serial number of a floppy disk to ensure that you have the original disk in drive A. Because you should never have to work with original disks, you can use this book's companion disk utility command, SETSER#.EXE, to assign the original disk's serial number to the current disk. To assign a serial number, select the desired drive as the default drive and then invoke SETSER# with the desired serial number as shown here:

```
A:\> SETSER#  1234-5678 <ENTER>
```

Listing SETSER#.EXE

The utility command SETSER#.EXE resides on the companion disk that accompanies this book.

SETSER#.EXE

Huge Partitions Can Waste Huge Amounts of Space

DOS 4 was the first DOS version to allow partitions larger than 32Mb. With DOS 4, a partition can contain 512Mb. If you are using DOS 5, a partition can contain up to 2Gb! To support these large partitions, DOS increases the number of sectors in each disk cluster. As discussed in Tip 503, every file on your disk requires at least one disk cluster. The larger the cluster size, the larger the amount of wasted space on your disk. When you first partition and format your disk, use CHKDSK to determine the disk's cluster size. If the cluster size is larger than 4096, strongly consider further dividing the disk into smaller partitions. Otherwise, you'll end up wasting a lot of disk space.

Pay Attention to Early Signs of an Imminent Disk Failure

In most cases, a hard disk will give you early signs that it is failing, rather than just suddenly stopping. Some of the error signals will be obvious. The disk will experience read, write, or seek errors that are detected by DOS. Other signals may be more subtle. For example, your disk may become noisy, or you may have to power your system off and on several times before it boots, or files or programs may take longer to load. As a rule, the more often you execute the CHKDSK command, the greater your chance of early disk error detection. Pay attention to your disk's subtle signals. If any of these warning signals occur, make sure you have a complete set of backup disks.

Rewriting the Master Boot Record

Tip 351 discusses the master boot record in detail. In addition to containing your disk's partition information, the master boot record contains the instructions used to boot your computer (actually the instructions that select the bootable partition). If your system fails to boot, these instructions may have been overwritten by an errant program, a disk error, or a virus. If you are using DOS 5, the FDISK command lets you restore these instructions if you use the /MBR switch as shown here:

```
A> FDISK /MBR <ENTER>
```

When you specify the /MBR switch, FDISK will restore the instructions without changing any of the partition table information.

Getting Back to Drive C from an Empty Floppy Drive

If your system prompt uses $P to display the current directory and you select an empty floppy drive as the current drive, DOS will display the following error message:

```
Not ready reading drive A
Abort, Retry, Fail?
```

If you select the Abort option, DOS will repeatedly display the error message. If you insert a floppy disk in the drive, you can select either Abort or Retry to continue. If you don't have a floppy disk handy, select the Fail option. DOS will change your prompt to the following:

```
Current drive is no longer valid>
```

From this prompt you can select the drive you desire. By using the Fail option in this way, you don't have to find a floppy disk to continue.

Viewing Your Disk Drive Information

There may be times when you need to determine specifics about the current drive. One way to view disk specifics is to invoke CHKDSK. However, depending on your disk size, CHKDSK may take considerable time to execute. As a solution, invoke the companion disk utility command SHOWDRV.EXE as shown here:

```
C:\> SHOWDRVS <ENTER>
Drive       Size          Available      Sector       Cluster
Letter      Bytes         Bytes          Size         Size
C:          200065024     3912700        512          4096
```

Using SHOWDRV, you can quickly display specifics about your disk.

SHOWDRV.EXE

The utility command SHOWDRV.EXE resides on the companion disk that accompanies this book.

Solving Disk Errors on PCs that Stand on Their Sides

Tip 850 discusses how placing a PC next to or under your desk can free workspace. In the past, some users who have placed PCs on their sides have encountered disk errors. Here's why. The low-level formatting process lays down the information your disk controller uses to locate tracks and sectors on the disk. If you perform low-level formatting on your disk with the PC chassis flat and then turn the disk on its side, the disk controller may have problems locating its layout information. If you plan to place a PC in a vertical stand, first perform a low-level format operation on the disk with the PC standing vertically.

A Simplified FORMAT Command for Use in Batch Files

By default, when you format a floppy disk, FORMAT will prompt you to insert a disk in the drive and enter a volume label if you did not specify one; then FORMAT asks you whether you want to format a second disk. If you are using DOS 4 or 5, you can add the /AUTOTEST switch to your FORMAT command to eliminate these prompts. The following batch file, FASTFMAT.BAT, uses the /AUTOTEST switch to format the floppy disk in drive A:

```
@ECHO OFF
FORMAT A: /AUTOTEST
```

Before you invoke FASTFMAT, make sure you have a disk in drive A; neither the batch file nor FORMAT will prompt you for one. If you need to add other switches to the FORMAT command, such as /S or /4, do so.

To use FORMAT /AUTOTEST switch, you must be using DOS 4 or higher.

A Faster FORMAT Command that Adds a Disk Label

Tip 428 describes how to use FORMAT's /AUTOTEST under DOS 4 and 5 to perform a format operation for which FORMAT displays minimum system prompts. In some cases, however, you may want to ensure that the user specifies a disk volume label. If you are using DOS 4, use FORMAT's /SELECT switch to suppress FORMAT's prompts other than the request for a disk volume label. The following batch file, V4FMTLBL.BAT, illustrates how you would use FORMAT's /SELECT switch to prompt the user for a volume label if the user does not specify one in the batch command line:

```
@ECHO OFF
IF '%1'=='' FORMAT A: /SELECT
IF NOT '%1'='' FORMAT A: /V:%1 /SELECT
```

To use FORMAT's /SELECT switch to prompt for a volume name, you must be using DOS 4. If you are using DOS 5, using the /SELECT switch directs FORMAT to place the file MIRROR.FIL on the target disk.

Displaying Partition Table Information with UNFORMAT

Tip 369 discusses disk partitions in detail. If you are using DOS 5, you can use UNFORMAT's /PARTN and /L switches to display the partition table information as shown here:

```
C:\> UNFORMAT C: /PARTN /L <ENTER>
Hard Disk Partition Table display.

Drive # 636h has 815 cylinders, 15 heads, 32 sectors (from BIOS).
```

The following table is from drive 80h, cylinder 0, head 0, sector 1:

```
Type  Total_size       Start_partition  End_partition
Rel#  Bytes   Sectors  Cyl Head  Sector Cyl  Head  Sector HUGE  Boot
      191M    391168   0   1     1      814  14    32     32
```

Using the DOS output redirection operator, you may want to print a copy of your partition table information by entering the command shown here:

```
C:\> UNFORMAT C: /PARTN /L > PRN <ENTER>
```

To use the UNFORMAT command, you must be using DOS 5.

Determining the Last Drive

The CONFIG.SYS LASTDRIVE entry lets you specify the drive letter of the last valid drive that DOS can reference. If you are creating a batch file that uses SUBST to assign

a directory to a logical drive, you may need to determine the last available drive letter. The companion disk that accompanies this book provides the utility command LASTDRIV.EXE that returns an exit status value that corresponds to the last drive letter where the value 0 corresponds to A, 1 to B, and so on up to value 25, which corresponds to Z. The following batch commands use LASTDRIV to verify whether a drive letter greater than E exists:

```
@ECHO OFF
LASTDRIV
IF ERRORLEVEL 5 GOTO DRIVE_F_OR_MORE
REM Other commands here
```

The utility command LASTDRIV.EXE resides on the disk that accompanies this book.

LASTDRIV.EXE

Determining the Next Available Logical Drive Letter

Tip 453 discusses the SUBST command that lets you use logical drive letters to abbreviate directory names. If you are assigning logical drives for use in a batch file, the batch file should not make assumptions about the next available drive letter. Instead, your batch file should use the companion disk utility NEXTLOG.EXE, which assigns the drive letter of the next available logical drive to the environment entry NEXT_LOGICAL. If no logical drives are available, the entry is undefined. The following batch commands use NEXTLOG to determine the next available logical drive. The batch file then uses the SUBST command to assign the directory C:\DOS to the logical drive.

```
@ECHO OFF
NEXTLOG
IF '%NEXT_LOGICAL%'=='' GOTO NO_LOGICAL_DRIVES
SUBST %NEXT_LOGICAL% C:\DOS
ECHO Drive used %NEXT_LOGICAL%
SET NEXT_LOGICAL=
GOTO DONE
:NO_LOGICAL_DRIVES
ECHO No available logical drives
:DONE
```

If NEXTLOG successfully adds the environment entry, it returns the exit status 0. If the environment is full, it returns the exit status 1.

NEXTLOG.EXE

The utility command NEXTLOG.EXE resides on the companion disk that accompanies this book.

Am I Connected to Network Drives?

If you work in a local area network environment, you may have files on a local drive as well as on a remote network drive. In most cases, before you can use the network, you must log on. If you have been working on and off of the network, you can use the companion disk utility NETDRIVE.EXE to display the network drives, if any, to which you are connected, as shown here:

```
C:\> NETDRIVE <ENTER>
Drive F:
Drive G:
```

By using NETDRIVE in this way, you won't try to log on to the network if you are already connected.

NETDRIVE.EXE

The utility command NETDRIVE.EXE resides on the companion disk that accompanies this book.

Fixing the Probable Non-DOS Disk Error

As discussed in Tip 644, every DOS disk type has a unique identifier called a media descriptor. DOS stores the media descriptor in the first byte of the file allocation table (the FAT). If a DOS application displays the following error message, the media descriptor value may have been corrupted, possibly by a virus:

```
Probable Non-DOS disk
```

If this error message occurs, you may be able to display and edit the media descriptor value by using DEBUG. To do so, invoke DEBUG from the DOS prompt:

```
C:\> DEBUG <ENTER>
```

When DEBUG displays its hyphen prompt, issue one of the commands listed in Table 434a to load the start of the file allocation table into memory.

Table 434a. DEBUG Commands to Load the Start of the File Allocation Table into Memory

Disk	DEBUG Command
A	L 100 0 1 1
B	L 100 1 1 1
C	L 100 2 1 1

Next, use the following Enter command to view the disk's media descriptor value:

```
-E 300 <ENTER>
1234:01000 F0:
```

The byte value listed should correspond to one of the media descriptor values listed in Table 434b.

Table 434b. Media Descriptor Values for Different Disk Types

Disk Type	Media Descriptor
1.44Mb or 2.88Mb	F0
Hard disk	F8
720Mb or 1.2Mb	F9
320Kb	FA
180Kb	FC
360Kb	FD
160Kb	FE
320Kb	FF

If the value does not match one of the media descriptors listed, type the correct media descriptor for the disk type and press ENTER. If the value is correct, simply press ENTER. If you changed the media descriptor value, issue one of the commands listed in Table 434c to write the descriptor back to disk.

If the correction works, you were lucky! If it does not, you'll probably have to format your disk and restore backup copies of your files.

Table 434c. DEBUG Commands to Write the Updated File Allocation Table Back to Disk

Disk	DEBUG Command
A	W 100 0 1 1
B	W 100 1 1 1
C	W 100 2 1 1

Displaying the File Allocation Table Type

As Tip 405 discusses depending on your disk type, DOS uses 12- or 16-bit file allocation table entries. When you partition a hard disk, you normally want to keep the partition sizes such that DOS will use

the 16-bit FAT. To help you determine your disk's FAT type, the companion disk that accompanies this book contains the utility command FAT_TYPE.EXE, which displays the file allocation table type for the current disk as shown here:

```
C:\> FAT_TYPE <ENTER>
Current file allocation type: 16-bit.
```

If you are using FAT_TYPE from within a DOS batch file, FAT_TYPE also returns the value 12 or 16, depending on the FAT type, as an exit status value.

FAT_TYPE.EXE

The utility command FAT_TYPE.EXE resides on the companion disk that accompanies this book.

Quickly Selecting a Drive or Directory

If you work within the DOS shell, you know that you can quickly select a disk drive by holding down the CTRL key and pressing the corresponding drive letter. Tip 311 explains how the ANSI driver lets you assign commands to different key combinations. Using the following ANSI escape sequences, you can direct DOS to select drive A (from the DOS prompt) if you press ALT-A, drive B if you press ALT-B, and so on:

```
SET SAVE_PROMPT=%PROMPT%
PROMPT $E[0;30;"A:$_"p
PROMPT $E[0;48;"B:$_"p
PROMPT $E[0;46;"C:$_"p
PROMPT %SAVE_PROMPT%
SET SAVE_PROMPT=
```

Tip 495 uses SUBST to create logical drive letters for your commonly used directories. Using escape sequences similar to those listed above, you can quickly change directories by using an ALT-*key* combination.

A Low-Disk-Space Warning

Depending on your batch file commands, you sometimes may want the batch file to warn you when your disk space drops below a specific level.

The companion disk that accompanies this book contains the utility command DISKLOW.EXE that returns the exit status value 1 if the current disk space is less than the value specified and returns 0 otherwise. Specify the disk size in kilobytes. Table 437 lists several example DISKLOW commands.

Table 437. Sample DISKLOW Commands

Command	Disk Space Tested
DISKLOW 256	256Kb
DISKLOW 1024	1,024Kb or 1Mb
DISKLOW 4096	4,096Kb or 4Mb

The following batch commands use DISKLOW to notify you when disk space falls below 2Mb:

```
@ECHO OFF
DISKLOW 2048
IF ERRORLEVEL 1 GOTO NOTIFY_USER
REM Other commands here
```

DISKLOW.EXE

The utility command DISKLOW.EXE resides on the companion disk that accompanies this book.

Is This Drive a CD-ROM?

In many ways, a CD-ROM drive behaves similarly to a DOS disk. You can select the CD-ROM drive as the current disk, select directories on the drive, or run programs or copy files the disk contains. However, you cannot create files on the drive. In your batch files, therefore, you may need to change drives if a batch file command will create a file. To help you determine whether the current drive is a CD-ROM, your batch files can use the companion disk utility ISCDROM.EXE. If the current drive is a CD-ROM, the program returns the exit status value 1; otherwise, it returns the exit status value 0. The following batch commands use ISCDROM to determine whether the current drive is a CD-ROM:

```
@ECHO OFF
ISCDROM
IF ERRORLEVEL 1 ECHO Drive is a CD-ROM
IF NOT ERRORLEVEL 1 ECHO Drive is not a CD-ROM
```

The utility command ISCDROM.EXE resides on the companion disk that accompanies this book.

ISCDROM.EXE

For a Single-Drive Copy Operation, Use XCOPY

If your system has a single floppy drive and you need to copy one floppy disk's contents to another, you can do so by using the drives' logical A and B names. The following COPY and XCOPY commands would both work:

```
C:\> COPY A:*.* B:*.* <ENTER>
C:\> XCOPY A:*.* B:*.* <ENTER>
```

If you are copying more than one file, the best way to perform this operation is to use XCOPY. The COPY command copies only one file's contents at a time. As a result, you must repeatedly exchange the floppy disks between drives A and B. XCOPY, on the other hand, reads as many files into memory as it can before prompting you to exchange disks. In addition, if you need to copy files that reside in subdirectories, XCOPY's /S switch lets you do just that.

Handling a Spill on a Floppy Disk

Although most computer books warn users to keep sodas and other drinks away from their PCs, it is almost inevitable that a soda can or coffee cup will tip over on a desk, possibly on top of a 5 1/4-inch floppy. If the liquid gets on only the disk envelope and jacket, use a napkin or paper towel to gently blot up the spill. If the spill gets on the disk media, drying and leaving the disk sticky, do not use the disk. Instead, follow the steps presented in Tip 417 to remove the disk from the jacket. Next, holding the disk by its hub, run a soft stream of warm water over the disk's surface. After the disk dries, gently insert the disk in a new jacket (again following the steps presented in Tip 417). Copy the information on the floppy disk to a new disk.

Removable Disk Media

If you have a PC at home and at the office, you have probably experienced the frustration of having a file you desperately need at the other location. With the decrease in the cost of disk storage media, many users are choosing removable hard drives or hard drive cartridges. The following illustration shows a commonly used disk cartridge and a removable drive:

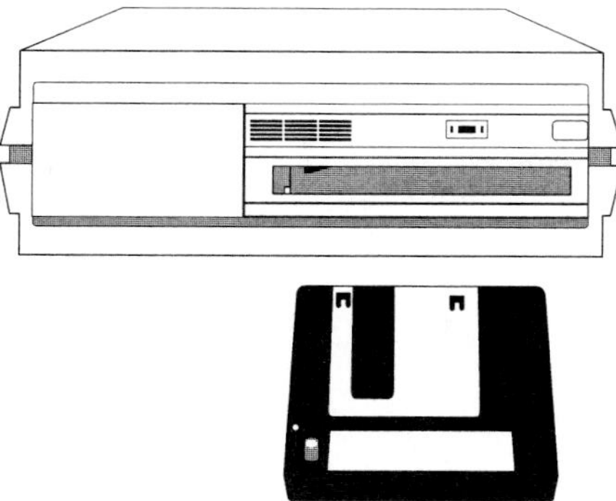

Recently, hard drive cartridges capable of providing more than 90Mb of disk space have become readily available. Although you need to treat the media with care, you can quickly be on the road with the files or programs you need. If you work on projects at home and at the office and you don't want to carry your PC or a handful of floppy disks with you, removable hard disk media provide an excellent alternative.

PART 5

Directory

Viewing Directories in Lowercase

By default, DIR displays directory listings using uppercase letters. Beginning with DOS 5, DIR lets you view directories using lowercase letters. To do so, invoke DIR using the /L switch as shown here:

```
C:\> DIR /L <ENTER>
```

If you always want to display your filenames in lowercase letter, assign the /L switch to the DIRCMD environment entry in your AUTOEXEC.BAT file by using SET as shown here:

```
SET DIRCMD=/L
```

If you want to be able to display directory listings in uppercase or lowercase letters, leave the DIRCMD entry alone and use DOSKEY to create a macro named LODIR, as shown here, that displays the directory listing in lowercase letters:

```
C:\> DOSKEY LODIR=DIR /L <ENTER>
```

To display a directory listing in lowercase, you must be using DOS 5.

Renaming a Directory

The RENAME command lets you change a file's name. RENAME, however, does not let you rename a directory. If you want to change the name of a directory, one way to do so is by creating a new directory, copying to the directory the files from the current directory and then removing the old directory and its files. Unfortunately, not only is this process time consuming, it may fail if your disk does not have enough space to hold the duplicate files. If you are using DOS

5, you can rename a directory by using the DOS shell. To do so invoke DOSSHELL from the DOS prompt as shown here:

```
C:\> DOSSHELL <ENTER>
```

Next, press the TAB and arrow keys to highlight the desired directory name from the list of directories. Press the ALT-F keyboard combination to select the File menu and choose the Rename option. DOS will display the Rename Directory dialog box as shown here:

Rename Directory

Current name: DOSTIPS

New name. .

OK Cancel Help

Type the desired directory name and press ENTER. DOS will rename your directory as desired. To exit the DOS shell, press F3.

Cleaning Up Your Root Directory

As a rule, the only two files that should reside in your hard disk's root directory are CONFIG.SYS and AUTOEXEC.BAT. All other root directory entries should correspond to directories. If your root directory contains other files, move the files to an appropriate directory. If you move the file COMMAND.COM from the root directory, you must place a SHELL= entry in your CONFIG.SYS file that describes the file's location. After you move all other files from the root, examine the PATH command in your AUTOEXEC.BAT file. If the PATH command includes the root directory, remove the directory from the path. Because the root no longer contains files, there is no reason for DOS to search it.

How Many Files Should a Directory Contain?

DOS provides directories to help you organize the files on your disk. Although most users know they should create and use directories, they don't always know when they should further divide a directory into additional subdirectories.

For most application programs, such as WordPerfect or Lotus 1-2-3, you cannot move the program files to additional directories, because the programs look for files in specific locations. If you were to move the files, the programs would not work. However, with respect to your program data, you can better organize the files by creating additional directories.

The number of files you place in a directory should be controlled by your goal of preventing disk fragmentation (see Tip 347). When a directory becomes fragmented, its corresponding sectors are dispersed across your disk, thereby requiring more time for the drive to read the directory. To determine how many entries a directory can hold before becoming fragmented, divide the disk's cluster size by 32 (the size of a directory entry) as shown here:

$$\text{Directory Entries} = \frac{\text{Disk cluster size}}{32}$$

Using The CHKDSK command, you can display a disk's cluster (allocation unit) size as shown here:

```
C:\> CHKDSK <ENTER>

Volume DOS 5 DISK  created 04-18-1992 4:43p
Volume Serial Number is 16F6-3B73

 200065024 bytes total disk space
   4276224 bytes in 3 hidden files
   1638400 bytes in 380 directories
 178151424 bytes in 8354 user files
  15998976 bytes available on disk

      4096 bytes in each allocation unit
     48844 total allocation units on disk
      3906 available allocation units on disk
    655360 total bytes memory
    541744 bytes free
```

Given a 4,096-byte cluster, the number of entries a directory can hold without becoming fragmented is the following:

$$\text{Entries} = \frac{4096}{32} = 128$$

If your directory becomes fragmented, your system performance will suffer every time DOS must search the directory.

Optimizing Directory Order in Your Command Path

When you issue a command, DOS first checks whether the command is internal. If it is, DOS executes it. If it is not internal, DOS searches the current or the specified directory for a matching COM, EXE, or BAT file. If DOS finds a matching file, DOS executes it; otherwise, DOS starts searching the directories listed in the command path.

The PATH command defines your command path. If you examine your AUTOEXEC.BAT file, you will usually find a PATH command. When you first installed DOS on your system, the PATH command probably contained only the DOS directory. As you installed other software, the installation programs probably added entries to the path. Today, most users' command paths reference several directories.

When DOS searches the command path, it searches the entries in order, from first to last. You should examine your current command path to make sure the directories that appear at the start of the command path are the directories most likely to contain your commonly used commands. If the most commonly used directories are not first, change the PATH command. Otherwise, DOS will spend considerable time searching unnecessary directories.

Moving COMMAND.COM from the Root Directory

As Tip 444 explains, the only two files that should reside in your disk's root directory are AUTOEXEC.BAT and CONFIG.SYS. By using the CONFIG.SYS SHELL entry, you can direct DOS to use the copy of COMMAND.COM that resides in your disk's DOS directory. This way, you can clean up the root directory, freeing disk space by eliminating the duplicate COMMAND.COM. The following SHELL entry directs DOS to use the copy of COMMAND.COM that resides in the DOS directory:

```
SHELL=C:\DOS\COMMAND.COM  C:\DOS  /P
```

The entry tells DOS where to locate COMMAND.COM and what value to assign to the COMSPEC environment entry (see Tip 8); then it tells DOS to execute AUTOEXEC.BAT. If you want to increase the environment size, you can do so using the SHELL entry (see Tip 13).

Displaying Directory and Subdirectory Listings

The DIR command displays the directory listing for files on your disk. In the past, DIR displayed information only about files residing in the current or specified directory. Under DOS 5, however, the /S switch directs DIR to display information about files residing in subdirectories as well. For example, the following DIR command displays the files that reside in the current directory as well as files that reside in subdirectories beneath the current directory:

```
C:\SUBDIR> DIR /S <ENTER>
```

If the current directory is the root, or if you specify the root directory as shown next, DOS will display the directory listing for every file on your disk:

```
C:\SUBDIR> DIR \*.* /S <ENTER>
```

The following DOSKEY command creates a macro named SUBDIR that uses the DIR /S switch:

```
C:\> DOSKEY SUBDIR=DIR /S <ENTER>
```

To use the DIR /S switch or DOSKEY, you must be using DOS 5 or higher.

Managing the DOS Directory

Virtually every DOS user includes the DOS directory in the command path. Thus, for almost every external command you execute, DOS searches the DOS directory. By managing the files the DOS directory contains, you can improve system performance. The directory contains several files that most users won't need regularly. To improve performance, you can move these files into other subdirectories or onto a floppy disk. The following DOS files are needed only by users requiring international DOS support:

COUNTRY.SYS	EGA.SYS	NLSFUNC.COM
DISPLAY.SYS	EGA.CPI	KEYB.COM
KEYBOARD.SYS	4201.CPI	4208.CPI
5202.CPI	LCD.CPI	PRINTER.SYS

The following files are needed only by users wanting to use the DOS 5 shell:

DOSSHELL.VID	DOSSHELL.COM	DOSSHELL.EXE
DOSSHELL.GRB	DOSSWAP.EXE	DOSSHELL.HLP
DOSSHELL.INI		

The following programs are needed only by users wanting to program in BASIC:

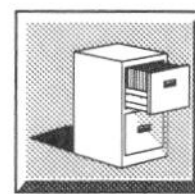

QBASIC.HLP	GORILLA.BAS	MONEY.BAS
NIBBLES.BAS	REMLINE.BAS	

If you don't plan to use EDIT or EDLIN, you can move the following files:

EDLIN.COM	EDIT.COM	EDIT.HLP
QBASIC.EXE		

DOS 5 includes several files with the TXT or LST extension. After you have read or printed these files, you should consider moving or deleting them too. By eliminating unneccessary files from the DOS directory, you decrease the amount of time DOS spends searching through files, which improves your system performance.

TIP 450 Copying an Entire Directory to Floppy Disks

Users often need to copy files that reside in a directory on their hard disk to one or more floppy disks. Because they need a way to continue the copy operation when the floppy disk fills up, users must use the ATTRIB and XCOPY commands. To begin, select the directory containing the files you want to copy by using the CHDIR command. Next, issue the following ATTRIB command to set the archive attribute of each file. The XCOPY command will later use the archive attribute to determine which files it has and has not copied.

```
C:\SUBDIR> ATTRIB +A *.* /S <ENTER>
```

The /S switch directs ATTRIB to also set the attribute for files that reside in subdirectories beneath the directory. You should only include this switch if you are using DOS 3.3 or higher.

Next, place a floppy disk in drive A and issue the following XCOPY command:

```
C:\> XCOPY *.* A: /M /S <ENTER>
```

As XCOPY successfully copies a file, it will remove the file's archive required attribute. As before, the /S switch directs XCOPY to copy files that reside in subdirectories beneath the directory. When the floppy disk fills up, DOS will display the following message:

```
Insufficient disk space
```

Insert a new floppy disk in drive A and repeat the previous XCOPY command. Because XCOPY has been changing each file's archive attribute, it knows where to continue the copy operation. Depending on the number and size of files you are copying, you may have to issue the XCOPY command for several floppy disks.

Defining DOS 5 DIR Command Options

Beginning with DOS 5, the DIR command supports several command switches that control the order, files, and directories DIR uses to display directory listings. Table 451 briefly describes these switches.

After you select the switch combination you want to use regularly, you can assign the switches to the DIRCMD environment entry. For example, the following SET command assigns DIRCMD the /L and /O:N switches (see Tip 454 for other switches for /O), directing DIR to display the directory list in lowercase letters, sorted by name:

```
C:\> SET DIRCMD=/L /O:N <ENTER>
```

Most users will place a similar SET command in their AUTOEXEC.BAT file.

To use the DIRCMD environment entry, you must be using DOS 5.

Table 451. DOS 5 DIR Command-line Switches

Switch	Purpose
/P	Directs DIR to pause on each screenful of files until the user presses a key
/W	Directs DIR to display filenames only
/A	Directs DIR to display only files matching the attributes specified
/O	Specifies the desired sort order
/B	Directs DIR to display filenames only
/S	Directs DIR to display files stored in lower-level subdirectories
/L	Directs DIR to display the directory listing in lowercase letters

Hiding a Directory

If you are using DOS 5, you can use the ATTRIB command to hide a file (preventing the file from appearing in directory listings or being affected by DOS commands) as shown here:

```
C:\> ATTRIB +H FILENAME.EXT <ENTER>
```

To unhide the file at a later time, you can use ATTRIB as follows:

```
C:\> ATTRIB -H FILENAME.EXT <ENTER>
```

Unfortunately, ATTRIB does not let you hide and unhide directories. However, the companion disk that accompanies this book provides the utility command HIDEDIR.EXE that lets you hide and unhide a directory. To hide a directory named data, you would invoke HIDEDIR as follows:

```
C:\> HIDEDIR +H DATA <ENTER>
```

To later unhide the directory, you can use HIDEDIR as follows:

```
C:\> HIDEDIR -H DATA <ENTER>
```

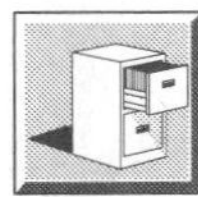

HIDEDIR.EXE does not support wildcards.

The utility command HIDEDIR.EXE resides on the companion disk that accompanies this book.

HIDEDIR.EXE

Abbreviating Long Directory Names with SUBST

As the number of directories on your disk increases, so too will the length of your directory names. If you have several directory paths you commonly use, you can use the SUBST command to abbreviate the path name by using an unused drive letter. For example, the following SUBST command abbreviates the directory C:\1001DOS\BATCH as drive E:

```
C:\> SUBST E: C:\1001DOS\BATCH <ENTER>
```

After you perform the substitution, you can refer to the directory by using drive E as shown here:

```
C:\> DIR E: <ENTER>
```

Users with many software packages installed have very long command paths. By abbreviating command path directories with drive letters, you can increase the number of entries in the path. If you do so, your AUTOEXEC.BAT file will contain several SUBST commands that define the abbreviations, followed by a PATH command that uses the abbreviations as shown here:

```
SUBST E C:\DOS
SUBST F C:\WINDOWS
SUBST G C:\BORLANDC
PATH E;F;G
```

If you plan to use disk drive letters higher than E, such as F, G, and so on, as previously shown you must include a LASTDRIVE= entry in your CONFIG.SYS file that corresponds to the last drive you plan to reference.

Sorting Directory Listings with DOS 5

If you are using DOS 5, the DIR command lets you specify the order in which you want files displayed. To display a sorted directory listing, you must use the /O switch with one of the order values specified in Table 454.

The following command directs DIR to display the files sorted by name:

```
C:\> DIR /O:N <ENTER>
```

DIR lets you specify the multiple sort order values. For example, the following command directs DIR to display files sorted by size, followed by directories:

```
C:\> DIR  /O:-GS <ENTER>
```

To use the DIR order switches, you must be using DOS 5.

Table 454. DOS 5 DIR sort options

Sort Value	Order
N	Sort by name A to Z
-N	Sort by name Z to A
E	Sort by extension A to Z
-E	Sort by extension Z to A
D	Sort by date oldest to newest
-D	Sort by date newest to oldest
S	Sort by size smallest to largest
-S	Sort by size largest to smallest
G	Display directory names before files
-G	Display filenames before directories

Removing Unused Directory Entries

When you delete a *file*, DOS does not actually remove the file from disk, but rather, DOS marks the file's disk space and directory entry as available for reuse. DOS marks a *directory* entry as available for reuse by assigning extended ASCII value 229 (the Greek letter σ) to the first character of the filename in the directory listing. When you create new files in the directory, DOS reuses the entries on a first-come, first-served basis. Unfortunately, when DOS searches the directory for a specific file, it must search through each of these unused entries, which is a time-consuming process. If you delete several files from a directory for which your don't anticipate creating other files, you can perform the following steps to remove the unused entries:

Use XCOPY to copy the directory's contents to a new directory as shown here:

```
C:\> XCOPY  \DIRNAME\*.*  \NEW  /S <ENTER>
```

Use the DEL command to delete the current directory files (or use the companion disk KILLTREE utility discussed in Tip 456).

Use RMDIR to remove the directory.

Use XCOPY to copy the temporary directory back to the previous directory and delete the temporary directory or use the DOS 5 shell to rename the temporary directory with the previous directory's name.

See Tip 486 to learn how to determine how many unused entries reside in a specific directory.

Killing a Directory Tree

One of the most time-consuming tasks users have to perform is deleting an entire directory tree. The companion disk that accompanies this book contains the utility

program KILLTREE.EXE that deletes a specified directory as well as the subdirectories the directory contains. The following command, for example, deletes a directory named OLDDIR, as well as subdirectories within the directory:

```
C:\> KILLTREE \OLDDIR <ENTER>
```

KILLTREE.EXE

The utility program KILLTREE.EXE resides on the companion disk that accompanies this book.

Checking a Directory for Fragmented Files

If your programs seem to take increasingly longer to start, or if your files are slow to load, the files on your disk may be fragmented. A fragmented file is a file whose contents are dispersed across your disk, as opposed to residing in consecutive storage locations.

The following illustration shows a contiguous and a fragmented file:

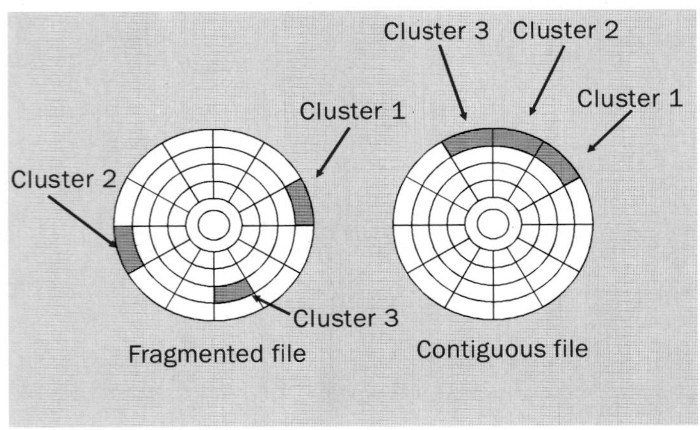

Fragmented files decrease your system performance because your disk drive has to look in more than one place for the data. The following CHKDSK command lets you examine a directory for fragmented files:

```
C:\> CHKDSK *.* <ENTER>
```

CHKDSK lets you examine only one directory's files at a time. If a file is fragmented, CHKDSK will display a message similar to the following, describing the number of fragmented clusters:

```
FILENAME.EXT Contains n non-contiguous blocks
```

If your disk contains a large number of fragmented files (more than 10 percent), you should correct the fragmentation by using a third-party software program or the BACKUP, FORMAT, or RESTORE commands discussed in Tip 347.

Displaying Only Directory Names

By default, when you issue the DIR command, it displays both file and directory names. If you are using DOS 5, you can use the DIR /A switch to display only subdirectory names as shown here:

```
C:\> DIR /A:D <ENTER>
```

The following DOSKEY command creates a macro named DIRSONLY that uses the DIR /A switch to display only directories:

```
C:\> DOSKEY DIRSONLY=DIR /A:D <ENTER>
```

If you are not using DOS 5, you can create the following batch file, DIRSONLY.BAT, that also displays only directories:

```
@ECHO OFF
DIR %1 | FIND "<DIR>"
```

Defining a Data File Search Path with APPEND

The PATH command lets you define a list of directories within which you want DOS to search for BAT, COM, and EXE files. Depending on your directory organization, you may have a set of directories that contain your commonly used data files.

The APPEND command lets you define a collection of directories within which DOS searches for your data files. The format of the APPEND command is very similar to PATH; you simply specify the directories you want DOS to search, with directory names separated by semicolons.

For example, the following APPEND command directs DOS to search three specific directories:

```
C:\> APPEND C:\LOTUS;C:\LOTUS\DATA;C:\LOTUS\BUSINESS <ENTER>
```

In this case, if DOS does not find the file in the current or specified directory, DOS will first search the directory LOTUS and then the LOTUS subdirectories DATA and BUSINESS. By defining data file search in this way, you can eliminate the need to change directories or specify complete path names for your commonly used files.

Improving Performance with FASTOPEN

Each time DOS opens a file, it must search the disk for the file's directory entry. Because disks are mechanical, they are much slower than the computer's electronic components. As a result, directory search operations are time consuming. If you tend to use the same files more than once, you can improve your system performance by using the FASTOPEN command.

Each time DOS opens a file, FASTOPEN records the file's directory location in a table in memory. If you use the file a second time, FASTOPEN can locate the file's directory information much faster by

using its table in RAM. If the table does not contain an entry for the file, DOS must perform the slower disk-based directory search.

FASTOPEN lets you track up to 999 files. In most cases, 50 files is more than sufficient. Remember that FASTOPEN does not make every file open operation faster—only those for files you open more than once. The following FASTOPEN command directs DOS to track up to 50 files on drive C:

```
C:\> FASTOPEN C:=50 <ENTER>
```

FASTOPEN requires DOS 3.3 or higher. If you are using DOS 4, install FASTOPEN by using the INSTALL entry in your CONFIG.SYS file. If you are using DOS 5 and have support for the upper-memory area, install FASTOPEN by using LOADHIGH.

If you use a third-party disk package to unfragment your disk, make sure you immediately reboot your system. *See Tip 357 for more information.*

A Directory Copy Batch File

Tip 450 discussed how to use the ATTRIB and XCOPY commands to copy an entire directory of files to one or more floppy disks. The following batch file, DIRCOPY.BAT, automates this process by taking advantage of XCOPY's exit status values:

```
@ECHO OFF
IF '%1'=='' GOTO NO_PARAMS
IF '%2'=='' GOTO NO_PARAMS
ATTRIB +A  %1 /S
:LOOP
XCOPY %1 %2 /S /W
IF NOT ERRORLEVEL 4 GOTO DONE
IF ERRORLEVEL 4 IF NOT ERRORLEVEL 5 GOTO LOOP
IF ERRORLEVEL 5 GOTO ERROR
:NO_PARAMS
ECHO Must specify source and destination
GOTO DONE
:ERROR
```

```
ECHO Error writing to disk
:DONE
```

Each time a floppy disk becomes full, the batch file will display the message "Insufficient disk space" and then prompt you to press any key to continue. When these messages appear, insert a new floppy disk in the drive and press any key to continue. To use DIRCOPY, you must invoke the batch file with a file specification and floppy drive as shown here:

```
C:\> DIRCOPY  *.*  A: <ENTER>
```

If the files you want to copy reside in a different directory, include the directory name as shown:

```
C:\> DIRCOPY C:\DATA\*.*  A: <ENTER>
```

When to Use . and ..

Each time you create a subdirectory, DOS places two entries in the directory: "." and ".." as shown here:

```
C:\TEMP> DIR <ENTER>

 Volume in drive C has no label
 Volume Serial Number is 16F6-3B73
 Directory of C:\TEMP

.          <DIR>      03-19-92   5:10a
..         <DIR>      03-19-92   5:10a
        2 file(s)           0 bytes
                     43778048 bytes free
```

These two entries are actually abbreviations for the current directory and the parent directory (the directory one level immediately above the current directory). The most common use of the ".." abbreviation is to move up one level in the directory tree. For example, if the current directory is C:\LOTUS\DATA, the following CHDIR command selects the directory one level up (C:\LOTUS):

```
C:\LOTUS\DATA> CHDIR .. <ENTER>
C:\LOTUS>
```

You can, however, use the abbreviations to simplify DOS commands. Assume again that the current directory is C:\LOTUS\DATA. To copy the file BUDGET.DAT from the current directory to the directory C:\LOTUS, you can use the following COPY command:

```
C:\LOTUS\DATA> COPY BUDGET.DAT C:\LOTUS <ENTER>
```

You can also use the ".." abbreviation to achieve the same result:

```
C:\LOTUS\DATA> COPY BUDGET.DAT .. <ENTER>
```

The current directory abbreviation is not used as often as the parent directory abbreviation. The following command illustrates how you might use the current directory icon to copy the file BUDGET.DAT from the current directory to the subdirectory BACKUP, which also resides in the current directory:

```
C:\LOTUS> COPY BUDGET.DAT .\BACKUP <ENTER>
```

Because the following (shorter) command is equivalent, most commands can omit the current directory abbreviation:

```
C:\LOTUS> COPY BUDGET.DAT BACKUP <ENTER>
```

Does This Directory Contain Files?

As you create batch files that perform various disk and directory operations, you sometimes will need to test whether the current directory contains files. The companion disk that accompanies this book contains the utility command ANYFILES.EXE that returns the exit status value 1 if the current directory contains files and returns 0 otherwise. The following batch commands illustrate how you would use ANYFILES:

```
@ECHO OFF
ANYFILES
IF NOT ERRORLEVEL 1 GOTO NO_FILES
REM Other commands here
```

Just because ANYFILES returns the exit status 0 doesn't mean the directory is empty. You need to test for subdirectories as well (see Tip 463).

ANYFILES.EXE

The utility command ANYFILES.EXE resides on the companion disk that accompanies this book.

Tip 464 Does This Directory Contain Subdirectories?

Tip 463 presents the utility command file ANYFILES.EXE that lets your batch files test whether the current directory contains any files. In a similar way, the companion disk that accompanies this book contains the utility command ANYDIRS.EXE that returns the exit status value 1 if the current directory contains subdirectories other than . and .. and returns 0 otherwise. The following batch commands illustrate how you might use ANYDIRS:

```
@ECHO OFF
ANYDIRS
IF ERRORLEVEL 1 GOTO DIRECTORIES
XCOPY *.* A:
GOTO DONE
:DIRECTORIES
XCOPY *.* A: /S
:DONE
```

The utility command ANYDIRS.EXE resides on the companion disk that accompanies this book.

ANYDIRS.EXE

Directories Consume Disk Space, Too

Does your disk have empty directories? If the answer is yes, you may be surprised how much disk space you are wasting. A directory is a list of file entries, containing the file's name, size, date and time stamp, starting disk location, and attributes. Each directory entry consumes 32 bytes. DOS stores directories on your disk, and allocates disk space to hold the directories only in clusters. When you create a directory, DOS automatically allocates a cluster of disk space to hold the directory's entries. If the directory is empty, the cluster is unused. If your directory is large, DOS may allocate several clusters to hold the entries. Using the CHKDSK command, shown here, you can determine just how much space your directories consume:

```
C:\> CHKDSK <ENTER>

Volume Serial Number is 16F6-3B73

 200065024 bytes total disk space
     81920 bytes in 3 hidden files
   1318912 bytes in 300 directories
 154308608 bytes in 6985 user files
  44355584 bytes available on disk

      4096 bytes in each allocation unit
     48844 total allocation units on disk
     10829 available allocation units on disk

    655360 total bytes memory
    584992 bytes free
```

If you have any empty directories that don't exist for a specific purpose, remove the directories to free disk space.

Testing the Current Directory

As your batch files become more complex, you sometimes will need to test the current directory. Tip 657 describes how to use the utility command SETDIR to save the current directory to the named parameter %DIRECTORY% that you can test in your batch files. The companion disk that accompanies this book provides the utility command ISCURDIR.EXE that lets your batch files compare the current directory to a specified directory. If the current directory matches the specified directory, the command returns the exit status 1; otherwise, it returns the value 0. The following batch commands, for example, use ISCURDIR to test whether the current directory is DOS:

```
@ECHO OFF
ISCURDIR C:\DOS
IF ERRORLEVEL 1 GOTO DOS_DIRECTORY
REM other commands here
```

ISCURDIR.EXE

The utility command ISCURDIR.EXE resides on the companion disk that accompanies this book.

Discarding Your Empties

As Tip 465 explains, empty directory entries consume a cluster of disk space. Thus, you should remove unused entries that don't exist for a specific purpose. To help you locate unused entries, the companion disk that accompanies this book provides the utility command DIREMPTY.EXE that searches the current disk for empty directories. When DIREMPTY encounters an empty directory, it displays the directory's path name on the screen. To locate empty directories, invoke DIREMPTY from the DOS prompt as shown here:

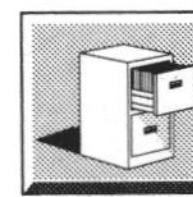

```
C:\> DIREMPTY <ENTER>
```

The utility command DIREMPTY.EXE resides on the companion disk that accompanies this book.

DIREMPTY.EXE

Adding WINDOWS to Your Command Path as You Need It

Most users have Windows installed on their disk. If you do, examine the WINDOWS directory and note the number of files the directory contains. If the WINDOWS directory is in your command path, DOS must continually search through all of the files the directory contains. As an alternative, you can create the following batch file, STARTWIN.BAT, that adds the WINDOWS directory to the command path before it invokes Windows and then removes the directory from the command path when Windows completes.

```
@ECHO OFF
SET SAVE_PATH=%PATH%
PATH C:\WINDOWS;%PATH%
WIN
PATH %SAVE_PATH%
SET SAVE_PATH=
```

By adding and removing WINDOWS on the command path as needed, you can improve your system's overall performance.

A More Selective File Delete Operation

Tip 496 explains how to use DEL's /P switch to selectively delete files. Although using the /P switch lets you control which files you delete, you have to respond individually for each file. If you want to delete all of the remaining files, DEL does not provide an option to let you do so. The companion disk that accompanies this book contains the utility command SELERASE.EXE that performs a one-by-one delete operation similar to DEL's. However, this command provides an additional option.

To selectively delete files, invoke SELERASE as follows:

```
C:\> SELERASE *.* <ENTER>
```

The SELERASE command will display each matching filename followed by this prompt:

```
D(elete), L(eave), R(est)
```

If you type **D**, SELERASE will delete the file. If you type **L**, SELERASE will leave the file on disk. If you type **R**, SELERASE will delete the remainder of the matching files.

SELERASE.EXE

The utility command SELERASE.EXE resides on the companion disk that accompanies this book.

Display Two Directory Listings Side by Side

You sometimes may want to display the directory listing for two directories side by side. The companion disk that accompanies this book provides the utility command TWO_DIR.EXE that

displays a sorted directory listing of the two directories that you specify. For example, to display directory listings of your DOS and WINDOWS directories, you would invoke TWO_DIR as follows:

```
C:\> TWO_DIR  C:\DOS C:\WINDOWS <Enter>

 Directory of C:\DOS              Directory of C:\WINDOWS
.         <DIR> 07-22-91          .          <DIR> 01-02-92
..        <DIR> 07-22-91          ..         <DIR> 01-02-92
EGA       SYS    4885 04-09-91    SYSTEM     <DIR> 01-02-92
FORMAT    COM    32911 04-09-91   GLOSSARY   HLP    44773 12-17-91
NLSFUNC   EXE    7052 04-09-91    SETUP      EXE    405248 12-17-91
COUNTRY   SYS    17069 04-09-91   SETUP      HLP    50891 12-17-91
DISPLAY   SYS    15792 04-09-91   WINHELP    EXE    253616 12-17-91
EGA       CPI    58873 04-09-9    WINHELP    HLP    38555 12-17-91
HIMEM     000    11552 04-09-91   WINTUTOR   EXE    114688 12-17-91
KEYB      COM    14986 04-09-91   CONTROL    HLP    127592 12-17-91
KEYBOARD  SYS    34697 04-09-9    CHORD      WAV    24982 12-17-91
MODE      COM    23537 04-09-91   NETWORKS   WRI    45568 12-17-91
```

Using the MORE command, you can view the directory listings a screenful at a time as shown here:

```
C:\> TWO_DIR C:\DOS C:\TEMP | MORE <ENTER>
```

The utility command TWO_DIR.EXE resides on the companion disk that accompanies this book.

TWO_DIR.EXE

Getting APPEND's Directory Search Settings

Tip 557 and Tip 558 describe how to use APPEND's /X and /PATH switches to enhance APPEND's processing. Sometimes a batch file may need to change APPEND's settings before executing a specific program. Ideally, the batch file should restore APPEND's original settings before it ends. The following DEBUG script file, APP_MODE.SCR, creates a command file named APP_MODE.COM that returns an exit status whose bits specify the current setting as listed in Table 471:

Table 471. Bit Meanings of the Exit Status Value Returned by APP_MODE.COM

Bit Set	Meaning
1	APPEND is applied to file requests that include a drive specifier.
2	APPEND is applied to file requests that include a directory specifier.
3	APPEND creates an environment entry.
4	APPEND is applied to Int 21H functions 4BH and 4EH.

APP_MODE.SCR

```
N APP_MODE.COM   <ENTER>
A 100            <ENTER>
MOV AX,B706      <ENTER>
INT 2F           <ENTER>
MOV CL,4         <ENTER>
MOV AL,BH        <ENTER>
SAR AL,CL        <ENTER>
MOV AH,4C        <ENTER>
INT 21           <ENTER>
                 <ENTER>
R CX             <ENTER>
F                <ENTER>
W                <ENTER>
Q                <ENTER>
```

Use DEBUG as follows to create the command file APP_MODE.COM:

```
C:\> DEBUG < APP_MODE.SCR <ENTER>
```

Conditional Execution Based on File Size

You sometimes may need to execute a specific command for files in the current directory whose size is equal to or larger than a given size. For example, you might want to compress all files larger than

Table 472. Metacharacters Supported by the FOR_SIZE Command

Metacharacter	Purpose
$F	Filename minus extension
$E	Extension only
$F.$E	Filename.Extension

64K. The companion disk that accompanies this book contains the FOR_SIZE utility command that executes a command for files larger than a specified size. The format of the FOR_SIZE command is as follows:

```
C:\> FOR_SIZE  SizeInBytes  Command <ENTER>
```

The command supports the metacharacters listed in Table 472.

For example, the following commands display the names of all files in the current directory that are larger than 30,000 and 65,000 bytes, respectively:

```
C:\> FOR_SIZE 30000 ECHO $F.$E <ENTER>
C:\> FOR_SIZE 65000 ECHO $F.$E  A: <ENTER>
```

The utility command FOR_SIZE.EXE resides on the companion disk that accompanies this book.

FOR_SIZE.EXE

An Easy CHDIR Command

Many new users are confused about when they need to precede the directory name with a backslash and when they can just specify the directory name. The batch file EZCD.BAT lets the user type just name of the directory they desire as shown here:

```
C:\> EZCD DirectoryName <ENTER>
```

The batch file, shown here, first looks for the directory within the current directory. If the directory is found, the batch file selects it. Otherwise, the batch file searches for the directory within the other directories. If the directory is still not found, the batch file displays a directory not found message.

```
@ECHO OFF
IF '%1'=='' GOTO DONE
SETDIR
SET SAVE_DIRECTORY=%DIRECTORY%
IF EXIST %1\NUL CD %1 > NUL
SETDIR
IF NOT %DIRECTORY%==%SAVE_DIRECTORY% GOTO DONE
IF EXIST \%1\NUL CD \%1
:DONE
```

The batch file uses the SETDIR utility command presented in Tip 657 to determine whether the current directory has changed.

Salvaging a Damaged Directory

Sometimes a disk error may leave a subdirectory damaged. When this occurs, CHKDSK will display a message similar to the following:

```
Unrecoverable error in directory
Convert directory to a file (Y/N)?
```

Should this message appear, restart your system and repeat the CHKDSK command to determine whether the error will go away. If the error persists, repeat the CHKDSK command with the /F switch as shown:

```
C:\> CHKDSK /F <ENTER>
```

When CHKDSK displays the error message, type **Y**. CHKDSK will create the file in the root directory. Use DEL to erase this file. Because the directory's files no longer reside in a directory, CHKDSK will display the lost-cluster message shown here:

```
nnn lost allocation units found in nn chains.
Convert lost chains to files (Y/N)?
```

Type **Y** to create the files. CHKDSK will place the files in the root directory, using filenames with the format FILEnnnn.CHK. Use the TYPE command to display each file's contents. If the files contain ASCII text, you can rename and reuse them. If the files contain unrecognizable text, copy them to a floppy disk, renaming each using the EXE or COM extension. Try executing the command with the floppy disk as the default drive. By following these procedures, you may be able to correctly identify program files you would otherwise have had to delete.

Dumping Root Directory Entries Using DEBUG

Tip 367 discusses how to use DEBUG to load and display your disk's boot sector. In a similar way, you can load and display the disk sectors containing your disk's root directory. To begin, place a floppy disk containing files or directory entries in drive A. Next, depending on the drive's type, issue the corresponding DEBUG L(oad) and D(ump) commands listed in Table 475. The D(ump) commands listed in Table 475 display the entire directory. If the listing scrolls past you too quickly, use the length 100 (L100).

Table 475. DEBUG L(oad) and D(ump) Commands for Loading and Displaying Root Directory Sectors

Disk Type	Load Command	Dump Command
360Kb	L 100 0 5 7	D 100 L E00
720Kb	L 100 0 B 7	D 100 L E00
1.2Mb	L 100 0 F E	D 100 L 1C00
1.44Mb	L 100 0 13 E	D 100 L 1C00

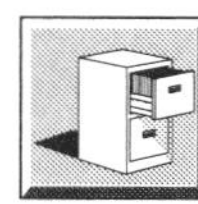

Each L(oad) command loads sectors at location 100 (hexadecimal format) from drive A (0). The two numbers at the end of the command specify (in hexadecimal format) the starting disk sector and the number of sectors desired. The D(ump) commands direct DEBUG to display memory locations beginning at offset 100, displaying the number of bytes specified.

To display the root directory entries on your hard drive, run the BOOTINFO utility command presented in Tip 366 to determine the root directory's starting sector as well as a count of the number of sectors the root directory requires. Use the utility command BASECHG discussed in Tip 78 to convert the values to hexadecimal format. Next, invoke DEBUG, changing the L(oad) command to read the desired sectors from drive C (2). As before, use the D(ump) command to display the sectors.

Tip 476 Renaming Root Directory Entries Using DEBUG

Tip 475 explained how to load and display the sectors containing your disk's root directory. Likewise, Tip 129 shows how to enter values into specific memory locations using DEBUG's E(nter) command. By combining these two techniques, you can (carefully) rename root directory entries. Before you try this operation with your hard disk, practice on a floppy whose contents you don't require. Assume, for example, you are using a 360Kb floppy in drive A whose root directory contains the following entries:

```
 Volume in drive A has no label
 Volume Serial Number is 2D73-1BC9
 Directory of A:\

COMMAND  COM     47845 04-09-91    5:00a
AUTOEXEC BAT       358 07-24-92   11:05p
CONFIG   SYS       401 07-24-92   11:03p
OLDDIR       <DIR>     07-27-92    8:02p
        4 file(s)      48604 bytes
                      239616 bytes free
```

Use the following DEBUG commands to load and display the disk's root directory sectors:

```
-L 100 0 5 7 <ENTER>
-D 100 L E00 <ENTER>
165F:0100  49 4F 20 20 20 20 20 20-53 59 53 27 00 00 00 00   IO      SYS'....
165F:0110  00 00 00 00 00 00 00 28-89 16 02 00 96 82 00 00   .......(........
165F:0120  4D 53 44 4F 53 20 20 20-53 59 53 27 00 00 00 00   MSDOS   SYS'....
165F:0130  00 00 00 00 00 00 00 28-89 16 23 00 12 92 00 00   .......(..#.....
165F:0140  43 4F 4D 4D 41 4E 44 20-43 4F 4D 20 00 00 00 00   COMMAND COM ....
165F:0150  00 00 00 00 00 00 00 28-89 16 48 00 E5 BA 00 00   .......(..H.....
165F:0160  41 55 54 4F 45 58 45 43-42 41 54 20 00 00 00 00   AUTOEXECBAT ....
165F:0170  00 00 00 00 00 00 A6 B8-F8 18 77 00 66 01 00 00   ..........w.f...
165F:0180  43 4F 4E 46 49 47 20 20-53 59 53 20 00 00 00 00   CONFIG  SYS ....
165F:0190  00 00 00 00 00 00 76 B8-F8 18 78 00 91 01 00 00   ......v...x.....
165F:01A0  4F 4C 44 44 49 52 20 20-20 20 20 10 00 00 00 00   OLDDIR      .....
165F:01B0  00 00 00 00 00 00 EC A0-FB 18 7A 00 00 00 00 00   ..........z.....
165F:01C0  00 00 00 00 00 00 00 00-00 00 00 00 00 00 00 00   ................
.
.
.
```

Assuming you want to rename the directory entry OLDDIR as NEWDIR, write down the hexadecimal values for each letter in the new name. Next, use the following Enter command to enter the new name:

```
-E 1A0 4E 45 57 <ENTER>
```

You have now updated the values in memory only. To update the disk, you must issue a DEBUG W(rite) command, whose format is identical to L(oad) with the exception that you replace the L with a W. The following DEBUG W(rite) command writes the updated information back to disk:

```
-W 100 0 5 7 <ENTER>
```

Use DEBUG's Q(uit) command to return to DOS.

Editing disk sectors using DEBUG can quickly destroy the information on your disk if you are not careful. If you make a mistake while editing, your best bet is to Q(uit) DEBUG and start again. Make sure you practice this operation on several floppy disks before you try it on your hard disk.

A Double Directory Listing

If you are using DOS 5, the DIR command provides many different capabilities. One of the capabilities it does not provide, however, is the ability to produce a side-by-side, or double, directory listing. The companion disk that accompanies this book contains the utility command DDIR.EXE, which displays a double directory listing as shown here:

```
C:\> DDIR <ENTER>
.           <DIR>       07-22-91      ..         <DIR>      07-22-91
EGA        SYS       4885 04-09-91    FORMAT     COM       32911 04-09-91
NLSFUNC    EXE       7052 04-09-91    COUNTRY    SYS       17069 04-09-91
DISPLAY    SYS      15792 04-09-91    EGA        CPI       58873 04-09-91
HIMEM      000      11552 04-09-91    KEYB       COM       14986 04-09-91
KEYBOARD   SYS      34697 04-09-91    MODE       COM       23537 04-09-91
SETVER     EXE      12007 04-09-91    ANSI       SYS        9029 04-09-91
DEBUG      EXE      20634 04-09-91    EDLIN      EXE       12642 04-09-91
EMM386     EXE      91742 04-09-91    FASTOPEN   EXE       12050 04-09-91
FDISK      EXE      57224 04-09-91    MEM        EXE       39818 04-09-91
```

To print a double directory listing, redirect DDIR's output to your printer as shown here:

```
C:\> DDIR > PRN <ENTER>
```

DDIR.EXE

The utility command DDIR.EXE resides on the companion disk that accompanies this book.

How DOS Locates a File's FAT Entries

Tip 407 describes how DOS uses the file allocation table (or FAT) to track a file's clusters on disk. The following example illustrates the file allocation table entries for three files. Using the FAT, you can traverse the cluster chains to determine which clusters correspond to each file.

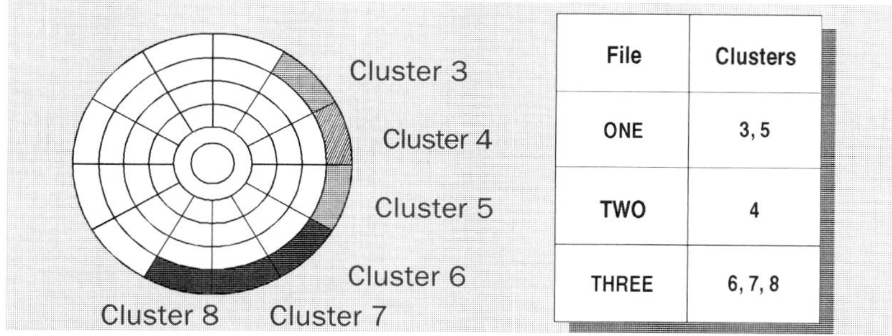

File	Clusters
ONE	3, 5
TWO	4
THREE	6, 7, 8

What the file allocation table entry does not tell you, however, is which cluster is the start of each file's cluster chain. DOS stores the file's starting cluster number in the file's 32-bit directory entry. The following illustration shows the directory entries for the files shown in the previous example. As you can see, using the directory entry, you can determine the starting cluster number, which you can then use to traverse the file allocation table cluster chain.

Name	Size	Date	Time	Starting cluster
ONE	2048	8-1-91	6:01p	4
TWO	4096	8-1-91	6:02p	3
THREE	6144	8-1-91	6:03p	6

Directory entries

Cluster	Next cluster
2	0
3	5
4	FFF8
5	FFF8
6	7
7	8
8	FFF8

File allocation table

Processing a List of Directories

Tip 593 explains how to use the companion disk utility NEXTFILE.EXE to process a list of files. Similarly, the companion disk utility NEXTDIR.EXE lets your batch files process a list of directories. The command examines the CURRENT_DIR environment entry and changes the entry to the directory name that follows the current name in the directory list. If the entry is not defined, NEXTDIR returns the first directory in the list. If no directories follow the current directory, NEXTDIR undefines the CURRENT_DIR entry.

The following batch file commands use NEXTDIR to perform a directory listing of each directory in your disk's root:

```
@ECHO OFF
CD \
SET CURRENT_DIR=
:LOOP
NEXTDIR
IF '%CURRENT_DIR%'=='' GOTO DONE
DIR %CURRENT_DIR%
GOTO LOOP
:DONE
```

If NEXTDIR successfully adds the entry to the environment, it returns the exit status 0; otherwise, it returns the exit status 1.

NEXTDIR.EXE

The utility command NEXTDIR.EXE resides on the companion disk that accompanies this book.

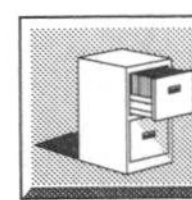

Expanding and Collapsing DOS Shell Directories

When you display the directory tree within the DOS 5 shell, by default, the shell displays only the names of directories that reside in your disk's root. As you examine the directories, you will find that many of the directory folders contain a plus sign (+) indicating that the directory contains lower-level subdirectories. The directories whose folders don't contain the plus sign don't have lower-level subdirectories.

To view the next level of directory names, click the plus sign with your mouse or highlight the directory name and press the plus key. To view every level of subdirectory, highlight the directory name and press the asterisk key (*). When you are done viewing a directory's branches, you can collapse the branches by highlighting the directory and pressing the minus key or by clicking the directory folder's minus key. If you want to expand your disk's entire directory tree, press the CTRL-* keyboard combination, or highlight the root directory and press the asterisk.

Each of the keyboard combinations listed in this tip correspond to options on the Shell's Tree menu.

How Many Subdirectories Does This Directory Contain?

As your batch files become more complex, you sometimes may want to execute specific commands for each subdirectory in the current directory. Tip 479 explains how to use the companion disk utility command NEXTDIR to obtain the name of the next directory on your disk. Before you use NEXTDIR, you may first want to know the number of subdirectories. Thus, the companion disk that accompanies this book provides the utility command DIRCOUNT.EXE that assigns the number of current directory subdirectories to the environment entry DIR_COUNT. The following batch file commands use DIRCOUNT to display the number of subdirectories:

```
@ECHO OFF
DIRCOUNT
ECHO  The number of subdirectories is %DIR_COUNT%
SET DIR_COUNT=
```

The DIRCOUNT utility does not include the directory abbreviations "." and ".." in its count.

If DIRCOUNT successfully adds the environment entry, it returns the exit status value 0; otherwise, if the environment is full, it returns the staus value 1.

DIRCOUNT.EXE

The utility command DIRCOUNT.EXE resides on the companion disk that accompanies this book.

Working with Files that Reside in Different Directories

You sometimes may need to copy, delete, or print files that reside in different directories. Using the DOS 5 shell, you can do so in one step. To start, select the shell's Options menu. If the Select Across Directories option is not preceded by a diamond, select the option. The Options menu should appear as shown here:

```
Options
 Confirmation...
 File Display Options...
•Select Across Directories
 Show Information...
•Enable Task Swapper
 Display...
 Colors...
```

To select the files from different directories, select the directory with which you want to begin.

Next, use the techniques discussed in Tip 606 to select the desired files in the directory. Change to the next directory, repeating this process for each of the desired files. You can then use the File menu to move, copy, delete, or print the files.

Controlling the Shell's Directory Tree Order

By default, the DOS 5 shell displays files sorted by name in A-to-Z order. Sometimes you may want to display the files sorted using a field other than the name, or perhaps not sorted at all. To change the order the shell uses to display files, select the Options menu and choose File Display Options. The shell will display the File Display Options dialog box shown here:

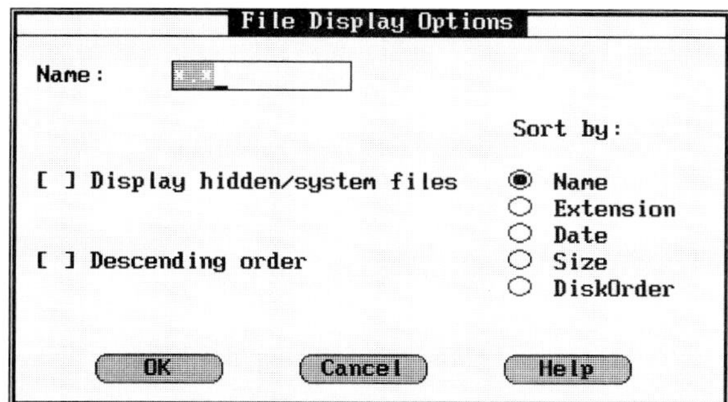

Select the desired sort option by clicking on the option with your mouse or by pressing the TAB key to select the sort fields and then selecting the desired order with the keyboard arrow keys. If you want the shell to display the list in descending order (Z to A), click the Descending order check box with your mouse, or press the TAB key to select the box and press the SPACEBAR. The shell will display an X in the box. Next, select the OK option. Note that the last field in the sort options, DiskOrder, does not sort the filenames but, rather, displays them in the order they appear in the directory on your disk.

Quickly Selecting All the Files in a Directory

If you are using the DOS 5 shell, you can perform file operations on all the files in a directory, such as copying or deleting all the files, by invoking the filename and choosing the Select All options or by pressing the CTRL-/ keyboard combination. When you choose the Select All option, the shell will highlight all of the files in the current directory. While you are selecting files for a file operation, if you decide to cancel the operation, you can use the File menu Deselect All option to cancel your previous file selections.

Labeling Your Floppy Disks

You should assign a label to your floppy disks that describes the disks' contents in a meaningful way. Unfortunately, because disk labels are so small, you can write only a small amount of information on the label. As an alternative, you can use the batch file LISTFLOP.BAT to print a compressed listing of the files on your disk:

```
@ECHO OFF
ECHO Esc(s16.66H > PRN
ECHO Esc(s8.5V > PRN
DIR /W > PRN
```

In this case, the batch file was written for an HP LaserJet. The escape sequences select a compressed font. The batch file then uses DIR /W to create a directory listing five files wide. You can print the listing and attach the printout to a disk envelope as shown here:

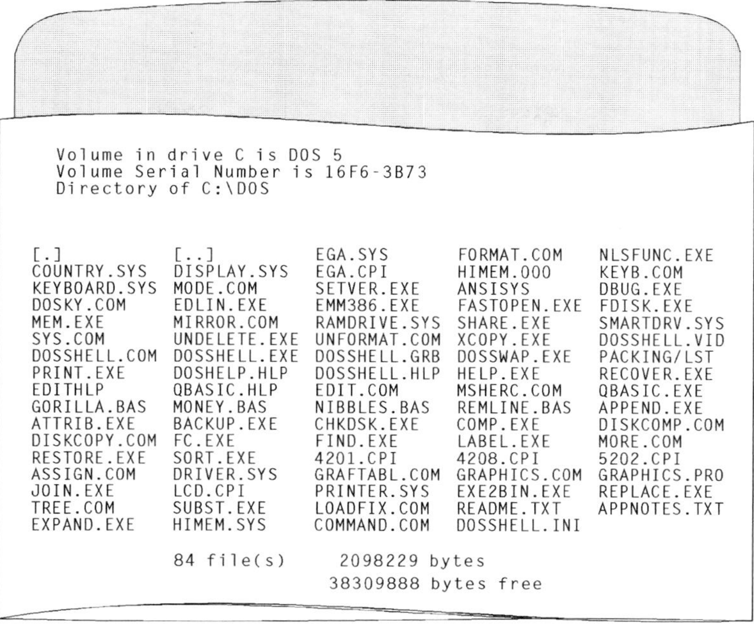

```
Volume in drive C is DOS 5
Volume Serial Number is 16F6-3B73
Directory of C:\DOS

[.]            [..]           EGA.SYS        FORMAT.COM     NLSFUNC.EXE
COUNTRY.SYS    DISPLAY.SYS    EGA.CPI        HIMEM.000      KEYB.COM
KEYBOARD.SYS   MODE.COM       SETVER.EXE     ANSISYS        DBUG.EXE
DOSKY.COM      EDLIN.EXE      EMM386.EXE     FASTOPEN.EXE   FDISK.EXE
MEM.EXE        MIRROR.COM     RAMDRIVE.SYS   SHARE.EXE      SMARTDRV.SYS
SYS.COM        UNDELETE.EXE   UNFORMAT.COM   XCOPY.EXE      DOSSHELL.VID
DOSSHELL.COM   DOSSHELL.EXE   DOSSHELL.GRB   DOSSWAP.EXE    PACKING/LST
PRINT.EXE      DOSHELP.HLP    DOSSHELL.HLP   HELP.EXE       RECOVER.EXE
EDITHLP        QBASIC.HLP     EDIT.COM       MSHERC.COM     QBASIC.EXE
GORILLA.BAS    MONEY.BAS      NIBBLES.BAS    REMLINE.BAS    APPEND.EXE
ATTRIB.EXE     BACKUP.EXE     CHKDSK.EXE     COMP.EXE       DISKCOMP.COM
DISKCOPY.COM   FC.EXE         FIND.EXE       LABEL.EXE      MORE.COM
RESTORE.EXE    SORT.EXE       4201.CPI       4208.CPI       5202.CPI
ASSIGN.COM     DRIVER.SYS     GRAFTABL.COM   GRAPHICS.COM   GRAPHICS.PRO
JOIN.EXE       LCD.CPI        PRINTER.SYS    EXE2BIN.EXE    REPLACE.EXE
TREE.COM       SUBST.EXE      LOADFIX.COM    README.TXT     APPNOTES.TXT
EXPAND.EXE     HIMEM.SYS      COMMAND.COM    DOSSHELL.INI

               84 file(s)      2098229 bytes
                              38309888 bytes free
```

If you are using an Epson-compatible printer, change the batch file as shown here:

```
@ECHO OFF
EPSON171 > PRN
DIR /W > PRN
```

Determining the Number of Unused Directory Entries

Tip 455 shows you how to remove unused directory entries in your commonly used directories to improve the performance of directory search operations. If you are using DOS 5, you can use the following UNDELETE command to list the unused entries in the current directory:

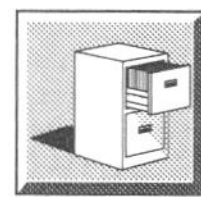

```
C:\> UNDELETE /DOS /LIST <ENTER>
```

UNDELETE will display the unused entries on your screen.

To use the UNDELETE command, you must be using DOS 5.

How Much Disk Space Am I Wasting?

As discussed in Tip 503, because DOS allocates disk space in clusters, small files can waste a considerable amount of disk space. To help you better recognize the amount of wasted space, the companion disk that accompanies this book provides the utility command WASTED.EXE that examines the current directory files and lists the amount of disk space each file wastes and the total amount of space consumed by the directory's files as shown here:

```
C:\> WASTED <ENTER>
Filename.One      Size: nnnnn bytes  Wasted: nnnn bytes
Filename.Two      Size: nnnnn bytes  Wasted: nnnn bytes
Filename.Thr      Size: nnnnn bytes  Wasted: nnnn bytes
Filename.Fou      Size: nnnnn bytes  Wasted: nnnn bytes
```

Use WASTED to examine your commonly used directories; then remove as many space wasters as you can.

WASTED.EXE

The utility command WASTED.EXE resides on the companion disk that accompanies this book.

Some Programs Use TMP Instead of TEMP

As Tip 12 describes, many applications, such as DOS and Windows, use the TEMP environment entry to determine where to create temporary files. By assigning TEMP to a RAM drive, you can improve an application's performance by decreasing the amount of time needed to open files. In addition, some programs use an environment entry named TMP for this same purpose. If you run several applications regularly, determine whether the program uses TEMP or TMP. The following AUTOEXEC.BAT commands assign TEMP and TMP to a RAM drive named drive D:

```
SET TEMP=D:\
SET TMP=%TEMP%
```

As you can see, the commands assign the desired drive to TEMP and then use the TEMP entry's value to set TMP.

Periodically Cleaning Up After the DOS 5 Shell

As Tip 12 explains, as the DOS 5 shell executes, it creates temporary files in the directory specified by the TEMP environment entry. If TEMP is not defined, the shell creates the files in the DOS directory, sometimes because the system is turned off with the shell on, or perhaps because tasks running in the shell leave files in either the DOS or TEMP directory. Thus, check these directories periodically for files with the BAT, TMP, or SWP extensions; you can probably delete the files. The batch files will normally have a base name that uses four hexadecimal digits followed by the letters DOSC (for instance, 0123DOSC.BAT) Use the TYPE command to display the file's contents before you delete the file.

Displaying the Current Directories for Each Disk

DOS keeps track of the current directory for every drive in your system. If you are having difficulty running a program because the program can't find its data files, use the companion disk utility command LISTDIRS.EXE, which displays the current directory for each of your disk's available drives:

```
C:\> LISTDIRS <ENTER>
A:\
B:\
C:\1001DOS
D:\DATA
E:\
```

LISTDIRS.EXE

The utility command LISTDIRS.EXE resides on the companion disk that accompanies this book.

Saving and Restoring All Current Directories

As Tip 490 explains, DOS keeps track of the current directory for each of your disk drives. Tip 650 presents the utility commands PUSHDIR and POPDIR that your batch files can use to save and restore the current directory. Sometimes, however, you may want your batch files to save and later restore the current directory for every drive in your system in just one step. The following batch commands use the utility command LISTDIRS.EXE, presented in Tip 432, to write the directory names to a file. The batch file then uses the command FILECMD, presented in Tip 104, to restore each directory.

```
@ECHO OFF
LISTDIRS > C:\SAVEDIRS.DAT
```

```
REM Other commands here
FILECMD C:\SAVEDIRS.DAT CHDIR
DEL C:\SAVEDIRS.BAT
```

As your batch files become more complex, saving and restoring your current directories in one step can be very convenient.

Quickly Moving Up Directory Levels

The command CD.. moves you up one level in the directory tree. You can use the following CD command to move up two levels in the directory tree:

```
C:\SOMEDIR\SOMELVL> CD ..\.. <ENTER>
```

You can use the following CD command to move up three levels in the directory tree:

```
C:\SOMEDIR\SOMELVL\LEVEL> CD ..\..\.. <ENTER>
```

To simplify this process, you can use the following batch file UP.BAT, which lets you move up directory levels:

```
@ECHO OFF
IF '%1'=='..' CD ..
IF '%1'=='...' CD ..\..
IF '%1'=='....' CD ..\..\..
IF '%1'=='.....' CD ..\..\..\..
IF '%1'=='......' CD ..\..\..\..\..
```

The following table lists several sample uses of UP.BAT and the function of each:

Command	Function
UP ..	Moves up one level
UP ...	Moves up two levels
UP	Moves up three levels

The batch file UP.BAT allows you to move up five directory levels in one step.

Moving Up Directory Levels with DOSKEY

Tip 492 presents the batch file UP.BAT that lets you quickly move up several directory levels in one step. If you are using DOS 5, you can create the following DOSKEY macros that achieve the same result:

```
C:\> DOSKEY ..=CD .. <ENTER>
C:\> DOSKEY ...=CD ..\.. <Enter
C:\> DOSKEY ....=CD ..\..\.. <ENTER>
```

After you define these macros, you can move up one or two levels in the directory tree by invoking the macros as shown here:

```
C:\SOMEDIR\SOMELVL\LEVEL> .. <ENTER>
C:\SOMEDIR\SOMELVL> ... <ENTER>
```

To use DOSKEY macros, you must be using DOS 5.

Creating the UTIL Directory

Your DOS directory contains many commands you will rarely use. Because the DOS directory normally appears at the start of the command path, these files slow operations that search for external commands. To speed operations, in your DOS directory create a directory called UTIL and copy the seldom-used files to this directory. Next, in your AUTOEXEC.BAT file append the directory name as shown here:

```
PATH C:\DOS;C;\BATCH;C:\WINDOWS;C:\DOS\UTIL
```

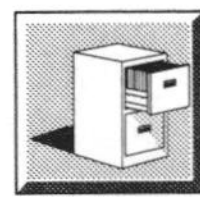

With the directory placed at the end of the command path, the files have minimal impact on command search operations and yet are readily accessible if you need them.

Using Logical Drives for Quick Directory Changes

Tip 453 describes how to abbreviate long directory names by using the SUBST command. If you have several directories that you regularly switch among, you can use SUBST to assign the directory names to logical drive letters as shown here:

```
C:\> SUBST E: C:\DOS      <ENTER>
C:\> SUBST F: C:\WINDOWS <ENTER>
C:\> SUBST G: C:\WP51     <ENTER>
```

After you define these logical drives, you can quickly change directories by selecting the corresponding drive. For instance, the following two commands produce equivalent results, but it is much easier and faster to use the second form:

```
C:\> CD C:\WINDOWS <ENTER>
C:\> F: <ENTER>
```

To use a logical drive letter higher than E, you must place a LASTDRIVE entry in your CONFIG.SYS file.

PART
6

File

Selective File Deletions

If you are using DOS 4 or later, the DEL /P switch lets you selectively delete files from a directory. When you use the /P switch, DEL displays the following message to verify you really want to delete a file:

```
FILENAME.EXT, Delete (Y/N)?
```

If you type **Y**, DOS will delete the file. If you type N, DOS will leave the file on disk.

To selectively delete files from your directory, you can combine the /P switch and the DOS wildcards as shown in the following command:

```
C:\> DEL *.* /P <ENTER>
```

In this case, DOS will display the name of each file in the directory, asking you if you want each file. In this way, you can selectively delete files.

To use the /P switch, you must be using DOS 4 or later.

Creating a SAFEDEL Command

If you are using DOS 4 or later, you can use the DEL /P switch to selectively delete files (See Tip 497). If you are using DOS 4, create the following SAFEDEL.BAT batch file, which uses /P to verify file deletions:

```
@ECHO OFF
:GET_NEXT_FILE
SHIFT
```

```
IF '%0'=='' GOTO DONE
DEL %0 /P
GOTO GET_NEXT_FILE
:DONE
```

Using the SAFEDEL batch file, you can specify wildcards, or place multiple filenames on the command line as shown here:

```
C:\> SAFEDEL  FILENAME.ONE  FILENAME.TWO  *.BAK <ENTER>
```

Place the batch file in a directory whose name is included in your command path.

If you are using DOS 5, use the DOSKEY command to create a command named SAFEDEL as shown here:

```
C:\> DOSKEY SAFEDEL=DEL $1 /P <ENTER>
```

If you plan on using SAFEDEL on a regular basis, add the previous DOSKEY command to your AUTOEXEC.BAT file, defining the SAFEDEL command each time your system starts.

To use the DEL /P switch, you must be using DOS 4 or later. To use the DOSKEY command, you must be using DOS 5.

Protecting AUTOEXEC.BAT

When you install a software package, most installation routines make changes to your AUTOEXEC.BAT, normally making changes to the PATH command. In some cases, however, errors in an installation program may overwrite your computer's AUTOEXEC.BAT file. To prevent your AUTOEXEC.BAT from being overwritten, create a second batch file in your disk's root directory named AUTOSAVE.BAT that contains the commands you would normally place in your AUTOEXEC.BAT file. Within your AUTOEXEC.BAT file, you simply invoke the second batch file by using the CALL command as shown here:

```
CALL AUTOSAVE
```

When your system starts, DOS will invoke AUTOEXEC.BAT normally, which will in turn invoke the batch file AUTOSAVE.BAT, which customizes your system. After you install a program, note the changes the installation has made to the AUTOEXEC.BAT file and make the same changes to the file AUTOSAVE.BAT, restoring AUTOEXEC.BAT to the one-line command previously shown.

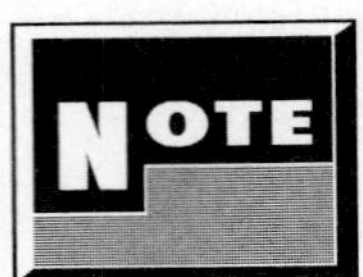

If you have a batch directory, you should consider placing the batch file AUTOSAVE.BAT in that directory as opposed to the root directory (see Tip 444).

Creating and Selecting a Directory in One Step

In most cases, when you create a directory, you immediately select the same directory by using the CHDIR command. If you are using DOS 5, you can use DOSKEY to create a macro named MDCD (make directory, change directory) that creates and then selects the specified directory as shown here:

```
C:\> DOSKEY MDCD=MD $1 $T CD $1 <ENTER>
```

To create and select a directory named TIPS, you would use the MDCD macro as follows:

```
C:\> MDCD TIPS <ENTER>
```

If you are not using DOS 5, you can create a batch file named MDCD.BAT that contains the following commands:

```
@ECHO OFF
MD %1
CD %1
```

If you use the batch file MDCD.BAT, place the batch file in a directory whose name is in your command path.

Creating Extended ASCII Characters

The PC uses ASCII characters to represent letters, numbers, and symbols. The letters "A" through "Z," for example, correspond to the ASCII values 65 through 90; the letters "a" through "z" correspond to the ASCII values 97 through 122. There are 128 ASCII characters that correspond to the values 0 through 127. In addition to the ASCII character set, the PC supports 128 extended ASCII characters, whose values are shown in Table 500.

As Tip 50 discusses, you can use extended ASCII characters to display boxes around batch file messages. As Tip 506 explains, you can include extended ASCII characters in your filenames. To enter an extended ASCII character from your keyboard, hold down the ALT key and type the extended ASCII value by using the numeric keypad that appears to the far right of your keyboard. After you type the last number, release the ALT key, and the extended ASCII character should appear.

If you are entering extended ASCII characters from an editor or word processor, the steps you must perform may differ. Refer to the documentation that accompanies your software.

Table 500. The Extended ASCII Characters

128	Ç	141	ì	154	Ü	167	º	180	┤	193	┴	206	╬	219	█	232	ϕ	244	⌠
129	ü	142	Ä	155	¢	168	¿	181	╡	194	┬	207	╧	220	▄	233	θ	245	⌡
130	é	143	Å	156	£	169	⌐	182	╢	195	├	208	╨	221	▌	234	Ω	246	÷
131	â	144	É	157	¥	170	¬	183	╖	196	─	209	╤	222	▐	235	δ	247	≈
132	ä	145	æ	158	Pt	171	½	184	╕	197	┼	210	╥	223	▀	236	∞	248	°
133	à	146	Æ	159	*f*	172	¼	185	╣	198	╞	211	╙	224	α	237	∅	249	•
134	å	147	ô	160	á	173	¡	186	║	199	╟	212	╘	225	β	238	∈	250	·
135	ç	148	ö	161	í	174	<<	187	╗	200	╚	213	╒	226	Γ	239	∩	251	√
136	ê	149	ò	162	ó	175	>>	188	╝	201	╔	214	╓	227	π	240	≡	252	η
137	ë	150	û	163	ú	176	░	189	╜	202	╩	215	╫	228	Σ	241	±	253	^{2}
138	è	151	ù	164	ñ	177	▒	190	╛	203	╦	216	╪	229	σ	242	≥	254	■
139	ï	152	ÿ	165	Ñ	178	▓	191	┐	204	╠	217	┘	230	μ	243	≤	255	
140	î	153	Ö	166	ª	179	│	192	└	205	═	218	┌	231	τ				

Faster File Deletions Without MIRROR

The DOS 5 MIRROR command increases your chances of successfully recovering an inadvertently deleted file by recording information about each file you delete in the file PCTRACKR.DEL, which resides on your disk. When you use MIRROR, you increase the amount of time required to delete a file because time is needed to record the information about the deleted file. If you delete only one or two files, MIRROR's overhead is hard to detect. However, if you delete a large directory, MIRROR's overhead is considerable. So if you are deleting a directory you don't need to undelete, you might consider removing MIRROR before you make the deletion by using the /U switch as shown here:

```
C:\> MIRROR /U <ENTER>
```

After the deletion is complete, you can reinstall MIRROR.

To use the MIRROR command, you must be using DOS 5.

Splitting Redirected Input

The DOS pipe command lets you redirect one program's output to become a second program's input. Sometimes, however, you may first want to view or file the redirected input. For example, the following command redirect's the output of DIR to become the input of the SORT command:

```
C:\> DIR | SORT <ENTER>
```

The companion disk that accompanies this book contains a utility command named SPLIT.EXE that lets you split a command's output to a file, screen, or printer while still using the output for redirection. For example, the following command redirects DIR's output to SORT, but it first splits the output to the printer:

```
C:\> DIR | SPLIT PRN | SORT
```

If you only specify SPLIT without a file or device name, SPLIT will display the output to the screen.

SPLIT.EXE

The file SPLIT.EXE resides on the companion disk that accompanies this book.

Small Files Don't Save Disk Space

When you issue the DIR command, DIR displays the size of each file in bytes. Although the file size tells you the amount of information the file contains, it does not tell you the amount of disk space the file consumes on disk. When you create a file or increase a file's size, DOS allocates disk space in clusters or allocation units. Typically, the cluster size for a hard disk is 2,048 or 4,096 bytes. Use the CHKDSK command to display your disk's cluster size as shown here:

```
C:\> CHKDSK <ENTER>

Volume DOS 5 DISK  created 04-18-1992 4:43p
Volume Serial Number is 16F6-3B73

 200065024 bytes total disk space
   4276224 bytes in 3 hidden files
   1638400 bytes in 380 directories
 178151424 bytes in 8354 user files
  15998976 bytes available on disk

      4096 bytes in each allocation unit
     48844 total allocation units on disk
      3906 available allocation units on disk

    655360 total bytes memory
    541744 bytes free
```

Regardless of your file's size, DOS allocates a cluster of space. If, for example, you create a 1-byte file, DOS allocates an entire cluster of disk space. Assuming that your disk uses 4,096 byte clusters, 1 byte of the cluster will be used, while 4,095 bytes are unused and available for future use. If you increase the file's size at a later time, DOS will use up part of the unused cluster. However, if the file's size never changes, the unused portion of the cluster will always remain unused. The point to remember is that a small file size listed in the directory doesn't necessarily mean that your file consumes only a small amount of disk space. Regardless of the file's size, the file will always consume at least one disk cluster.

Listing Today's Files

As the number of files you create increases, so does the likelihood of misplacing a file. The companion disk that accompanies this book includes the command TODAYS.EXE that displays the name of each file you have created in the current directory today. Use the command as follows to display the files:

```
C:\> TODAYS <ENTER>
```

To display the files you created on a different disk or directory, you must first select the drive or directory as the default.

```
C:\> TODAYS B: <ENTER>
```

TODAYS.EXE

The utility command file TODAYS.EXE resides on the companion disk that accompanies this book.

Copying a Large File

The XCOPY and COPY commands let you copy one or more files. These commands work very well until you need to copy a file larger than the floppy disk to which you

need to copy the file. As Tip 509 explains, you can use this book's companion disk IMPLODE and EXPLODE utilities to compress the file before copying it to a floppy disk, later expanding the file on the target hard disk. As an alternative, you can use the BACKUP and RESTORE commands to split the disk into pieces, each of which resides on a specific disk. The following BACKUP command, for example, copies the file FILENAME.BIG from the current directory to the floppy disk in drive A:

```
C:\> BACKUP  FILENAME.BIG  A: <ENTER>
```

When the floppy disk fills, BACKUP will prompt you to enter a second disk. Do so and press ENTER. When you are ready to copy the file from floppy to a hard disk, use the following RESTORE command:

```
C:\> RESTORE  A:  FILENAME.BIG <ENTER>
```

RESTORE will build the file on the hard disk, piece by piece, one floppy disk at a time.

Using Extended ASCII Characters in Your Filenames

Tip 16 explains the extended ASCII character set and how you can view these characters by using the companion disk ASCII utility command. When you create files and directories, you sometimes may want to use the extended ASCII characters. For example, if you have a directory whose contents you don't want another user to access, consider placing the extended ASCII blank character (extended ASCII 255) at the end of the directory name. When another user attempts to access the directory, the access will fail because the user is unaware of the hidden character.

```
C:\> CHDIR \PRIVATE <ENTER>
Invalid directory
```

When you want to access the directory, include the hidden character in the directory name by holding down the ALT key and typing the value 255 on the numeric key pad; then release ALT.

```
C:\> CHDIR \PRIVATE<ALT+255> <ENTER>
```

By including extended ASCII characters in this way you may prevent another user's access. Note, however, that if a user runs a shell program such as the DOS 5 shell or Windows, that lets the user graphically select a directory, the user can bypass this protection scheme.

Tip 507 Moving a File from One Directory to Another

When you organize your directories, you will often move a file from one directory to another. Using only DOS commands, you must first copy the file to the new directory and then delete the existing file, a two-step process. The companion disk that accompanies this book includes the FILEMOVE.EXE utility that lets you quickly move a file from one directory to another as shown here:

```
C:\> FILEMOVE FILENAME.EXT \NEWDIR\FILENAME.EXT <ENTER>
```

FILEMOVE.EXE

The utility command file FILEMOVE.EXE resides on the companion disk that accompanies this book.

Tip 508 Protecting Files with the DOS 5 MIRROR Command

The DOS 5 MIRROR command lets you increase the likelihood of successfully recovering an inadvertently deleted file. MIRROR is a memory-resident command that records to the file PCTRACKR.DEL information about each file you delete. If you need to later undelete a file, the

DOS 5 UNDELETE command will record use the information recorded by MIRROR. If you are using DOS 5, place an entry similar to the following in your AUTOEXEC.BAT file:

```
MIRROR /TC-100
```

The /TC entry directs MIRROR to track files you delete on drive C. The value 100 specifies the number of files MIRROR will track. MIRROR lets you track from 1 to 999 files. In most cases, the value 100 is more than sufficient.

In addition to tracking information about the files you delete, MIRROR will copy your disk's file allocation table and root directory contents that can later be used by the UNFORMAT command should you inadvertently format your hard disk.

To use the MIRROR command, you must be using DOS 5.

Compressing and Decompressing Files

Over time, your hard disk will begin to collect many large files that you may not use regularly. To reduce the amount of disk space these files consume, you can compress the files into a smaller form, later decompressing the files when you need to use them. The companion disk that accompanies this book contains two programs, IMPLODE.EXE and EXPLODE.EXE, that compress and decompress a file. To compress a file, use IMPLODE as shown here:

```
C:\> IMPLODE FILENAME.EXT FILENAME.CMP <ENTER>
```

As a rule, use the CMP extension to represent a compressed file. After you successfully compress a file, you can delete the file using DEL.

When you later need to use the file, decompress it using EXPLODE as shown here:

```
C:\> EXPLODE FILENAME.CMP FILENAME.EXT <ENTER>
```

After you successfully explode a file, you can delete the compressed version using DEL. As Tip 503 explains, compressing a file whose size is smaller than your disk's cluster size will not save disk space.

The files IMPLODE.EXE and EXPLODE.EXE reside on the companion disk that accompanies this book.

IMPLODE.EXE
EXPLODE.EXE

Tip 510 Hiding and Unhiding Files Under DOS 5

If you are using DOS 5, the ATTRIB command lets you hide a file, protecting the file from most directory operations and preventing DIR from displaying information about the file in the directory listing. To hide a file using ATTRIB, use the +H switch as shown here:

```
C:\> ATTRIB +H FILENAME.EXT <ENTER>
```

When you hide a file, you cannot accidentally delete the file using DEL; however, if you know the file exists, you can display its contents using TYPE or even execute the file if it is a COM, EXE, or BAT file. To later unhide the file, use the -H switch as shown here:

```
C:\> ATTRIB -H FILENAME.EXT <ENTER>
```

If you plan to hide and unhide files regularly, consider creating the following DOSKEY macros:

```
DOSKEY  HIDE=ATTRIB +H $1
DOSKEY  UNHIDE=ATTRIB -H $1
```

To use the ATTRIB command to hide and unhide files, you must be using DOS 5 or higher.

Undelete Files Immediately

Whether you use the DOS 5 UNDELETE command or a different, third-party disk utility, it is essential that you undelete an inadvertently deleted file immediately after you delete the file. If you run other programs or copy other files to the disk, you risk overwriting the deleted file's contents, making the undeletion impossible. When you delete a file's contents, DOS does not actually erase the file's contents from disk. Instead, DOS marks the disk space that previously held the file's content available for use by other files. If you create other files, DOS will very likely use the space, overwriting the previous file.

One of the most common mistakes users make when they inadvertently delete files is to copy an undeleted utility to their hard disk, overwriting the deleted file's contents on disk. As in Tip 344 shows, you should store an undelete utility on a floppy disk, from which you can undelete other files.

To undelete files using UNDELETE, you must be using DOS 5. If you are not, you can use third-party disk utility software to undelete files.

Understanding the CONFIG.SYS FILES Entry

Each time a program opens a file, DOS places information about the file in a table of file entries. The CONFIG.SYS FILES entry specifies the number of entries the file table can hold. The file table not only holds information about the current program's file's, but also about memory-resident programs that can open files. In other words, the CONFIG.SYS FILES entry controls the number of files DOS can open system wide.

If you don't specify a value for the FILES entry, DOS uses the default value of 8. Because DOS predefines the first five file handles to the standard devices (stdin, stdout, stderr, stdaux, and stdprn), eight file handles would allow your program to open only three additional files. At a minimum, you should set FILES to 20.

If you are running a larger database program, the program may require 40 to 50 file handles (a handle is an index entry into the file table). DOS lets you specify a value up to 255. Each entry requires 64 bytes of memory. In general, 30 to 40 handles should be sufficient for most uses. If your system displays messages stating it cannot open a file and you know the file exists, try increasing the number of file handles.

Protecting Files with Read-Only Attributes

The ATTRIB command lets you set various file attributes. One of the attributes you should learn to use right away is the read-only attribute. A read-only file is a file whose contents DOS can read and use but cannot change or delete. By setting a file to read-only status, you reduce the possibility that the file will be accidentally deleted or overwritten. To set a file to read-only status, use ATTRIB with the +R switch as shown here:

```
C:\> ATTRIB +R FILENAME.EXT <ENTER>
```

If you try to delete a read-only file, DOS will display the message shown here:

```
C:\> DEL FILENAME.EXT <ENTER>
Access denied
```

Many users protect files such as CONFIG.SYS and AUTOEXEC.BAT by setting the files to read-only status. Other candidates for read-only files include your EXE and COM files whose contents never change.

If you need to change the contents of, or delete, a file you have set to read-only status, you must first remove the read-only attribute by using ATTRIB with the -R switch as shown here:

```
C:\> ATTRIB -R FILENAME.EXT <ENTER>
```

ATTRIB fully supports the DOS wildcard characters.

Displaying the Name of Every File on Your Disk

DOS provides you with several different ways to list the names of every file on your disk. First, if you are using DOS 5, you can use the following DIR command:

```
C:\> DIR \*.* /S <ENTER>
```

If you are not using DOS 5, you can display a graphical representation of your directory structure as well as the files each directory contains by using the following TREE command:

```
C:\> TREE C:\ /F <ENTER>
```

The following ATTRIB command displays each filename preceded by its attributes and directory name:

```
C:\> ATTRIB C:\*.*  /S <ENTER>
```

Last, using the /V switch, you can direct CHKDSK to display the name of every file on your disk:

```
C:\> CHKDSK /V <ENTER>
```

Copying Small Files from the Keyboard

As you work with DOS, you sometimes will want to quickly create a small batch file. The fastest way to do so is by using the COPY command to copy the file's contents directly from the keyboard as you type. Assume, for example, you want to create a simple two-line batch file named SIMPLE.BAT that issues the DATE and TIME commands. To begin, issue the following COPY command:

```
C:\> COPY CON SIMPLE.BAT <ENTER>
```

The device name CON tells DOS you want to copy the file from the keyboard. When you press ENTER to execute the command, DOS moves the cursor to the start of the next line in preparation for you to type the file's contents. Type the DATE and TIME commands as shown here:

```
C:\> COPY CON SIMPLE.BAT <ENTER>
DATE <ENTER>
TIME <ENTER>
```

Next, you must tell DOS that you are done entering information by pressing the F6 (end-of-file) key. When you press F6, DOS will display ^Z (pronounced control Z). Press ENTER to end the copy operation as shown here:

```
C:\> COPY CON SIMPLE.BAT <ENTER>
DATE <ENTER>
TIME <ENTER>
^Z   <ENTER>
        1 file(s) copied

C:\>
```

Using this technique, you can quickly create most small files.

Viewing the First *n* Lines of a Text File

The TYPE command lets you display the contents of an ASCII file on your screen. Many times, however, you may not want to view a file's entire contents. The companion disk that accompanies this book includes a utility program named FIRST.EXE that displays the first *n* lines of a file. If you invoke FIRST without specifying a line count as shown next, FIRST, by default, displays the first 10 lines of the file:

```
C:\> FIRST < FILENAME.EXT <ENTER>
```

The following command, for example, displays the first 100 lines of a file:

```
C:\> FIRST 100 < FILENAME.EXT <ENTER>
```

If the number of lines specified exceeds the number of lines in the file, FIRST will display the entire file.

The utility command FIRST.EXE resides on the companion disk that accompanies this book.

FIRST.EXE

Assigning Line Numbers to a Text File

If you are working with text files, you sometimes may want to precede the file's contents with line numbers. The companion disk that accompanies this book provides the utility program LINENBR.EXE that assigns line numbers to a text file. Invoke LINENBR as follows:

```
C:\> LINENBR FILENAME.EXT > NEWFILE.EXT
```

If you don't redirect LINENBR's output, LINENBR will display its output to the screen.

The utility program LINENBR.EXE resides on the companion disk that accompanies this book.

LINENBR.EXE

Setting a File's Date and Time Stamp

Each time you create or change a file, DOS assigns the current date and time to the file's directory entry. You sometimes may want to change the date and time stamp assigned to a file without actually changing the file's contents. One way to do this is by using the COPY command. For example, assume you want to set the date and time stamp for a file named FILENAME.EXT to the current date and time. You would issue the following COPY command:

```
C:\> COPY  FILENAME.EXT/B+CON/A  FILENAME.EXT <ENTER>
```

The /B switch directs DOS to perform a binary file copy operation.

The /A switch directs COPY to treat CON as an ASCII device. The plus sign directs COPY to append the contents you type at the keyboard to the previous file. Last, the second occurrence of the name FILENAME.EXT tells COPY the name of the target file. When you press ENTER to execute the command, your screen will display the following:

```
C:\> COPY  FILENAME.EXT/B+CON/A  FILENAME.EXT <ENTER>
FILENAME.EXT
CON
```

Because you don't want to change the file in any way, press the F6 (end-of-file) function key and press ENTER. Your screen will display the following:

```
C:\> COPY  FILENAME.EXT/B+CON/A  FILENAME.EXT <ENTER>
FILENAME.EXT <ENTER>
CON <ENTER>
^Z  <ENTER>
     1 file(s) copied
```

Because you did not change the file's contents, only the file's date and time stamp will change. If you want to assign a date and time stamp using other than the current date and time, select the desired date and time with DATE and TIME, update the file's data and time stamp as shown, and then restore the original date and time.

Setting Several Files' Date and Time Stamps

Tip 518 discusses how you can change one file's date and time stamps with COPY. If you have several files whose date and time stamps you want to change, you can use the CHGSTAMP utility program provided on this book's companion disk. CHGSTAMP sets the date and time stamp of files specified to the current date and time. The following CHGSTAMP command, for example, sets the date and time stamp for every file in the current directory:

```
C:\> CHGSTAMP *.* <ENTER>
```

As discussed in Tip 518, to use a specific date and time, use DATE and TIME to select the date and time and then invoke CHGSTAMP.

After CHGSTAMP ends, use DATE and TIME to restore the original date and time.

The utility command CHGSTAMP.EXE resides on the companion disk that accompanies this book.

CHGSTAMP.EXE

Leave the System File Attribute for DOS Use Only

If you are using DOS 5, the ATTRIB command lets you set or clear a file's system attribute. Likewise, some third-party disk utilities let you manipulate the system attribute. As a general rule, leave the use of the *system* attribute to DOS. If you don't want a file to appear in a directory listing or to be affected by directory commands, set the *file's* hidden attribute. When you start manipulating the system

attribute, you risk inadvertently changing the attributes of IO.SYS or MSDOS.SYS, the two key system files DOS needs to start.

Verifying a Critical File Copy Operation

Tip 18 discusses the use of the VERIFY command to ensure that data you have written to disk has been correctly recorded. Use of the VERIFY command imposes considerable system overhead, which slows down your system performance. Most users typically leave disk verification disabled. If you copy a critical file by using COPY or XCOPY, you can include the /V switch to direct DOS to verify the copy operation as shown here:

```
C:\> COPY FILENAME.ONE FILENAME.TWO /V <ENTER>
```

By using the /V switch in this way, you gain the benefits of disk verification for the duration of the copy operation without introducing the constant overhead of disk verification.

Making Your File Names More Meaningful

DOS filenames consist of two parts: an up-to-8-character base name that describes the file's contents and an up-to-3-character extension that describes the file's type. As you create files, take full advantage of all 11 characters to create meaningful names. Although most users only use the letters A through Z in their filenames, DOS also lets you use numbers and the following characters:

```
~ ! @ # $ ^ & ( ) - _ { } '
```

Note how the use of these characters lets you create meaningful filenames:

1992TAX.RPT	PHONE#S.DAT	PROFITS!.$$$
APR&MAY.EXP	KEY_ACCT.LST	(SOLD) .DAT

Displaying a Directory's Deleted Files

Tip 511 discusses in detail the steps DOS performs when it deletes a file. If you are using DOS 5, you can use the UNDELETE command to unerase an inadvertently deleted file. To view the names of deleted files in a directory, invoke UNDELETE with the /LIST switch as shown here:

```
C:\> UNDELETE /LIST <ENTER>
```

The UNDELETE command will list the names of the deleted files and tell you whether the files can be undeleted. If the directory contains several files that cannot be undeleted, you can remove the corresponding directory entries as discussed in Tip 455.

To use the UNDELETE command, you must be using DOS 5.

Abbreviating COPY Commands

The COPY command copies the contents of one file's contents to another. Although users use this command regularly, most users type a longer command than they need. COPY requires you to specify a source and target filename as shown here:

```
C:\> COPY SOURCE.EXT TARGET.EXT <ENTER>
```

When you copy a file from one directory to another, or from one disk to another, and you don't want to change the filename, you can considerably reduce your typing by taking advantage of COPY's default filenames. For example, assume you want to copy the file TESTFILE.EXT from the current directory to drive A. One way is to specify the source and target filenames as shown here:

```
C:\> COPY TESTFILE.EXT A:TESTFILE.EXT <ENTER>
```

As an alternative, you can use wildcards as shown here:

```
C:\> COPY TESTFILE.EXT A:*.* <ENTER>
```

However, if you don't specify a filename or wildcards, by default COPY will use the same name for the target file as for the source file. Thus, the following COPY command is equivalent to the previous commands:

```
C:\> COPY TESTFILE.EXT A: <ENTER>
```

If you don't specify a filename when you copy a file from one disk or directory to another, COPY uses the same filename for the target as you have specified for the source. For example, the following command copies the file TESTFILE.EXT from the directory SUBDIR to the current directory with the same name TESTFILE.EXT:

```
C:\> COPY \SUBDIR\TESTFILE.EXT <ENTER>
```

By taking advantage of COPY's use of the source filename, you can reduce the length of your copy commands that copy files from one drive or directory to another.

Know When to Use RECOVER

As you work with DOS, a power loss or disk error may leave a file damaged. When you later try to use the file, DOS may display a message telling you that it encountered an error while reading from or writing to the file. In such instances, the RECOVER command may help you salvage part of the file. The following illustration shows a file containing several undamaged sectors, followed by a damaged sector, and then several more undamaged sectors:

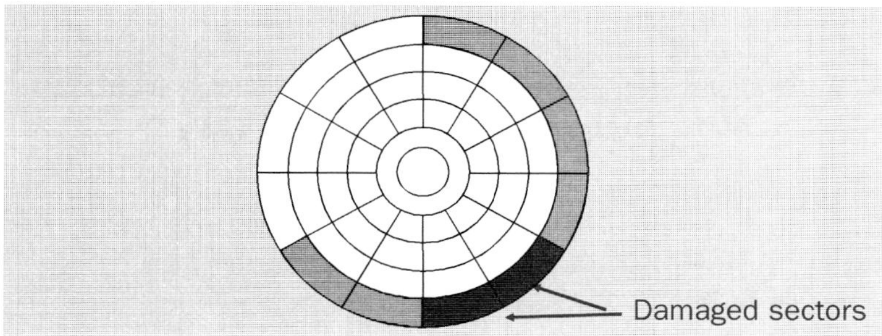

When you attempt to use the file, DOS can't get past the damaged sectors. The RECOVER command will salvage the file's sectors up to the damaged sector, discarding the file contents that follow. If the damaged sector occurs near the start of the file, you won't be able to salvage much. If the damaged sector appears near the end of the file, you may save considerable data. Think of RECOVER as a last-ditch attempt to rescue your data. You are much better off restoring a backup copy of the file. Should you need to recover part of a file, invoke RECOVER as shown here:

```
C:\> RECOVER FILENAME.EXT <ENTER>
```

Never invoke RECOVER with a file that is not damaged.

Because the type of file error discussed here is rare, most users will never require RECOVER. If you are setting up a system for a new user, consider removing the RECOVER command from the disk to avoid user confusion with UNDELETE.

Understanding the Asterisk (*) Wildcard

Although most users have used the asterisk wildcard with DIR, DEL, or COPY, many don't really understand how the wildcard behaves. Consider the following DIR command:

```
C:\> DIR *.* <ENTER>
```

In this case, DIR will test the name of every file in the current directory.

The following command directs DIR to display listings for files residing in the DOS directory that begins with the word *DISK*:

```
C:\> DIR \DOS\DISK*.*

 Volume in drive C has no label
 Volume Serial Number is 16F6-3B73
 Directory of C:\DOS

DISKCOMP COM      10652 04-09-91   5:00a
DISKCOPY COM      11793 04-09-91   5:00a
        2 file(s)       22445 bytes
                     48533504 bytes free
```

Some users might guess the following DIR command would display the directory listing for DISKCOPY and DISKCOMP:

```
C:\> DIR D*CO*.*
```

However, when DOS encounters the asterisk wildcard character in either a filename or extension, DOS ignores all of the characters that follow the asterisk. In the previous DIR command, for example, DOS ignores the characters CO* that follow the first asterisk. The DIR command in this case displays the following files:

```
C:\> DIR D*CO*.*

 Volume in drive C has no label
 Volume Serial Number is 16F6-3B73
 Directory of C:\DOS

DISPLAY  SYS      15792 04-09-91   5:00a
DEBUG    EXE      20634 04-09-91   5:00a
DOSKEY   COM       5883 04-09-91   5:00a
DOSSHELL VID       9462 04-09-91   5:00a
DOSSHELL COM       4623 04-09-91   5:00a
DOSSHELL EXE     235484 04-09-91   5:00a
DOSSHELL GRB       4421 04-09-91   5:00a
DOSSWAP  EXE      18756 04-09-91   5:00a
DOSHELP  HLP       5650 06-09-92   3:20p
DOSSHELL HLP     161763 04-09-91   5:00a
DISKCOMP COM      10652 04-09-91   5:00a
DISKCOPY COM      11793 04-09-91   5:00a
```

```
DRIVER   SYS        5409 04-09-91   5:00a
DOSSHELL INI       13675 07-16-92  10:09p
       14 file(s)       523997 bytes
                      48529408 bytes free
```

The point to remember is that once DOS encounters the asterisk wildcard in a filename or extension, any characters that follow the asterisk are meaningless.

Using REPLACE to Update Files on Your Disk

One of the least-understood DOS commands, REPLACE, can be very convenient when you need to update files on your hard disk. As you work with files in directories, periodically you will end up with duplicate copies of program files on your hard disk. If you later receive an update to such a file on a floppy disk, REPLACE makes lets you easily and quickly update every occurrence of the program file on your disk. For example, assume the floppy disk in drive A contains the program file SOMEPROG.EXE. The following REPLACE command replaces every occurrence of the file on your hard disk with the new file:

```
C:\> REPLACE  A:SOMEPROG.EXE  C:\  /S <ENTER>
```

If you include the /P switch, REPLACE will prompt you individually for each file, asking you if you want to perform the replacement. If you note the directory names listed, you can later delete the duplicate files, if necessary, to free disk space.

Performing a Selective File Delete Operation

When you clean up the files that reside in your directory, you sometimes may want to select specific files for deletion. One of the easiest ways to do so is using the DOS 5 shell. To begin, invoke the shell and select the directory desired. Next, select the files you want to delete. If you are using a mouse, you can select files by holding down the CTRL key and clicking the names of the desired files. If you aren't

using a mouse, press the SHIFT-F8 keyboard combination. The shell will display the message Add in the status bar. To select a file, highlight the file by using your arrow keys and press the space bar. If you accidentally select a wrong file, simply press the space bar a second time. After you have selected the desired files, press DEL. The shell will display a dialog box asking you to verify the file deletion. Select OK.

By default, the shell will prompt you to verify each file's deletion individually. Using the Options menu Confirmation option, you can disable the Confirm on Delete dialog box. By deleting files from within the shell, you can visually watch and manage your changes to the directory.

Viewing a File with PGUP and PGDN

The TYPE command lets you display the contents of an ASCII file. There may be times when, depending on the file's contents, it would be more convenient to traverse the file's contents using the PGUP and PGDN keys. If you use an editor to view the file, you run the risk of inadvertently changing the file's contents. The DOS 5 shell, however, provides a way to view files (as read only) while still using PGUP and PGDN. To view a file using the shell, select the file's directory and then highlight the file by pressing the TAB and arrow keys. By default, unless you have changed the shell's "explicit selection" setting as Tip 728 shows, the shell automatically selects the highlighted file. Next, select the File menu View option or press F9. The shell will display the file's contents, letting you traverse the file using the PGUP and PGDN keys. When you are done viewing the files, press ESC.

Moving One or More Files

Tip 507 discusses moving a file from one directory to another. If you need to move several files from one directory to another, a convenient way to do so is to use the DOS 5 shell. To begin, select the directory containing the files you want to move. Next select the files you

want to move (see Tip 606 for a discussion of how to select files). Next, select the File menu and choose Move, or simply press the F7 function key. The shell will display a dialog box asking you for the desired directory. Type the directory name and press ENTER. The shell will copy the file to the new directory. If the copy operation is successful, the shell will delete the file. If a file already exists in the new directory with the same name as a file you want to move, the shell will display a dialog box asking you if you want to overwrite the existing file. To overwrite the file select Yes; otherwise, select No.

Mouse-Driven File Copy and Move Operations Within the DOS 5 Shell

As you know, you can copy files using the DOS 5 shell's File menu. Tip 530 discusses moving files within the shell. By using a mouse, you also can generally move or copy a file. To copy a file, for example, select the file or files you want to copy. Next, hold down the mouse button and drag the files to the desired disk drive icon or directory. When you release the mouse button, the shell will display a dialog box asking you to confirm the operation. To move files using the mouse, perform the same steps, but hold down the ALT key while you drag the mouse.

Performing an Incremental Backup Operation

Tip 354 describes how to back up every file on your hard disk to a floppy disk. Because of the tremendous storage capacity of hard disks, backing up an entire hard disk can be a time-consuming task. Luckily, however, you don't have to perform a complete disk backup operation on a regular basis; you need to back up only those files you have created or changed since the last backup operation. Ideally, you should perform an incremental backup operation for your new and changed files daily.

Because you normally don't create or change a large number of files each day, the backup operation can be completed quickly. Use the following scenario to perform your backup operations. At the start of each month, perform a complete disk backup operation. On the remaining days of the month, use the following BACKUP command to perform an incremental backup operation:

```
C:\> BACKUP C:\*.* A:/S/A/M <ENTER>
```

Searching Your Disk for Specific Files

Tip 340 discusses how you can search your disk for specific files by using the DOS 5 DIR command. Using the DOS shell, you can quickly search your disk for files. When the shell lists matching files, you can select the files and perform a specific file operation. For example, you can search your disk for files with the BAK extension. When the shell lists the files, you can select the files and quickly delete them. To use the shell to search for files, select the File menu and choose Search. The shell will display a dialog box prompting you for the desired filename. Type a filename or wildcard combination and press ENTER. The shell will search your disk and display a dialog box listing matching files. You can then select files and manipulate them using File menu options.

Selectively Assigning File Attributes

Several of the tips presented in this book discuss how you set or clear file attributes by using the ATTRIB command. Using the DOS 5 shell, you can selectively assign or clear file attributes. To begin, select the directory containing the desired files. Following the steps discussed in Tip 606, select the files you desire. Next, select the File menu and choose Change Attributes. The shell will display a dialog box prompting you for the attributes you want to change. Each option on the dialog box works

as a toggle, meaning that if you select an option, the shell changes the file's attribute to the opposite of its current setting. Highlight a desired attribute and press the space bar. After the attributes are selected, select OK. The shell will display a dialog box asking you if you want to change files individually or all at once. Select the option you desire and press ENTER.

Viewing a File's Contents in Hexadecimal and ASCII Formats

The TYPE command lets you view an ASCII file's contents on your screen. There may be times, however, when you not only want to view the file's standard ASCII characters, but the hidden characters such as carriage returns and line feeds. Using the DOS 5 shell, you can view a file's ASCII and hexadecimal contents at the same time. To begin, go to the shell and select the directory containing the desired file. Next, use the TAB and arrow keys to highlight the filename. Select the File menu and choose View File Contents. The shell will display the file's ASCII-format contents. Select the Display menu and choose Hex. The shell will divide the screen into three parts. The first part contains byte offsets, the second the file's hexadecimal-format contents, and the third the file's ASCII-format contents. In the file's hexadecimal-format contents, the value 0D corresponds to a carriage return and 0A to a line feed.

Displaying a File's Last Lines

The TYPE command lets you display an ASCII file's contents on your screen display. Tip 516 describes how to use the companion disk FIRST utility to display the first *n* lines. The companion disk also includes the LAST utility, which displays the last *n* lines of a file. For example, the following command displays the last five lines of your CONFIG.SYS file:

```
C:\> LAST 5 < CONFIG.SYS <ENTER>
```

If you do not specify the number of lines, as shown here, LAST, by default, uses the value 10:

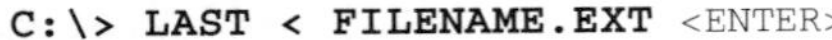

```
C:\> LAST < FILENAME.EXT <ENTER>
```

LAST.EXE

The utility program LAST.EXE resides on the companion disk that accompanies this book.

Displaying File Contents or Command Output in Uppercase Letters

Tip 61 discusses the utility program LOWER.COM that lets you display a file's contents or a command's output in lowercase letters. Similarly, the following DEBUG script file, UPPER.SCR, creates a command file named UPPER.COM that uses uppercase letters:

UPPER.SCR

```
N UPPER.COM    <ENTER>
A 100          <ENTER>
JMP 103        <ENTER>
DB '?'         <ENTER>
MOV AH,3F      <ENTER>
MOV BX,0       <ENTER>
MOV CX,1       <ENTER>
MOV DX,102     <ENTER>
INT 21         <ENTER>
CMP AX,0       <ENTER>
JE  12A        <ENTER>
MOV AL,[102]   <ENTER>
CMP AL,61      <ENTER>
JL  122        <ENTER>
CMP AL,7A      <ENTER>
JG  122        <ENTER>
```

```
SUB AL,20       <ENTER>
MOV DL,AL       <ENTER>
MOV AH,02       <ENTER>
INT 21          <ENTER>
JMP 103         <ENTER>
MOV AH,4C       <ENTER>
INT 21          <ENTER>
<ENTER>
R CX            <ENTER>
2E              <ENTER>
W               <ENTER>
Q               <ENTER>
```

Use the DEBUG command as follows to create the command file UPPER.COM:

```
C:\> DEBUG < UPPER.SCR <ENTER>
```

The following command displays the contents of the AUTOEXEC.BAT file in uppercase letters:

```
C:\> UPPER < \AUTOEXEC.BAT <ENTER>
```

Searching Files for Specific Text

As the number of files on your disk increases, there may be times when you can't recall which file contains your desired text. If your files contain ASCII text, such as batch files, you can search the files for the matching text using the FIND command as shown here:

```
C:\> FIND "text" *.* <ENTER>
```

For example, if you want to search for the name Richard, you can use FIND as shown here:

```
C:\> FIND "Richard" *.* <ENTER>
```

Note that FIND searches files only in the current directory or the directory specified. Likewise, FIND is case sensitive, meaning that it considers "Richard" and "RICHARD" as different text.

Counting the Number of Lines in a File or Redirected Input

Although the DIR command tells you a file's size in bytes, DIR gives you little other information about the file's size in terms of lines or words. Thus, the companion disk that accompanies this book includes the utility program LINECNT.EXE. The following command, for example, uses LINECNT to display a count of the number of lines in the file AUTOEXEC.BAT:

```
C:\> LINECNT < \AUTOEXEC.BAT <ENTER>
```

Similarly, the following command displays a count of the number of lines output by the DIR command:

```
C:\> DIR | LINECNT <ENTER>
```

LINECNT.EXE

The utility command LINECNT.EXE resides on the companion disk that accompanies this book.

Adding a Margin to Text Files

When you print a text file by using PRINT or COPY or by redirecting output to the printer, the text appears very close to the left edge of the page. If, for example, you want to place the printout in a binder, the holes you punch may interfere with the text. The following DEBUG script file, MARGIN.SCR, creates a utility command named MARGIN.COM that adds a one-tab margin to its redirected input:

```
N MARGIN.COM <ENTER>
A 100        <ENTER>
JMP 103      <ENTER>
DB '?'       <ENTER>
MOV DL,9     <ENTER>
MOV AH,2     <ENTER>
INT 21       <ENTER>
MOV AH,3F    <ENTER>
MOV BX,0     <ENTER>
MOV CX,1     <ENTER>
MOV DX,102   <ENTER>
INT 21       <ENTER>
CMP AX,0     <ENTER>
JE  134      <ENTER>
MOV DL,[102] <ENTER>
CMP DL,A     <ENTER>
JNE 12E      <ENTER>
MOV AH,2     <ENTER>
MOV DL,9     <ENTER>
INT 21       <ENTER>
MOV DL,[102] <ENTER>
MOV AH,2     <ENTER>
INT 21       <ENTER>
JMP 109      <ENTER>
MOV AH,4C    <ENTER>
INT 21       <ENTER>
             <ENTER>
R CX         <ENTER>
38           <ENTER>
W            <ENTER>
Q            <ENTER>
```

MARGIN.SCR

Use the DEBUG command as follows to create MARGIN.COM:

```
C:\> DEBUG < MARGIN.SCR <ENTER>
```

Use MARGIN.COM with the DOS redirection operators as shown here:

```
C:\> MARGIN < FILENAME.EXT > PRN <ENTER>
```

A One-Step Undelete Operation

When MIRROR's file tracking is not active, using the UNDELETE command forces you to type the first letter of the name of each file you want undeleted. Alternatively, you can invoke the UNDELETE command with the /ALL switch as shown here:

```
C:\SUBDIR> UNDELETE /ALL <ENTER>
```

Rather than prompting you for the first letter of each filename, UNDELETE will use the characters #, %, &, and - followed by the numbers 0 through 9 and then the letters A through Z. After the UNDELETE command ends, you can use RENAME at your convenience to restore correct filenames.

By using the /ALL switch with UNDELETE, you can perform undelete operations much faster.

A Simple Virus Checker

Before a virus can attack your system, the virus must attach itself to a program or batch file. When you later execute the program, the virus gets loaded into your computer's memory. The companion disk that accompanies this book contains the utility command 1STVIRUS.EXE that you can use as your first line of defense against viruses. To use 1STVIRUS, invoke the command with a filename as shown here:

```
C:\> 1STVIRUS Filename.Ext <ENTER>
```

As shown here, the command displays a unique value for the program, which you need to write down:

```
C:\> 1STVIRUS Filename.Ext <ENTER>
Value: 1021
```

You can later invoke the 1STVIRUS command from within a batch file, including the file's value. If the file's current value does not match the value specified, the file has been changed, possibly because of a virus. In this case, 1STVIRUS will return the exit status value 1, indicating a change. If the file's value and the specified value match, 1STVIRUS returns the exit status 0. The following batch file commands illustrate how you might use 1STVIRUS:

```
@ECHO OFF
1STVIRUS Filename.Ext 1021
IF ERRORLEVEL 0 SomeCommand
IF ERRORLEVEL 1 GOTO PossibleVirus
REM Other commands here
```

Computer viruses are very complex and sophisticated programs. The 1STVIRUS utility program is only one tool you can use to defend your PC. For the best protection, use a third-party virus-protection package. If a program file is already infected, 1STVIRUS cannot detect the virus; 1STVIRUS can detect only changes to program files that occur after you obtain the file's unique value.

1STVIRUS.EXE

The utility command 1STVIRUS.EXE resides on the companion disk that accompanies this book.

Counting the Number of Words in an ASCII File

Tip 539 presents the LINECNT utility, which displays a count of the number of lines in an ASCII file or redirected input. Similarly, the companion disk that accompanies this book includes the utility program WORDCNT.EXE, which displays a count of the number of words in a file. A word is any string of characters separated by a space, tab, or carriage return. To use WORDCNT to count the number of words in the ASCII file BOOK.RPT, use WORDCNT as follows:

```
C:\> WORDCNT < BOOK.RPT <ENTER>
```

WORDCNT.EXE

The utility command WORDCNT.EXE resides on the companion disk that accompanies this book.

Moving the File WINA20.386 from Your Root Directory

When you perform the DOS 5 upgrade on a 386 computer or higher, the upgrade places the read-only file WINA20.386 in your disk's root directory. Windows uses this file to switch between virtual DOS applications while it is running in enhanced mode. As Tip 447 explains, the only files your root directory should contain are AUTOEXEC.BAT and CONFIG.SYS. To move the file WINA20.386 from your root directory (ideally to your Windows directory), perform these steps:

1. Move the file WINA20.386 from the root to the desired directory.
2. Edit the file CONFIG.SYS and add the following entry:

```
SWITCHES=/W
```

3. Edit the Windows file SYSTEM.INI and place the following entry immediately after the [386Enh] entry:

```
[386Enh]
DEVICE=C:\WINDOWS\WINA20.386
```

4. Restart your system by pressing CTRL-ALT-DEL.

Replacing a Word or Phrase Throughout an ASCII File with EDIT

As you work with large batch files or other ASCII files, you sometimes may need to replace several occurrences of a word or phrase throughout a file. Using the DOS 5 EDIT command, you can do so very quickly. To begin, invoke EDIT with the desired filename as shown here:

```
C:\> EDIT Filename.Ext <ENTER>
```

Next, press ALT-S to select the search menu and choose Change. EDIT will display a dialog box prompting you for the text you want to change. Type the text and press the TAB key (not ENTER). Next, type the desired replacement word or phrase. By default, EDIT considers uppercase and lowercase letters as the same input. If you want EDIT to perform a case-sensitive operation, press the TAB key to select the Match Upper/Lowercase option and then press the space bar. Again by default, EDIT will match text that appears within another word. For example, if the text to replace is the word *book*, EDIT will match *bookstore* as well. If you want EDIT to match only whole words, press TAB to select the Whole Word option and press the space bar. Last, EDIT lets you individually confirm the replacement of each match (by using the Find and Verify option), or you can direct EDIT to automatically change every match (using the Change All option). Press the TAB key to select one of these options and press ENTER.

Copying the Files You Created Today to Floppy Disk

Tip 948 explains that the companion disk utility SETDATE.EXE assigns the current date to an environment entry named DATE. The following batch file, CPTODAYS.BAT, uses the named parameter %DATE% to back up the files you created or changed today to the floppy disk in drive A:

```
@ECHO OFF
SETDATE
BACKUP C:\*.* A: /S /L:%DATE%
SET DATE=
```

A TYPE Command with Batch File Support

The TYPE command lets you display the contents of an ASCII file on your screen. If you invoke TYPE with a filename that does not exist, TYPE displays the following error message:

```
C:\> TYPE Filename.Ext
File not found - FILENAME.EXT
```

When you invoke TYPE from the DOS prompt, you are instantly aware of the error and can correct it. However, if you invoke TYPE from within a batch file and the file specified is not found, the batch file has no way of knowing that the TYPE command failed. In other words, TYPE does not provide an exit status value. Luckily, the companion disk that accompanies this book contains the utility command BAT_TYPE.EXE that, like TYPE, displays an ASCII file's contents but, unlike TYPE, provides the exit status values listed in Table 547.

Table 547. Exit Status Values Supported by the BAT_TYPE Command

Exit Status	Meaning
0	Operation succeeded.
1	File was not found.
2	Path was not found.

The following batch commands illustrate how you might use BAT_TYPE:

```
@ECHO
IFNOT '%1'==" BAT_TYPE %1
IF ERRORLEVEL 1 GOTO ERROR
REM Other commands here
```

The utility command BAT_TYPE.EXE resides on the companion disk that accompanies this book.

BAT_TYPE.EXE

Using EDLIN to Replace a Word or Phrase Throughout an ASCII File

Tip 545 discusses how to replace a word or phrase by using EDIT, the DOS 5 screen editor. If you are not yet using DOS 5, you can perform similar operations by using EDLIN. To use EDLIN to replace a word or phrase throughout a document, invoke EDLIN specifying the desired filename as shown here:

```
C:\> EDLIN Filename.Ext <ENTER>
```

EDLIN will display its asterisk prompt. Next, use the following replacement command (R) to replace the word or phrase:

```
1,#R OldText^ZNewText <ENTER>
```

To generate the ^Z characters, press the F6 function key. For example, to replace the word *DOS* with *MS-DOS*, you would use the following command:

```
*1,#RDOS^ZMS-DOS <ENTER>
```

In this case, EDLIN will automatically replace each occurrence of the word *DOS*. If you want EDLIN to prompt you before each replacement, include a question mark in the command as shown here:

```
*1,#?RDOS^ZMS-DOS <ENTER>
```

TIP 549 Understanding How EXE and COM Files differ

Files with the EXE and COM extensions contain executable programs and commands. Many users ask why a specific file uses one or the other. Actually, the programmer who creates the program is the one who decides on the extension. For best performance, the programmer will normally try to create files in the COM format. However, the programmer must satisfy the COM file restrictions:

- A COM program's instructions and data must be less than 64Kb.
- A COM program's instructions cannot use a far call to subroutines outside of the code segment.

The COM file contains an exact copy of the information DOS will load into memory. Thus, a COM file will begin execution slightly faster than an EXE file. When you execute an EXE file, on the other hand, DOS must allocate areas in memory for the program's instructions, data, and stack and then load the EXE file, making adjustments for the various memory locations. The process of adjusting for memory locations is called relocation and results in some system overhead when a program starts. Ideally, for best performance, every program would be a COM file. Unfortunately, most programs are simply too large to fit the COM format.

Some DOS versions include a command named EXE2BIN that converts an EXE file to the COM format (because of the differences in their format, you cannot simply rename an EXE file as COM). The EXE2BIN command is a programmer's utility. You should not use it yourself to convert files. In most cases, if a program can meet the COM requirements, the programmer who created it will choose the COM format.

If you try to convert an EXE file that does not meet the COM requirements, EXE2BIN will display an error message as shown here:

```
C:\> EXE2BIN SOMEPROG.EXE SOMEPROG.COM <ENTER>
File cannot be converted
```

Backup Logs Make Files Easier to Find

Tip 354 discusses how you can make a complete backup of your disk. Likewise, Tip 532 discusses making incremental backups. Depending on the size and number of files on your hard disk, you may end up with a considerable number of backup floppies. Should you ever need to restore a specific file, locating the file on your backup disks can be a difficult task. One way to make the take easier is to create a backup log file that lists the files stored on each floppy disk. To begin, create a directory named BACKUP, within which you will store the log file:

```
C:\> MKDIR \BACKUP <ENTER>
```

Next, when you invoke the BACKUP command, include the /L switch to tell BACKUP the name of the log file you want to create. Your command to perform a complete disk backup operation will become the following:

```
C:\> BACKUP C:\*.* A: /S /L:C:\BACKUP\BACKUP.LOG <ENTER>
```

Likewise, your incremental backup command becomes the following:

```
C:\> PRINT C:\BACKUP\BACKUP.LOG <ENTER>
```

To prevent your backup log from becoming too long, delete the log file before performing each compete disk backup operation.

Repairing Cross-Linked Files

If you turn off your computer while a program other than DOS is active, or if you experience a power outage, two files may become cross linked. To track your files on disk, DOS uses a table of disk clusters

called the file allocation table, or FAT. The FAT tracks available disk locations, which locations are in use by which files, and unusable locations marked as damaged by FORMAT. When two files become cross linked, one of the files mistakenly thinks it owns the storage locations that belong to another file. The only way to detect cross-linked files is by using the CHKDSK command as follows:

```
C:\> CHKDSK /F <ENTER>
```

If a file is cross linked, CHKDSK will display the following message:

```
FILENAME.EXT
Is cross-linked on allocation unit nn
```

When a file is cross linked, the file normally loses part of its previous contents. Thus, CHKDSK typically displays the following error message as well:

```
nnn lost allocation units found in n chains
Convert lost chains to files (Y/N)?
```

Type **Y** to recover the lost file chains. CHKDSK will create one or more files in the root directory whose names have the form FILE0000.CHK, FILE0001.CHK, and so on. Use the TYPE command to display each file's contents. If the file contains recognizable text, use RENAME to assign it a meaningful name. Otherwise, delete the file. Next, to correct the cross link, follow the procedures listed here.

For ASCII or word processing files, follow this steps:

- ❑ Copy the two cross-linked files to a different disk or directory.
- ❑ Delete the two cross-linked files.
- ❑ Copy the files back from the directory on the disk you used in the first step.
- ❑ If the files are ASCII or word processing files, edit the files to determine which file contains the correct contents. Remove the invalid contents from the second file.
- ❑ If one of the files created by CHKDSK (FILEnnnn.CHK) contains information belonging to one of the cross-linked files, edit the file and merge the appropriate data.

For executable files, note the following:

- ❑ Executing a command file that has been cross linked is dangerous because the program may now contain unrelated instructions from two commands. Depending on the instructions, the program could inadvertently damage your disk or files.
- ❑ Delete both of the files in question and restore the originals from your backup disks.

Copying Zero-Length Files

Depending on your application programs, a directory sometimes may contain a file whose size is zero bytes, such as the one shown here.

```
FILENAME EXT          0 12-31-90   12:00p
```

If you try to copy the file with the COPY command, the command will fail, displaying the following error message:

```
C:\> COPY FILENAME.EXT FILENAME.NEW <ENTER>
     0 file(s) copied
```

To copy a zero-length file, use the XCOPY command as shown here:

```
C:\> XCOPY FILENAME.EXT FILENAME.NEW <ENTER>
```

Understanding XCOPY's (F=File, D=Directory) Prompt

Several of the tips presented in this book recommend times when you should use the XCOPY command instead of COPY. Tip 524 discusses shortcuts you can use when you issue the COPY command. Each of these techniques also supports XCOPY. For example, the following command copies files in the current directory that have the BAT extension to the directory BATCH that resides in the root:

```
C:\> XCOPY *.BAT  \BATCH <ENTER>
```

Because the copy destination does not specify a filename and extension, XCOPY uses the source filename and extension as it copies files to the directory. Such a command allows you to quickly copy files from one directory to another. However, if the target directory does not exist, XCOPY will display the following prompt:

```
Does FILENAME specify a filename
or directory name on the target
(F=file, D=directory)?
```

XCOPY displays this prompt because it doesn't know whether you want to place the files in a directory or to combine all the files into one large file. If you want XCOPY to combine all of the specified files into one large file, press F. If XCOPY displays this message because you misspelled the target directory name, press CTRL-C to end the command and then retype the correct command at the DOS prompt.

Creating a Monthly Backup Batch File

Tip 354 discusses the process of backing up your entire hard disk to floppy disks by using the BACKUP command. Ideally, you should perform a complete disk backup operation at least once a month. To simplify this process, create the following batch file, COMPLETE.BAT:

```
@ECHO OFF
REM Make sure a directory named BACKUP exists
REM to hold the log file.
MKDIR C:\BACKUP > NUL

REM If a previous log file exists, rename it.
IF EXIST C:\BACKUP\BACKUP.LOG REN C:\BACKUP\BACKUP.LOG *.SAV

REM Perform the backup.
BACKUP C:\*.*  A: /S /L:C:\BACKUP\BACKUP.LOG
```

At the start of each month, invoke the batch file as follows:

```
C:\> COMPLETE <ENTER>
```

The batch file assumes you are using formatted floppy diskettes. If your diskettes aren't formatted, change the BACKUP command to include the /F switch.

Creating an Incremental Backup Batch File

Tip 532 discusses how you perform incremental backup operations to back up only those files created or changed since the last backup operation. Ideally, you should perform incremental backup operations daily. Because incremental backup operations copy only changed or new files, the backup operation completes quickly. To make incremental backup operations easier, create the following batch file FASTBU.BAT:

```
@ECHO OFF
REM Perform the backup.
BACKUP C:\*.*  A: /S /A /M /L:C:\BACKUP\BACKUP.LOG
```

To perform an incremental backup operation, invoke the batch file from the DOS prompt as shown here:

```
C:\> FASTBU <ENTER>
```

Changing a File's Date and Time Stamp

Tip 518 discusses one method of changing an existing file's date and time stamp to the current system date and time. Although Tip 518 works well if you are working interactively at the keyboard, there is

an easier method that is well suited for use in DOS batch files. The following COPY command changes the date and time setup of the file Filename.Ext:

```
C:\. COPY /B Filename.Ext+ <ENTER>
Filename.Ext
    1 file(s) copied
```

Using this copy technique, you can create the following batch file, STAMP.BAT, that sets a file's date and time stamp to the current date and time:

```
@ECHO OFF
IF NOT '%1'==''  COPY /B %1+
IF '%1'=='' ECHO You must specify a filename
```

If you are using DOS 5, the following DOSKEY command creates a similar macro:

```
C:\> DOSKEY STAMP=IFNOT '$1'=='' COPY /B $1+ <ENTER>
```

Controlling APPEND's Directory Search for Complete Pathnames

Tip 459 discusses how to use the APPEND command to create a data file search path. By default, DOS uses the data file search list every time it fails to open a file. By default, DOS uses the data file search path even when you precede the filename with a drive letter and directory path. In most cases, if the user specifies a directory path, the user is probably looking for a specific file. Thus, APPEND should probably not use a different file. Using APPEND's /PATH switch, you can restrict data file searches to those cases when the user does not precede the filename with a drive letter or directory path. To restrict data file search operations in this way, include the switch /PATH:OFF the first time you invoke APPEND as shown here:

```
C:\> APPEND C:\DATA;C:\FILES /PATH:OFF <ENTER>
```

The /PATH:OFF switch directs APPEND not to perform data file search operations when the user precedes the filename with a directory path.

Increasing the Number of Programs that Support Data File Search Operations

Tip 459 discusses how to use the APPEND command to define a data file search path. Using APPEND's /X switch, you can increase the number of operations for which DOS will use the data file search path. By default, DOS uses the data file search path for the following DOS system services:

Int 21H function 0FH Open File
Int 21H function 3DH Open File Handle
Int 21H function 23H Get File Size

If you invoke APPEND by using the /X:ON switch, DOS will use the data file search for the following system services as well:

Int 21H function 11H Find First Entry
Int 21H function 4EH Find First File
Int 21H function 4BH Execute Program

Because /X:ON directs DOS to use the date file search path for the execute program system service, DOS will locate and execute programs that reside in the data file search path, just as if the file's directory were listed in the command path created by PATH.

To use the /X:ON switch, you must specify it the first time you invoke APPEND as shown here:

```
C:\> APPEND  C:\DATA;C:\FILES /X:ON <ENTER>
```

Restoring a Specific File from Your Backup Disks

Several of the tips presented in this book discuss file backup operations. Should you ever need to restore a file from your backup disks, use the backup log file (see Tip 550) to locate the disk containing the file. Next, place the floppy disk in drive A and issue the following RESTORE command:

```
C:\> RESTORE A: Filename.Ext <ENTER>
```

If you don't have a backup log file, you will have to search the backup disks for the file. If the file has not changed since the last complete disk backup operation, place the first backup disk in drive A and issue the previous command. If the file changes regularly, place the last backup disk in drive A and issue the previous RESTORE command.

If this method does not find the file, continue to work backward through your backup disks until RESTORE finds the file.

Excluding Files from a Specific Command

As you execute commands, you sometimes may want a command to ignore one or more files in the directory. For example, you may want to copy to drive A all files except those with the BAK extension. The companion disk that accompanies this book includes the utility command EXCEPT.EXE that lets you apply a command to all files in a directory except those specified. For example, to copy all files except those with the BAK extension, you would issue the following command:

```
C:\> EXCEPT *.BAK COPY *.* A: <ENTER>
```

Similarly, the following command deletes all but one file:

```
C:\> EXCEPT Filename.Ext DEL *.* <ENTER>
```

The third parameter in the EXCEPT command line must be the wild card combination for which you want to execute the command.

The utility command EXCEPT.EXE resides on the companion disk that accompanies this book.

EXCEPT.EXE

Changing Date and Time Stamps for Multiple Files

Tip 518 describes how to quickly update a file's date and time stamp by using COPY. If you are using DOS 5, the following DOSKEY STAMPS macro lets you update the time stamps of several files at one time:

```
C:\> DOSKEY STAMPS=FOR %I IN ($*) DO COPY /B %i+ <ENTER>
```

If you are not using DOS 5, the following batch file, STAMPS.BAT, achieves the same result:

```
@ECHO OFF
:LOOP
SHIFT
IF '%0'=='' GOTO DONE
FOR %%I IN (%0) DO COPY /B %%I+
GOTO LOOP
:DONE
```

Using either the macro or the batch file, you can update several files as shown here:

```
C:\> STAMPS Filename.One Filename.Two Filename.Thr <ENTER>
```

You can also use STAMPS with wildcard characters as follows:

```
C:\> STAMPS *.* <ENTER>
```

Searching Your Disk for Duplicate Files

As the number of files you place on your disk increases, so does your likelihood of duplicating one or more files. If you are using DOS 5, the shell provides you with an easy way to search for duplicate files. To begin, start the DOS shell and press ALT-V to Select the view menu. Next, select the All Files options. The shell will divide your screen into two parts. The left side contains specifics about the currently highlighted file, and the right side contains a sorted listing of every file on your disk. Using your keyboard arrow, PGUP, and PGDN keys, you can quickly search through the list for duplicates. If two files with the same name exist, individually highlight each file. The shell will display the file's directory in the file details that appear on the left side of your screen. By pressing the DEL key, you can delete the highlighted file.

Replacing Text in a File

When you work with ASCII text files, you sometimes may need to replace or remove text. The companion disk that accompanies this book provides the utility command CHG_TXT.EXE that lets you change or delete specific text from a file. For example, to replace the text "K. Jamsa" with "Kris Jamsa" throughout the file named Filename.Ext, you would use CHG_TXT as follows:

```
C;\> CHG_TXT "K. JAMSA"  "KRIS JAMSA" < Filename.Ext <ENTER>
```

In this case, CHG_TXT will write its output to the screen. To save the output to a file, redirect CHG_TXT's output to a file as shown here:

```
C:\> CHG_TXT "Old" "New" < OLDFILE.EXT > NEWFILE.EXT <ENTER>
```

The utility command CHG_TXT.EXE resides on the companion disk that accompanies this book.

CHG_TXT.EXE

Don't Use the Same Filename on Opposite Sides of a DOS I/O Redirection Operator

When you issue commands from the DOS prompt, DOS lets you use multiple I/O redirection operators. For example, the following command sorts the contents of the file named Filename.Ext, redirecting the sorted output to the file Filename.SRT:

```
C:\> SORT < Filename.Ext > Filename.SRT <ENTER>
```

When you use the DOS I/O redirection operators, do not place the same filename on opposite sides of an operator; doing so will cause you to lose the information the file contains. For example, the following SORT command attempts to sort the file Filename.Ext, writing the command's output (the sorted contents) to the same filename:

```
C:\> SORT < Filename.Ext > Filename.Ext <ENTER>
```

Unfortunately, when you execute the command, the output redirection operator directs DOS to overwrite the specified file. Thus, DOS overwrites the file Filename.Ext, destroying the file's contents and leaving the command no data to sort.

Executing a Specific Command for Current Directory Files with Specific Attributes

You sometimes may need to execute a command for files that have specific attributes. The companion disk that accompanies this book provides the utility command FOR_ATTR.EXE that executes a command for files that match the specified file attributes. The format of the FOR_ATTR command is as follows:

FOR_ATTR Attributes Command

Specify the attributes just as you would for ATTRIB. For example, the attributes +R-H-A select read-only files whose hidden and archive attributes are not set. The FOR_ATTR command supports the metacharacters specified in Table 565.

For example, the following command copies the current directory files whose read-only and archive attributes are both set to drive A:

```
C:\> FOR_ATTR  +R+A  COPY $F.$E  A: <ENTER>
```

Table 565. Metacharacters Supported by the FOR_SIZE Command

Metacharacter	Purpose
$F	Filename minus extension
$E	Extension only
$F.$E	Filename.Extension

The utility command FOR_ATTR.EXE resides on the companion disk that accompanies this book.

FOR_ATTR.EXE

Defining a Default File Specification

Tip 451 discusses how to use the DOS 5 DIRCMD environment entry to specify your desired format or file attributes for DIR commands that don't specify otherwise. Using this same technique, you can specify a default file specification that DIR uses if you don't specify otherwise. For example, assume most of the files you work with have the extension RPT (for report). The following DIRCMD entry directs DIR to display only these files unless you specifically include a filename or wildcard in the DIR command line:

```
C:\> SET DIRCMD=*.RPT <ENTER>
```

To use the DIRCMD environment entry, you must be using DOS 5 or higher.

Removing Stubborn Directories

As you clean up the directories on your disk, you sometimes may encounter a stubborn directory that DOS just won't let you remove. Instead, the following message appears:

```
C:\> RMDIR STUBBORN <ENTER>
Invalid path, not directory,
or directory not empty
```

If this error message appears and a listing of the directory shows no files, the directory probably contains one or more hidden files. If you are using DOS 5, use the following ATTRIB command to examine the directory entries:

```
C:\STUBBORN> ATTRIB *.* <ENTER>
```

If a file exists with the hidden or system attribute, use ATTRIB to remove the attribute and then move or delete the files. If you are not using DOS 5, use the FOR_ATTR command discussed in Tip 565 to display the files as shown here:

```
C:\> FOR_ATTR +S ECHO $F.$E has system set <ENTER>
C:\> FOR_ATTR +H ECHO $F.$E has hidden set <ENTER>
```

If a file has the hidden file attribute set, use the UNHIDE utility presented in Tip 905 to remove the attribute. If a file has a system file attribute set, use the NOSYSTEM command presented in Tip 565 to remove the attribute.

Removing a File's System Attribute

Tip 510 discusses the use of DOS file attributes in detail. As this tip explains, you should reserve the system file attribute for use by DOS. Even so, you may periodically encounter user files for which a user has set the system attribute. If you are using DOS 5, you can use the following ATTRIB command to remove the file's system attribute:

```
C:\> ATTRIB -S Filename.Ext <ENTER>
```

If you are not using DOS 5, you can use the command file NOSYSTEM.EXE provided on the companion disk that accompanies this book. The following NOSYSTEM command removes the system attribute from a file named Filename.Ext:

```
C:\> NOSYSTEM Filename.Ext <ENTER>
```

The NOSYSTEM command does not support DOS wildcards.

The utility command NOSYSTEM.EXE resides on the companion disk that accompanies this book.

NOSYSTEM.EXE

A Simple Encryption Filter

Encryption is a process of encoding information in a form that is not easily read or translated. If, for example, you have an office memo you don't want others to read, you can encrypt the file using a password only you know. The companion disk that accompanies this book provides a simple encription command, ENCRYPT.EXE, that encrypts its input using the password you specify. For example, the following command uses ENCRYPT to encrypt the file MEMO.NTS by using the password "My Password":

```
C:\> ENCRYPT "My Password" < MEMO.NTS > MEMO.ENC <ENTER>
```

When you need to use the file, you can decrypt the file by using the following command:

```
C:\> ENCRYPT "My Password" < MEMO.ENC > MEMO.NTS <ENTER>
```

The password you type must match the original letter for letter (uppercase and lowercase format must correspond as well).

Do not forget the password you use to encrypt the file. Without the password, you cannot decrypt the file.

The utility command ENCRYPT.EXE resides on the companion disk that accompanies this book.

ENCRYPT.EXE

File Size Dictates Whether You Use COPY or XCOPY

The COPY and XCOPY commands both let you copy a file's contents. The file size determines whether you should choose COPY or XCOPY. If the file is less than 64Kb, use COPY. Because COPY is an internal DOS command, it will execute faster than XCOPY, which DOS must load from disk. If the file is larger than 64Kb, use XCOPY. As discussed in various tips in this book, a performance goal is to reduce the number of disk I/O operations that the computer must perform. When you use XCOPY to copy a large file, XCOPY allocates as much memory as is currently available and then reads the file, if possible, in one step. In this way, XCOPY considerably reduces the number of disk I/O operations required, thus speeding completion of the command.

When Copying Multiple Files, Use XCOPY

Tip 570 discusses the file-size criteria you should take into account when choosing between COPY and XCOPY. If you are copying more than one file, use XCOPY. A performance goal is to reduce the number of disk I/O operations. When you use COPY to copy multiple files, COPY performs the operation one file at a time. XCOPY, on the other hand, reads as many files as it can into memory and then writes those files to the target disk. By performing file copy operations in this way, XCOPY reduces the number of disk I/O operations required, which speeds the command's execution.

Quickly Moving, Copying, or Deleting ASCII Text with EDIT

As you work with ASCII files, you sometimes may need to move, copy, or delete a large block of text in the file. An easy way to do so is with the DOS 5 EDIT command. To begin, invoke EDIT with the desired filename:

```
C:\> EDIT Filename.Ext <ENTER>
```

Next, use the keyboard's arrow, PGUP, and PGDN keys to locate the desired text. Using your keyboard, hold down the SHIFT key and use the arrow keys to highlight the desired text. Next, press the ALT-E keyboard combination to invoke EDIT's Edit menu. To delete the text, select the clear option or press DEL. If you want to copy text to a different location, select Copy or Press CTRL-INS. If you want to move the text, select Cut or press SHIFT-DEL. If you are copying or moving text, move to the location in the document where you want to place the text. Then press ALT-E to select the Edit menu and choose the Paste option or press SHIFT-INS to place text in the document. If you want to copy the text several times, repeatedly press SHIFT-INS.

What Files Are Open?

As discussed in Tip 131, DOS uses a job file table to track the current program's open files and a system file table to track system files. The CONFIG.SYS FILES entry controls the size of the system file table. To help you better understand the system file table, the companion disk that accompanies this book contains the utility command SYSFILES.EXE that displays the files open throughout the system. To view the files, invoke SYSFILES from the DOS prompt as shown here:

```
C:\> SYSFILES <ENTER>
```

If you invoke SYSFILES from a batch file, the program returns an exit status value corresponding to the number of open files.

SYSFILES.EXE

The utility command SYSFILES.EXE resides on the companion disk that accompanies this book.

Redirecting stderr's Output to a File

Tip 130 and Tip 132 describe how to redirect stderr's output to the NUL device and to your printer. Sometimes, however, you may simply want to file stderr's output. The companion disk that accompanies this book provides the utility command ERRTOLOG.EXE that temporarily redirect's stderr's output to a file named STDERR.LOG. The following command illustrates how you might use ERRTOLOG.EXE:

```
C:\> ERRTOLOG SomeProg [Parameters] <ENTER>
```

ERRTOLOG supports DOS I/O redirection, however you must use the DOSKEY metacharacters $B, $G, $L, and GG.

ERRTOLOG.EXE

The utility command ERRTOLOG.EXE resides on the companion disk that accompanies this book.

Redirect Files More than Just Batch

Often you need to automate common tasks. In many such instances, DOS batch files meet your needs. In some cases, however, you can more fully automate a process by creating redirect files. A redirect file is similar to a batch file in that it contains one or more commands. However, unlike a batch file, a redirect file may also include a sequence of keystrokes that are required by a specific command. For example, the following redirect file, EXAMPLE.RED (the RED stands for redirect), contains several DOS commands as well as the DEBUG commands to create the command file YESORNO.COM:

```
DEBUG > NUL         <ENTER>
N YESORNO.COM       <ENTER>
A 100               <ENTER>
MOV AH,0            <ENTER>
INT 16              <ENTER>
MOV AL,0            <ENTER>
CMP AH,15           <ENTER>
JE  112             <ENTER>
CMP AH,31           <ENTER>
JE  114             <ENTER>
JMP 100             <ENTER>
MOV AL,1            <ENTER>
MOV AH,4C           <ENTER>
INT 21              <ENTER>
                    <ENTER>
R CX                <ENTER>
18                  <ENTER>
W                   <ENTER>
Q                   <ENTER>
                    <ENTER>
CLS                 <ENTER>
REM Do you want to print a directory listing? <ENTER>
YESORNO             <ENTER>
IF ERRORLEVEL 1 DIR > PRN                     <ENTER>
DEL YESORNO.COM <ENTER>
EXIT                <ENTER>
```

To execute the redirect file, redirect it to COMMAND.COM as shown here:

```
C:\> COMMAND < EXAMPLE.RED <ENTER>
```

The commands will execute just as if you had invoked them from the DOS prompt. All redirect files must end with an EXIT command to terminate the command processor. By including carriage returns after each command, the following redirect file displays the system date and time without prompting you to press ENTER:

```
DATE        <ENTER>
            <ENTER>
TIME        <ENTER>
            <ENTER>
EXIT        <ENTER>
```

Finding Lines in a File that Contain Specific Text

As the number of batch, DEBUG script, and redirect files (see Tip 575) on your disk increases, you sometimes will want to search these ASCII files for specific commands or text. The FIND command lets you examine an ASCII file or redirected input for specific text. You can use the FIND command in two ways. First, you can invoke FIND with a filename as shown here:

```
C:\> FIND "Text" Filename.Ext <ENTER>
```

Second, you can invoke FIND by using redirected input as shown here:

```
C:\> SomeProg | FIND "Text" <ENTER>
C:\> FIND "Text" < SomeFile.Ext <ENTER>
```

The following command, for example, uses FIND to display each DEVICE entry in your CONFIG.SYS file:

```
C:\> FIND "DEVICE"  C:\CONFIG.SYS <ENTER>
```

Likewise, this batch file displays the name of each current directory batch file and each line within the batch file that uses the CALL command:

```
@ECHO OFF
FOR %%I in (*.BAT) DO FIND "CALL" %%I
```

The following command uses FIND to display the names of subdirectories within the current directory:

```
C:\> DIR | FIND "<DIR>" <ENTER>
```

Extracting Specific Lines of Redirected Input

Tip 516 presents the utility command FIRST.EXE that extracts the first *n* lines of redirected input. Tip 536 presents the utility command LAST.EXE that extracts the last *n* lines of redirected input. Sometimes, however, the text you desire may fall in the middle of a file. The companion disk that accompanies this book contains the utility command MIDDLE.EXE that extracts a specific number of lines beginning at the line number you specify. For example, the following command would extract 15 lines of text beginning at line 10:

```
C:\> SomeProg | MIDDLE 10 15
```

Likewise, this command would display lines 3 through 10 of your CONFIG.SYS file:

```
C:\> MIDDLE 3 7 < C:\CONFIG.SYS  (ENTER)
```

The utility command MIDDLE.EXE resides on the companion disk that accompanies this book.

MIDDLE.EXE

Solving FIND's Case Sensitivity

As described in Tip 576, the FIND command lets you search a file or redirected input for specific text. By default, FIND performs a case-sensitive search, meaning FIND doesn't consider uppercase and lowercase letters as the same input. If you are using DOS 5, however, you can use FIND's /I switch to direct FIND to ignore the case of letters as shown here:

```
C:\> FIND /I "Text" Filename.Ext <ENTER>
```

or

```
C:\> SomeProg | FIND /I "Text" <ENTER>
```

If you are not using DOS 5, however, you can use the UPPER utility command presented in Tip 537 to first convert the text to uppercase letters and then use FIND to search for an uppercase equivalent of the text as shown here:

```
C:\> Someprog | UPPER | FIND "text" <ENTER>
```

Counting the Number of Occurrences of Specific Text in a File or Redirected Input

As described in Tip 576, the FIND command lets you locate specific text in a file or redirected input. Sometimes, however, you may not want to view the lines that contain the text, but instead want to count the number of lines in the file or redirected input that contains the text. Using FIND's /C switch, you can direct FIND to display only the number of lines containing the specified text. The following batch file, DIRCOUNT.BAT, uses FIND /C to display a count of the number of subdirectories in the current directory:

```
@ECHO OFF
DIR | FIND /C "<DIR>"
```

A Better Text Count Utility

Tip 579 explains how to use FIND's /C switch to display the number of lines containing specified text. If you are searching files for text from within a batch file, a

more useful utility would return an exit status value corresponding to the number of files containing the specified text. The companion disk that accompanies this book contains the utility command TXTLINES.EXE that returns as an exit status the number lines containing the desired text. If the text is not found, TXTLINES returns the exit status 0. Otherwise, TXTLINES's exit status value corresponds to the number of lines containing the text. If more than 255 lines contain the text, the exit status value remains at 255. The following batch file commands illustrate how you could use TXTLINES to search a file for the text "DEVICE":

```
@ECHO OFF
TXTLINES "DEVICE" Filename.Ext
IF ERRORLEVEL 1 GOTO Text_Found
REM Other commands here
```

TXTLINES does not perform a case-sensitive search. Like FIND, TXTLINES also supports redirected input.

The utility command TXTLINES.EXE resides on the companion disk that accompanies this book.

TXTLINES.EXE

Locating Lines of a File or Redirected Input that Don't Contain Specified Text

Tip 576 explains how to use the FIND command to display lines of text from a file or redirected input that contain specific text. Sometimes you may want to display the lines that don't contain the text. Using FIND's /V switch, you can do just that. The following FIND command, for example, directs FIND to display the names of current directory files only, ignoring subdirectory entries:

```
C:\> DIR | FIND /V "<DIR>" <ENTER>
```

Note that your screen will display the volume information, subdirectory name, and count of the number of files found. To exclude this information, change the command in the batch file FILEONLY.BAT as shown here:

```
@ECHO OFF
DIR | FIND /V "<DIR>" | FIND /V "e"
```

Cutting and Pasting (Moving) ASCII Text with EDLIN

Tip 564 describes how to move or copy ASCII text with the DOS 5 EDIT command. If you are not using DOS 5 but need to quickly move or copy text in an ASCII file, you can use EDLIN, the DOS line editor. To do so, you must use EDLIN's C(opy) and M(ove) commands, whose format is shown here:

```
[Startline],[Endline],TargetLine[,NumberOfCopies]C
[Startline],[Endline],TargetLine M
```

All EDLIN commands work by using line numbers. Startline specifies the starting line number of the desired text. If you don't specify a line number, EDLIN uses the current line. Likewise, Endline specifies the line number of the last line in the desired text. As before, if you don't specify a line number, EDLIN uses the current line. TargetLine specifies the line number to which you want the text moved or copied. If you are copying text, NumberOfCopies tells EDLIN how many copies to make. If you don't specify a value, EDLIN makes one copy. The following C(opy) command, for example, copies lines 1 through 5 to line 20:

```
*1,5,20,C <ENTER>
```

By specifying the number of copies desired, the following command places four copies of the text at line 20:

```
*1,5,20,4C <ENTER>
```

Although most people agree that EDLIN is archaic, using it to copy ASCII text in this way is still easier and faster than using many powerful word processors.

Comparing ASCII Files

As the number of ASCII files (batch, DEBUG script, and redirection files) on your disk increases, you may have a large number of files on your disk with the BAK extension that contain changes to previous versions of your files. If you want to know the differences between the file's current contents and the contents of the previous file, use the FC command as shown here:

```
C:\> FC Filename.Ext Filename.BAK <ENTER>
```

Assume, for example, that your disk contains the files APPOINT.DAT and APPOINT.BAK that contain your current and previous appointments. Using FC, you can quickly locate the lines that differ as shown here:

```
C:\> FC APPOINT.DAT APPOINT.BAK  <ENTER>
```

Displaying the Line Numbers in a File that Contain Specific Text

Tip 576 describes how to use the FIND command to locate and display the lines of text in a file that contain specific text. In many cases, you will want to know the line number that corresponds to each

line containing the text. Using the /N switch as follows, you can direct FIND to display the corresponding line numbers of each line in your CONFIG.SYS file that contains the DEVICE entry:

```
C:\> FIND /N "DEVICE" C:\CONFIG.SYS <ENTER>
```

Locating the First Occurrence of Text in a File or Redirected Input

As discussed in Tip 576, the FIND command lets you display each line of a file or redirected input that contains specific text. Unfortunately, the FIND command does not return a status value you can use in your DOS batch files. The companion disk that accompanies this book contains the utility command FIND1ST.EXE that searches a file for occurrences of the specified text. If the text is found, FIND1ST returns the exit status value 1 and assigns the environment entry FIND1ST to the line number that corresponds to the first occurrence. If the text is not found, FIND1ST returns the exit status value 255. The following batch file commands search the file Filename.Ext for the word *Test*; if the word is found, the batch file uses the named parameter %FIND1ST% with the MIDDLE command to display the corresponding line:

```
@ECHO OFF
FIND1ST "Test"
IF ERRORLEVEL 255 GOTO DONE
MIDDLE %FIND1ST% 1
SET FIND1ST=
:DONE
```

FIND1ST.EXE

The utility command FIND1ST.EXE resides on the companion disk that accompanies this book.

Displaying the Line Numbers of Lines that Differ Between Two Files

Tip 583 describes how to compare and display the differences between two ASCII files by using the FC command. In many cases, you will also want to know the line numbers of the lines that differ. Using FC's /N switch, you can direct FC to display the line numbers of each differing line. Assuming that the files SALES.CUR and SALES.OLD contain the following information:

Sales.Old	
Johnson	1400
Smith	1233
Owens	1000
Garle	933
Adams	1503
Brown	1500

Sales.Cur	
Johnson	1400
Smith	1233
Owens	1000
Garle	740
Adams	1503
Brown	1500

Using FC with the /N switch, you can quickly identify the lines that differ, and their line numbers, as shown here:

```
C:\> FC /N  SALES.CUR  SALES.OLD <ENTER>
Comparing files SALES.CUR and SALES.OLD
***** SALES.CUR
    3:  Owens   1000
    4:  Garle    740
    5:  Adams   1503
***** SALES.OLD
    3:  Owens   1000
    4:  Garle    933
    5:  Adams   1503
*****
```

As you can see, FC lists the differing line (line 4) along with the line before and after, so you can see the differing line in context in both files.

Controlling FC's Case Sensitivity

As discussed in Tip 583, the FC command lets you compare ASCII files, displaying the file's differences on your screen. By default, FC performs a case-sensitive comparison, which means it treats lowercase characters as different input from uppercase letters. For example, assume that the files NAME.DAT and NAMES.OLD contain the following information:

Names.Dat		**Names.Old**	
Johnson	1400	JOHNSON	1400
Smith	1233	SMITH	1233
Owens	1000	OWENS	1000
Garle	933	GARLE	933
Adams	1503	ADAMS	1503
Brown	1500	BROWN	1500

By default, performing a case-sensitive comparison, FC will note the following differences:

```
C:\> FC NAMES.OLD NAMES.DAT <ENTER>
Comparing files NAMES.OLD and NAMES.DAT
***** NAMES.OLD
Johnson 1400
Smith   1233
Owens   1000
Garle    933
Adams   1503
Brown   1500
```

However, using FC's /C switch, which directs FC to ignore the case of letters, FC finds that all the files are the same:

```
C:\> FC /C NAMES.OLD NAMES.DAT <ENTER>
Comparing files NAMES.OLD and NAMES.DAT
FC: no differences encountered
```

You Can't Hide from CHKDSK

Tip 510 describes how to use the DOS 5 ATTRIB command to hide a file. Tip 452 presents the utility command HIDEDIR that lets you hide directories. However, even when you hide files and directories, you can't hide them from CHKDSK. If you invoke CHKDSK using the /V switch shown here, CHKDSK will display the name of every file on your disk, hidden or not:

```
C:\> CHKDSK /V <ENTER>
```

A Batch File FIND Command

As described in Tip 538, the FIND command lets you search a file or redirected input for specific text. If you are using FIND within a DOS batch file, however, FIND does not provide an exit status value that your batch files can test with IF ERRORLEVEL. The companion disk that accompanies this book provides the utility command FINDEXIT.EXE that behaves identically to the FIND command with the exception that FINDEXIT returns one of the exit status values listed in Table 589.

Table 589. Exit Status Values Returned by FINDEXIT

Exit Status	Meaning
0	Successful operation: no match
1	Successful operation: match
2	Invalid syntax
3	File not found

The following batch commands illustrate how you might use FINDEXIT:

```
@ECHO OFF
FINDEXIT 702 - PHONE.DAT
IF NOT ERRORLEVEL 1 GOTO NO_MATCH
IF ERRORLEVEL 1 IF NOT ERRORLEVEL 2 GOTO MATCH
IF ERRORLEVEL 2 IF NOT ERRORLEVEL 3 GOTO SYNTAX_BAD
IF ERRORLEVEL 3 GOTO FILE_NOT_FOUND
REM Other commands here
```

FINDEXIT.EXE

The utility command FINDEXIT.EXE resides on the companion disk that accompanies this book.

Understanding Files Whose Extensions End with an Underscore

If you have purchased the DOS 5 upgrade and have displayed a directory listing of the disk, you will find that many of the file's extensions end with an underscore as shown here:

```
C:\> DIR A: <ENTER>
 Volume in drive A is DISK      1
 Volume Serial Number is 1966-0205
 Directory of  A:\

COMMAND  CO_      34493 04-09-91   5:00a
EGA      SY_       4107 04-09-91   5:00a
FORMAT   CO_      23835 04-09-91   5:00a
 :        :         :        :        :
IO       SY_      25191 04-09-91   5:00a
```

```
MSDOS     SY_      31567 04-09-91    5:00a
        11 File(s)        9216 bytes free
```

To fit the files on the upgrade program floppy disks, the DOS 5 upgrade program stores the files in a compressed format. When you perform the upgrade, the installation program automatically expands these files. If you inadvertantly delete one of the DOS files and need to copy the file from one of the original disks, you will have to expand the file yourself. To expand a DOS 5 upgrade file, use the DOS 5 EXPAND command. The following EXPAND command, for example, expands the file UNDELETE.EX_ from drive A to the DOS directory:

```
C:\> EXPAND A:UNDELETE.EX_ C:\DOS\UNDELETE.EXE (Enter)
```

If you are using DOS 5, make sure you place EXPAND.EXE on your emergency disk, discussed in Tip 344.

Are Two Files the Same?

If you have two files whose contents you think are the same, perform these steps to find out. First, compare the file's size and date and time stamps in the directory listing. Next, use the COMP command to compare the file's contents as shown here:

```
C:\> COMP Filename.One Filename.Two <ENTER>
```

If the file contents are identical, COMP will display the following message:

```
Files compare OK
```

If the files are the same, delete one of them; otherwise, you are wasting disk space.

If the files are different, COMP will display the byte offsets in the files where their contents differ, as well as the values that differ, as shown here:

```
Compare error at OFFSET 0
File 1 = 41
File 2 = 42
Compare error at OFFSET F
File 1 = FA
File 2 = F0
```

COMP will display up to 10 differences. By default, prior to DOS 5, COMP displays the offsets and values in hexadecimal format. Tip 592 discusses how to make COMP'S output more meaningful.

In addition to using COMP to determine whether two files are identical, many users invoke COMP after a critical file copy operation to verify that the operation was successful, as shown here:

```
C:\> COPY CRITICAL.EXT  A:*.* <ENTER>
    1 file(s) copied

C:\> COMP CRITICAL.EXT  A:*.* <ENTER>
Files compare ok
Compare more files (Y/N)?
```

A More Meaningful File Comparison

Tip 591 explains how to use the COMP command to determine whether the contents of two files is the same. Prior to DOS 5, COMP displayed the offsets of files that differ, as well as the bytes that differ, in hexadecimal format. Although the hexadecimal output lets you know that the files differ, if you aren't a programmer who regularly works in hexadecimal format, the output is probably meaningless. Beginning with DOS 5, however, COMP displays the offsets and difference in decimal format. In addition, COMP has several additional command-line switches, listed in Table 592, that help improve the understandability of its output.

In addition to the switches listed in Table 592, you can use the /C switch to direct COMP to ignore the case of ASCII characters.

Table 592. DOS 5 COMP Command-Line Switches

Switch	Purpose
/A	Directs COMP to use ASCII to display the characters that differ
/L	Directs COMP to display the line number of lines that differ

Processing a List of Files

As the complexity of your batch files increases, you sometimes will want to execute commands using a list of files. The DOS FOR command lets you execute one command for a set of files. To enhance the capabilities of your batch files, you can use the companion disk utility command NEXTFILE.EXE. NEXTFILE examines the CURRENT_FILE environment entry and changes the entry so that it contains the filename that follows the current filename in the directory list. If CURRENT_FILE is not defined, NEXTFILE assigns the first file in the directory list. If no files follow the name specified, NEXTFILE removes the CURRENT_FILE entry. The following batch file, SHOWLIST.BAT, uses NEXTFILE.EXE to display the name of each file in the directory list:

```
@ECHO OFF
SET CURRENT_FILE=
:LOOP
NEXTFILE
IF '%CURRENT_FILE%'=='' GOTO DONE
ECHO The current file is %CURRENT_FILE%
GOTO LOOP
:DONE
SET CURRENT_FILE=
```

If NEXTFILE successfully adds the entry to the environment it returns the exit status value 0. Otherwise, NEXTFILE returns the exit status 1.

The utility command NEXTFILE.EXE resides on the companion disk that accompanies this book.

NEXTFILE.EXE

Processing Files by Age

If your batch files perform backup or other file management operations, you sometimes may want the oldest file in a directory. To help you find the oldest file, the

companion disk utility command OLDFILE.EXE assigns the name of the oldest file in the current directory to the OLDEST_FILE environment entry. If no files exist in the directory, OLDFILE undefines the OLDEST_FILE entry. The following batch commands display the name of the oldest file in the current directory:

```
@ECHO OFF
OLDFILE
IF '%OLDEST_FILE%'=='' ECHO No files found
IF NOT '%OLDEST_FILE%'=='' ECHO The oldest file %OLDEST_FILE%
SET OLDEST_FILE=
```

If two or more files have the same date, OLDFILE selects the first file encountered and returns the exit status value 255. Otherwise, if OLDFILE successfully creates the entry, it returns the exit status value 0. If the environment is full, OLDFILE returns the exit status value 1.

OLDFILE.EXE

The utility command OLDFILE.EXE resides on the companion disk that accompanies this book.

Backing Up Your CONFIG.SYS and AUTOEXEC.BAT Files

Many magazines and books present batch files that copy your AUTOEXEC.BAT and CONFIG.SYS files to a backup location each time your system starts. Most of these batch files keep only one or two copies of each file. Unfortunately, when users experience errors after changing their AUTOEXEC.BAT or CONFIG.SYS file, they may have to reboot several times. If the batch file saves only two copies of your AUTOEXEC.BAT or CONFIG.SYS file, the backup copies will be overwritten. The following batch file, SAVEAUTO.BAT, saves up to five copies of your AUTOEXEC.BAT and CONFIG.SYS files:

```
@ECHO OFF
IF EXIST C:\BACKUP\CONFIG.001 REN C:\BACKUP\CONFIG.001*.000
```

```
IF EXIST C:\BACKUP\CONFIG.002 REN C:\BACKUP\CONFIG.002 *.001
IF EXIST C:\BACKUP\CONFIG.003 REN C:\BACKUP\CONFIG.003 *.002
IF EXIST C:\BACKUP\CONFIG.004 REN C:\BACKUP\CONFIG.004 *.003
COPY \CONFIG.SYS C:\BACKUP\*.004
IF EXIST C:\BACKUP\AUTOEXEC.000 DEL C:\BACKUP\AUTOEXEC.000
IF EXIST C:\BACKUP\AUTOEXEC.001 REN C:\BACKUP\AUTOEXEC.001*.000
IF EXIST C:\BACKUP\AUTOEXEC.002 REN C:\BACKUP\AUTOEXEC.002*.001
IF EXIST C:\BACKUP\AUTOEXEC.003 REN C:\BACKUP\AUTOEXEC.003 *.002
IF EXIST C:\BACKUP\AUTOEXEC.004 REN C:\BACKUP\AUTOEXEC.004 *.003
COPY \AUTOEXEC.BAT C:\BACKUP\*.004
```

The batch file requires that the directory C:\BACKUP exist on your disk. The batch file stores the backup copies in files with the extensions 000 through 004, where the file with the 000 extension contains the oldest copy of the file and 004 contains the newest.

Parsing a Path Name

A path name consists of four parts: a drive, directory, filename, and extension. As the complexity of your batch files increases, you sometimes may need to break a path name into its component parts. The companion disk utility command PARSE.EXE breaks a path name into its four parts, assigning the parts to the environment entries DRIVE, SUBDIR, FILENAME, and EXTENSION. If the path name does not contain a drive or directory, PARSE uses the current drive or directory. The following batch file, SHOWNAME.BAT, displays the different parts of the file you specify in the command line:

```
@ECHO OFF
IF '%1'=='' GOTO DONE
PARSE %1
ECHO Drive %DRIVE%
ECHO Directory %SUBDIR%
ECHO Filename %FILENAME%
ECHO Extension %EXTENSION%
:Done
```

If PARSE successfully assigns the environment entries, it returns the exit status value 0. If the environment is full, PARSE returns the value 1.

PARSE.EXE

The utility command PARSE.EXE resides on the companion disk that accompanies this book.

Processing the Smallest File

If your batch files perform file copy or other directory management operations, you sometimes may want the smallest file in a directory. To help you find it, the companion disk utility command SMAFILE.EXE assigns the name of the smallest file in the current directory to the SMALLEST_FILE environment entry. If no files exist in the directory, SMAFILE undefines the SMALLEST_FILE entry. The following batch commands display the name of the smallest file in the current directory:

```
@ECHO OFF
SMAFILE
IF '%SMALLEST_FILE%'=='' ECHO No files found
IF NOT '%SMALLEST_FILE%'=='' ECHO The smallest file
    %SMALLEST_FILE%
SET SMALLEST_FILE=
```

If two or more files have the same size, SMAFILE selects the first file encountered and returns the exit status value 255. Otherwise, if SMAFILE successfully creates the entry, it returns the exit status 0. If the environment is full, SMAFILE returns the exit status 1.

SMAFILE.EXE

The utility command SMAFILE.EXE resides on the companion disk that accompanies this book.

Processing the Largest File

If your batch files perform file copy or other directory management operations, you sometimes may want the largest file in a directory. To help you find it, the companion disk utility command BIGFILE.EXE assigns the name of the largest file in the current directory to the BIGGEST_FILE environment entry. If no files exist in the directory, BIGFILE undefines the BIGGEST_FILE entry. The following batch commands display the name of the largest file in the current directory:

```
@ECHO OFF
BIGFILE
IF '%BIGGEST_FILE%'=='' ECHO No files found
IF NOT '%BIGGEST_FILE%'=='' ECHO The largest file %BIGGEST_FILE%
SET BIGGEST_FILE=
```

If two or more files have the same size, BIGFILE selects the first file encountered and returns the exit status value 255. Otherwise, if BIGFILE successfully creates the entry, it returns the exit status 0. If the environment is full, BIGFILE returns the exit status 1.

The utility command BIGFILE.EXE resides on the companion disk that accompanies this book.

BIGFILE.EXE

Clearing a File's Attributes

Several of the tips presented in this book show ways you can set or clear file attributes. Sometimes, however, you may want to clear all of a file's attributes at one time. To do so, you can use the companion disk utility command CLRATTR.EXE. The following CLRATTR command, for example, clears the attributes of the file FILENAME.EXT:

```
C:\> CLRATTR FILENAME.EXT <ENTER>
```

If you use the CLRATTR command, you don't have to remember ATTRIB's command-line switches. Also, if you are not using the DOS 5 ATTRIB command, CLRATTR gives you control over the hidden and system attributes.

The utility command CLRATTR.EXE resides on the companion disk that accompanies this book.

CLRATTR.EXE

Obtaining the Next Archive File

Tip 593 presents the NEXTFILE utility, which assigns to the environment entry CURRENT_FILE the name of the next file in the directory list that follows the entry's current filename. Similarly, the companion disk utility command NEXTARCH.EXE assigns to the environment entry NEXT_ARCHIVE the name of the next file in the directory list whose archive attribute is set. If the NEXT_ARCHIVE entry is not currently defined, NEXTARCH uses the first file in the directory. If no files exist, NEXTARCH removes the environment entry. The following batch file uses NEXTARCH to copy each current directory file whose archive attribute is set to drive A, without changing the attribute:

```
@ECHO OFF
SET NEXT_ARCHIVE=
:LOOP
NEXTARCH
IF '%NEXT_ARCHIVE%'=='' GOTO DONE
XCOPY %NEXT_ARCHIVE% A:
GOTO LOOP
:DONE
SET NEXT_ARCHIVE=
```

If NEXTARCH successfully creates the environment entry, it returns the exit status value 0; if the environment is full, NEXTARCH returns the value 1.

The utility command NEXTARCH.EXE resides on the companion disk that accompanies this book.

NEXTARCH.EXE

Obtaining the Next Hidden File

Tip 600 presents the companion disk NEXTARCH utility, which assigns to the environment entry NEXT_ARCHIVE the name of the next file in the directory list whose archive attribute is set. Similarly, the companion disk utility command NEXTHIDE.EXE assigns to the environment entry NEXT_HIDDEN the name of the next file in the directory list whose hidden attribute is set. If the NEXT_HIDDEN entry is not currently defined, NEXTHIDE uses the first file in the directory. If no files exist, NEXTHIDE removes the environment entry. The following batch file uses NEXTHIDE to display the name of each hidden file in the root directory:

```
@ECHO OFF
SET NEXT_HIDDEN=
:LOOP
NEXTHIDE
IF '%NEXT_HIDDEN%'=='' GOTO DONE
ECHO %NEXT_HIDDEN%
GOTO LOOP
:DONE
SET NEXT_HIDDEN=
```

If NEXTHIDE successfully creates the environment entry, it returns the exit status value 0; if the environment is full, NEXTHIDE returns the value 1.

The utility command NEXTHIDE.EXE resides on the companion disk that accompanies this book.

NEXTHIDE.EXE

Obtaining the Next Read-Only File

Tip 600 presents the companion disk NEXTARCH utility, which assigns to the environment entry NEXT_ARCHIVE the name of the next file in the directory list whose archive attribute is set. Similarly, the companion disk utility command NEXTREAD.EXE assigns to the environment entry NEXT_READONLY the name of the next file in the directory list whose read-only attribute is set. If the NEXT_READONLY entry is not currently defined, NEXTREAD uses the first file in the directory. If no files exist, NEXTREAD removes the environment entry. The following batch file uses NEXTREAD to display the name of each read-only file in the current directory:

```
@ECHO OFF
SET NEXT_READONLY=
:LOOP
NEXTREAD
IF '%NEXT_READONLY%'=='' GOTO DONE
ECHO %NEXT_READONLY%
GOTO LOOP
:DONE
SET NEXT_READONLY=
```

If NEXTREAD successfully creates the environment entry, it returns the exit status value 0; if the environment is full, NEXTREAD returns the value 1.

The utility command NEXTREAD.EXE resides on the companion disk that accompanies this book.

NEXTREAD.EXE

Obtaining the Next System File

Tip 600 presents the companion disk NEXTARCH utility, which assigns to the environment entry NEXT_ARCHIVE the name of the next file in the directory list whose archive attribute is set. Similarly, the companion disk utility command NEXTSYST.EXE assigns to the environment entry NEXT_SYSTEM the name of the next file in the directory list whose system attribute is set. If the NEXT_SYSTEM entry is not currently defined, NEXTSYST uses the first file in the directory. If no files exist, NEXTSYST removes the environment entry. The following batch file uses NEXTSYST to display the name of each system file in the root directory:

```
@ECHO OFF
CD \
SET NEXT_SYSTEM=
:LOOP
NEXTSYST
IF '%NEXT_SYSTEM%'=='' GOTO DONE
ECHO %NEXT_SYSTEM%
GOTO LOOP
:DONE
SET NEXT_SYSTEM=
```

If NEXTSYST successfully creates the environment entry, it returns the exit status value 0; if the environment is full, NEXTSYST returns the value 1.

The utility command NEXTSYST.EXE is on the companion disk that accompanies this book.

NEXTSYST.EXE

How Many Files Does the Current Directory Contain?

As the complexity of your batch files increases, you sometimes may need to determine the number of files in the current directory. Thus, the companion disk that accompanies this book provides the utility command FILECNT.EXE that assigns the count of the number of current directory files (not files or directories) to the environment entry FILE_COUNT. The following batch file commands use FILECNT.EXE to display the number of files in the current directory listing:

```
@ECHO OFF
FILECNT
ECHO The number of files is %FILE_COUNT%
SET FILE_COUNT=
```

If FILECNT successfully adds the environment entry, it returns the exit status 0; otherwise, if the environment is full, it returns the exit status value 1. FILECNT only counts file entries. It does not count subdirectories.

FILECNT.EXE

The utility command FILECNT.EXE resides on the companion disk that accompanies this book.

Understanding the File Creation Error Message

As you copy files to different drives, you may see one of the following error messages:

```
Insufficient disk space
File creation error
```

Table 605. The Number of Root Directory Entries Supported by Different Disk Types

Disk Type	Root Directory Entries
360Kb	112
720Kb	112
1.2Mb	224
1.44Mb	224
Hard disk	512

The Insufficient disk space error message occurs when the disk simply doesn't have enough free disk space to hold the file. The file creation error message normally occurs when you are copying the file to the root directory and the root does not have room for any more directory entries. As shown in Table 605, the root directory can store only a fixed number of file and subdirectory entries.

If you try to exceed the number of root directory entries, DOS will display the file creation error message. This error message is common for RAM drives, which, as discussed in Tip 375, provide support for 64 root directory entries unless you specify otherwise.

Selecting Specific Files within the DOS Shell

Several tips presented throughout this book have taught you how to perform file operations within the DOS 5 Shell. Most of the file operations allow you to use multiple files. To select multiple files within the Shell, first select the directory desired. If you are using a mouse, you can select files by holding down the CTRL key and clicking on the desired files. If you aren't using a mouse, press the SHIFT-F8 keyboard combination. The Shell will display the status bar message Add. To select a file, highlight the file using your arrow keys and press the space bar. If you accidentally select a wrong file, simply press the space bar a second time. After you have selected the desired files, perform the desired operation.

Using FIND to Number the Lines of a File

Tip 581 describes how the FIND command's /V switch directs FIND to locate each line in a file that does not contain a specified string. The /N switch directs FIND to display the corresponding line numbers. The following DOSKEY macro, NUMBER, uses FIND to number the lines of a file that don't contain the uncommon string "QWERTY12345":

```
C:\> DOSKEY NUMBER=FIND /V/N "QWERTY12345" $1 <ENTER>
```

If you are not using DOS 5, the following batch file, NUMBER.BAT, uses FIND to also number the specified file:

```
@ECHO OFF
IF NOT '%1'=='' FIND /V/N "QWERTY12345" %1
```

To display the line numbers of your AUTOEXEC.BAT file, for example, invoke NUMBER as shown here:

```
C:\ NUMBER C:\AUTOEXEC.BAT <ENTER>
```

Using FIND to Display a File's Line Count

Tip 607 uses the FIND command to number the lines in a file. The following DOSKEY macro, FILELINE, uses FIND to display a count of the number of lines in a file:

```
C:\> DOSKEY FILELINE=FIND /V/C "QWERTY12345" $1 <ENTER>
```

The command uses FIND to search for lines that do not contain the uncommon string "QWERTY12345". If you are not using DOS 5, the following batch file, FILELINE.BAT, achieves the same result:

```
@ECHO OFF
IF NOT '%1'=='' FIND /V/C "QWERTY12345" %1
```

To use DOSKEY, you must be using DOS 5. If a file, such as FILELINE.BAT, happens to contain the string "QWERTY12345", the line count will be incorrect. If this occurs, change the string to something unique.

Finding a File's True Name

As your batch files increase in complexity, they sometimes may need to determine the complete path name of a file that resides in the current directory. The DOS 5 TRUENAME command provides one way to do just that. TRUENAME is an internal DOS command that, given a filename, displays (to stdout) the file's complete path name. For example, assuming the current directory is DOS, TRUENAME will display the following information for the file FORMAT.COM:

```
C:\DOS> TRUENAME FORMAT.COM <ENTER>
C:\DOS\FORMAT.COM
```

If you are using a logical disk drive name to abbreviate a directory path, you can use TRUENAME to determine the file's actual directory. Tip 697 shows you how to assign TRUENAME's output to a named parameter whose contents you can use in your DOS batch files.

To use the TRUENAME command, you must be using DOS 5.

Looking for a Lost File

As you learned in Tip 340, if you are using DOS 5, you can use the DIR /S command to search your disk for a lost file. If you are not using DOS 5, you can use the companion disk utility LOOKFOR.EXE to search your disk for a file. For example, assume that you have misplaced a file named BUDGET.DAT. The following LOOKFOR command searches your hard disk for the file:

```
C:\ LOOKFOR BUDGET.DAT  <ENTER>
```

LOOKFOR.EXE does not support wild cards. When using LOOKFOR you can only search for one specific file name at a time.

LOOKFOR.EXE

The utility command LOOKFOR.EXE resides on the companion disk that accompanies this book.

Viewing a File's ASCII Contents

Files with the COM and EXE extensions contain binary program instructions. If you try to display or print one of these file's contents with TYPE or PRINT, you will see lots of unrecognizable character combinations. In addition to the program instructions, ASCII messages are embedded in these files. You can learn a lot about a command by studying its error messages. The companion disk that accompanies this book contains the utility command VIEWASCI.EXE that lets you view a file's ASCII messages. For example, the following command shows the contents of COMMAND.COM:

```
C:\> VIEWASCI COMMAND.COM <ENTER>
```

To reduce the possibility of binary instruction values that happen to form a sequence of ASCII characters, VIEWASCI shows only strings of five characters or more.

The utility command VIEWASCI.EXE resides on the companion disk that accompanies this book.

VIEWASCI.EXE

Finding Empty Files on Your Disk

Periodically, because a program fails or is terminated prematurely, your disk will end up with zero-length or empty files. The following DOSKEY macro, EMPTIES, searches your disk for empty files, displaying their names a screenful at a time:

```
C:\> DOSKEY EMPTIES=DIR \*.* /S $B FIND " 0 " $B FIND /V "e"
$B MORE <ENTER>
```

To view the names of your empty files, invoke the macro from the DOS prompt as shown here:

```
C:\> EMPTIES <ENTER>
```

To use DOSKEY macros, you must be using DOS 5.

Compressing Your Files Reduces Modem Transmission Times

Tip 509 presents the utility commands IMPLODE and EXPLODE that let you compress and later uncompress a file. If you are exchanging files with another user and the user has these same utilities,

you should first compress files before you transmit them. At the receiving end, the other user can decompress the files. If, for example, you compress a file to 50 percent of its original size, you also decrease your transmission time by 50 percent. As Tip 840 explains, many modems incorporate data compression. However, by first compressing the files yourself, you start with a better file size.

Several third-party and shareware programs exist that let you compress multiple files into one large executable program file. When you later execute the program, it decompresses the individual files. Thus, you have to transmit only one file, and the remote user does not need a program to decompress the files; the executable programs will do that automatically.

Viewing BASIC Program Files

Files with the BAS extension contain BASIC programs you can run with QBASIC, GWBASIC, or BASICA, depending on your DOS version. If you try to view one of these files by using the TYPE or PRINT commands, you may see a screen or page full of unrecognizable character combinations. Most BASIC programs are stored in a condensed format called tokenized form. When you load the file into BASIC to run or edit it, BASIC converts the file to a readable format. By default, when you later save the program to a file on disk, BASIC stores the file in the tokenized format. Within BASIC you can use the SAVE command to save the file in an ASCII format as shown here:

```
SAVE "Filename.ASC",A
```

The ,A that follows the filename directs BASIC to store the file in ASCII format. By using the extension ASC, you won't overwrite the existing tokenized file that uses the BAS extension.

Are Your Files Really Readable?

Many users invoke the CHKDSK command to examine the state of their disks. CHKDSK examines the disk's file allocation tables and directories for inconsistencies. Even if CHKDSK does not report

errors, however, your files may not be fully accessible. CHKDSK does not actually examine the sectors containing each file's data. Thus, CHKDSK may report that your disk is error free, and yet your next command may result in the following error message:

```
Data error reading drive n:
```

To avoid this problem, use the following batch file, CHKFILES.BAT, which actually reads the disk sectors that correspond to every file in a specified directory:

```
@ECHO OFF
COPY %1\*.* NUL
```

If the batch file cannot read a disk sector, it will display the previous error message. Disk sector read errors are an early warning to impending disk problems. If such errors occur, you should immediately back up your disk. If you have several commonly used directories, you might invoke the CHKFILES batch file from within your AUTOEXEC.BAT file to examine each directory's files as shown here:

```
CALL CHKFILES C:\DATA
CALL CHKFILES C:\WORDPROC
CALL CHKFILES C:\SPRDSHET
```

Handling Utility Name Conflicts

DOS 5 provides UNDELETE and UNFORMAT utilities. If you have other third-party disk utility programs, the utility names may conflict. If you want to ensure that the third-party commands execute before these two DOS 5 disk utilities, you have three choices. First, if you don't need them, you can delete the DOS 5 disk utilities. Second, you can ensure that the name of the directory containing the third-party disk utilities precedes the DOS directory name in the directory path. Third, you can use the DOSKEY macro to assign the commands to the third-party utilities as shown here:

```
C:\> DOSKEY UNDELETE=C:\DISKUTIL\UNDELETE <ENTER>
C:\> DOSKEY UNFORMAT=C:\DISKUTIL\UNFORMAT <ENTER>
```

Performing a Safe File Copy Operation

Unless a file is a read-only (or a hidden or system) file, its contents can be overwritten by a COPY command. To prevent accidental file overwrites, you can use the REPLACE command to perform your copies. If you include the /P switch, REPLACE will display the following message before overwriting an existing file:

```
Do you want to replace drive:filename.ext?
```

If you type **Y**, REPLACE will overwrite the file; if you type **N**, REPLACE will leave the file unchanged. The following DOSKEY command creates a macro named SAFECOPY that uses REPLACE to perform copy operations:

```
C:\> DOSKEY SAFECOPY=REPLACE $* /P <ENTER>
```

If you are not using DOS 5, you can create the batch file SAFECOPY.BAT that performs the same processing:

```
@ECHO OFF
REPLACE %1 %2 /P
```

EDIT Relies on QBASIC.EXE

As discussed in Tip 449, there are many files that you can remove from your DOS directory to free disk space and improve the performance of operations that search the DOS directory for external commands. If you don't plan to program in BASIC, you may be considering erasing the files with the BAS extension as well as the QBASIC.EXE and QBASIC.HLP files. If you plan to use EDIT, the DOS 5 full-screen editor, however, you need to leave QBASIC.EXE. If you try to invoke EDIT without the QBASIC.EXE file in the command path, EDIT will display the following error message:

```
C:\> EDIT FILENAME.EXT <ENTER>
Cannot find file QBASIC.EXE
```

EDIT Does Not Create a Backup Copy

If you have used EDLIN or a word processor to edit an existing file, the edit typically saves a copy of the file's original contents in a second file that uses the BAK (for backup) extension. Should you decide after editing a file that you wish you hadn't made the file changes, you can use the BAK file to restore the file's original contents. If you are using EDIT, the DOS 5 full-screen editor, however, you need to use care, because EDIT does not make a copy of the file's original contents. After you edit and save changes to a file with EDIT, the file's original contents are lost. If you are going to use EDIT to edit an existing file, make your own backup copy of the file, as follows, before you begin:

```
C:\> COPY FILENAME.EXT *.BAK <ENTER>
```

A Better-Fit File Copy

Tip 450 discusses how to use the XCOPY command to copy files that reside in the current directory to a floppy disk. By directing XCOPY to clear file archive attributes as it successfully copies files, you can quickly resume a file copy operation after the floppy disk fills. Unfortunately, XCOPY has a problem: XCOPY copies the files in the same order as the files appear in the directory. Assume that the floppy disk has 90,000 bytes of available space, and the next file to be copied requires 100,000 bytes. Because the file does not fit, the XCOPY command will end, even if 20 other files containing a total of 1,000 bytes, which would all fit on the disk, remain to be copied.

To make better use of the remaining disk space, you can use the companion disk utility command NEXTCOPY.EXE, which helps your batch files to copy the next files whose archive attributes are set to the floppy disk. For example, if you are performing an XCOPY operation that copies every file in the current directory and the floppy disk fills, you can continue the operation using NEXTCOPY as shown here:

```
C:\> NEXTCOPY *.* A: <ENTER>
```

If NEXTCOPY successfully locates a file that will fit on the disk, NEXTCOPY will assign the file's name to the environment entry NEXTCOPY. Your batch file can loop repeatedly, copying the files

until NEXTCOPY removes the environment entry. Note that unlike XCOPY, NEXTCOPY does not support a /S switch that tells it to copy files from subdirectories; NEXTCOPY supports only the current directory. After NEXTCOPY assigns the empty string, place a new floppy disk in the drive and repeat the XCOPY command.

NEXTCOPY.EXE

The utility command NEXTCOPY.EXE resides on the companion disk that accompanies this book.

Removing a File's Hidden Attribute

Tip 471 presented the companion disk utility command NOSYSTEM.EXE that removes the system attribute from the file specified. In a similar way, there may be times when you want to remove a file's hidden attribute. If you are using DOS 5, you can use the following ATTRIB command to remove the file's hidden attribute:

```
C:\ ATTRIB -H Filename.Ext <ENTER>
```

If you are not using DOS 5, you can use the command file NOHIDDEN.EXE provided on the companion disk that accompanies this book. The following NOHIDDEN command removes the hidden attribute from a file named Filename.Ext:

```
C:\ NOHIDDEN Filename.Ext <ENTER>
```

The NOHIDDEN command does not support DOS wildcards.

NOHIDDEN.EXE

The utility command NOHIDDEN.EXE resides on the companion disk that accompanies this book.

PART 7

Discarding Command Messages

Using the @ECHO OFF command, your batch files can direct DOS to suppress the display of command names as the batch file executes. By preventing the display of command names in this way, your batch files can better control the screen's appearance. Unfortunately, many commands display messages on the screen as they execute. For example, consider the following batch file that copies the files AUTOEXEC.BAT and CONFIG.SYS from the current disk's root directory to a floppy disk in drive A:

```
@ECHO OFF
COPY \AUTOEXEC.BAT A:
COPY \CONFIG.SYS A:
```

Although the batch file disables the display of command names as they execute, it does not prevent the display of messages by the COPY command. For instance, when you execute the batch file, it displays the following messages:

```
1 file(s) copied
1 file(s) copied
```

To prevent the display of such messages, you can redirect a command's output to the NUL device as shown here:

```
@ECHO OFF
COPY \AUTOEXEC.BAT A: > NUL
COPY \CONFIG.SYS A: > NUL
```

When you redirect a program's output to the NUL device in this way, DOS simply discards the output. In the case of the previous batch file, the "1 file(s) copied" message will not appear.

Sounding Your Computer's Bell

Often you will want to sound your computer's built-in speaker during a batch file's execution to notify the user of a specific event. One way to do so is by using the command file SPEAKER.COM created by the following DEBUG script file, SPEAKER.SCR:

```
N SPEAKER.COM <ENTER>
A 100         <ENTER>
MOV AH,2      <ENTER>
MOV DL,7      <ENTER>
INT 21        <ENTER>
MOV AH,4C     <ENTER>
INT 21        <ENTER>
              <ENTER>
R CX          <ENTER>
A             <ENTER>
W             <ENTER>
Q             <ENTER>
```

SPEAKER.SCR

Use DEBUG as follows to create the command file SPEAKER.COM:

```
C:\> DEBUG < SPEAKER.SCR <ENTER>
```

After the command exists, you can use it within your batch file as shown here:

```
@ECHO OFF
SPEAKER
ECHO About to do something important...
PAUSE
REM Other commands here
```

In some cases, you may want to sound the speaker several times. One way to do so is by invoking SPEAKER within the FOR command. The following FOR command, for example, sounds the speaker three times:

```
FOR %%I IN (1 2 3) DO SPEAKER
```

What Is Today's Date?

As you create more complex batch files, you may want to determine the current date. For example, on the fifteenth and thirtieth of each month you may perform a complete disk backup operation. On a different date you may want your computer to remind you of a specific event. The following DEBUG script file, TODAY.SCR, creates a command file named TODAY.COM that returns the current day's date as an exit status value in the range 1 through 31:

TODAY.SCR

```
N TODAY.COM <ENTER>
A 100       <ENTER>
MOV AH,2A   <ENTER>
INT 21      <ENTER>
MOV AL,DL   <ENTER>
MOV AH,4C   <ENTER>
INT 21      <ENTER>
            <ENTER>
R CX        <ENTER>
A           <ENTER>
W           <ENTER>
Q           <ENTER>
```

Use DEBUG as follows to create the command file TODAY.COM:

```
C:\> DEBUG < TODAY.SCR <ENTER>
```

The following batch file illustrates how you can use TODAY.COM to test for the fifteenth of the month:

```
TODAY
IF ERRORLEVEL 15 IF NOT ERRORLEVEL 16 GOTO 15TH
REM Other commands here
```

What Day of the Week Is Today?

When you create batch files to automate tasks, it's often necessary for them to determine the current day and then to continue their processing accordingly. The following DEBUG script file, TODAYIS.SCR, returns an exit status value corresponding to the current day of the week, where Sunday corresponds to the exit status 0, Monday to 1, and so on through Saturday, which is equal to 6:

```
N TODAYIS.COM <ENTER>
A 100         <ENTER>
MOV AH,2A     <ENTER>
INT 21        <ENTER>
MOV AH,4C     <ENTER>
INT 21        <ENTER>
              <ENTER>
R CX          <ENTER>
8             <ENTER>
W             <ENTER>
Q             <ENTER>
```

TODAYIS.SCR

Use DEBUG as follows, to create the command file TODAYIS.COM:

```
C:\> DEBUG < TODAYIS.SCR
```

The following batch file uses the TODAYIS command to display a greeting to the user:

```
@ECHO OFF
TODAYIS
IF ERRORLEVEL 0 IF NOT ERRORLEVEL 1 ECHO Have a great Sunday
IF ERRORLEVEL 1 IF NOT ERRORLEVEL 2 ECHO Have a great Monday
IF ERRORLEVEL 2 IF NOT ERRORLEVEL 3 ECHO Have a great Tuesday
IF ERRORLEVEL 3 IF NOT ERRORLEVEL 4 ECHO Have a great Wednesday
IF ERRORLEVEL 4 IF NOT ERRORLEVEL 5 ECHO Have a great Thursday
IF ERRORLEVEL 5 IF NOT ERRORLEVEL 6 ECHO Have a great Friday
IF ERRORLEVEL 6 ECHO Have a great Saturday
```

Using this same technique, your batch files can determine the current day and execute programs (such as backup operations) accordingly.

Is It AM or PM?

Just as you may sometimes want your batch files to determine the current day (see Tip 625), you may sometimes want your batch files to determine whether it is AM or PM, so they can display appropriate user messages. The following DEBUG script file, AM_PM.SCR, returns the exit status value 0 if the current time is AM and the exit status value 1 if the current time is PM:

AM_PM.SCR

```
N AM_PM.COM <ENTER>
A 100       <ENTER>
MOV AH,2C   <ENTER>
INT 21      <ENTER>
CMP CH,C    <ENTER>
JGE 10D     <ENTER>
MOV AL,0    <ENTER>
JMP 10F     <ENTER>
MOV AL,1    <ENTER>
MOV AH,4C   <ENTER>
INT 21      <ENTER>
            <ENTER>
R CX        <ENTER>
13          <ENTER>
W           <ENTER>
Q           <ENTER>
```

Use DEBUG as follows to create the command file AM_PM.COM:

```
C:\> DEBUG < AM_PM.SCR <ENTER>
```

The following batch file uses AM_PM to display a user message:

```
@ECHO OFF
AM_PM
IF NOT ERRORLEVEL 1 ECHO Have a great morning!
IF ERRORLEVEL 1 ECHO Have a great day!
```

What Month Is It?

As you use batch files to automate more operations, you often will want the batch file to determine the current month. The following DEBUG script file, MONTH.SCR, creates a command named MONTH.COM that returns an exit status value in the range 1 to 12 corresponding to the current month:

```
N MONTH.COM <ENTER>
A 100       <ENTER>
OV AH,2A    <ENTER>
INT 21      <ENTER>
MOV AL,DH   <ENTER>
MOV AH,4C   <ENTER>
INT 21      <ENTER>
            <ENTER>
R CX        <ENTER>
A           <ENTER>
W           <ENTER>
Q           <ENTER>
```

MONTH.SCR

Use DEBUG as follows to create the command file MONTH.COM:

```
C:\> DEBUG < MONTH.SCR <ENTER>
```

The following batch file assumes you have files named EVENTS.JAN, EVENTS.FEB, and so on that contain important events (such as birthdays, and anniversaries) for a specific month. The batch file uses MONTH.COM to determine the current month and then displays the corresponding file.

```
@ECHO OFF
MONTH
IF ERRORLEVEL 1 IF NOT ERRORLEVEL 2 TYPE EVENTS.JAN
IF ERRORLEVEL 2 IF NOT ERRORLEVEL 3 TYPE EVENTS.FEB
IF ERRORLEVEL 3 IF NOT ERRORLEVEL 4 TYPE EVENTS.MAR
.   .
.   .
.   .
IF ERRORLEVEL 12 TYPE EVENTS.DEC
```

Creating Readable Batch Files

DOS batch files allow you to simplify difficult operations by grouping (or abbreviating) a series of commands in a single batch file. When you create a batch file, one of the most important steps you must perform is documenting the batch file to explain what it does. The REM command lets you place a single-line remark within your batch file. When DOS encounters a REM command in your batch file, it ignores the line, continuing the batch file's execution with the next command. You should place one or more REM commands before every command in your batch file to explain the command's purpose. Then if the batch file is read at a later time, the comments will fully explain the batch file's purpose and processing.

When you include REM commands in your batch file, it may become slightly cluttered, making it more difficult to read. Use blank lines in the batch file to separate various commands. The blank lines will improve the batch file's readability. DOS ignores any blank lines it encounters in a batch file. The following sample AUTOEXEC.BAT illustrates the use of REM and blank lines to improve the batch file's readability:

```
@ECHO OFF
REM AUTOEXEC.BAT
REM Created by Kris Jamsa 12-25-92
REM Last Change - Added SHARE 01-01-93

REM Set the command prompt to the current drive and directory
REM followed by a greater than character
PROMPT $p$g

REM Define the command path
PATH C:\DOS;C:\WINDOWS;C:\DOSHELP

REM Set the TEMP entry to the fast RAM drive D
SET TEMP=D:\

REM Invoke the SHARE command for network support
SHARE
```

Using IF ERRORLEVEL with DOS Commands

The IF ERRORLEVEL command lets your batch files test the exit status value of the previous program. Several of the DOS commands provide support for exit status values. Table 629 lists the exit status values used by various DOS commands.

Table 629. Exit Status Values

DOS Command	Exit Status	Meaning
BACKUP	0	Successful backup operation
	1	No files found to back up
	2	File sharing conflicts prevented a complete backup
	3	User termination via CTRL-C
	4	Fatal processing error
DISKCOMP	0	Disks are the same
	1	Disks are not the same
	2	User termination via CTRL-C
	3	Fatal disk error
	4	Initialization error
DISKCOPY	0	Successful copy operation
	1	Nonfatal disk error
	2	User termination via CTRL-C
	3	Fatal disk error
	4	Initialization error
FORMAT	0	Successful format operation
	3	User termination via CTRL-C
	4	Fatal disk error
	5	User termination via FORMAT'S "Proceed with Format (Y/N)?" prompt

Table 629. Exit Status Values (continued)

DOS Command	Exit Status	Meaning
GRAFTABL	0	Character set successfully loaded
	1	Previously loaded set replaced
	2	File access error
	3	Invalid command line
	4	Invalid DOS version
KEYB	0	Keyboard template successfully loaded
	1	Invalid keyboard code, code page, or syntax
	2	Keyboard definition file not found
	4	Error accessing CON device
	5	Requested code page not prepared
REPLACE	0	Successful replacement
	2	Source files not found
	3	Directory not found
	5	Access denied
	8	Insufficient RAM
	11	Invalid command line
	15	Invalid disk
	22	Invalid DOS version
RESTORE	0	Successful file restoration
	1	No files found to restore
	3	User termination via CTRL-C
	4	Fatal disk error
SETVER	0	Successful version assignment
	1	Invalid command line
	2	Invalid filename
	3	Insufficient RAM
	4	Invalid version number
	5	Entry not found
	6	System files not found
	7	Valid drive
	8	Too many parameters

Table 629. Exit Status Values (continued)

DOS Command	Exit Status	Meaning
	9	Missing parameters
	10	Error reading System files
	11	System file is corrupt
	12	System files don't support version numbers
	13	Insufficient version table space
	14	Error writing to system files
XCOPY	0	Successful file copy operation
	1	No files found
	2	User termination via CTRL-C
	3	Initialization error
	4	Disk write error

What Year Is This?

TIP 630

Depending on your computer type, when your CMOS battery dies, you may not be aware of it. In many cases, your only clue is that the system date is set to January 1, 1980. The following YEAR.SCR DEBUG script file creates a command named YEAR.COM that returns the last two digits of the year, such as 92, as an exit status value:

```
N YEAR.COM <ENTER>
A 100      <ENTER>
MOV AH,2A  <ENTER>
INT 21     <ENTER>
SUB CX,76C <ENTER>
MOV AX,CX  <ENTER>
MOV AH,4C  <ENTER>
INT 21     <ENTER>
           <ENTER>
R CX       <ENTER>
E          <ENTER>
```

YEAR.SCR

```
W           <ENTER>
Q           <ENTER>
```

Use the DEBUG command as follows to create the command file YEAR.COM:

```
C:\> DEBUG < YEAR.SCR <ENTER>
```

The following batch file commands illustrate how you would use YEAR.COM to test for a bad CMOS battery in your AUTOEXEC.BAT file:

```
YEAR
IF ERRORLEVEL 80 IF NOT ERRORLEVEL 81 GOTO BAD_YEAR
```

Echoing Blank Lines to the Screen

Using the ECHO command, your batch files can display a message to the user on the screen. To make the message easier to read, you may need to include blank lines in the message. Unfortunately, if you include in a batch file an ECHO command that contains no text, ECHO will not display a blank line, but rather its current state of command-name suppression (either on or off) as shown here:

```
C:\> ECHO <ENTER>
ECHO is on
```

Luckily, there are several ways to display a blank line by using ECHO. The most common way is to place the extended ASCII value 255 (which corresponds to a blank) in ECHO's command line. Because the extended ASCII value 255 does not actually appear on the screen, most books and magazines use the letters <ALT+255> to represent it as shown here:

```
ECHO <ALT+255>
```

You can enter extended ASCII values from the keyboard by holding down the ALT key and typing the extended ASCII value from the numeric keypad. In addition to using the extended ASCII character 255 to echo blank lines, you can place any of the following characters immediately next to ECHO to produce a blank line:

```
ECHO.
ECHO[
ECHO]
ECHO+
ECHO/
ECHO\
ECHO;
ECHO,
```

Sounding the Computer's Speaker in ECHO and PAUSE Commands

The ECHO command lets your batch file display messages to the user. The PAUSE command displays a message and then suspends the batch file's execution until the user presses a key. Depending on your batch file's execution, you sometimes may want the batch file to sound your computer's built-in speaker to get the user's attention. One way to sound the speaker is to include the CTRL-G character in the message displayed by ECHO or PAUSE. The following batch file, BELLS.BAT, sounds the computer's speaker three times. Create the batch file by copying it from the CON device. To generate the character ^G, hold down the CTRL key and press G. To generate the ^Z character, hold down the CTRL key and press Z, or press the F6 function key:

```
C:\> COPY CON BELLS.BAT        <ENTER>
ECHO Bell ^G Bell ^G Bell ^G <ENTER>
^Z                             <ENTER>
            1 File(s) copied
```

When you execute the batch file, it will display the message "Bell Bell Bell," sounding the computer's speaker three times.

A Better PAUSE Command

The PAUSE command lets your batch files display a message to the user, suspending the batch file's execution until the user presses a key. Unfortunately, if the batch file contains the ECHO OFF command, DOS will not display the user message, showing instead only the following message:

```
Press any key to continue...
```

The following DEBUG script file, NEWPAUSE.SCR, creates a PAUSE-like command that displays the user message when ECHO OFF is active:

NEWPAUSE.SCR

```
N NEWPAUSE.COM <ENTER>
A 100          <ENTER>
JMP 123        <ENTER>
DB A,D,'Press any key to continue...',A,D,'$' <ENTER>
MOV Cl,[80]    <ENTER>
MOV BX,82      <ENTER>
CMP CL,1       <ENTER>
JE 139         <ENTER>
MOV AH,2       <ENTER>
MOV DL,[BX]    <ENTER>
INT 21         <ENTER>
DEC CX         <ENTER>
INC BX         <ENTER>
JMP 12A        <ENTER>
MOV AH,9       <ENTER>
MOV DX,102     <ENTER>
INT 21         <ENTER>
MOV AH,8       <ENTER>
INT 21         <ENTER>
CMP AL,0       <ENTER>
JE 141         <ENTER>
MOV AH,4C      <ENTER>
INT 21         <ENTER>
               <ENTER>
R CX           <ENTER>
4C             <ENTER>
W              <ENTER>
```

```
Q                    <ENTER>
```

Use the DEBUG command as follows to create the command file NEWPAUSE.COM:

```
C:\> DEBUG < NEWPAUSE.SCR <ENTER>
```

Within your batch files, you can use NEWPAUSE as shown here:

```
@ECHO OFF
NEWPAUSE message
REM Other commands here
```

A Different PAUSE Command

By default, the PAUSE command suspends a batch file's execution until a user presses any key. The following DEBUG script file PAWSE.SCR, creates a command file named PAWSE.COM that displays a user message and then suspends the batch file's execution until the user presses ENTER (as opposed to any key):

PAWSE.SCR

```
N PAWSE.COM <ENTER>
A 100       <ENTER>
JMP 120     <ENTER>
DB A,D,'$'  <ENTER>
DB 'Press Enter to continue...$' <ENTER>
MOV AH,9    <ENTER>
MOV DX,105  <ENTER>
INT 21      <ENTER>
MOV AH,8    <ENTER>
INT 21      <ENTER>
CMP AL,D    <ENTER>
JNE 127     <ENTER>
MOV AH,9    <ENTER>
MOV DX,102  <ENTER>
INT 21      <ENTER>
```

```
MOV AH,4C     <ENTER>
INT 21        <ENTER>
              <ENTER>
R CX          <ENTER>
3A            <ENTER>
W             <ENTER>
Q             <ENTER>
```

Use DEBUG as follows to create the command file PAWSE.COM:

```
C:\> DEBUG < PAWSE.SCR <ENTER>
```

Within your batch files, you can replace the internal DOS PAUSE command with PAWSE.COM. Note that if the batch file has invoked the ECHO OFF command, the only message PAWSE.COM will display is the message for the user to press ENTER to continue. In other words, PAWSE behaves identically to the PAUSE command.

Using SHIFT to Enhance DEL

Most DOS commands, such as DEL and TYPE, let you specify only one filename or wildcard combination at a time in your command line. By creating simple batch files, you can expand many DOS commands to support multiple command-line filenames. The following batch file MYDEL.BAT deletes each file specified in the command line:

```
@ECHO OFF
:GET_NEXT_FILE
SHIFT
IF '%0'=='' GOTO DONE
DEL %0
GOTO GET_NEXT_FILE
:DONE
```

Using MYDEL, you can delete several files or wildcard combinations as shown here:

```
C:\> MYDEL FILENAME.ONE FILENAME.TWO *.BAK <ENTER>
```

The batch file uses SHIFT to delete each file specified, one at a time.

Merging Batch Files

As discussed in Tip 503, small files consume a considerable amount of disk space. One of the most common types of these files is small batch files. If you have several small batch files, you should consider combining the files into one large file named BATCH.BAT. When you invoke BATCH, you include the name and parameters for the desired batch file as shown here:

```
C:\> BATCH MYDEL *.BAK <ENTER>
```

Within BATCH.BAT, you first SHIFT the parameters one position and then test for the desired batch file as shown here:

```
@ECHO OFF
SHIFT
IF '%0'=='MY_DEL' GOTO MY_DEL
IF '%0'=='MY_TYPE' GOTO MY_TYPE
GOTO NO_MATCH

REM Other batch commands here
```

You then just merge your batch file into BATCH.BAT as shown here:

```
:MY_DEL
REM Place the batch file commands here
GOTO DONE
```

After you merge the smaller batch files in this way, you can delete the smaller batch files, freeing disk space.

A More Flexible PAUSE Command

The PAUSE command displays a message and suspends a batch file's execution until the user presses a key. Tip 633 presents the NEWPAUSE command that suspends a batch file's execution until the user presses ENTER. The companion disk that accompanies this book contains a utility command named RESPONSE.EXE that displays a message similar to PAUSE and then waits for the user to press one of the letters specified in the command. The command then returns an exit status value that corresponds to the letter selected. The following command illustrates how a batch file would use RESPONSE:

```
RESPONSE "Do you want to (R)epeat or (Q)uit?" "RrQq"
```

The first set of quotation marks contains the message to be displayed. The second set contains the desired keystrokes. If the user presses **R**, RESPONSE displays the value 0. For the letters r, Q, and q, RESPONSE will return the exit status values 1, 2, and 3, respectively:

```
@ECHO OFF
RESPONSE "Do you want to (C)ontinue or (Q)uit?" "CcQq"
IF ERRORLEVEL 0 IF NOT ERRORLEVEL 2 GOTO CONTINUE
IF ERRORLEVEL 2 GOTO QUIT
REM Other commands here
```

RESPONSE.EXE

The utility command RESPONSE.EXE resides on the companion disk that accompanies this book.

Using CTTY and NUL to Discard Batch File Messages

The ECHO OFF command lets your batch files suppress the display of command names as the commands execute. As described in Tip 622, you can redirect a command's output to the NUL device to prevent the command's output from appearing on the screen. If your batch file does not require user I/O, and if it does not invoke programs that require user input, you can disable the display of command names and messages by using CTTY NUL command at the start of the batch file. The CTTY command selects the device DOS should use for input and output operations. After the batch file assigns CTTY to NUL, no output is written to the screen, and keyboard input is ignored. In other words, the user can't end the batch file using the CRTL-C keyboard combination. The following batch file illustrates the use of CTTY NUL:

```
@ECHO OFF
CTTY NUL
PAYROLL
TAXES
CTTY CON
```

As you can see, the batch file must enable console output by using the CTTY CON command before ending, or the user will have to restart the system to perform normal input and output operations.

Accessing the DOS Prompt from Your Batch File

Many users create powerful menu-driven batch files that provide menu options for each of the tasks a user performs. Periodically, however, the user may need to access the DOS prompt to execute a specific command. If you invoke COMMAND.COM in your batch file, DOS will temporarily

suspend the batch file, displaying the DOS prompt. For example, the following batch file issues the DATE command, followed by COMMAND, and then TIME:

```
@ECHO OFF
DATE
COMMAND
TIME
```

When DOS encounters COMMAND, it will suspend the batch file and display the DOS prompt. The user is then free to execute any commands from the DOS prompt. When the user is ready to continue with the batch file's execution, the user must issue the EXIT command from the DOS prompt as shown here:

```
C:\> EXIT <ENTER>
```

In the case of the previous batch file, DOS will continue the execution with the TIME command.

A Partial Suspend

The PAUSE command suspends a batch file's execution until the user presses any key to continue. The following DEBUG script file, DELAY10.SCR, creates a command file named DELAY10.COM that suspends a batch file's execution for 10 seconds or until the user presses any key to continue:

DELAY10.SCR

```
N DELAY10.COM <ENTER>
A 100         <ENTER>
JMP 103       <ENTER>
DB 0          <ENTER>
MOV AH,2C     <ENTER>
INT 21        <ENTER>
ADD DH,A      <ENTER>
CMP DH,3C     <ENTER>
JL  112       <ENTER>
SUB DH,3C     <ENTER>
MOV [102],DH  <ENTER>
INT 21        <ENTER>
```

```
CMP DH,[102]   <ENTER>
JNE 116        <ENTER>
MOV AH,4C      <ENTER>
INT 21         <ENTER>
               <ENTER>
R CX           <ENTER>
22             <ENTER>
W              <ENTER>
Q              <ENTER>
```

Use the DEBUG command as follows to create the command file DELAY10.COM:

```
C:\> DEBUG < DELAY10.SCR <ENTER>
```

The following illustrates how a batch file might use DELAY10:

```
@ECHO OFF
ECHO About to print the directory listing
DELAY10
DIR > PRN
```

Understanding ERRORLEVEL Testing

Many DOS commands as well as many of the DEBUG script files presented in this book use an exit status that can be tested by your batch files. To test an exit status value, the batch file should invoke the command and then use IF ERRORLEVEL as shown here:

```
SomeCommand
IF ERRORLEVEL Value DOS_Command
```

When DOS encounters an IF ERRORLEVEL command, it compares the exit status value of the previous command with the value specified immediately after IF ERRORLEVEL. If the exit status value is equal to or greater than the ERRORLEVEL value, DOS executes the command specified.

Note that DOS will execute the specified command if the previous command's exit status is equal to or greater than the specified value. Thus, you need to consider the order in which you test exit status values. For example, the following batch file commands incorrectly test FORMAT's exit status values:

```
@ECHO OFF
FORMAT A:
IF ERRORLEVEL 0 GOTO SUCCESSFUL
IF ERRORLEVEL 3 GOTO USER_CTRL_C
IF ERRORLEVEL 4 GOTO FATAL_ERROR
IF ERRORLEVEL 5 GOTO USER_N
REM Other commands here
```

In this case, because all of FORMAT's status values are greater than or equal to zero, the first IF command always evaluates to true. Thus, regardless of how FORMAT ends, the batch file branches to the SUCCESSFUL label. To solve this problem, change the batch commands to test status values in the opposite order as shown here:

```
@ECHO OFF
FORMAT A:
IF ERRORLEVEL 5 GOTO USER_N
IF ERRORLEVEL 4 GOTO FATAL_ERROR
IF ERRORLEVEL 3 GOTO USER_CTRL_C
IF ERRORLEVEL 0 GOTO SUCCESSFUL
REM Other commands here
```

Using REM to for Non-Comment Purposes

Tip 628 discusses the importance of using REM statements in your batch files to explain their contents, and Tip 11 discusses using REM statements in CONFIG.SYS files.

In addition to using REM for documentation, you can use it to prevent DOS from executing a batch file command or processing a specific CONFIG.SYS entry. For example, assume your CONFIG.SYS file contains the following entries:

```
FILES=30
BUFFERS=35
LASTDRIVE=G
DEVICE=C:\DOS\RAMDRIVE.SYS 256 512 64 /A
```

Next, assume you want to temporarily remove the RAM drive created by the RAMDRIVE.SYS device driver. One way to do so is to remove the corresponding DEVICE entry from CONFIG.SYS and restart DOS. Unfortunately, when you later want to use the RAM drive, you must remember the contents of the previous DEVICE entry. A better solution is to disable the entry by preceding the entry with REM as shown here:

```
FILES=30
BUFFERS=35
LASTDRIVE=G
REM DEVICE=C:\DOS\RAMDRIVE.SYS 256 512 64 /A
```

When DOS encounters the REM, it will ignore the entry. Using REM in this same way, you can also disable commands in a batch file.

Combining Two IF ERRORLEVEL Commands for an Exact Test

As discussed in Tip 641, you need to be careful when you use IF ERRORLEVEL in your batch files because DOS considers any value a match if it is greater than or equal to the value specified. By combining two IF ERRORLEVEL commands, however, your batch files can test for an exact exit status value. For example, the following batch commands test for exact values of 0, 1, and 2:

```
SOMEPROG
IF ERRORLEVEL 0 IF NOT ERRORLEVEL 1 ECHO ZERO
IF ERRORLEVEL 1 IF NOT ERRORLEVEL 2 ECHO ONE
IF ERRORLEVEL 2 IF NOT ERRORLEVEL 3 ECHO TWO
```

The first IF ERRORLEVEL tests whether the value is equal to or greater than the value specified. If the result of the test is true, the second IF ERRORLEVEL tests to see whether the value is not greater than the first value specified. For example, assume a program exits with an exit status of 0. The first test, IF ERRORLEVEL 0, evaluates as true. The second test, IF NOT ERRORLEVEL 1, also evaluates to true because the exit status 0 is not 1 or higher. By combining two IF ERRORLEVEL tests in this way, you can test for an exact exit status.

TIP 644 What Kind of Disk Is This?

To help DOS, your programs, and your batch files determine the disk type, DOS assigns each disk a media descriptor value. Table 644 lists the various media descriptor values and disk types.

The following DEBUG script file, MEDIA.SCR, creates a command file named MEDIA.COM that returns the current drive's media descriptor value as an exit status:

MEDIA.SCR

```
N MEDIA.COM     <ENTER>
A 100           <ENTER>
MOV AH,1B       <ENTER>
INT 21          <ENTER>
MOV AL, [BX]    <ENTER>
MOV AH,4C       <ENTER>
INT 21          <ENTER>
                <ENTER>
R CX            <ENTER>
A               <ENTER>
W               <ENTER>
Q               <ENTER>
```

Use DEBUG as follows to create the command file MEDIA.COM:

```
C:\> DEBUG < MEDIA.SCR <ENTER>
```

The following batch command illustrates how you might use MEDIA.COM in your batch files:

```
@ECHO OFF
```

```
MEDIA
IF ERRORLEVEL 248 IF NOT ERRORLEVEL 249 GOTO HARD_DISK
REM Other commands here
```

Table 644. Drive Media Descriptors

Hexadecimal	Decimal	Disk Type
F0	240	1.44Mb
F8	248	Hard disk
F9	249	720Kb or 1.2Mb
FC	252	180Kb
FD	253	360Kb
FE	254	160Kb
FF	255	320Kb

Testing Your IF ERRORLEVEL Logic

As your batch files increase in complexity, they will take considerable advantage of the IF ERRORLEVEL command. Unfortunately, it is sometimes difficult to completely test your batch file's IF ERRORLEVEL commands. The companion disk that accompanies this book contains the utility command ERRORLVL.EXE that returns an exit status value in the range 0 to 255. To use ERRORLVL in your batch files, simply invoke it with the value you want to test as shown here:

```
ERRORLVL value
```

For example, the following batch commands test the IF ERRORLEVEL processing for an exit status of 5:

```
ERRORLVL 5
IF ERRORLEVEL 1 IF NOT ERRORLEVEL 2 GOTO ONE
    :
IF ERRORLEVEL 5 GOTO FIVE
REM other commands here
```

The utility command ERRORLVL.EXE resides on the companion disk that accompanies this book.

Invoking a Second Batch File with CALL or COMMAND /C

Invoking a second batch file from a batch file isn't as easy as it might seem. If the second batch file occurs at the end of the current batch file, you can invoke the batch file by name. For example, the following batch file invokes the DATE and TIME commands followed by a batch file named SECOND.BAT:

```
@ECHO OFF
DATE
TIME
SECOND
```

A problem occurs, however, when the second batch file is in the middle of the batch file as shown here:

```
@ECHO OFF
DATE
SECOND
TIME
```

When DOS encounters the batch file SECOND, DOS will execute the commands the batch file contains. Unfortunately, when the batch file SECOND ends, DOS will return control to the DOS prompt, as opposed to continuing the batch file's execution with the TIME command. If you are using DOS 3.3 or higher, you can solve this problem by invoking the batch file by using CALL as shown here:

```
@ECHO OFF
DATE
CALL SECOND
TIME
```

If you are using a DOS version lower than 3.3, invoke the file by using COMMAND /C as shown here:

```
ECHO OFF
DATE
COMMAND /C SECOND
TIME
```

If the second batch file you are invoking uses batch parameters, simply include the parameters after the batch filename as you normally would.

Testing Multiple Conditions in Your Batch Files

The IF command lets your batch files compare the contents of one string of characters to another. For example, the following command tests whether the value in the batch parameter %1 contains the word BLUE:

```
IF '%1'=='BLUE' GOTO BLUE_BACKGROUND
```

The IF command is case sensitive, meaning that if the user specifies the color *blue* in lowercase letters, the previous IF command will evaluate to false. To account for this case sensitivity, you have two choices. One choice is to include several IF commands for the most common cases of the word *blue* as shown here:

```
IF '%1'=='BLUE' GOTO BLUE_BACKGROUND
IF '%1'=='Blue' GOTO BLUE_BACKGROUND
IF '%1'=='blue' GOTO BLUE_BACKGROUND
```

Alternatively, you can combine the FOR command and IF commands as shown here:

```
FOR %%B IN (BLUE Blue blue) DO IF '%%B'=='%1' GOTO
     BLUE_BACKGROUND
```

In this case, the FOR command will perform the test by using IF for each of the different combinations. If a match occurs, the batch file will branch to the specified label. If no match occurs, the batch file continues execution with the next command. By using the FOR command to test various cases in this way, you reduce the number of commands the batch file must contain.

Tip 648 Building Batch Files on the Fly

As discussed in Tip 503, small files consume more space on your disks than you might expect. Batch files are some of the most common small files.

In some cases, one of your batch files may need a second, small batch file to perform specific processing. For example, the following batch file DELETE.BAT invokes a second batch file named DELFILE.BAT:

```
@ECHO OFF
FOR %%I IN (%1) DO CALL DELFILE %%I
```

The batch file DELFILE.BAT displays a filename and asks the user whether the file is to be deleted. If the user responds with Y, the batch file deletes the file; otherwise, the batch file leaves the file unchanged. The batch file, shown here, uses the command YESORNO.COM created in Tip 649:

```
ECHO Delete %1 (Y/N)?
YESORNO
IF ERRORLEVEL 1 DEL %1
```

In this case, two batch files are required. Although each batch file is small, both consume a cluster of disk space. Rather than requiring that the batch file DELFILE.BAT exists, the batch file DELETE.BAT can create DELFILE.BAT when it starts, use the batch file, and then delete the file before it ends. The following batch file illustrates how you would create a second batch file on the fly by using ECHO:

```
@ECHO OFF
ECHO ECHO Delete %%1 (Y/N)? > DELFILE.BAT
```

```
ECHO YESORNO >> DELFILE.BAT
ECHO IF ERRORLEVEL 1 DEL %%1 >> DELFILE.BAT

FOR %%I IN (%1) DO CALL DELFILE %%I
DEL DELFILE.BAT
```

When the batch file begins, it redirects the output of several ECHO commands to create the second batch file. Note that the batch file uses %%1 in the ECHO commands that build DELFILE.BAT. When DOS encounters the double percent sign, DOS converts it to %1, which is the proper text to write to the batch file. If the batch file had instead used %1, DOS would have substituted the first batch parameter.

By building batch files on the fly in this way, you eliminate a batch file's dependence on a second batch file, and you reduce the amount of disk space consumed by small batch files.

Prompting the User for a Yes or No Response

There are times when, in your batch files, you want to prompt a user for a yes or no response to a question. This can be done with a command file called YESORNO.COM. It prompts the user for a Y (yes) or N (no) response, returning the exit status 1 if the user types Y and the exit status 0 if the user types N. The command ignores all other keystrokes. The following DEBUG script file, YESORNO.SCR, creates the command file YESORNO.COM:

YESORNO.SCR

```
N YESORNO.COM <ENTER>
A 100         <ENTER>
MOV AH,0      <ENTER>
INT 16        <ENTER>
MOV AL,0      <ENTER>
CMP AH,15     <ENTER>
JE  112       <ENTER>
CMP AH,31     <ENTER>
JE  114       <ENTER>
JMP 100       <ENTER>
MOV AL,1      <ENTER>
```

```
MOV AH,4C        <ENTER>
INT 21           <ENTER>
                 <ENTER>
R CX             <ENTER>
18               <ENTER>
W                <ENTER>
Q                <ENTER>
```

Use the DEBUG command as follows to create the command file YESORNO.COM:

```
C:\> DEBUG < YESORNO.SCR <ENTER>
```

The following batch commands illustrate the use of YESORNO:

```
@ECHO OFF
ECHO Do you want to continue (Y/N)?
YESORNO
IF NOT ERRORLEVEL 1 GOTO Done
ECHO You said yes!
:Done
```

Tip 650 Saving and Restoring the Current Directory

As they execute, many batch files change the current directory. Ideally, unless the batch file's purpose is to change the current directory, it should restore the original directory before it ends. The companion disk that accompanies this book contains two utility programs—PUSHDIR.EXE and POPDIR.EXE—that save and later restore the current directory. The following batch file illustrates the use of these utilities:

```
@ECHO OFF
REM Save current directory
PUSHDIR
REM Change directory and issue a command
CHDIR \SOMEDIR
```

```
SOMEPROG
REM Restore the original directory
POPDIR
```

Each time you execute the PUSHDIR command, PUSHDIR searches the root directory on drive C for a file named SAVEDIR.DAT. If the file exists, PUSHDIR appends the current directory to the file. If the file does not exist, PUSHDIR creates it. When you later execute the POPDIR command, POPDIR also searches for the same file, selecting and removing the last directory the file contains. Each time you execute a PUSHDIR command, you should later execute a corresponding POPDIR command. Depending on your batch file's processing, you may execute several PUSHDIR commands followed later by several POPDIR commands.

The utility commands PUSHDIR.EXE and POPDIR.EXE reside on the companion disk that accompanies this book.

PUSHDIR.EXE
POPDIR.EXE

A Different Type of ECHO Command

The ECHO command lets your batch files display messages to the user. After ECHO displays a message, it advances the cursor to the start of the next line with a carriage-return linefeed. You may want your batch files to display a message without advancing the cursor, however. The following DEBUG script file, NEW_ECHO.SCR, creates the command file NEW_ECHO.COM that allows your batch files to do just that:

```
N NEW_ECHO.COM      <ENTER>
A 100               <ENTER>
MOV BX,80           <ENTER>
INC BX              <ENTER>
CMP BYTE [BX],D     <ENTER>
JNE 103             <ENTER>
MOV BYTE [BX],24    <ENTER>
```

```
MOV AH,9           <ENTER>
MOV DX,82          <ENTER>
CMP DX,BX          <ENTER>
JG  117            <ENTER>
INT 21             <ENTER>
MOV AH,4C          <ENTER>
INT 21             <ENTER>
                   <ENTER>
R CX               <ENTER>
1B                 <ENTER>
W                  <ENTER>
Q                  <ENTER>
```

Use DEBUG as follows to create the command file NEW_ECHO.COM:

```
C:\> DEBUG < NEW_ECHO.SCR <ENTER>
```

The following illustrates how your batch files might use NEW_ECHO:

```
@ECHO OFF
NEW_ECHO Do you want to continue (Y/N)?
YESORNO
REM Other commands
```

Determining Whether HIMEM.SYS Is Installed

As discussed in Tip 221, before DOS can use extended memory, you must install the HIMEM.SYS device driver. The following DEBUG script file, CHKHIMEM.SCR, creates a command file named CHKHIMEM.COM that tests whether the driver is installed. If the driver is installed, the command returns the exit status 1. If the driver is not installed, the command returns the exit status 0.

```
N CHKHIMEM.COM <ENTER>
A 100          <ENTER>
MOV AX,4300    <ENTER>
INT 2F         <ENTER>
CMP AL,80      <ENTER>
JNE 10D        <ENTER>
MOV AL,1       <ENTER>
JMP 10F        <ENTER>
MOV AL,0       <ENTER>
MOV AH,4C      <ENTER>
INT 21         <ENTER>
               <ENTER>
R CX           <ENTER>
13             <ENTER>
W              <ENTER>
Q              <ENTER>
```

CHKHIMEM.SCR

Use DEBUG as follows to create the command file CHKHIMEM.COM:

```
C:\> DEBUG < CHKHIMEM.SCR <ENTER>
```

If you have a program that requires HIMEM.SYS, you can invoke the program from a batch file that first uses CHKHIMEM to verify that the driver is installed. If the driver is not installed, CHKHIMEM displays a message directing the user to install it—or better yet, the batch file could modify CONFIG.SYS to add the HIMEM.SYS entry and then restart the system to install the driver.

Saving and Restoring the Current Drive

In Tip 650 you learned how you can save the current directory. What about the current drive, however? As they execute, many batch files change the current drive. Ideally, unless the batch file's purpose is to change the drive, it should restore the original drive before it ends. The companion disk that accompanies this book contains two utility programs, PUSHDRV.EXE and POPDRV.EXE, that save and later restore the current drive. The following batch file illustrates how you use these utilities:

```
@ECHO OFF
REM Save current drive
PUSHDRV
REM Change drive and issue a command
D:
SOMEPROG
REM Restore the original drive
POPDRV
```

Each time you execute the PUSHDRV command, PUSHDRV searches the root directory on drive C for a file named SAVEDRV.DAT. If the file exists, PUSHDRV appends the current drive to the file. If the file does not exist, PUSHDRV creates it. When you later execute the POPDRV command, POPDRV searches for the same file, selecting and removing the last drive the file contains. Each time you execute a PUSHDRV command, you should later execute a corresponding POPDRV command. Depending on your batch file's processing, you may execute several PUSHDRV commands followed later by several POPDRV commands.

PUSHDRV.EXE
POPDRV.EXE

The utility commands PUSHDRV.EXE and POPDRV.EXE reside on the companion disk that accompanies this book.

Getting a Function Key Response

As you increase the complexity of your batch files, there will be times when you will want to display a menu of options and wait for the user to press a specific key. The following DEBUG script file, F1TOF10.SCR, creates a command file named F1TOF10.COM that waits for the user to press one of the function keys. The command then returns an exit status value from 1 through 10 corresponding to the key pressed:

F1TOF10.SCR

```
N F1TOF10.COM <ENTER>
A 100         <ENTER>
MOV AH,0      <ENTER>
INT 16        <ENTER>
CMP AH,3B     <ENTER>
JL   100      <ENTER>
CMP AH,44     <ENTER>
JG   100      <ENTER>
SUB AH,3A     <ENTER>
MOV AL,AH     <ENTER>
MOV AH,4C     <ENTER>
INT 21        <ENTER>
              <ENTER>
R CX          <ENTER>
17            <ENTER>
W             <ENTER>
Q             <ENTER>
```

Use DEBUG as follows to create the command file F1TOF10.COM:

```
C\> DEBUG < F1TOF10.SCR <ENTER>
```

The following batch commands illustrate how you might use F1TOF10.COM:

```
@ECHO OFF
:LOOP
ECHO            F1   DIR Command
ECHO            F2   FORMAT Command
ECHO            F3   DISKCOPY Command
ECHO            F4   Quit
:GET_KEY
F1TOF10
IF ERRORLEVEL 1 IF NOT ERRORLEVEL 2 GOTO F1
IF ERRORLEVEL 2 IF NOT ERRORLEVEL 3 GOTO F2
IF ERRORLEVEL 3 IF NOT ERRORLEVEL 4 GOTO F3
IF ERRORLEVEL 4 IF NOT ERRORLEVEL 5 GOTO F4
GOTO GET_KEY
:F1 DIR
PAUSE
GOTO LOOP
:F2
FORMAT A:
GOTO LOOP
```

```
:F3
DISKCOPY A: B:
GOTO LOOP
:F4
```

Understanding Named Parameters

If you are using DOS 3.3 or higher, DOS lets your batch files access environment entries by using named parameters. Environment entries take the form EntryName=Value. A named parameter is nothing more than the EntryName surrounded by percent signs: %EntryName%. For example, the following batch commands display the contents of three common environment entries—PATH, PROMPT, and COMSPEC:

```
@ECHO OFF
ECHO The current path is %PATH%
ECHO The current prompt is %PROMPT%
ECHO The current COMSPEC is %COMSPEC%
```

When DOS encounters a named parameter in a batch file, it searches the environment for a matching entry. If one is found, the named parameter is replaced with the entry's value. Otherwise, DOS assigns the named parameter an empty value. Several of the batch file tips presented in this book take advantage of named parameters.

To use named parameters, you must be using DOS 3.3 or higher.

Using Named Parameters to Store and Restore Environment Entries

Tip 655 describes how DOS versions 3.3 and higher can use named parameters within batch files to access environment entries. Sometimes you may change environment entries in your batch files, as in the following example:

```
PROMPT $E[0;67;"CLS"$_p
PROMPT $E[0;68;"DIR"$_p
PROMPT $P$G
```

The last command restores the prompt to the current drive and directory, followed by a greater-than symbol. Unfortunately, if you have previously customized your prompt to something different, your prompt is now changed. A better batch file would have first saved the original prompt and later restored the prompt, using named parameters as shown here:

```
@SET SAVE_PROMPT=%PROMPT%
PROMPT $E[0;67;"CLS"$_p
PROMPT $E[0;68;"DIR"$_p
PROMPT %SAVE_PROMPT%
@SET SAVE_PROMPT=
```

Several of the tips presented in this book provide commands that help your batch files take advantage of named parameters.

To use named parameters, you must be using DOS 3.3 or higher.

Assigning the Current Directory as an Environment Entry

The companion disk that accompanies this book includes a utility command named SETDIR.EXE that assigns the current directory to an environment entry named DIRECTORY. After your batch file saves the current directory, it can perform its processing, later restoring the original directory by using the named parameter %DIRECTORY%. The following batch commands illustrate how you would use SETDIR:

```
@ECHO OFF
SETDIR
REM other commands
CD %DIRECTORY%
SET DIRECTORY =
```

If SETDIR cannot assign the current directory to the environment entry, SETDIR returns the exit status value 1. Otherwise, SETDIR returns the exit status value 0.

SETDIR.EXE

The utility command SETDIR.EXE resides on the companion disk that accompanies this book.

Saving the Current System Time to a Named Parameter

The companion disk that accompanies this book provides a handy utility command, SETTIME.EXE, that assigns the current hours and minutes to an environment entry named TIME. The following batch file commands use SETTIME to display the current hours and minutes:

```
@ECHO OFF
SETTIME
ECHO The current system time is %TIME%
SET TIME=
```

If SETTIME cannot assign the current time to the environment, SETTIME returns the exit status value 1. Otherwise, SETTIME returns the exit status value 0.

The utility command SETTIME.EXE resides on the companion disk that accompanies this book.

SETTIME.EXE

Assigning the System Date to an Environment Entry

The companion disk that accompanies this book contains the utility command SETDATE.EXE that assigns the current date in the form mm-dd-yy to an environment entry named DATE. The following batch commands use the named parameter %DATE% to list the names of current directory files that were created today:

```
@ECHO OFF
SETDATE
DIR | FIND %DATE%
```

If SETDATE cannot assign the environment entry, it returns the exit status 1. Otherwise, SETDATE returns the exit status 0.

The utility command SETDATE.EXE resides on the companion disk that accompanies this book.

SETDATE.EXE

Assigning the Current Drive to an Environment Entry

The companion disk that accompanies this book includes the utility command SETDRIVE.EXE that assigns the current drive letter and a colon to an environment entry named DRIVE. The following batch commands save the current drive using SETDRIVE, changes the drive to drive A, displays a directory listing, and then restores the original drive using the %DRIVE% named parameter:

```
@ECHO OFF
SETDRIVE
A:
DIR
%DRIVE%
SET DRIVE=
```

If SETDRIVE cannot assign the drive to an environment entry, SETDRIVE returns the exit status value 1; otherwise, SETDRIVE returns 0.

SETDRIVE.EXE

The utility program SETDRIVE.EXE resides on the companion disk that accompanies this book.

Using Drop-Down Shadow Boxes to Improve Message Appearance

Tip 500 discusses how using extended-ASCII characters improves the appearance of your batch file messages and menus by letting you put output in a box as shown here:

```
            MENU
   F1 Directory Listing
   F2 CHKDSK Command
   F3 Quit
```

By using the extended ASCII block characters, you can also create shadow boxes. The following batch file commands illustrate how to create a simple shadow box:

```
@ECHO OFF
ECHO
ECHO               MENU
ECHO      F1 Directory Listing
ECHO      F2 CHKDSK Command
ECHO      F3 Quit
ECHO
ECHO
ECHO
```

As you can see, the batch file uses thin extended ASCII characters to draw the box and thick characters to produce the shadow. Use the table of characters presented in Tip 30 to determine the values of the characters you desire.

Quitting a Batch File

When you create complex batch files, often they will perform a specific set of commands and then branch to an ending label by using a command such as GOTO DONE, as shown here:

```
:SomeLabel
FirstCmd
SecondCm
ThirdCmd
GOTO DONE
REM Other commands
:DONE
```

As an alternative, you can create a second batch file named QUIT.BAT that contains only the following label:

```
:DONE
```

Instead of using GOTO to branch to a specific label, your batch file can invoke QUIT as follows:

```
:SomeLabel
FirstCmd
SecondCm
ThirdCmd
QUIT
```

If you invoke a second batch file without using CALL or COMMAND /C, DOS will execute the second batch file's commands without returning control to the original batch file. In the case of QUIT.BAT, your batch file's execution will simply end, as you desire.

The advantage of ending your batch file by using QUIT.BAT, as opposed to GOTO DONE, is you can customize QUIT.BAT so that all your batch files end the same way, possibly by clearing the screen or restoring the original drive and directory. In addition, you can change QUIT.BAT to execute a specific command passed to it by the batch file as shown here:

```
IF NOT '%1'=='' %1
:DONE
```

Ways to Test for Missing Parameters

As your batch files increase in complexity, you will probably make extensive use of the parameters %0 through %9, which let the user specify values with which the batch file works. If your batch files make use of, or depend on, batch parameters, you should use the IF command to verify that the user has specified values for the parameters. When a user does not specify a value for a parameter, DOS assigns the parameters the null, or empty, value. The most common way to test for an empty parameter value is by using the IF command as follows:

```
IF '%1'=='' GOTO NO_PARAMETER
```

In this case, if the user does not specify a value for %1, the following parameter substitution occurs:

```
IF ''=='' GOTO NO_PARAMETER
```

Because the two strings are equal, the condition evaluates are true, and the batch file branches control to the NO_PARAMETER label. If the user specifies a value for %1, the IF condition will fail.

As you read other batch files, you may see conditions similar to the following:

```
IF %1X==X GOTO NO_PARAMETER
```

This condition also tests for an empty %1. In this case, if %1 is empty, the condition changes to the following:

```
IF X==X GOTO NO_PARAMETER
```

As before, if the user specifies any value for %1, the condition fails.

Although both ways of testing for an empty parameter work, the first method is recommended because its use is more common and the least confusing to new users.

Redirecting Input from the CON Device

Tip 638 explains how to use the command CTTY NUL to redirect a batch file's input and output to the NUL device. This tip states that you would normally use this technique only for batch files that don't require user input or output. However, by redirecting a command's input or output to the CON device, you can use this technique to discard messages for interactive batch files as well.

For example, the following batch file begins by issuing the CTTY NUL command. Next, it copies several files. Because the NUL device is the current output source, COPY's messages do not appear. The batch file then invokes the EDIT command, redirecting the command's input to the keyboard. After EDIT ends, the batch file resumes its processing, eventually issuing the command CTTY CON to restore normal processing.

```
@ECHO OFF
CTTY NUL
COPY *.* \BACKUP
EDIT < CON
REM other commands
CTTY CON
```

Admittedly, you could have used CTTY to enable and disable console I/O throughout the batch file's processing, but doing so would require additional commands.

Faster Command Execution

If your batch files repeatedly invoke external commands, you can improve performance by copying the commands to a RAM disk and then changing the batch file to invoke the commands from the RAM disk. Before DOS can execute an external command, DOS must load the command from disk into memory. Because the RAM disk is much faster than the mechanical hard drive, the program will execute much faster.

Building on the DEBUG Script Files

Tip 503 explains that small files can actually consume a considerable amount of disk space. Throughout this book, tips present many small DEBUG script files. If you have a DEBUG script file you use with only a particular batch file, you might consider letting the batch file create the DEBUG script file on the fly, later deleting the file before the batch file ends. Tip 649 presents the DEBUG script YESORNO.SCR. The following batch file illustrates how you can build a similar DEBUG script file on the fly:

```
@ECHO OFF
ECHO N YESORNO.COM   > YESORNO.SCR
ECHO A 100          >> YESORNO.SCR
ECHO MOV AH,0       >> YESORNO.SCR
ECHO INT 16         >> YESORNO.SCR
ECHO MOV AL,0       >> YESORNO.SCR
ECHO CMP AH,15      >> YESORNO.SCR
ECHO JE  112        >> YESORNO.SCR
ECHO CMP AH,31      >> YESORNO.SCR
ECHO JE  114        >> YESORNO.SCR
ECHO JMP 100        >> YESORNO.SCR
ECHO MOV AL,1       >> YESORNO.SCR
ECHO MOV AH,4C      >> YESORNO.SCR
ECHO INT 21         >> YESORNO.SCR
ECHO.               >> YESORNO.SCR
ECHO R CX           >> YESORNO.SCR
ECHO 18             >> YESORNO.SCR
ECHO W              >> YESORNO.SCR
ECHO Q              >> YESORNO.SCR

DEBUG < YESORNO.SCR

ECHO Do you want to continue (Y/N)?
YESORNO
IF ERRORLEVEL 1 ECHO You said yes
IF NOT ERRORLEVEL 1 ECHO You said no
DEL YESORNO.SCR
DEL YESORNO.COM
```

By creating DEBUG script files in this way on the fly, your batch files will take slightly longer to execute, but you will save disk space.

XCOPY Is the Batch File Command of Choice

When you issue a COPY command from the DOS prompt and the command fails, possibly either because a file or path could not not be found, COPY displays an error message that makes you instantly aware of the error. Within a batch file, however, such an error cannot be detected because COPY does not return an exit status value. Thus, if your batch files need to detect and respond to errors, use the XCOPY command, which returns one of the exit status values listed in Table 667.

The following batch commands illustrate how you might use XCOPY in a batch file:

```
@ECHO OFF
XCOPY %1 %2
IF ERRORLEVEL 1 GOTO ERROR
REM Other commands here
```

Table 666. Exit Status Values Returned by XCOPY

Exit Status	Meaning
0	File copy operation succeeded.
1	No files were found to copy.
2	File copy operation was terminated by CTRL-C.
4	Initialization error prevented copy operation.
5	Disk write error occurred during copy operation.

Saving an Event's Time

As your batch files execute, you sometimes may want to save the time at which a specific event occurred. The companion disk that accompanies this book contains two utility programs, PUSHTIME.EXE and POPTIME.EXE, that save and later restore the current time. The utility command PUSHTIME.EXE records the current time in a file that is later read by POPTIME. POPTIME, in turn, assigns the time to the environment entry POP_TIME. The following batch file illustrates the use of these utilities:

```
@ECHO OFF
REM Save current time
PUSHTIME
SOMEPROG
REM Obtain the event's starting time
POPTIME
ECHO Program began at %POP_TIME%
REM Get current time
ENVTIME
ECHO Program ended at %CURRENT_TIME%
SET POP_TIME=
SET CURRENT_TIME=
```

Each time you execute the PUSHTIME command, PUSHTIME searches the root directory on drive C for a file named SAVETIME.DAT. If the file exists, PUSHTIME appends the current time to the file. If the file does not exist, PUSHTIME creates it. When you later execute the POPTIME command, POPTIME also searches for the same file, selecting and removing the last time the file contains and assigning the time to the environment entry POP_TIME. Each time you execute a PUSHTIME command, you should later execute a corresponding POPTIME command. Depending on your batch file's processing, you may execute several PUSHTIME commands followed later by several POPTIME commands.

The utility commands PUSHTIME.EXE and POPTIME.EXE reside on the companion disk that accompanies this book.

PUSHTIME.EXE
POPTIME.EXE

A Locator Batch File

If you work in an office, many times you will be pulled away from your desk for meetings and other reasons. The following BASIC program, IM_AT.BAS, lets you display a message on your screen telling others where you can be reached:

```
INPUT "Where are you going"; W$
INPUT "Phone Number"; P$
INPUT "Return at"; E$
CLS
WHILE INKEY$ = ""
 ROW = RND * 25
 COLUMN = RND * 50
 IF ROW < 1 THEN ROW = 1
 IF ROW > 22 THEN ROW = 22
 IF COLUMN < 1 THEN COLUMN = 1
 LOCATE ROW, COLUMN
 PRINT "I'm at: "; W$
 LOCATE ROW + 1, COLUMN
 PRINT "If you need me, call: "; P$
 LOCATE ROW + 2, COLUMN
 PRINT "I'll be back at: "; E$
 START = TIMER
 WHILE (START + 5 > TIMER)
 WEND
 CLS
WEND
SYSTEM
```

Use the following command to run the program:

```
C:\> QBASIC IM_AT.BAS <ENTER>
```

When you invoke the batch file, it prompts you for your location, a phone number, and your estimated time of return. Your screen will then display a message that tells where you are and where you can be reached. Every 5 seconds the message moves to a different screen location to prevent screen burn in. To end the display, press any key.

To use QBASIC, you must be using DOS 5. If you are using a different DOS version, invoke the program by using GWBASIC or BASICA.

When to Use the NOT Operator

Several of the batch files presented in this book make use of the NOT operator in IF commands. The IF command lets you test whether or not a specific condition is true, such as whether a batch parameter is equal to a specific value or the exit status of the previous program is greater than or equal to a specific value. If the condition specified is true, DOS executes the specified command. Sometimes, however, you may want DOS to execute a command when a condition is not true. For example, if a program's exit status is not greater than or equal to a specific value, you may want a batch file to branch to a specific location. The NOT operator lets you test for and issue a command when a condition is not true. For example, several of the DEBUG script files presented in this book return the exit status value 1 if a specific program or device driver is installed; otherwise, the commands return the exit status 0. The easiest way to test for the exit status value 0 is to use the NOT operator as shown here:

```
IF NOT ERRORLEVEL 1 GOTO EXIT_STATUS_ZERO
```

In this case, the NOT operator makes the previous command read, "if the exit status is not greater than or equal to 1, branch to a specific label." The only exit status that is not greater than or equal to one is 0.

Using Named Parameters to Create Batch Subroutines

Programmers often complain because batch files don't support subroutines or GOSUB and RETURN statements. If you are using DOS 3.3 or higher, however, you can use named parameters to simulate subroutines. Subroutines are unique in that after a subroutine executes, it returns control to the location that immediately follows the command that invoked it. The following batch file, SUBDEMO.BAT illustrates how you can simulate subroutines by using the named parameter %RETURN%:

```
@ECHO OFF
SET RETURN=WRITE_CHECKS
GOTO PAYROLL
:WRITE_CHECKS
SET RETURN=UPDATE_LEDGER
GOTO CHECKS
:UPDATE_LEDGER
SET RETURN=DONE
GOTO LEDGER

:PAYROLL
REM Payroll commands here
GOTO %RETURN%

:CHECKS
REM Check processing commands here
GOTO %RETURN%

:LEDGER
REM Ledger processing commands here
GOTO %RETURN%

:DONE
```

Notice that before invoking a subroutine with the GOTO statement, the label to which the subroutine is to return control is assigned to the RETURN environment entry. When the subroutine is done, it

returns to the desired label by using the command GOTO %RETURN%. Although to the purist such processing is far from actual subroutine use, it does provide an easy way to reuse commands without having to duplicate the commands throughout the batch file.

@ECHO OFF Isn't Required

Almost every batch file begins with the @ECHO OFF command, which directs DOS to suppress the display of command names as the batch file executes. When you create short batch files, keep in mind that you can suppress the display of a batch command by preceding the command itself with the @ character. For example, the following batch file prints a directory listing of the files on your disk:

```
@DIR > PRN
```

By preceding the command with the @ character, you eliminate the need for @ECHO OFF, which lets you create the batch file faster, keeps the batch file simpler, and results in one less command DOS must execute. If your batch files are only a few lines long, consider simply preceding each command with the @ character as shown.

To use the @ character with commands other than ECHO, you must be using DOS 3.3 or higher.

How DOSKEY Macros Differ from Batch Files

DOSKEY macros and DOS batch files both allow you to execute one or more commands by typing a name at the DOS prompt and pressing ENTER. However, there are differences between the two, as listed here:

- There is no limit to the number of commands a batch file can contain. A DOSKEY macro, however, cannot exceed 127 characters.
- DOS batch files reside on disk. DOSKEY macros reside in RAM. Because RAM is much faster, an equivalent macro will execute faster than its batch file counterpart.
- Pressing CTRL-C lets you end a batch file's execution. Pressing CTRL-C with a DOSKEY macro ends only the current command.
- DOSKEY macros do not have a command equivalent to SHIFT, which moves parameters one position left.
- DOSKEY macros do not support a command similar to GOTO, which lets you branch to a different location.
- DOSKEY macros do not support a command similar to ECHO OFF, which lets you disable command name display.
- You can invoke a batch file from within a DOSKEY macro, but you cannot invoke a macro from within a batch file. Macros can be invoked only from the keyboard.
- DOSKEY macros do not support named parameters.

To use DOSKEY, you must be using DOS 5.

Be Aware of REM and Redirection

Tip 642 discusses how to use the REM command to suppress execution of a command in a batch file. When you suppress a command in this way, or when you comment your macros, you need to be aware of the redirection operators. For example, assume you use REM to comment out a command that redirects a copy of the directory listing to the file DIR.LST as shown here:

```
REM DIR > DIR.LST
```

When DOS encounters the command in your batch file, DOS assumes you want REM's output redirected to the file DIR.LST. Because REM does not generate output, the file will be empty. Similarly,

the following batch file comment creates an error because DOS tries to redirect REM's output using the DOS pipe (|):

```
REM This batch file uses the pipe (|) operator
```

Executing Several Commands on the Same Line

Tip 92 discusses how to execute several commands at the same time by using DOSKEY. If you are not using DOS 5, you can create the following batch file, MULT.BAT, that lets you execute several commands on the same line:

```
@ECHO OFF
:OUTER_LOOP
IF '%1'=='' GOTO DONE
SET COMMAND=
:INNER_LOOP
  IF '%1'=='' GOTO DO_COMMAND
  IF '%1'=='&' GOTO DO_COMMAND
  SET COMMAND=%COMMAND% %1
  SHIFT
GOTO INNER_LOOP
:DO_COMMAND
IF NOT '%COMMAND%'=='' %COMMAND%
SHIFT
GOTO OUTER_LOOP
:DONE
```

To use MULT.BAT, separate commands with an ampersand (&) as shown here:

```
C:\> MULT CLS & DATE & TIME <ENTER>
```

In this case, DOS will execute the CLS, DATE, and TIME commands.

A Better Way to Compare Strings

The IF command lets your batch file compare two strings. These comparisons are case-sensitive; that is, IF doesn't consider uppercase and lowercase characters as the same input. The companion disk that accompanies this book contains the utility command STRCOMP.EXE that compares two strings without regard to case. If the strings are equal, STRCOMP returns the exit status 0. If the first string is longer than the second, STRCOMP returns the value 1. If the second string is longer, STRCOMP returns the value 2. Unlike IF, STRCOMP considers uppercase and lowercase characters as the same input. The following batch commands use STRCOMP to determine whether %1 is equal to MONTHLY:

```
@ECHO OFF
IF '%1'=='' GOTO NO_PARAMETER
STRCOMP %1 MONTHLY
IF NOT ERRORLEVEL 1 GOTO MONTHLY
REM other commands here
```

STRCOMP.EXE

The utility command STRCOMP.EXE resides on the companion disk that accompanies this book.

Waiting for a Key in the Range 0 through 9

As your batch files become more complex, you will likely want to present menus of options to which the user can respond. The following DEBUG script file, 0_THRU_9.SCR, creates a command file

named 0_THRU_9.COM that waits for the user to press a key in the range 0 through 9 and then returns an exit status value in the same range:

```
N 0_THRU_9.COM <ENTER>
A 100          <ENTER>
MOV AH,8       <ENTER>
INT 21         <ENTER>
CMP AL,30      <ENTER>
JL  102        <ENTER>
CMP AL,39      <ENTER>
JG  102        <ENTER>
SUB AL,30      <ENTER>
MOV AH,4C      <ENTER>
INT 21         <ENTER>
               <ENTER>
R CX           <ENTER>
12             <ENTER>
W              <ENTER>
Q              <ENTER>
```

0_THRU_9.SCR

Use DEBUG as follows to create the command file 0_THRU_9.COM:

```
C:\> DEBUG < 0_THRU_9.SCR <ENTER>
```

The following batch commands illustrate how you might use 0_THRU_9:

```
@ECHO OFF
:LOOP
CLS
ECHO 1 DIR Listing
ECHO 2 VER Command
ECHO 3 VOL Command
ECHO 4 Quit
:GET_KEY
0_THRU_9
IF ERRORLEVEL 1 IF NOT ERRORLEVEL 2 GOTO DIR
IF ERRORLEVEL 2 IF NOT ERRORLEVEL 3 GOTO VER
IF ERRORLEVEL 3 IF NOT ERRORLEVEL 4 GOTO VOL
IF ERRORLEVEL 4 IF NOT ERRORLEVEL 5 GOTO DONE
GOTO GET_KEY
:DIR
DIR
PAUSE
```

```
GOTO LOOP
:VER
VER
PAUSE
GOTO LOOP
:VOL
VOL
PAUSE
GOTO LOOP
:DONE
```

Waiting for a Letter from A through Z

Often you will create menu-driven batch files. The following DEBUG script file, A_THRU_Z.SCR, creates a command file named A_THRU_Z.COM that waits for the user to press a key in the range A through Z; the command then returns an exit status value in the range 0 through 25 that corresponds to each letter:

A_THRU_Z.SCR

```
N A_THRU_Z.COM <ENTER>
A 100          <ENTER>
MOV AH,8       <ENTER>
INT 21         <ENTER>
CMP AL,41      <ENTER>
JL  102        <ENTER>
CMP AL,5A      <ENTER>
JG  102        <ENTER>
SUB AL,41      <ENTER>
MOV AH,4C      <ENTER>
INT 21         <ENTER>
               <ENTER>
R CX           <ENTER>
12             <ENTER>
W              <ENTER>
Q              <ENTER>
```

Use DEBUG as follows to create the command file A_THRU_.COM:

```
C:\> DEBUG < A_THRU_Z.SCR <ENTER>
```

The following batch commands illustrate how you would use A_THRU_Z.COM:

```
@ECHO OFF
:LOOP
CLS
ECHO A DIR Listing
ECHO B VER Command
ECHO C VOL Command
ECHO Z Quit
:GET_KEY
A_THRU_Z
IF ERRORLEVEL 0 IF NOT ERRORLEVEL 1 GOTO DIR
IF ERRORLEVEL 1 IF NOT ERRORLEVEL 2 GOTO VER
IF ERRORLEVEL 2 IF NOT ERRORLEVEL 3 GOTO VOL
IF ERRORLEVEL 25 GOTO DONE
GOTO GET_KEY
:DIR
DIR
PAUSE
GOTO LOOP
:VER
VER
PAUSE
GOTO LOOP
:VOL
VOL
PAUSE
GOTO LOOP
:DONE
```

The DEBUG script file A_THRU_Z supports only uppercase letters. It does not support lowercase letters.

Move Batch File Remarks for Best Performance

As discussed in Tip 628, you should use the REM command to provide detailed comments about your batch files. Many batch files, therefore, will begin with a series of REM commands that provide details about the batch file as shown here:

```
@ECHO OFF
REM ******************************************
REM **      S O M E F I L E . B A T         **
REM **                                      **
REM ** Written by: Kris Jamsa               **
REM ** Date Written: 8-23-92                **
REM ** Function: Performs some specific     **
REM **    task to make the PC easier.       **
REM **                                      **
REM ******************************************
```

These REM commands provide an example of a well-documented batch file. Unfortunately, when you execute the batch file, these commands slow the batch file's execution because DOS must read them. To speed up processing, move such comments to the end of your batch file so you don't incur their overhead when the batch file starts, or use GOTO to branch around the commands as shown here:

```
@ECHO OFF
GOTO START
REM ******************************************
REM **      S O M E F I L E . B A T         **
REM **                                      **
REM ** Written by: Kris Jamsa               **
REM ** Date Written: 8-23-92                **
REM ** Function: Performs some specific     **
REM **    task to make the PC easier.       **
REM **                                      **
REM ******************************************
:START
```

Resuming a Batch File's Execution at a Specific Time

Tip 658 describes you the utility command SETTIME that assigns the current hours and minutes to an environment entry named TIME. Using SETTIME, the following batch commands illustrate how you can suspend a batch file's execution until a specific time:

```
@ECHO OFF
SET START_TIME=12:30
:LOOP
SETTIME
IF NOT %TIME%==%START_TIME% GOTO LOOP
REM Other commands here
```

The batch file begins by using SET to create a second named parameter, %START_TIME%. The commands then use the utility program SETTIME to assign the current hours and minutes to the environment entry TIME. The batch file loops, assigning the current time to the named parameter TIME. When the named parameters TIME and START_TIME are equal, the batch file continues execution.

Testing for an Existing File

Several of the batch files presented in tips in this book allow the user to specify files they want the batch file to manipulate. For example, the following batch file, TYPE_3.BAT, lets the user specify in the command line up to three files whose contents the user wants to display:

```
@ECHO OFF
IF NOT '%1'=='' TYPE %1
IF NOT '%2'=='' TYPE %2
```

```
IF NOT '%3'=='' TYPE %3
```

In this case, if the user specifies the name of a file that does not exist, the batch file still attempts to display the file's contents, resulting in the following error message:

```
File not found
```

A better batch file would use the IF EXIST command, which causes DOS to check your disk to verify that the specified file exists before attempting to display the file's contents. If the file exists, DOS executes the specified command. Otherwise, DOS proceeds with the next batch file command. If you precede the word EXIST with the NOT operator, you can direct DOS to execute the command if the given file does not exist. The format of the IF EXIST command is as follows:

IF NOT EXIST Filename.Ext SomeCommand

The following batch file commands illustrate how you would change TYPE_3.BAT to use IF EXIST:

```
@ECHO OFF
IF NOT '%1'=='' IF EXIST %1 TYPE %1
IF NOT '%2'=='' IF EXIST %2 TYPE %2
IF NOT '%3'=='' IF EXIST %3 TYPE %3
```

Hiding a Batch File's Processing

Many users create small working batch files for other users, only to have the user make changes that cause the batch file to fail. If the batch file is fairly small, you can use the following technique to make it much more difficult for users to modify the file. Assume, for example, you have created the four line batch file LISTDIR.BAT as shown here:

```
@ECHO OFF
DIR > PRN
FFLPT1
DEL LISTDIR.BAT
```

Use DEBUG as follows to note the file's ASCII representation.

```
C:\> DEBUG LISTDIR.BAT <Enter>
-D 100
28F0:0100  40 45 43 48 4F 20 4F 46-46 0D 0A 44 49 52 20 3E   @ECHO OFF..DIR >
28F0:0110  20 50 52 4E 0D 0A 46 46-4C 50 54 31 20 3E 20 50    PRN..FFLPT1 > P
28F0:0120  52 4E 0D 0A 44 45 4C 20-4C 49 53 54 44 49 52 2E   RN..DEL LISTDIR.
28F0:0130  42 41 54 0D 0A 1A 1A 1A-1A 1A 1A 1A 1A 1A 1A 1A   BAT.............
28F0:0140  1A 1A 1A 1A 1A 1A 1A 1A-1A 1A 1A 1A 1A 1A 1A 1A   ................
28F0:0150  1A 1A 1A 1A 1A 1A 1A 1A-1A 1A 1A 1A 1A 1A 1A 1A   ................
28F0:0160  1A 1A 1A 1A 1A 1A 1A 1A-1A 1A 1A 1A 1A 1A 1A 1A   ................
28F0:0170  1A 1A 1A 1A 1A 1A 1A 1A-1A 1A 1A 1A 1A 1A 1A 1A   ................
-Q
```

Use SHIFT-PRTSC to print a copy of the DEBUG screen. Next, count the number of bytes the batch file uses up to the last carriage return and linefeed (0D 0A) which in this case is 35 (hexadecimal). Exit DEBUG. Using your printout, create the DEBUG script file, LISTDIR.SCR similar to the following:

```
N LISTDIR.BAT            <ENTER>
E 100 40 45 43 48 4F 20 4F 46 46 0D 0A 44 49 52 20 3E <ENTER>
E 110 20 50 52 4E 0D 0A 46 46 4C 50 54 31 20 3E 20 50 <ENTER>
E 120 52 4E 0D 0A 44 45 4C 20 4C 49 53 54 44 49 52 2E <ENTER>
E 130 42 41 54 0D 0A     <ENTER>
R CX                     <ENTER>
35                       <ENTER>
W                        <ENTER>
Q                        <ENTER>
```

LISTDIR.SCR

Next, the batch file you create for the user becomes the following:

```
@ECHO OFF
DEBUG < LISTDIR.SCR
LISTDIR
```

Because the batch file LISTDIR.BAT exists only briefly, the user probably won't figure out how to view, let alone change, the file.

Cleaning Up Before Turning Off

If you are using a RAM drive to store files, you need to copy the files to a hard or floppy disk before you turn off your computer, or the files will be lost. If you are using SMARTDRV's write-behind cache capabilities, you may want to invoke the command SMARTDRV /C before turning off your computer to flush the buffers to disk. The following batch file, TURN_OFF.BAT, contains commands to copy the RAM drive contents from drive D to the directory RAMDRIVE to flush the SMARTDRV buffer and to delete files in the directory TEMP:

```
@ECHO OFF
COPY D:\*.* C:\RAMDRIVE
ECHO Y | DEL C:\TEMP
SMARTDRV /C
```

By creating a batch file similar to TURN_OFF.BAT, you can place in the batch file those command's you want to run each time you turn off your system.

An Environment Parse Utility

As the complexity of your batch files increases, you sometimes may need to extract specific characters from an environment entry or a command-line entry. For example, assume the named parameter %TODAY% contains "Tuesday January 12, 1993," and you want to use only the month, day, and year. The companion disk that accompanies this book contains the utility command MID$.EXE that lets you extract specific characters from a command, assigning them to an environment entry named MID$. The format of the MID$ command is as follows:

MID$ String FirstCharacter Count

The *FirstCharacter* parameter specifies the index value (character position) of the first character to extract. The *Count* parameter specifies the number of characters you want to extract. To extract the characters "January 12, 1993" from the named parameter %TODAY%, you would invoke MID$ as follows:

```
MID$ %TODAY% 9 16
```

If successful, MID$ will assign the result to the environment entry MID$ and will return an exit status value of 0. If the environment is full, MID$ will return the exit status value 1.

The utility command MID$.EXE resides on the companion disk that accompanies this book.

MID$.EXE

Controlling a File Copy Operation

As discussed in Tip 450, by combining the ATTRIB and XCOPY commands, you can copy an entire directory of files to floppy disk. Unfortunately, to do so you must change each file's attributes. As an alternative, you can use the following batch file, DIR_COPY.BAT, that uses the utility command NEXTFILE.EXE presented in Tip 593:

```
@ECHO OFF
SET CURRENT_FILE=
:LOOP
NEXTFILE
IF '%CURRENT_FILE%'=='' GOTO DONE
:TRY_AGAIN
XCOPY '%CURRENT_FILE%' A:
IF ERRORLEVEL 1 GOTO DISK_FULL
GOTO LOOP

:DISK_FULL
ECHO Place a new floppy disk in drive A
PAUSE
```

```
GOTO TRY_AGAIN

:DONE
```

The batch file copies files one at a time from the current directory to drive A. If the floppy disk in drive A fills, the batch file prompts you to insert another disk. Because the CURRENT_FILE entry contains the file to copy, the batch file can easily continue the operation.

TIP 686 Is Task Switching Active?

Tip 738 discusses DOS 5 task swapping. You sometimes may not want a particular program to run. For example, many disk utilities that modify the file allocation table should not be run while other tasks are active unless they are knowledgeable of, and can prevent, task switching. The following DEBUG script file, TASKCHK.SCR, creates a command file named TASKCHK.COM that returns the exit status value 1 if task switching is active and returns 0 otherwise:

TASKCHK.SCR

```
N TASKCHK.COM <ENTER>
A 100         <ENTER>
MOV AX,4B02   <ENTER>
MOV BX,0      <ENTER>
MOV ES,BX     <ENTER>
MOV DI,0      <ENTER>
INT 2F        <ENTER>
MOV AL,1      <ENTER>
CMP AH,0      <ENTER>
JE 116        <ENTER>
MOV AL,0      <ENTER>
MOV AH,4C     <ENTER>
INT 21        <ENTER>
              <ENTER>
R CX          <ENTER>
1A            <ENTER>
W             <ENTER>
Q             <ENTER>
```

Use DEBUG as follows to create the command file TASKCHK.COM:

```
C:\> DEBUG < TASKCHK.SCR <ENTER>
```

The following batch commands use TASKCHK to determine whether task switching is active and, if it is, to prevent a command from running:

```
@ECHO OFF
TASKCHK
IF ERRORLEVEL 1 GOTO ACTIVE
SomeProg
GOTO DONE
ACTIVE
ECHO Cannot run while task switching is active.
:DONE
```

Getting a Response from the User

Often you will want your batch files to obtain a response from the user, such as the user's name or desired file. The companion disk that accompanies this book provides the utility command ASK_USER.EXE that prompts the user for specific information, assigning the result to the environment entry USER. The following batch file prompts the user for a desired filename and, if the file exists, displays it by using the TYPE command:

```
@ECHO OFF
ASK_USER What file do you want to see?
IF NOT '%USER%'=='' IF EXIST %USER% TYPE %USER%
IF NOT '%USER%'=='' IF NOT EXIST %USER% ECHO No such file
```

If ASK_USER successfully places the entry in the environment, it returns the exit status 0. If the environment is full, ASK_USER returns the exit status 1.

The utility command ASK_USER.EXE resides on the companion disk that accompanies this book.

ASK_USER.EXE

Determining the Length of a String of Characters

As your batch files become more complex, there may be times when you need the batch file to determine the length of a string. For example, if your batch file prompts the user for a filename using the ASK_USER utility presented in Tip 687, you may want to insure the filename does not exceed 12 characters (8.3). As such, the companion disk that accompanies this book provides the utility command LENGTH.EXE that returns the length of the first command line argument as an exit status. The command skips leading and trailing white space characters, returning the length of the first command line parameter. For example, the following batch command returns the length of the word Hello:

```
LENGTH Hello
```

Because LENGTH only examines the first parameter, the following command also returns the length of the word Hello:

```
LENGTH Hello World!
```

LENGTH.SCR

The utility command LENGTH.EXE resides on the companion disk that accompanies this book.

Storing the DOS Version as an Environment Entry

If you create batch files for other users, you sometimes may need to determine the current DOS version before you execute a specific command. To help your batch files determine the current version number,

the companion disk that accompanies this book contains the utility command DOSVER.EXE that stores the major and minor DOS version numbers in the environment entry DOS_VERSION. The following batch commands illustrate how you might use DOSVER:

```
@ECHO OFF
DOSVER
IF %DOS_VERSION%==5.0 GOTO DOS_5
IF %DOS_VERSION%==4.1 GOTO DOS_41
REM Remainder of commands
```

If DOSVER successfully adds the environment entry, DOSVER returns the exit status 0. If the environment is full, DOSVER returns the exit status 1.

The utility command DOSVER.EXE resides on the companion disk that accompanies this book.

DOSVER.EXE

Saving and Restoring Specific Information

As your batch files become more complex, you sometimes may need to save and later restore specific information. The companion disk that accompanies this book provides the utility commands PUSHINFO.EXE and POPINFO.EXE that let your batch files save and later restore specific information. In this case, POPINFO places the information in the environment entry POP_INFO. The following batch file illustrates how you use these utilities:

```
@ECHO OFF
REM Save some specific information
PUSHINFO A:\PUBLIC\DATA
REM Other batch commands
REM Restore the information
POPINFO
```

Each time you execute the PUSHINFO command, PUSHINFO searches the root directory on drive C for a file named SAVEINFO.DAT. If the file exists, PUSHINFO appends the information to the file. If the file does not exist, PUSHINFO creates it. When you later execute the POPINFO command, POPINFO also searches for the same file, selecting and removing the last entry the file contains. Each time you execute a PUSHINFO command, you should later execute a corresponding POPINFO command. Depending on you batch file's processing, you may execute several PUSHINFO commands followed later by several POPINFO commands.

PUSHINFO.EXE
POPINFO.EXE

The utility commands PUSHINFO.EXE and POPINFO.EXE reside on the companion disk that accompanies this book.

What Files Have I Changed Today?

As you work throughout the day, you may create or change many files. If you are using DOS 5, you can use the following batch file, CHGTODAY.BAT, to list those files you have created or changed today:

```
@ECHO OFF
SETDATE
DIR C:\*.* /A:A /S | FIND "%DATE%
SET DATE=
```

The batch file uses the utility command SETDATE.EXE presented in Tip 659.

To use DIR's /A and /S switches, you must be using DOS 5.

Testing Whether a Directory Exists

Tip 681 explains how to test whether a file exists by using the IF EXIST command. DOS lets your batch files test whether a directory exists. If you know a few secrets, you can also use the IF EXIST command to test for a directory's existence. To use IF EXIST to test whether a directory exists, place the name of a DOS device immediately after the directory name, as if the device were a file within the directory. For example, the following batch commands use the NUL device to test whether the directories DOS and NOPE exist:

```
@ECHO OFF
IF EXIST C:\DOS\NUL ECHO DOS directory exists
IF EXIST C:\NOPE\NUL ECHO NOPE directory exists.
```

Placing Your Batch Files in the Command Path

As the number of batch files you use regularly increases, you will want to place the batch files in a directory whose name is in your command path, to make the batch files easier to execute. In most cases, you will want to create a directory named BATCH, within which you place your batch files. Next, edit your AUTOEXEC.BAT file, adding the BATCH directory to your command path, similar to the following:

```
PATH  C:\DOS;C:\WINDOWS;C:\BATCH
```

This book presents many batch files and commands you can create using DEBUG. By placing these commands in the BATCH directory, and by including the directory name in your command path, you make the commands very easy to use.

Building on a Named Parameter

When you execute commands from within a DOS batch file, you can pass information to the commands using the batch paramters %1 through %1 as shown here:

```
@ECHO OFF SomeCommand %1 %2 %3 %4 %5 %6 %7 %8 %9
```

Although the batch parameters allow your batch files to pass information to the commands, you are still restricted to nine arguments. If you are using DOS 3.3 or higher, a better solution is build a named paramter that contains the entire command line. The following batch commands, for example, loop though all of the batch file's parameters, assigning them to the the named parameter ARGUMENT:

```
@ECHO OFF
SET ARGUMENT= SHIFT
:LOOP
IF '%0'=='' GOTO DONE
SET ARGUMENT=%ARGUMENT% %0
GOTO LOOP
:DONE
ECHO The command line arguments were: %ARGUMENT%
```

A Timed Prompt with a Default Character Response

As the complexity of your batch files increases, you sometimes will want to prompt the user for a response for which you know the most likely response. The companion disk that accompanies this

book provides the utility command ASK_CHAR.EXE that prompts the user for a character response and provides a default choice. If the user fails to respond within 30 seconds, the command returns the default choice. For example, the following batch file uses ASK_CHAR to prompt the user for a Y or N response; if the user fails to respond within 30 seconds, the batch file uses the default Y response:

```
@ECHO OFF
ECHO Print directory list (Y/N)?
:LOOP
ASK_CHAR Y
IF ERRORLEVEL 89 GOTO YES
REM Check for lowercase y
IF ERRORLEVEL 121 GOTO YES
IF ERRORLEVEL 78 GOTO NO
REM Check for lowercase n
IF ERRORLEVEL 110 GOTO NO
GOTO LOOP
:YES
DIR > PRN
:NO
```

ASK_CHAR returns an exit status value matching the ASCII value that corresponds to the key pressed. Thus, you need to test for uppercase and lowercase letters.

The utility command ASK_CHAR.EXE resides on the companion disk that accompanies this book.

ASK_CHAR.EXE

A Timed Prompt with a Default Scancode Response

Tip 695 uses the companion disk utility command ASK_CHAR.EXE to prompt the user for a character response, returning the exit status for a default character response if the user fails to respond

within 30 seconds. Similarly, the utility command ASK_SCAN.EXE lets your batch files prompt the user for a scancode, returning an exit status that matches the default scancode if the user fails to respond within 30 seconds. The advantage of using ASK_SCAN over ASK_CHAR is that you don't have to test for uppercase and lowercase letters. The disadvantage is that you must know the corresponding scancodes. The following batch commands prompt the user for a Y or N response, returning the exit status code for N if the user fails to respond within 30 seconds:

```
@ECHO OFF
ECHO Print directory list (Y/N)?
:LOOP
ASK_SCAN 49
IF ERRORLEVEL 21 GOTO YES
IF ERRORLEVEL 49 GOTO NO
GOTO LOOP
:YES
DIR > PRN
:NO
```

ASK_SCAN.EXE

The utility command ASK_SCAN.EXE resides on the companion disk that accompanies this book.

Creating a Named Parameter with TRUENAME

Tip 609 presents the DOS 5 TRUENAME command that returns the complete path name for a file residing in the current directory. The following batch file, TNAME.BAT, uses TRUENAME to create the named parameter %TRUENAME%:

```
@ECHO OFF
NEW_ECHO SET TRUENAME=> 1
TRUENAME %1 | FIND ":" > 2
COPY 1+2 3.BAT
```

```
CALL 3.BAT
DEL 1
DEL 2
DEL 3.BAT
```

The batch file uses the NEW_ECHO utility presented in Tip 651 to create a temporary single-line file containing only the text "SET TRUENAME=". Next, the batch file uses TRUENAME to determine the "true name" of the desired file, redirecting the output to a second temporary file. Using the COPY command, the batch file creates a third temporary file, 3.BAT, that contains a single SET command. Using the CALL command, the batch file executes the SET command and then later deletes the temporary files. In this case, to display the path name for the file Filename.Ext, you would invoke the batch file as shown here:

```
C:\> TNAME Filename.Ext <ENTER>
```

To use the TRUENAME command, you must be using DOS 5.

Adding an Automatic Modem Hangup Command

Tip 112 explains how to create the batch file AUTODIAL.BAT that lets you automatically make phone calls with your PC. After you place the phone call, you have to hang up your phone manually. By adding the Hayes modem command ATH to the batch file, you can let the batch file automatically hang up. The following batch commands illustrate how you would place a call, letting the batch file hang up the phone when the call is complete:

```
@ECHO OFF
MODE COM1 1200 > NUL
IF '%1'=='ALLEN' ECHO ATDT555-1212 > COM1
PAUSE Press any key to hang up
ECHO ATH > COM1
```

A Timed Environment Response

Tip 687 presents the utility command ASK_USER.EXE that prompts the user for a response and then assigns the response to the USER environment entry. The companion disk utility command ASK_ENV.EXE lets your batch files prompt for a response. However, if the user does not respond to the prompt within 30 seconds, the command assigns the default value. The following batch commands illustrate how you can use ASK_ENV to prompt the user for a specific batch file you want to run at system startup:

```
@ECHO OFF
ASK_ENV MYAUTO.BAT
CALL %USER%
SET USER=
```

The batch file assigns its result to the environment entry USER. If the batch file successfully adds the environment entry, it returns the exit status value 0. If the environment is full, it returns 1.

ASK_ENV.EXE

The utility command ASK_ENV.EXE resides on the companion disk that accompanies this book.

Saving and Restoring the Environment

When a batch file makes changes or additions to environment entries, the batch file should clean up after itself, restoring the environment to its original contents before ending. The following batch commands illustrate how your batch files can do just that:

```
@ECHO
REM Save the environment to SAVE.ENV
SET > SAVE.ENV
REM Other batch commands
REM Restore the environment
FILECMD SAVE.ENV SET
```

When the batch file begins, it redirects the current environment settings to the file SAVE.ENV. Later, the batch file uses the command FILECMD, presented in Tip 104, to restore the environment entries.

Using Colons to Comment Your Batch Files

Tip 628 describes how to document your batch files by using the REM command. Recently, many computer magazines have presented tips that use colons, rather than REM, to comment batch files. For example, the following batch file uses colons to start each comment:

```
@ECHO OFF
: Name: SAMPLE.BAT
: Written by: K. Jamsa
: Date written: 9-01-92
: Purpose: Illustrates the use of colons for comments
```

When DOS encounters the colon at the start of a line in a batch file, DOS considers the line to be a label and ignores it. Thus, you can successfully document your batch files by using either colons or REM. The problem with using colons is you may create a conflict between one of your comments and an actual label in the batch file that you reference with GOTO. To avoid such conflicts, you should normally use REM.

Where Did Your Day Go?

Many users create batch files that display menu options for their commonly used applications. By taking advantage of the SETDATE (Tip 659) and SETTIME (Tip 658) commands, you can change the batch file slightly to log the date and time you started and ended each program. At the end of the day, you can print the log file to find out where you are spending your time. Within the batch file, you probably have labels corresponding to each application. The following batch commands illustrate how you can time a command's use:

```
@ECHO OFF
:LOOP
ECHO            F1    DIR Command
ECHO            F2    FORMAT Command
ECHO            F3    DISKCOPY Command
ECHO            F4    Quit
:GET_KEY
F1TOF10
IF ERRORLEVEL 1 IF NOT ERRORLEVEL 2 GOTO F1
IF ERRORLEVEL 2 IF NOT ERRORLEVEL 3 GOTO F2
IF ERRORLEVEL 3 IF NOT ERRORLEVEL 4 GOTO F3
IF ERRORLEVEL 4 IF NOT ERRORLEVEL 5 GOTO F4
GOTO GET_KEY
:F1
SETDATE
SETTIME
ECHO DIR at %DATE% %TIME% >> C:\EVENT.LOG
DIR
PAUSE
GOTO LOOP
:F2
SETDATE
SETTIME
ECHO FORMAT at %DATE% %TIME% >> C:\EVENT.LOG
FORMAT A:
GOTO LOOP
:F3
SETDATE
SETTIME
ECHO DISKCOPY at %DATE% %TIME% >> C:\EVENT.LOG
```

```
DISKCOPY A: B:
GOTO LOOP
:F4
```

In this case, the batch file records its entries in the root directory file EVENT.LOG. You should use an appropriate filename and directory. At the end of each day or week, you can print and delete the current log file. By tracking your program use in this way, you can better understand how your day is spent.

Testing a Parameter's First Letter with FOR

Tip 647 presents the FOR command that lets you repeat a specific command for a set of files. If you precede a filename listed in the set of files with a forward slash, FOR will treat the filename as two parameters: one containing the first letter of the filename and one containing the letters that follow. For example, the following FOR command will echo the entries "F" and "ilename.Ext":

```
@ECHO OFF
FOR %%I IN (/Filename.Ext) DO ECHO %%I
```

Unfortunately, if the number of character combinations is large, you may have to use several FOR commands. The following batch commands use FOR to test only the parameter's first letter:

```
@ECHO OFF
FOR %%I IN (/%1) DO IF %%I==B GOTO BLUE
FOR %%I IN (/%1) DO IF %%I==b GOTO BLUE
REM Remainder of commands here
```

In this case, the first FOR command tests for an uppercase B, and the second command tests for a lowercase b.

Using a Disk's Serial Number

Tip 421 discusses disk serial numbers, which are used beginning with DOS version 4. If your batch files work with floppy disks, you sometimes may need to verify that a specific floppy disk is still in the drive. One way to do so is to use the disk's serial number. The companion disk that accompanies this book provides the utility command ENVSER#.EXE that assigns the serial number of the current disk to the environment entry SERIAL#. The following batch commands illustrate how you can use ENVSER# to save and later test a disk's serial number:

```
@ECHO OFF
A:
ENVSER#
SET SAVE#=%SERIAL#%
REM other commands
ENVSER#
IF NOT %SAVE#%==%SERIAL#% GOTO DIFFERENT_DISK
REM Remainder of commands here
```

If ENVSER# successfully adds the environment entry, it returns the exit status 0. If the environment is full, it returns the status 1.

To use disk serial numbers, you must be using DOS 4 or higher.

ENVSER#.EXE

The utility command ENVSER#.EXE resides on the companion disk that accompanies this book.

A Combined File or Directory Rename Operation

You can use the RENAME command to change the name of a DOS file. Tip 443 describes how to use the DOS shell to rename a directory. The following batch file, RENBOTH.BAT, lets you rename a file or directory:

```
@ECHO OFF
IF '%1'=='' GOTO NO_PARAMS
IF '%2'=='' GOTO NO_PARAMS
IF NOT EXIST %1 IF NOT EXIST %1\NUL GOTO NO_FILE
IF EXIST %2 GOTO FILE_EXISTS
IF EXIST %2\NUL GOTO FILE_EXISTS

ECHO ON ERROR GOTO FAILED > RENBOTH.BAS
ECHO NAME "%1" AS "%2" >> RENBOTH.BAS
ECHO SYSTEM >> RENBOTH.BAS
ECHO FAILED: >> RENBOTH.BAS
ECHO PRINT "Rename operation failed" >> RENBOTH.BAS
ECHO SYSTEM >> RENBOTH.BAS

QBASIC /RUN RENBOTH.BAS
DEL RENBOTH.BAS
GOTO DONE

:NO_PARAMS
ECHO Must specify source and target
GOTO DONE

:NO_FILE
ECHO No file or directory named %1
GOTO DONE

:FILE_EXISTS
ECHO %2 already exists
```

```
:DONE
```

As you can see, the batch file builds a BASIC program that uses BASIC's NAME statement to rename the directory. This batch file was created to use QBASIC, which comes with DOS 5. If you are using a different DOS version, change the batch file to use GWBASIC or BASICA.

Comparing One Number to Another

Using the IF command, you can test whether the characters in one string are identical to those in another. When you are working with numbers, however, you sometimes may need to determine whether one value is less than or greater than another. For example, Tip 958 presents the utility command DOSVER that assigns the DOS version to an environment entry named DOS_VERSION. In most cases, your batch files will use the entry to determine whether the current version number is greater than or equal to a specific version. The companion disk that accompanies this book provides the utility command NBRCOMP.EXE that lets your batch files compare two numbers. If the numbers are equal, NBRCOMP returns the value 0. If the first number is larger, NBRCOMP returns the exit status value 1. If the second number is larger, NBRCOMP returns the exit status value 2.

The following batch commands illustrate how you can use NBRCOMP to determine whether the current DOS version is DOS 4 or higher:

```
@ECHO OFF
DOSVER
NBRCOMP %DOS_VERSION% 4
IF ERRORLEVEL 0 IF NOT ERRORLEVEL 1 ECHO DOS 4
IF ERRORLEVEL 1 IF NOT ERRORLEVEL 2 ECHO Later than DOS 4
```

NBRCOMP.EXE

The utility command NBRCOMP.EXE resides on the companion disk that accompanies this book.

Hiding Batch Command Display with ANSI.SYS

Tip 622 discusses how to redirect a command's output in your batch files to the NUL device to discard the output. Tip 638 discusses how to use the CTTY command to discard all batch output. However, there are times when you cannot use CTTY NUL. As an alternative, if you have installed the ANSI.SYS driver, you can disable the display of batch output by using the driver to select a black foreground on a black background. The following batch file uses the escape sequence Esc[8m to select concealed text, and then later, after command execution is complete, the file uses the escape sequence Esc[0m to restore normal text attributes:

```
@ECHO OFF
ECHO Esc[8m
REM Other commands
ECHO Esc[0m
```

The batch file uses the letters Esc to represent the unprintable ASCII escape character. In your batch file, you must use the actual ASCII character as discussed in Tip 34.

Handling Case-Sensitive Batch Parameters

Several of the tips presented in this book discuss ways to test case-sensitive parameters in your batch files. One way to do so is by using the DOS environment. When you create an environment entry, DOS converts the entry's name to uppercase letters. For example, if you issue the following SET command, DOS will create an uppercase environment entry named FILE:

```
C:\> set file=filename.ext <ENTER>
```

The following batch file tests for the specification of one of the colors red, green, or blue. To accomplish this, the batch file creates an environment entry that uses the name specified by the first batch parameter, %1:

```
@ECHO OFF
IF '%1'=='' GOTO NO_PARAMETER
SET %1=%1
IF NOT '%BLUE%'=='' GOTO BLUE
IF NOT '%RED%'=='' GOTO RED
IF NOT '%GREEN%'=='' GOTO GREEN
GOTO BAD_PARAMETER
REM Other commands here
SET %1=
```

To better understand how the batch file works, experiment with the following batch file, SETTEST.BAT:

```
@ECHO OFF
IF NOT '%1'=='' SET %1=%1
SET
```

Invoke SETTEST.BAT with different parameters and note the environment entries it creates.

A Musical Pause Command

Tip 192 described how to produce music with your PC by using BASIC's SOUND statement. The following batch file, MPAUSE.BAT, builds, on the fly, a BASIC program that displays the command-line message you specify and then plays a tune until the user presses a key:

```
@ECHO OFF
ECHO DATA 262,1,294,2,330,2,350,2,392,2,440,2,494,1>MPAUSE.BAS
ECHO DATA 494,1,440,2,392,2,350,2,330,2,294,2,262,1>>MPAUSE.BAS

ECHO DO  >> MPAUSE.BAS
ECHO FOR I = 1 TO 14   >> MPAUSE.BAS
```

```
ECHO      READ FREQ, DURATION  >> MPAUSE.BAS
ECHO      SOUND FREQ, DURATION >> MPAUSE.BAS
ECHO NEXT I  >> MPAUSE.BAS
ECHO RESTORE >> MPAUSE.BAS
ECHO LOOP UNTIL NOT INKEY$ = ""  >> MPAUSE.BAS
ECHO SYSTEM  >> MPAUSE.BAS

ECHO %1 %2 %3 %4 %5 %6 %7 %8 %9
QBASIC /RUN MPAUSE

DEL MPAUSE.BAS
```

If you want to use a musical pause in one of your batch files, invoke MPAUSE with the CALL command. The following batch commands, for example, use MPAUSE to play a tune until the user presses a key to print a directory listing:

```
@ECHO OFF
CALL MPAUSE Turn your printer on-line
DIR > PRN
```

By editing the DATA statement used in the BASIC program MPAUSE.BAS, you can make MPAUSE play back any tune you desire.

Debugging Your Batch Files

When you create complex batch files, sometimes a batch file simply won't work. When this occurs, you have to find out what's wrong. The process of locating and correcting errors in your batch files is called debugging. To debug your batch files, follow these steps:

- Place a REM command in front of ECHO OFF (producing REM ECHO OFF). As the batch file executes, watch the commands displayed on the screen to ensure that the commands are executing as you expect.
- If the batch file is long, use the utility command presented in Tip 901 to echo output to the printer so you can examine the printout to verify that the correct commands are executing.

- ❑ Double-check your IF ERRORLEVEL commands. Remember that DOS will execute the corresponding command if the previous command's exit status is greater than or equal to the value specified.
- ❑ If necessary, throughout the batch file place ECHO commands that display messages informing you of the batch file's processing.
- ❑ Add REM statements to the batch file that explain the batch file's processing in detail. You'll be surprised how often you'll find the batch file's error by reading the REM statement as you view each step.

Turning DEBUG ECHO Statements On and Off

Tip 710 discusses steps you should follow when you debug your batch files. The following batch commands illustrate how you might use the ECHO command to display messages describing the batch file's processing. The batch file debugs the ASKIT.BAT file presented in Tip 206.

```
@ECHO OFF
IF '%1'=='' GOTO DONE

REM Create the file ASKIT.BAT on the fly.
ECHO ECHO Run %%1 (Y/N)? > ASKIT.BAT
ECHO YESORNO >> ASKIT.BAT
ECHO IF ERRORLEVEL 1 %%1 >> ASKIT.BAT

REM View the file's contents to make sure it is correct.
TYPE ASKIT.BAT

REM Display the current path
PATH

REM View the files the batch file examines
FOR %%I IN (%PATH%) DO ECHO %%I\%1

FOR %%I IN (%PATH%) DO IF EXIST %%I\%1 CALL ASKIT %%I\%1
```

```
DEL ASKIT.BAT
:DONE
```

When users think they have a batch file working, they often immediately remove the ECHO commands. Unfortunately, more often than not, a second error appears, causing the users to wish they had left the ECHO commands in place. To avoid this problem, place debug ECHO statements in your batch file in the following form:

IF NOT '%DEBUG%'=='' ECHO Some Message

The command checks to see whether the named parameter DEBUG is defined and, if it is, echoes the message. The following batch commands modify the previous batch commands to use this format:

```
@ECHO OFF
IF '%1'=='' GOTO DONE

REM Create the file ASKIT.BAT on the fly.
ECHO ECHO Run %%1 (Y/N)? > ASKIT.BAT
ECHO YESORNO >> ASKIT.BAT
ECHO IF ERRORLEVEL 1 %%1 >> ASKIT.BAT

REM View the file's contents to make sure it is correct.
IF NOT '%DEBUG%'=='' TYPE ASKIT.BAT

REM Display the current path
IF NOT '%DEBUG%'=='' PATH

REM View the files the batch file examines
IF NOT '%DEBUG%'=='' FOR %%I IN (%PATH%) DO ECHO %%I\%1

FOR %%I IN (%PATH%) DO IF EXIST %%I\%1 CALL ASKIT %%I\%1

DEL ASKIT.BAT
:DONE
```

If you are debugging a batch file and you want the messages echoed, place the following SET command at the start of the batch file:

```
SET DEBUG=TRUE
```

The IF statements in the batch file will now evaluate as true, causing the ECHO statements to execute. If you are debugging the batch file, place the following command at the start of the batch file:

```
SET DEBUG=
```

When you are at last sure the batch file is correct, you can remove the IF commands. If your batch file modifies or relies on environment entries, you can use this same format, as follows, to display the environment:

```
IF NOT '%DEBUG%'=='' SET
```

Is Windows Active?

Windows, as many other programs do, lets you temporarily exit to the DOS prompt to issue commands. In most cases, you don't want to temporarily exit a program and then issue a memory-resident command, but because many people do use DOS this way, the companion disk that accompanies this book provides the utility command CKWINDOW.EXE that lets your batch files test whether Windows is currently active. If Windows is active, CKWINDOW returns the exit status value 1. If Windows is not active, CKWINDOW returns 0. The following batch commands use CKWINDOW to determine whether Windows is active:

```
@ECHO OFF
CKWINDOW
IF ERRORLEVEL 1 GOTO WINDOWS_ACTIVE
REM Other commands here
```

If you don't want certain commands to execute if Windows is active, invoke the commands only from a batch file that uses CKWINDOW as shown.

CKWINDOW.EXE

The utility command CKWINDOW.EXE resides on the companion disk that accompanies this book.

How DOS Determines Batch Parameters

When you execute a batch file, DOS assigns the first nine command-line parameters to %1 through %9. How does DOS select these parameters? Read on.

The most common way users distinguish between parameters is by separating the parameters with spaces or tabs:

```
C:\> TEST A B C <ENTER>
```

Batch files, however, let you separate parameters with other characters besides spaces. These characters include commas, semicolons, or equal signs. DOS processes the parameters even if you enclose them in quotation marks:

```
C:\> TEST "A;B;C" <ENTER>
```

To see how DOS assigns parameters, create the batch file TEST.BAT that contains the following instructions:

```
@ECHO OFF
ECHO Parameter 1 is %1
ECHO Parameter 2 is %2
ECHO Parameter 3 is %3
ECHO Parameter 4 is %4
ECHO Parameter 5 is %5
ECHO Parameter 6 is %6
ECHO Parameter 7 is %7
ECHO Parameter 8 is %8
ECHO Parameter 9 is %9
```

You can then use TEST.BAT to discover how DOS interprets your command line. TEST.BAT will display each parameter on its own line.

The DOS Major Version Number as an Exit Status

Tip 958 presents the utility command DOSVER.EXE that assigns the DOS version to the environment entry DOS_VERSION. In some cases, you may find it more convenient to word the version number as an exit status. The following DEBUG script file, DOSMAJOR.SCR, creates the command file DOSMAJOR.COM that returns the major DOS version as an exit status:

DOSMAJOR.SCR

```
N DOSMAJOR.COM <ENTER>
A 100          <ENTER>
MOV AX,3000    <ENTER>
INT 21         <ENTER>
MOV AH,4C      <ENTER>
INT 21         <ENTER>
               <ENTER>
R CX           <ENTER>
9              <ENTER>
W              <ENTER>
Q              <ENTER>
```

Use DEBUG as follows to create the command file DOSMAJOR.COM:

```
C:\> DEBUG < DOSMAJOR.SCR <ENTER>
```

The following batch commands use DOSMAJOR to verify that the user has DOS version 4 or higher:

```
@ECHO OFF
DOSMAJOR
IF NOT ERRORLEVEL 4 GOTO WRONG_VERSION
REM Other commands here
```

The DOS Minor Version Number as an Exit Status

Tip 714 creates the command file DOSMAJOR.COM that lets your batch files determine the current major DOS version number by using an exit status. In a similar way, the following DEBUG script file, DOSMINOR.SCR, creates the command file DOSMINOR.COM that returns the minor DOS version number (the revision number) as an exit status:

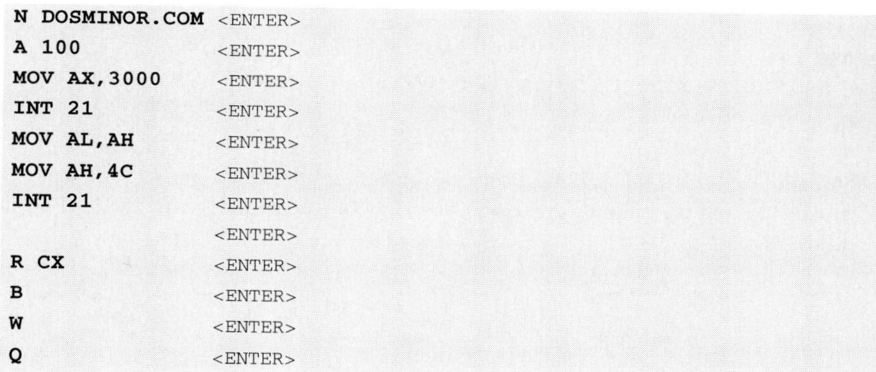

```
N DOSMINOR.COM <ENTER>
A 100          <ENTER>
MOV AX,3000    <ENTER>
INT 21         <ENTER>
MOV AL,AH      <ENTER>
MOV AH,4C      <ENTER>
INT 21         <ENTER>
               <ENTER>
R CX           <ENTER>
B              <ENTER>
W              <ENTER>
Q              <ENTER>
```

DOSMINOR.SCR

Use DEBUG as follows to create the command file DOSMINOR.COM:

```
C:\> DEBUG < DOSMINOR.COM <ENTER>
```

Depending on your DOS version and the original equipment manufacturer (OEM) from whom you got DOS, DOSMINOR may return the minor version number 3, for example, as either 3 or 30. Experiment with DOSMINOR on your system and create your batch commands accordingly.

Testing Whether a Batch Parameter Contains Wildcards

You sometimes may want a batch file to behave differently if the user specifies a wildcard combination as a parameter. Using the FOR command, your batch files can test whether a parameter contains wildcards as shown here:

```
@ECHO OFF
FOR %%I IN (%1) DO IF NOT %%I==%1 GOTO WILDCARD
REM Other commands here
```

The FOR command expands wildcard characters into matching filenames, one file at a time. If you use FOR to expand %1 and the value assigned to FOR's variable is not equal to %1, then %1 originally contained a wildcard.

A Windows Batch File

If you are using Windows, you may sometimes wish you could issue specific DOS commands immediately before Windows starts. If you are using Windows in 386 enhanced mode, you can. Each time you start Windows in 386 enhanced mode, Windows searches for the batch file WINSTART.BAT. If the batch file exists, Windows executes its contents; otherwise, Windows just starts. Add your desired commands to this batch file.

Be Aware of Redirection in Your IF Commands

As you use IF EXIST commands in your batch files, you need to be aware of how DOS treats redirected commands. For example, the following IF command tests whether the file FILENAME.EXT exists. If the file does not exist, DOS writes a directory to the file.

```
IF NOT EXIST FILENAME.EXT DIR > FILENAME.EXT
```

At first glance, the command seems simple enough. Unfortunately, the command does not behave as you would expect. When DOS first examines the command, DOS notes the redirection operator and opens the file FILENAME.EXT. As a result, the IF command will always evaluate to false because the file exists. Thus, an IF command that tests for a file created as a result of redirection in the current command will always evaluate to true.

How to Determine Whether a Batch File Has Already Run

Depending on the processing the batch file performs, you sometimes may want a file to execute only once per user session. To accomplish this, simply place an entry in the environment the first time the batch file runs. Your batch file can use the IF command to test for the entry's existence. If the entry exists, the batch file can assume it has already run. If the entry does not exist, the batch file can execute. The following batch commands use the entry HAS_RUN to control the batch file's execution:

```
@ECHO OFF
IF NOT '%HAS_RUN%'=='' GOTO ALREADY_RAN
SET HAS_RUN=YES
REM Other commands here
```

ECHO Versus TYPE

The following batch file uses the ECHO command to display several messages to the user:

```
@ECHO OFF
ECHO This is the company's payroll batch files. Before
ECHO you begin you must have the authorization password.
ECHO.
ECHO Next, you must have access to the printers in room
ECHO B-2 in order to print ledgers and checks.
ECHO.
ECHO When you finish updating the pay statements, you will
ECHO be asked to update the ledger. More instructions will
ECHO appear at that time.
REM Other batch commands here
```

To improve their batch file performance, many users recommend that you place such messages in an ASCII file whose contents is displayed by using the TYPE command as shown here:

```
@ECHO OFF
TYPE INSTRUCT.DAT
REM Other batch commands here
```

However, although the TYPE command may cause the batch file to execute slightly faster, it also results in a second file. As discussed in Tip 503, a goal is to reduce the number of such small files on your disk because of the disk space they consume. In most cases, therefore, use ECHO to display messages; the slight performance loss probably outweighs the amount of disk space consumed.

Have I Been Shelled?

Depending on your batch file's commands, there may be times when you don't want the batch file to execute if the user has temporarily exited the program to the DOS

prompt. The companion disk that accompanies this book contains the utility command CKSHELL.EXE that returns the exit status 1 if a program has shelled to a temporary DOS prompt and returns 0 if the user is at the original DOS prompt. The following batch commands use CKSHELL to determine whether the user is at a temporary DOS prompt:

```
@ECHO OFF
CKSHELL
IF ERRORLEVEL 1 ECHO Shelled prompt
IF NOT ERRORLEVEL 1 ECHO Original DOS prompt
```

The utility command CKSHELL.EXE resides on the companion disk that accompanies this book.

CKSHELL.EXE

Running a Batch File Once a Day

Depending on your batch file's processing, you sometimes may want a particular batch file to run only once a day, regardless of whether the user reboots the computer. One way to accomplish this is to use the PUSHDATE and POPDATE commands presented in Tip 726. For example, when the following batch file starts, it uses POPDATE to get the date stored in the file SAVEDATE.DAT. If the date matches today's date, the batch file has already been run and won't run again; otherwise, the batch file can execute. The batch file then uses PUSHDATE to place the date back in the file.

```
@ECHO OFF
REM Get date from file
POPDATE
IF '%POP_DATE%'=='' GOTO NOT_RUN_YET
REM Get today's date
SETDATE
IF NOT '%POP_DATE%'=='%DATE%' GOTO NOT_RUN_YET
GOTO ALREADY_RUN
:NOT_RUN_YET
```

```
SomeCMD
:ALREADY_RUN
PUSHDATE
```

If you use PUSHDATE and POPDATE in this way, the file SAVEDATE.DAT will always exist on your disk. The file is needed to prevent the batch file's second execution.

Testing for a Windows 386 DOS Window

Just as there are times when you don't want a batch file to execute specific commands if Windows has temporarily shelled to a DOS prompt, there may be times when you don't want commands to execute from within a Window 386 DOS window. The companion disk that accompanies this book provides the utility command INWINDOW.EXE that returns the exit status 1 if you are running in a Windows DOS window and returns 0 otherwise. The following batch commands use INWINDOW to determine whether the batch file is running from the DOS prompt or from within the Windows DOS window:

```
@ECHO OFF
INWINDOW
IF ERRORLEVEL 1 ECHO In DOS Window
IF NOT ERRORLEVEL 1 ECHO Not in Window
```

INWINDOW.EXE

The utility command INWINDOW.EXE resides on the companion disk that accompanies this book.

Be Aware of Redirection with FOR

As discussed in Tip 718, DOS does not treat I/O redirection in IF EXIST commands as you might guess. The same is true of the FOR command. Consider the following FOR command, which tries to use MORE to display the contents of three files:

```
@ECHO
FOR %%I IN (A.DAT B.DAT C.DAT) DO MORE < %%I
```

At first glance, you would expect FOR to display each file's contents one at a time. When you execute this command, however, the command fails, and DOS displays this message:

```
File not found
```

The reason the command fails is because when DOS first examines the command, DOS evaluates the redirected input first. DOS first converts the name %%I to %I and searches your disk for a matching file. Because no such file exists, the command fails, and DOS displays the error message stating that a file was not found.

Handling I/O Redirection Problems with FOR and IF EXIST

As discussed in Tip 718, because DOS evaluates I/O redirection first, the following IF EXIST command will always evaluate to true:

```
IF EXIST FILENAME.EXT DIR >> FILENAME.EXT
```

As discussed in Tip 724, again because DOS evaluates I/O redirection first, the following FOR command will always fail:

```
FOR %%I IN (A.DAT B.DAT C.DAT) DO MORE < %%I
```

The easiest way to solve redirection problems is to create a batch file that executes the desired command and that you can invoke with CALL. The following batch file, FOR_OK.BAT, solves the previous error by on the fly creating a batch file named IOFOR.BAT that executes the following command:

```
MORE < %1
```

Before the batch file completes, the batch file deletes IOFOR.BAT, as shown here:

```
@ECHO OFF
ECHO MORE %%I IN (A.DAT B.DAT C.DAT) DO CALL IOFOR %%I
DEL IOFOR.BAT
```

Saving the Current Date

As they execute, many batch files need to access the current date. The companion disk that accompanies this book contains two utility programs, PUSHDATE.EXE and POPDATE.EXE, that save and later restore the current date. The utility command PUSHDATE.EXE records the current date in a file that is later read by POPDATE. POPDATE, in turn, assigns the date to the environment entry POP_DATE. The following batch file illustrates the use of these utilities:

```
@ECHO OFF
REM Save current date
PUSHDATE
REM Change the date to 12-25-93 and issue a command
DATE 12-25-93
SOMEPROG
REM Restore the original date
POPDATE
DATE %POP_DATE%
SET POP_DATE=
```

Each time you execute the PUSHDATE command, PUSHDATE searches the root directory on drive C for a file named SAVEDATE.DAT. If the file exists, PUSHDATE appends the current date to the file. If the file does not exist, PUSHDATE creates it. When you later execute the POPDATE command, POPDATE also searches for the same file, selecting and removing the last date the file contains and assigning the date to the environment entry POP_DATE. Each time you execute a PUSHDATE command, you should later execute a corresponding POPDATE command. Depending on your batch file's processing, you may execute several PUSHDATE commands followed later by several POPDATE commands.

The utility commands PUSHDATE.EXE and POPDATE.EXE reside on the companion disk that accompanies this book.

PUSHDATE.EXE
POPDATE.EXE

PART 8

Tip 727 Improving the DOS 5 Shell's Performance

If you are using the DOS 5 shell, one of the most frustrating events occurs when you change disk drives and the shell reads the disk's directory structure. Depending on the number of files and directories on your disk, reading the directory structure can be time consuming. If you have two disks whose contents you use regularly, you can eliminate the directory read operations by joining the two disks together with the JOIN command. To join two disks, you must create an unused directory on one of the two disks.

Assume, for example, that you use drives C and A regularly. You can create a directory named JOIN_A on drive C and then use the JOIN command to JOIN the disks, as shown here:

```
C:\> MKDIR \JOIN_A <ENTER>
C:\> JOIN A: C:\JOIN_A <ENTER>
```

When you later invoke the DOS shell, you can select the directory JOIN_A to access the files stored on the disk in drive A. Because you don't actually change drives, the shell won't perform the time-consuming directory read operations. When you are done using the shell, you can remove the JOIN as follows:

```
C:\> JOIN A: /D <ENTER>
```

Tip 728 Disabling the Shell's Automatic File Selection

By default, when you use the DOS shell, the shell automatically selects the first file in the directory list. If you use the arrow keys to scroll through the file list, the shell automatically selects the file you

highlight. If you leave a file highlighted and then accidently press a key such as DEL, the shell will delete the file. To prevent this problem, you can disable the shell's automatic selection of a file by editing the file DOSSHELL.INI and locating the line containing the explicitselection entry. Change the entry's setting from disabled to enabled. Exit the editor and restart the shell. The shell will no longer automatically select a file. Instead, you must explicitly select files.

Temporarily Exiting the DOS Shell (or Windows)

When you invoke the DOS shell, DOS reads your disk's current directory tree. Depending on the number of files on your disk, the directory read operation can be time consuming. If you are working within the shell and find you need to execute one or more DOS commands from the prompt, don't permanently exit the shell. Instead, press the SHIFT-F9 keyboard combination to temporarily access the DOS prompt. After you execute your commands, use the EXIT command as shown here to return to the shell:

```
C:\> EXIT <ENTER>
```

DOS will redisplay the shell exactly as you left it. By temporarily exiting the shell in this way, you avoid the time-consuming startup directory read operation.

If you are using Microsoft Windows, you can select the DOS Prompt icon from the Windows Main Group to temporarily access the DOS prompt. When you are ready to resume Windows, type EXIT at the DOS prompt.

Never turn off your computer or restart DOS when you have temporarily exited the shell, Windows, or other applications in this way. If you do and the application has open files, you may damage or destroy the files.

Understanding Shell Files and Disk Types

When you display the file list and directory tree within the DOS 5 shell, DOS will precede each filename with a specific icon type and may display different disk drive icons. Table 730a describes the file icon types.

Table 730b describes the disk icon types.

Table 730a. DOS Shell File Icons

File Icon	File Type
	Executable EXE, COM, or BAT file
	Nonexecutable file

Table 730b. Disk Icon Types

Disk Icon	Disk Type
	Floppy disk drive
	Hard disk drive
RAM	RAM drive
NET	Network drive
CD	CD-ROM

If you highlight an executable file and press ENTER, the shell will immediately execute the command. As Tip 731 explains, the shell lets you associate a nonexecutable file type with a specific program. If you later highlight a file whose extension matches the type specified and then press ENTER, the shell will execute the corresponding command.

Associating a File with an Application

If you are using the DOS 5 shell, the shell lets you associate a file type with a specific program. A file type is a specific file extension such as LTR, DAT, or TXT. After you associate a file type with a program, each time you highlight a file of that type from within the file list and press ENTER, the shell will execute the associated program, using the selected file as its input. For example, to associate files with the DAT extension with EDIT in the DOS 5 editor, highlight a file of the desired type. Next, select the File menu Associate option. The shell will display its Associate Dialog box, prompting you for the desired command. In this case, you would type **EDIT** and press ENTER. When you later highlight a file with the DAT extension and press ENTER, the shell will automatically invoke EDIT. To later change or remove an association, perform these same steps. When the shell prompts you for a command, type the desired command, or delete the current command if you no longer want an association.

Customizing the Shell's Screen Colors

If you work within the DOS shell, you may find that periodically changing the shell's color relieves the strain on your eyes. To change the shell colors, select the Options menu and choose Colors. The shell will display the Color Scheme dialog box shown here:

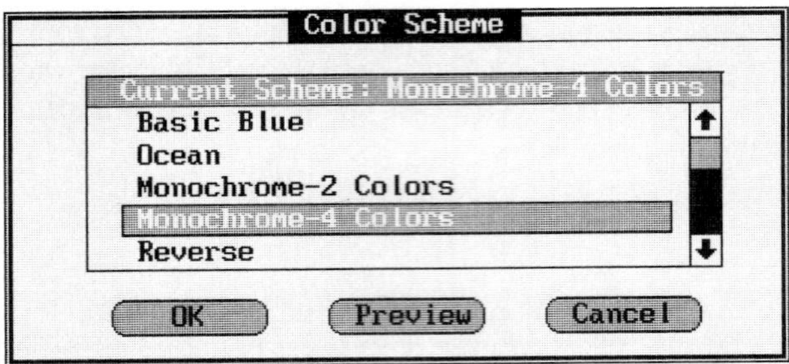

Before you select a color, highlight the color and select the Preview option (either by using your mouse or by pressing the TAB key to highlight the option and then pressing ENTER). The shell's colors will temporarily change to match the selected color. If you want to use the color, select OK. Otherwise, preview a different color or select Cancel.

Controlling the Shell's Confirmations

Be default, the DOS 5 shell displays a confirmation dialog box each time you attempt to delete or replace files or you perform file copy or move operations with your mouse. For example, if you select several files for deletion, the shell will display the Delete File Confirmation dialog box shown here:

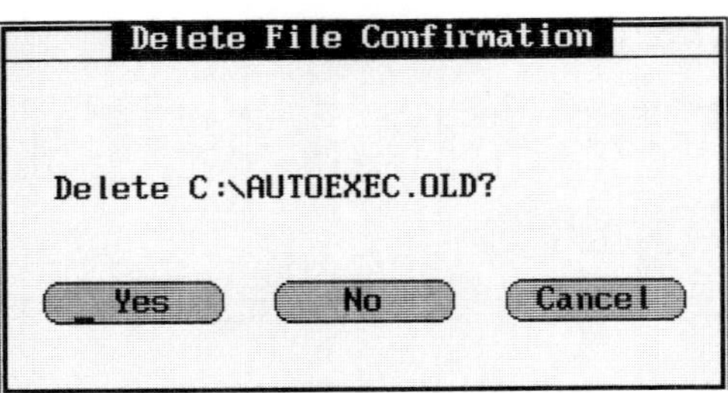

Although confirmation boxes may prevent you from inadvertently deleting or overwriting key files, there are times when having to respond to the boxes can really slow you down. If you are about to perform an operation you don't want confirmed, disable the confirmation by selecting the Options menu Confirmation option. The shell will display its Confirmation dialog box, shown here:

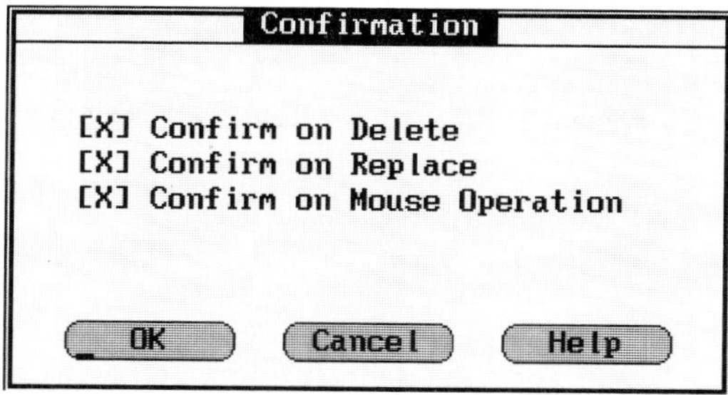

To disable a confirmation, remove the option's check mark, either by clicking the option using your mouse or by pressing the TAB key to highlight the option and pressing the SHIFT-SPACEBAR key combination. In general, having the confirmation options enabled is a safer way to operate.

Fast Program Execution in the DOS Shell

When you double-click your mouse on or highlight a file with the executable file icon and press ENTER, the shell will execute the program. Using this technique, you can quickly execute files that reside in the current directory. If the program you desire resides in a different directory, you can select the directory and execute the command, or you can select the File menu and choose Run. The shell, in turn, will display the Run dialog box shown here:

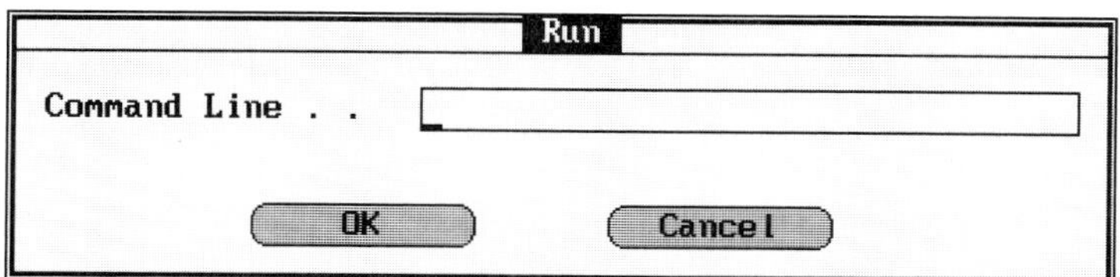

Type the desired command and press ENTER. Using the shell's Run dialog box, you can execute even internal DOS commands.

Be Aware of the Shell's Hidden File Display

If you are using the DOS 5 shell, you can direct the shell to display the names of hidden files in its directory list. To do so, select the Options menu and choose File Display Options. The shell will display the File Display Options dialog box shown in Tip 483. Next, to display hidden files, click the Display hidden/system files box with your mouse, or press the TAB key to select the box and press the SPACEBAR. If the box contains an X, the shell will display files in the directory tree regardless of whether the file's hidden or system attributes are set.

Although displaying hidden and system files gives you the actual list of files the directory contains, it puts the files at risk. Should you later highlight the filename and press DEL, the shell will delete the files. If you were to delete the hidden files IO.SYS or MSDOS.SYS, you will render your system unbootable. As a rule, therefore, you shouldn't display hidden or system files.

Displaying Only a Program List

If you are setting up a system for a first-time user, you can provide a completely menu-driven interface by using the DOS 5 shell. To begin, include the DOSSHELL command in the user's AUTOEXEC.BAT. Next, invoke the shell, select the Options menu, and initially disable the task swapper. From the shell's View menu, select the Program List option. The shell will change its display to include only the group titles in its Main group as shown in the following illustration:

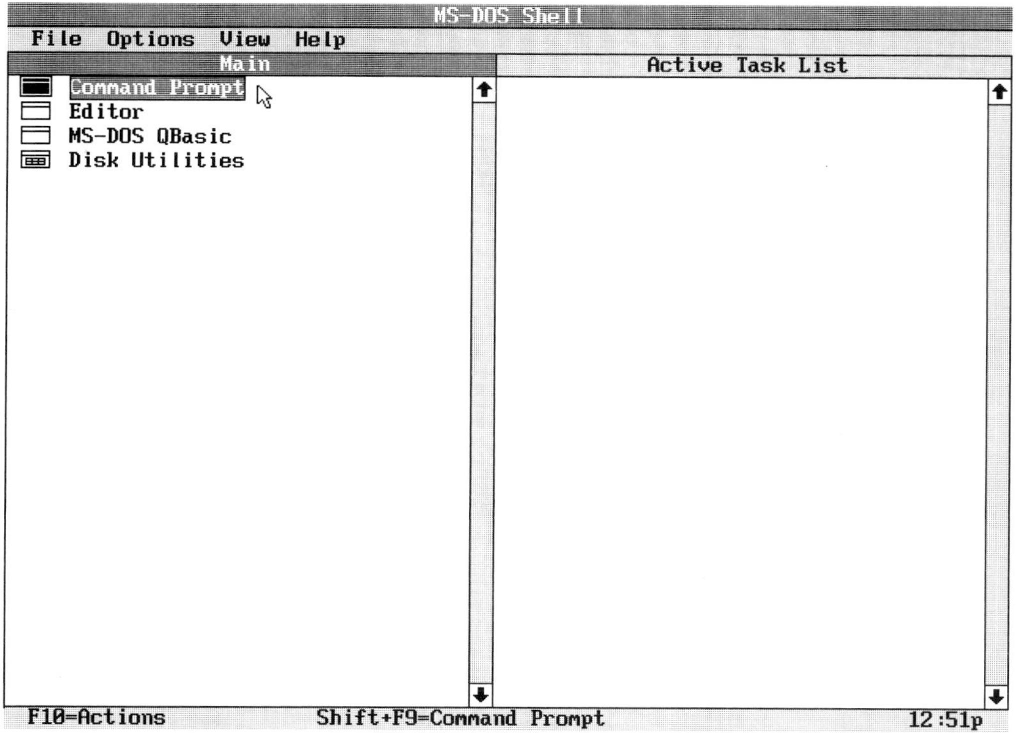

Tip 746 describes how to add entries to the shell's menu. By displaying the shell in this way, new users can work with DOS in a very straightforward manner.

What Is Multitasking?

TIP 737

Multitasking describes the computer's ability to perform more than one task, or job, at a time. If you are using Windows, for example, you can have several programs running at the same time. The advantage multitasking provides is that by running several programs at the same time, the computer is always kept busy, which helps you get your money's worth. A PC has only one processor, so a PC, in fact, can really do only one thing at a time. When Windows is multitasking, only one program runs at any given instant. However, the processor quickly switches between each program. Because the processor switches so fast, the programs appear to be running simultaneously.

The DOS 5 shell does not perform multitasking. Instead, the shell provides a task swapper that lets you load up to 15 programs into memory at one time. Unlike with a multitasking operating system, which quickly switches the processor from one program to the next, you must select one application you want to run. The shell's task swapper will temporarily copy the other programs to disk (a process called swapping). When you later want to use a different (loaded) program, you must press the CTRL-ESC keyboard combination to activate the shell and then select the desired program. The task swapper will copy the current program to disk (swap it) and then read in the desired program. Because disk operations are inherently slow, so is task swapping.

The advantage task swapping provides is that you don't have to end the current program, closing its files, just to quickly run a second program so you can look up some information. Instead, you can temporarily swap the first program to disk.

How to Task Swap

If you are using the DOS 5 shell, enabling task swapping lets you load several programs into memory at one time. Tip 737 discusses task swapping and multitasking. To use the task swapper, select the shell's Options menu. If the Enable Task Swapper option is not preceded by a diamond, select the option. When task swapping is enabled, the Options menu will appear as shown here:

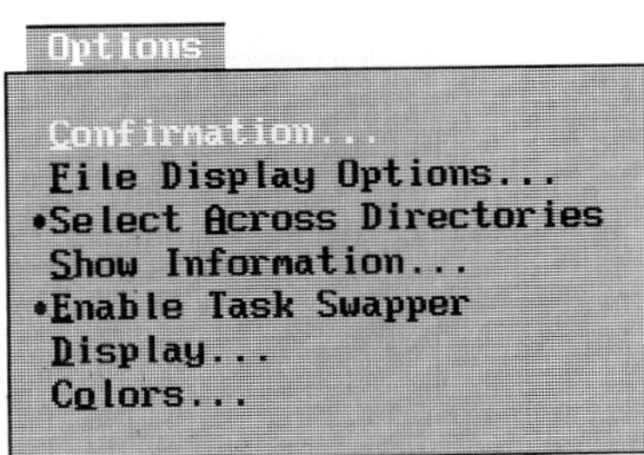

The shell will add a new section on your screen, titled Active Task List. This list will contain the names of programs that are loaded into memory. To better understand how the task swapper works, run the editor from the shell's Main group list. When EDIT displays its opening screen, press the CTRL-ESC

key combination. The shell will reappear on your screen, and EDIT will appear in the active task list. You can now use the shell to perform other operations. When you are ready to resume working with EDIT, highlight EDIT in the active task list and press ENTER. When you are done using EDIT, exit the program normally, and the shell will appear.

When you are running a program and want to switch back to the shell, press CTRL-ESC. Always exit the program in the normal manner when you are done.

Always End Programs Normally When Task Swapping

Tip 738 discusses how to use the DOS 5 task swapper. Task swapping is convenient because it lets you leave files open in one program while quickly switching to another. Always make sure you exit programs normally when you are task swapping to ensure that data is stored correctly on disk. Never turn off your computer while tasks are active; doing so risks the files that the tasks had open. The shell itself will not let you exit while tasks are active. If you try, the shell will display the following dialog box telling you that tasks are active:

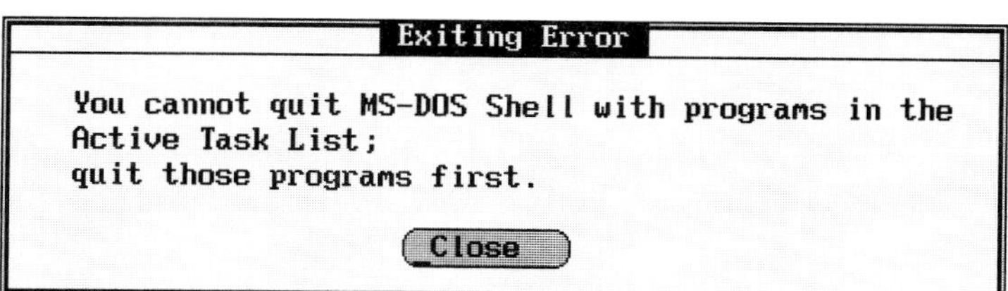

Be sure not to open the same file from within two different tasks at the same time. Doing so could corrupt the file's contents.

Ending a Hung Task

If you are using DOS 5 task swapping and a task fails, hanging the session, press the CTRL-ESC keyboard combination to return to the shell. Next, highlight the task in the active task list and press the DEL key. The shell will display a Warning dialog box similar to the one shown here asking you to verify that you really want to end the task. Select OK.

Never use this technique to end a task that is not hung that has open files. Doing so may damage the file's contents.

Quickly Switching Between Active Tasks

Tip 738 explains that to use DOS 5 task switching to switch between tasks, you can press CTRL-ESC to return to the shell and then select the desired task. A faster technique may be to hold down the ALT key and then press TAB. When you do, the shell will display a title bar on a blank screen that contains the name of the next task in the active task list. If the task name displayed matches the task you desire, press ENTER, and the shell will quickly switch to the task. Otherwise, continue to hold down the ALT key pressing TAB until the desired task name appears.

Customizing the DOS 5 Shell with DOSSHELL.INI

If you are using the DOS 5 shell, you have probably selected several shell options to customize the shell as you desire. The shell stores your selections in a file named DOSSHELL.INI that resides in the DOS directory. INI is short for initialization. The shell reads the DOSSHELL.INI file each time it starts. Using the PRINT command, print a copy of the file's current contents:

```
C:\> PRINT C:\DOS\DOSSHELL.INI <ENTER>
```

Also make a copy of the file on a floppy disk as shown here and store it in a safe location:

```
C:\> COPY C:\DOS\DOSSHELL:INI A: <ENTER>
```

If you examine the printout, you will find that DOSSHELL.INI contains several one-line entries that control various shell options and several longer entries that describe the shell's group and program entries. By editing the file DOSSHELL.INI, you can change the shell settings and entries. However, do not edit the file unless you have a backup copy you can later restore if necessary.

Editing DOSSHELL.INI

Tip 742 explains that the DOS 5 shell stores its configuration information in a file named DOSSHELL.INI. Using an editor, you can make changes to this file that affect the shell's settings or entries. As discussed in Tip 742, never edit the file DOSSHELL.INI unless you have a backup copy. The best way to edit the file is by using the EDIT command. Several of the file's lines may contain up to 256 characters. Some editors and word processors may not support lines this long. Also, by using EDIT, you ensure that the file remains a pure ASCII file. A word processor may insert formatting codes that, while understandable to the word processor, cause the DOS shell to fail.

Increasing the PC's Task-Swapping Speed

Tip 738 discusses task swapping using the DOS 5 shell. Because the task swapper must continually move programs to or from disk, the disk's slow mechanical nature makes task swapping slow. One way to improve task-swapping performance is to create a large RAM drive in extended or expanded memory and then set the TEMP environment entry to point to the drive. When the shell needs to swap a program, the RAM drive lets it do so much faster. The shell actually makes intelligent decisions about where to swap. If you assign the TEMP entry to a floppy drive, for example, the shell will not swap to the drive, but rather to its default swap directory (C:\DOS). If you plan to use DOS task swapping, use the TEMP environment entry to improve performance.

Faster Task Switching Using Shortcut Keys

Tip 738 discusses DOS 5 task switching in detail; you can switch from the current program back to the shell by pressing the CTRL-ESC keyboard combination. Tip 741 describes how the shell lets you cycle through the names of active tasks by pressing ALT-TAB. By pressing ALT-ESC, you can cycle through the tasks themselves. If you have specific programs you switch to regularly, the fastest way to select the task is to assign a specific shortcut key combination to the task. After you assign the shortcut key combination, you can quickly select the task for execution, or if the task is active, quickly switch to the task itself. To assign a shortcut key to a task, you must create a program entry for the task, as Tip 746 discusses. In the Program Item Dialog box shown here, assign the desired shortcut key combination:

```
Add Program
Program Title . . . .
Commands . . . . . .
Startup Directory . .
Application Shortcut Key
[X] Pause after exit          Password . .
OK    Cancel    Help    Advanced...
```

The shell will not let you select a shortcut key that is already in use or one of the key combinations listed here:

CTRL-C	CTRL-[	SHIFT-CTRL-M	SHIFT-CTRL-[
CTRL-M	CTRL-5*	SHIFT-CTRL-1	SHIFT-CTRL-5*
CTRL-I	CTRL-H	SHIFT-CTRL-H	

*Indicates the numeric keypad number 5

Adding Program Entries to the Shell's Program List

If you have several programs you commonly run from within the DOS 5 shell, you can make the programs easier to use by assigning them to the shell's program list. To create a program entry, select the shell's Main icon. Next, select the File menu and choose New. The shell will display the New Program Object dialog box shown here:

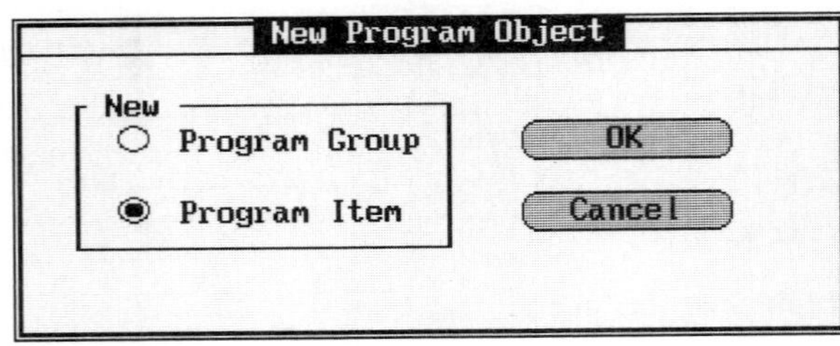

Select the Program Item option and choose OK. The shell will display the Add Program dialog box shown here:

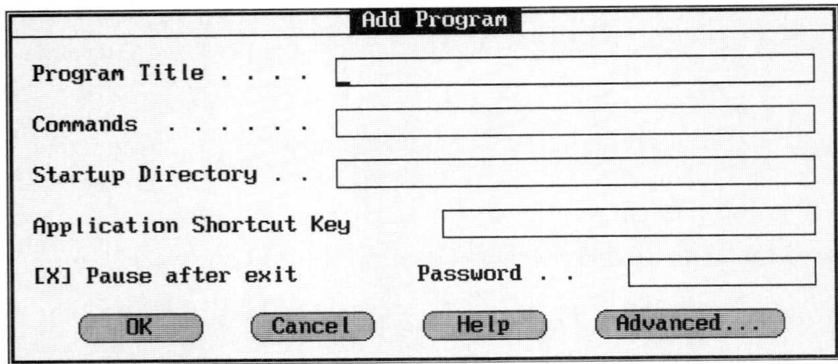

Table 746 describes the values you should use for each dialog box entry.

After you have completed the program items, select OK.

Table 746. Values to Assign to Program Items

Option	Value to Assign
Program title	Enter the title you want to appear in the shell's task list.
Commands	Enter the commands required to execute the program.
Startup directory	If the command must be run from a specific directory, enter the complete path to the directory.
Application Shortcut key	See Tip 758.
Pause after exit	See Tip 747.
Password	See Tip 748.
Advanced button	See Tip 757.

Pausing a Program's Output in the DOS 5 Shell

By default, every time a program ends, the shell displays a message asking you to press any key to continue before the shell returns to the shell interface. In many cases, when you end a program such as your word processor, you simply want the program to end and the shell to reappear. To make this happen, you must create a program entry for the desired program, as Tip 746 explains. When the shell displays the Add Program dialog box shown in Tip 746, disable the Pause after exit option by removing the option's X. To invoke the program in the future, you must use the program entry. The shell will no longer display the prompt telling you to press any key to continue.

Adding Password Protection to Shell Program Items

When you create a program group or program item within the DOS shell, the shell lets you specify a password the user must type to use the items. After you assign a password, each time the user selects the program item, the shell will display the Password dialog box shown here:

Password

Enter Password:

OK   Cancel   Help

If the user does not correctly enter the password, the user cannot use the item. Note that the password does not prevent a knowledgeable user from running the program simply by specifying the File menu Run option, bypassing your password protection. With novice users, however, some protection is provided. Should you ever forget your password, see Tip 749.

Handling a Forgotten Program Item Password

Tip 748 describes how to password-protect DOS 5 shell program items. Should you forget a password, edit the file DOSSHELL.INI as Tip 743 shows. Locate the program item entry in the file for the corresponding command. Remove the line containing the password entry. When you later restart the shell, edit the program item and assign a new password.

Controlling the Shell's Screen Resolution

If you have a color monitor, the shell, by default displays its output in 25 lines of 80 columns. If you are using an EGA or VGA monitor, however, you can direct the shell to use 43- or 50-line mode. To do so, display the shell's Options menu and select the Display option. The shell will display the Screen Display Mode Dialog box as shown here:

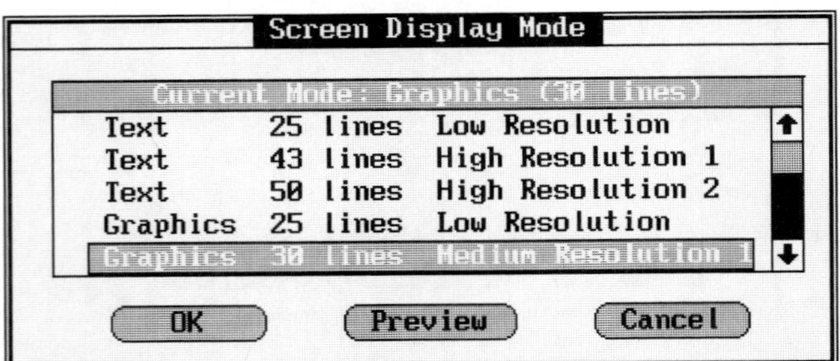

Using your keyboard arrow keys or mouse, select the desired mode and choose OK.

Editing a Shell Program Item

As you create program items, you sometimes may need to change an entry, perhaps to add a parameter as Tip 752 explains or to change a password. To do so, highlight the desired program items by clicking the item with your mouse or by pressing the TAB key and using your arrow keys. Next, select the File menu and choose Properties. The shell will display the Program Item Properties dialog box. Change the entries as required and select OK. Note that if the item has a password assigned to it, you must enter the password before you can edit the entry.

Using Command-line Parameters with Program Entries

Tip 748 describes how to create program entries within the DOS 5 shell. Often you may want the user to pass parameters to a command. To support parameters, place the symbols %1 through %9 in the program's command line. The following illustration shows how you would use %1 to pass a filename to the EDIT command:

Program Item Properties

Program Title . . . . Edit

Commands . . . . . . EDIT %1

Startup Directory . .

Application Shortcut Key

[X] Pause after exit   Password . .

OK   Cancel   Help   Advanced...

After you complete the other fields in the Add Program dialog box and select OK, the shell will display the dialog box shown next, asking you for information about the parameters:

Program Item Properties

Fill in information for % 1 prompt dialog.

Window Title . . . .

Program Information .

Prompt Message . . .

Default Parameters . .

OK   Cancel   Help

Table 752 describes the values you should assign to each field.

The following illustration shows the dialog box the shell might display for the EDIT command:

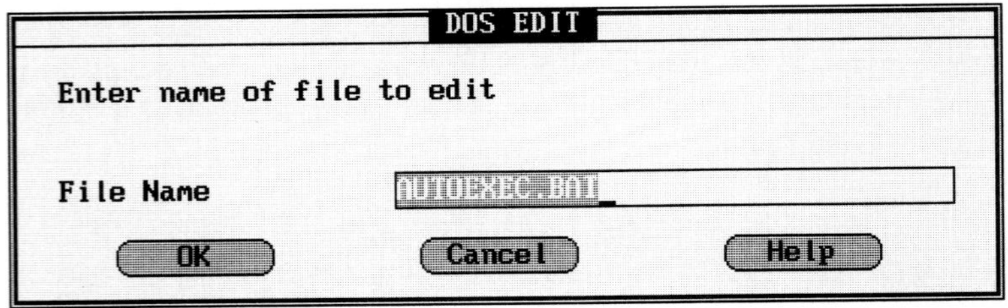

Table 752. Dialog Box Field Descriptions

Field	Contents
Window title	Enter the title the shell displays in the dialog box it uses to prompt the user for parameters. The title can contain up to 23 characters.
Program information	Enter up to 106 characters describing the information the user should type.
Prompt message	Enter the characters the shell displays to prompt the user for the required parameters. You can enter up to 18 characters.
Default parameters	Enter a string of wildcard characters, the letters %L for the last parameter used by the user for this command, or %F for the selected file.

Organize Your Program Entries

Tip 746 describes how to add program entries to the DOS 5 shell. As the number of program entries increases, you will eventually want to group related program entries into program groups, much like you would use directories on your disk to organize files. To create a program group, select the program list. Next, select the shell's File menu and choose New. The shell will display the New Program Object dialog box shown here:

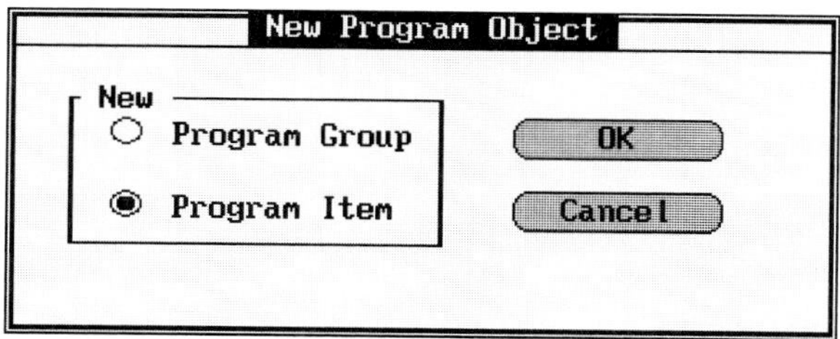

Select Program Group and choose OK. The shell will display the Add Group dialog box shown here:

Add Group

Required

Title . . . .

Optional

Help Text . .

Password . .

OK Cancel Help

Table 753 lists the values you should assign to each entry.

After you create a program group, you can select the group and then follow the steps discussed in Tip 746 to create entries in the group.

Table 753. Values to Assign to Program Group Entries

Entry	Value
Title	Enter the group title that will appear in the shell menu. The title can contain up to 23 characters.
Help Text	Enter up to 255 characters that describe the group and its entries should the user highlight the entry and choose Help.
Password	Enter up to 20 characters as a password that must be entered before accessing the group.

Reorder Your Program Group Icons

If you invoke programs from within the DOS 5 shell by using program groups, order the program entries from most commonly used to least commonly used. To reorder program entries, select the entry

you want to move. Next, select the File menu and choose Reorder. Highlight the program entry before which you want the item moved and press ENTER. The shell will move the program entry as desired.

Moving Shell Program Entries

Tip 753 discusses how to create program groups within the DOS 5 shell to organize your program entries. After you create one or more program groups, you will probably want to move entries from one group to another. To move a program entry, highlight the entry and select the File menu Copy option. Next, select the program group you desire. Highlight the entry before which you want the second entry copied and press ENTER. Last, highlight the original entry in the first group and select Delete. The shell will display the Delete Item dialog box shown here:

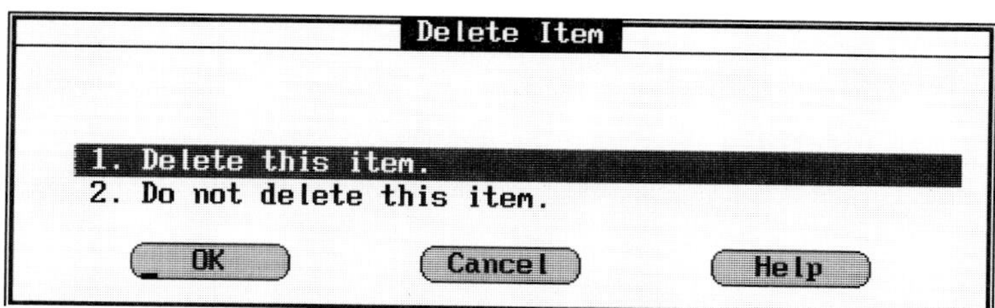

Select the Delete this item option and choose OK.

Creating a Program Group for Backup Operations

If you work within the DOS 5 shell, you can create a program group to simplify your monthly and incremental backup operations. To begin, from within the shell's Main group, create a program group named Disk Backup as Tip 753 shows. Next, select the new program group. Using the File menu's New option, create a program entry named Daily Backup as shown here:

```
                        Add Program
Program Title . . . .   Daily Backup
Commands  . . . . . .   BACKUP C:\*.* A: /S /A /M /L:C:\BAC_
Startup Directory . .
Application Shortcut Key
[X] Pause after exit         Password . .
   OK        Cancel        Help        Advanced...
```

Next, create a second program entry named Monthly Backup as shown here:

```
                        Add Program
Program Title . . . .   Monthly Backup
Commands  . . . . . .   BACKUP C:\*.* A: /S /L:C:\BACKUP\BA_
Startup Directory . .
Application Shortcut Key
[X] Pause after exit         Password . .
   OK        Cancel        Help        Advanced...
```

Both of the BACKUP commands assume you are using a backup log file, as Tip 550 explains. If you are not, remove the /L switch from the commands.

Preventing a Program Switch Operation

Tip 738 describes how to use the DOS 5 shell's task-switching capabilities. Sometimes, however, you may not want to switch from a specific program. To prevent such task switching, you must create a program entry for the program as Tip 746 explains. With the Add Program dialog box active, select the Advanced option. The shell will display the Advanced dialog box shown here:

```
                              Advanced
Help Text
Conventional Memory   KB Required
XMS Memory  KB Required               KB Limit
Video Mode  (•) Text     Reserve Shortcut Keys [ ] ALT+TAB
            ( ) Graphics                       [ ] ALT+ESC
[ ] Prevent Program Switch                     [ ] CTRL+ESC
        OK              Cancel             Help
```

To prevent a program switch, check the Prevent Program Switch option or select the option and press the SPACEBAR.

The Prevent Program Switch option will prevent a switch from the program only if you invoke it by using the program entry. If you invoke the program by using the File menu Run option or by simply selecting the program file and pressing ENTER, *you cannot prevent the task switch.*

Reserving Shortcut Keys

As Tip 745 shows, the DOS 5 shell uses the key combinations listed in Table 758 for task switching.

If your program also requires the use of one of these keystrokes, you can disable the shell's use of the keys. To do so, you must create a program entry for the program as Tip 746 explains. With the shell's Add Program dialog box displayed, select the Advanced option. The shell will display the Advanced dialog box (as Tip 757 shows).

To reserve shortcut keys for the program, click the required key combination with the mouse or highlight the entry and press the SPACEBAR.

You can reserve only the program's use of shortcut keys; you must invoke the program by using the program entry. If you invoke the program by using the File menu's Run option or by simply selecting the program file and pressing ENTER, *you cannot reserve the shortcut keys.*

Table 758. Task-Switching Keystrokes

Key Combination	Purpose
ALT-TAB	Cycles through the active tasks, displaying the task name in a dialog box
ALT-ESC	Cycles through the active tasks, displaying the task's current screen
CTRL-ESC	Switches control back to the shell's task list

Loading a Task Without Executing It

Tip 738 discusses how you can execute a program within the DOS 5 shell, later switching from and back to the shell or to a different application. If you highlight a file in the file list and press ENTER, the shell will execute the program, displaying the program's output on your screen. If you later switch from the program, the shell will display the program's name in the active task list. Sometimes, however, you may want to add a program to the active task list, but not immediately run the program. To do so, select the program filename from the file list and press the SHIFT-ENTER keyboard combination. The shell will place the program's name in the Active Task list as you desire.

Add Online Help to Program Entries

Tip 746 describes how to create DOS 5 shell program entries. Tip 753 describes how to create program groups. When you create a program group, the shell's Add Group dialog box, shown in Tip 753, lets you add up to 255 characters of help text that explains the group's entries and purpose to the user should the user highlight the entry and press F1 for help. Similarly, when you create a program entry, you can select the Add Programs dialog box's Advanced option and then type help text in the Advanced dialog box, shown in Tip 757.

As you enter help text, you can type it in as one long line of text. When the shell later displays the text, the shell will automatically format the text with the Help dialog box. If, for any reason, you need to format the text yourself by adding carriage returns and line feeds, type the characters **^M**—press the caret key (^) followed by **M**. Each time the shell encounters the characters **^M**, it will execute a carriage return and line feed in the help text.

Specify Minimum Memory Requirements for Program Entries

Tip 746 describes how to create program entries within DOS 5 shell. Tip 738 describes how to use the shell's task-swapping capabilities. Depending on your programs, you sometimes may want to specify the minimum amount of conventional or extended memory a specific program must have before the task swapper can run the program. To do so, you must create a program entry for the program. From the Add Program dialog box, shown in Tip 746, select the Advanced option. The shell will display the Advanced dialog box, which is shown in Tip 757.

Type the required memory amounts in kilobytes. By default, the shell uses a minimum of 128Kb for conventional memory. The XMS options let you specify the program's minimum extended memory

requirements as well as the maximum amount (the limit) the program can request. By default, the shell uses 0Kb for the amount of extended memory that must be available before a program can run. The XMS limit specifies the maximum amount of extended memory (or less, if the system has less extended memory).

If you try to run a program for which you have defined memory requirements and insufficient memory is available, the shell will display the Program Error dialog box shown here:

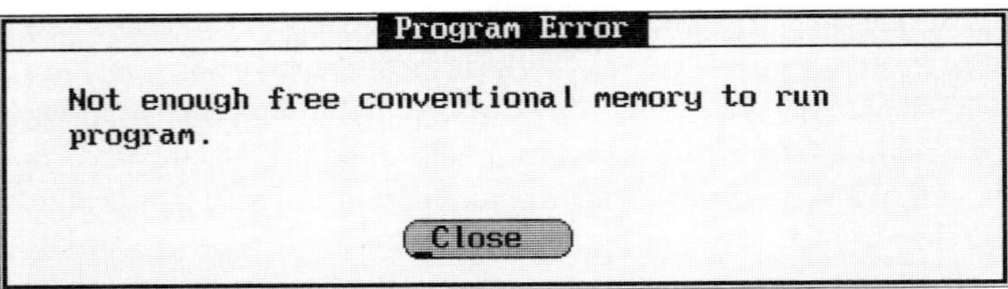

You Don't Have to Wait for the Shell

Each time you start the DOS 5 shell or switch disk drives, the shell displays the dialog box shown here, which tells you it is reading files in the directory tree:

```
Reading Disk Information . . .

Files Read:                 310
Directories Read:            18
```

Unfortunately, if the number of files on your disk is large, the amount of time DOS takes to read your directory tree can be considerable. Luckily, however, you don't have to wait for the shell. Instead, you can begin your operations, possibly selecting a program from the program list or executing a different menu option. The shell will continue reading the directory as time permits.

Using the Shell's Online Help

If you are using the DOS 5 shell and you can't recall how to perform a specific task, invoke the shell's online help facility by selecting the Help menu. The shell will display the pull-down Help menu shown here:

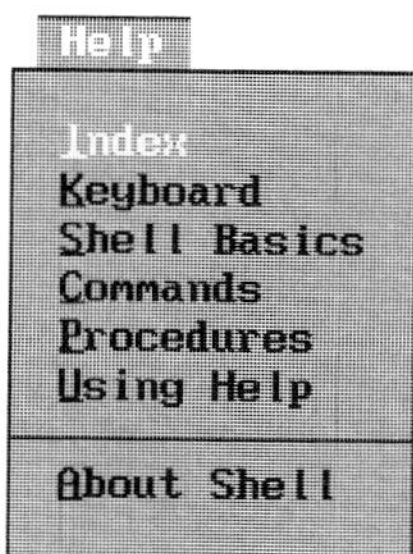

Table 763a describes each Help menu option.

Table 763a. The DOS 5 Shell Help Menu Options

Menu Option	Help
Index	Provides access to every help topic
Keyboard	Discusses common keyboard operations as well as commonly used keyboard combinations
Shell Basics	Walks you through the use of the shell, discussing the operations you'll use regularly
Commands	Explains each menu option
Procedures	Describes the steps you must perform for common operations
Using Help	Explains how to use the shell's online help
About Help	Displays the shell's copyright information

When you select a menu option, the shell will display related text. Some topics in the text appear in a different color; if you double-click one of these topics with your mouse, or press your TAB key to highlight a topic and press ENTER, the shell will display additional help. At the bottom of every help screen, the shell displays a list of buttons you can double-click with your mouse or highlight by pressing the TAB key and pressing ENTER. Table 763b describes these buttons.

If you are using the DOS 5 shell, you can find the answer to most of your questions in the shell's online help.

Table 763b. Button Uses Within the DOS 5 Shell's Online Help

Button	Purpose
Close	Ends a help session returning control to the shell
Back	Returns to the help screen displayed immediately before the current screen
Keys	Displays the shell's keyboard help
Index	Displays the shell's help index screen
Help	Displays the shell's help text about the help screen

PART
9

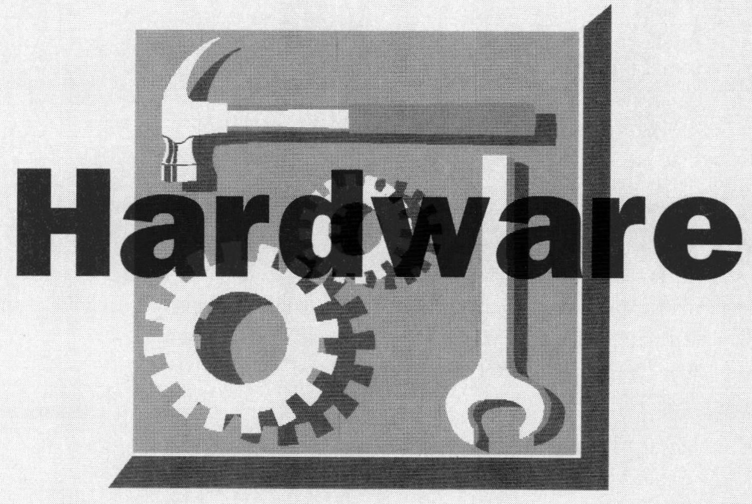
Hardware

Understanding Serial and Parallel Ports

A port is a cable connection at the back of your computer's chassis. Two of the most common port types are serial and parallel ports. The primary difference between those two port types is the way they exchange information. Serial ports transmit data one bit at a time over a single wire. Parallel ports, on the other hand, transmit data a byte at a time over eight wires. Because parallel ports can send more data at one time, they are much faster than serial ports. The following illustration shows how serial and parallel ports appear on the back of your system chassis:

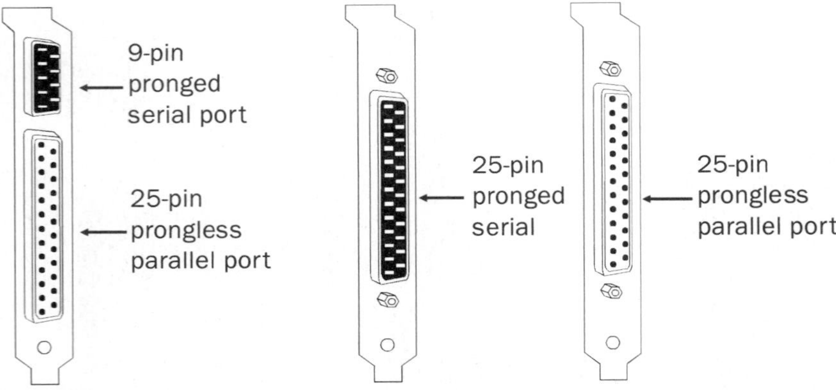

Most printers support a serial or parallel interface. If your printer is currently connected to a serial port, find out whether you can connect it to a parallel port. You will have to buy a parallel cable (about $20), but the performance you will gain is well worth the cost.

Determining Your Video Type from Its Connector

If you are using another user's computer and you need to quickly determine whether the computer has a VGA or EGA monitor, examine the cable that connects the monitor to the back of your computer.

As shown here, EGA monitors typically connect to a 9-pin port, and VGA monitors use a 15-pin port:

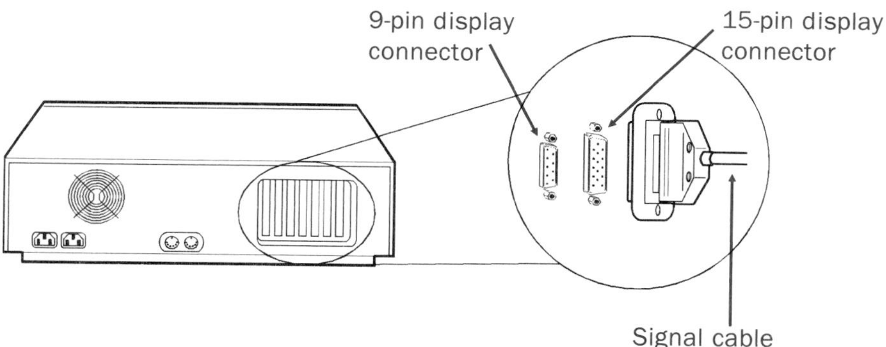

Adding a Serial or Parallel Port

Most computers ship with one serial and one parallel port. Depending on your printer requirements, you sometimes may want to add a second or possibly a third parallel printer. Likewise, you may want to add multiple serial ports, possibly for use with a printer, modem, mouse, or other hardware device. DOS supports three parallel ports, named LPT1, LPT2, and LPT3, and four serial devices, COM1 through COM4. When you add a new parallel or serial board to your computer, you must specify the

device name by which the computer recognizes the device. To do so, you select a specific setting on the board, using either a specific DIP switch setting or jumper combination. The following illustration shows jumpers and DIP switches:

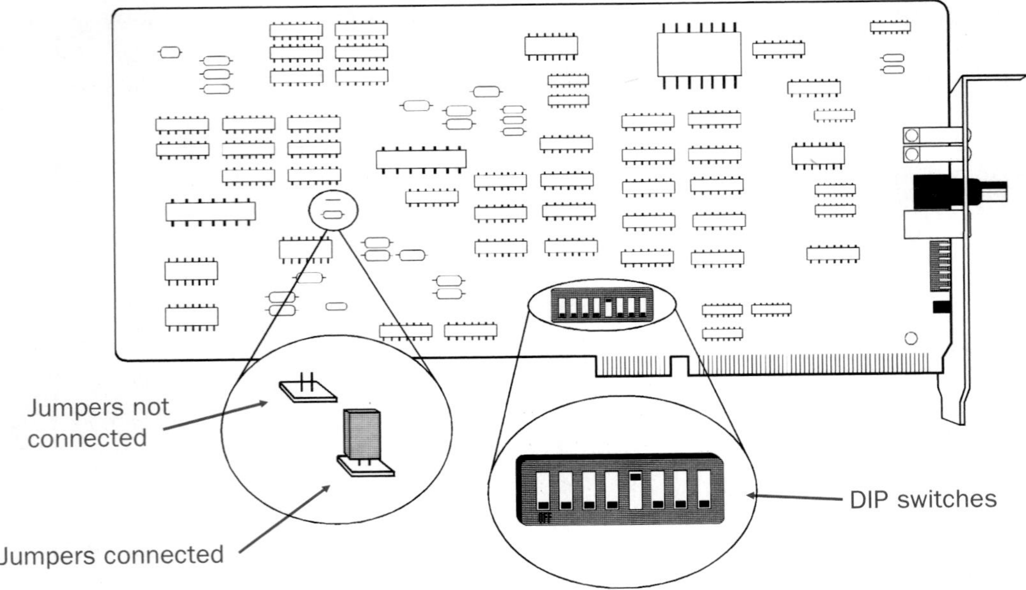

The documentation that accompanies your board should specify the proper settings for each device.

To set DIP switches, use a small screwdriver or ballpoint pen. If you are setting jumper switches, be careful not to damage the jumper pins.

Is a Math Coprocessor Right for You?

Many users purchase a math coprocessor for their system and are then disappointed when Windows, for example, doesn't seem to run faster. Here's how a math coprocessor works. Although the PC's CPU provides instructions for addition, subtraction, and multiplication, it does not include instructions for

performing square root or trigonometric operations such as sine, cosine, and tangent. To perform such operations, the CPU must build upon its normal instructions. A math coprocessor is a second chip that contains instructions for such advanced operations. If you are running a scientific program or design program such as AutoCAD that performs complex mathematical operations, the program can take advantage of the math coprocessor's instructions and, as a result, will execute faster. It's important to note, however, that not all programs can use a math coprocessor. Before you purchase one, make sure your software will support it. If you are using a 486DX, the processor provides the math instructions. If you are using a 486SX, however, the mathematical instructions are not included, so you will need to purchase a coprocessor.

Understanding Startup Beep Codes

Each time you turn on your computer, the PC runs its power-on self-test (Post) to test its internal components. If Post encounters an error, it may display an error message on your screen, or it may sound a series of beeps. Table 768a lists the meanings of the fatal beep codes sounded by the Phoenix BIOS and Phoenix Compatible BIOS chips. The beep codes are written as x-y-z; for instance, 2-3-1 means that the PC will sound two beeps and then delay, sound three beeps and then delay, and then sound one more beep.

Table 768a. Meanings of the Phoenix BIOS Post Fatal Error Beep Messages

Beep Code	Meaning
1-1-3	Error in accessing CMOS
1-1-4	Error in BIOS checksum
1-2-1	Failure of programmable internal timer
1-2-2	Failure in initializing DMA
1-2-3	Failure in accessing DMA page register
1-3-1	Failure in verifying RAM refresh
1-3-3	Failure of first 64Kb RAM chip
1-3-4	Failure of first 64Kb RAM chip even/odd logic

Table 768a (continued). Meanings of the Phoenix BIOS Post Fatal Error Beep Messages

Beep Code	Meaning
1-4-2	Parity error in first 64Kb RAM chip
2-*-*	Failure of bit in first 64Kb RAM chip
3-1-1	Failure of slave DMA register
3-1-2	Failure of master DMA register
3-1-3	Failure of master interrupt mask register
3-1-4	Failure of slave interrupt mask register
3-2-4	Failure of keyboard controller
3-3-4	Failure of screen initialization
3-4-1	Failure of screen retrace

Table 768b lists the meanings of the nonfatal beep codes.

Table 768b. Meaning of the Phoenix BIOS Post Nonfatal Error Beep Messages

Beep Codes	Meaning
4-2-1	Failure of timer interrupt test
4-2-2	Failure of shutdown test
4-2-3	Failure of A20 gate
4-2-4	Unexpected protected mode interrupt
4-3-1	Failure of RAM test above 64Kb
4-3-3	Failure of internal timer channel 2
4-3-4	Failure of time-of-day clock
4-4-1	Failure of serial port
4-4-2	Failure of parallel port
4-4-3	Failure of math coprocessor

Understanding the PC's Port Use

To communicate with different devices, the computer often reads information from, or writes information to, storage locations called ports. Each device must have a unique port address. Table 769 lists the common port addresses used for EISA systems (see Tip 57). PS/2 microchannel port use will differ.

When you install new hardware, you may need to specify a port address. You can use Table 769 to avoid possible conflicts. To select a port address for a hardware board, you may have to set jumpers or DIP switches as discussed in Tip 766.

Table 769. Port Use for EISA-Based PCs

Port Address	Use
00H-1FH	DMA controller
20H-3FH	Interrupt controller
40H-5FH	Timer
60H-6FH	Keyboard
70H-7FH	Real-time clock
80H-9FH	DMA page registers
A0H-BFH	Interrupt controller 2
C0H-DFH	DMA controller 2
F0H-FFH	Math coprocessor
1F0H-1FFH	Hard disk
200H-220H	Joystick game adapter
270H-27FH	LPT2
2B0H-2DFH	Alternate EGA
2E0H-2E7H	COM4
2E8H-2EFH	COM3
2F8H-2FFH	COM2

Table 768 (continued). Port Use for EISA-Based PCs

Port Address	Use
300H-31FH	Network/prototype cards
378H-37FH	LPT1
380H-38FH	SDLC
390H-39FH	Cluster adapter
3B0H-3BFH	Monochrome display
3C0H-3CFH	EGA
3D0H-3DFH	CGA
3F0H-3F7H	Floppy disk
3F0H-3FFH	COM1
400H-4FFH	DMA
500H-7FFH	Port-aliasing ports 100H-3FFH
800H-8FFH	CMOS
900H-8FFF	Reserved for port-aliasing ports 100H-3FFH
9FFFH-FFFFH	Reserved

Why a FAX/Modem Is a Good Investment

If you are used to working with laser printer documents, it doesn't take very many rolled up faxes before you become frustrated with fax output. Unfortunately, when you price plain-paper fax machines, you will quickly find that you can put up with rolled up paper. Luckily, by using a fax/modem board, you can receive faxes via your computer, printing them with your system printer. If you have a document stored on disk, you can use the fax/modem to send the document to another fax. Unfortunately, you can't use the fax/modem to fax documents not stored in your computer. However, the ability to receive faxes on plain paper makes the fax/modem board well worth the cost. You can purchase a fax/modem for $150 or less; plain-paper fax machines still cost several thousand

dollars. Most fax/modem boards come with software that allows them to send and receive faxes in the background while you use the PC to perform other operations.

When You Need a Surge Suppressor

A surge suppressor is an electronic device that sits between your wall outlet and your computer; in other words, you plug the surge suppressor into a wall outlet and then plug your computer into the surge suppressor. The following illustration shows the two most common surge suppressor types:

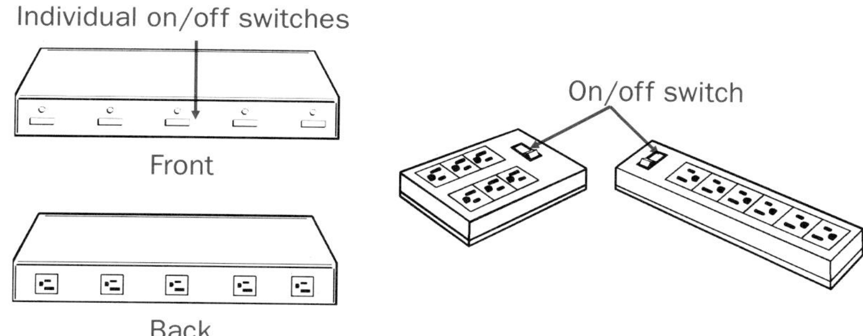

Suppressors exist to prevent surges of electricity, called spikes, from traveling down electrical wires and reaching your computer. Spikes can quickly destroy your computer investment.

If you are planning to plug in your computer, you want a surge suppressor. You don't have to spend a fortune to get a good suppressor. Make sure, however, that the suppressor you buy has Underwriters Laboratory approval. Many users find a flat surge suppressor that sits on top of the chassis, beneath the monitor, to be convenient because its switches let them easily control their various hardware devices.

Understanding Video Resolution

When you display images on your screen, the screen's resolution controls how sharp the image appears. To produce an image, your screen illuminates thousands of small picture elements, called pixels. The more pixels your screen can illuminate, the sharper the image. The number of pixels on the screen defines the screen's resolution. The following illustration shows the number of horizontal and vertical pixels for common video display types:

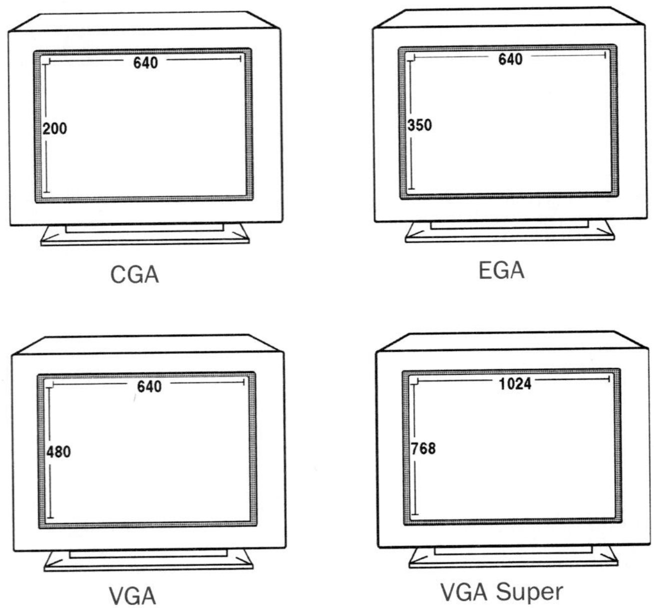

If you are considering purchasing a new video system, resolution is only one consideration (see Tip 798).

What Is a UART?

As Tip 764 discusses, serial devices exchange information one bit at a time over a single wire. Each serial board contains a chip called the UART—universal asynchronous receiver transmitter. The UART is the chip responsible for overseeing serial communication. Just as you might consider the CPU to be the computer's electronic brain, you can consider the UART to be the brain of the serial board.

When sending information, the BIOS places a byte of data into the UART's transfer holding register. When the UART is ready to send the data, it moves the byte into the data shift register. The UART then places onto the wire, one bit at a time, the contents of its transfer shift register (preceded and followed by the appropriate number of start and stop bits). The receiving serial port also contains a UART. In the case of the receiver, the UART takes bits off the wire, one bit at a time (removing the start and stop bits), placing the data into the receiver shift register. When the entire byte has been received, the UART moves the data into a receiver data register, which is then accessed by the BIOS.

Should a data transmission error occur, the UARTs set flags within their status registers, indicating the error to the BIOS. Thus, serial device communication can be thought of as occurring UART to UART. The UART is often the controlling factor in determining how fast serial devices can communcate.

Understanding Parity

In discussing memory chips or serial communications, one of the terms that always comes up is parity, often preceded by the word *even, odd,* or *none.* Parity is an error-detection technique that helps identify single-bit errors. Each byte of memory, for example, has a corresponding parity bit. The parity bit controls whether an even or odd number of bits are 1's. For example, if memory uses even parity, the number of bits in the byte of memory, plus the parity bit, should add up to an even number. The following illustration shows the even parity settings for various values; in each case, the number of bits that are 1's adds up to an even value as shown in Table 774.

Table 774. Even Parity Settings

Data Bits	Parity	Number of 1's Bits
01101101	1	6
00000000	0	0
01010101	0	4
11111111	0	8
11111110	1	8

When the PC stores a value in memory, it sets the parity bit as necessary to obtain the correct parity. When the PC later reads the memory, it calculates the value's parity a second time. If the parity is no longer correct, one of the bits has changed in error (the chip may be going bad), and a parity error has occurred. By continually checking for parity errors, the PC can quickly detect a faulty memory chip.

When the PC uses a serial device, such as a modem, parity is again used to detect transmission errors. If even parity is being used and an odd number of 1's bits occurs, a transmission error has occurred, and the data needs to be re-sent. Odd parity is identical with the exception that the parity bit ensures that an odd number of 1's bits are used. It doesn't matter whether you use even or odd parity so long as the devices communicating use the same parity type.

Parity can detect only single-bit errors. For example, if you are using even parity and a memory location contains 01010101, the parity bit is zero. If two of the bits changes due to an error, yielding 10010101, the parity is still even, and the error is not detected. As Tip 124 and Tip 862 explain, the PC uses other techniques to detect such errors. The advantage of parity is that it can be calculated very quickly.

Determining Board Type

Tip 57 discusses PC buses in detail. The boards you plug into expansion slots can be 8-, 16-, or 32-bit boards. To make best use of your expansion slots, you should place

each board in a slot designed specifically for the board's size. In other words, you shouldn't waste a 32-bit slot on an 8-bit board if you can help it. To help you distinguish among board types, examine the connectors shown here:

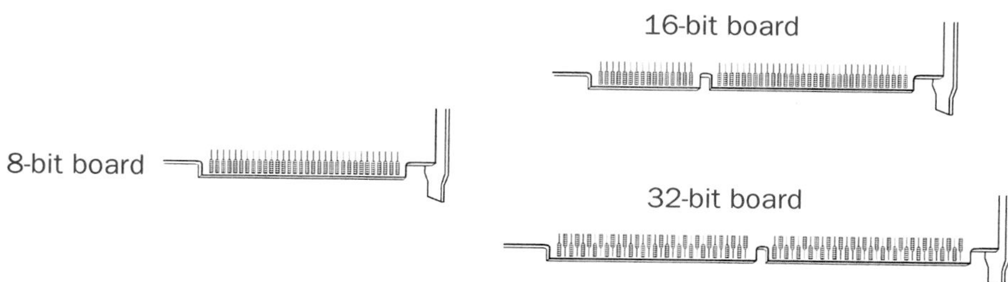

Use this illustration to determine your board type.

What Is DMA?

TIP 776

DMA is an abbreviation for direct memory access. The DMA controller is a computer chip with the ability to move data from a device to a specific location in memory or from memory to a device without using the CPU. In early computers, if the operating system needed to store information to or read information from disk, the CPU had to move the information to or from memory itself, a time-consuming operation. When the CPU was overseeing this data transfer, it could not perform other operations, such as executing programs. Essentially, everything came to a halt until the transfer was completed. A DMA chip can move information between memory and a device without the CPU's intervention. Most disk input and output, for example, occurs via DMA. In general, the BIOS tells the DMA controller the operation to perform and then continues processing, allowing the CPU to perform other tasks. When the DMA transfer is complete, the DMA controller interrupts the CPU, telling it that the operation is complete. Because the CPU was free to work on other tasks during the data transfer, performance speed is increased.

A DMA channel is a bus (or set of wires) used by the DMA controller to transfer data between the I/O device and memory. The 286 and higher computers provide seven DMA channels as described in Table 776.

Table 776. AT-Based Computer DMA Channel Use

DMA Channel	Use
0	Available for 8-bit transfers
1	Available for 8-bit transfers
2	Floppy disk controller
3	Available for 8-bit transfers
4	Cascade for DMA channels 0 to 3
5	Available for 16-bit transfers
6	Available for 16-bit transfers

As you can see, DMA channel 4 provides cascading for channels 0 to 3. Each DMA controller supports four channels. The 8-bit controller for channels 0 to 3 feeds into channel 4 of the 16-bit controller. This process is called cascading. When you set up a hardware device, you may have to specify a DMA channel. Use the channel use specified in Table 776 as your guide.

Understanding the Flags Register

Almost all of the DEBUG script files presented in this book use assembly language instructions to create the command files. Many of the commands use instructions such as JG or JL that tell the PC to jump to a specific instruction if the result of a comparison is greater than (JG) or less than (JL) than a specified value. Each time the PC executes an instruction, the PC places specific information about the machine's state in a special storage location called the flags register. As shown in the following illustration, different bit settings within the flags register indicate the occurrence of specific events:

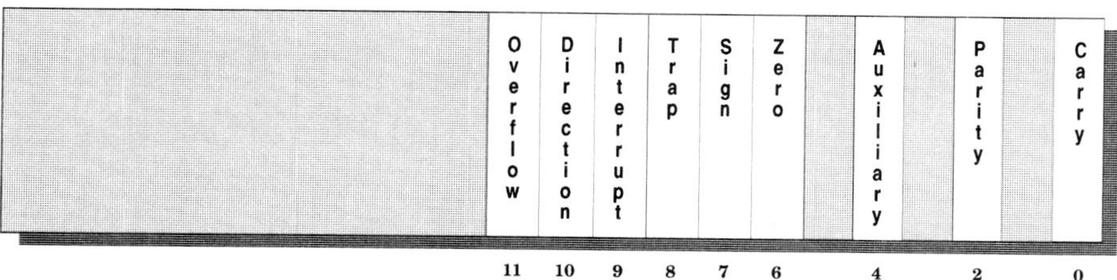

Table 777 briefly describes each flag.

When you create DEBUG script files, you can use the flags register to determine whether a specific event has occurred and, if so, to branch to the corresponding set of instructions.

Table 777. Meaning of Each Flag in the Flags Register

Flag	Meaning If Set
Carry	Indicates that the previous arithmetic operation resulted in an arithmetic carry
Parity	Indicates that the previous arithmetic operation resulted in an even number of bits
Auxiliary Carry	Indicates that an adjustment is required following a BCD arithmetic operation
Zero	Indicates that the previous arithmetic operation had a result of zero
Trap	Used for trapping in a debugger
Interrupt	Enables and disables maskable interrupts
Direction	Controls the direction of string operations such as STOS
Overflow	Indicates that the previous arithmetic operation resulted in an arithmetic overflow

What Is the Clock$ Device?

If you issue the MEM /DEBUG command, you will see a device driver for the CLOCK$ device. The CLOCK$ driver is one of the device drivers DOS installs when it loads IO.SYS during system startup. DOS uses the CLOCK$ driver to set file date and time stamps and to control the current system date and time. If you are writing programs, you can open the CLOCK$ driver and read from it a 6-byte entry that contains the days, hours, minutes, and seconds since January 1, 1980.

Understanding Chip Types

If you examine the chips connected to your PC's motherboard, you may see three different types of chips. The most common chip uses two rows of pins called a dual in-line package (or DIP). If you examine the chip closely, you may find that the pins are numbered. If so, insert the chip so that the pin numbers match the chip receptacle numbers. If the pins are not numbered, use the documentation that accompanies the chip to note the orientation of the chip's notch relative to the board.

The second chip type (and the type normally used by a 386 or 486 processor) is called a pin grid array (or PGA). A PGA is normally square, with pins on all four edges. When you insert the chip, match pin numbers or the alignment of the chip's notched corner.

The third type of chip, a leadless chip carrier (or LCC), does not have visible pins. To insert an LCC chip, you treat the chip much like a piece of a jigsaw puzzle, aligning and inserting the entire chip into a socket. The common chip types are shown here:

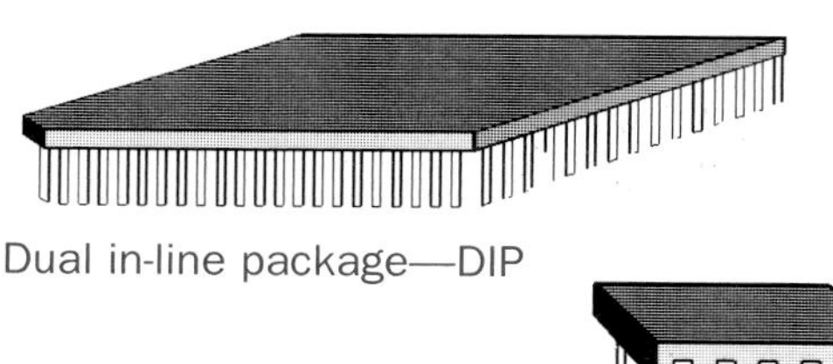

Dual in-line package—DIP

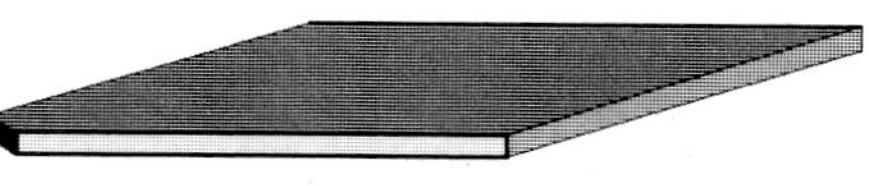

Leadless chip carrier—LCC

Pin grid array—PGA

Removing a Chip

TIP 780

Tip 779 presents the different types of chips you may encounter when you open your computer's chassis. If you upgrade your CPU type or purchase math coprocessor or other chips, you may have to remove an exiting chip before you can insert the new chip. One of the best $20 purchases you can make is to buy a computer tool set from your computer dealer. The tool set should contain a chip extractor similar to the one shown here. By sliding the extractor under both ends of the chip, you should be able to gently remove the chip from the socket by first extracting one end and then the other.

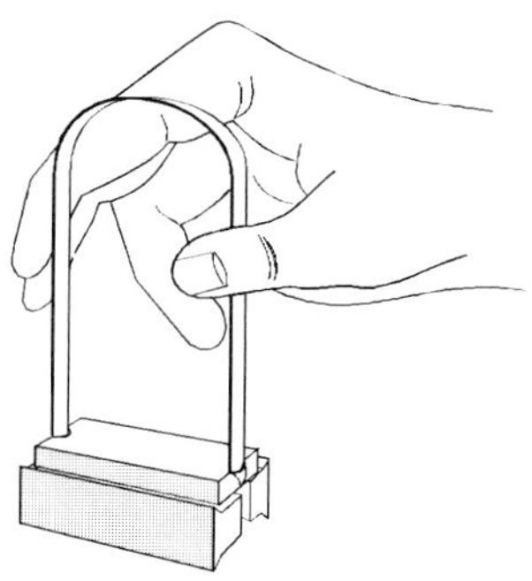

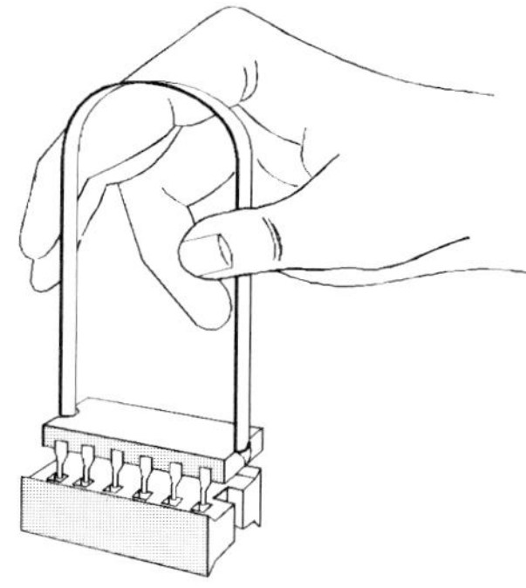

In addition to the chip extractor, you might consider purchasing an inexpensive screw driver and bend its top at a 90 degree angle as shown in the previous illustration. By sliding the screw driver tip between the chip and its mounting, you should be able to loosen even the most difficult chips.

Be Aware of Bent Pins When You Insert Chips

Tip 779 explains how to insert different types of chips into their sockets. Each of the pins on a chip is used to send or receive a specific electronic signal. When you insert a chip, you need to make sure each pin actually goes into its socket. One of the most common problems users experience when inserting chips is a bent pin, illustrated here:

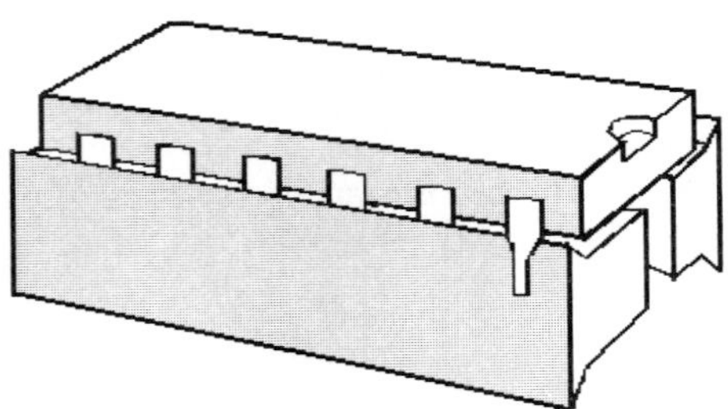

If a chip has a bent pin, the chip will not work. Depending on the chip's function and the pin's use, the PC may immediately detect the error, or the PC may fail intermittently at a later time. When you insert chips, examine the chip closely to ensure that no pins are bent. If a pin is bent, gently remove the chip as discussed in Tip 780. Next, carefully straighten the pin by using a small screwdriver. Be very careful not to break the pin. Should the pin break, you must replace the chip.

A First Look Inside Your Computer's Chassis

As a rule, new users should leave their computer's chassis closed. Opening the chassis before you feel comfortable with the computer's normal operation will only result in more intimidation. Most of your computer's boards should have been previously installed by your computer's manufacturer. If a board needs to be installed, have an experienced user assist you.

When you are ready to open your computer's chassis, follow these steps. First, unplug the chassis. Next, unscrew the chassis lid from your computer and gently slide the cover off the chassis as shown here:

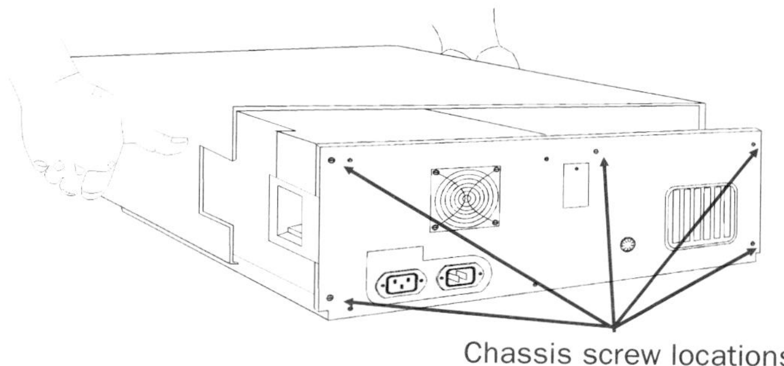

As you slide the cover off of your chassis, make sure the lid does not catch on any of the computer's internal cables. When you remove the cover, your system's components should look similar to those shown in the next illustration. Several of the Tips presented in this book take a close look at the various system components.

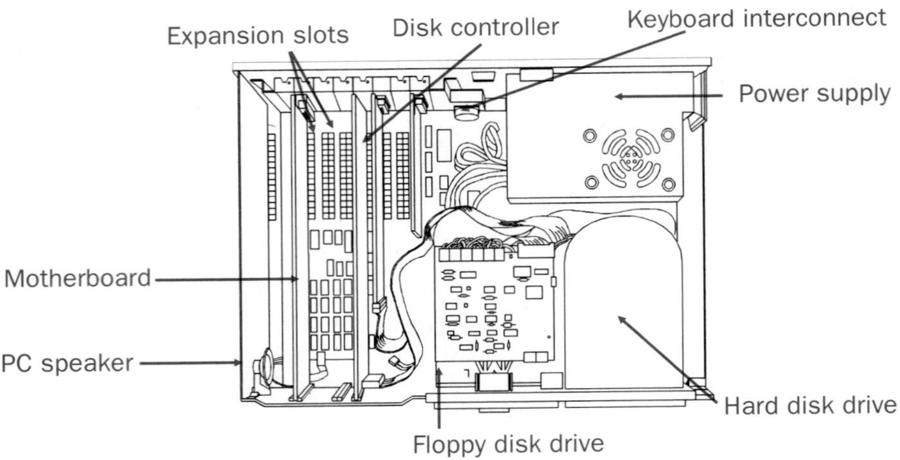

A Closer Look at Your Computer's Motherboard

Tip 782 presents an overview of your computer's internal system components. At the bottom of your chassis, beneath your disk drives, is a large circuit board, called the motherboard, that contains the CPU, expansion slots, memory, and other various chips. Although the layout of chips on your motherboard may differ, most motherboards will contain the components shown here:

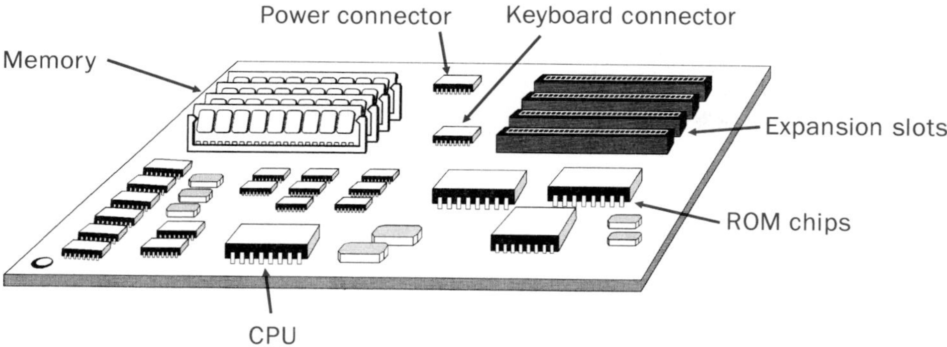

If your computer's chassis is open, use the preceding diagram to identify the components.

Understanding RS-232C Serial Cables

As Tip 764 discusses, serial devices can connect to a 9-pin or 25-pin connector. To help you better understand the serial interface, the pin assignments used for various RS-232C serial connections are illustrated here:

Pin,	Function
1	Not used
2	Transmit data
3	Receive data
4	Request to send
5	Clear to send
6	Data set ready
7	Ground
8	Carrier detect
9	Transmit clock +
10	Not used
11	Transmit clock -
12	Not used
13	Not used
14	Not used
15	Not used
16	Not used
17	Not used
18	Receive clock +
19	Not used
20	Data terminal ready
21	Not used
22	Ring indicator
23	Not used
24	Not used
25	Receive clock

1 2 3 4 5
6 7 8 9

Pin,	Function
1	Carrier detect
2	Receive data
3	Transmit data
4	Data terminal ready
5	Ground
6	Data set ready
7	Request to send
8	Clear to send
9	Ring indicator

If you have an older hardware device, the device may require specific signals on different pins. Using the preceding illustration, you can determine the custom cable required. The documentation that accompanies your hardware device should specify its pin use.

Understanding the Function of an Uninterruptable Power Supply

As Tip 771 explains, you should protect your computer equipment by plugging it into a surge suppressor. A surge suppressor protects your equipment from potentially fatal power surges. A surge suppressor, however, does not prevent loss of power. To prevent power loss, you must plug your computer into an uninterruptable power supply, or UPS. A UPS is much more expensive than a surge suppressor, typically costing several hundred dollars. Should a power loss occur, the UPS will normally provide up to 15 minutes of power. The goal of a UPS is to give you time to end your programs in an orderly manner so you don't lose files or data. Because of their cost, most users will not purchase a UPS. However, if you have a network server that contains information shared by several users, plugging the server into a UPS is a smart and cost-justifiable way to protect your data.

Understanding the SCSI Interface

Tip 764 discusses the parallel and serial ports that let you attach various devices to your computer. Over the past few years, a new device interface, the SCSI (pronounced SCUZZY), is becoming a convenient way to connect to the computer external devices that require high speed. The SCSI uses 50 wires. A SCSI port on the back of the PC is shown here:

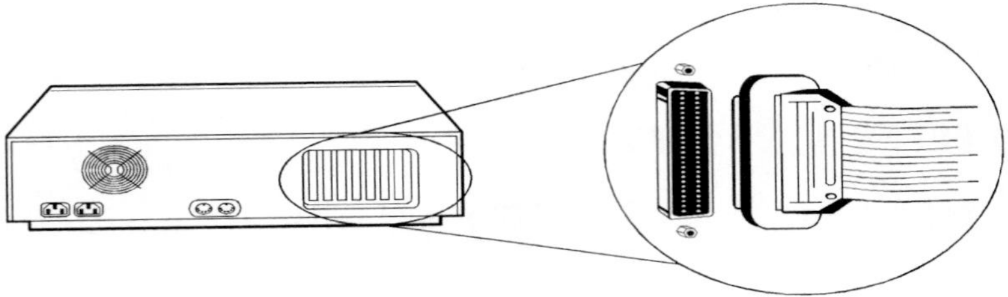

Devices commonly connected to the SCSI port include external hard disks, CD-ROM devices, scanners, and tape drivers. The SCSI is unique from other ports in that it lets you connect up to seven devices to the port. Actually, one device connects to the port, and the second device connects to the first. Thus, your CD-ROM can connect to your scanner, which connects to your external hard disk, which in turn connects to the SCSI port.

Understanding Start and Stop Bits

If you use a modem to perform serial communication, you have undoubtedly encountered the terms start and stop bits. Tip 86 explains, when two serial devices communicate, they must agree on the speed they will use as well as other parameters. Serial communication is often called asynchronous communication because the two devices that communicate don't use a common clock that coordinates the intervals at which the data is sent and received. Thus, the receiver monitors the line waiting for data. The receiving device doesn't know when data may arrive. When no information is being sent, the line maintains a constant state (either a 1 or a 0). The start bit causes a change in the line's state, to tell the receiver, "Here comes some data." When the receiver gets the start bit, it starts sampling the line at the interval corresponding to the baud rate to determine each data bit's value. The stop bit simply provides the receiving device with a chance to catch up in preparation for the next data's start bit. The number of stop bits may be 1, 1.5, or 2.

Just as with baud rates and parity, the sending and receiving devices must agree on the number of stop bits. The following illustration of a data packet surrounded by start, parity, and stopy bits shows how a data packet might appear on the line:

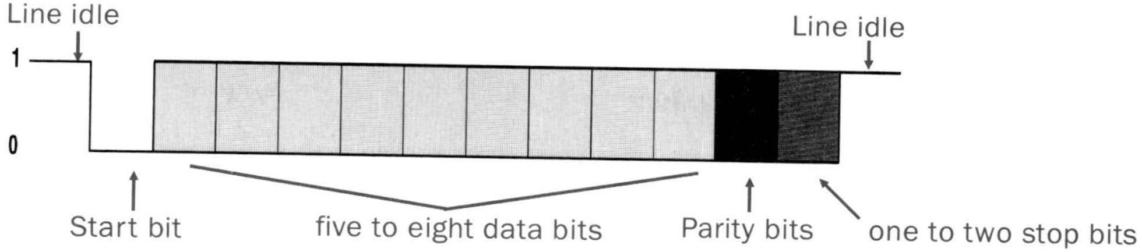

What Type of Processor Do I Have?

Tip 60 describes the differences among various processor types. As you create batch files, you can take advantage of different program capabilities if you know the current processor type. The following DEBUG script file, CPU_TYPE.SCR, creates a command file named CPU_TYPE.COM that returns the exit status value listed in Table 788 that corresponds to the current processor type:

CPU_TYPE.SCR

```
N CPU_TYPE.COM        <ENTER>
A 100                 <ENTER>
PUSHF                 <ENTER>
MOV AX,0              <ENTER>
PUSH AX               <ENTER>
POPF                  <ENTER>
PUSHF                 <ENTER>
POP AX                <ENTER>
CMP AH,F0             <ENTER>
JNZ 114               <ENTER>
NOP                   <ENTER>
NOP                   <ENTER>
MOV AL,00             <ENTER>
JMP 14A               <ENTER>
NOP                   <ENTER>
MOV AX,F000           <ENTER>
```

```
PUSH AX                   <ENTER>
POPF                      <ENTER>
PUSHF                     <ENTER>
POP AX                    <ENTER>
CMP AH,0                  <ENTER>
JNZ 127                   <ENTER>
NOP                       <ENTER>
NOP                       <ENTER>
MOV AL,2                  <ENTER>
JMP 14A                   <ENTER>
NOP                       <ENTER>
DB 0F,20,C0               <ENTER>
DB 66,8B,D8               <ENTER>
DB 66,35,00,00,00,20      <ENTER>
DB 0F,22,C0               <ENTER>
DB 0F,20,C0               <ENTER>
DB 66,3B,C3               <ENTER>
DB 75,07                  <ENTER>
DB 90,90                  <ENTER>
DB B0,03                  <ENTER>
DB EB,06                  <ENTER>
DB 90                     <ENTER>
DB 0F,22,C3               <ENTER>
MOV AL,4                  <ENTER>
POPF                      <ENTER>
MOV AH,4C                 <ENTER>
INT 21                    <ENTER>
                          <ENTER>
R CX                      <ENTER>
4F                        <ENTER>
W                         <ENTER>
Q                         <ENTER>
```

Use DEBUG as follows to create the command file CPU_TYPE.COM:

```
C:\> DEBUG < CPU_TYPE.SCR <ENTER>
```

Table 788. Exit Status Values Returned by CPU_TYPE.COM

Exit Status	CPU Type
0	8088
1	80186
2	80286
3	80386
4	80486

Understanding Data Bits

Serial communication occurs on a single wire, one bit at a time. When a device sends information, it does so using a group of bits typically called a packet. This data packet contains one start bit (see Tip 787), several data bits, a parity bit (see Tip 774), and normally, 1 or 2 stop bits (see Tip 787). The two communicating devices must agree on the number of data bits sent per packet. The number typically ranges from 5 to 8. The following illustration shows a complete data packet:

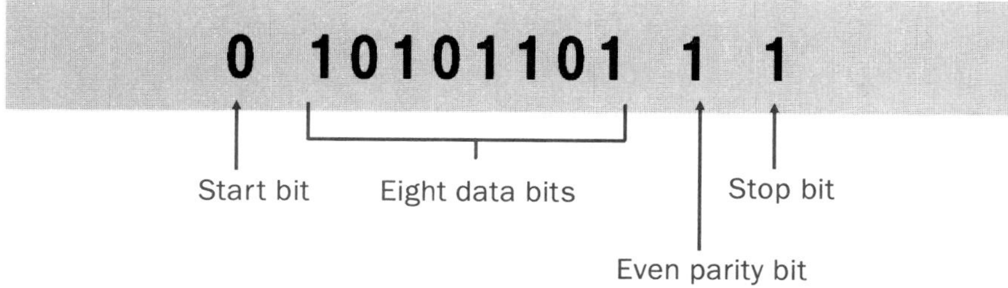

What Is Change-Line Support?

When you use removable media, such as a floppy disk, you are free to remove or exchange the media almost at any time. To help DOS detect such media changes, many drives set a status signal when the media may possibly have been changed. In the case of a floppy drive, the change-line signal would occur if you unlatched and latched the drive. Not all floppy drives support change-line signaling. The following DEBUG script file, CHGLINE.SCR, creates the command file CHGLINE.COM that returns the exit status value 1 if the current drive supports change-line signaling and returns 0 otherwise:

CHGLINE.SCR

```
N CHGLINE.COM.     <ENTER>
A 100              <ENTER>
MOV AH,19          <ENTER>
INT 21             <ENTER>
MOV AH,15          <ENTER>
MOV DL,AL          <ENTER>
INT 13             <ENTER>
AND AX,200         <ENTER>
JZ 115             <ENTER>
MOV AL,1           <ENTER>
JMP 115            <ENTER>
MOV AL,0           <ENTER>
MOV AH,4C          <ENTER>
INT 21             <ENTER>
                   <ENTER>
R CX               <ENTER>
19                 <ENTER>
W                  <ENTER>
Q                  <ENTER>
```

Use DEBUG as follows to create the command file CHGLINE.COM:

```
C:\> DEBUG < CHGLINE.SCR <ENTER>
```

The following DEBUG commands illustrate how you might test drive A for change-line support:

```
@ECHO OFF
A:
```

```
CHGLINE
IF ERRORLEVEL 1 ECHO change line supported
IF NOT ERRORLEVEL 1 ECHO no change line support
```

If your drive does not provide change-line support, use the utility command DISKFLSH.COM presented in Tip 356 to flush all disk buffers before you change floppy disks.

What Is a Null Modem Cable?

Tip 784 describes the pins used by serial ports. When serial devices communicate, they send and receive messages over a single wire. Several third-party software programs let you copy files between computers by connecting their serial ports with a null modem cable.

Examine the serial port pins shown here:

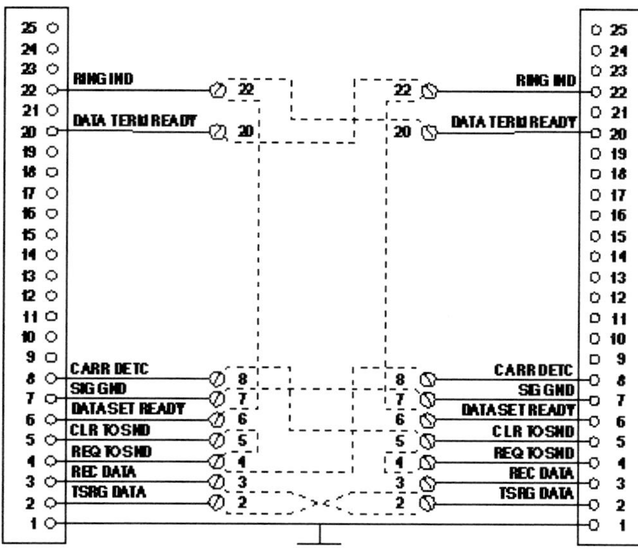

In this illustration, pin 2 is used to transmit the data that pin 3 is used to receive. A null modem cable is simply a cable that at one end switches pins 2 and 3, thus allowing information sent from one computer on pin 2 to arrive at the receiving computer on pin 3.

You need to use a null modem cable only when you want to connect two computers through their serial ports.

TIP 792

A Closer Look at UARTs

Tip 773 discusses the UART (universal asynchronous receiver/transmitter) in detail. The UART oversees the PC's serial communication. Like most PC components, the UART has evolved since the original 8450 chip in the IBM PC. The PC AT used a faster 16450 chip. Today, a far superior 16550 chip is most common. Unlike older UARTs, which buffered 1 byte of information at a time, the 16550 can hold up to 16 bytes. Thus, a program can fill the UART buffer and then perform other tasks. The UART will send each of the buffered bytes on its own. At the receiving end, the UART can buffer up to 16 incoming characters. In short, this character buffering capability lets the UART perform a lot of data communications work on its own. If you require high-speed communication, or if you are using serial communications in a multitasking environment such as Windows, the 16550 will give you better performance. Upgrading to the 16550 is as easy as exchanging boards. To determine your UART type, examine your serial card for the number 8450, 16450, or 16550.

What Is the Multimedia PC?

Multimedia will be the driving force behind the next PC revolution. The multimedia PC combines text, sound, and video to create an information-presentation system. Recently, many advertisements for hardware and software products claim compatibility with the multimedia PC. The following illustration shows the hardware components of the multimedia PC used for products that run in such a configuration:

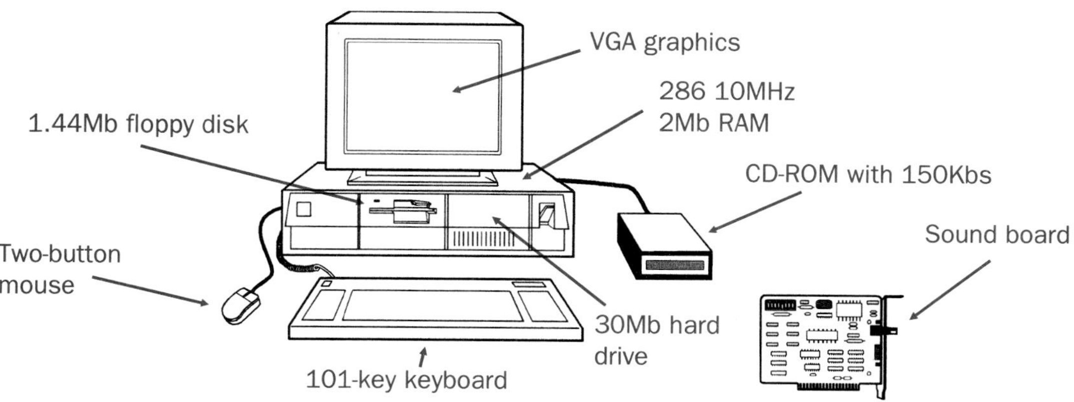

If you are upgrading components in preparation for multimedia, use the values listed in the preceding illustration as the minimum specifications.

How Much Power Does Your PC Have Left?

Tip 807 discusses the power supply in detail. Depending on their type, power supplies generally produce 65 to 200 watts. If you are upgrading your system, you need to take into account the number of watts you really need. Table 794 lists common hardware devices and their power requirements.

If you are using over 80 percent of your power supply's capacity, you should consider an upgrade. As Tip 970 shows, replacing a power supply is quite easy.

Table 794. Power Requirements of Commonly Used Devices

Device	Power Requirement
Motherboard	20 to 35 watts
Hard drive (5 1/4 inch)	15 to 30 watts
Hard drive (3 1/2 inch)	5 to 15 watts
Floppy drive (5 1/4 inch)	5 to 15 watts
Floppy drive (3 1/2 inch)	5 watts
CD-ROM	20 to 20 watts
Expansion board (short card)	5 watts
Expansion board (full size)	10 to 15 watts
Memory	5 watts per Mb

Slots Full? Don't Sacrifice the Video Board

Depending on your PC type, you may have a combination of 8-, 16-, and 32-bit expansion slots. When your expansion slots are full, someone may move your video board from a 16-bit to an 8-bit slot (many video boards have switches or jumpers that control this bus connection). If your video board is in an 8-bit slot but supports a 16-bit interface, move it to a 16-bit slot if at all possible. By using the 16-bit slot, you double the amount of information that can be sent to your video card at one time, which reduces the number of bus cycles that the video board requires.

What Makes EISA and MCA Buses Better?

As Tip 57 explains, a bus is a collection of wires used to send information. The EISA bus is the 32-bit bus found in 386 and 486 PCs and compatibles. The MCA bus is the 32-bit microchannel architecture bus found in IBM's PS/2 computers. Because these two buses are 32-bit buses, they can send much more information in a shorter period of time. In addition, these two bus types support bus mastering, which eliminates the processor's need to manage bus operations. In the past, when the processor needed to send information to, or get information from, a device, the processor oversaw the transfer of information on the bus. Depending on the speed of the device, the processor sometimes spent a considerable amount of time waiting for a response. The EISA and MCA buses transfer the bus management responsibilities from the processor to the desired hardware board. This technique, called bus mastering, gives the board temporary control of the bus, allowing the processor to continue with its own task. When the data transfer is complete, the board relinquishes control of the bus.

What's a Turbo Board?

If you are using a computer with an older processor, you have three ways to upgrade. First, you can simply purchase a new system. With the constant decreases in price, this solution is becoming quite popular. Second, you can replace your system motherboard. With this solution, you don't have to purchase new disk drives and so on. However, unless you are really proficient with the PC, you will want someone else to perform the upgrade for you. The third upgrade technique is to add a turbo board to your system. A turbo board is a board that you insert in an expansion slot and that either replaces or supplements your existing processor. In many cases, you will remove your existing CPU and plug into its slot a cable to the turbo board as shown here:

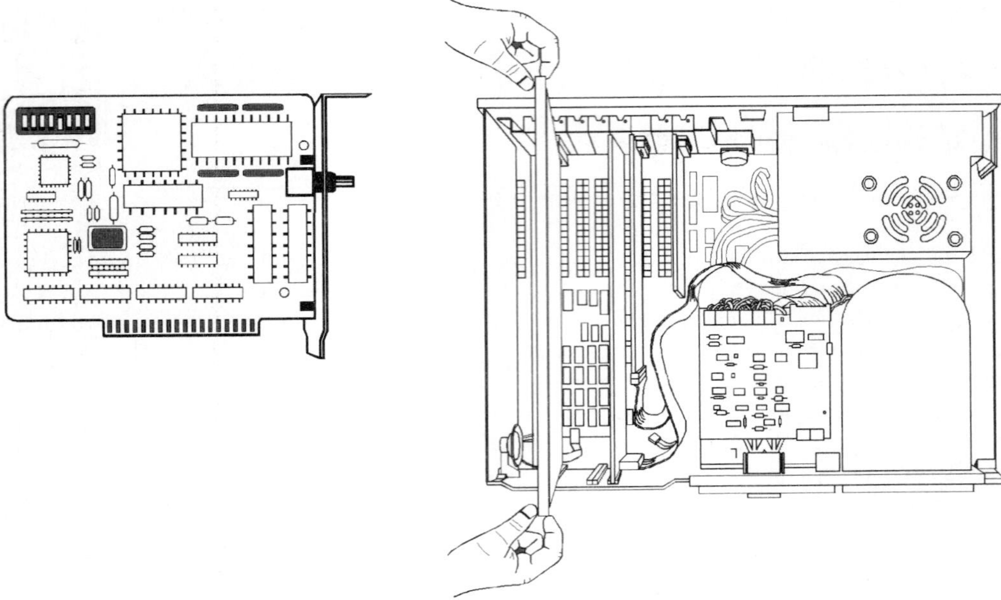

For the novice user, turbo boards provide a relatively easy way to upgrade the processor. Unfortunately, they have several drawbacks. First, unless it provides its own system board memory, the turbo board must use the system board memory on your motherboard that was originally installed for your slower processor. If the turbo board has its own memory, its cost increases, which makes it about as expensive as a motherboard upgrade. For the same money, you will be happier with a motherboard upgrade.

Understanding Video Frequencies

To produce an image on your screen, the monitor illuminates individual dots on the screen called pixels. The monitor has only a fixed amount of time to spend with each pixel to illuminate each dot. The monitor begins the pixel display at the upper-left corner of the screen. The monitor's electron gun quickly scans each row of the monitor from left to right. When the beam reaches the right edge of the screen, the gun briefly turns off its beam, moves down one line, and returns to the left edge of

the screen to restart the pixel illumination process. The process of moving the beam back to the screen's left edge is called horizontal retracing. When the beam reaches the bottom-right corner of the screen, the gun again turns off the beam and moves the beam back to the upper-left corner, a process called vertical retracing. The following illustration shows the horizontal and vertical retrace operations:

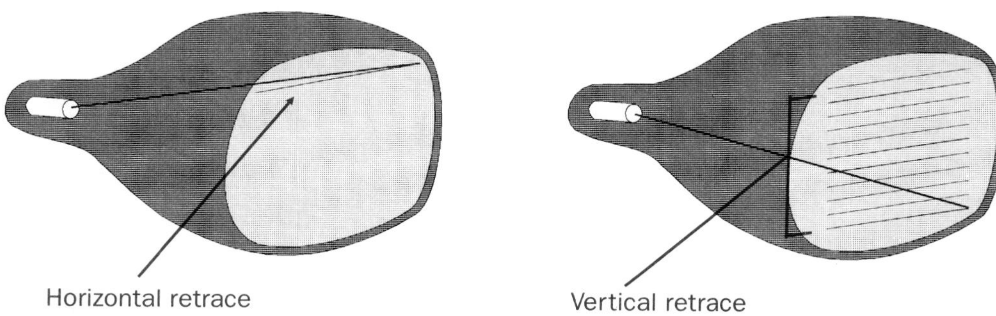

To prevent screen flicker, the monitor refreshes your screen 60 or more times per second. Unfortunately, as screen resolution increases, it becomes more difficult for the monitor to successfully illuminate every pixel within the update interval. As Tip 799 shows, inexpensive monitors have turned to a technique called interlacing to display very-high-resolution images. When you shop for a monitor, be sure that the monitor supports refresh frequencies sufficient for the picture quality you desire.

Understanding Video Interlacing

When high resolution is used, such as in the XGA's 1,024-by-768 mode, it becomes impossible for the monitor to draw the screen image 60 times per second. Thus, some interlaced monitors draw the screen image in two passes. The first pass refreshes the even-numbered lines, and the second pass refreshes the odd-numbered lines. Using interlacing, the monitor can simulate more screen updates. Because of the high resolution, the lines are so close together that, to the eye, the every-other-line refreshing is normally hard to detect. However, some individual's eyes are more sensitive to such screen updates. If screen resolution and sharpness is a high priority, you will want to purchase a noninterlaced monitor. However, the noninterlaced monitor will be more expensive. If you are shopping, place a

noninterlaced and an interlaced monitor side by side and decide whether or not you find the interlaced monitor distracting.

TIP 800 Understanding How Your Monitor Works

Your screen displays text or graphics by illuminating small picture elements, or pixels. To accomplish this, the monitor uses an electron gun that illuminates small phosophorus regions on your screen. Once illuminated, a phosphor glows for a brief period of time. To continually appear on your screen, the phosphors must be repeatedly refreshed. The following illustration shows how a typical monitor works:

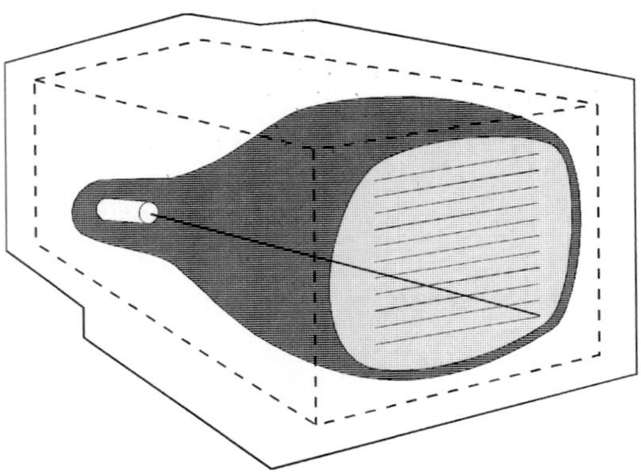

To produce different colors, different phosphor types are used that, when illuminated, appear in different colors. To illuminate these different phosphor types, the monitor actually use three different electron beams: one for each of the colors red, green, and blue. An RGB monitor is a monitor that uses red, green, and blue to produce pixel colors. The combination of these three phosphors—red, green, and blue—on your screen, when illuminated, determines the pixel color. The number of pixels determines the sharpness of an image; to increase image sharpness, the number of pixels must be increased. Tip 798 discusses the problem of refreshing a large number of pixels in the short period of time required to prevent screen flicker.

Understanding Trinitron Monitors

As Tip 798 discusses, most color monitors use three electron guns (one each for red, green, and blue). Normally, these three guns are arranged in a triangle. A Trinitron monitor, however, arranges the electron guns in a straight line. Unlike standard monitors, whose resolution is fixed by the monitor's dot pitch (see Tip 802), the Trinitron monitor uses vertical strips to separate similar colors. The spacing between the strips dictates the screen's sharpness. When you are shopping for a monitor, do not purchase the monitor until you have placed it side by side with the most expensive monitor available and run the same program on each to compare picture quality.

Understanding the Monitor's Dot Pitch

As Tip 798 explains, your monitor typically contains sets of three phosphor types for the colors red, green, and blue. As shown here, the monitor's dot pitch is the distance between two successive phosphors of the same color:

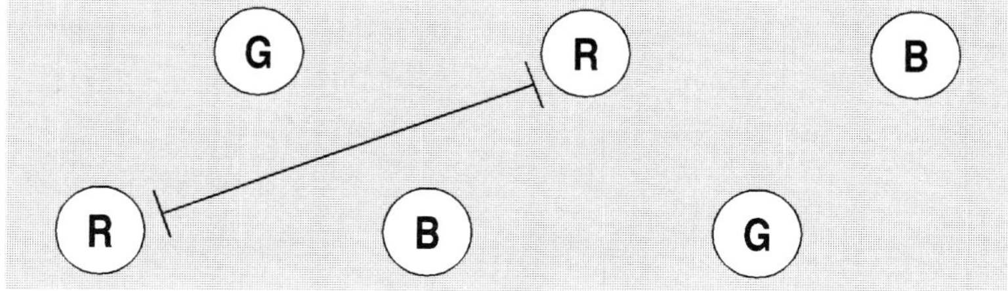

The lower a monitor's dot-pitch value, the sharper the image that appears on the screen.

More 386 Types

As Tip 230 explains, the 386SX is a 386 processor that uses a 16-bit bus. Likewise, a 386DX is a 386 processor that uses a 32-bit bus. If you look closely at computer advertisements, you may see two new chip names: the 386SL and the 386SLC. The 386SL is a low-power 386SX processor designed for battery-powered lap-top computers where power consumption is a premium concern. The chip contains several enhancements that essentially let it hibernate when not in use in order to conserve power. The 386SLC adds an 8K cache to the 386SL chip and also boosts the system speed. In fact, the 386SLC processor can perform nearly as well as a 33MHz 386DX.

Understanding Interrupt Requests (IRQs)

When you add a new hardware board to your system, you normally have to configure the board's interrupt request (IRQ) line. Here's what an IRQ is. Each of your hardware boards performs a specific task, such as controlling the disk, printer, or mouse. When the board has completed its processing, it needs a way to tell the CPU that the task is done. Interrupt request lines (or channels) are wires that run from the expansion slots to an interrupt controller. Each board in your system is assigned a unique interrupt request line. When a board needs to interrupt the processor, the board continually sends a signal down the interrupt request line until the interrupt is acknowledged. Table 804a lists the IRQ line uses for the 8088. Table 804b lists the IRQ line uses for 286 and higher computers.

Table 804a. IRQ Line Use in 8088 Computers

IRQ	Device
0	Timer
1	Keyboard
2	Cascade
3	COM2
4	COM1
5	Hard disk controller
6	Floppy disk controller
7	LPT1
NMI	Parity check

Table 804b. IRQ Line Use in 286 and Higher Computers

IRQ	Device
0	Timer
1	Keyboard
2	Cascaded
3	COM2
4	COM1
5	LPT2
6	Floppy disk controller
7	LPT1
8	Real-time clock
9	PC network
10	Available
11	Available
12	PS/2 mouse
13	Math coprocessor
14	Hard disk controller
15	Available
NMI	Parity

Understanding Cascaded IRQ's

As Tip 804 describes, hardware devices use IRQs to inform the CPU that they have completed a task. The 8088 computer supports 8 IRQs, and the 286 and higher computers support 15. If you look at IRQ2 in Table 804a, you'll find the word *cascade.* To provide support for 15 interrupt requests, the 286 provides two interrupt controller chips (Intel 8259A). If you examine IRQ2 in Table 804b, you will find that it contains the word *cascaded.* When IRQ2 is active, it tells the PC that one of the IRQ lines from 8 through 15 is active. In other words, IRQ line 2 serves a unique function, selecting IRQ lines 0 through 7 when it is inactive and 8 through 15 when active.

Your system may include a board that has been set to IRQ2. For compatibility, the line for IRQ9 has been mapped to the slot position previously used by IRQ2. Thus, if a board is set to IRQ2, it actually uses the line for IRQ9, essentially transparently as far as the user is concerned.

Assigning IRQ Values

When you install a new hardware device, you may need to assign the board's IRQ settings. Tip 804 lists the IRQ settings for 8088 and 80286 and higher computers. If the board appears in Table 804a or 804b, use the IRQ value specified. If the board is not listed, you will have to determine an available IRQ line. It's important to note that IRQ lines 0 through 7 correspond to 8-bit boards, and lines 8 through 15 correspond to 16-bit boards. You cannot, therefore, assign one of the IRQ values from 8 through 15 to an 8-bit card.

What Do Power Supplies Really Do?

If you look inside your PC's chassis, the largest device you will find is the power supply. The power supply takes power from your wall outlet and then distributes the correct amount from your computer's hardware boards. The power at your wall outlet uses alternating current (AC) at 110 to 120 volts. Alternating current reverses direction at fixed intervals. The following illustration shows how AC current would appear on an electrician's scope:

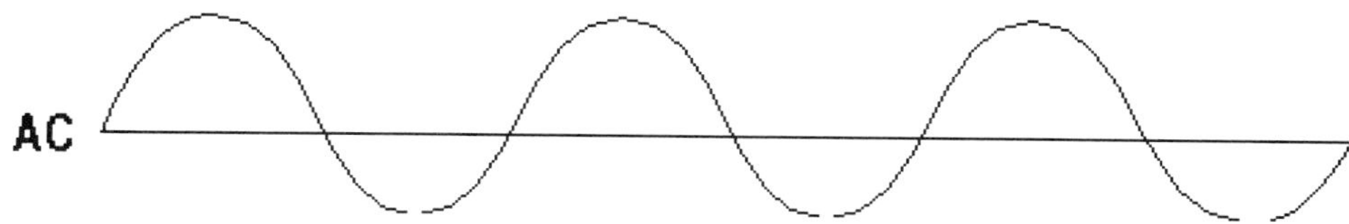

Within the PC however, hardware boards use direct current (DC), which travels in only one direction. The following illustration shows how direct current would appear on a scope:

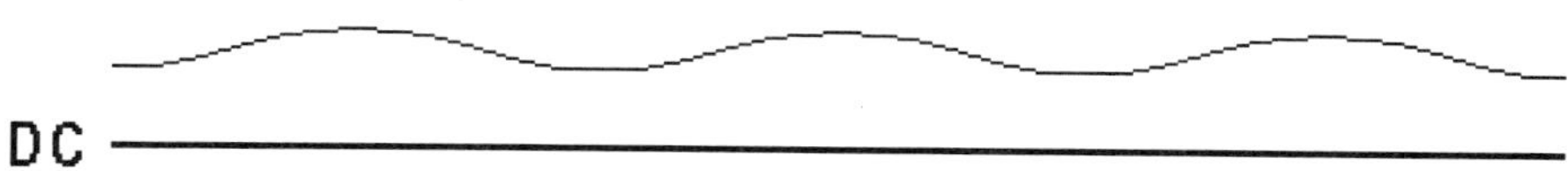

Your power supply consists of three primary components: A transformer that converts the line voltage to match that required by the PC's power supply, a rectifier that converts the AC voltage to DC, and a filter that smooths the signal, which can then be distributed to your hardware devices.

Sound Board Buying Suggestions

Tip 809 discusses sound boards in detail. If you are considering purchasing a sound board, use the following as your buyer's guide:

- Is the sound card compatible not only with your hardware, but with your existing or anticipated software? Typically, for software compatibility, the board should be Sound Blaster or Ad-Lib compatible.
- What is the board's sampling rate? There are three common sampling rates: 11.025KH, 22.05KHz, and 44.1KHz. For multimedia capability, you need a minimum of 22.05KHz. Your stereo plays CDs at 44.1KHz. The higher the sampling rate, the better the quality.
- What is the board's sample size? There are three common sample sizes: 8, 12, and 16 bits. The higher the sample size, the higher the quality.
- Does the board include MIDI support? If you plan to use a MIDI device (see Tip 847), you will need a MIDI port. By purchasing a sound board with a MIDI port, you reduce the number of devices you must buy and install.
- Does the board play in monaural or stereo? A monaural board can play only one sound at a time. Some stereophonic boards can play as many as 20 sounds simultaneously.

What Is a Sound Board?

PCs contain built-in speakers. Many of the tips presented in this book use the speaker to generate a beep. In Tip 74, you create the command file SIREN.COM that uses the speaker to produce a siren-like noise. The PC's speaker can be used to produce a wide range of sounds, including music. However, if you will be using your PC for multimedia, you will want to install a sound card. A sound card is a hardware board you install in your system that can produce high-quality, even stereophonic, sound. The sound can be generated by a program or played back from a sound file stored on a disk or CD. (A CD storing sound files differs from a CD you play in a stereo.

However, some CD-ROM drives can read both.) As the following illustration shows, a sound card typically contains jacks for external speakers, possibly a microphone jack, a MIDI, stereo inputs, and a CD-ROM audio input:

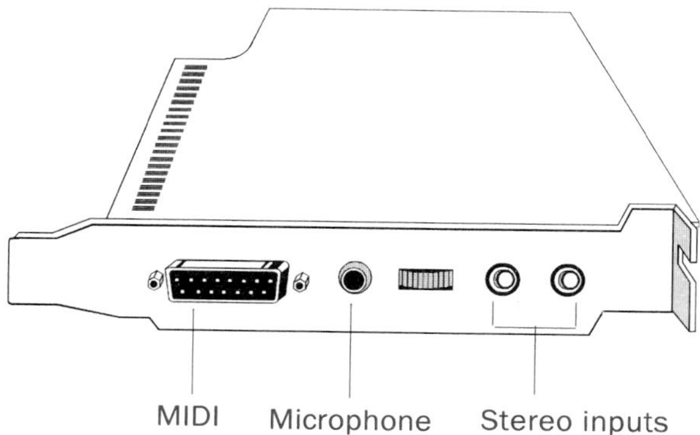

Tip 808 provides a sound board buyer's guide. To ride the coming multimedia wave, you'll want to add a sound board to your PC shopping list.

How Does a Sound Board Work?

As Tip 809 explains, a sound board lets your PC play high-quality sound such as music or special sound effects. As the following illustration shows, sound is normally represented in analog wave form:

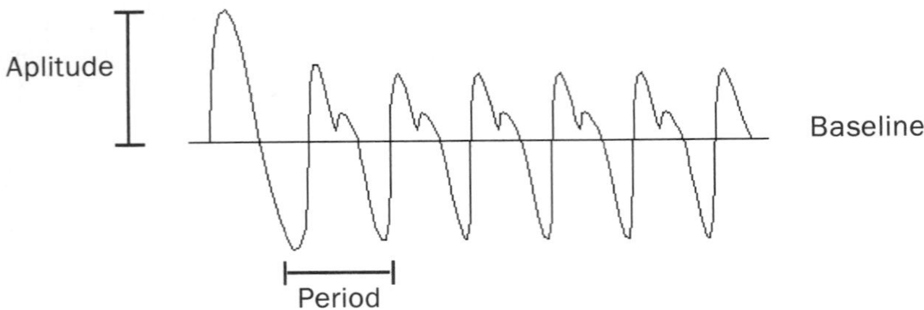

PC's, however, do not use analog signals. Instead, a sound board records sounds and converts them into a digital format that it stores on disk. The sound board contains an analog-to-digital converter that changes the sound's representation into a digital format that the PC can understand and manipulate. To perform this conversion, the analog-to-digital converter examines the sound wave at fixed intervals. This process, called sampling, eventually dictates the sound's quality. The more frequently the sampling occurs, the better the resultant quality.

Eventually, to play back the sound, the sound board converts the signal back to analog format, this time using an analog-to-digital converter, and then sends it to a speaker, amplifier, or other analog device.

How Do Bus Cycles Differ from CPU Clock Cycles?

As Tip 53 shows, the CPU clock cycle establishes your computer's speed. In a 25MHz 386 computer, for example, the CPU's clock cycles 25 million times per second, or every 40 nanoseconds. A bus cycle, on the other hand, specifies the amount of time required for the CPU to request data on the bus and then for the data to arrive. Ideally, the CPU places its request for data on the bus during the first CPU clock cycle, and the data appears on the bus during the second clock cycle. Thus, a bus cycle requires at least two processor clock cycles. Assuming a 25MHz 386 computer, a bus cycle could complete every 80 nanoseconds. Unfortunately, if the data has not been made available from memory, the processor must wait—entering the notorious wait state. To reduce the number of wait states, computers use high-speed memory caches as discussed in Tip 228 and memory organization techniques such as interleaving (see Tip 262).

Understanding Font Cartridges

Font cartridges provide you with one way to add fonts to a laser printer. Font cartridges contain the various fonts in ROM. You insert font cartridges into the front of your printer. The steps you must follow to insert and remove the cartridges vary depending on your printer type.

Normally, you must take your printer off line before adding or removing the cartridge, placing the printer back on line when you are done. When you insert the cartridge, you will eventually hear the cartridge snap into place. As shown here, font cartridges have connectors that attach to the printer:

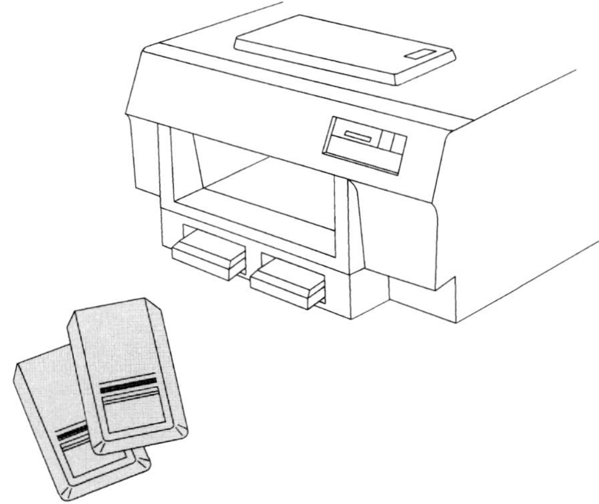

Over time, if you continually insert and remove the cartridges, these connectors may become damaged.

If you are shopping for fonts, you will find that software-based (downloadable) fonts are much more economical than font cartridges.

Identifying the Motherboard's Electrical Components

Several of the tips presented in this book examine various motherboard components, such as the processor, BIOS, and memory. If you take a closer look at your motherboard, you will find several of the electrical components shown here:

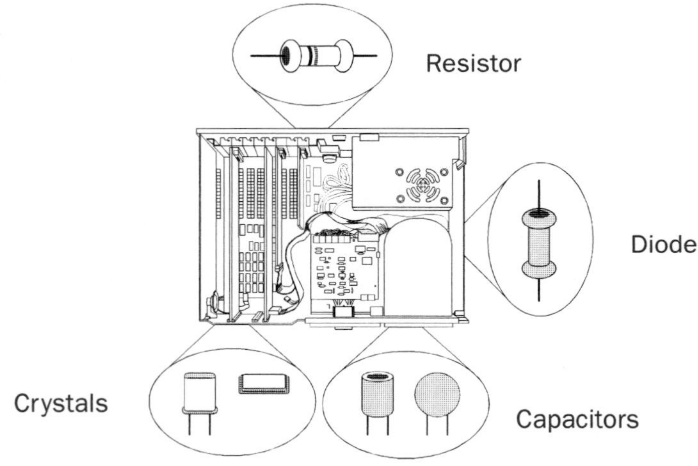

Table 813 briefly describes the function of each electrical component.

Table 813. Functions of Common Motherboard Electrical Components

Component	Function
Crystals	Generate clock signals that occur at fixed intervals
Capacitors	Store energy; normally used to smooth signals between components
Diodes	Normally used as a rectifier to convert AC to DC
Resistors	Used to change a signal's voltage by increasing current resistance

Understanding DX2 Processors

Tip 60 describes the difference between DX and SX chips. Tip 803 describes SL chips, which require less power for laptop and notebook computers. Recently, manufacturers have started to advertise 486DX2 chips. As Tip 53 describes, your computer's clock speed is restricted to the speed at which your devices can operate. In most cases, the processor is capable of running at speeds faster than the computer's clock rate. The 486DX2 processors are designed to exploit this fact. When the processor performs external operations (communicates with other devices), the processor does so using the normal clock speed, such as 25MHZ. Internally, however, the DX2 chip operates at twice (X2) the normal clock speed (50MHz). If you are currently using a 25MHz 486 computer, you can probably purchase a DX2 upgrade, with which you simply replace your existing processor.

How Scanners Scan

Scanners let you convert pages of text, images, or even photographs to a machine-readable form on disk. Scanners work very much like copy machines. The scanner projects a light on the image, which is reflected back to photosensitive cells. The number of cells controls the scanner's resolution. Each cell generates a signal that corresponds to the strength of the reflected image, which, in turn, is stored on disk. To produce color images, scanners must individually reflect the colors red, green, and blue against the image, recording the intensity of the reflected signal. The following illustration shows the two common scanner types: a hand-held scanner that costs a few hundred dollars and a flat-bed scanner that costs up to $2000.

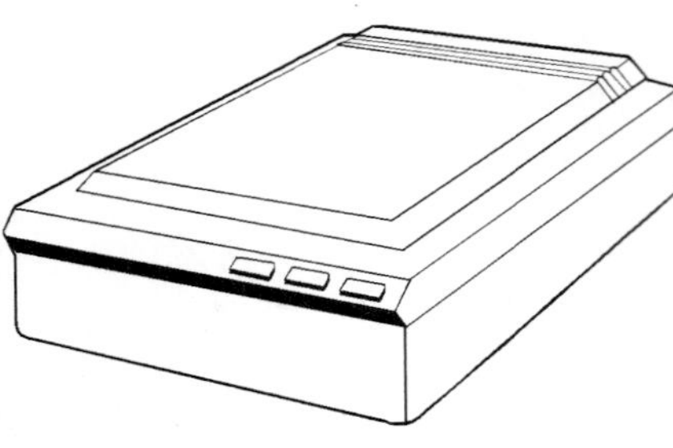

Hand-held scanner

Flatbed scanner

Most scanners come with software programs that let you edit or, in some cases, automatically enhance the scanned image.

Speakers Are a Must When You Purchase a Sound Board

Tip 809 discusses PC sound boards, which let your systems play high-quality audio. Sound boards do not have built-in speakers. When you purchase a sound board, you should buy speakers as well. Otherwise, you will be forced to play back the sound through the PC's speaker, which will defeat your sound board's purpose. When you purchase speakers, pay attention to the speaker's shielding. Speakers contain a fairly large magnet, which, if not shielded, can damage your disks or distort your video display. Although the speakers can be battery powered, if you plan to use the speakers regularly, purchase an AC adapter that lets you plug in the speakers (the cost is less than $10). Also, purchase speakers that contain external volume controls. In most cases, you should be able to find speakers that meet your needs for less than $35. The following illustration shows a PC using external speakers:

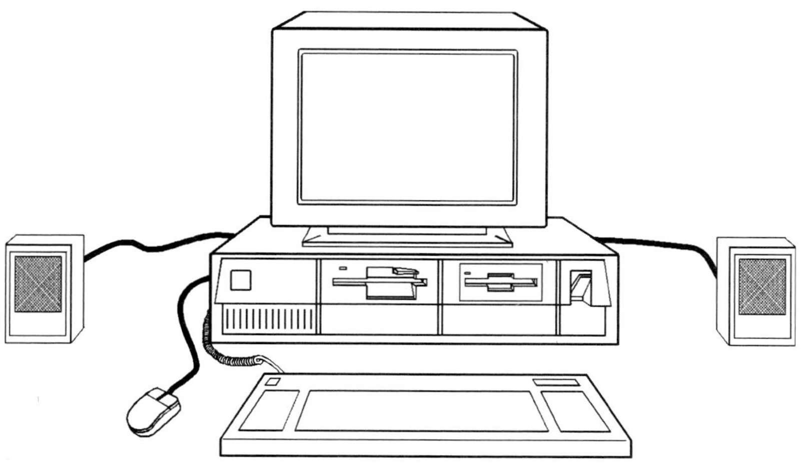

What Is ZIF?

TIP 817

Tip 779 presents several different chip types. When you insert and remove chips, you need to be very careful not to damage one of the chip's pins. To help you perform CPU upgrades, many computer manufacturers now provide zero-insertion force (ZIF) sockets. As shown here, a ZIF socket uses a lever to insert and lock the chip into place or to extract the chip. ZIF sockets are a first step toward user-friendly chip upgrades.

How Do the Processors Really Differ?

Tip 60 discusses several of the differences among various processors, including such fundamental differences as processor speeds, addressing capabilities, and coprocessor requirements. As discussed in Tip 821, transistors are used to control the flow of current. Table 818 lists the number of transistors used in each processor type.

Table 818. Approximate Transistor Counts in Different Processor Types

Processor	Transistor Count
8088	Nearly 30,000
80286	Nearly 130,000
80386	Nearly 250,000
80486	Nearly 1,250,000

How Many COM Ports Can You Really Have?

Beginning with DOS version 3.3, DOS lets you use four serial ports: COM1, COM2, COM3, and COM4. Unfortunately, you can't use all four ports at the same time. If you examine the table of IRQ entries in Tip 804, you will find that the PC does not provide IRQ lines for COM3 and COM4. Instead, COM1 and COM3 share a line, as do COM2 and COM4. This means that you can use either COM1 or COM3, but not both. Likewise, you can use either COM2 or COM4, but not both.

What Is a Bit BLT?

As you examine advertisements for video accelerators, one of the categories you may find compared is bit block transfers, or bit blts. To display an image, the PC represents each piece of the image by bits in memory. The PC performs bit blt operations to move a window from one location to another, to quickly change the cursor's appearance, to drop down a menu, or to quickly scale fonts.

When you compare bit blt operations, convert the speeds specified to a meaningful value such as pixels per second. Many graphics accelerator boards can reach speeds of 20 million pixels per second.

What Is a Transistor?

In the computer's "dinosaur era" (the 1940s and 1950s), tubes were used to store bits of information. In the later 1950s, the vacuum tube was replaced by a solid-state electronic device called a transistor. The transistor is so named because it transfers current across a resistor. The transistor is the work horse of the computer chip. An integrated circuit is a chip containing many transistors. A chip's degree of integration (small, large, very large, and so on) is determined by the number of transistors per chip. Table 821 lists the number of transistors required for various integration types.

Table 821 lists the approximate number of transistors in each common PC processor type.

Table 821. The Number of Transistors per Common Chip Classifications

Integration	Number of Transistors
Medium-scale integration (MSI)	500 or less
Large-scale integration (LSI)	500 to 10,000
Very-large-scale integration (VLSI)	10,000 to 100,000
Ultra-large-scale integration (ULSI)	More than 100,000

Tip 822 Decoding the AMI BIOS Number

If you are using an American Megatrend BIOS, your computer screen will display information about the BIOS each time your system starts, as shown here:

```
Abbb-CCCC-MMDDYY-Kv
```

The letter value that appears for the letter A corresponds to one of the BIOS types listed in Table 822.

The letters *bbb* are replaced with an abbreviation of the motherboard type for which the system was designed. The digits *CCCC* provide a model number. The digits *MMDDYY* indicate the BIOS date. The digit *v* indicates the keyboard BIOS version number. If you have questions regarding BIOS compatibility, use these fields to decode your BIOS type and version number.

Table 822. AMI BIOS Types

Type	BIOS Type
D	BIOS with built-in diagnostics
E	BIOS with built-in setup
S	BIOS with built-in extended setup

Tip 823 Playing Audio CDs with Your PC

CD-ROM discs are similiar in size and appearence to the audio CD discs that you play on your stereo. In fact, both disc types store information by stamping onto the discs a series of 1's and 0's. However, the actual file formats on the discs differ. After all, PC discs are meant to store files in a format

understandable by DOS, and audio discs are meant to be played back by a stereo. However, several software programs exist that can read audio discs. Using these, your PC can play back the audio files, as background music, as you perform other tasks. If you are shopping for a CD-ROM drive, make sure you get a program that lets the drive read audio discs.

A Quick Way to Determine Pin 1

When you attach a cable to a hardware board, you have to pay attention to both the cable and the card to make sure you match pin 1 on the card to the appropriate slot on the cable. In many cases, both the cable and the slot are numbered to help you. By matching the numbers, you will correctly connect the cable. If the card's pins are not numbered, you can use the solder that appears on the opposite side of the card as a clue. The following illustration shows the solder marks on the back of a card. As a standard, most hardware cards use a square solder for pin 1.

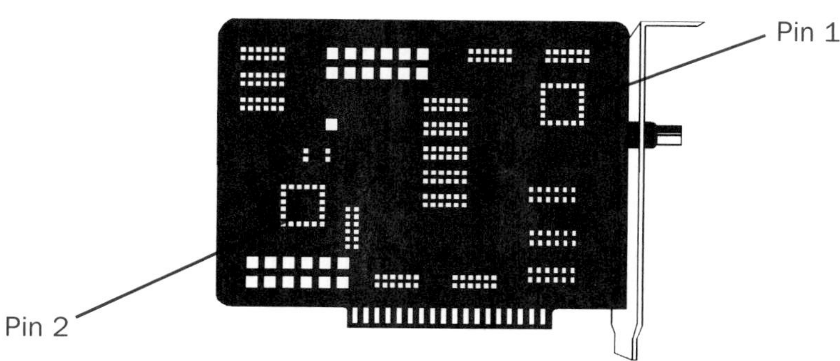

If you find the square solder, you've found pin 1.

Understanding Your Video Board's Components

Several of the tips presented in this book discuss your PC's video operations in detail. A video board and its common components are illustrated here:

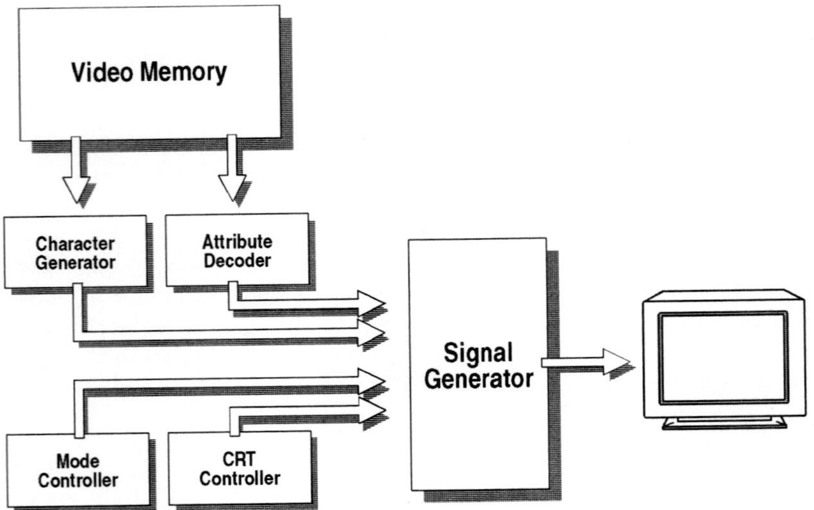

Table 825 lists the functions of each video board component.

Several of the tips presented in this book use these video components. By having a basic knowledge of their function, you will better understand the tips.

Table 825. The Functions of Common Video Board Components

Video Board Component	Function
Video memory	Holds the text and attributes or image and colors that appear on the screen
CRT controller	Generates the horizontal and vertical signals, displays the size and position of the cursor, controls which region of the video buffer is displayed, and performs other miscellaneous functions
Attribute decoder	Converts text attributes and graphic colors into signals to drive the video display
Mode controller	Controls the video display mode and timing signals that correspond to the mode
Character generator	Converts the characters stored in the video buffer into signals used to drive the video display
Signal generator	Combines the signals and timing frequencies generated by other video board components into the actual signals that produce the video display

Identifying Pin 1 on a Ribbon Cable

This tip describes how to locate pin 1 on most board connectors. If you are using a ribbon cable and the cable's connectors aren't numbered, most cables either darken or increase the size of the wire area that corresponds to pin 1. As shown in the following illustration, the darkened cable identifies pin 1.

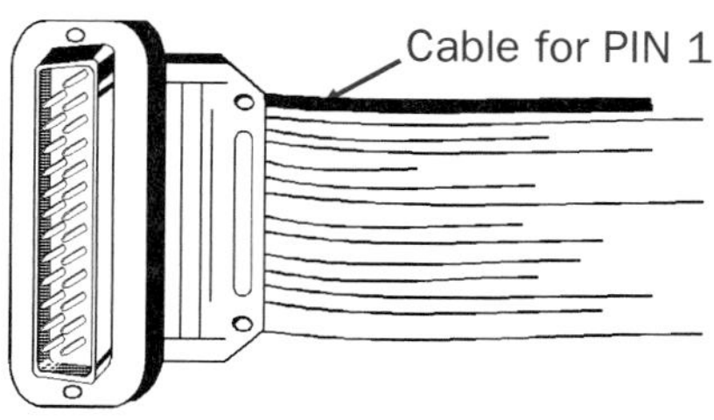

Using the CD-ROM Drive's Speaker Port

To support sound and animation, CD-ROM drives play a major role in multimedia applications. In the near future, many new multimedia applications will find their way into offices and homes. Although the use of sound is essential to the multimedia experience, users working near the multimedia workstation may be annoyed by the sound. Luckily, however, many CD-ROM drives provide a speaker port into which you can plug headphones, as well as a volume control.

By connecting headphones to a CD-ROM drive, you can prevent the sound of a multimedia presentation from disturbing others.

Understanding MIDI Files

Tip 847 introduces MIDI and the role of MIDI in multimedia applications. When most users hear the term MIDI, they visualize a recording studio filled with instruments. Although you may never create your own MIDI sound files, you may use MIDI files in multimedia presentations. As Tip 143 explains, WAV files, which contain actual digitized sound waves, can quickly consume your entire disk; a minute of sound recorded in waveform can require 1Mb of disk space. MIDI files, on the other hand, are much smaller. The same minute of sound recorded in MIDI format would probably require less than 10Kb.

The most common MIDI device is the electronic keyboard. However, MIDI saxaphones, flutes, drums, and so on are also available. When you record sound from a MIDI device, you actually record messages that describe the device's current operation. For example, if you hold down the key of C on an electronic keyboard, a message such as "C key down" is recorded. When you later release the key, a message such as "C key up" is recorded. When you play back a MIDI file, a synthesizer on your sound board converts these messages to actual sounds, which can be played through your speakers.

Storing sounds in message format makes MIDI files much smaller than their WAV counterparts. Unfortunately, you cannot use MIDI files to record and play back voices.

Solving the Unrecognizable Character Problem

If you are using a serial printer, or if you are using a modem and strange-looking characters appear on your printout or screen, the problem most likely is an incorrect baud rate. Tip 86 discusses baud rates in detail, and Tip 787 discusses start bits and stop bits. If you are connecting a serial device for the first time and strange characters appear, check the serial port's communication settings by using the companion disk utility COM_PORT.EXE as shown here:

```
C:\> COM_PORT  COM1: <ENTER>
Baud: 1200
Parity: N
Data bits: 8
Stop bits: 1
```

Compare the settings to the required settings specified in the documentation that accompanies the device. If the device worked in the past and now suddenly does not, check your AUTOEXEC.BAT file to ensure that a software installation has not changed or removed a MODE command that configures the corresponding serial port.

The utility command COM_PORT.EXE resides on the companion disk that accompanies this book.

COM_PORT.EXE

Swapping COM1 and COM2

As Tip 950 discusses, you sometimes may want to trick DOS into swapping its assignments for LPT1 and LPT2. Similarly, you also may sometimes want to swap COM1 and COM2. The following DEBUG script file, SWAPCOM.SCR, creates a command file named SWAPCOM.COM that swaps COM1 and COM2:

SWAPCOM.SCR

```
N SWAPCOM.COM      <ENTER>
A 100              <ENTER>
MOV AX,40          <ENTER>
MOV DS,AX          <ENTER>
MOV AX, WORD [0]   <ENTER>
MOV BX, WORD [2]   <ENTER>
MOV WORD [0], BX   <ENTER>
MOV WORD [2], AX   <ENTER>
MOV AH,4C          <ENTER>
INT 21             <ENTER>
                   <ENTER>
R CX               <ENTER>
17                 <ENTER>
W                  <ENTER>
Q                  <ENTER>
```

Use DEBUG as follows to create the command file SWAPCOM.COM:

```
C:\> DEBUG < SWAPCOM.SCR <ENTER>
```

To swap the COM1 and COM2 assignments, invoke SWAPCOM from the DOS prompt as shown here:

```
C:\> SWAPCOM <ENTER>
```

Distinguishing EISA and ISA Boards

Tip 57 briefly discusses the differences between the ISA and EISA buses. If you are exchanging boards between computers, you need to pay attention to the board type: ISA or EISA. The EISA bus supports boards created for either the EISA or ISA bus. To recognize the difference between EISA and ISA boards, examine the board's edge connectors as shown here:

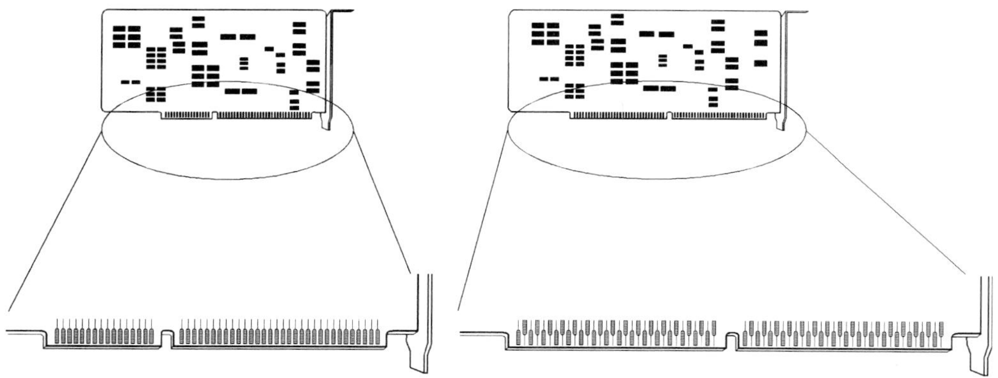

You can place an ISA board into an EISA bus, but not vice versa.

No Room for a Mouse?

With the popularity of mouse-driven programs such as Windows, almost every new PC comes with a mouse. Thus, most users are finding the mouse a common extension of their right (or left) arm. If you fall into this category, you may find notebook PCs frustrating because sometimes you just can't use the mouse (in an airplane, for example). As a solution, buy a trackball that connects to the side of your laptop computer as shown in the following illustration:

The trackball works the same way as a mouse, moving the cursor on your screen. Unlike a mouse, however, you don't have to move the trackball. Instead, you simply spin the ball with your fingers.

A Better Mouse Trap

If your work space is cramped, you probably have several piles of printouts, books, and disks near your computer. To prevent these piles from crushing your mouse, consider attaching a mouse trap (the name may differ) to your monitor, where you can store your mouse as shown here when it is not in use:

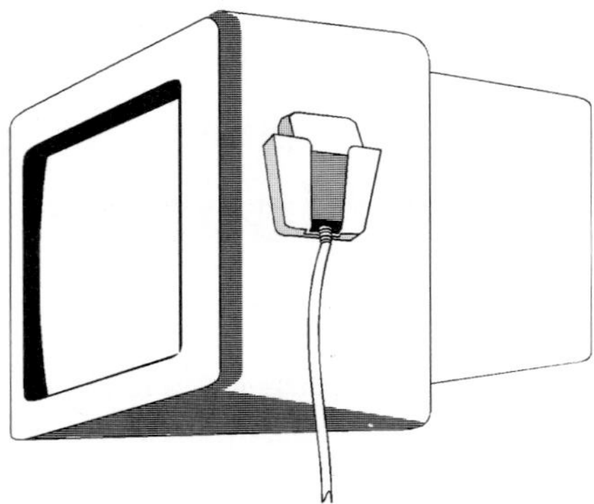

By placing your mouse in such a trap, you prevent it from being crushed, and you can quickly locate it when you need it.

Understanding Modem Lights

If you have an external modem, your modem probably has several of the lights shown here:

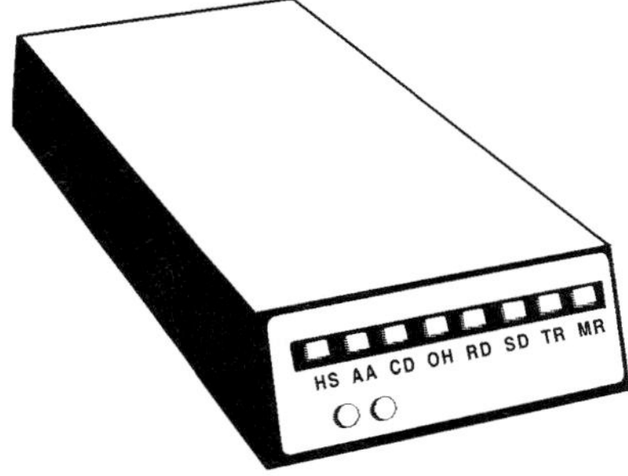

By understanding when the modem illuminates these lights, you can greatly increase your understanding of modem operations. Table 834 lists each light's purpose.

Serial Port Loopback Testing

If you are connecting a modem or printer to a serial port and you are experiencing problems, the problem may be the port itself. To test the port, you need to purchase a loopback connector from your computer retailer. The loopback connector connects the port's incoming and outgoing wires so that any data the port sends out is sent back to the port. Most modem communication software packages provide a loopback test. With your loopback connector in place, start the test. In most cases, the test can be as simple as verifying that the letters you type on the keyboard are sent the port, received, and then correctly displayed. If the letters are not correct, the loopback test has failed, and your culprit is very likely your serial port.

Table 834. Meanings of an External Modem's Control Lights

Light	Purpose
HS	The modem's high-speed light. The modem illuminates this light when it is communicating at its highest-possible speed.
AA	The modem's auto-answer light. The modem illuminates this light when it will answer incoming phone calls.
CD	The modem's carrier detect light. The modem illuminates this light when it is successfully connected to a remote computer. The carrier detect light should be illuminated during your entire remote session.
OH	The modem's off hook light. The modem illuminates this light whenever it has taken control of the phone line.
RD	The modem's receive data light. The modem illuminates this light each time the remote computer sends you data.
SD	The modem's send data light. The modem illuminates this light each time your computer sends data.
TR	The modem's terminal ready light. The modem illuminates this light when it receives a data terminal-ready signal from your computer, which is ultimately generated by your communications software.
MR	The modem's modem ready light. The modem illuminates this light when it has power and is ready to operate.

Determining Pin 1 on a Board Socket

Several tips presented in this book discuss how to determine your board or chip orientation by quickly finding pin 1's location. If you are inserting a chip into an unnumbered socket, examine the socket for a small notch similar to the one shown in the following illustration. The end with the notch always corresponds to the end of the chip that contains pin 1.

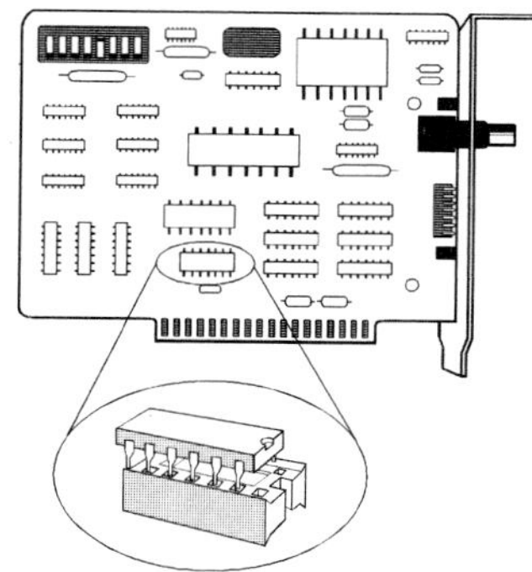

Be Aware of CD-ROM IRQ Conflicts

Tip 804 discusses IRQs (interrupt requests) in detail. If you are adding a SCSI-based CD-ROM to your system, be aware that the CD-ROM will probably use IRQ 5, the IRQ used by LPT2. If your system is using a printer connected to LPT2, you will need to select a different IRQ for the CD-ROM. Because the SCSI adapter is probably a 16-bit device, you can use an IRQ in the range IRQ 8 through 15.

What Is a 486SLC?

Tip 803 discusses the 386SL and 386SLC. Recently, many computer advertisements have listed a chip called the 486SLC. The 486SLC is a 32-bit processor that uses a 16-bit bus. The 486SLC uses the 486SX instruction set, but it does not have a floating-point processor. Like the 386SL and 386SLC, the 486SLC contains logic that lets it hibernate while not in use, thus saving power. Like the 386SLC, the 486SLC contains an internal 8Kb cache to improve its performance. Because its pins are compatible with the 386SC, upgrading to the 486SLC is easy.

Unlike the 486SX, which uses 32-bit addressing (4Gb address space), the 486SLC uses 24-bit (16Mb address space).

TIP 839 Controlling a Hand Scanner

Tip 815 introduces the scanning process. Because of their affordable price, hand-held scanners are becoming very popular. One of the difficulties of using a hand-held scanner is scanning a straight line. If you scan images regularly, consider building a simple scanner guide to be used as shown here:

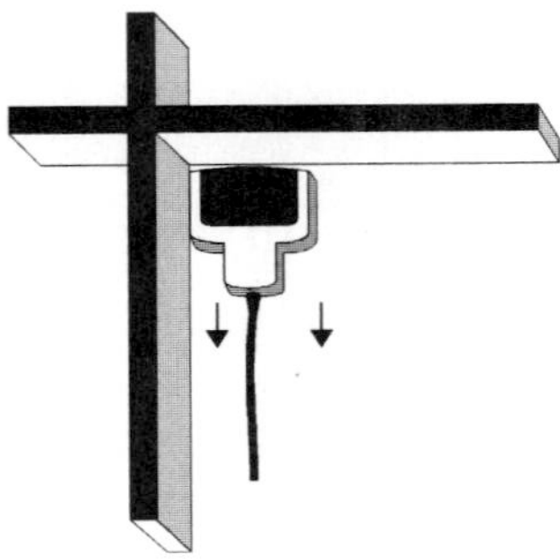

TIP 840 What Is an MNP Modem?

When you shop for a modem, a term you may encounter is MNP, an abbreviation for Microcom Networking Protocol. A protocol is really nothing more than an agreed upon means of communicating. To increase their data communication speed, two MNP modems may use data compression techniques. Because one modem is compressing while another is decompressing, both modems must agree on the technique used—the protocol. In the past, MNP protocol levels 2

through 4 provided error detection and correction capabilities. MNP level 5, however, adds data compression to these capabilities. Using MNP level 5, compression levels greater than 2:1 can be achieved. The higher the compression level, the less data your modem must transmit, and hence, the lower the cost of the phone call.

What's Super About Super VGA?

When you shop for a computer, one of the decisions you'll have to make is whether to purchase a VGA or Super VGA card. Because Super VGA cards are more expensive, there is a tendency to assume that VGA is good enough. Here are the differences. A VGA's highest pixel resolution is 640 by 480. When using VGA in this resolution, you can simultaneously display up to 256 colors. Super VGA, on the other hand, has a maximum resolution of 1024 by 768. Within this resolution, Super VGA can display 256 colors. Because Super VGA's resolution is nearly double that of VGA, Super VGA produces a much clearer image. In addition to higher resolution, Super VGA also has faster refresh rates (see Tip 798). Unlike VGA, which can use a VGA monitor, Super VGA requires a more expensive multisync monitor.

As graphical user interfaces such as Windows become more powerful, the higher-resolution, faster Super VGA will be a must. If you are purchasing a new system, a Super VGA card should be on your list.

What Is a Video Accelerator?

Tip 767 discusses math coprocessors, which save your CPU from having to perform time-consuming mathematical operations. The math coprocessor contains specialized instructions that allow it to perform such operations much faster. Similarly, a video accelerator is a hardware board that contains

video coprocessors that provide specialized instructions for video operations. Tip 820 discusses bit blts (bit block transfers), which are common occurrences in graphical user interfaces such as Windows. Video accelerators contain instructions that allow them to perform such operations very quickly. Video accelerators are typically built using either a Weitek or S3 chip. S3 chips tend to provide better performance at a slightly higher price. Video accelerators typically contain a minimum of 512Kb of video RAM. The more memory the board contains, the more colors it can display simultaneously. If you are shopping for a video accelerator, don't settle for less than 1,280-by-1,024 pixel resolution. The accelerator should support this resolution in noninterlaced mode. The card also should refresh the screen 70 or more times per second.

Understanding Network Cable Types

If you are considering installing a local area network in your office, one of the decisions you will have to make is the type of cable used to connect the computers. The three factors that will influence your decision are speed, reliability, and cost. The three most common network types are coaxial, unshielded twisted pair, and shielded twisted pair, shown here:

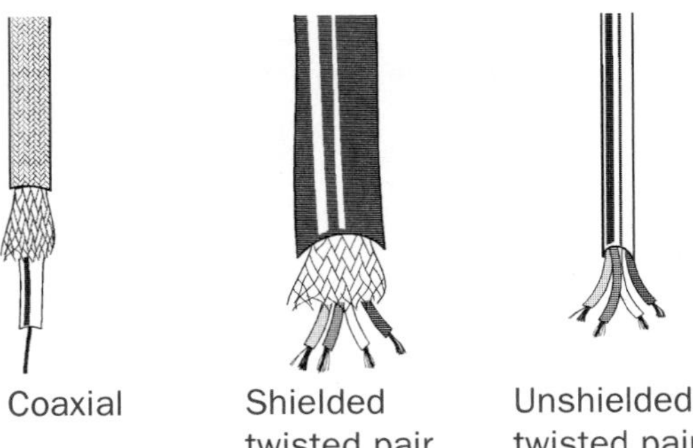

With respect to reliability, each of the different cable types have a different susceptibility to noise (electronic interference), in general because of the long antennae. The coaxial cable is the most protected. It uses a single wire covered (shielded) by a metal mesh that is further protected by bendable plastic coating. The metal mesh prevents noise from entering or leaving the cable, and the plastic

coating protects the mesh from water, spills, and other damage. Coaxial cable is the most expensive cable option.

At the opposite end of the cable spectrum is unshielded twisted pair, the least expensive cable but also the most susceptible to noise. Twisted pair is popular for networks because you can normally use existing phone wiring. Twisted pair uses two wires: one carrying a plus signal and one carrying a minus signal. The two wires are wrapped (twisted) around each other. Because the wires are twisted, noise that appears on one wire typically appears on the second, so the noise is canceled out. Unfortunately, phone wires can experience cross-talk, where they pick up another conversation, probably because wires have been stretched or worn. Because a twisted-pair network uses these same wires, such problems can cause network errors that are very difficult to troubleshoot.

To reduce the likelihood of the errors to which twisted pair is prone, shielded twisted-pair cables insulate the wire, preventing incoming or outgoing noise. Also, the wires are then covered by a flexible outer shield that protects them from damage.

What Is a 24-Bit Video Board?

If you examine advertisements for Super VGA and video accelerator cards, you will see the term 24-bit video. The 24 bits specifies the number of bits the board can use to represent each pixel's color. Assume, for example, you have 1-bit video. Each pixel can have the value 0 (off) or 1 (on). If you want more colors than black and white, you need to use more color bits per pixel. A 2-bit video can display 4 different colors (2^2). A 24-bit video card can display over 16 million different colors per pixel (2^{24}). In most cases, however, the cards don't contain nearly enough memory to do so. Here's why. Assume your card supports 1,280 by 1,024 pixels—that's 1,210,720 pixels. To use 24-bit color, the board must use 3 bytes per pixel (3 bytes equals 24 bits). That would mean your video card must have almost 4Mb of memory! So if you buy a 24-bit video card with 512Kb of memory, don't expect to see all 16,777,216 colors at once using the highest resolution.

What Is a Local Bus?

Tip 57 discusses the expansion bus that connects your CPU to your hardware boards. Compared to your CPU's clock speed, the bus speed is much slower. In the past, many video cards were designed for a 16-bit ISA bus slot. Not only did this mean that the video information the CPU sents to the card had to travel the slow bus, but it had to do so 16 bits at a time. Recently, new video boards have emerged that connect to the CPU's local bus, which means they can exchange data at the CPU's clock speed, using 32 bits at a time. The following illustration shows the local bus. Video boards that use the local bus will far outperform standard video cards.

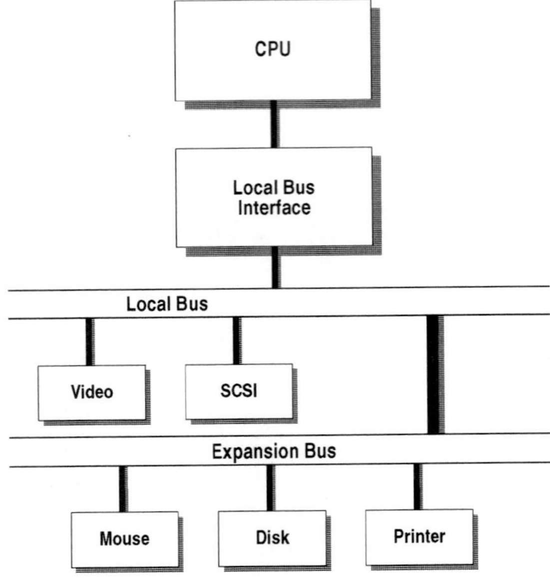

Depending on your PC type, the way you connect a card or chip to the local bus may differ. Before you buy a local bus card, make sure the card is compatible with your system.

Monitor Size Can Effect Resolution

With the recent popularity of high-resolution video cards, many users are upgrading from 14-inch monitors to 17-inch monitors. To understand why a larger monitor can improve resolution, compare the monitors' resolutions. The following illustration shows approximate image sizes on 14- and 17-inch monitors:

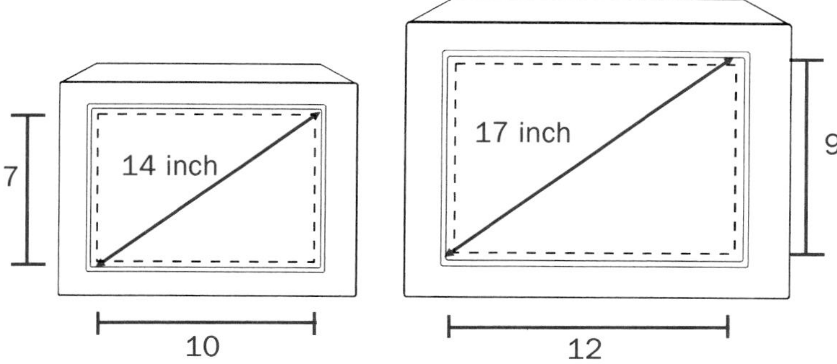

As Tip 802 discusses, a monitor's resolution is controlled by its dot pitch. Table 846 lists the dot-pitch size each monitor must support to meet different video resolutions.

As you can see, with a 14-inch monitor, the video card's resolution may exceed the monitor's resolution because of the dot-pitch required. Thus, if you plan to use high-resolution graphics, you probably should consider a 17-inch monitor.

Table 846. Monitor Dot-Pitch Sizes Required for Different Video Resolutions

Monitor	Resolution	Dot Pitch
14 inch	640 by 480	.39 mm
14 inch	1024 by 768	.25 mm
14 inch	1280 by 1024	.19 mm
17 inch	640 by 480	.47 mm
17 inch	1024 by 768	.29 mm
17 inch	1280 by 1024	.23 mm

Understanding MIDI

With the recent growth of multimedia products, many more products are advertising support for MIDI products. MIDI is an acronym for musical instrument digital interface. MIDI specifies the connectors, cables, and data formats that let you connect MIDI devices such as keyboards, synthesizers, or even drum machines to your PC. Once these are connected, you can record music from the MIDI to files on disk, edit the music with MIDI software, and later play the music back through the device. Most sound boards offer MIDI capabilities. If you plan to use MIDI devices, spend considerable time experimenting with the available software. Also, make sure the hardware board you select is compatible with the software.

Conference Room Presentations

If you are giving an on-screen presentation to a group of ten or more people, the first problem you will encounter is that most of the audience can't see your screen. If you give such presentations regularly, you might consider purchasing a video projection system. As shown here, such systems connect to your PC's video port, and you then place the screen on top of a slide projector that projects the screen image against a screen or wall.

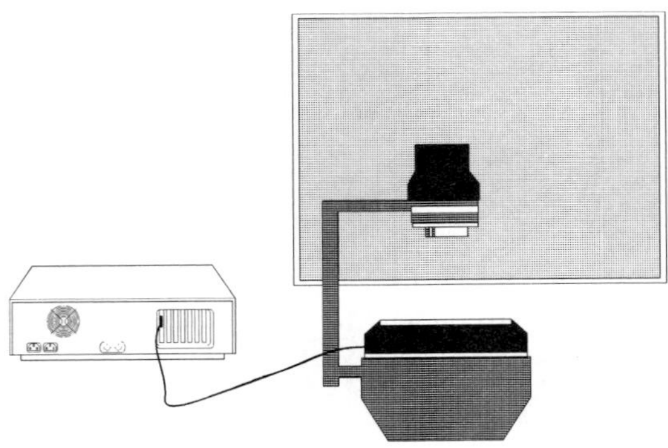

Although such projectors still range in price from $2000 to $5000, they are lightweight and compact, which makes them ideal for sales and marketing people who have to give presentations on the road. With the growth of multimedia presentation tools, you will see the use of such projection systems continue to grow.

A Better Mouse?

If you are new to mouse-driven environments or are setting up a system for someone who is, you may find the mouse not as user-friendly as everyone says it is. As an alternative to the conventional mouse, many computer stores sell a pen-based mouse. As shown here, you operate the pen-based mouse much like you write with a pen:

The pen-based mouse works identically to a normal mouse. As you move it, the mouse cursor moves on your screen. The pen-based mouse also contains small buttons that you click, just as with a conventional normal mouse. If you find the mouse frustrating, or if just want to a change, consider a pen-based mouse.

Vertical System Unit Stands Save Space

Many users now purchase tower-based PC systems as Tip 851 shows, not only because of their expansion capabilities, but because they fit neatly under a desk. Depending on your PC's chassis type,

you may be able to purchase and use a PC stand that allows your chassis to stand vertically, beside, or under your desk as shown here:

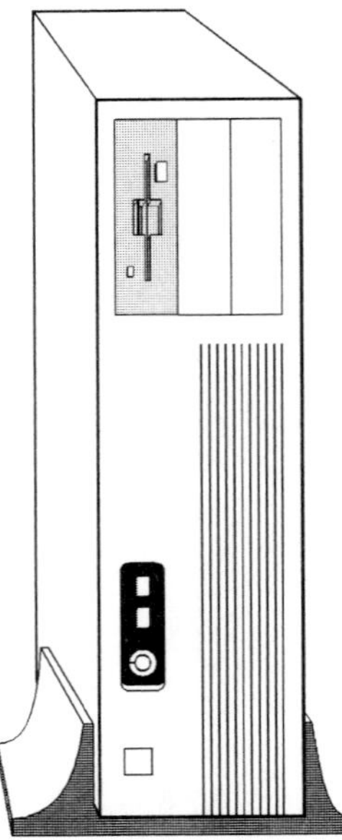

If you are working with minimal desk space, using a PC stand to stand your PC under your desk may free considerable desk space.

Tower PC's Solve Expansion Problems

The following illustration shows a standard PC chassis and a tower PC. Tower PC's have become very popular for two reasons. First, they let you move the PC chassis off of your desk top, freeing workspace (see Tip 850). Because you don't have to move the monitor and other items on your desk to access the tower PC's expansion slots, adding hardware boards to a tower PC is often easier than working with a standard PC chassis. Second, depending on the motherboard, many tower PC's normally provide more expansion capabilities than a standard PC. More important, the tower PC can provide more

drive bays for floppy or hard disk drives or an internal tape drive or CD-ROM. If you are considering a PC upgrade, take a close look at a tower PC.

In additon to full-size towers, you will find smaller tower PC's whose height is one-half to two-thirds that of a full-height tower. Before you purchase a tower of this height, make sure it can hold the number of drive bays you may require in the future.

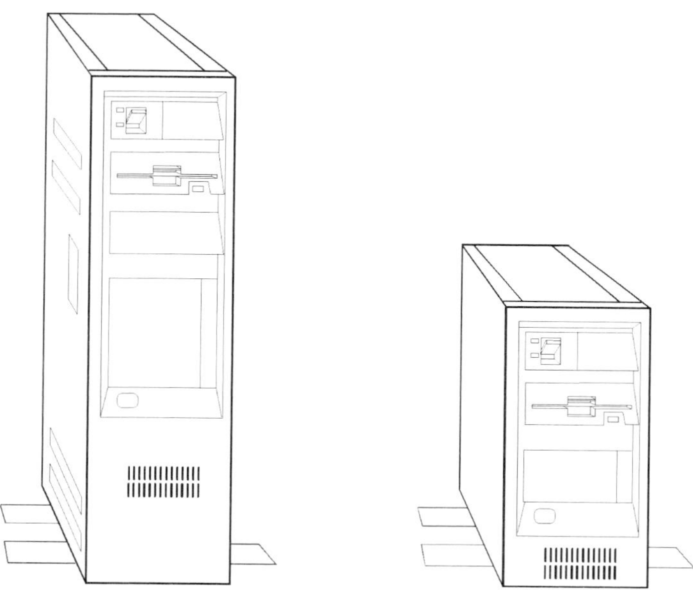

Does It Tilt?

TIP 852

When you are shopping for a monitor, one of the features you will want is the ability to rotate and tilt the display. Not only does the monitor movement let you adapt the monitor's position to your workspace, it also lets you move your display to compensate for glare that may change throughout the day. If you have already purchased a monitor that does not tilt, most computer stores sell tilting monitor stands, as shown here, that let you position your monitor as you desire:

TIP 853

Using a Monitor Stand

As discussed in Tip 850, using a vertical stand for your PC chassis lets you move your PC off of your desk, freeing workspace. If you are working in very cramped quarters, consider purchasing an elevated monitor stand as shown here:

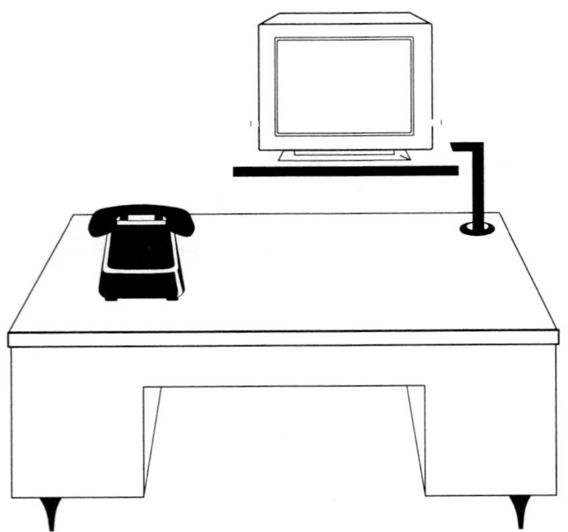

Using an elevated monitor stand, you can position the monitor so that you have a good view when you work with your PC, and you can later push the monitor out of the way when it's not in use. When you shop for such a stand, pay attention to the stand's mounting brackets; some brackets screw directly into your desk top, which may not be suitable.

Did You See the Light?

Tip 849 presents a pen-like mouse, which replaces the standard hand-held mouse with a mouse shaped much like a pen. The pen mouse provides an alternative for individuals who have difficulty operating a standard mouse. Another pointing device whose use is much less common than that of the mouse is the light pen. As shown in the following illustration, the light pen is a hand-held device, shaped much like a pen, one end of which can sense light:

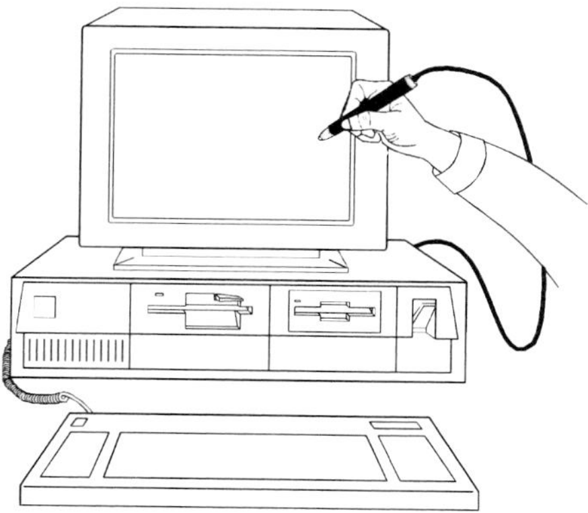

When you aim the light pen at different screen regions, the light pen card and driver determine the pen's screen position. As discussed in Tip 798, in displaying images on your screen, the monitor uses electron beams to continually refresh the image. The light sensor at the end of the pen responds to the pixel change in illuminosity when it is refreshed and notifies the light pen board. By considering the row and column of the monitor's electron guns when the light pen responds to the light change, the light pen driver can determine the pen's current screen position.

To use a light pen, you add a light pen expansion board and load a software driver. You do not need a different monitor or video card. If you are shopping for a light pen, keep your monitor type in mind. Some light pens work better with some monitors than others. Before you buy a light pen, make sure

your software will support it. Only a few light pens provide device drivers that allow the pen's use under Windows.

Understanding Mouse Resolution

Mouse resolution is measured in points per inch (ppi). Mouse resolution relates the movement of the mouse cursor on your screen to movement of the mouse on your mouse pad. For years, the resolution standard was 200 ppi. Most mice today support 400 ppi. A normal screen consists of 640 horizontal points by 480 vertical points. The advantage of the higher resolution is that you don't have to move the mouse as far on the mouse pad to obtain the same movement of the mouse cursor. If you are shopping for a mouse, make sure that a lower price doesn't mean lower resolution. Some mouse information uses the term "mickeys" to describe the mouse's resolution. In general, a mickey is equivalent to 1/200 of an inch.

Understanding CPU Step Numbers

If you examine the requirements of a software program closely, you may see a note such as "386 Step A1 Required." Like most software, CPU instructions often contain bugs, so new versions are periodically issued, each with a different version number. A CPU step is a version number. The letter, such as A or B, is the major version number, and the number that follows, such as 0 or 1, is the version revision number.

The only time you should worry about CPU step numbers is when you are purchasing a new system. Ask your retailer what the latest CPU step number is and what the step number is of the CPU in the system you plan to buy.

Finding Pin 1 on a Chip

TIP 857

Tip 824 describes how to locate pin 1 on an expansion board. Tip 826 describes how to locate pin 1 on a ribbon cable. To help you find pin 1 on a chip, most manufacturers place a notch above pin 1 as shown in the following illustration:

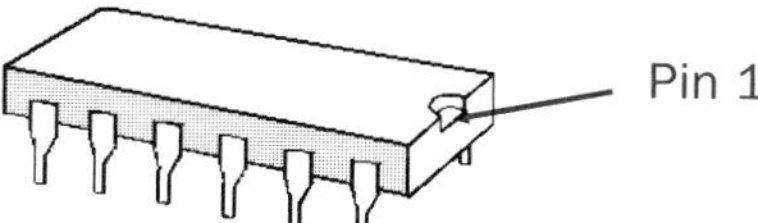

Monitor Position Can Be a Pain in the Neck

If you work at a PC all day and then go home with a stiff neck at night, the problem may be your monitor position. Most users place their monitors on top of the system unit. Depending on your desk and chair height, your monitor may be too high. Ideally, your monitor should be positioned beneath your head, so you look down to it at an angle of 15 to 20 degrees. If your monitor is too high, your neck and shoulder muscles have to stay tight all day to keep your head elevated. If you've experienced a stiff neck, try lowering your monitor.

Lower Back Pain? Check Your Chair Height

If you sit in front of a PC all day, your most important piece of hardware may be your chair. Sit in your chair in your normal sitting position. Note the angle of your thighs relative to the floor. Ideally,

your thighs should be parallel to the floor. If your hips are above your knees, your chair is too high. If your knees are above your hips, the chair is too low.

Tired Eyes? Be Aware of Monitor Glare

If you spend your days in front of a PC, headaches or bloodshot eyes are an indication that you need to adjust your monitor. One of the primary causes of eye strain is monitor glare. The easiest way to reduce glare from your monitor is to move the monitor so that all light sources are at 90-degree angles to your screen. If you cannot move the monitor away from the source of glare, consider purchasing a glare reflector that attaches to the front of your screen as shown in the following illustration:

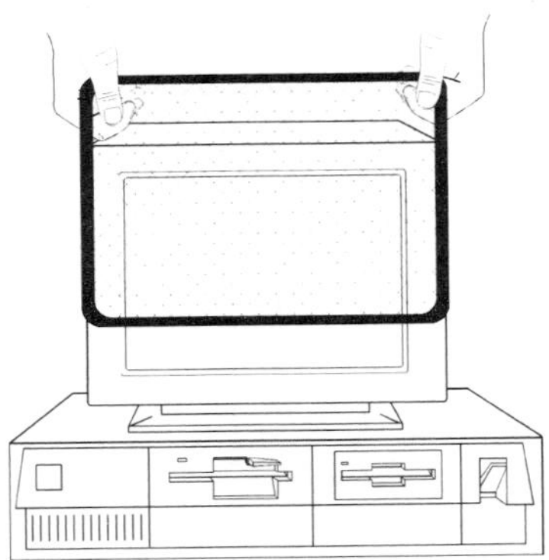

Before you buy an antiglare screen cover, try it out at your computer store. Some screens not only cut glare, but they also cut down the screen's intensity—which may cause even greater eye strain.

Understanding SCSI-2

TIP 861

Tip 786 introduces the small computer systems interface, or SCSI. Using a SCSI controller, you can attach up to seven SCSI devices to a high-speed bus. A 50-pin ribbon cable is most commonly used to connect a SCSI controller; IBM's microchannel architecture, however, uses a 60-pin cable. Because of standardization problems such as these and the related incompatibility problems they cause, SCSI devices have received a fair amount of bad press. Thus, a second SCSI specification, called SCSI-2, is emerging that provides two bus options. The first option uses the existing 50-pin bus, but doubles the bus transfer rate to 10Mb per second. The second option uses a wider, 68-pin cable to increase the number of data transfer lines to 32. This combination of a faster bus transfer rate and a larger number of data lines allows the second option to support data transfer rates of up to 40Mb per second.

The SCSI-2 specification provides backward compatibility to the existing SCSI standard. As you can see, SCSI-2 will greatly increase the speed of the already very fast SCSI.

What Is ECC?

Tip 774 describes how parity detects single-bit errors. ECC is an acronym for error-correcting code. Unlike parity, which simply detects errors, ECCs try to detect and *correct* errors. As Tip 403 discusses, your disk stores error-correcting codes for each sector; ECCs assign multiple parity checks to groups of bits. For example, assume there are three bits named A, B, and C. A simple ECC would use two parity bits: one for bits A and B and one for bits B and C. Assuming you are using even parity, the code would assign the values listed here to the parity bits:

A	B	C	Pab	Pbc
0	0	0	0	0
1	0	0	1	0
0	1	1	1	0
1	1	1	0	0

The following illustration shows how you can use these parity values not only to determine whether an error occurred, but also on which bit it occurred:

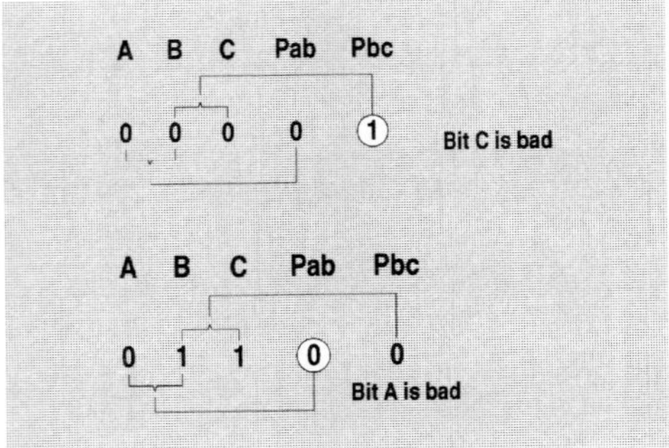

Once the ECC knows which bit is wrong, it can correct the error. It's important to note that the ECC algorithm presented here is quite simplistic (for understandability); most ECCs use very complex methods.

Understanding ROMs, PROMs, and EPROMs

Tip 216 discusses ROM, your computer's read-only memory. Unlike with RAM, you cannot change the contents of ROM, and the contents of ROM are not lost when you turn off your computer. The PC stores its BIOS on a ROM chip. When you first turn on your computer's power, the PC reads the startup instructions from ROM.

Two terms related to ROM are PROM and EPROM. PROM is an acronym for programmable read-only memory. A ROM chip contains fixed circuits that are prewired and cannot be changed. PROM, on the other hand, starts off as a generic chip. A special device called a PROM burner burns out the chip's desired circuitry. Because the chip's function is defined in this way, the generic chip is said to be programmable. Because once the circuits are burned in, they cannot be changed, and the chip is read only.

EPROM is an acronym for erasable programmable read-only memory. Like PROM, EPROM begins as a generic chip whose function is later burned in. However, unlike PROM, whose contents can never change, EPROM's logic can be erased and later reprogrammed. To do this, however, requires a special EPROM burner. As you can guess, the advantage of storing the BIOS on an EPROM is that new BIOS upgrades could simply be burned into the chip. However, the advent of memory technologies such as flash memory, discussed in Tip 258, may make EPROMs obsolete.

Controlling Your Modem's Auto-Answer Feature

Most modems support a feature called auto-answer that lets the modem answer incoming calls. If you use auto-answer, you can use the modem's S0 register to control on which ring number the modem answers the call. You can assign a value from 0 (don't answer) through 255. For example, the format of the ring assignment command that directs the modem to answer on the third ring is S0=3.

Specifying Your Modem's Comma Pause Wait

As Tip 173 discusses, placing a comma in the number that the modem is to dial directs the modem to pause briefly. The modem's S8 register contains a value in the range 0 through 255 that specifies how long the modem should pause (in seconds) when it encounters a comma. If, for example, you want the modem to pause for 10 seconds, issue the command S8=10.

Understanding the Effects of RF Noise

RF is an abbreviation for radio frequency. RF noise is stray electronic signals that can be produced by virtually any device you plug in. Some devices, however, such as a TV or radio, are bigger offenders than others. Within your PC, each of the millions of electronic components and wires can be affected by RF noise, essentially confusing the noise with a normal signal. Because such signals can crash your disk, reboot your system, or disconnect your modem, they can be very frustrating. The Federal Communications Commission, which polices RF noise, sets the minimum noise standards that computers, TVs, and other devices must meet. When you purchase computer equipment such as a monitor or printer, make sure the equipment has an FCC class A or B certification. Otherwise, the equipment may emit noise at levels capable of causing interference.

If your computer experiences intermittent errors, don't rule out the possibility of RF noise. Remove any devices that may be offenders away from your computer. Also, keep in mind that the long cables that connect your devices can serve as long antennae for picking up RF noise. See Tip 986 for a discussion of shielded cables.

PART 10

International

Is NLSFUNC Active?

If you use DOS code-page switching to toggle between international character sets, you know you must first install the memory-resident NLSFUNC command. If you have a batch file that performs code-page switching operations, your batch files can use the command CHKNLS.COM to determine whether NLSFUNC has been installed and, if it has not, to install it. The following DEBUG script file, CHKNLS.SCR, creates the command file CHKNLS.COM that returns the exit status value 1 if NLSFUNC is installed and returns 0 otherwise:

CHKNLS.SCR

```
N CHKNLS.COM   <ENTER>
A 100          <ENTER>
MOV AX,1400    <ENTER>
INT 2F         <ENTER>
AND AL,1       <ENTER>
MOV AH,4C      <ENTER>
INT 21         <ENTER>
               <ENTER>
R CX           <ENTER>
B              <ENTER>
W              <ENTER>
Q              <ENTER>
```

Use DEBUG as follows to create the command file CHKNLS.COM:

```
C:\> DEBUG < CHKNLS.SCR <ENTER>
```

The following command illustrates how a batch file would test whether NLSFUNC is installed, and if it is not, how it would install it:

```
CHKNLS
IF NOT ERRORLEVEL 1 NLSFUNC C:\DOS\COUNTRY.SYS
Rem Other commands here
```

Determining the Current User Code Page

If you use the DOS code-page switching capabilities to change from one international character set to another, your batch files may use the CHCP command. If a batch file changes the code page for a specific application, it should restore the original code page before it ends. The following DEBUG script file, USERCP.SCR, creates a command file named USERCP.COM that returns an exit status value that corresponds to the current code page:

USERCP.SCR

```
N USERCP.COM   <ENTER>
A 100          <ENTER>
JMP 110        <ENTER>
DW 1B5,352,354,35C,35F,361,0 <ENTER>
MOV AX,6601    <ENTER>
INT 21         <ENTER>
MOV SI,102     <ENTER>
CMP [SI],BX    <ENTER>
JE 121         <ENTER>
ADD SI,2       <ENTER>
JMP 118        <ENTER>
SUB SI,102     <ENTER>
MOV AX,SI      <ENTER>
SAR AX,1       <ENTER>
MOV AH,4C      <ENTER>
INT 21         <ENTER>
               <ENTER>
R CX           <ENTER>
2D             <ENTER>
W              <ENTER>
Q              <ENTER>
```

Use DEBUG as follows to create the command file USERCP.COM:

```
C:\> DEBUG < USERCP.SCR <ENTER>
```

USERCP.COM returns one of the exit status values listed in Table 868.

Table 868. Exit Status Value Returned by USERCP.COM

Exit Status	Code Page	Exit Status	Code Page
0	437	4	863
1	850	5	865
2	852	6	No user code page
3	860		

Once the batch file knows the original code page, it can store the value by using named parameters as discussed in Tip 655.

Which Keyboard Is Active?

The KEYB command lets you select an international keyboard template. After you have installed a keyboard template, you can select it or the default template by using the keyboard combinations listed in Table 869.

The following DEBUG script file, WHICHKBD.SCR, creates a command file named WHICHKBD.COM that returns the exit status value 0 if the default template is active and 1 if the user-defined template is active:

WHICHKBD.SCR

```
N WHICHKBD.COM     <ENTER>
A 100              <ENTER>
MOV AX,AD83        <ENTER>
INT 2F             <ENTER>
AND BL,1           <ENTER>
MOV AL,BL          <ENTER>
MOV AH,4C          <ENTER>
INT 21             <ENTER>
                   <ENTER>
R CX               <ENTER>
E                  <ENTER>
W                  <ENTER>
Q                  <ENTER>
```

Table 869. Keyboard Combinations Required to Select a Keyboard Template

Keyboard Template	Keyboard Combination
Default	CTRL-ALT-F1
User installed	CTRL-ALT-F2

Use DEBUG as follows to create the command file WHICHKBD.COM:

```
C:\> DEBUG < WHICHKBD.SCR <ENTER>
```

Toggling Between Keyboard Templates

Tip 869 discusses how to toggle between keyboard templates and how your batch files can determine which keyboard template is active. The following DEBUG script file, TOGGLEKB.SCR, creates a command file named TOGGLEKB.COM that toggles the current keyboard template. In other words, if the default template is active TOGGLEKB selects the user-installed keyboard, and vice versa:

```
N TOGGLEKB.COM    <ENTER>
A 100             <ENTER>
MOV AX,AD83       <ENTER>
INT 2F            <ENTER>
XOR BL,FF         <ENTER>
MOV AX,AD82       <ENTER>
INT 2F            <ENTER>
MOV AH,4C         <ENTER>
INT 21            <ENTER>
                  <ENTER>
R CX              <ENTER>
11                <ENTER>
W                 <ENTER>
Q                 <ENTER>
```

TOGGLEKB.SCR

Use the DEBUG command as follows to create the command file TOGGLEKB.COM:

```
C:\> DEBUG < TOGGLEKB.SCR <ENTER>
```

The following batch file uses the WHICHKBD utility created in Tip 869 to determine whether the default template is active; if the default template is not active, the file selects the default template using TOGGLEKB:

```
@ECHO OFF
WHICHKBD
IF ERRORLEVEL 1 TOGGLEKB
```

When and Why to Load GRAFTABL

Most international character sets make extensive use of the extended-ASCII values 128 through 255. If you are using an older monitor, several of these characters may be difficult to read. The GRAFTABL command loads memory-resident software that improves the display of such characters. If you are using DOS 4 and need to use GRAFTABL, load it by using the CONFIG.SYS INSTALL entry. If you are using DOS 5, use the LOADHIGH command. The following DEBUG script file, CHKGRAF.SCR, creates a command file named CHKGRAF.COM that you can use to determine whether GRAFTABL is installed; CHKGRAF returns the exit status 1 if GRAFTABL is installed and returns 0 otherwise:

CHKGRAF.SCR

```
N CHKGRAF.COM <ENTER>
A 100         <ENTER>
MOV AX,B000   <ENTER>
INT 2F        <ENTER>
AND AL,1      <ENTER>
MOV AH,4C     <ENTER>
INT 21        <ENTER>
              <ENTER>
R CX          <ENTER>
B             <ENTER>
W             <ENTER>
Q             <ENTER>
```

Use DEBUG as follows to create the command file CHKGRAF.COM:

```
C:\> DEBUG < CHKGRAF.SCR <ENTER>
```

The following batch file commands use CHKGRAF to determine whether GRAFTABL is installed; if GRAFTABL is not installed, the file installs it:

```
@ECHO OFF
CHKGRAF
IF NOT ERRORLEVEL 1 GRAFTABL
```

Under DOS 5, Use LOADHIGH for NLSFUNC, KEYB, and GRAFTABL

If you are an international user using DOS 5 with a 386 or higher computer, use the LOADHIGH command to install the NLSFUNC and KEYB commands and, if your monitor needs it (see Tip 871), the GRAFTABL command. By using LOADHIGH to execute these commands, you free conventional memory for your program use. The following batch commands illustrate how you might invoke these commands by using LOADHIGH from within your AUTOEXEC.BAT file:

```
LOADHIGH  C:\DOS\NLSFUNC   C:\DOS\COUNTRY.SYS
LOADHIGH  C:\DOS\KEYB  FR,850,C:\DOS\KEYBOARD.SYS
```

Viewing the International Symbol Sets

The CONFIG.SYS COUNTRY= entry lets you select an international symbol set that specifies the format DOS uses to display the current date and time, separate items in a list, separate digits, represent

currency, and so on. The file COUNTRY.SYS contains the symbol sets for each country. To help you better understand international symbol sets, the companion disk that accompanies this book provides the utility command SYMBOL.EXE that displays the current symbol set. To use SYMBOL, invoke it from the DOS prompt as shown here:

```
C:\> SYMBOL <ENTER>
Country code 1
Code page 437
Date format mm/dd/yy
Currency symbol $
Thousands separator ,
Decimal separator .
Date separator -
Time separator :
Data separator ,
Currency symbol precedes amount
Space between currency symbol and amount
Currency format 2 digits after decimal point
12 hour time format
```

SYMBOL.EXE

The utility command SYMBOL.EXE resides on the companion disk that accompanies this book.

Getting the Correct Date Format

As you know, depending on the current country code, DOS uses one of the three date formats shown in Table 874a.

If you are creating batch files that will distributed internationally, you should take date formats into account. The following DEBUG script file, DATEFMT.SCR, creates a command file named

Table 874a. DOS Date Formats

Code	Date Format
USA	mm dd yy
Europe	dd mm yy
Japan	yy mm dd

DATEFMT.COM that returns one of the exit status values listed in Table 874b that corresponds to the current country format:

```
N DATEFMT.COM <ENTER>
A 100         <ENTER>
JMP 12A       <ENTER>
DW 0,0,0,0,0,0,0,0,0,0 <ENTER>
DW 0,0,0,0,0,0,0,0,0,0 <ENTER>
MOV AX,6501   <ENTER>
MOV BX,FFFF   <ENTER>
MOV CX,28     <ENTER>
MOV DX,FFFF   <ENTER>
MOV DI,102    <ENTER>
INT 21        <ENTER>
ADD DI,7      <ENTER>
MOV AX,[DI]   <ENTER>
MOV AH,4C     <ENTER>
INT 21        <ENTER>
              <ENTER>
R CX          <ENTER>
44            <ENTER>
W             <ENTER>
Q             <ENTER>
```

DATEFMT.SCR

Use DEBUG as follows to create the command file DATEFMT.COM:

```
C:\> DEBUG < DATEFMT.SCR <ENTER>
```

Table 874b. Exit Status Values Returned by DATEFMT.COM

Exit Status	Code
0	USA
1	Europe
2	Japan

Understanding Code Page Types

Depending on your printer or screen type, you may have two types of code pages: hardware code pages and user-prepared code pages. Hardware code pages are built in to your device, installed by the manufacturer. User-prepared code pages are software-based code pages you download to the device by using the MODE command. If you examine the files in the DOS directory, you will see that the files with the CPI extension contain code page information. To determine the code pages currently available for the screen display, invoke the follow MODE command:

```
C:\> MODE CON /STATUS <ENTER>

Status for device CON:
----------
Columns=80
Lines=25

Active code page for device CON is 437
Hardware code pages:
  code page 437
Prepared code pages:
  code page 437
  code page 850
```

Installing code page support for a video display is fairly easy. Unfortunately, the printers for which DOS provides downloadable code pages is very limited. If you are purchasing a printer, make sure the printer comes with the hardware code pages you require or with downloadable code pages.

Understanding HP LaserJet International Symbol Sets

As discussed in Tip 911, a symbol set contains the actual symbols a font can display. To support international users, the HP LaserJet contains many country-specific symbol sets. Depending on the age and type of your printer, the number of international symbol sets you have may differ from those mentioned here. As discussed in Tip 912, you can select a symbol set from the HP LaserJet's control panel or use an escape sequence. Table 876 lists several international symbol sets and their corresponding escape sequences.

Table 876. HP LaserJet International Symbol Sets

Symbol Set	Identification	Escape Sequence
ISO 60 Norwegian 1	0D	Esc(0D
ISO 61 Norwegian 2	1D	Esc(1D
ISO 6 United Kingdom	1E	Esc(1E
ISO 25 French	0F	Esc(0F
ISO 69 French	1F	Esc(1F
HP German	0G	Esc(0G
ISO 21 German	1G	Esc(1G
HP Greek-8	8G	Esc(8G
ISO 15 Italian	0I	Esc(0I
ISO 14 JIS ASCII	0K	Esc(0K
ISO 57 Chinese	2K	Esc(2K
ISO 100 Latin 1	0N	Esc(0N
ISO 11 Swedish	0S	Esc(0S
HP Spanish	1S	Esc(1S
ISO 17 Spanish	2S	Esc(2S
ISO 10 Spanish	3S	Esc(3S
ISO 16 Portuguese	4S	Esc(4S
ISO 84 Portuguese	5S	Esc(5S
ISO 85 Spanish	6S	Esc(6S

Refreshing the Printer Code Page

Using the CHCP or the MODE command, you can assign a code page to your printer. Should the printer lose power or be reset, you can quickly restore the code page by using the MODE command as follows:

```
C:\> MODE LPT1 CODEPAGE REFRESH <ENTER>
```

Because MODE already knows what code page the printer should be using, you can simply refresh the device as opposed to having to prepare and select the code page.

PART 11

A Simple Page Eject for LPT1

When you redirect the output of a DOS command to the printer, you normally have to take the printer off line, press the form-feed button, and then place the printer back on line to view the page. The following DEBUG script file, FFLPT1.SCR, creates a command file named FFLPT1.COM that ejects a page from the printer attached to LPT1:

FFLPT1.SCR

```
N FFLPT1.COM <ENTER>
A 100        <ENTER>
MOV AX,C     <ENTER>
XOR DX,DX    <ENTER>
INT 17       <ENTER>
MOV AH,4C    <ENTER>
INT 21       <ENTER>
             <ENTER>
R CX         <ENTER>
B            <ENTER>
W            <ENTER>
Q            <ENTER>
```

Use DEBUG as follows to create the command file FFLPT1.COM:

```
C:\> DEBUG < FFLPT1.SCR <ENTER>
```

The following batch commands print a listing of the current directory and then eject the last page from the printer:

```
@ECHO OFF
DIR > PRN
FFLPT1
```

Selecting Landscape Mode on an HP Printer

Hewlett-Packard laser and inkjet printers let you print using portrait and landscape modes, which are illustrated here:

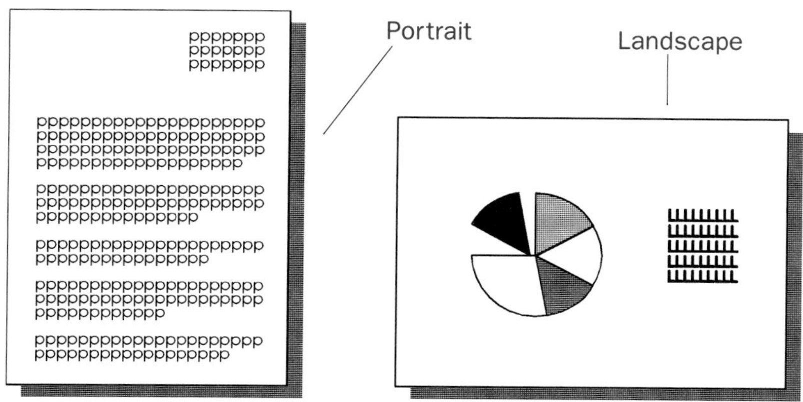

To select landscape mode, you must send the escape sequence Esc&l1O to your printer. The following DEBUG script file, HP_LAND.SCR, creates a command file named HP_LAND.COM that you can use to send the escape sequence to your printer:

```
N HP_LAND.COM <ENTER>
A 100         <ENTER>
JMP 108       <ENTER>
DB 1B,'&l1O$' <ENTER>
MOV AH,9      <ENTER>
MOV DX,102    <ENTER>
INT 21        <ENTER>
MOV AH,4C     <ENTER>
INT 21        <ENTER>
              <ENTER>
R CX          <ENTER>
13            <ENTER>
W             <ENTER>
Q             <ENTER>
```

HP_LAND.SCR

Use the DEBUG command as follows to create the command file HP_LAND.COM:

```
C:\> DEBUG < HP_LAND.SCR <ENTER>
```

After the HP_LAND command exists, you can use it as follows to send the escape sequence to the printer:

```
C:\> HP_LAND > PRN <ENTER>
```

Selecting Portrait Mode on an HP Printer

Tip 879 described how you select landscape mode on an HP printer. To select portrait mode, you must download the following escape sequence: Esc&l0O. The following DEBUG script file, HP_PORT.SCR, creates a command file named HP_PORT.COM whose output you can redirect to select portrait mode:

HP_PORT.SCR

```
N HP_PORT.COM <ENTER>
A 100         <ENTER>
JMP 108       <ENTER>
DB 1B,'&l0O$' <ENTER>
MOV AH,9      <ENTER>
MOV DX,102    <ENTER>
INT 21        <ENTER>
MOV AH,4C     <ENTER>
INT 21        <ENTER>
              <ENTER>
R CX          <ENTER>
13            <ENTER>
W             <ENTER>
Q             <ENTER>
```

Use the DEBUG command as follows to create the command file HP_PORT.COM:

```
C:\> DEBUG < HP_PORT.SCR <ENTER>
```

After the HP_PORT command exists, you can use it as follows to select portrait mode:

```
C:\> HP_PORT > PRN <ENTER>
```

Canceling All Jobs in the PRINT Queue

If you use the PRINT command to send files to your printer, you sometimes may need to cancel the printing of files in the print queue. Using the PRINT command, you can cancel the current jobs by using the PRINT /C switch as shown here:

```
C:\> PRINT /C <ENTER>
```

Similarly, the following DEBUG script file, ENDPRINT.SCR, creates a command file named ENDPRINT.COM that cancels all print jobs:

```
N ENDPRINT.COM <ENTER>
A 100          <ENTER>
MOV AX,0103    <ENTER>
INT 2F         <ENTER>
MOV AH,4C      <ENTER>
INT 21         <ENTER>
               <ENTER>
R CX           <ENTER>
9              <ENTER>
W              <ENTER>
Q              <ENTER>
```

ENDPRINT.SCR

Use the DEBUG command as follows to create the command file ENDPRINT.COM:

```
C:\> DEBUG < ENDPRINT.SCR <ENTER>
```

Customizing the PRINT Command

Several of the tips presented in this book use switches to customize the PRINT command. For example, the /B switch specifies the print buffer size, and /Q specifies print's queue size. PRINT also provides three switches you can use the first time you invoke it that control how much CPU time PRINT can consume.

So it can perform background printing while you issue other commands, PRINT actually shares the CPU with DOS or the active program. Because this CPU exchange occurs so fast, your PC appears to be performing two tasks at once. Actually, however, PRINT is controlling the CPU for several clock ticks and then relnquishing control of the CPU for a fixed number of clock ticks.The CPU clock ticks occur 18.2 times per second, or every 0.055 seconds.

By default, PRINT controls the CPU for 2 clock ticks (0.11 seconds) and then must relinquish control of the CPU for 8 ticks (0.44 seconds). Using PRINT'S /M switch, you can increase the number of clock ticks for which PRINT can control the CPU to a value in the range 1 through 255 (0.055 seconds through 14 seconds). If you make this value too large, your computer's other operations will slow to a near standstill. PRINT's /S switch controls the number of clock ticks PRINT must wait before it can resume control of the CPU. You can specify a value in the range 1 through 255 for /S.

PRINT's /U switch specifies the number of clock ticks PRINT waits before relinquishing control of the CPU if the printer is currently busy. The default value is 1, which means PRINT instantly relinquishes control of the CPU. You can specify a value in the range 1 through 255 for /U.

If you have a fast printer that contains large amounts of memory, consider increasing the amount of time for which PRINT can control the CPU by increasing the value of PRINT's /M switch. If you are more concerned with your system's responsiveness than with how fast your documents print, increase the value that corresponds to PRINT's /S switch. In most cases, you will leave the /U switch alone. Determining which switches provide the best performance for your system requires some experimentation. However, because you now know how each switch affects PRINT, you can begin your testing.

Temporarily Suspending the Print Queue

If you use the PRINT command to print files, sometimes while you are printing several files or a very long file, you wish to temporarily stop the printout—perhaps to print a document with your word processor. The following DEBUG script file, PRTSTOP.SCR, creates a command file named PRTSTOP.COM that suspends the print queue:

```
N PRTSTOP.COM <ENTER>
A 100         <ENTER>
MOV AX,0104   <ENTER>
INT 2F        <ENTER>
MOV AH,4C     <ENTER>
INT 21        <ENTER>
              <ENTER>
R CX          <ENTER>
9             <ENTER>
W             <ENTER>
Q             <ENTER>
```

PRTSTOP.SCR

Use the DEBUG command as follows to create the command file PRTSTOP.COM:

```
C:\> DEBUG < PRTSTOP.SCR <ENTER>
```

When you invoke PRTSTOP, it may take a moment for printing to actually stop, depending on the amount of memory in your printer (to which PRINT has already sent information).

Resuming Print Queue Operations

Tip 883 discussed how to temporarily suspend PRINT's queue operations by using the command file PRTSTOP.COM. When you are ready to resume PRINT's queue operations, you can issue the PRTGO command created by the following DEBUG script file PRTGO.SCR:

PRTGO.SCR

```
N PRTGO.COM    <ENTER>
A 100          <ENTER>
MOV AX,0105    <ENTER>
INT 2F         <ENTER>
MOV AH,4C      <ENTER>
INT 21         <ENTER>
               <ENTER>
R CX           <ENTER>
9              <ENTER>
W              <ENTER>
Q              <ENTER>
```

Use the DEBUG command as follows to create the command file PRTGO.COM:

```
C:\> DEBUG < PRTGO.SCR <ENTER>
```

Is LPT1 On?

If you are creating a batch file that uses LPT1, it should check LPT1's current status, and if the printer is not on, display a message to the user instructing them to turn it on. The following DEBUG script file, CHKLPT1.SCR, creates a command file named CHKLPT1.COM that returns the exit status value 1 if LPT1 is ready for output, or 0 otherwise:

```
N CHKLPT1.COM <ENTER>
A 100         <ENTER>
MOV AH,2      <ENTER>
XOR DX,DX     <ENTER>
INT 17        <ENTER>
MOV AL,0      <ENTER>
AND AH,40     <ENTER>
CMP AH,40     <ENTER>
JE 112        <ENTER>
INC AL        <ENTER>
MOV AH,4C     <ENTER>
INT 21        <ENTER>
              <ENTER>
R CX          <ENTER>
16            <ENTER>
W             <ENTER>
Q             <ENTER>
```

CHKLPT1.SCR

Use DEBUG as follows to create the command file CHKLPT1.COM as follows:

```
C:\> DEBUG < CHKLPT1.SCR <ENTER>
```

The following batch commands illustrate how you might use CHKLPT1:

```
CHKLPT1
IF NOT ERRORLEVEL 1 GOTO PRINTER_NOT_READY
DIR > PRN
GOTO DONE
REM Other commands
```

Echoing Screen Output to the Printer

Tip 32 explains how pressing the SHIFT-PRTSC keyboard combination directs your computer to print the screen's current contents. Similarly, pressing the CTRL-PRTSC keyboard combination directs the

PC to write all of the information it displays on your screen to your printer at the one time. For example, assume that you press the CTRL-PRTSC keyboard combination. Next, issue the DIR command. As DIR displays a list of your files on the screen, it also sends the identical list to the printer. The CTRL-PRTSC keyboard combination works as a toggle. To turn off printer echoing, simply press CTRL-PRTSC a second time.

By default, DOS echos the data to LPT1. If your printer is connected to COM1, you must first issue the following MODE command before you can perform printer echoing:

```
C:\> MODE LPT1:=COM1 <ENTER>
```

Printing Text in Compressed Mode on an HP LaserJet

By default, the HP LaserJet printer prints text at a size of 10 characters per inch. However, sometimes your text may not fit on a line. By default, the printer ignores the extra text. Using the escape sequence Esc(s16.66H, you can direct the printer to print in compressed mode, with 16.66 characters per inch. Likewise, using the escape sequence Esc(s8.5V, you can reduce the font height to 8.5 points (one point is 1/72 of an inch). The following batch file, LASERCMP.BAT, echos these escape sequences to your printer:

```
@ECHO OFF
ECHO Esc(s16.66H > PRN
ECHO Esc(s8.5V > PRN
```

After you execute the batch file, the printer will use the compressed font until you reset it or select a different font size.

To select the default font size, create a second batch file, echoing the escape sequence Esc(s10H and Esc(s12V.

The batch file uses the letters Esc to represent the unprintable ASCII escape character. In your batch file you must use the actual escape character as discussed in Tip 34.

An Alternate Print Screen for 43- or 50-Line Screens

As discussed in Tip 17, the MODE command lets you set an EGA monitor to a 43-line display and a VGA monitor to a 50-line display.

Unfortunately, when you select one of these modes, SHIFT-PRTSC operations (see Tip 32) no longer work correctly. However, the following DEBUG script file, FIXPRTSC.SCR, creates a command file named FIXPRTSC.COM that corrects the problem:

```
N FIXPRTSC.COM <ENTER>
A 100          <ENTER>
MOV AH,12      <ENTER>
MOV BL,20      <ENTER>
INT 10         <ENTER>
MOV AH,4C      <ENTER>
INT 21         <ENTER>
               <ENTER>
R CX           <ENTER>
A              <ENTER>
W              <ENTER>
Q              <ENTER>
```

FIXPRTSC.SCR

Use DEBUG as follows to create the command file FIXPRTSC.COM:

```
C:\> DEBUG < FIXPRTSC.SCR <ENTER>
```

Increase the Size of PRINT's RAM Buffer to Improve Performance

If you use the PRINT command to print ASCII files, such as your batch files or CONFIG.SYS, you can improve your system performance by increasing the size of the RAM buffer PRINT uses to store data.

When PRINT prints data, PRINT reads data from disk into memory and then sends the data to the printer as shown here:

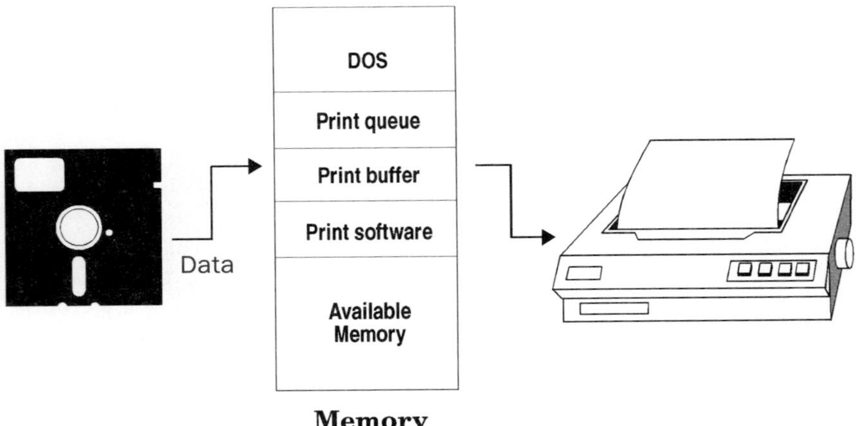

By default, PRINT uses a 512-byte buffer, roughly enough to hold one-eighth of a page of data. If your file is larger than this, PRINT must perform several disk read operations. Because the disk is a mechanical device, such operations are much slower than those performed by your computer's electronic components. The fundamental way to improve system performance is to minimize the number of slow disk I/O operations. With respect to the PRINT command, you can reduce the number of slow disk I/O operations by increasing PRINT's RAM buffer size with the /B switch. For example, the PRINT command allocates a 4,096 buffer, large enough to hold a page of information:

```
PRINT /B:4096
```

Because you can specify a buffer size only the first time you invoke PRINT (PRINT installs memory-resident code), most users specify the /B switch with PRINT in their AUTOEXEC.BAT file. If you don't use PRINT, don't include the PRINT command in your AUTOEXEC.BAT file; doing so will consume memory unnecessarily.

Specifying the Printer for the PRINT Command

The PRINT command provides a convenient way to print ASCII files such as batch files or CONFIG.SYS. The first time you invoke it, PRINT installs memory-resident software. In addition, PRINT displays the following message asking you for the name of the desired printer:

```
Name of list device [PRN]:
```

If you press ENTER, PRINT will select the default device PRN, which corresponds to your computer's first parallel port. If your printer is connected to a different device, such as the serial port COM1, you must type the device name and press ENTER. If you plan to use PRINT regularly, you can avoid this message by invoking PRINT from within your AUTOEXEC.BAT, using the /D switch to specify the desired device. For example, the following command directs PRINT to use LPT1 (PRN):

```
PRINT /D:LPT1
```

Likewise, this PRINT command directs PRINT to use COM1:

```
PRINT /D:COM1
```

If you invoke the PRINT from AUTOEXEC.BAT, include the /D switch to avoid having to select the printer device each time the system starts.

Allowing Print Screen Operations

Tip 904 describes how to create the utility command NOPRTSCR.COM that disables print screen opreations. Sometimes, however, you may want to temporarily reenable print screen operations. The following DEBUG script file, OKPRTSCR.SCR, creates the command file OKPRTSCR.COM that enables SHIFT-PRTSC operations that have been disabled with NOPRTSCR.COM:

OKPRTSCR.SCR

```
N OKPRTSCR.COM   <ENTER>
A 100            <ENTER>
MOV AX,50        <ENTER>
MOV DS,AX        <ENTER>
MOV BYTE [0],0   <ENTER>
MOV AH,4C        <ENTER>
INT 21           <ENTER>
                 <ENTER>
R CX             <ENTER>
E                <ENTER>
W                <ENTER>
Q                <ENTER>
```

Use DEBUG as follows to create the command file OKPRTSCR.COM:

```
C:\> DEBUG < OKPRTSCR.SCR <ENTER>
```

Sending a Carriage Return and Line Feed to Your Printer

In Tip 878 you use the DEBUG script file FFLPT1.SCR to create the command FFLPT1.COM that sends a form-feed character to your printer and ejects the current page. Sometimes, however, you may

want to print more information on the current page, separating the information by a few lines. The following DEBUG script file, CR_LF.SCR, creates a command file named CR_LF.COM that generates a carriage return that you can redirect to the printer:

```
N CR_LF.COM   <ENTER>
A 100         <ENTER>
MOV AH,2      <ENTER>
MOV DL,D      <ENTER>
INT 21        <ENTER>
MOV DL,A      <ENTER>
INT 21        <ENTER>
MOV AH,4C     <ENTER>
INT 21        <ENTER>
              <ENTER>
R CX          <ENTER>
E             <ENTER>
W             <ENTER>
Q             <ENTER>
```

CR_LF.SCR

Use DEBUG as follows to create the command file CR_LF.COM:

```
C:\> DEBUG < CR_LF.SCR <ENTER>
```

To send a carriage-return and line-feed combination to your printer, redirect the output of CR_LF as follows:

```
C:\> CR_LF > PRN <ENTER>
```

A Software-Based PrtSc Operation

Tip 32 discusses how you can press the SHIFT-PRTSC keyboard combination to print the current contents of your screen. The following DEBUG script file, SHFPRTSC.SCR, creates a command file named SHFPRTSC.COM that also performs a print screen operation:

SHFPRTSC.SCR

```
N SHFPRTSC.COM      <ENTER>
A 100               <ENTER>
INT 5               <ENTER>
MOV AH,4C           <ENTER>
INT 21              <ENTER>
                    <ENTER>
R CX                <ENTER>
6                   <ENTER>
W                   <ENTER>
Q                   <ENTER>
```

Use DEBUG as follows to create the command file SHFPRTSC.COM:

```
C:\> DEBUG < SHFPRTSC.SCR <ENTER>
```

The following batch commands perform a directory listing; use the SHFPRTSC command file to print the screen's current contents and the command file FFLPT1 (see Tip 878) to eject the page from the printer:

```
@ECHO OFF
DIR /W
SHFPRTSC
FFLPT1
```

How Many Parallel Ports Do I Have?

The PC allows you three parallel ports: LPT1, LPT2, and LPT3. The following DEBUG script file LPTCOUNT.SCR creates a command file named LPTCOUNT.COM that returns an exit status value in the range 0 through 3 that indicates the number of parallel ports available:

```
N LPTCOUNT.COM      <ENTER>
A 100               <ENTER>
MOV AX,40           <ENTER>
MOV DS,AX           <ENTER>
MOV AL,[11]         <ENTER>
MOV CL,6            <ENTER>
SAR AL,CL           <ENTER>
MOV AH,4C           <ENTER>
INT 21              <ENTER>
                    <ENTER>
R CX                <ENTER>
10                  <ENTER>
W                   <ENTER>
Q                   <ENTER>
```

LPTCOUNT.SCR

Use DEBUG as follows to create the command file LPTCOUNT.COM:

```
C:\> DEBUG < LPTCOUNT.SCR <ENTER>
```

The following batch commands illustrate how you can test for the number of printer ports by using LPTCOUNT.COM:

```
@ECHO OFF
LPTCOUNT
IF NOT ERRORLEVEL 1 GOTO NO_PARALLEL_PORTS
IF ERRORLEVEL 1 GOTO PARALLEL_AVAILABLE
REM Other commands here
```

Selecting Condensed Mode on an Epson-Compatible Printer

If you are using an Epson- or IBM-compatible printer, you can use the MODE command to specify the number of characters per line (80 or 132) and the number of lines per row (6 or 8). If you are

using DOS 3.3 or lower, the following command selects condensed print for a printer attached to LPT1:

```
C:\> MODE LPT1 132,8 <ENTER>
```

If you are using DOS 4 or higher, you can issue the following MODE command to select condensed print:

```
C:\> MODE LPT1: COLS=132 LINES=8 <ENTER>
```

To restore the normal print size, repeat the MODE command using 80 columns and 6 lines.

If you are using a printer that is not IBM or EPSON compatible, the printer probably supports an escape sequence that selects condensed print. Refer to the manual that accompanies your printer.

Removing Files from the Print Queue

In Tip 881, you create a command file named ENDPRINT.COM that cancels the printing of files in the print queue. If you instead want to remove a single file from the queue, you can do so by using the /C switch as shown here:

```
C:\> PRINT Filename.Ext /C <ENTER>
```

When PRINT encounters /C, it removes from the queue the file whose name precedes the switch as well as those files that follow. The following PRINT command uses the /C switch to remove three files from the queue:

```
C:\> PRINT ONE.DAT /C TWO.DAT THREE.DAT <ENTER>
```

If you want to cancel the printing of all files in the queue, you can use the utility command ENDPRINT.COM, or you can invoke PRINT with the /T switch as shown here:

```
C:\> PRINT /T <ENTER>
```

Replacing One Print Queue File with Another

Tip 881 describes how to use PRINT's /C switch to remove a file from the print queue. Sometimes you may want to replace a file that exists in the print queue with another file. To do so, you must combine PRINT's /C and /P switches. For example, the following PRINT command removes the file named OLDFILE.DAT from the queue and adds the file NEWFILE.DAT:

```
C:\> PRINT OLDFILE.DAT /C NEWFILE.DAT /P <ENTER>
```

In this case, the /C switch directs PRINT to remove the file OLDFILE.DAT, and /P directs PRINT to add the file NEWFILE.DAT.

Understanding the Parallel Interface

As Tip 764 discusses, parallel ports can transmit data much faster than a serial port because the ports transmit data 8 bits at a time as opposed to 1 bit at a time. Pin use for a 25-pin parallel port is shown here:

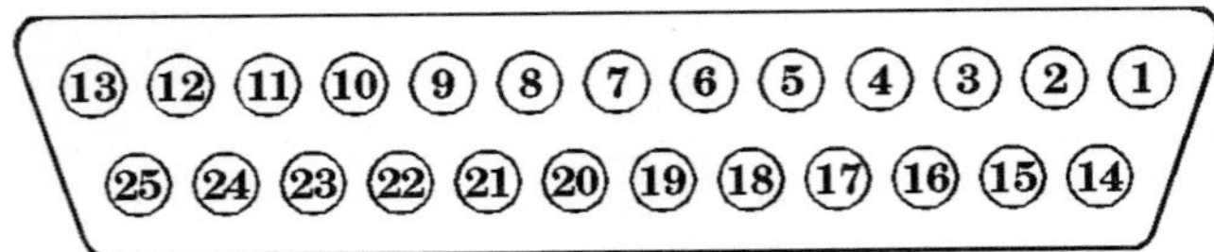

Pin	Function	Pin	Function	Pin	Function	Pin	Function
1	Strobe	8	Data bit 6	15	Error	22	Ground
2	Data bit 0	9	Data bit 7	16	Init printer	23	Ground
3	Data bit 1	10	Acknowledge	17	Select in	24	Ground
4	Data bit 2	11	Busy	18	Ground	25	Ground
5	Data bit 3	12	Paper empty	19	Ground		
6	Data bit 4	13	Select	20	Ground		
7	Data bit 5	14	Auto line feed	21	Ground		

Many newer printers use a special 36-pin interface called a Centronics connector, shown here:

Pin	Function	Pin	Function	Pin	Function	Pin	Function
1	Strobe	10	Acknowledge	19	Ground	28	Ground
2	Data bit 0	11	Busy	20	Ground	29	Ground
3	Data bit 1	12	Paper empty	21	Ground	30	Ground
4	Data bit 2	13	Select	22	Ground	31	Init printer
5	Data bit 3	14	Auto line feed	23	Ground	32	Error
6	Data bit 4	15	Not used	24	Ground	33	Ground
7	Data bit 5	16	Ground	25	Ground	34	Not used
8	Data bit 6	17	Ground	26	Ground	35	Not used
9	Data bit 7	18	+5 volts	27	Ground	36	Select in

If you are purchasing a new printer or printer cable, make sure the connector type matches your system.

Resetting Your HP Laser Jet Printer

Several of the tips presented in this book use escape sequences to select different LaserJet fonts, page orientations, and so on. One way to restore your printer to normal operations at a later time is simply to cycle the printer's power. An easier way, however, is to send the following escape sequence to your printer: EscE.

The following batch file, RESETLJ.BAT, uses the escape sequence to reset the printer:

```
@ECHO OFF
ECHO EscE > PRN
```

The batch file assumes the printer is attached to LPT1. If it is connected to a different port, replace LPT1 with the correct port name.

The batch file uses the letters "Esc" to represent the unprintable ASCII escape character. In your batch files, you must use the actual character, as discussed in Tip 34.

Extending the Life of Your Laser Printer's Toner Cartridge

If your are using a LaserJet printer, a toner cartridge normally lasts from 3,000 to 5,000 pages. When the toner becomes low, the printer may display a message on the front of its case to indicate the toner status. Should this message appear, unplug the printer, open the chassis, and remove the toner cartridge. Next, as shown here, shake the cartridge from left to right, spreading the remaining toner throughout the cartridge:

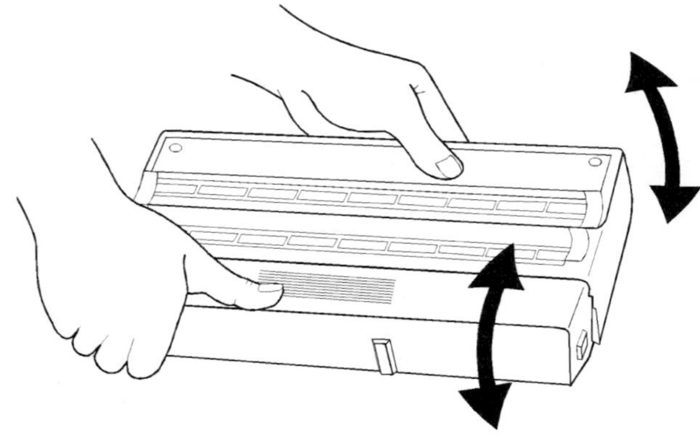

Using this technique, you can normally extend the cartridge's life by a few days.

Toggling Printer Echoing On and Off

Tip 886 describes how to toggle printer echoing on and off by pressing the CTRL-PRTSC keyboard combination. Depending on your batch file's execution, you sometimes may want the batch file to turn the printer itself on or off without requiring the user to press CTRL-PRTSC. The following DEBUG script file, PRTECHO.SCR, creates a command file named PRTECHO.COM that toggles printer echoing on and off:

PRTECHO.SCR

```
N PRTECHO.COM              <ENTER>
A 100                      <ENTER>
MOV AX,40                  <ENTER>
MOV DS,AX                  <ENTER>
MOV BX,1E                  <ENTER>
MOV WORD PTR [BX],7200     <ENTER>
MOV BX,1C                  <ENTER>
MOV BYTE PTR [BX],20       <ENTER>
MOV BX,1A                  <ENTER>
MOV BYTE PTR [BX],1E       <ENTER>
```

```
MOV AX,4C00                <ENTER>
INT 21                     <ENTER>
                           <ENTER>
R CX                       <ENTER>
1D                         <ENTER>
W                          <ENTER>
Q                          <ENTER>
```

Use DEBUG as follows to create the command file PRTECHO.COM:

```
C:\> DEBUG < PRTECHO.SCR <ENTER>
```

The following batch file commands use PRTECHO to echo a directory listing that appears on your screen to the printer as well:

```
@ECHO OFF
PRETCHO
DIR
PRTECHO
```

Adding Printer Memory Can Substantially Increase Your Performance

If you are using a laser printer, your printer can hold several megabytes of memory. There are two reasons to add memory to your system. The first is to hold software-based, or downloadable, fonts. The second is to improve your system's performance. The printer's mechanical nature makes it by far the slowest of all your computer devices. When you print a document, the PC sends the data to the printer, which in turn buffers the data in its internal memory. If the entire document fits in the printer's memory, the program sending the data can start performing other tasks. Otherwise, the program must wait for the printer to print the data currently in its memory buffer. By increasing the amount of memory in your printer, you allow programs to quickly download their data to the printer so they can be available to perform other tasks.

If you are using an HP LaserJet, you can determine how much memory your printer has by taking the printer off-line and then pressing the PRINT FONTS key for 3 seconds. The printout will also specify the number of pages your printer has printed in its lifetime.

A Fast Way to Print Multiple Copies

As discussed in Tip 902, printer memory lets your printer hold the document as it prints. If you are using an HP LaserJet printer, you can take advantage of this printer memory to quickly print multiple copies of a document. Normally, if you want to print multiple copies of a document, you tell your word processor the number of copies you desire, and the word processor oversees the printing of each copy, repeatedly sending the data to the printer—a slow process. However, using the escape sequence Esc&lCopies# you can direct your printer to generate the pages automatically—a much faster process. The following batch file, HPCOPIES.BAT, uses the escape sequence to set the number of copies to the value you specify in %1:

```
@ECHO OFF
IF '%1'=='' GOTO DONE
ECHO Esc&l%1# > PRN
```

To select two-copy mode, you would invoke the batch file as shown here:

```
C:\> HPCOPIES 2 <ENTER>
```

To restore one-copy mode, use HPCOPIES as follows:

```
C:\> HPCOPIES 1 <ENTER>
```

The batch file uses the letters "Esc" to represent the unprintable ASCII escape character. In your batch file you must use the actual escape character as discussed in Tip 34.

Disabling Print Screen Operations

Sometimes, when you are working with a notebook computer, for example, you may want to disable the SHIFT-PRTSC screen print operation to avoid inadvertent screen prints. The following DEBUG script file, NOPRTSCR.SCR, creates a command file named NOPRTSCR.COM that disables SHIFT-PRTSC:

```
N NOPRTSCR.COM    <ENTER>
A 100             <ENTER>
MOV AX,50         <ENTER>
MOV DS,AX         <ENTER>
MOV BYTE [0],1    <ENTER>
MOV AH,4C         <ENTER>
INT 21            <ENTER>
                  <ENTER>
R CX              <ENTER>
E                 <ENTER>
W                 <ENTER>
Q                 <ENTER>
```

NOPRTSCR.SCR

Use DEBUG as follows to create the command file NOPRTSCR.COM:

```
C:\> DEBUG < NOPRTSCR.SCR <ENTER>
```

Printing on Both Sides of Your Paper

Although some newer laser printers allow you to print on both sides, most of us are still using printers that don't. If you need to print only a few pages of text using both sides of the paper, and you own an HP LaserJet, try the following tip.

To begin, use the command file HP_MANUAL.COM to select manual output. Tip 941 tells you how to create this file. Next, print a page. After the printer ejects the page, turn the page over face down, as shown in Figure 905, and refeed the page back into the printer. Repeat this process for each page.

If you have to print a large document on both sides of the page, hope that your word processor provides the ability to print only odd or even pages. After you print the odd pages, place the paper back into the printer, face down, with page 1 on top, and then print the even pages.

Controlling End-of-Line Wrapping and Truncation for an HP LaserJet

By default, if the amount of text on your line exceeds the number of characters the HP LaserJet can print on the current line, the printer will truncate the text, discarding the additional characters. However, you sometimes may prefer the printer to wrap the text to the following line. Using the escape sequences listed in Table 906, you can select wrapping or truncation.

To help you perform these operations, the following DEBUG script file, WRAPTRUN.SCR, creates two command files, HPWRAP.COM and HPTRUNC.COM, whose output you can redirect to your printer to select text wrapping or truncation:

```
N HPWRAP.COM            <ENTER>
A 100                   <ENTER>
JMP 108                 <ENTER>
DB 1B,26,73,30,43,24    <ENTER>
MOV AH,9                <ENTER>
MOV DX,102              <ENTER>
INT 21                  <ENTER>
MOV AH,4C               <ENTER>
INT 21                  <ENTER>
                        <ENTER>
R CX                    <ENTER>
13                      <ENTER>
W                       <ENTER>
N HPTRUNC.COM           <ENTER>
E 105 31                <ENTER>
W                       <ENTER>
Q                       <ENTER>
```

WRAPTRUN.SCR

Use DEBUG as follows to create the command files HPWRAP.COM and HPTRUNC.COM:

```
C:\> DEBUG < WRAPTRUN.SCR <ENTER>
```

To select text wrapping, for example, you would use HPWRAP as follows:

```
C:\> HPWRAP > LPT1 <ENTER>
```

Table 906. Escape Sequences to Control Wrapping and Truncation on an HP LaserJet

Mode	Escape Sequence
Wrap text	Esc&x0C
Truncate text	Esc&1C

Restoring HP LaserJet Default Settings

Several of the tips presented in this book show you how to change HP LaserJet settings such as margins, lines per page, orientation, and so on. If another user has changed one or more of these settings, you may want to restore the originals. One way to do so is to power up your computer. A second way is to individually reset the changed settings. Table 907 lists the default values for several of these settings. You can use these values to restore the default settings.

Table 907. HP LaserJet Default Settings

Setting	Default Value
Top margin	0.5 inches
Bottom margin	0.5 inches
Left margin	0.25 inches
Right margin	0.25 inches
Page orientation	Portrait
Characters per inch	10
Lines per inch	6
Lines per page	60

Understanding Printer Fonts

A font is the type used to print characters. A font consists of three parts: a typeface, such as Courier; attributes, such as bold or italics; and a point size. Most laser printers support three types of fonts: internal, cartridge, and downloadable. Internal fonts are the fonts built in to the printer. Printers normally provide only a minimal number of internal fonts. Cartridge fonts are so named because they come stored in a cartridge that you actually plug into the front of your printer. The advantage of cartridge fonts is that they are easy to install. Unfortunately, if you have multiple printers, you have to buy multiple cartridges, which can become expensive. In addition, many cartridge manufacturers warn that cartridges have a fixed insertion lifetime. In other words, they can be inserted into and removed from a printer only so many times before they experience problems. Before you purchase a cartridge, verify its durability.

Downloadable fonts come as files on floppy disks. Using a program that accompanies the fonts, you download the fonts into the printer's memory. Software fonts are the least expensive. Their disadvantage is that each time you turn off the printer's power, you must reload the fonts from disk.

Leaving Through the Backdoor

If you are using an HP LaserJet, your printed pages normally eject and stack at the top of the printer. Depending on the number of pages you are printing, you may prefer that the printer ejects pages from the back, possibly stacking them in your own custom paper tray. To eject pages from the back of your printer, open the rear tray door at the back of the printer. As shown here, the printer will eject the pages from the rear:

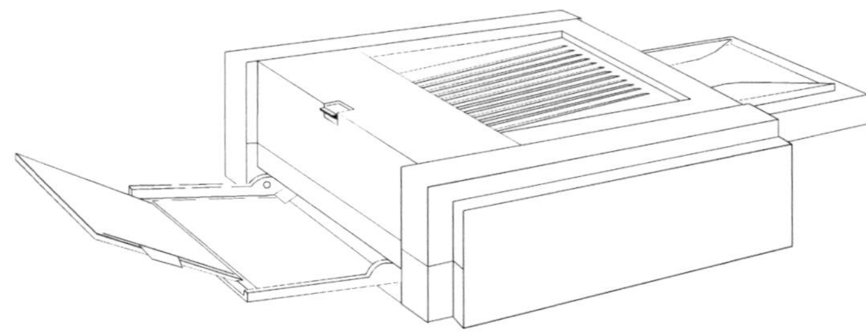

To resume normal printer operations, simply close the rear tray door.

What Is PCL?

PCL is an abbreviation for printer command language. PCL is the set of commands you can use to select various features on HP LaserJet printers. Several of the tips presented in this book use various escape sequences to direct the LaserJet to perform different tasks. These escape sequences constitute HP's PCL. Most PCL commands have the same format. The commands begin with an escape character; then a parameterized character such as &()* tells the printer the command's type and that parameters follow. Next, a lowercase group character identifies the specific command. This character is followed by a user value specific to the command and an uppercase command-termination character. Each new printer in the LaserJet series may add new PCL commands. However, each printer is backward-compatible, which means it supports the PCL commands of previous printers.

Understanding Symbol Sets

A symbol set is the collection of symbols a font can display. Most printers provide several different symbol sets that you can select for different purposes. Symbol sets may

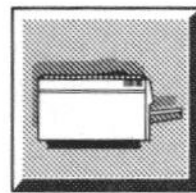

correspond to mathematical, legal, or even international symbols. Tip 876 lists common HP LaserJet international symbol sets. By default, the LaserJet uses the Roman-8 symbol set shown in Table 911.

Tip 913 discusses how you display the LaserJet's current symbol set. Tip 912 discusses how to select a different symbol set.

Table 911. The Roman-8 Symbol Set

NUL 0	DLE 16	32	0 48	@ 64	P 80	‘ 96	p 112	128	144	160	¯ 176	â 192	Å 208	Á 224	Þ 240
SOH 1	DC1 17	! 33	1 49	A 65	Q 81	a 97	q 113	129	145	À 161	Ý 177	ê 193	î 209	Ã 225	þ 241
STX 2	DC2 18	" 34	2 50	B 66	R 82	b 98	r 114	130	146	Â 162	ý 178	ô 194	Ø 210	ã 226	· 242
ETX 3	DC3 19	# 35	3 51	C 67	S 83	c 99	s 115	131	147	È 163	° 179	û 195	Æ 211	Đ 227	μ 243
EOT 4	DC4 20	$ 36	4 52	D 68	T 84	d 100	t 116	132	148	Ê 164	Ç 180	á 196	å 212	ð 228	¶ 244
ENQ 5	NAK 21	% 37	5 53	E 69	U 85	e 101	u 117	133	149	Ë 165	ç 181	é 197	í 213	Í 229	¾ 245
ACK 6	SYN 22	& 38	6 54	F 70	V 86	f 102	v 118	134	150	Î 166	Ñ 182	ó 198	ø 214	Ì 230	— 246
BEL 7	ETB 23	’ 39	7 55	G 71	W 87	g 103	w 119	135	151	Ï 167	ñ 183	ú 199	æ 215	Ó 231	¼ 247
BS 8	CAN 24	(40	8 56	H 72	X 88	h 104	x 120	136	152	´ 168	¡ 184	à 200	Ä 216	Ò 232	½ 248
HT 9	EM 25	) 41	9 57	I 73	Y 89	i 105	y 121	137	153	` 169	¿ 185	è 201	ì 217	Õ 233	ª 249
LF 10	SUB 26	* 42	: 58	J 74	Z 90	j 106	z 122	138	154	^ 170	¤ 186	ò 202	Ö 218	õ 234	º 250
VT 11	ESC 27	+ 43	; 59	K 75	[91	k 107	{ 123	139	155	¨ 171	£ 187	ù 203	Ü 219	Š 235	« 251
FF 12	FS 28	, 44	< 60	L 76	\ 92	l 108	| 124	140	156	˜ 172	¥ 188	ä 204	É 220	š 236	■ 252
CR 13	GS 29	- 45	= 61	M 77	] 93	m 109	} 125	141	157	Ù 173	§ 189	ë 205	ï 221	Ú 237	» 253
SO 14	RS 30	. 46	> 62	N 78	^ 94	n 110	~ 126	142	158	Û 174	ƒ 190	ö 206	ß 222	Ÿ 238	± 254
SI 15	US 31	/ 47	? 63	O 79	_ 95	o 111	▒ 127	143	159	£ 175	¢ 191	ü 207	Ô 223	ÿ 239	255

Selecting a Symbol Set

To select a symbol set on an HP LaserJet:

1. Place the printer off line.
2. Hold down the control panel MENU button until the SYM SET message appears.
3. Press the control panel plus (+) and minus (-) keys to display the name of the desired symbol set.
4. Press the control panel ENTER button to select the option.
5. Place the printer back on line.

The LaserJet also lets you select a symbol set by using an escape sequence. Table 912 lists common symbol sets and their corresponding escape sequences.

Table 912. HP LaserJet Symbol Sets and Their Corresponding Escape Sequences

Symbol Set	Identification	Escape Sequence
HP Math-7	0A	Esc(0A
HP Line Draw	0B	Esc(0B
HP Roman Extension	0E	Esc(0E
HP Math 7	0M	Esc(0M
HP Math-8	8M	Esc(8M
HP Math-8a	0Q	Esc(0Q
OCR A	0O	Esc(0A
OCR B	1O	Esc(1O
USASCII	0U	Esc(0U
HP Legal	1U	Esc(1U
OEM-1	7U	Esc(7U
HP Roman-8	8U	Esc(8U
PC-8	I0U	Esc(10U
HP Pin Font	15U	Esc(15U
HP Pin Fonta	2Q	Esc(2Q

Displaying the Current Symbol Set

Tip 911 discusses symbol sets. Tip 912 describes how to select different HP LaserJet symbol sets from the control panel and by using escape sequences. To print a page containing the current symbol set, hold down the control panel PRINT FONTS key for three seconds. The LaserJet will print a page similar to the one shown here containing the symbol set name as well as its corresponding symbols.

```
Page Count=66600
Program ROM Datecode=19861203, Internal Font ROM Datecode=19860611
Auto Continue=OFF
Installed Memory=512 Kbytes
Symbol Set=IBM-US
Menu Items:
   Copies=1, Manual Feed=OFF, Font Source=I, Font Number=01,
   Form=60 Lines
Parallel I/O



 !"#$%&'()*+,-./0123456789:;<=>?@ABCDEFGHIJKLMNOPQRSTUVWXYZ[\]^_`abcdefghijklmno
!"#$%&'()*+,-./0123456789:;<=>?@ABCDEFGHIJKLMNOPQRSTUVWXYZ[\]^_`abcdefghijklmnop
"#$%&'()*+,-./0123456789:;<=>?@ABCDEFGHIJKLMNOPQRSTUVWXYZ[\]^_`abcdefghijklmnopq
#$%&'()*+,-./0123456789:;<=>?@ABCDEFGHIJKLMNOPQRSTUVWXYZ[\]^_`abcdefghijklmnopqr
$%&'()*+,-./0123456789:;<=>?@ABCDEFGHIJKLMNOPQRSTUVWXYZ[\]^_`abcdefghijklmnopqrs
%&'()*+,-./0123456789:;<=>?@ABCDEFGHIJKLMNOPQRSTUVWXYZ[\]^_`abcdefghijklmnopqrst
&'()*+,-./0123456789:;<=>?@ABCDEFGHIJKLMNOPQRSTUVWXYZ[\]^_`abcdefghijklmnopqrstu
'()*+,-./0123456789:;<=>?@ABCDEFGHIJKLMNOPQRSTUVWXYZ[\]^_`abcdefghijklmnopqrstuv
()*+,-./0123456789:;<=>?@ABCDEFGHIJKLMNOPQRSTUVWXYZ[\]^_`abcdefghijklmnopqrstuvw
)*+,-./0123456789:;<=>?@ABCDEFGHIJKLMNOPQRSTUVWXYZ[\]^_`abcdefghijklmnopqrstuvwx
*+,-./0123456789:;<=>?@ABCDEFGHIJKLMNOPQRSTUVWXYZ[\]^_`abcdefghijklmnopqrstuvwxy
+,-./0123456789:;<=>?@ABCDEFGHIJKLMNOPQRSTUVWXYZ[\]^_`abcdefghijklmnopqrstuvwxyz
,-./0123456789:;<=>?@ABCDEFGHIJKLMNOPQRSTUVWXYZ[\]^_`abcdefghijklmnopqrstuvwxyz{
-./0123456789:;<=>?@ABCDEFGHIJKLMNOPQRSTUVWXYZ[\]^_`abcdefghijklmnopqrstuvwxyz{|
./0123456789:;<=>?@ABCDEFGHIJKLMNOPQRSTUVWXYZ[\]^_`abcdefghijklmnopqrstuvwxyz{|}
/0123456789:;<=>?@ABCDEFGHIJKLMNOPQRSTUVWXYZ[\]^_`abcdefghijklmnopqrstuvwxyz{|}~
0123456789:;<=>?@ABCDEFGHIJKLMNOPQRSTUVWXYZ[\]^_`abcdefghijklmnopqrstuvwxyz{|}~■
123456789:;<=>?@ABCDEFGHIJKLMNOPQRSTUVWXYZ[\]^_`abcdefghijklmnopqrstuvwxyz{|}~■
23456789:;<=>?@ABCDEFGHIJKLMNOPQRSTUVWXYZ[\]^_`abcdefghijklmnopqrstuvwxyz{|}~■ !
3456789:;<=>?@ABCDEFGHIJKLMNOPQRSTUVWXYZ[\]^_`abcdefghijklmnopqrstuvwxyz{|}~■ !"
456789:;<=>?@ABCDEFGHIJKLMNOPQRSTUVWXYZ[\]^_`abcdefghijklmnopqrstuvwxyz{|}~■ !"#
56789:;<=>?@ABCDEFGHIJKLMNOPQRSTUVWXYZ[\]^_`abcdefghijklmnopqrstuvwxyz{|}~■ !"#$
6789:;<=>?@ABCDEFGHIJKLMNOPQRSTUVWXYZ[\]^_`abcdefghijklmnopqrstuvwxyz{|}~■ !"#$%
789:;<=>?@ABCDEFGHIJKLMNOPQRSTUVWXYZ[\]^_`abcdefghijklmnopqrstuvwxyz{|}~■ !"#$%&
89:;<=>?@ABCDEFGHIJKLMNOPQRSTUVWXYZ[\]^_`abcdefghijklmnopqrstuvwxyz{|}~■ !"#$%&'
9:;<=>?@ABCDEFGHIJKLMNOPQRSTUVWXYZ[\]^_`abcdefghijklmnopqrstuvwxyz{|}~■ !"#$%&'(
:;<=>?@ABCDEFGHIJKLMNOPQRSTUVWXYZ[\]^_`abcdefghijklmnopqrstuvwxyz{|}~■ !"#$%&'()
;<=>?@ABCDEFGHIJKLMNOPQRSTUVWXYZ[\]^_`abcdefghijklmnopqrstuvwxyz{|}~■ !"#$%&'()*
<=>?@ABCDEFGHIJKLMNOPQRSTUVWXYZ[\]^_`abcdefghijklmnopqrstuvwxyz{|}~■ !"#$%&'()*+
 ÀÂÈÊËÎÏ´`ˆ¨˜ÙÛ£¯Ýý°ÇçÑñ¡¿¤£¥§ƒ¢âêôûáéóúàèòùäëöüÅîØÆåíøæÄìÖÜÉïßÔÁÃãÐðÍÌÓÒÕõŠšÚŸÿ
ÀÂÈÊËÎÏ´`ˆ¨˜ÙÛ£¯Ýý°ÇçÑñ¡¿¤£¥§ƒ¢âêôûáéóúàèòùäëöüÅîØÆåíøæÄìÖÜÉïßÔÁÃãÐðÍÌÓÒÕõŠšÚŸÿÞ
ÂÈÊËÎÏ´`ˆ¨˜ÙÛ£¯Ýý°ÇçÑñ¡¿¤£¥§ƒ¢âêôûáéóúàèòùäëöüÅîØÆåíøæÄìÖÜÉïßÔÁÃãÐðÍÌÓÒÕõŠšÚŸÿÞþ
ÈÊËÎÏ´`ˆ¨˜ÙÛ£¯Ýý°ÇçÑñ¡¿¤£¥§ƒ¢âêôûáéóúàèòùäëöüÅîØÆåíøæÄìÖÜÉïßÔÁÃãÐðÍÌÓÒÕõŠšÚŸÿÞþ·
ÊËÎÏ´`ˆ¨˜ÙÛ£¯Ýý°ÇçÑñ¡¿¤£¥§ƒ¢âêôûáéóúàèòùäëöüÅîØÆåíøæÄìÖÜÉïßÔÁÃãÐðÍÌÓÒÕõŠšÚŸÿÞþ·µ
ËÎÏ´`ˆ¨˜ÙÛ£¯Ýý°ÇçÑñ¡¿¤£¥§ƒ¢âêôûáéóúàèòùäëöüÅîØÆåíøæÄìÖÜÉïßÔÁÃãÐðÍÌÓÒÕõŠšÚŸÿÞþ·µ¶
ÎÏ´`ˆ¨˜ÙÛ£¯Ýý°ÇçÑñ¡¿¤£¥§ƒ¢âêôûáéóúàèòùäëöüÅîØÆåíøæÄìÖÜÉïßÔÁÃãÐðÍÌÓÒÕõŠšÚŸÿÞþ·µ¶¾
Ï´`ˆ¨˜ÙÛ£¯Ýý°ÇçÑñ¡¿¤£¥§ƒ¢âêôûáéóúàèòùäëöüÅîØÆåíøæÄìÖÜÉïßÔÁÃãÐðÍÌÓÒÕõŠšÚŸÿÞþ·µ¶¾—
´`ˆ¨˜ÙÛ£¯Ýý°ÇçÑñ¡¿¤£¥§ƒ¢âêôûáéóúàèòùäëöüÅîØÆåíøæÄìÖÜÉïßÔÁÃãÐðÍÌÓÒÕõŠšÚŸÿÞþ·µ¶¾—¼
`ˆ¨˜ÙÛ£¯Ýý°ÇçÑñ¡¿¤£¥§ƒ¢âêôûáéóúàèòùäëöüÅîØÆåíøæÄìÖÜÉïßÔÁÃãÐðÍÌÓÒÕõŠšÚŸÿÞþ·µ¶¾—¼½
ˆ¨˜ÙÛ£¯Ýý°ÇçÑñ¡¿¤£¥§ƒ¢âêôûáéóúàèòùäëöüÅîØÆåíøæÄìÖÜÉïßÔÁÃãÐðÍÌÓÒÕõŠšÚŸÿÞþ·µ¶¾—¼½ª
¨˜ÙÛ£¯Ýý°ÇçÑñ¡¿¤£¥§ƒ¢âêôûáéóúàèòùäëöüÅîØÆåíøæÄìÖÜÉïßÔÁÃãÐðÍÌÓÒÕõŠšÚŸÿÞþ·µ¶¾—¼½ªº
˜ÙÛ£¯Ýý°ÇçÑñ¡¿¤£¥§ƒ¢âêôûáéóúàèòùäëöüÅîØÆåíøæÄìÖÜÉïßÔÁÃãÐðÍÌÓÒÕõŠšÚŸÿÞþ·µ¶¾—¼½ªº«
ÙÛ£¯Ýý°ÇçÑñ¡¿¤£¥§ƒ¢âêôûáéóúàèòùäëöüÅîØÆåíøæÄìÖÜÉïßÔÁÃãÐðÍÌÓÒÕõŠšÚŸÿÞþ·µ¶¾—¼½ªº«■
Û£¯Ýý°ÇçÑñ¡¿¤£¥§ƒ¢âêôûáéóúàèòùäëöüÅîØÆåíøæÄìÖÜÉïßÔÁÃãÐðÍÌÓÒÕõŠšÚŸÿÞþ·µ¶¾—¼½ªº«■»
£¯Ýý°ÇçÑñ¡¿¤£¥§ƒ¢âêôûáéóúàèòùäëöüÅîØÆåíøæÄìÖÜÉïßÔÁÃãÐðÍÌÓÒÕõŠšÚŸÿÞþ·µ¶¾—¼½ªº«■»±
¯Ýý°ÇçÑñ¡¿¤£¥§ƒ¢âêôûáéóúàèòùäëöüÅîØÆåíøæÄìÖÜÉïßÔÁÃãÐðÍÌÓÒÕõŠšÚŸÿÞþ·µ¶¾—¼½ªº«■»±
Ýý°ÇçÑñ¡¿¤£¥§ƒ¢âêôûáéóúàèòùäëöüÅîØÆåíøæÄìÖÜÉïßÔÁÃãÐðÍÌÓÒÕõŠšÚŸÿÞþ·µ¶¾—¼½ªº«■»±
ý°ÇçÑñ¡¿¤£¥§ƒ¢âêôûáéóúàèòùäëöüÅîØÆåíøæÄìÖÜÉïßÔÁÃãÐðÍÌÓÒÕõŠšÚŸÿÞþ·µ¶¾—¼½ªº«■»±  À
°ÇçÑñ¡¿¤£¥§ƒ¢âêôûáéóúàèòùäëöüÅîØÆåíøæÄìÖÜÉïßÔÁÃãÐðÍÌÓÒÕõŠšÚŸÿÞþ·µ¶¾—¼½ªº«■»±  ÀÂ
```

Understanding Font Components

Several of the tips presented in this book discuss font operations. Although the multiplicity of fonts may make fonts seem complex, they actually are quite easy to understand. In the simplest sense, a font is a set of characters and symbols. Each font has a unique name and unique characteristics such as size, spacing, style, stroke weight, and pitch. Tip 911 discusses symbol sets in detail, Tip 916 discusses font sizes, and Tip 915 discusses font spacing. The font's style is how it appears, other than size (for example, italics). The font's stroke weight defines each character's thickness (darkness) on the page; a bold font, for example, has a different stroke weight than a normal font. The font pitch is the number of those characters that will fit in an inch of space.

Understanding Character Spacing

A font's spacing indicates the amount of space each character on a page consumes. There are two spacing types: fixed and proportional. In a fixed-space font, every character receives the same amount of space.

> `This paragraph uses a fixed-space font. As you can see, each character consumes the same amount of space, regardless of the character's size. Fixed-space fonts more closely resemble typewriter output.`

In comparison, this book's text uses a proportional-spaced font. The amount of space characters in a proportional space font consume is directly proportional to the character's width. As you can see, the selection of proportional or fixed space can have a dramatic affect on your document's appearance.

Understanding Font Sizes

As Tip 914 shows, fonts have unique sizes. Font sizes are described in terms of points; a point is 1/72 of an inch. The following illustration shows several font sizes:

10 point font

12 point font

18 point font

24 point font

48 point font

72 point font

Font sizes can be fixed or scalable. You cannot change the size of a fixed-sized font. Depending on your software, you can increase or decrease the size of a scalable font to meet your needs. Before you purchase fonts, make sure you can use the font with your software and printer.

Creating HP LaserJet Macros

Throughout this book you have sent various PCL escape sequences to the LaserJet printer to select different printer attributes. There may be times, however, when you want the printer to select different characteristics on a per-page basis. One way to do so is by creating downloadable printer macros. If you use a software program such as WordPerfect or Lotus 1-2-3, you already know that a macro is a series of recorded keystrokes you can play back as required to perform a specific task. In a similar way, a LaserJet macro contains one or more PCL escape sequences. When you record a LaserJet macro, the printer stores the macro in its memory.

You must assign each macro a unique number. When you later want to use the macro, you simply refer to it by number. To record a macro, you send an escape sequence that directs the printer to start recording. You then send the PCL commands to be assigned to the macro, followed by an escape sequence that ends the recording. The following escape sequences illustrate the macro recording for macro number 1:

Esc&f1Y	Create macro #1
Esc&f0X	Begin recording
PCL escape sequences here	
Esc&f1X	End recording

The following batch file, AUTHOR.BAT, creates macro number 1, assigning to it the commands necessary to place your name at the top of each page:

```
@ECHO OFF
ECHO Esc&f1YEsc&f0X > PRN
ECHO Esc&f0S > PRN
ECHO Esc&a0HEsc&a0VDocument by: Kris Jamsa > PRN
ECHO Esc&f1S > PRN
ECHO Esc&f1X > PRN
```

In this case, the batch file listing uses the letters "Esc" to represent the unprintable ASCII escape character. Within your batch file, you must use the actual escape character.

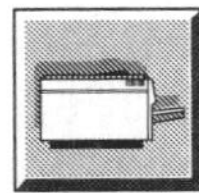

Executing an HP LaserJet Macro

Tip 917 explains how to create an HP LaserJet macro that lets you automatically print your name at the top of a page. To execute the macro, you must first select the macro by using the following escape sequence:

```
Esc&f#Y
```

Next, you must issue the following escape sequence to execute the command:

```
Esc&f2X
```

For example, to execute macro 1, you use the following escape sequence:

```
Esc&f1Y
Esc&f2X
```

Executing a macro is only one way to play back a macro. When you execute a macro, any page or printer settings the macro makes remain in effect after the macro ends.

Calling an HP LaserJet Macro

Tip 917 describes how to record HP LaserJet macros. Tip 918 describes how to execute a LaserJet macro. As discussed in Tip 918, when you execute a macro, any changes the macro makes to page and printer settings remain in effect after the macro ends. If you have a macro that performs a specific task, but then does not clean up after itself (leaving settings changed), you can call the macro rather than executing it. If you call a macro, any changes to printer or page settings persist only while the macro

is executing. After the macro's execution ends, the previous settings are restored. To call a macro in this way, first use the following escape sequence to select the macro:

```
Esc&f#Y
```

Next, use the following escape sequence to call the macro:

```
Esc&f3X
```

The following escape sequences call macro 1, created in Tip 917:

```
Esc&f1Y
Esc&f3X
```

Executing a LaserJet Macro for Every Printed Page

Tip 917 explains how to record LaserJet macros. Sometimes you may want the printer to execute your macro each time it prints a page. For example, you might want to print a document version classification on each page. To do so, you must first select the macro by using the following escape sequence:

```
Esc&f#Y
```

Next, use the following escape sequence to direct the LaserJet to execute the macro for each printed page:

```
Exc&f4X
```

The following escape sequences direct the LaserJet to execute macro 1 (created in Tip 917) with each printed page:

```
Esc&f1Y
Esc&f4X
```

Making Your LaserJet Macros Reset-Resistant

Tip 917 describes how to create LaserJet macros. By default, the macros you create are temporary, which means a printer reset operation will erase them. To protect your macros from reset operations, first use the following escape sequence to select the macro:

```
Esc&f#Y
```

Next, issue the following escape sequence:

```
Esc&f10X
```

For example, the following escape sequence makes macro 1 created in Tip 917 permanent (at least until you turn off the printer's power):

```
Esc&f1
Esc&f10x
```

If you want to change the macro's status from permanent to temporary, select the macro using escape sequence Esc&f#Y and then issue the following escape sequence:

```
Esc&f9X
```

Making macros permanent is a way to protect the macros from users who, on a shared printer, tend to reset the printer.

Removing LaserJet Macros from the Printer's Memory

Tip 917 describes how to record LaserJet macros where you see how the printer stores macros in its internal memory. If your printer has a limited amount of memory, or if you no longer require a specific macro, you can remove the macro from memory. To do so, first issue the following escape sequence to select the macro:

```
Esc&f#Y
```

Next, issue the following escape sequence to remove the macro from memory:

```
Esc&f8X
```

For example, to remove macro 1 from the printer's memory, you would use the following escape sequences:

```
Esc&f1Y
Esc&f8X
```

The previous escape sequences will remove a macro from memory regardless of whether the macro is permanent or temporary. If you want to remove all temporary macros from memory, use the following escape sequence:

```
Esc&f7X
```

To delete all permanent macros, use the following escape sequence:

```
Esc&f8X
```

Controlling Italics on an Epson-Compatible Printer

If you are using a dot-matrix printer, the printer is probably Epson compatible. Using the printer escape sequences listed in Table 923, you can turn the use of italics on and off.

To make these escape sequences easy to use, the following DEBUG script file, EPSONITA.SCR, creates the command files ITALON.COM and ITALOFF.COM, whose output you can redirect to your printer to control italics:

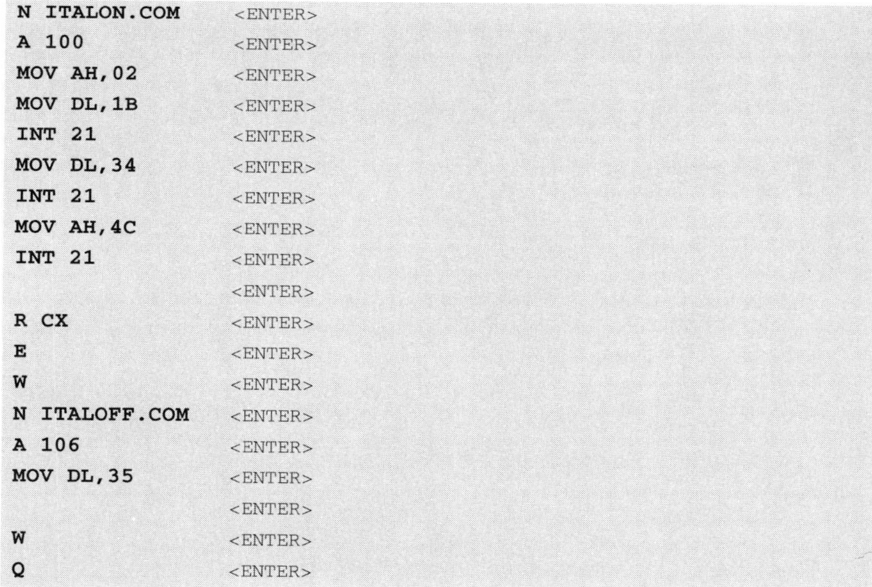

```
N ITALON.COM    <ENTER>
A 100           <ENTER>
MOV AH,02       <ENTER>
MOV DL,1B       <ENTER>
INT 21          <ENTER>
MOV DL,34       <ENTER>
INT 21          <ENTER>
MOV AH,4C       <ENTER>
INT 21          <ENTER>
                <ENTER>
R CX            <ENTER>
E               <ENTER>
W               <ENTER>
N ITALOFF.COM   <ENTER>
A 106           <ENTER>
MOV DL,35       <ENTER>
                <ENTER>
W               <ENTER>
Q               <ENTER>
```

EPSONITA.SCR

Table 923. Controlling Italics on an Epson-Compatible Printer

Italics	Escape Sequence
On	Esc4
Off	Esc5

Use DEBUG as follows to create the command files:

```
C:\> DEBUG < EPSONITA.SCR <ENTER>
```

The following batch file, ITALDIR.BAT, uses these two commands to print a directory listing in italics:

```
@ECHO OFF
ITALON > PRN
DIR  > PRN
ITALOFF > PRN
```

Controlling Underlining on an Epson-Compatible Printer

If you are using a dot-matrix printer, the printer is probably Epson compatible. Using the printer escape sequences listed in Table 924, you can turn your printer's use of underlining on and off.

To make these escape sequences easier to use, the DEBUG script file on the following page, EPSONUND.SCR, creates the command files UNDON.COM and UNOFF.COM, whose output you can redirect to your printer to control underlining:

Table 924. Controlling Underlining on an Epson-Compatible Printer

Underlining	Escape Sequence
On	Esc-<SOH>
Off	Esc-<NUL>

The <SOH> character is ASCII 1, and <NUL> is ASCII 0.

```
N UNDON.COM      <ENTER>
A 100            <ENTER>
MOV AH,2         <ENTER>
MOV DL,1B        <ENTER>
INT 21           <ENTER>
MOV DL,2D        <ENTER>
INT 21           <ENTER>
MOV DL,1         <ENTER>
INT 21           <ENTER>
MOV AH,4C        <ENTER>
INT 21           <ENTER>
                 <ENTER>
R CX             <ENTER>
12               <ENTER>
W                <ENTER>
N UNDOFF.COM     <ENTER>
A 10A            <ENTER>
MOV DL,0         <ENTER>
                 <ENTER>
W                <ENTER>
Q                <ENTER>
```

EPSONUND.SCR

Use DEBUG as follows to create the command files:

```
C:\> DEBUG < EPSONUND.SCR <ENTER>
```

The following batch file, UND_DIR.BAT, uses UNDON and UNDOFF to print an underlined directory listing:

```
@ECHO OFF
UNDON > PRN
DIR > PRN
UNDOFF > PRN
```

Tip 925 Controlling Proportional and Fixed-Space Printing on an Epson-Compatible Printer

Tip 915 discusses the difference between proportional and fixed-spaced fonts. If you are using a dot-matrix printer, you can probably use the Epson-printer escape sequences listed in Table 925 to turn proportional printing on and off.

To make these escape sequences easier to use, the following DEBUG script file, EPSONPRO.SCR, creates the command files PROPON.COM and PROPOFF.COM, whose output you can redirect to your printer to control proportional spacing:

EPSONPRO.SCR

```
N PROPON.COM      <ENTER>
A 100             <ENTER>
MOV AH,2          <ENTER>
MOV DL,1B         <ENTER>
INT 21            <ENTER>
MOV DL,70         <ENTER>
INT 21            <ENTER>
MOV DL,1          <ENTER>
INT 21            <ENTER>
MOV AH,4C         <ENTER>
INT 21            <ENTER>
                  <ENTER>
R CX              <ENTER>
12                <ENTER>
W                 <ENTER>
N PROPOFF.COM     <ENTER>
A 10A             <ENTER>
MOV DL,0          <ENTER>
                  <ENTER>
W                 <ENTER>
Q                 <ENTER>
```

Use DEBUG as follows to create the command files PROPON.COM and PROPOFF.COM:

```
C:\> DEBUG < EPSONPRO.SCR
```

The following batch file, PROPDIFF.BAT, uses PROPON and PROPOFF with DIR to illustrate the differences between proportional and fixed-space printing:

```
@ECHO OFF
PROPON > PRN
DIR
PROPOFF > PRN
DIR
```

Table 925. Controlling Proportional Spacing on an Epson-Compatible Printer

Proportional Printing	Escape Sequences
On	Escp<SOH>
Off	Escp<NUL>

The <SOH> character in ASCII 1, and <NUL> is ASCII 0.

Select Elite or Pica Type on an Epson-Compatible Printer

Pica type is the large type on a typewriter, measuring 10 characters per inch. Elite type is the smaller type, measuring 12 characters per inch. If you are using a dot-matrix printer, you can probably use the escape sequences listed in Table 926 to select pica or elite print.

To make these escape sequences easier to use, the following DEBUG script file, EPSONPIE.SCR, creates the command files PICA.COM and ELITE.COM, whose output you can redirect to your printer to select Pica or Elite type:

EPSONPIE.SCR

```
N PICA.COM          <ENTER>
A 100               <ENTER>
MOV AH,02           <ENTER>
MOV DL,1B           <ENTER>
INT 21              <ENTER>
MOV DL,50           <ENTER>
INT 21              <ENTER>
MOV AH,4C           <ENTER>
INT 21              <ENTER>
                    <ENTER>
R CX                <ENTER>
E                   <ENTER>
W                   <ENTER>
N ELITE.COM         <ENTER>
A 106               <ENTER>
MOV DL,4D           <ENTER>
                    <ENTER>
W                   <ENTER>
Q                   <ENTER>
```

Use DEBUG as follows to create the command files PICA.COM and ELITE.COM:

```
C:\> DEBUG < EPSONPIE.SCR <ENTER>
```

Table 926. Selecting Pica or Elite Type on an Epson-Compatible Printer

Print Type	Escape Sequence
Pica	EscP
Elite	EscM

Controlling the Number of Characters per Inch on an Epson-Compatible Printer

The number of characters per inch (cpi) your printer prints controls whether the text appears normal or compressed. If you are using a dot-matrix printer, you can probably use the Epson printer ASCII sequences listed in Table 927 to select compressed (17.1 cpi) or normal (10 cpi) mode.

To make these ASCII sequences easier to use, the following DEBUG script file, EPSONCPI.SCR, creates the command files EPSON1O.COM and EPSON171.COM, whose output you can redirect to your printer to control the number of characters per inch:

```
N EPSON10.COM    <ENTER>
A 100            <ENTER>
MOV AH,2         <ENTER>
MOV DL,12        <ENTER>
INT 21           <ENTER>
MOV AH,4C        <ENTER>
INT 21           <ENTER>
                 <ENTER>
R CX             <ENTER>
A                <ENTER>
W                <ENTER>
N EPSON171.COM   <ENTER>
A 102            <ENTER>
MOV DL,F         <ENTER>
                 <ENTER>
W                <ENTER>
Q                <ENTER>
```

EPSONCPI.SCR

Table 927. ASCII Codes to Control the Number of Characters Per Inch on an Epson-Compatible Printer

Characters per Inch	ASCII
10	<DC2> (r)
17.1	<SI> (o)

Use DEBUG as follows to create the command files EPSON1O.COM and EPSON171.COM:

```
C:\> DEBUG < EPSONCPI.SCR <ENTER>
```

The following batch commands print a directory listing using 17.1 and then 10 characters per inch:

```
@ECHO OFF
EPSON171 > PRN
DIR > PRN
EPSON10 > PRN
DIR > PRN
```

Controlling Enlarged Print on an Epson-Compatible Printer

If you are using a dot-matrix printer, you can probably use the ASCII sequences listed in Table 928 to turn enlarged printing on and off.

To make these ASCII sequences easier to use, the following DEBUG script file, EPSONBIG.SCR, creates the command files BIGON.COM and BIGOFF.COM, whose output you can redirect to your printer to control enlarged print:

EPSONBIG.SCR

```
N BIGON.COM       <ENTER>
A 100             <ENTER>
MOV AH,2          <ENTER>
MOV DL,E          <ENTER>
INT 21            <ENTER>
MOV AH,4C         <ENTER>
INT 21            <ENTER>
                  <ENTER>
R CX              <ENTER>
A                 <ENTER>
W                 <ENTER>
```

```
N BIGOFF.COM      <ENTER>
A 102             <ENTER>
MOV DL,14         <ENTER>
                  <ENTER>
W                 <ENTER>
Q                 <ENTER>
```

Use DEBUG as follows to create the command files BIGON.COM and BIGOFF.COM:

```
C:\> DEBUG < EPSONBIG.SCR <ENTER>
```

The following batch commands use BIGON and BIGOFF to print a directory listing with a title:

```
@ECHO OFF
BIGON > PRN
VOL > PRN
BIGOFF > PRN
DIR > PRN
```

Table 928. Controlling ASCII Codes on Epson-Compatible Printers

Enlarged Print	ASCII
On	<SO> (n)
Off	<DC4> (t)

Controlling Double-Strike Print Operations on an Epson-Compatible Printer

If you are using a dot-matrix printer, you can probably use the Epson-printer escape sequences listed in Table 929 to turn double-strike mode on and off. Double-strike mode darkens your printed text by directing the printer to print each line twice. However, using double-strike mode slows down your printer operations by almost 50 percent.

To make these escape sequences easier to use, the following DEBUG script file, EPSONDBL.SCR, creates the command files DBLSTON.COM and DBLSTOFF.COM, whose output you can redirect to your printer to control double-strike operations:

EPSONDBL.SCR

```
N DBLSTON.COM    <ENTER>
A 100            <ENTER>
MOV AH,02        <ENTER>
MOV DL,1B        <ENTER>
INT 21           <ENTER>
MOV DL,47        <ENTER>
INT 21           <ENTER>
MOV AH,4C        <ENTER>
INT 21           <ENTER>
                 <ENTER>
R CX             <ENTER>
E                <ENTER>
W                <ENTER>
N DBLSTOFF.COM   <ENTER>
A 106            <ENTER>
MOV DL,48        <ENTER>
                 <ENTER>
W                <ENTER>
Q                <ENTER>
```

Use DEBUG as follows to create the command files DBLSTON.COM and DBLSTOFF.COM:

```
C:\> DEBUG < EPSONDBL.SCR <ENTER>
```

Table 929. Controlling Double-Strike Mode on an Epson-Compatible Printer

Double Strike	Escape Sequence
On	EscG
Off	EscH

Controlling Emphasized Printing on an Epson-Compatible Printer

If you are using a dot-matrix printer, you can probably use the escape sequences listed in Table 930 to turn emphasized printing on and off. Emphasized printing makes text bold.

To make these escape sequences easier to use, the following DEBUG script file, EPSONEMP.SCR, creates two command files, EMPHON.COM and EMPHOFF.COM, whose output you can redirect to your printer to control emphasized print:

```
N EMPHON.COM   <ENTER>
A 100          <ENTER>
MOV AH,02      <ENTER>
MOV DL,1B      <ENTER>
INT 21         <ENTER>
MOV DL,45      <ENTER>
INT 21         <ENTER>
MOV AH,4C      <ENTER>
INT 21         <ENTER>
               <ENTER>
R CX           <ENTER>
E              <ENTER>
W              <ENTER>
N EMPHOFF.COM  <ENTER>
A 106          <ENTER>
MOV DL,46      <ENTER>
               <ENTER>
W              <ENTER>
Q              <ENTER>
```

EPSONEMP.SCR

Use DEBUG as follows to create the command files EMPHON.COM and EMPHOFF.COM:

```
C:\> DEBUG < EPSONEMP.SCR <ENTER>
```

Table 930. Controlling Emphasized Printing on Epson-Compatible Printers

Emphasized Printing	Escape Sequence
On	EscE
Off	EscF

Bringing Your Printer Ribbon Back to Life

If your printer ribbon runs dry and you don't have a replacement ribbon readily available, don't fret. By removing your ribbon from the printer and evenly spraying the ribbon with WD-40, you can cause ink to run back into the dry track. As you spray the ribbon, rewind the ribbon using a screwdriver so you can spray all of it. Don't soak the ribbon: spray only enough WD-40 to get the job done. As an added bonus, the WD-40 provides good lubrication for your print head.

Selecting 66 Lines Per Page on an HP LaserJet

By default, the HP LaserJet prints 60 lines per page. Depending on what you are printing, you may sometimes want the LaserJet to print 66 lines per page. The LaserJet provides escape sequences that let you select 60 or 66 lines per page. As shown in Table 932, the escape sequence you use also depends on the current line size (the characters per line).

The following batch file, for example, selects 66 lines per page and 132 characters per line:

```
@ECHO OFF
ECHO Esc&l17.27CEsc(s16.66H  > PRN
```

Table 932. Escape Sequences to Select Different Page and Line Lengths on an HP LaserJet Printer

Lines per Page	Characters per Line	Escape Sequence
60	80	EscE
60	96	Esc(s0p12H
60	132	Esc(s16.66H
66	80	Esc&l7.27C
66	96	Esc&l7.27CEsc(s0p12H
66	132	Esc&l7.27CEsc(s16.66H

The batch file uses the characters Esc to represent the unprintable ASCII escape character. In your batch files you must use the actual escape character as discussed in Tip 34.

Performing a Printer Engine Test on an HP LaserJet

If you have an HP LaserJet printer that is experiencing dropouts or other printer errors, locate the printer's engine test button shown here:

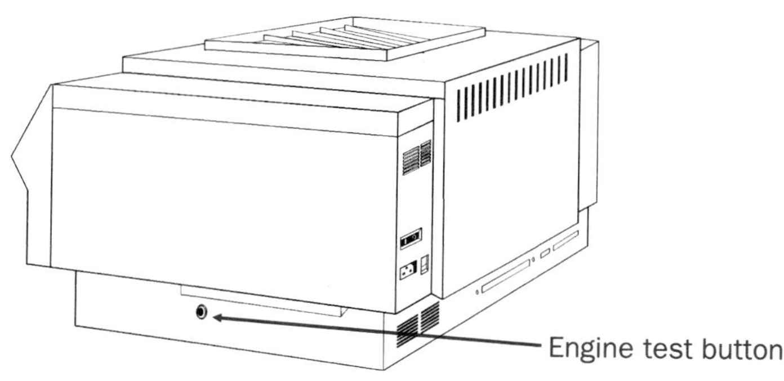

Using a pen or other narrow object, press the engine test button. Your printer should print a page containing a series of long narrow lines. If your printer does not, it is experiencing engine problems.

Understanding How a Laser Printer Works

Many users think that a laser printer uses a laser to burn an image into a sheet of paper. Actually, the laser never comes in contact with the paper. The following illustration shows the path your paper travels through the laser printer:

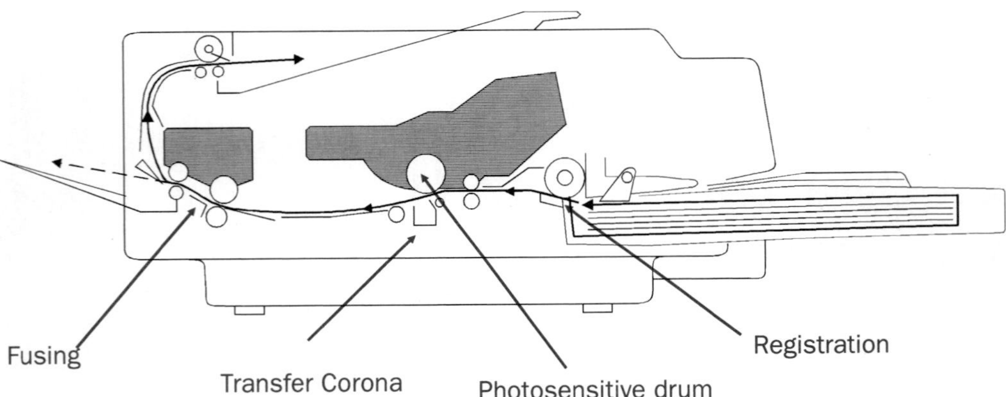

To begin, the printer grabs a piece of paper from the sheet feeder. The printer first applies an electrical charge to the paper that will later attract toner. At this same time, the laser is scanning the printer's photosensitive drum, applying precise signals to the drum that correspond to the characters to be printed (the laser's only role). After the laser has applied signals to the drum, the printer releases toner, which is attracted to the drum's charged areas, creating the letters to be printed. As the paper passes under the drum, the toner is transferred to the paper. The paper then passes through its final stage, in which high-intensity lamps permanently fuse the toner to the page.

To summarize, the laser's role in printing is simply to apply precise signals to the printer's photosensitive drum; the signals correspond to the desired characters.

Understanding PCL Coordinates

As Tip 910 describes, PCL is Hewlett-Packard's printer command language. Many of the tips presented in this book use PCL escape sequences to direct the LaserJet to perform various operations. Several tips use PCL escape sequences to move the cursor to specific page locations or to shade different regions. Before you can perform these operations, you need to understand PCL's page coordinate system. To begin, PCL divides the page into square grids, 1/300 of an inch in width and height. Many books and magazines refer to these grids as dots. Each dot on the page has a corresponding x,y coordinate. The following example illustrates the various dot coordinates:

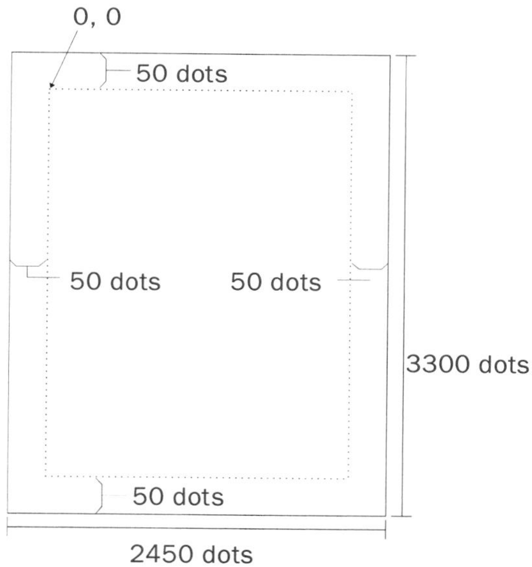

Each page you print using an HP printer has a 50-dot right and left border outside of which the printer is unable to print. If you position the cursor in the border area and attempt to print text or graphics, the printer will ignore the data.

As shown in Table 935, PCL provides two escape sequences you can use to move the cursor to a specific x and y location.

Table 935. PCL Escape Sequence to Move the Cursor to a Specific x,y Dot Coordinate

Cursor Movement	Escape Sequence
Move to x coordinate	Esc*pRowX
Move to y coordinate	Esc*pColumnY

The following batch file, MIDDLE.BAT, uses the PCL escape sequences to print the message "Middle" along the left margin, near the middle of your page:

```
@ECHO OFF
ECHO. > PRN
ECHO Esc*p1600YMiddle > PRN
```

Moving the Cursor Relative to Its Current Position

Tip 935 describes how to move the cursor relative to its current position by using PCL escape sequences; you move the cursor to specific dot locations on the page grid. PCL also provides escape sequences that let you move the cursor relative to its current location. Actually, you use the same escape sequences as shown in Tip 935. To move the cursor relative to its current position, precede the dot value with a plus (+) or minus (-) sign. Table 936 shows several different ways to move the cursor relative to its current position.

Table 936. PCL Escape Sequences to Move the Cursor Relative to Its Current Position

Escape Sequence	Cursor Movement
Esc*p+10X	Ten dots to the right
Esc*p-15Y	Fifteen dots up
Esc*p-25X	Twenty-five dots to the left
Esc*p+1Y	One dot down

Working with LaserJet Decipoints

In Tip 935 you learned how to work with PCL dots, each of which are 1/300 of an inch. If you need finer resolution, the LaserJet lets you work with decipoints which are 1/720 of an inch (a point is 1/72 of an inch). Table 937 lists the PCL escape sequences to position the cursor at different decipoint locations.

The following batch commands use these escape sequences to display the message "Middle Bottom" centered at the bottom of your page:

```
@ECHO OFF
ECHO Esc&a2300HEsc&a7000VMiddle Bottom > PRN
```

As was the case in with dot movement discussed in Tip 936, you can move the cursor in relative decipoints by preceding the values with a plus or minus sign.

In this case, the batch used the letters "Esc" to represent the the unprintable ASCII escape character. Within your batch file, however, you must use the actual escape character.

Table 937. PCL Escape Sequences to Move the Cursor to a Specific x,y Dot Coordinate

Cursor Movement	Escape Sequence
Move to x coordinate	Esc&aRowH
Move to y coordinate	Esc&aColumnV

Controlling LaserJet Carriage-Return, Line-Feed, and Form-Feed Interpretation

By default, when the LaserJet receives a carriage-return, line-feed, or form-feed character, the LaserJet performs the corresponding operation. The LaserJet, however, lets you customize its response by using the escape sequences shown in Table 938.

Table 938. LaserJet Character Translation Escape Sequences

Escape Sequence	Original Character CR	LF	FF
Esc&k0G	CR	LF	FF
Esc&k1G	CR+LF	LF	FF
Esc&k2G	CR	CR+LF	CR+FF
Esc&k3G	CR+FF	LF+FF	CR+FF

Using the LaserJet Stack to Save and Restore the Cursor Position

Several of the tips presented throughout this book have used PCL escape sequences to position the cursor. As you use PCL escape sequences to position the cursor for different purposes, there may be

times when you want to save the cursor's position before performing a specific set of PCL commands. To help you save the cursor position, the LaserJet provides a stack, upon which you can place up to 20 cursor positions. To save the cursor position on the stack, you perform a push operation. Table 939 lists the escape sequences required to perform push and pop operations.

The following batch commands illustrate how to use the push and pop operations. The batch file begins by printing text "Starting Position." Next, the batch file performs a push operation to save the cursor position. The batch file then moves the cursor to the middle of the page and prints the message "Middle Position." Last, the batch file pops the original cursor position and prints the message "Ending Position."

```
@ECHO OFF
ECHO Starting Position > PRN
ECHO Esc&f0S > PRN
ECHO Esc&a2700HEsc&a4000VMiddle Position > PRN
ECHO Esc&f1S > PRN
ECHO Ending Position > PRN
```

When you execute the batch commands, the printer will print the messages "Starting Position" and "Ending Position" one beneath the other. Because ECHO generates a carriage return and line feed, a blank line exists between the two lines of text.

In this case, the batch file listing uses the letters "Esc" to represent the unprintable ASCII escape character. Within your batch file, however, you must use the actual escape character.

Table 939. PCL Escape Sequences to Push and Pop the Current Cursor Position

Operation	Escape Sequence
Push cursor position	Esc&f0S
Pop cursor position	Esc&f1S

Selecting Paper Sizes on an HP LaserJet

Using the LaserJet's manual paper-feed slot, you can use different paper sizes. The two most common paper sizes are letter size (8 1/2 by 11 inches) and legal size (8 1/2 by 14 inches). The following DEBUG script file, HPPAPER.SCR, creates two command files, HPLTR.COM and HPLEGAL.COM, whose output you can redirect to your printer to select a paper size:

HPPAPER.SCR

```
N HPLTR.COM                    <ENTER>
A 100                          <ENTER>
JMP 109                        <ENTER>
DB 1B,26,6C,36,36,50,24        <ENTER>
MOV AH,9                       <ENTER>
MOV DX,102                     <ENTER>
INT 21                         <ENTER>
MOV AH,4C                      <ENTER>
INT 21                         <ENTER>
                               <ENTER>
R CX                           <ENTER>
14                             <ENTER>
W                              <ENTER>
N HPLEGAL.COM                  <ENTER>
E 105 38,34                    <ENTER>
W                              <ENTER>
Q                              <ENTER>
```

Use DEBUG as follows to create the command files HPLTR.COM and HPLEGAL.COM:

```
C:\> DEBUG < HPPAPER.SCR <ENTER>
```

Assuming that you have a long document, you can select legal mode as shown here and then print the document:

```
C:\> HPLEGAL > PRN      <ENTER>
C:\> PRINT DOCUMENT.BIG <ENTER>
```

Controlling Paper Feed on an HP LaserJet

An HP LaserJet printer can get its paper from the paper tray, or it can use the manual feed. Depending on your applications, you sometimes may want to control which paper source the printer uses. The following DEBUG script file, HPSOURCE.SCR, creates two command files, HPTRAY.COM and HPMANUAL.COM, whose output you can redirect to the printer to control the LaserJet's paper source:

```
N HPTRAY.COM              <ENTER>
A 100                     <ENTER>
JMP 108                   <ENTER>
DB 1B,26,6C,31,48,24      <ENTER>
MOV AH,9                  <ENTER>
MOV DX,102                <ENTER>
INT 21                    <ENTER>
MOV AH,4C                 <ENTER>
INT 21                    <ENTER>
                          <ENTER>
R CX                      <ENTER>
13                        <ENTER>
W                         <ENTER>
N HPMANUAL.COM            <ENTER>
E 105 32                  <ENTER>
W                         <ENTER>
Q                         <ENTER>
```

HPSOURCE.SCR

Use DEBUG as follows to create the command files HPTRAY.COM and HPMANUAL.COM:

```
C:\> DEBUG < HPSOURCE.SCR <ENTER>
```

The following command uses HPMANUAL.COM to select the LaserJet's manual feed:

```
C:\> HPMANUAL > PRN <ENTER>
```

Toner Cartridge Refills Make Sense

If you are using a laser printer, your toner cartridge will normally be good for between 3,000 and 5,000 sheets of paper. To replace your cartridge with a new one will cost between $90 and $100. However, many companies can refill your cartridge or sell you recharged cartridges for around $40. In many cases, the recharged cartridge will contain more toner than a new one would. Also, if you would like a specific toner color, you can probably request it. Before your cartridge runs out of toner, check the advertisements at the back of a computer magazine to see where to order a replacement cartridge. When your cartridge runs out of toner, use the replacement cartridge and send yours out to be refilled or recharged.

Understanding Laser Printer Components

Several of the tips presented in this book make reference to various laser printer components. You will be able to change your cartridge, clean your machine, and troubleshoot more easily if you know the location of the components in your printer shown here:

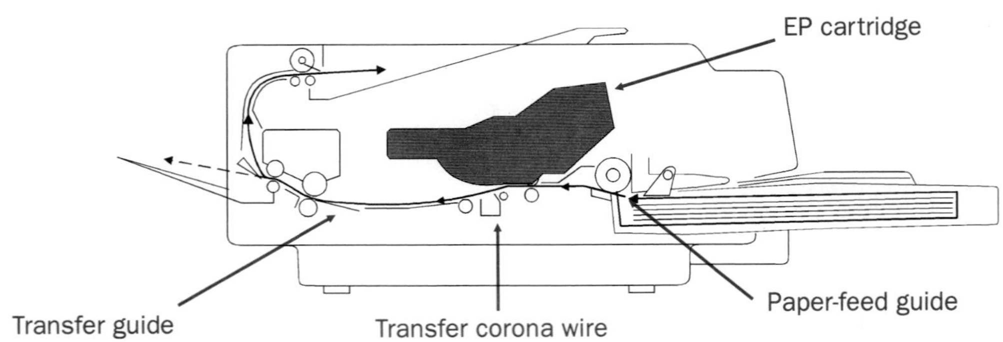

Table 943 describes each component's purpose.

Table 943. Functions of Various Laser Printer Components

Printer Component	Function
EP cartridge	Contains the photosensitive print drum and toner
Paper feed guide	Guides paper past the EP cartridge to the fusing station
Transfer corona wire	Negatively charges the paper so it attracts the toner
Transfer guide	Guides the paper past the corona wire

Understanding Dot-Matrix Printers

Tip 934 describes how a laser printer produces a printed page. This tip examines dot-matrix printers. The dot-matrix printer, as its name implies, prints a character by using a box of dots. The following illustration shows how the printer might create the letters *DOS:*

Depending on the printer type, a dot-matrix printer has a print head containing 9 to 24 vertical pins. As the head moves across the page, the printer pushes different pins against the print ribbon to produce dots corresponding to different letters. Because the character heights produced by 9- and 24-pin heads are the same, a 24-pin print head uses more dots per character, which results in a higher-quality printout. As shown in the following illustraion, the 24-pin print head can produce a sharper image.

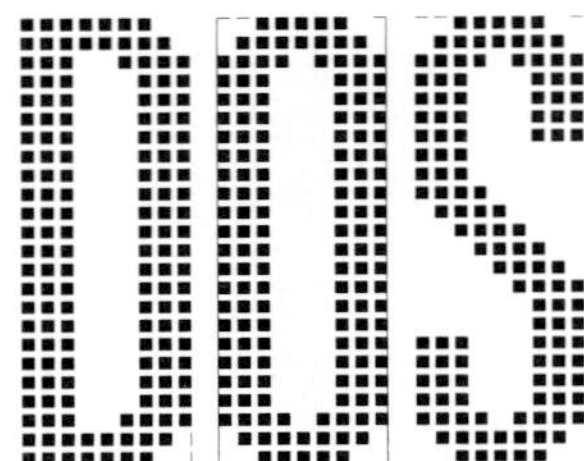

No Matter How Hard You Try, You Have to Use LPT1

As Tip 766 explains, when you install a serial or parallel card, you use switches on the card to specify whether the card corresponds to LPT1, 2, or 3 or COM1 through COM4. If, for some reason, you don't want the parallel port LPT1, you are out of luck.

Regardless of how you set the switches on your parallel port cards, DOS always selects and treats one of the ports as LPT1; you just can't get around it. If, for example, you set two parallel cards in LPT2 and LPT3, to DOS the cards become LPT1 and LPT2. Thus, if you try to eliminate LPT1 by typing another port, you cannot.

Solid Color Printing Is Easier than You Would Guess

By default, printers print black text on white paper. This is because the toner or ribbon you are using is black. Most computer and office supply stores, however, sell paper in almost every color. Likewise,

printing in a color other than black is simply a matter of using a colored laser toner or different-color ink jet or changing to a colored ribbon. The back pages of most computer magazines list sources where you can order colored toner, ink cartridges, or ribbons to meet your needs.

Has PRINT Been Installed?

TIP 947

Several of this book's tips discuss PRINT's command-line switches. Because PRINT installs memory-resident software, you can specify several of the switches only the first time you invoke PRINT. If PRINT has already been installed, the switches will be ignored. The following DEBUG script file, PRINTCHK.SCR, creates a command file named PRINTCHK.COM that returns the exit status value 1 if PRINT has been installed and returns 0 otherwise:

```
N PRINTCHK.COM <ENTER>
A 100          <ENTER>
MOV AX,0100    <ENTER>
INT 2F         <ENTER>
AND AL,1       <ENTER>
MOV AH,4C      <ENTER>
INT 21         <ENTER>
               <ENTER>
R CX           <ENTER>
B              <ENTER>
W              <ENTER>
Q              <ENTER>
```

PRINTCHK.SCR

Use DEBUG as follows to create the command file PRINTCHK.COM:

```
C:\> DEBUG < PRINTCHK.SCR <ENTER>
```

If you plan to print files from within the DOS shell, you must first install PRINT. The following batch file, STARTSHL.BAT, uses PRINTCHK to determine whether PRINT has been installed. If PRINT has not been installed, the batch file installs it. The batch file then starts the DOS shell.

```
@ECHO OFF
PRINTCHK
IF NOT ERRORLEVEL PRINT /D:LPT1 /B:4096
DOSSHELL
```

Have You Pushed Printer Speed to the Limit?

In general, two factors in addition to your printer's internal mechanics can influence the speed at which your documents print. If your printer has a sufficient amount of internal memory (typically, more than 1Mb for good performance), programs can send the data to the printer's memory and can continue without having to wait for the data to print. The second factor controlling print speed then is the rate at which the computer can send the data. If you are using a serial printer, the top speed is normally 9600 baud, or at best about 960 characters per second. If you are using a serial connector and your printer can support a parallel cable, use the parallel cable, over which data can be sent at 10Kb characters per second.

If you repeatedly wait for large or complex graphics printouts, you might consider upgrading your printer to support the SCSI interface, over which data can be sent at rates of 5 to 10Mb. Currently, printers that support the SCSI interface are more expensive than printers that have a standard parallel interface.

Selecting Spacing on an Epson-Compatible Printer

If you are using an Epson-compatible printer, you can redirect the output of the commands DBLSPACE.COM and SNGSPACE.COM to select double- and single-spaced output. The following DEBUG script file, EPSONSPA.SCR, creates the two command files:

EPSONSPA.SCR

```
N SNGSPACE.COM   <ENTER>
A 100            <ENTER>
MOV AH,02        <ENTER>
MOV DL,1B        <ENTER>
INT 21           <ENTER>
MOV DL,31        <ENTER>
```

```
INT 21                  <ENTER>
MOV AH,4C               <ENTER>
INT 21                  <ENTER>
                        <ENTER>
R CX                    <ENTER>
E                       <ENTER>
W                       <ENTER>
N DBLSPACE.COM          <ENTER>
A 106                   <ENTER>
MOV DL,32               <ENTER>
                        <ENTER>
W                       <ENTER>
Q                       <ENTER>
```

Use DEBUG as follows to create the command files DBLSPACE.COM and SNGSPACE.COM:

```
C:\> DEBUG < EPSONSPA.SCR <ENTER>
```

The following batch commands illustrate how you might use these commands to control spacing:

```
@ECHO OFF
DBLSPACE > PRN
SomeProg
SNGSPACE > PRN
```

Swapping LPT1 and LPT2

TIP 950

As Tip 32 discusses, you can use the MODE command to direct DOS to send output for LPT1 to COM1. MODE does not, however, let you swap two parallel ports. For example, if your computer has two parallel printers attached to LPT1 and LPT2, MODE does not let you switch which printer DOS uses as the default printer. However, you can use the following DEBUG script file, SWAPPRNS.SCR, to create a command file named SWAPPRNS.COM that exchanges the two printer assignments:

SWAPPRNS.SCR

```
N SWAPPRNS.COM      <ENTER>
A 100               <ENTER>
MOV AX,40           <ENTER>
MOV DS,AX           <ENTER>
MOV AX, WORD [8]    <ENTER>
MOV BX, WORD [A]    <ENTER>
MOV WORD [8], BX    <ENTER>
MOV WORD [A], AX    <ENTER>
MOV AH,4C           <ENTER>
INT 21              <ENTER>
                    <ENTER>
R CX                <ENTER>
17                  <ENTER>
W                   <ENTER>
Q                   <ENTER>
```

Use DEBUG as follows to create the command file SWAPPRNS.COM:

```
C:\> DEBUG < SWAPPRNS.SCR <ENTER>
```

To exchange the printer assignments, invoke SWAPPRNS from the DOS prompt or from within a DOS batch file as shown here:

```
C:\> SWAPPRNS <ENTER>
```

Who Is Using Which Ports?

Tip 769 explains that the computer communicates with various devices through its ports and lists the port values that common devices use. Tip 950 and Tip 830 explain how to swap the parallel ports LPT1 and LPT2 and how to swap the serial ports COM1 and COM2. To help you view these device's current port settings, the companion disk that accompanies this book provides the utility command PORTUSE.EXE. If you invoke PORTUSE from the DOS prompt, it will display the current port assignments as shown here:

```
C:\> PORTUSE <ENTER>
Device     Port
```

```
LPT1:     378
LPT2:     278

COM1:     3F8
COM2:     2F8
COM3:     3E8
```

If a port assignment is not correct, use the utility commands SWAPPRNS.COM or SWAP-COM.COM to correct the assignment.

The utility command PORTUSE.EXE resides on the companion disk that accompanies this book.

PORTUSE.EXE

Why Parallel Printers Don't Require Baud Settings

Tip 86 discusses baud in detail. When two serial devices communicate, they must agree on the transmission speed. Serial devices must coordinate their communication in this way because they exchange information one bit at a time over a single wire. Parallel printers, on the other hand, don't require such data communication settings. Why? The following illustration shows a parallel port's pin use:

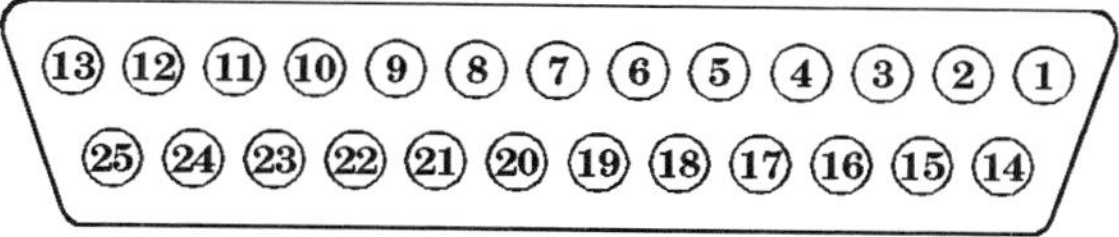

In addition to using eight wires for exchanging data, parallel devices also use several wires that coordinate data communication. Table 952 describes the use of these wires.

Table 952. Wire Use for Data Communication Coordination by Parallel Devices

Wire	Purpose
Strobe	Output
Data bit 0	Output
Data bit 1	Output
Data bit 2	Output
Data bit 3	Output
Data bit 4	Output
Data bit 5	Output
Data bit 6	Output
Data bit 7	Output
Acknowledge	Printer acknowledgment
Busy	Printer busy
Paper end	Printer out of paper
Select	Input
Auto feed	Output
Error	Printer error
Initialize	Printer initialization
Select input	Output
Data bit 0	Input
Data bit 1	Input
Data bit 2	Input
Data bit 3	Input
Data bit 4	Input
Data bit 5	Input
Data bit 6	Input
Data bit 7	Input

Because parallel devices can use the wires to coordinate communication, there is no need for other data communication settings to provide this capability. Parallel devices do require more wires. However, parallel devices communicate much faster than serial devices.

The Portable Printer

TIP 953

A natural extension of the growth in the use of laptop and notebook computers is the notebook printer. For less than $550, you can buy portable printers that fit in your briefcase and still give you room for your notebook PC. These portable printers, illustrated here, can weigh as little as 2 1/2 pounds and require less space than 4 inches by 12 inches by 2 inches:

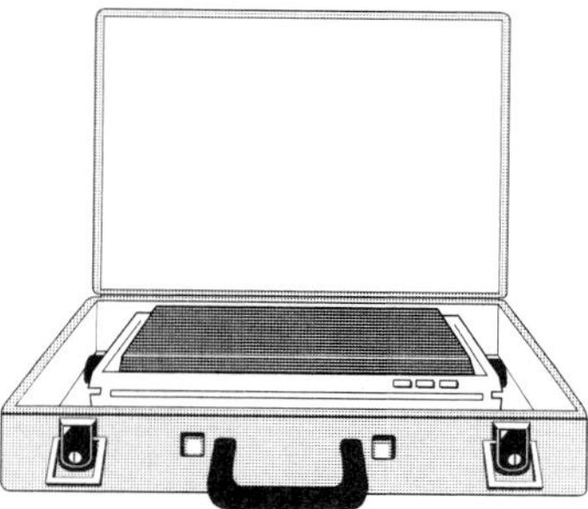

Although you must manually insert paper, portable printers let you print letters, reports, memos, and even contracts while you are on the road.

One-Way Printing on a DeskJet Printer

Normally, the HP DeskJet printer prints as the head moves right and while the head moves back to the left margin. Depending on the image you are trying to print (boxed output is notorious for creating problems), the left and right printing may cause the image to be misaligned. The following DEBUG script file, DIRECT.SCR, creates two command files, RIGHTPRT.COM and LEFTRIGH.COM, that control the direction the DeskJet prints:

DIRECT.SCR

```
N RIGHTPRT.COM          <ENTER>
A 100                   <ENTER>
JMP 108                 <ENTER>
DB 1B,26,6B,31,57,24    <ENTER>
MOV AH,9                <ENTER>
MOV DX,102              <ENTER>
INT 21                  <ENTER>
MOV AH,4C               <ENTER>
INT 21                  <ENTER>
                        <ENTER>
R CX                    <ENTER>
13                      <ENTER>
W                       <ENTER>
N LEFTRIGH.COM          <ENTER>
E 105 30                <ENTER>
W                       <ENTER>
Q                       <ENTER>
```

Use DEBUG as follows to create the command files RIGHTRT.COM and LEFTRIGH.COM:

```
C:\> DEBUG < DIRECT.SCR <ENTER>
```

The following command uses RIGHTPRT to direct the DeskJet to print only when the head is moving right:

```
C:\> RIGHTPRT > LPT1 <ENTER>
```

TIP 955 Paper Makes a Difference

If you are using an ink-jet printer, you will be amazed how different print appears on different paper types. In fact, if you are preparing a resume, report, or some other document, experiment with different paper weights and qualities. Many colored papers, such as stationery, are created by bonding together paper particles. If you are going to print on such paper, first take several sheets and rub them together on your desk top. Rub hard but do not bend the paper. In so doing, you will smooth out many of the fibers, which will result in a sharper print image.

Performing a Printer Test with MSD.EXE

If your system contains Windows 3.1, you can use the utility program MSD.EXE to display information about your system. In addition, MSD lets you perform a printer test. To test your printer, invoke MSD.EXE from the DOS prompt. Next, select the Utilities menu and choose Test Printer. MSD will display the test printer screen shown here:

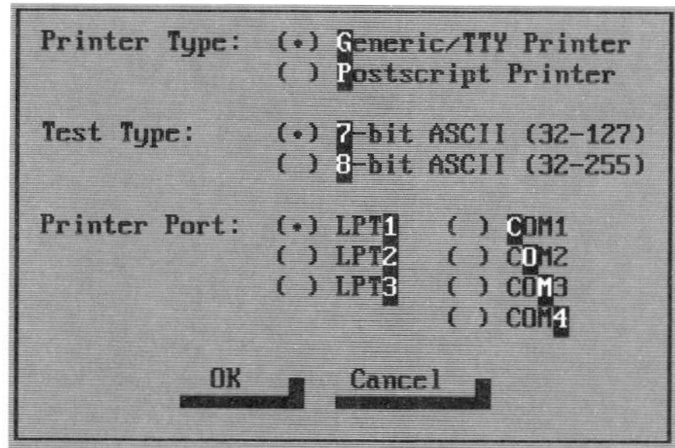

Using your mouse or the keyboard arrow keys and TAB, select the desired options. If your printer supports it, the 8-bit ASCII printout gives you a convenient table listing the extended ASCII characters. Select the OK option to perform the test. If an error occurs, MSD will display a message describing the error.

Displaying Your Printer Status

Tip 885 presents the utility command CHKLPT1.COM that returns your printer's current status as an exit value. Tip 951 presents the utility PORTUSE that displays your current printer port

assignments. The companion disk utility command SHOWLPT.EXE combines these two utilities to display the status of your parallel ports as shown here:

Port	Port Address	Online	Paper Out	Error	I/O	Time Out	Ack
LPT1	0378	Yes	No	No	No	No	No
LPT2	—	—	—	—	—	—	—
LPT3	—	—	—	—	—	—	—

If you are experiencing problems with your parallel printer, use the SHOWLPT utility to troubleshoot your system.

SHOWLPT.EXE

The utility command SHOWLPT.EXE resides on the companion disk that accompanies this book.

Sharing Printers

If you work in an office that does not have a local area network yet shares printers, your printer may be connected to a switch box similar to the one shown here:

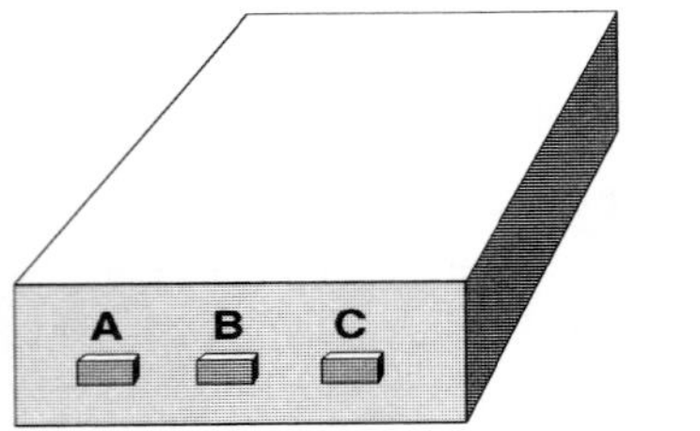

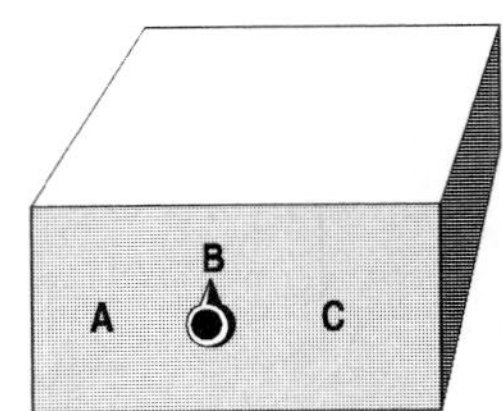

When different users need to print, they simply set the switch to their computer. Although such a switch lets several users share a printer, the switching process can be time consuming. As an alternative, for a few hundred dollars you can purchase an electronic switch that automatically switches between

computers as data is received. If the printer is currently in use, many of these electronic switches contain memory to which the incoming data can be stored. If printer contention is a problem in your office, an electronic switch may be the solution.

Adding Memory to an HP LaserJet

As discussed in Tip 902, adding memory to your printer improves your system performance because programs can send information to the printer, which in turn stores the information until it's printed, allowing the program to continue. If you are using an HP LaserJet, adding memory is very easy. First, you must buy a card containing the amount of additional memory you require. The LaserJet supports only one add-on memory card. Next, unplug your printer and locate the memory expansion slot illustrated here:

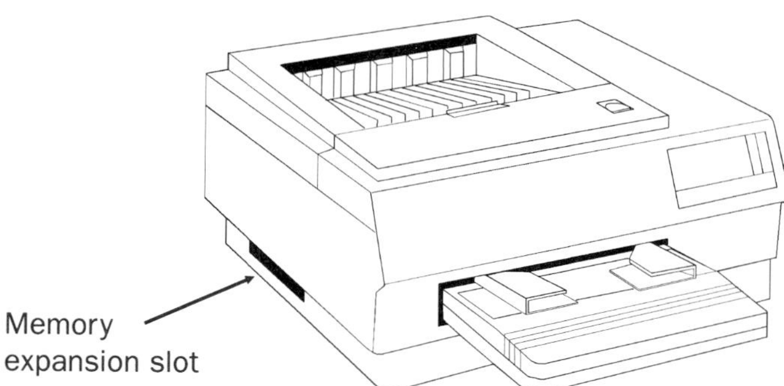

Unscrew the slot cover and gently insert the board, connecting it to the printer's system board port. Replace the slot cover and plug in your printer. Follow the steps discussed in Tip 902 to determine your system's new memory amount.

Serial Printer Settings

As Tip 764 discusses, if you are attaching a printer to a serial port, you have to specify correct data communications settings for the port. The MODE command does just that. The documentation that accompanies your printer should specify the correct data communication settings. Place a MODE command in your AUTOEXEC.BAT that assigns the settings each time your system starts. If you don't have your manual available, the following MODE command illustrates the settings used by most laser printers:

```
C:\> MODE COM1 96,N,8,1 <ENTER>
```

PART 12

Maintenance

Cleaning Your Monitor

In most offices, monitors become magnets for dust and smoke. Several companies sell spray cleaners specifically for monitors. Be careful of the type of cleaner you use on your monitor; some will leave a film that makes the monitor hard to see. Always turn your monitor off before cleaning it and never spray the cleaning solution directly onto the screen. Instead, spray the solution onto a rag and then wipe the screen. Normally, a little rubbing alcohol and a soft cloth will do a great job cleaning your screen.

Computers Need Fresh Air Too

As they operate, computers generate a significant amount of heat. Within the chassis, the computer has a fan that circulates air, allowing the hot air to escape. Most monitors have vents that allow the hot air to escape out the top. Always make sure these vents are open (not covered) so the heated air can escape.

Never place books or printouts on top of the monitor where they may block the vent. Likewise, never place the computer's chassis so close to a wall or desk that the fan becomes blocked. If your computer cannot vent the hot air, you risk not only damaging your equipment, but you also create a serious fire hazard.

Cleaning Your Keyboard

Although it's very easy for dust and other particles to fall between the keys of your keyboard, you will normally cause more harm than good by trying to clean the

keyboard. For the most part, restrict your cleaning inside the keyboard to the particles you can easily blow out from between the keys. Many computer stores sell small cartridge air blowers with noses small enough to fit between the keys. Some users successfully vacuum their keyboards by taping a small straw to their vacuum cleaner nozzle. If you want to vacuum the keyboard in this way, disconnect the keyboard from your computer and vacuum it away from your disks. To clean the keys themselves, use a Q-Tip and rubbing alcohol. The alcohol is also a good way to clean the keyboard chassis.

Cleaning an HP InkJet Print Head

If you are using an HP InkJet printer, the ink may sometimes collect on the cartridge's print head, causing your printouts to blur or appear messy. As shown here, gently wipe the print head with a Q-Tip you have soaked in rubbing alcohol:

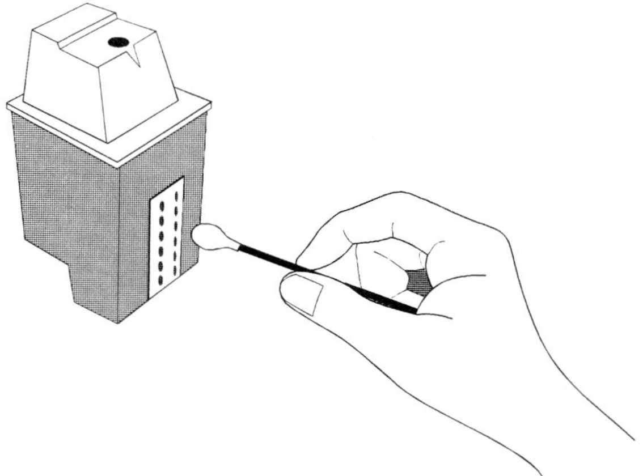

The ink should easily wipe off of the head.

Troubleshooting an Intermittent Hardware Error

If hardware devices such as your screen or printer sometimes behave strangely, but for the most part works, follow these steps to isolate the cause of the error:

1. If the error occurs only when you attempt to perform a specific operation, the problem may be in your software. If the device requires a unique driver, make sure the device driver is the latest version by contacting the company's technical support staff and providing them with the driver's filename and date and time stamp. Next, make sure the program you are using supports the device.
2. Check the cable that connects the device to your computer to make sure it is securely attached at both ends.
3. Unplug your computer and check the board inside your computer's chassis. Make sure the board is completely inserted in a bus slot.
4. Try replacing the cable that connects the device. The cable may be damaged.
5. Watch for static electricity or power drops when you turn on lights or other devices such as an air conditioner. If such power drops occur, you will need to contact an electrician.
6. If the problem persists, your computer or device probably needs servicing.

Protecting Your Computer Investment

One of the most important steps you should take when you purchase new hardware or software is recording the product's serial number, price, and information about the company from which you purchased the product in a log. When you purchase a large hardware device, such as a printer or scanner, also photograph the device. Next, place your log and photos in a safe location. Should your

computer ever be stolen or damaged by fire, you will need this information for your insurance claims. Note that most insurance policies don't reimburse you for development or data-entry time. To protect yourself against loss of custom programs or data, keep current backup copies at a location away from your computer.

Changing Your Computer's CMOS Battery

The PC contains a battery-powered chip called the CMOS chip that contains your computer's setup information (disk type, date, memory types and amounts, and so on). If, each time your system starts, your screen displays a message about invalid SETUP information, you probably need to replace the CMOS battery. To do so, unplug your system and open the computer chassis. As shown here, there are two types of CMOS batteries: an actual small replaceable battery, and a battery pack within which you can place four AA batteries.

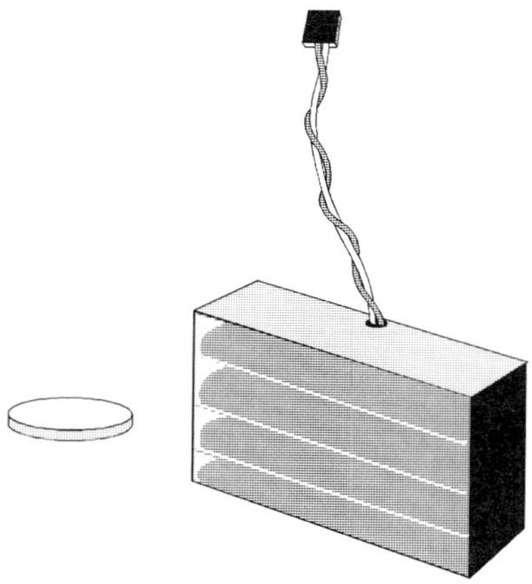

If your computer uses the small replaceable battery, slip the old battery out and slip the new battery in. If you are using a battery pack, simply replace the batteries within the pack. Close up your computer chassis, plug in the chassis, and start your system. You may have to enter your system settings one more time.

Cleaning the Edge Connectors on a Hardware Board

Before you install a hardware board in one of your computer's expansion slots, examine the board's edge connectors to ensure that they are clean. The edge connectors contain small copper strips that electronically connect the board to your computer's internal bus. If the edge connectors aren't clean, they may cause the board to malfunction. To clean the connectors, use a little rubbing alcohol and a Q-Tip, letting the connectors dry before inserting the board, or use a pencil eraser as shown here:

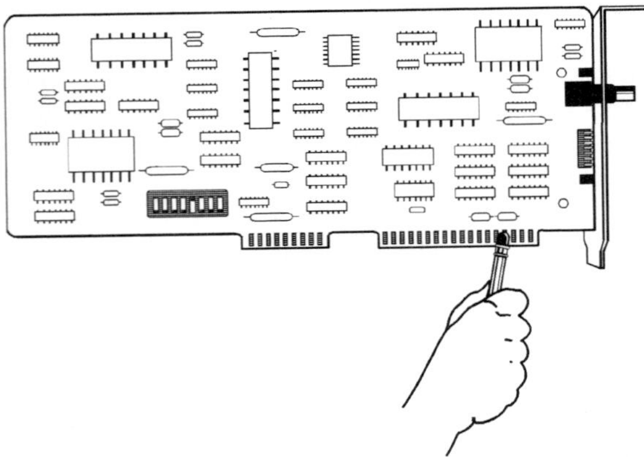

If you use an eraser, make sure you remove from the board any small pieces of rubber that break off.

Be Aware of Plastic Computer Covers

Many users have plastic covers they faithfully place on their computers at the end of each day to prevent dust from collecting on and within the computer. Although such covers are an excellent way to keep

your computer clean, they can potentially cause problems by trapping heat inside your computer. As discussed in Tip 973, running your computer produces a great amount of heat that escapes through vents near the top of your monitor and at the back of your computer's chassis.

If you turn off your computer and immediately cover it with plastic, a considerable amount of heat is trapped. If you use plastic covers, turn your computer off and let is cool down for a few minutes before you cover it.

Replacing or Upgrading Your Power Supply

Tip 794 explains how to estimate your PC's power requirements. If your current power supply is too small, or if your power supply fails (when you turn on your computer's power, you don't hear the fan), you can replace your power supply yourself. To begin, unplug your system unit and remove the lid. Next, note the size of your existing power supply. Although the new power supply may provide more power, it cannot exceed the current power supply's size. Next, gently move cables and note which cables are plugged into which devices. I strongly recommend you draw and label a picture or label the cables themselves. Unplug the current power supply's cables, unscrew the power supply, and remove the power suppy from your system chassis. Before you insert the new power supply, make sure the voltage selector is set for the United States (for 110 to 120 volts). Insert the supply, connect the power supply to the chassis, and plug in each device once again. Place the cover on the chassis, plug in your system, and turn on the power. The first noise you should hear is the power supply's fan. If one of your devices does not work, check the power cables and also the controller ribbon cables; it's not uncommon to accidentally loosen a controller cable while replacing the power supply.

Recognizing Floppy Disk Cables

When you open your computer's chassis, you will see one or more large, flat, ribbon cables. These cables connect your hard and floppy disks to the disk controller. As you work within the chassis, adding

drives or changing your power supply, you may need to use these cables. Likewise, if after working within your chassis, one of your drives does not work, one of these cables may have come loose. A floppy disk drive ribbon cable is shown here:

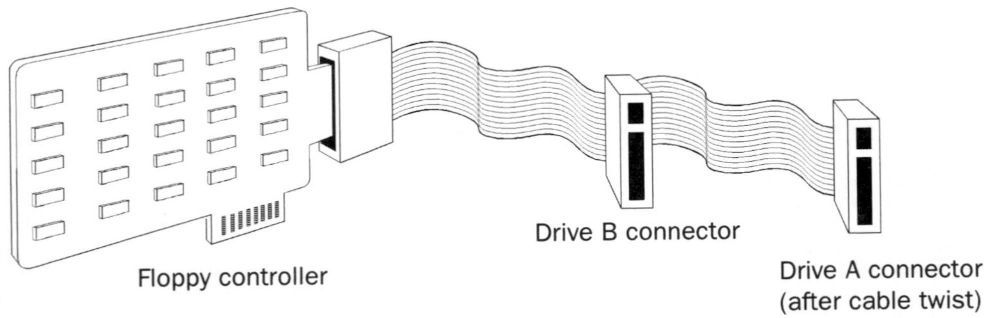

The floppy cable has a connector for drives A and B. Each connector is notched at one end to prevent you from plugging in the cable backward. If a drive is not working, examine the ribbon cable's connection to the disk controller and then to the drive itself.

Are Your Toner Cartridges Getting Poor Mileage?

Many Laser printer and toner cartridge advertisements state that a cartridge should print from 3,000 to 5,000 copies. Actually, the number of pages a cartridge can print is a function of page *contents,* not page *count.* If you tend to print pages containing dense graphics or bold text, you will obviously use toner faster. However, if you normally print a variety of page types, your cartridge should last its advertised page count. If your toner does not, you may need to adjust your printer's print density knob, which controls the amount of toner the printer applies per page. The location of the print density knob depends on your printer type. The following illustration shows the location of the print density knob in an HP LaserJet Series II printer:

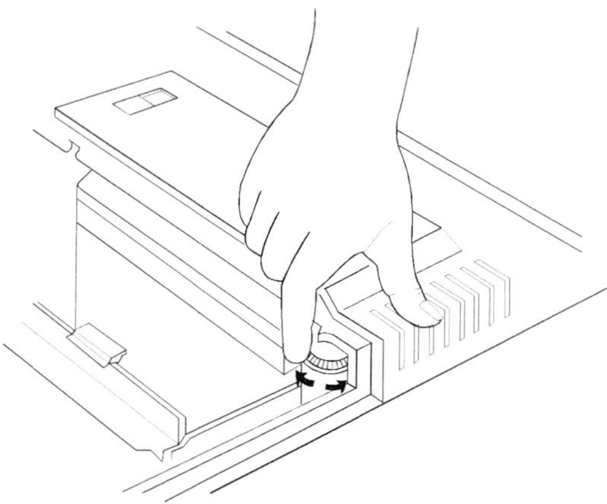

Refer to your printer documentation to determine how your print density knob behaves. In the case of a LaserJet, a setting of 1 selects the darkest print (and uses toner the fastest) and 9 selects the lightest. Most users select a density of 5.

Heating and Cooling Considerations

Almost every computer comes with instructions that tell you to keep the PC in the temperature range 50 to 100F. For most users, the PC's temperature never merits a second thought. However, excessive cold or heat can have a fatal impact on your PC's internal components. Here are some considerations you should keep in mind. If your PC has been in your car or a very cold office building, do not turn on the PC until it has had a chance to adjust to normal room temperature (which should be in the PC's operating temperature range). When the PC is exposed to extreme cold, its internal components will contract. If you turn on your computer while it is extremely cold, the heat immediately generated by the electronic signals can result in a thermal shock that can damage or destroy the PC's chips or circuitry.

When your PC is exposed to extreme heat, on the other hand, its internal components expand. As you add expansion boards or more memory to your system, you increase the number of heat sources, which in turn raises the temperature within your chassis. The first symptoms of excessive heat are

intermittent errors that occur because of signal crosstalk on the expanded circuits. If your PC is exposed to direct sunlight or other heat sources, move the PC. If your PC's chassis feels warm, consider changing your power supply to one with a larger fan to improve its ventilation and decrease its internal temperature. If your system starts to experience intermittent errors, don't rule out temperature problems.

Tip 974 Reducing the Static Electricity Threat

Everyone has experienced a static shock with walking across carpet and touching a doorknob. Such static shocks typically produce between 3,000 and 5,000 volts (you don't get hurt because the amperage of such a shock is low). The chips in your computer can be destroyed by as little as 1,000 to 2,000 volts (to them, the amperage doesn't matter). Depending on the season, your carpet, and the weather, the possibility of static electricity damaging your computer varies. Static electricity can destroy your computer's key electronic components in an instant. If you even suspect static electricity exists, take the following steps to reduce the danger to your computer equipment:

- Increase the humidity level by using a humidifier or add a source of evaporation such as an aquarium or plants you must regularly water.
- Place an antistatic mat beneath your keyboard.
- Wear an antistatic wrist strap while working inside your computer chassis.
- Always place boards in antistatic bags when they are not in use.
- Never stack one board on top of another while working inside the chassis.
- Place an antistatic floor mat beneath your desk, on top of your carpet.
- Regularly use an antistatic spray on your carpet.

Tip 975 Cleaning the LaserJet

When cleaning your LaserJet printer, you need to be concerned with only four areas: the transfer corona wire, transfer guide, transfer guide lock tray, and paper feed guide.

Before you begin, unplug your printer. If the printer has been running, let it cool down. You will need a Q-Tip, a bottle of rubbing alcohol, and a damp cloth. Clean each area as follows:

First, clean the transfer corona wire:

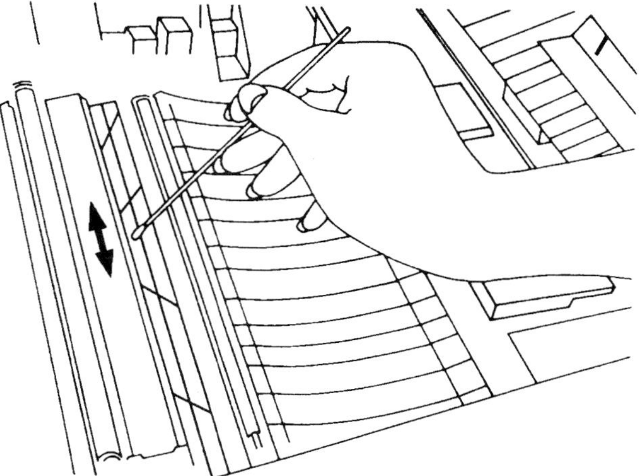

Then clean the transfer guide:

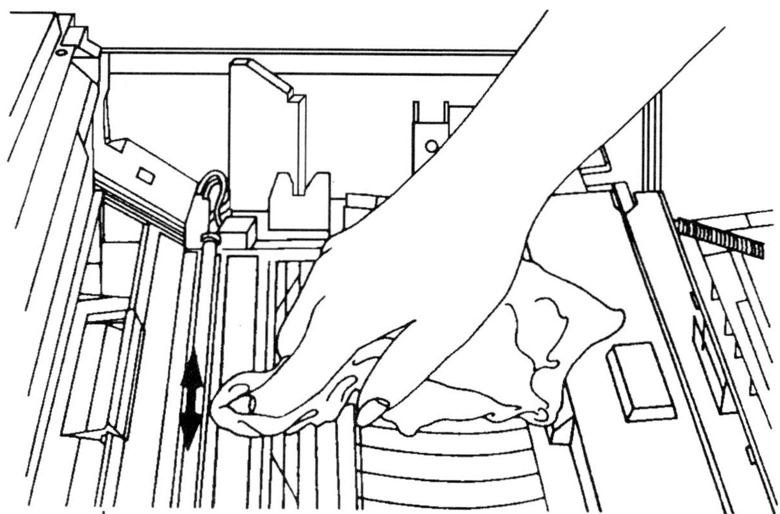

Next, clean the transfer guide lock tray:

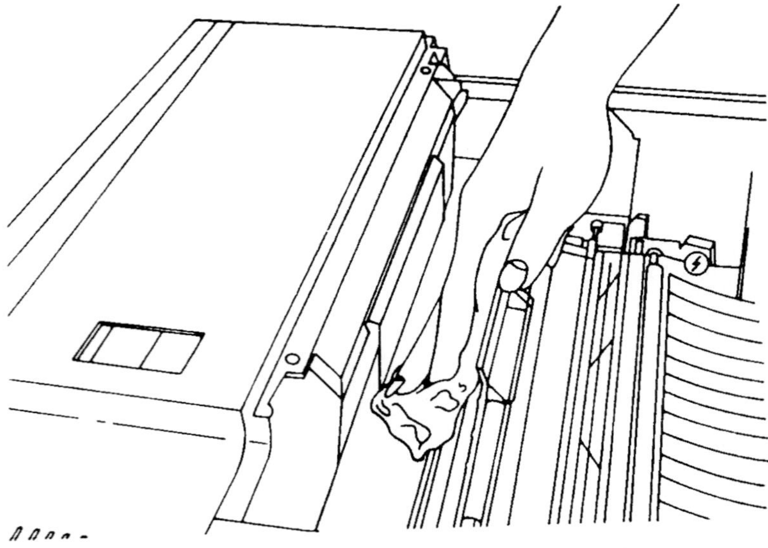

Finally, clean the paper guide:

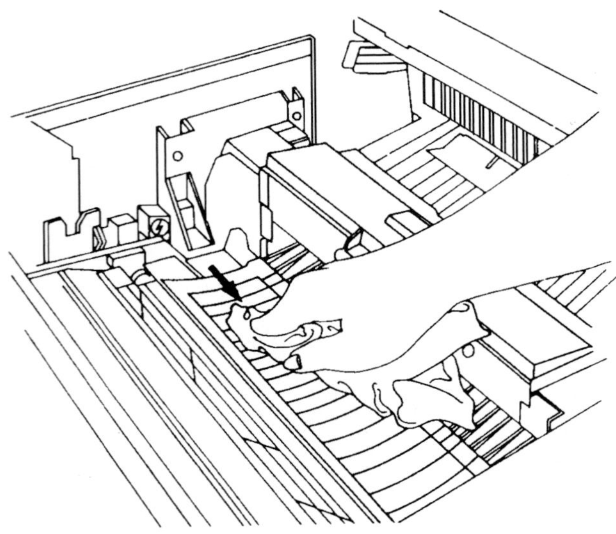

Correcting Vertical Fade on LaserJet Printouts

Shown here is a LaserJet printout that is suffering from vertical fade:

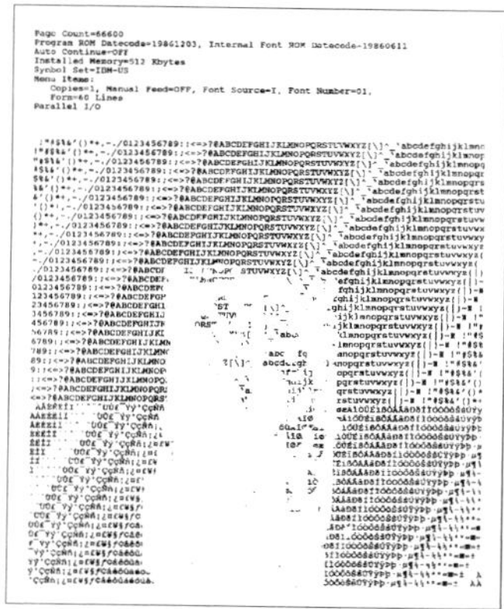

Page Count=66600
Program ROM Datecode=19861203, Internal Font ROM Datecode=19860611
Auto Continue=OFF
Installed Memory=512 Kbytes
Symbol Set=IBM-US
Menu Items:
Copies=1, Manual Feed=OFF, Font Source=I, Font Number=01,
Form=60 Lines
Parallel I/O

Vertical fade occurs most often when the amount of toner in the printer's EP cartridge is low. If vertical fade occurs, first make sure the toner density (see Tip 972) is set to a proper level (5 should be sufficient). If the problem persists, shake the EP cartridge as discussed in Tip 900 to extend the life of your cartridge; see Tip 942 for information about toner cartridge refills.

Correcting Toner Dropout on LaserJet Printouts

The following illustration shows a LaserJet printout that is suffering from toner dropout:

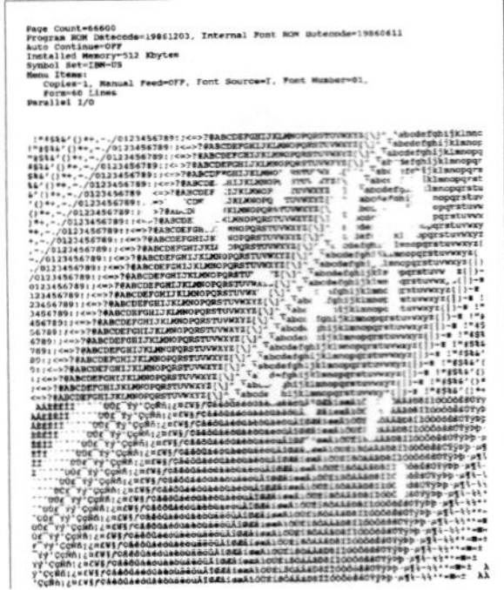

Toner dropout occurs most often when your printer's corona wire is dirty. As discussed in Tip 943, the corona wire is responsible for applying a negative charge to the paper, causing the paper to attract toner. As discussed in Tip 975, clean the corona wire using a Q-Tip and rubbing alcohol. If the dropout persists, try using a different type of paper. If the dropout still remains, the photosensitive cell inside the printer's EP cartridge may be damaged.

Correcting Vertical Streaking on a LaserJet Printout

Shown here is a LaserJet printout that is suffering from vertical streaking:

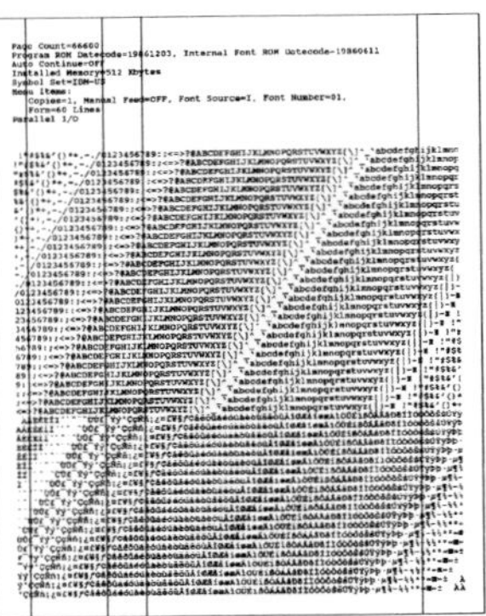

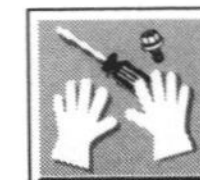

Vertical streaking occurs most often when the photosensitive drum inside the printer's EP cartridge has been scratched. Unfortunately, if the drum is scratched, you must replace the cartridge. In some cases, the streaks may occur as a result of toner buildup on the surface of the fuser roller cleaning pad. Make sure you replace the fuser roller cleaning pad each time you install a new toner cartridge.

Correcting Staining on a LaserJet Printout

The following illustration shows a LaserJet printout that is suffering from staining:

Toner stains normally occur as a result of toner buildup on the transport rollers. To clean the transport rollers, unplug your printer, open its cover, and let it cool down. Next, using a cloth and a little rubbing alcohol, clean the roller. You may actually be able to spin the roller slightly as you clean it. If the stains persist after you clean the transport rollers, try cleaning the fuser toner cleaning pad shown in Tip 978.

Be Aware of Battery Memory on Laptop and Notebook Computers

If you are using a battery-powered laptop or notebook computer, how and when you charge the PC's battery can have a big impact on how long you can run your PC using the battery. Rechargable batteries such as those used by PCs, cellular phones, and video recorders suffer from a unique characteristic known as battery memory or memory effect.

Assume that you have a battery that is supposed to power your system for up to four hours. If everyday you use the system for an hour and then recharge the battery, the battery will actually consider its life to be one hour! As a rule, you should always let your battery drain completely before recharging it, although in some cases, completely draining your battery is impossible.

The memory effect won't occur if you recharge your battery once or twice without draining it; the memory effect occurs after multiple recharge operations. If you normally drain your battery before recharging it, you won't experience problems. If you don't drain your battery, learn to work faster or plan on buying a new battery.

A Closer Look at the U-Plug

Almost all of your hardware devices use the U-type plug shown here:

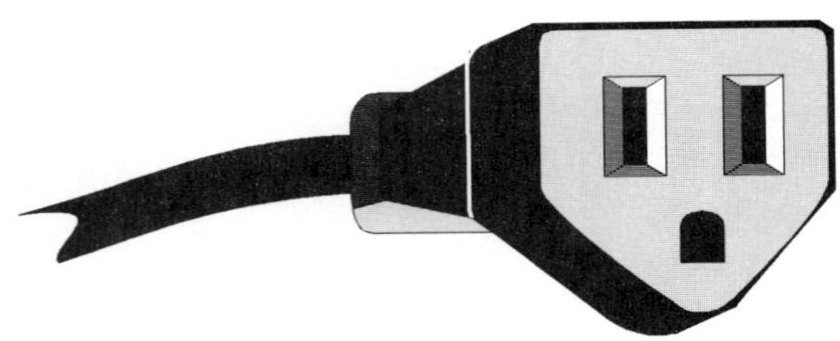

As shown, the U-plug has three connectors: two parallel blades that carry current and a cylindrical connector that provides grounding. The ground connector provides a means of discarding stray electrons. Not only does the ground connector protect your computer from line noise, it also reduces the possibility of radio frequency interference (RFI) from nearby devices.

Never plug one of your device's U-plugs into an extension cord that does not provide three-way connection. Doing so places your devices in danger of electrical damage.

Understanding Twin Plugs with Ground Connects

Tip 981 describes the U-plug used by most of your computer's devices. The U-plug's ground connector protects your devices from line noise and RFI. If, for some reason, the only available outlet does not provide a ground connect, plug your device's U-plug into a twin plug that provides a ground wire and then connect the ground wire to the outlet as shown here:

By connecting the ground cable to the wall outlet, you achieve the same result provided by a U-plug.

Use an Outlet Analyzer to Solve Power Problems

If your PC won't power up, but a fan plugged into the same wall outlet works, the problem may be the wall outlet's wiring. One of the devices you should add to your PC toolbox is an outlet analyzer. As shown here, you simply plug the analyzer into the wall outlet. If the outlet is correctly wired, the analyzer will illuminate a series of lights or sound a specific tone. If the outlet is not correctly wired, the analyzer may illuminate a different set of lights you can use to determine the cause of the problem.

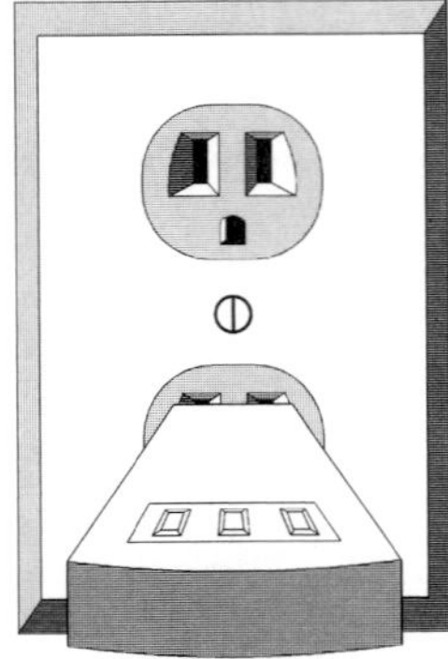

You can purchase an outlet analyzer at most electrical supply stores for less than $10.

Understanding Polarized Plugs

Tip 981 discusses the U-plug, which is the most common electrical plug used by your computer. In some cases your devices may use a polarized plug as shown here:

As you can see, one of the blades of the polarized plug is larger than the others, restricting you to inserting the plug in only one direction. The larger blade corresponds to the outlet's neutral wire, and the narrow blade corresponds to the hot wire. Never force a polarized plug into an outlet or extension cord that was designed for normal blades. The polarized plug exists to force hot and neutral to appear on specific wires.

Securing Your Cables Often Corrects Intermittent Errors

When you first install a hardware device, there is a tendency for many users to quickly connect a cable to try out the board. Unfortunately, most users never go back to make sure the cable is securely attached to the board. As the following illustration shows, most cables have screws you should screw into the board's receptacle to hold the board in place.

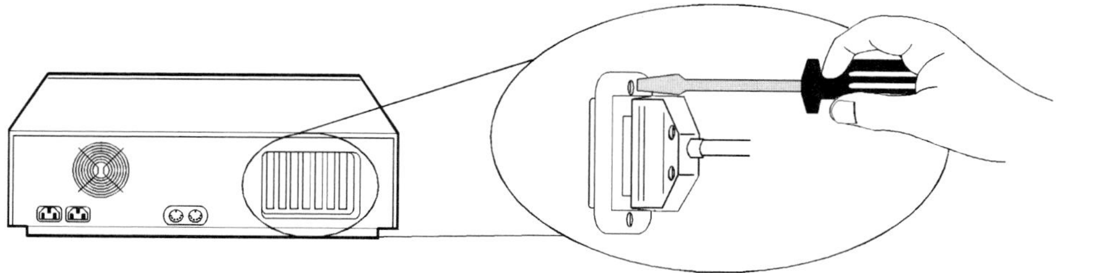

In many cases, when a working video display, mouse, keyboard, printer, or other device starts to experience errors, the cable has loosened from the board.

TIP 986 Shielded Versus Unshielded Cables

When you shop for cables, you may first wonder why one parallel or serial cable costs so much more than another. In most cases, the answer is shielding. To prevent radio frequency interference (RFI), which is noise that disrupts the cable's signals, a shielded cable is surrounded by a metallic shield. This works as a protective ground for transient signals. In many cases, you can get away with using unshielded cables. However, if you have many cables that run in the same area, or if cables run near other powerful devices, you should strongly consider shielded cables. If a device starts experiencing intermittent errors, and the cable is securely attached to the cord, don't rule out RFI noise as a possible cause.

TIP 987 Label Your Cables as Soon as You Buy Them

Because many different cable types use 25-pin connectors, it can be very difficult to determine a cable's type without taking the cable apart. When you purchase a cable, attach labels on each plug that describe the cable's type and purpose as shown here:

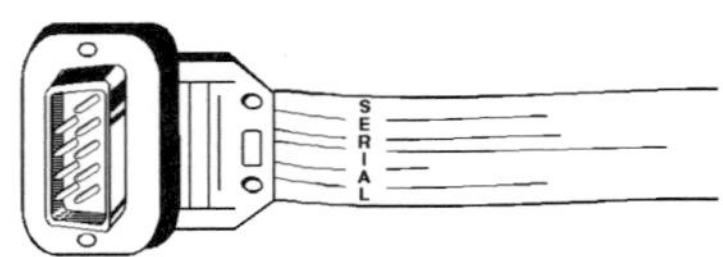

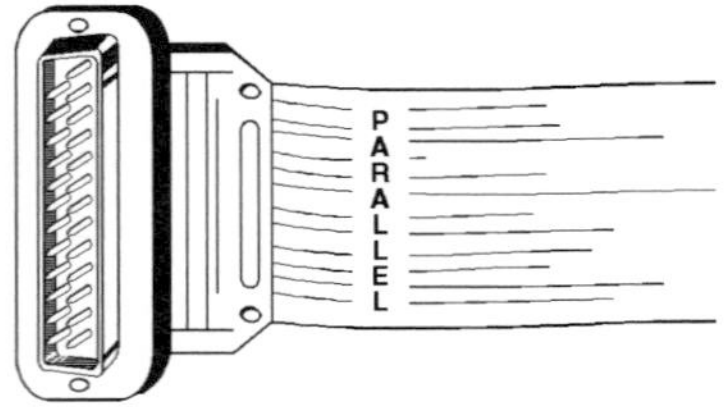

By labeling each cable in this way, you will save considerable time in the future troubleshooting what turns out to be an error caused by the use of the wrong cable type.

Vacuums Can Be Useful for Cleaning Your Printer

Regardless of whether you are using a laser or a tractor-feed dot-matrix printer, the printer will eventually accumulate paper scraps and paper dust. In most cases, if you try to clean out the paper dust by using a cloth, you will, more than likely, move the dust into printer areas where it is impossible to remove. To avoid this problem, unplug the printer and move it away from any disks. Next, as shown here, attach a straw to the end of your vacuum nozzle and vacuum out the paper dust.

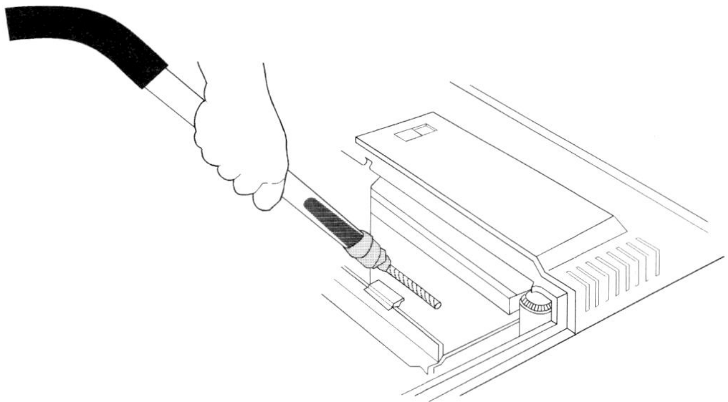

Solving Printer Paper Perforation Tears

If you are using a tractor-feed printer to print multiple-page forms or other long documents and the form's tractor feed perforations tend to tear and jam as shown in the following illustration, your problem may simply be paper weight.

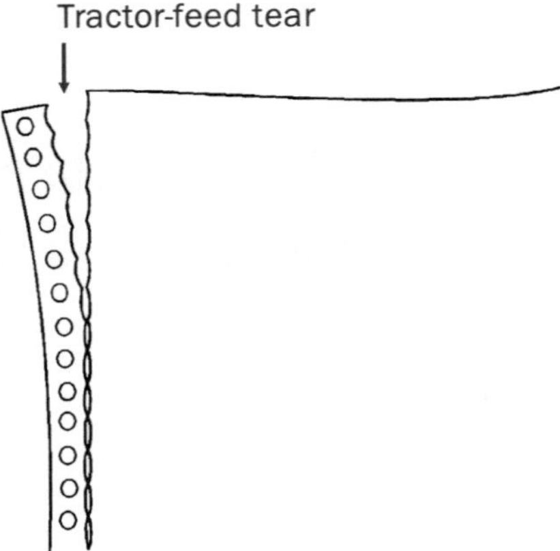

Most printer tractor feeds were designed to pull paper only a few inches from a nearby paper stack. Unfortunately, in many offices, tractor feeds often have to lift several pages at a time from a box of paper that sits on the floor.

Paper jams that occur as a result of perforation tears are the printer's way of telling you that you are asking it to do too much. If such tears occur, move the paper closer to the tractor feed.

Be Careful with What You Use to Clean Pins and Connectors

Unlike most of your computer's components, connector pins are one of the few items you should not clean. If a connector has not been used and is dusty, simply blow on the connector to remove as much dust as possible. If you try to clean the connector with a Q-Tip or cloth, you are likely to create connector problems. Likewise, cleaning solvent may cause a residue that interferes with the pin's connection.

How to Correct Print Streaking or Dropout for a Dot-Matrix Printer

Tip 944 discusses dot-matrix printers and how the printer creates images by firing specific pins (depending on your printer type, the print head has either 9 or 24 pins). If your printouts have streaks, either your print head or another component in your printer has an ink accumulation. In many cases, if you can locate the ink, you can rub it off by using a folded business card. If your printer has dropouts, one or more of the pins is not firing. If possible, remove the print head as shown here.

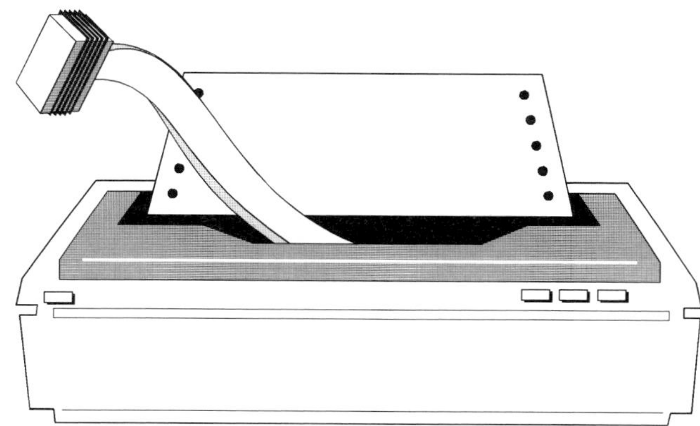

Next, first clean the head with a Q-Tip and rubbing alcohol. Then spray the head with a little WD-40.

If dropouts continue, your printer will require servicing.

Moving Your Laser Printer

Tip 993 presents several steps you should take before you move your computer. If you are moving a laser printer, follow these guidelines. First, remove the printer's toner cartridge, wrap it in a large plastic bag, and then separately box the cartridge. Toner cartridges are notorious for spilling during a move. By isolating the cartridge, you prevent spilled toner inside your printer. Next, remove the printer's paper tray, fill it with paper so it's less likely to get crushed, and then box it separately. Should the box containing your printer get set on its edge, it won't rest on the paper tray. Last, make sure you box the printer's power and data cables with the printer itself so they don't get lost.

Moving Your PC

If you are moving your PC, use the following checklist as a guide:

- ❑ Park your disk heads before turning off your computer with the utility presented in Tip 345.
- ❑ Make a diagram of your computer's current cabeling before you disconnect the cables. Tape the diagram to your computer's chassis.
- ❑ Stop by your computer retailer and ask for cardboard inserts to place in your floppy drives. Moving the computer with a floppy disk in the drive may cause more harm than good.
- ❑ Label the contents of each box or place a packing list in each box so you don't forget to unpack cables.
- ❑ If you don't have your original packing boxes, see whether a local dealer can provide some.
- ❑ Label the boxes as fragile and use "This Side Up" messages.

How Should You Turn Off Your Computer?

Many magazine articles suggest you should not turn off your PC by using its power switch because you will wear out the switch. Instead, most recommend you plug your PC into a surge suppressor and

use the surge suppressor's on/off switch. If this scheme forces you to use a surge suppressor, then I agree; every PC should be protected by a surge suppressor. With respect to wearing out the PC's power switch, however, unless you shut off your PC's power every 15 minutes, your PC's processor will probably be long obsolete before your power supply switch wears out. Admittedly, the switch, like every other component in your system, may eventually fail. However, dollar for dollar, the power supply is one of the least-expensive PC components to replace.

Cleaning a CD-ROM Disc

Tip 398 introduces CD-ROM drives and discs. As you learned, information is stored on the CD-ROM disc by stamping the information into the disc's surface. These pits are then covered with a protective coating. As such, if your CD-ROM disc has finger prints or other smudges, you can simply wipe them off with a damp cloth. Should a soda or other substance get spilled on the disc, simply run the disc under some cool water and wipe off the spill. As you can see, CD-ROM discs are much less susceptable to damage from spills that floppies.

Cleaning Your Mouse

Several tips in this book present cleaning techniques. With respect to your mouse, the only time you should have to worry about cleaning it is if its rubber ball starts to stick. Otherwise, leave the mouse alone. Should you need to clean the mouse, turn the mouse over and open the area that holds the rubber ball as shown here:

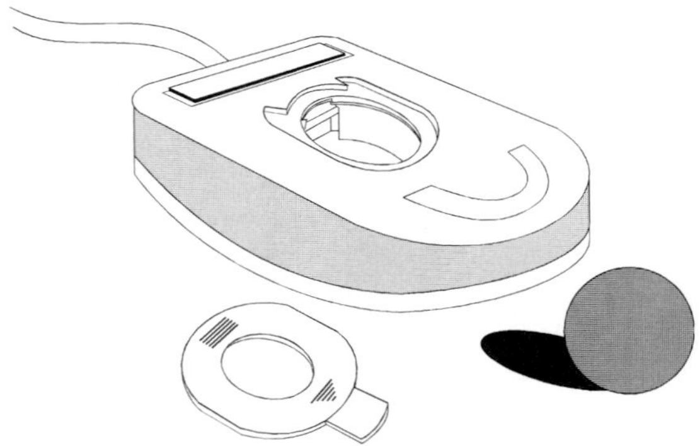

Using a damp cloth, clean the rubber ball. Next, disconnect the mouse from your PC. If the mouse movement area (the area in which the ball normally resides) contains dust, blow out the dust. If necessary, gently clean the area with a Q-Tip and rubbing alcohol. Let the area dry. Reinsert the ball, ensuring that it moves freely. Plug the mouse back into your PC.

Understanding Reliability

As you read computer advertisements, you will encounter the terms MTBF and MTTR. MTBF is an abbreviation for mean (average) time between failures. A device's MTBF gives you an indication of how long you can use your device before (statistically speaking) it will fail. Depending on the advertisement, MTBF may be listed in thousands of hours or in years. A year has approximately 8,760 hours. MTTR is an abbreviation for mean (average) time to repair. A device's MTTR gives you an indication of the time it will probably take to repair the device should it fail. MTTR is measured in hours.

Because hardware servicing can be expensive, it's important to understand and appreciate a device's MTBF and MTTR values.

Be Aware of Damaged or Bad Power Supply Cables

The following illustration shows the four power cables that lead from a typical power supply:

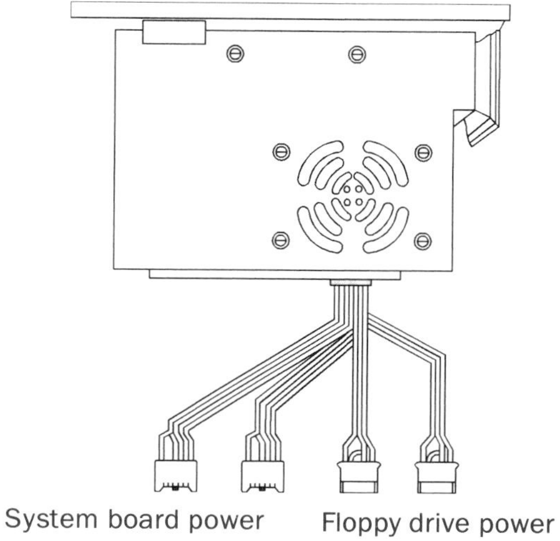

One of the cables plugs into your motherboard and one plugs into your hard disk, and two cables are available for floppy drives, a tape drive, or an internal CD-ROM.

If your system does not boot, or if one of your devices does not respond, check the power cables. First, make sure the cables are plugged in completely. Second, all of the cables are identical, so you can exchange cables between devices as you troubleshoot. If you find a bad cable and have an unused cable available, use the available cable. If you don't have an unused cable, have your power supply serviced or simply replace it. Do not attempt to service the power supply yourself. Doing so can be very dangerous.

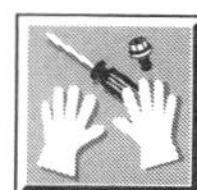

Understanding System Burn-In

If one of your computer components is going to fail, more than likely it will do so in the first 24 hours of use. Thus, most manufacturers put your computer components through 24 to 72 hours of operational testing, called a burn-in. Before you purchase a computer, ask about the manufacturer's burn-in process. Many manufacturers individually burn in components. Although your motherboard and parallel port both get burned in, they may not get burned in together. Ideally, all of your system components should be burned in together. If they are, your integrated system will be more likely to work when you get it.

If your salesperson can't describe the manufacturer's burn-in process for you, talk to someone who can. There's nothing more frustrating than unpacking a new system that does not work.

Extended Warranties: An Opinion

Many computer manufacturers and retailers offer extended warranties that, for $200 to $300 dollars per year, cover your computer's components in case of a breakdown. Often, your disk drive will be your computer's most expensive item (other than, perhaps, your monitors). The cost of your disk is probably close to $300.

As Tip 763 discusses, if your PC is going to fail, it will probably do so in the first few days. When PCs fail, normally just one item fails, not every expensive component. In many cases, you are better off pocketing the money you would spend on a warranty and keeping it available for replacements. If your city has a PC user group, contact it. Most user groups have hardware experts who can help you fix most problems. If your city doesn't have a user group and you don't have a friend who is an expert, the extended warranty may be right for you.

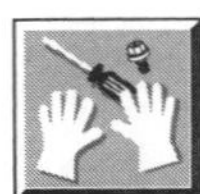

To find out about PC user groups in your area, contact:

Association of PC User Groups
1730 M. Street, N.W.
Washington, D.C. 20036

Be Careful Where You Place a PC Stand or Tower PC

Tip 850 discusses how using a PC stand can free space on your desk. Tip 851 discusses tower PC systems. If you use a vertical stand or tower PC system, keep the area around the PC as clean as possible. In most cases when you use a stand, the PC's fan will be close to your carpet or floor. If the area is not kept clean, the fan will continually pull dust, animal hair, or carpet fuzz into your computer. If the PC sits close to a carpet, move the PC before you vacuum. Not only does the vacuum possess a strong motor that can destroy your disks, but vacuuming can build up large amounts of static electricity.

Never place a PC on its side without using a stand; the stand not only elevates the PC from the floor (and hence dust and static), it keeps the PC from tipping over.

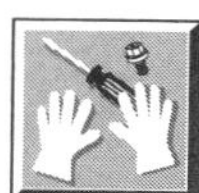

Index

B

C

D

E

F

G

H

L

M

N

Q

R

S

T

U

V

W

X

Y

Z